MACKINTOSH
MACINTOSH - MCINTOSH

Descendants of
Alexander-1 MacIntosh

with the
KIFF CONNECTION

Revised Edition

Frances Sterling Drisko

HERITAGE BOOKS
2012

HERITAGE BOOKS
AN IMPRINT OF HERITAGE BOOKS, INC.

Books, CDs, and more—Worldwide

For our listing of thousands of titles see our website
at
www.HeritageBooks.com

Published 2012 by
HERITAGE BOOKS, INC.
Publishing Division
100 Railroad Ave. #104
Westminster, Maryland 21157

International Standard Book Numbers
Paperbound: 978-0-7884-5447-9
Clothbound: 978-0-7884-9213-6

MACK INTOSH   MAC INTOSH   MC INTOSH

This book is dedicated to

the memory of my father
Charles Lee STERLING
(1890 – 1942)

and my husband
George Dolbey DRISKO
(1917 – 1994)

MACKINTOSH   MAC INTOSH   MC INTOSH

If you want to know WHAT you are,
Look to yourself –

If you want to know WHO you are,
Look to your ancestors.

They cleared the land,
Built the roads,
Founded the churches,
Fought the Wars.

THEY ARE YOU !!!

Anonymous

MACKINTOSH   **MAC INTOSH**   **MC INTOSH**

This work is a revised edition of the 1993 book which I compiled entitled

" MACKINTOSH, MAC INTOSH, MC INTOSH
Descendants of Alexander-1 MAC INTOSH
and his wife
Clara YOUNKHAUSE / JUNGHANS

It contains a vast amount of new information,
as well as corrections and updated information from the first edition.
In some families there is data to the 10th Generation

I am indebted to many people for the sharing of their history,
and the stories about the families they knew and loved.

In doing the research for this volume , it became evident to me that
I should include the KIFF/ MC INTOSH connection, and have dedicated an
entire section of this book to my research of the KIFF lines. .

Thousands of names
and those with considerable data include:
AYRES, BOETTGER, CEASE
CONGDON, CLEVELAND, COVERT
FREEMAN,GREENOUGH, HOWE
LYON, SIMMONS, SMITH
TANNER, THOMAS
and WILLIAMS

This edition to be titled:

MACKINTOSH, MAC INTOSH, MC INTOSH
with the
KIFF CONNECTION

MACKINTOSH   MAC INTOSH   MC INTOSH

EPITAPHS

Genealogists spend a great deal of time in cemeteries .
Here are a couple of gravestone inscriptions that I liked

The dear departed's gone before,
To that unknown and silent shore.
We hope to meet in Heaven above,
Where all is purity and love.

Marker on a small headstone in a family cemetery in Jordan, NY.

Grieve not, nor speak of me with tears,
But laugh and talk of me as if I were beside you …
I loved you so
'Twas Heaven here with you

Anonymous

I do not fear to tread the path that those I love have long since trod ;
I do not fear to pass the gates and stand before the living God,
In this world's fight I've done my part; If God be God he knows it well;
He will not turn his back on me and send me down to blackest Hell.
Because I have not prayed aloud and shouted in the market place,
Tis what we do, not what we say, that makes us worthy of his grace.

MACKINTOSH   MAC INTOSH   MC INTOSH

Tale of Contents

MACKINTOSH   MAC INTOSH   MC INTOSH

Abbreviations

ca - about or around
s/o - son of
dau/o – daughter of
marr.   - marriage
div. - divorce
Co. - county
EOL - end of line

MACKINTOSH   MAC INTOSH   MC INTOSH

A Brief History of the Name

Scotland's highland history can only be traced from around the middle of the 9th Century, although many legends have arisen around their Chiefs and their Clans.

Written records , other than church records, were not common in that time period, so very little is really known of the Scots regarding their way of life. Modern stories have been written, and movies made, but they may be more fiction that fact.

There are the stones of the Picts, but not much else. Most often the important dates and events were passed from one generation to another by " word of mouth ". It is through these oral traditions that we have learned about the Celtic people in Scotland from the 5th to the 8th Centuries. It appears that the most intriguing feature of their life was the " kin " or family. From the " kin ", it grew into a " clan " system. The head of the " kin " was a very powerful man, and was looked upon by everyone as a father figure. He demanded loyalty, even to the point of laying down ones' own life for the " kin ". He called his kinsfolk his " clan ".

A clan / clan is the Gaelic word for " children ". The clan members took the name of their "Chief ", usually placing the prefix of MAC or MC in front of it. MAC means " son of " and is found in numerous Scottish names.

The **MAC KIN TOSHES** are traced to the original Clan Chattan (The Clan of the Cats). The earliest authentic ancestry is traced to the Royal House of Duff. Skeagh/Shaw of Duff (MAC DUFF) was the 2nd son of Constantine, the 3rd Earl of Fife, and was appointed Constable of Inverness Castle in 1163.

He became known as **MAC AN TOSEICH** . Toseich is Gaelic for " chief " or " headman ". **A MAC AN TOSEICH** means the son of such a functionary. He became the 1st of the name and the progenitor of a long line.

MACKINTOSH   MAC INTOSH   MC INTOSH

The First American Generation

1. **ALEXANDER-**[1] **MAC INTOSH**, the founder of this branch of the MACKINTOSH - MAC INTOSH – MC INTOSH clan, and the immigrant, is believed to have been born 2 Feb 1724 at Urquhart, Inverness-shire, Scotland, and came to America about 1740. He was most certainly descended from the Scottish Clan MACKINTOSH.

He was a seafaring man. It is believed that his parents began the journey to the New World with him , but died en route.

He married **Clara-**[2] **YOUNKHAUSE/YONKHANS/JUNGHANS** ++, a Palatine, who arrived in America with her parents around 1738. She was a native of Germany, and was born there on 10 June 1725. She was the daughter of Mattheus-[1] JUNGHANS/ JUNGHAUS and his wife Margaretha SEITTER(S).

Alexander-[1] MAC INTOSH, and his wife , settled first near Pine Plains (NY) , at a place locally called Hammertown, in Dutchess County. He purchased land there on 18 April 1764. In 1786 he bought land of George CLINTON, and then possibly later moved to Delaware County, NY.

Information derived from the Amenia Church Records (New York Genealogical and Biographical Records – Vol. 35, page 110) and HUNTTING'S *" Little Nine Partners "* state that Clara MACKENTESH, wife of Alexander, was a member of the Round Top Church at Bethel (Pine Plains). Many members of their family were baptized there.

Page 152 of the *"Little Nine Partners"* states that " Alexander MC INTOSH – who married Clara YOUNKHANS and lived on the Samuel S. TANNER farm – it is said that he went to Albany, on foot, in 1760 for the communion service used in this church (the Red Church at Pulvers). This tradition as to date is probably correct, but the communion service was bought for the Lutheran Round Top Church. The purchase was made twelve years before the Red Church was built. Furthermore the record of the Round Top commenced at this date – 1760 – and the service of the Lord's Supper immediately follows when there was a need for these communion pieces, and they were repeatedly used ."

The *" History of Dutchess County "* (page 316) stated " and old church, built by the Moravians, or as some believe, by the Dutch Reformed Society, once stood a mile or more East of Pine Plains, near Hammertown, in the vicinity of the old burying ground." " Alex. MC INTOSH brought over the communion service and presented it to the church."

Children of Alexander-[1] MAC INTOSH and Clara YOUNKHAUSE/JUNGHANS:
Surname **MAC INTOSH**

+ 2.   **ALEXANDER II**   born ca 1757 New York; baptized 1759
                                   married Rachel TANNER   +++
                                   died 1836

    +++   Note: The will of William TANNER, Sr. mentions daughter
                   Rachel TANNER McIntosh – 11-29-1785 and 4-11-1786

MACKINTOSH   MAC INTOSH   MC INTOSH
The First American Generation

Children of Alexander-[1] MAC INTOSH and Clara JUNGHANS, continued:
Surname **MAC INTOSH**

+ 3.   **SIMON** (twin)   born 17 June 1761 Pine Plains, NY
married Sarah Sager Phelps BATES
died 8 Jan 1853 (gs) Kortright, Delaware Co., NY
buried Bloomville Cemetery

+ 4.   **JOHN** (twin)   born 17 June 1761 Pine Plains, NY
married Sarah _____
died _____

+ 5.   **MAGDALENA**   born 1762-64 Amenia, Dutchess Co., NY
baptized 21 June 1764
married Samuel S. TANNER
died ca 1789 Pine Plains

+ 6.   **RACHEL**   born 4 Aug 1766 ; baptized 12 Oct 1766
married Samuel S. TANNER (as his 2nd wife)
died 13 Oct 1845 Pine Plains, NY
buried Bethel, Dutchess County, NY

++ Ancestry of Clara-2 YOUNKHAUSE/ JUNGHANS

Clara-[2] YOUNKHAUSE/YOUNGHANS/JUNGHANS was born 10 June 1725 at Flacht, Neckarkreis, Wuerttenberg, Germany. She came to America with her parents Mattheus/Matthias-[1] YOUNKHAUSE (etc) and Margarete/Margaretha SEITTER.

Clara was baptized at Ancram (NY) on 8 May 1746. She married Alexander MAC INTOSH before 1757.

Clara , born 10 June 1725 was one of 9 children. Her siblings were Magdalena Sybilla; Margaretha born 10 Oct 1723, who married Henrich HOFFMAN; Margaretha born June 1727; Christianus possibly born 5 Dec 1728; Georg Leonhardt born 20 Dec 1729, who married Maria UHL 9 June 1751; Regina born 21 Dec 1731 who married Michael RAU/RAUH/ROUW; Mattheus / Matthias born 16 Apr 1734 ; Magnus born 5 Sep 1737; and Henrich born 3 Feb 1740 NY, who married first to Sarah ____, and second to Anna Maria WEIDREWACHS.

Mattheus/Matthias-[1] YOUNKHAUSE/JUNGHANS (etc) was born 16 July 1692 in Germany, and was a blacksmith by trade. He probably came from Evangelisch, Flacht, Neckarkreis, Wurttenburg. He married Margaretha SEITTER(S) there on 11 Nov 1721. They both died around 1770.

Margaretha SEITTER(S) was the daughter of Hans SEITTER(S) and Magdalena Von MAURER, and was born 5 May 1700 in Evangelisch Flacht, Neckarkreis, Wurtetenburg, Germany.

Matthias JUNGHANS appeared on the Tax Lists for Northeast, NY in the years 1745-46. His son Hendrick was listed for 1771-74 and again in 1778-79.

The " History of Dutchess County (NY)" page 317 states " Henry YONKHONCE and a man named MONTROSS were among the early settlers " Younkhonce it is said was slain on his own domain by a war party of fierce Mohawk Indians, who were on their way to attack the Shekemeko settlement "

References: Census data 1790,1800,1810 Livingston and Rennsalaer, NY; Amenia Church Records; NY Genealogical and Biographical Records, Vol. 35, page 110; Bloomville Cemetery (NY);DAR Records; Extant Calendar of Wills, pub. by Colonial dames of NY 1896, page 398; American Genealogical & Biographical Index, Vol. 114, page 384.

2. **ALEXANDER-**[2] **MAC INTOSH**, son of Alexander—[1] MAC INTOSH , was born ca 1757, baptized 1759 Pine Plains, Dutchess County, New York.

He married Rachel-[2] TANNER before 1783. She was the daughter of William-[1] TANNER and Rachel DE LONG, and was born ____; died ca 1835.

William-[1] TANNER, a native of England, was one of the early settlers of the Town of Dover, Dutchess County, NY., according to the Commemorative Biographical Record for Dutchess County.

Alexander-[2] MAC INTOSH was a Revolutionary War soldier, and was residing in Livingston, Columbia County, NY. in 1800. He served under Captain William STEWART and Colonel Morris GRAHAM during the Revolution, an made application for a pension under the Act 0f 1832. He died in 1835 before the pension was granted.

Children of Alexander-[2] MAC INTOSH and Rachel TANNER:
Surname **MAC INTOSH**

+   **7. ALEXANDER III**   born ca 1783
                                     baptized 21 Sept 1783 Pine Plains
                                     married Catherine RAU/ROUW/ROW/RAUH 26 Apr 1804
                                                          at Gallatin, Columbia County, NY
                                     died _____

           8. Rachel Regina   born 25 Aug 1785
                                     baptized 16 Oct 1785 Pine Plains Round Top Church
                                     married _____
                                     died _____

           9. George   born ca 1788; died 9 May 1876 (88 gs)
                                     married Anna _____
                                     (she born March 1786; died 13 June 1849 (63-3-0-)
                                     buried Bethel, Pine Plains Cemetery
                          Note: name spelled Mc INTASH on the gravestone)

           10. Phebe   born 3 Sep 1791
                                     baptized 14 Feb 1792 Gallatin, Columbia County, Ny
                                     married _____
                                     died _____

           11. Margaret   born 7 Oct 1794; died 23 Jan 1872 (78-3-16 GS)
                                     never married   EOL

+   **12. ANNA/ANNE**   born 26 Aug 1796 Gallatin
                                     married William WEAVER 1 Jan/Jun1832 Gallatin Reformed Church
                                     died _____

Children on Alexander-[2] MAC INTOSH and Rachel TANNER:
Surname **MAC INTOSH**

13. Elizabeth	born 5 Nov 1798
	baptized 1799 Gallatin Reformed Church
	married John Leonard DUNDEE/DUNEE
14. Hannah	born 4 July 1801; died 14 Dec 1858 (57-5-10 gs)
	baptized 19 Aug 1801 Gallatin Reformed Church
	never married
	died 14 Dec 1858 (57-5-10 gs)
	buried Old Community Cemetery Hillsdale,NY
15. William	born ____ ca 1803
	baptized 9 Aug 1803 Gallatin Reformed Church
	married ____

Reference: Round Top Church Records, Pine Plains, NY, and Gallatin Reformed Church Records

3. SIMON[2] **MAC INTOSH**, brother of above, was born 17 June 1761 at Pine Plains, Dutchess County, NY. He had a twin brother, John.

Simon married Sarah (Sally) Sager PHELPS (possibly Bates) ca 1788 probably at Livingston, Columbia County, NY Sarah was the daughter of _____PHELPS and _____, and was born 16 Dec 1769; died 16 May 1834 (65-5 gs) in Delaware County, NY. They had ten children.

He served as a Private in the Revolutionary War as a member of the Dutchess County Militia, 6th Regiment; under Captain Silas HUSTED and Colonel Morris GRAHAM.

In 1790, Simon resided at Livingston, Columbia County, NY. In 1795 he received a soldier's grant of 240 acres near Bloomville, Delaware County, NY. The grant was payment for his Revolutionary War service. He and his family went to that area, sometime between 1795 and 1800, following marked trees. They made the trip by ox team.

In 1837 he, and six of his children and their families, left Delaware County and traveled by covered wagon to Armenia Mountain, Tioga County, PA. They were able to take only a few of their precious possessions to the area which is near Troy and Canton, PA.

Those few " precious household goods " included a handmade four drawer chest which was made of tiger maple and flame grain mahogany. The chest, has a deep top drawer and served as a crib for many babies. It is not known who made the chest which has been verified to be a New York piece made around 1800. Today, the chest still serves a member of the MAC INTOSH family. It has been handed down from generation to generation and has always been referred to as the " MAC INTOSH Chest " . It has been appraised and documented and will remain a part of the MAC INTOSH heritage.

Simon MAC INTOSH later returned to Kortright where he was residing in 1850 with his son Henry and family.

In MUNSELL'S " *History of Delaware County* " 1880, it states " he (Simon) died in Kortright on the 20th day of January 1853. (This information is erroneous as the correct date is 8 Jan 1853 gs) Simon MAC INTOSH in the 92nd year of his age. He came by marked trail and settled near where Jehial GREGORY now lives. His descendants are numerous in this county and Canton, PA" He is buried in the Bloomville Cemetery, along with his wife and other members of his family.

The Second American Generation

Of his ten children, two remained in Delaware County, NY, six moved to the Tioga and Bradford County areas of PA., and two removed to Western New York. Simon MAC INTOSHES service.in the Revolution was approved by the NSDAR; service having been shown by certificate of pay issued him (the original records were burned) by the Roster of Troops, printed in the NYS Archives, Volume 1 (Documents relating to the Colonial History of the State of New York, Volume 15.

Simon MAC INTOSH is also mentioned in the Dutchess County Militia (Land Bounty Rights) 6th Regiment. *" New York in the Revolution as Colony and State "*, Volume 1, page 249. From the University of the State of New York Library, Manuscripts and History Section, Albany, NY.

Children of Simon-[2] MAC INTOSH and Sarah Phelps BATES:
Surname **MAC INTOSH**

+	**16. CLARA/ CLARACY**	born 17 March 1789 Dutchess County, NY; died 22 Sep 1875 1 married Samuel CALDWELL/COLWELL 2 married _____ SHERWOOD
+	**17. JONATHAN**	born 25 Dec 1791; died 24 Jun 1867 Cattaraugus County, NY married Annise/Annis CRANE
+	**18. HENRY**	born ca 1793; died 1872 Bloomville, Delaware Co., NY married Mary Ann SMITH
	19. Catherine	born ca 1794-95 NY; died ca 1870 Canton, PA; never married EOL
+	**20. WILLIAM**	born 22 July 1796 Delaware County, NY married Elizabeth KIFF 23 May 1820 Kortright, Delaware, NY died 14 Jan 1879 Armenia, Bradford, PA buried COVERT Cemetery MAC INTOSH Hollow
+	**21. MATTHIAS**	born 23 Mar 1799; died 20 Oct 1822-25 married Sarah (Sally) LOCKWOOD 8 Jan 1824
+	**22. ALEXANDER**	born 17 Dec 1800 Kortright, Delaware, NY married Hannah GEROWE/JEROW died 23 March 1899 Canton, Bradford, PA
+	**23. GEORGE**	born ca 1803 Kortright, NY married Sarah (Sally) JACQUISH died 3 Oct 1877 Delaware Co, NY (cancer)
+	**24. SIMON, JR.**	born 25 March 1809 Kortright, NY; died 11 July 1887 Canton, PA married Esther SUTTON 11 July 1831 NY
+	**25. JULIA**	born __ April 1814 Kortright, NY; died 26 July 1869 (gs) married Alexander CEASE buried Old Burton FASSETT Farm, Tioga County, PA.

References: MAC INTOSH family records; DAR Records, Tioga Co., PA Historical records; Addie WATTS Crawford dec'd,History of Delaware County., NY; NY Cemetery Records Vol. 47, page 64; Park Cemetery, Canton, PA

MACKINTOSH   MAC INTOSH   MC INTOSH
The Second American Generation

History of Delaware County, NY   Town of Kortright   published 1898   page 477

" Simon MC INTOSH was an early resident, came from Dutchess County in the year 1800; his wife's name was BATES, also from Dutchess. They were blessed with seven sons, Jonathan, Henry, William, Matthias, Alexander, George and Simon, Jr. Of these Henry had two children, William and Emeline. William MC INTOSH is now living in Washington, DC. – the father of James H., a former school commissioner of our county, and A.W. MC INTOSH of Delhi, NY.

Emeline MC INTOSH, daughter of Henry, was the wife of the late Francis FULLER, and mother of Mrs. J. E. POWELL. George MC INTOSH, the younger son of Simon, and brother of Henry, lived for many years on Federal Hill, Town of Delhi, and was the father of Theophilus, the senior editor of the Delaware Republican. Other members of the family drifted to other parts of the country.

The Delaware Republican was started 12 May 1860 by STURDEVANT and MC INTOSH."

The Oneonta Star (undated)   " The Gunny Sack "   by Gerald " Gunny " GUNTHRUP

" Glen HARPER, our Delhi reporter, uncovered an interesting story about the MC INTOSH twins during a visit to the Bloomville area the other day.

Buried in the Bloomville Cemetery more than a hundred years ago, 8 Jan 1853 to be exact, are the remains of a Revolutionary soldier by the name of **Simon MC INTOSH**. Born in 1761 at Pine Plains, he was 92 years of age when he died.

Simon was an identical twin. He would come home on leave from the Army and his brother would replace him. Their looks were so similar that the substitution was never discovered.

Revolutionary soldiers received small pay and often it was long delayed. After the War, Simon finally received a soldiers' grant of 240 acres of land from the State of New York. This land was located near Bloomville, and Simon moved to this grant from Dutchess County about 1795, making the trip by ox team.

Simon's wife was Sarah Phelps, and she is buried beside him. Mr. and Mrs. MC INTOSH had 10 children, two of whom remained in Delaware County. The others moved to PA and Western NY.

Descendants now living in Delhi are Eugene POWELL, Miss Sarah POWELL, Mrs. Milton Henderson, Miss Katherine MC INTOSH, Harry A. MC INTOSH and Mrs. Jessie Burkett. "

Note: No one knows whether the above story, about Simon and his brother, is merely folk lore or fact, but it has been recanted over many, many years.

Note: A bronze plaque was secured from the War Department by Harry A. MC INTOSH of Delhi, NY in 1959. After the headstones of Simon and Sarah were cleaned and reset, the plaque was placed on a cement foundation in front of Simon's headstone in the Bloomville Cemetery.

Reference: Miss Katherine MC INTOSH, Bloomville, NY (now deceased)

MACKINTOSH   MAC INTOSH   MC INTOSH
The Second American Generation

4. JOHN-[2] MAC INTOSH, twin brother of above, was born 17 June 1761 at Pine Plains, Dutchess County, NY. He possibly married twice, his first wife being a Sarah ____. This is unconfirmed. A second wife may have been Elizabeth ESSELSTINE. She was the daughter of _____ ESSELSTINE and _____, and was born 8 May 1775 Columbia County, NY. Folk lore indicates that John-2 may have moved to the Albany area from Dutchess County, and had several children, including a son John. John-[2] MAC INTOSH died ca 1827.

Children of John-[2] MAC INTOSH and _____?:
Surname **MAC INTOSH**

      26. George   born ca 1810
      27. John, Jr.   born ca 1812; died 24 Mar 1862
           Note: Old Gravestones of Dutchess County, NY; page 194, # 444

Note: A John MAC INTOSH, Jr. and Catherine, his wife; John PHILLIPS and Marie, his wife; and John BATHRICKS, all of Delhi, Delaware County, NY. sold land in the Town of Red Hook and Dutchess County 16 Oct 1834.

5. MAGDALENA-[2] MAC INTOSH, sister of above, was born ca 1764, baptized 21 June 1764. (Amenia Church records)

She married Samuel S. TANNER ca 1782. He was the son of William TANNER and his second wife , Rachel DE LONG, and was born 4 April 1758 at the "Clove", Dutchess County, NY.; died _____. Magdalena died ca 1788 at Pine Plains, possibly the result of childbirth, and is buried in Bethel, Dutchess County, NY.

Childen of Magdalena-[2] MAC INTOSH and Samuel S. TANNER:
Surname **TANNER**

+	**28. WILLIAM**	born 4 Feb 1783 Pine Plains; died 14 Jan 1867 Columbia County, NY.
		1 married Margaret STREVER ca 1805
		(she born 22 Jan 1785; died 15 July 1830)
		2 married Mrs. Myra CARD Finch ca 1832
		3 married Betsey/Elizabeth DAVIS 15 July 1847
		all buried Pine Plains, Dutchess County, NY.
	29. Rachel	born 20 Mar 1784; died 28 Mar 1864, never married
		buried Evergreen Cemetery, Pine Plains, NY
+	**30. ALEXANDER**	born 20 Feb 1785 Pine Plains; died 9 Aug 1841
	(twin)	married Nancy C. MERRITT
		(she born 13 July 1786; died 17 Mar 1856)
	31. Margaret	born 20 Feb 1785; died 15 Feb 1823
	(twin)	married Samuel POTTER
+	**32. JOHN**	born 6 Mar 1788 Pine Plains; died 29 Jun 1869 Columbia Co., NY
		1 married Olive MERRITT 1813
		(she born ca _____; died ca 1822)
		2 married Mrs. Christina FINGAR Mosher 1823

6. RACHEL-[2] MAC INTOSH, sister of above, was born 4 Aug 1766, baptized 12 Oct 1766. (Amenia Church Records).

She married Samuel S. TANNER ca 1789, as his second wife. He had previously been married to her older sister Magdalena-[2] MAC INTOSH (above). He was the son of William TANNER and Rachel DE LONG and was born 4 Apr 1758, died 2 Oct 1832 Bethel, Dutchess County, NY.

Records show that Samuel TANNER and his wife Rachel, sold 434 acres in Lot 31 of Little Nine Partners, in the Town of Northeast, Dutchess County, NY for $ 709.69 to William RICHTER on 25 Dec 1802, recorded 19 July 1805 at 9 AM.

Rachel-[2] MAC INTOSH died 13 Oct 1845. They are both buried at Bethel, Dutchess County, NY.

Children of Rachel-[2] MAC INTOSH and Samuel S. TANNER:
Surname **TANNER**

+	**33. MARY MAGDALENA**	born 2 Nov 1790 Pine Plains; died 1864 married William T. WOOLDRIDGE
+	**34. JAMES** (twin)	born 12 Jan 1795 Pine Plains; died 11 Feb 1877 1 married Annis WALES/Anna WELLS 2 married Kate BURGER 3 married Sally KIPP buried Ancram Free Cemetery, Columbia County, NY
+	**35. REUBEN S.** (twin)	born 12 Jan 1795 Pine Plains; died _____ married Lydia RICHTER/REIGHTER 21 Jan 1824 resided Northeast, Dutchess County, NY; later New York City
+	**36. CLARISSA**	born 16 Jan 1797 Pine Plains; died 4 Dec 1877 married Adam A. STREVER ca 1819 (he born 24 Nov 1793; died 14 July 1866) buried Evergreen Cemetery, Pine Plains, NY
+	**37. ANTHONY**	born 13 Aug 1799 Pine Plains; died 14 Jan/Jun 1877 1 married Catherine (Kate) SIMMONS (she born 30 Jan 1802; died 3 Feb 1834) 2 married Mrs. Mary Eliza SIMMONS Call buried Knickerbocker Ground # 101
+	**38. HENRY**	born 9 Nov 1801 Pine Plains; died ____ 1 married Eliza HINSDALE 2 married Catherine SNYDER Shadic (widow of Peter SHADIC)
+	**39. SAMUEL S.**	born 6 Aug 1804 Pine Plains; died 7 Feb 1891 1 married Fannie STREVER 16 Jan 1834 (she born 4 Aug 1807; died 9 Oct 1835) 2 married Mary Betsey/Elizabeth LOWN ca 1835 (she born 2 Mar 1814; died 30 Nov 1846 (32y8mo28da)) 3 married Julia SHELDON 15 Nov 1847
+	**40. MORRIS**	born 6 Apr 1807 Pine Plains; died 30 December 1877 Columbia Co. married Sally Ann SNYDER 24 Nov 1832 at Reformed Church, Claverack, NY

Children of Rachel-[2] MAC INTOSH and Samuel S. TANNER, continued:
Surname **TANNER**

41. Almyra/ Almira   born 24 May 1810 Pine Plains; died ____ (living 1881)
    (twin)   married Jeremiah LOWN 2 Apr 1836 Pine Plains, Dutchess, NY
                        (he born ca 1807; died after 1860) no issue   EOL

42. Eliza/Elizabeth   born 24 May 1810 Pine Plains; died ____
    (twin)   married Andrew CASE (he born ca 1810; died ____) EOL

References: Descendants of William TANNER by Peter SILVERNAIL; Commemorative Record of Dutchess Co., NY; Russell CHRISTIE, Ethel MILLER, Robert SIMMONS per Howard SMITH(now dec'd), Bella Vista, AK; Old Gravestones of Dutchess County, page 200; LDS-IGI-NY- Tanner ; Bethel Cemetery Records, Pine Plains, NY

MACKINTOSH   **MAC INTOSH**   **MC INTOSH**

7. ALEXANDER-[3] MAC INTOSH, III, son of Alexander-[2] MAC INTOSH (Alexander-[1]) and Rachel TANNER, was born ___ 1783; baptized 21 Sep 1783 at Pine Plains Round Top Lutheran Church (NY).

He married Catherine/Catharina ROUW/RAUH/RAU/ROE/ROU on 26 April 1804 at Gallatin, Columbia County, NY. She was the daughter of ____ ROUW, etc. and ____, and was born ca 178_; died ____. It is uncertain when Alexander-3 MAC INTOSH died, but he was still living and residing in Gallatin according to the 1850 Federal Census.

Children of Alexander-[3] MAC INTOSH and Catherine ROUW:
Surname **MAC INTOSH**

43. Maria	born ____ 1808; died ____	
	baptized 25 Mar 1808 Gallatin Reformed Church, Columbia Co., NY	
44. Geasie	born ____ 1810; died ____	
	baptized 15 May 1810 Gallatin Reformed Church	
45. John Herman	born ____ 1814; died ____	
	baptized 13 Mar 1814 Gallatin Reformed Church	

References: Baptismal Records of Round Top Church, and Gallatin Reformed Church

12. ANNE/ANNA-[3] MAC INTOSH, sister of above, was born 26 August 1796 at Gallatin, Columbia County, NY. She married William WEAVER on 1 Jan/June 1832 at the Gallatin Reformed Church. He was the son of _____ WEAVER and ____, and was born ____; died ____. Anne/Anna -[3] MAC INTOSH died ____.

Child of Anne/Anna-[3] MAC INTOSH and William WEAVER:
Surname **WEAVER**

46. Ambrose	born 15 Sep 1833; died ____

Reference: Gallatin Church Records

16. CLARA/CLARACY-[3] MAC INTOSH, daughter of Simon-[2] MAC INTOSH (Alexander-[1]) and Sarah PHELPS , was born 17 Mar 1789 at Livingston, Columbia County, NY.

She married first to Samuel CALDWELL on ____ 18__. He was the son of William CALDWELL and Polly WALTNER, and was born ca ____, baptized 3 July 1796, Cobbleskill Reformed Church, Schoharie County, NY.; died ____. She married second to ____ SHERWOOD.

According to the 1870 Federal Census for Armenia, PA., Clara was residing with her brother-in-law Alexander CEASE. Her age was listed as 80 and stated that she was a retired housekeeper. She died 22 Sep 1875 at Ward Township, Armenia, PA.

Child of Clara-[3] MAC INTOSH and Samuel CALDWELL:
Surname **CALDWELL**

+	**47. MARY**	born ca 1823, NY; died ____
		married James MC DONALD
		(he born ca 1823; died 28 May 1894)

17. JONATHAN-³ MAC INTOSH, brother of above, was born 25 December 1791, Delaware County, New York. It is unclear as to whether or not he married ca 1809 to a first wife, and there is no further data that this researcher can find regarding Adelaide or her husband Orson PRATT.

He married Annis CRANE of Homer, Cortland County, NY on " Wednesday evening 14 Feb 1817, Jonathan MAC INTOSH of Kortright and Miss Annis CRANE of Homer were married by B S CAMPBELL, Esq. at Preble, Cortland County, NY." (Reference: Cortland County Marriages 1815-21) She was the daughter of John CRANE and Anise KING, and was born 18 May 1791 at Hartford, CT.; died 5 Oct 1856 at Cadiz, Cattaraugus, NY.

Jonathan-³ MAC INTOSH and his wife settled in Cortland County, NY; later moving to Humphrey and Great Valley in Cattaraugus County, NY. In 1860 Jonathan-³ MAC INTOSH resided with his son George-⁴ at Olean, Cattaraugus County, NY, where he died 24 June 1867.

Child of Jonathan-³ MAC INTOSH and _____?_____:
Surname **MAC INTOSH**

48. Adelaide Miranda	born 7 July 1810, NY; died 20 April 1884	
	married Orson PRATT	

Children of Jonathan-³ MC INTOSH and Annis CRANE:
Surname **MAC INTOSH**

	49. Fidelia	born 7 Feb 1819, NY; died 2 Nov 1908 Great Valley, NY
		1 married William ALLEN (resided Richmond, McHenry, IL 1850)
		Children: Harriet S-⁵ born ca 1848 IL, and Charles W-⁵ ALLEN born ca 1849 IL.
		2 married Joseph CHOLLETTE
+	**50. RULUF CRANE**	born 23 Aug 1820,NY; died 26 Mar 1896 Knights Landing, CA
		married Helen Theodosia MOREY Feb 1847
		(she born 1828, NY; died ____ Knights Landing, Stanislaw Co., CA)
	51. Chauncey	born 19 Nov 1821; died 30 March 1827 EOL
+	**52. GEORGE SIMON**	born 25 June 1823 McGrawville, Cortland County, NY
		1 married Sarah A. PATTERSON 9 Nov 1859
		(she born 11 June 1832; died 1 Nov 1874)
		(she dau/o William PATTERSON and Anna CARPENTER)
		2 married Addie PATTERSON 1 Dec 1875
		(she born ____; died 1894, no issue)
		died 23 Oct 1884 Olean, Cattaraugus County, NY
+	**53. MARIETTE/ MARYETTE**	born 23 Sep 1824 Cortland Co., NY; died _____ IL
		married Alexander CHASE
		(he born ca 1823 Great Valley, Cattaraugus Co., NY; died _____)
		(he s/o Orrin CHASE and Sophia DILLINGHAM)
+	**54. EDWIN JONATHAN**	born 6 Nov 1826 Cortland Co., NY; died 1909 San Joaquin Valley, CA
		1 married Melancy D. MINOR ca 1861
		(she born 5 Jan 1835, MA; died 24 July 1871) Woodbridge, CA
		2 married Lydia BLAKESLEE July 1876
	55. Ruth	born 3 June 1828, NY; died 24 Sep 1830 EOL
+	**56. SI(L)VERTUS DARWIN**	born 13 May 1831 Homer Cortland Co., NY , NY;
		married Susan Cornelia PRATT 5 Jan 1861
		died 8 Jan 1886 Allegany, Cattaraugus, NY
	57. Albertus	born 13 Nov 1832, NY; died 19 May 1833 EOL
+	**58. SARAH**	born 29 Oct 1834, NY; died 11 Dec 1904
		married George REYNOLDS

References: 1860 Federal Census Cattaraugus County, NY, Addie WATTS Crawford (dec'd), Canton, PA

18. HENRY-^{3} MAC INTOSH, brother of above, was born ca 1793-94 at _____, Dutchess County, NY. He married Mary Ann SMITH on _____ at _____, NY. She was the daughter of Benjamin SMITH (1767 – 1823) and Polly _____ (1774 – 1843), and was born ca 1797 NY ; died 3 July 1889.

Henry-^{3} MAC INTOSH lived and died in Delhi, Delaware County, and was a carpenter, furniture maker and farmer. He was quite well educated for his time. He had a small library and was an avid reader. He had some renown as a mathematician and made almanacs for his neighbors and friends. He was well respected and had a high reputation in his community. He owned a 108 acre farm on McArthur Hill, not far from his father Simons' farm. Henry-^{3} MAC INTOSH died 22 Apr 1872. He and his wife are buried at Bloomville, Delaware Co., NY.

Note: Mary Ann SMITH had sisters: Sally Ann SMITH who married William BAKER;: and Polly Ann SMITH (born 9 Oct 1807; died Feb 1892) who married Joel H. MILLER (born 27 June 1809,died 14 Feb 1894) and resided in Otsego County, NY

Children of Henry-^{3} MAC INTOSH and Mary Ann SMITH:
Surname **MAC INTOSH**

+	**59. WILLIAM** **MC ARTHUR**	born 16 Apr 1818 Delhi, NY; died 16 Dec 1900 married Catherine BURNSIDE (she born ca 1812, NY; died 29 July 1895, NY) buried Riverside Cemetery, Bloomville, Delaware County, NY
+	**60. EMELINE**	born 7 Nov 1821 Delhi; died 11 Dec 1893 Delhi, NY 1 married John BURNSIDE (brother of Catherine) (he born _____; died 17 May1851) 2 married Francis FULLER (as his 2nd wife) (he born 24 Jul 1827; died 31 July 1885)

Note: Francis FULLER 1st married a Betsey Ann ___. She born 3 May 1828; died 19 Sept 1853.
They had a son Stephen E. FULLER, born May 1851.

	61. John	born _____; died young	EOL

20. WILLIAM-^{3} MAC INTOSH, brother of above, was born 22 July 1796 at _____, Delaware, NY. He married Elizabeth-^{3} KIFF on 23 March 1820 in Delaware Co., NY. She was the daughter of Andrew-^{2} KIFF (George-^{1}) and Mary MABIE (Marie JUNTEAU , a French Canadian girl adopted by the MABIE family of Westchester County, NY) Andrew KIFF was a Revolutionary War soldier. Elizabeth-^{3} KIFF was born 20 July 1802 in Schoharie County, NY; died 13 Dec 1879 Armenia Township, PA.

They moved from Kortright, Delaware County, NY to Ward Township, Tioga County, PA. William and his brother Matthias, operated a sawmill on the Tioga River from 1853- 1868.

William-^{3} MAC INTOSH died 14 June 1879. He and his wife, one son, and two granddaughters, are buried in a small family cemetery in MC INTOSH Hollow, on Armenia Mountain, Tioga County, PA.

Children of William-^{3} MAC INTOSH and Elizabeth-3 KIFF:
Surname **MAC INTOSH**

+	**62. CAROLINE**	born 22 Aug 1821 Kortright, NY; died 9 Jul 1858 Canton, PA married Lewis P. WILLIAMS 3 Dec 1839 (he born 29 Jan 1816; died 3 Nov 1885) buried Alba Cemetery, Alba, Bradford, PA
+	**63. SARAH JANE**	born 23 Jan 1823; died 1888 1 married _____ TANNER 16 Oct 1846 2 married Alonzo GREENO (he born 28 June 1812; died 15 Mar 1850; buried Alba, PA)

Children of William-[3] MAC INTOSH and Elizabeth-[3] KIFF, continued:
Surname **MAC INTOSH**

+	**64. CHARLOTTE**	born 16 Sep 1824; died ____ married Daniel RANDALL 8 Oct 1846	
	65. Andrew	born 30 Jan 1826; died 23 Jan 1827	EOL
+	**66. HARRIET**	born 8 Mar 1827; died ____ married Lorenzo THOMAS 24 Nov 1848 (he born ca 1826; died 25 Aug 1879 KS))	
+	**67. MICHAEL EDEN**	born 6 Dec 1830; died 19 Apr 1918 Harbor Springs, MI married Martha Helen LONGLEY/LONGWELL 15 Jul 1854 Tonawanda, NY (she born ca 1838; died 1900 MI)	
+	**68. SUSAN**	born 13 Mar 1834; died ca 1889 married John RANDALL	
	69. William K.	born 6 Dec 1835; died 29 Nov 1854 killed by a falling tree - buried MC INTOSH Hollow Cemetery, PA	
	70. Beland/Belair	born ca 1836; died 20 June 1837	EOL
+	**71. ELIZA ANN**	born 8 May 1837/38; died 2 May 1907 married N. Byron CASE ca 1855 Troy, Bradford, PA	
+	**72. FERNANDO**	born 27 Aug 1840; died 1918 married Rose LYON of Wellsboro, PA (she born ca 1844; died 1935)	
+	**73. LEWIS H.**	born 20 June 1843; died 1918 (age 75) Clarion, MI. married Norminda SMITH of MI (they divorced ca ____) (she born ca 1849, PA; died 1893 Clarion, MI)	
+	**74. ROSALTHEA AMANDA**	born May 1844; died ____ married Frank CURE of TX / OK	
	75. Isabel Ann	born ca 1846-47; died young	EOL
+	**76. LUCY DELPHINE**	born 13 Aug 1849; died 17 Oct 1922 Canton, PA married Hugh CRAWFORD 17 Apr 1865 Troy, PA	
+	**77. ESTELLA**	born 13 Oct 1850; died ca 1927 Horseheads, NY married James HOWE 15 Nov 1868 buried Canton, Bradford Co., PA	

References: Addie WATTS Crawford (dec'd), and Arlayne BOETTGER Lipchinsky, Harbor Springs, MI (dec'd) Family records and letters. Note: There were reportedly two more children – but have no information on them.

The Third American Generation

Ancestry of Elizabeth-3 KIFF

George-¹ KIFF, a sea captain, came to America with his wife, at an early date. Soon after their arrival his wife died. He was left with two sons, Andrew-² KIFF and George-² KIFF.

Andrew-² KIFF was born ca 1760, possibly at Boston, MA; and died 6 June 1825 at Bloomville, Delaware County, New York, and is buried at Riverside Cemetery, Bloomville..

He married Mary MABIE ca ____ at New Bedford , Westchester County, NY. where he had gone at the end of the Revolutionary War . Mary MABIE, born ca 1763 , originally named Marie JUNTEAU, was the adopted daughter of the MABIE family of Westchester County. She died 4 Aug 1835 at age 72.

The Revolutionary War service of Andrew-2 KIFF was listed in " New York in the Revolution" and appears on a receipt roll in the Military Secretary's Office, War Dept., Washington, DC.

The " History of Delaware County" by W.W. MUNSELL, published 1888, page 236 stated " Andrew KIFF stood on picket and helped guard WASHINGTON'S camp during the Revolutionary War."

The Will of Andrew -² KIFF of Kortright, NY – dated 1 May 1825, probated 31 Jan 1827, mentions his daughter Elizabeth-3 MC INTOSH. (Delaware County Wills) Andrew-2 KIFF was a hotel-keeper in the Town of Kortright (Kiffville) Delaware County, NY

Children of Andrew-² KIFF and Mary MABIE:
Surname **KIFF**

1. James	born ca 1784; married Elizabeth MUNGER (d/o John MUNGER)
2. Lyman	born ca 1788
3. Jemima	born 8 Apr 1790/91 ; married William COVERT
4. Phoebe	born 11 Apr 1792; married John-2 LYON
5. Dr. William	born 1793-94; married Jane WALKER
6. Andrew III	born ca 1797; married Rebecca ____
7. Peter	born 1800-01; 1 married Jemima LYON; 2 married Abigail; and 3 Harriet H __
8. ELIZABETH	born 20 July 1802; died 13 Dec 1879 Armenia Twsp. PA
	married **William-³ MAC INTOSH**
9. Erastus	born ca 1804; married Sarah (Sally) PALMER

Reference the KIFF Section in this book beginning on Page ____

21. MATTHIAS-³ MAC INTOSH, brother of above, was born 23 March 1799 at Northeast, Dutchess County, NY.

He married Sarah (Sally) LOCKWOOD on 8 January 1824 at Kortright, Delaware, NY. She was the daughter of _____ LOCKWOOD and _____, and was born 25 January 1803 Kortright, and died 9 Feb 1882 in Covington, Tioga, PA.

MATTHIAS-³ MAC INTOSH, and his wife, resided in or near Kortright, NY until 1835 when they moved to MC INTOSH Hollow, Tioga County, PA. According to the 1840 Federal Census they were residing in the Town of Sullivan (# 231) Tioga Co., PA. He was listed as an early settler of Ward Township.

Matthias-³, and his brother William, operated a sawmill there from 1853-68. Later he moved to a farm near Covington, where he died 20 Oct 1885.

Children of Matthias-³ MAC INTOSH and Sally LOCKWOOD:
Surname **MAC INTOSH**

78. Angeline	born 27 Mar 1826 Kortright; died 28 Aug 1854 Ward Twsp. PA
79. Ira B.	born 16 Dec 1828 Kortright; died 12 Jan 1830 Kortright, NY EOL
+ **80. HENRY**	born 18 Oct 1830 Kortright; died 13 Apr 1891 Colton,
	St. Lawrence Co., NY
	married Clarissa/Clara DOUGLAS 23 Oct 1864 at Newburyport, MA

MACKINTOSH   MAC INTOSH   MC INTOSH
The Third American Generation

Children of Matthias-[3] MAC INTOSH and Sally LOCKWOOD, continued:
Surname **MAC INTOSH**

	81. Rachel	born 30 Nov 1832 Kortright; died 22 Apr 1874 Ward Twsp, Tioga, PA

   81. Rachel   born 30 Nov 1832 Kortright; died 22 Apr 1874 Ward Twsp, Tioga, PA
   married George MC INTOSH Sep 1854
   (he born ca 1823; died _____; unrelated)

+ **82. FANNY C.**   born 12 Feb 1834 Kortright; died 24 Sep 1897 Alba, Bradford, PA
   married Charles E-[4] KIFF 5 Nov 1854
   (he s/o Erastus-[3] KIFF and Sarah (Sally) PALMER)

+ **83. ANDREW**   born 4 Sep 1836 Ward Twsp, PA; died 20 Dec 1879 W. Covington, PA
   married Ida Ophelia JENNINGS 2 May 1869 Wellsboro, Tioga, PA
   (she born 5 Apr 1851 Covington; died 10 May 1927 Elmira, NY)

   84. James   born 5 July 1839 Ward Twsp; died 28 May 1847 Ward Twsp, PA

   85. Adelbert   born 25 Dec 1842 Ward Twsp.; died 10 May 1862 W. Covington, PA

+ **86. LEWIS**   born 12 Oct 1846 Ward Twsp; died 2 Nov 1936 Mansfield, Tioga, PA
   LOCKWOOD   married Rosa-[8] KLOCK 1 Aug 1872
   (she dau/o Edwin KLOCK and Mary PETRIE)
   (she born 30 June 1855; died 17 May 1927)

References: Descendants of Matthias-[3]; Thomas R. MC INTOSH, Harrisburg, PA; Family records and photos

History of Tioga County, PA   Ward Township

The following article appeared in the paper " The Valley Dollar Saver " Westfield, PA 29 June 1966

" William MC INTOSH, Simon MC INTOSH and Matthias MC INTOSH settled in what is now known as McIntosh Hollow, in the Township of Ward, in the year 1837.

Harry COOVERT settled near them about the same time. James LYON, Andrew KNIFFIN, Erastus KIFF, William R. LYON, Daniel HAGER, John PURVIS, Waterman GATES and others, soon thereafter located in the township. A number of these were from Delaware County, NY.

The first election was held in 1852, at the house of William R. LYON. The first schoolhouse in the township was made of logs. It was located in McIntosh Hollow, and was erected in the year 1838. Erastus KIFF built a sawmill in 1863. A Farmers' Grange was established in the year 1879. The first schools in the township were taught at private houses. Rev. John SPAULDING was the first clergyman who preached in the township.

Among the first teachers were Mary WELSH and Susannah BASCOMB. Mr. WOOD erected a sawmill in Ward, in the year 1844. William MC INTOSH erected one a few years later. There are several religious organizations in the township, but no church edifices. The schoolhouses are used for religious services.

Tracy O. HOLLIS, A.J.TEETER, John KIFF, A.P. GRAY, Miles FURMAN, Stephen SEGAR, Hugh CRAWFORD, H.R. WILCOX are a few of the prominent businessmen and farmers of the township.

It should be borne in mind that Fallbrook was not taken from Ward until Aug 1864. During the Rebellion, Fallbrook and Ward, with a total voting population of 148, furnished either by commutation, substitution or drafted men, 366 persons for the Union Armies."

16

MACKINTOSH   MAC INTOSH   MC INTOSH
The Third American Generation

The following article appeared in the Canton (PA) Independent Sentinel in the year 1910

OUR TOWN KNOWN AS CANTON CORNERS IN 1837
written by Simon L-[4] MC INTOSH

Having been requested to write a short sketch of "Canton Corners" , the name by which our village was first known, I will try to describe it as it appeared over seventy years ago.

My father, with his wife and 5 children, left their home in Delaware County, New York State, and settled on Armenia Mountain, which was then (in 1837) a dark wilderness, inhabited chiefly by wild animals.

Here my father found an old log house which had been deserted by some unlucky earlier settler. Having arranged what few household goods we had in this house, my father (Alexander-[3] Mc I), Alexander CEASE, and myself started out to find Canton Corners. We traveled about a mile through the woods, came to the brow of a mountain, where a dug way led down the mountain side. At the foot of this dug way we found a clearing with an old log house in its center, from which the road led through woods and laurel swamps down the Troy road, which it joined at about where the house of William CHAPMAN now stands. As we approached nearer the Corners, we saw a small old log house standing on what is now ROCKWELL'S Mill, where the weighing scales are now located. Back of this was a well built red mill. Near the rear of the mill was another small wood colored house in which lived ROCKWELL, father of Elias ROCKWELL, grandfather of Jacob ROCKWELL and great grand-father of Robert and George ROCKWELL.

On the south side of Mill Creek was a large, two story frame building, used for a shop, on the west end of which was a large over-shot wheel 16 feet diameter which furnished the power to drive the machinery. Beyond this, as far as the eye could see, and extending down to the main road, were thick heavy woods. This building afterwards converted into a dwelling house, sometimes called the "Bee-Hive" because so many families moved in and swarmed out of it.

Opposite to where the house of Giles COONS now stands, on the east side of Troy Street, was a double log house, used as a schoolhouse. This was the beginning of the educational institutions in our city. It was not quite so convenient as our present school building since the upper grade pupil was obliged to reach the classroom by climbing a ladder, that being the only means of getting into the upper room. The fame of Canton Corners as an educational center was even at this time abroad in the land, and pupils came to this school from what is now called Grover, but which at that time had not yet received a name.

All that section of the town known as Center Street, and where the Methodist Church and schoolhouse now stands, was covered with woods and briars.

The next house on Troy Street at that time was a little old frame house which occupied the space where Mr. Herrick THOMAS' residence now stands, and which was occupied by a Mr. John ROSE. On the spot where T. BURK & Co.'s store now stands was the "Old Red Tavern", and a large barn and stable for stage horses occupied the corner on which the MANLEY block now stands. The proprietor of the "Old Red Tavern" at that time was a Mr. Samuel CUMMINGS. The space occupied by SECRIST & HICKOCK'S law office then held a Blacksmith shop, across the street was KENDALL'S wagon shop.

John GRIFFEN lived in a small house where Mr. WERLINE'S house is now. Further down the street David GRANTIER lived in a frame building on the west side of the street. Mr. GRANTIER also has a sawmill in the ravine just below where the railroad crosses.

Where the BULLOCK Block now stands, John C. ROSE had a small store.

After his death there were no stores in Canton for a year or more, and people went

17

to Troy to trade. Troy being at that time half as large as it is now. Soon after this Barnett WOOD built a little one-horse store which was located about where CLAYTON'S tin shop now is.

Calvin SELLARD had a blacksmith shop about where the Dr. BROOKS residence is now situated.

On the spot occupied by Milton FASSETT"S residence there stood an old dilapidated church, which fell into disuse for public worship. This was repaired and moved to where the present schoolhouse now stands and was used for many years as a schoolhouse.

When the present school building was erected, the old church was moved to its present location on the east side of Center Street. It can be easily recognized by the decoration on the gable which resembles a Lady's fan. Additions have since been added to the original building and it has been converted into a dwelling house. This building, the David GRANTIER house and the "Bee-Hive" must be nearly one hundred years old."

Simon L. MC INTOSH

22. ALEXANDER-³ MAC INTOSH, brother of above, was born 17 Dec 1800 at Delaware County, NY He married Hannah GEROWE/JEROW of Newburgh, Orange County, NY on _____ at _____. She was possibly the daughter of Daniel GEROWE and ____, and was born 1798-1800; died 1881.

Alexander-³ MAC INTOSH and his wife, move to Bradford County, PA when Alexander's father and other family members migrated from New York State. They resided at Union Township, Tioga County, PA. in 1840 (Family #179) and then moved to Canton , Bradford County, PA according to the 1860 Census. Alexander-³ MAC INTOSH died at Canton, PA on 23 March 1899.

Children of Alexander-³ MAC INTOSH and Hannah GEROWE:
Surname **MAC INTOSH**

87. Simon L.	born 14 Sep 1827 Orange Co., NY; died 26 May 1915 Canton, PA
	1 married Elizabeth _____(possibly divorced 1883)
	(she born ca 1835; died _____)
	2 married _____; 3 married Matilda _____
	(she born Feb 1842; died 3 July 1910)

Note: There is no indication that he had any children. The 1900 Census lists him as a Civil War pensioner. He served in Company K, 15th New York Engineers. He is buried at Maple Grove Cemetery, Canton, PA

Obituary for Simon L. MC INTOSH, published in the Towanda (PA) Daily Review 28 May 1915:
" Simon MC INTOSH, known far and wide as " Uncle Simon" died at his home in Spring Brook (Canton) 26 May 1915 at age 88, from old age. He was a pleasant, affable old gentleman, a poet and musical genius of considerable ability and one whose love for children attracted them in large numbers when he made his appearance on the street with his novel musical toys, his drum, guitar and dancing figures , made remarkable by the fact that he was the whole orchestra, made possible by his own mechanical contraption which he managed to play with his feet, hands and mouth. He was a Vet of the Civil War and had an excellent war record, and his death severs one of the last links of Canton present and Canton when the Little Red Tavern was about the only building at Canton Corners. His poems were published in the newspapers and his one on the "First Visit of the Martha Washington", the first steam locomotive to run through Canton, was an excellent effort."

	88. Julia A.	born ca 1830 NY; died ____
+	**89. ABIGAIL WEEKS**	born 10 July 1832, NY; died 13 Jan 1888 Elkland, PA
	"Abbie'	married Perry H. HARDING 7 Oct 1852 Canton, PA
		(he born 29 Nov 1830; died 1884)
		(he s/o Dr. Theodore HARDING and Rosalinda SOPER)
	90. Jonathan	born ca 1835, NY; died _____
	91. Emily C.	born ca 1837-38; died _____ no issue EOL
	"Emma"	married David H. BEARDSLEY
		(he born ca 1831; died _____ ; a carpenter)

The Third American Generation

23. GEORGE-³ MAC INTOSH, brother of above, was born ___ ___ 1803, Delaware County, New York. He married Sarah (Sally) JACQUISH on _____ at _____, NY. She was the daughter of John JACQUISH ++ and Catherine WHEATON, and was born 16 Aug 1801 Kortright, Delaware Co., NY; died 28 Dec 1864. According to the State of New York Census for 1855, George-³ MAC INTOSH was a farmer, his son Theophilus was a printer; and they resided on Federal Hill, Town of Delhi, Delaware County, NY.

George-³ MAC INTOSH died 3 Oct 1877 (age 75) and is buried in Delhi , NY. The will of John JAQUISH of Delhi, NY (dated 9-13-1842) and probated 3-28-1846, mentions a daughter Sarah, wife of George MAC INTOSH. (Delaware (NY) County Wills).

Children of George-³ MAC INTOSH and Sally JACQUISH:
Surname **MAC INTOSH**

+	**92. THEOPHILUS FLETCHER**	born 30 Nov 1829; died 29 Oct 1901 Delhi, NY married Frances Susan KEELER (she born 25 Sep 1833; died 9 Dec 1896) (she dau/o Hon. Stephen KEELER and _____)
	93. Perry H.	born ca 1831; died 1913 CA.; never married EOL <small>Note: A mention in the local paper stated that : Perry H. MAC INTOSH had returned to Delhi from Chico, CA in June 1876 for a visit, after an absence of 22 years</small>
	94. Adelia Ann (Delia)	born 25 Apr 1834; died 1879 Delhi, NY no issue EOL married A. Levander HAGAR 13 Dec 1875 Delaware Co., NY
+	**95. SOPHRONIA**	born 23 May 1837; died ca 1898 Delhi, NY married Joel B. CARPENTER 22 Jan 1867 Delhi Methodist Church
+	**96. OLIVE W.** (twin)	born ca 1839; died _____ married Reuben H. DART 23 Jan 1864 Delhi, NY
	97. Walter O. (twin)	born ca 1839; died 5/15 Mar 1866 Wilborn, FL never married EOL

Note: John-⁵ JACQUISH (John-⁴; ³; Henry-²;¹), father of Sally-⁶ JACQUISH MacIntosh, was born 17 June 1754 and was a native of New Jersey. According to the "Biographical Review- The Leading Citizens of Delaware County, NY:" "He was the son of a French sailor who made visits to the US but never settled in America." That seems unlikely. Mr. JACQUISH spent the early years of his life in NYC , but afterward became an honored resident of Delaware County. In the Revolutionary War he served 7 years 9 months and a day being Orderly Sergeant in General POOR"S Brigade and an active participant in the battles of Monmouth, Saratoga and Yorktown, besides being in many minor engagements. He also served with General SULLIVAN in his campaign against the Indians. "

He married Catherine WHEATON ca 1780, and died 3 Aug 1845. His wife was the daughter of Joseph WHEATON and Margrieta MABEE, and was born 15 Nov 1761; died 8 Sep 1842. John JACQUISH was a harness maker. He applied for and received land grants in Delaware County, NY for his War service, residing in Delhi until his death .

24. SIMON-³ MAC INTOSH, Jr., brother of above, was born 2 March 1809 (gs) at Kortright, Delaware County, New York. He married Esther SUTTON on ____ 1831 at ____, NY. She was the daughter of Samuel SUTTON and Esther BARRETT, and was born 12 Apr 1808 Roxbury, NY; died 10 July 1878 (gs) aged 70 years, 2 months, and 28 days, in Canton, Bradford County, PA.

According to the US Federal Census for 1850, Simon-³ Jr. and Esther resided at Troy, PA and in 1860 he resided at Canton , PA where his occupation was listed as that of a farmer. He died 11 Jul 1887, aged 78 years, 4 months and 9 days. He and his wife are buried in Park Cemetery, Canton, Bradford, PA.

MACKINTOSH   MAC INTOSH   MC INTOSH
The Third American Generation

Children of Simon-[3] MAC INTOSH, Jr. and Esther SUTTON:
Surname **MAC INTOSH**

+   **98. SARAH ADELINE**   born 22 Feb 1833 Delhi, Delaware, NY
            (twin)   married Charles STERLING 15 Apr 1856 at Troy , PA by the
                                              Rev C. MC DOUGAL
                                    (he born 4 Apr 1827, NY; died 31 Dec 1899 Canton, PA)
                                    (he s/o Charles STERLING and Elizabeth TYLER)
                                    died 4 Aug 1865 Susquehanna Depot, PA (age 32-5-23)
                                    buried Park Cemetery, Canton, PA

+   **99. MARY CAROLINE**   born 22 Feb 1833 Delhi, NY; died 17 Sep 1914
            (twin)   married Henry GREENOUGH 2 Jan 1854 at Granville, PA by
                                              the Rev. J. W. BROWN

     100. Clara Wright   born 22 June 1835 Delhi, NY; died 14 Apr 1837 PA   EOL

+   **101. ELIZABETH**   born 28 Nov 1838 Ward Township, Tioga, PA
              JANE   1 married James H. WHITEHEAD 24 May 185_ at Elmira, NY
                                              by the Rev J. W. BROWN
                                    2 married Charles STERLING 16 Apr 1867
                                    died 19 May 1896 Addison, New York; buried Park Cemetery

+   **102. ELECTA**   born 8 Oct 1841 Ward Township. , Tioga, PA; died 9 Jan 1929
              ADELIA   married Silas Newton DANN 10 Jan 1866 at Granville, PA by the
                                              Rev O. C. WILLIS
                                    (he born 28 Mar 1839 Greenfield, Luzerne, PA; died 27 Feb 1894)
                                    (he s/o Harvey DANN and Azuba MC MULLEN)

     103. Isabel Adelaide   born ca 1842-43; died young

+   **104. GEORGE**   born 8 Feb 1844 Ward, PA; died before 1934 Williamsport, PA
        WASHINGTON   married S. Louise WISE 15 Nov 1866 at Newberry, PA by the
                                              Rev. FINNEY
                                    (she born ca 1848; died 1934 Williamsport, PA)
              Note: He was a Civil War veteran, having served with Company M of the 24th New York Cavalry,

     105. John Sutton   born 29 Oct 1847 Canton, PA; died ____

+   **106. CHARLES**   born 20 May 1852, Troy, PA; died _____
          MELVIN   married Emma MELLOR _____; divorced before 1880
                                    (she born 1859 England; died 1923 Canton, PA)

25. JULIA ANN-[3] **MAC INTOSH**, sister of above, was born 15 April 1814 at ____ Delaware County,
NY.   She married Alexander H. CEASE ca 1838. He was the son of _____ CEASE and _____, and was
born 1 Sep 1812 at Delaware County, NY; died 22 March 1891 near McIntosh Hollow, Tioga, PA. He was
accidentally killed while hunting bear. He is buried at the Burton FASSET Cemetery, AKA the Cummings
Cemetery, Armenia Township, Bradford County, PA.

Julia-[3] MAC INTOSH died 26 July 1869 (age 55-3-11). Alexander CEASE married second to a Sarah
Ann _____ on Dec 1869. She was born ca 1813-14, died 10 Sep 1871 (aged 57) . His third wife was a
Betsey ____ (possibly HOLL), born ca 1812 PA ; living at Armenia 1880.

MACKINTOSH   MAC INTOSH   MC INTOSH
The Third American Generation

Children of Julia Ann-[3] MAC INTOSH and Alexander CEASE:
Surname **CEASE**

	107. Sarah C.	born ca 1839; died 3 Apr 1861 (age 22)	EOL

+   **108. JAMES LEROY**   born ca 1841-42; died ____; Civil War veteran
married Amanda MOORE ca 1865
(she born July 1848, PA; died _____)
(she dau/o Harriet-3 KIFF and Israel MOORE)

   109. George S.   born Aug 1846, PA; died 10 July 1861 (14-11-22)   EOL

   110. Fanny Esther   born ca 1848, PA; died ____
married Justice E. BROOKS
(he born ca 1840, PA; died ____)
(he s/o James BROOKS and Mary EASTMAN)
Children: James G-5 born ca 1867, and Betsey-5 BROOKS born ca 1873

+   **111. NELSON PRINCE**   born Feb 1850 PA; died 1921
married Margaret (Mag) EATON
(she born May 1848, PA; died ca 1924)

+   **112. SIDNEY T.**   born 24 Nov 1854 , PA; died 9 Mar 1914 Harbor Springs, MI
married Mary-[5] MAC INTOSH (#253) 15 Sep 1875
(she dau/o Michael-[4] MAC INTOSH and Helen LONGLEY)

   113. Lucy Lillian   born ca 1857-58 , PA; died _____

References: Info on Leroy, George and Nelson CEASE from Lysle CEASE (descendant) Info on Sidney CEASE from Mildred CEASE BOETTGER (dau); other data from Arlayne BOETTGER Lipchinsky (Dec'd) ; Census Data and family bibles

The following is a letter from Herman-[5] CEASE (Sidney T-[4], Alexander-[3,] etc) to his niece , which she received 20 Oct 1945. She was a descendant of both Alexander-[1] MAC INTOSH and Alexander-[1] CEASE.

" The CEASE 'tree' of which you, of course, are a scion, rooted insofar as this country is concerned (began) supposedly in the settlement of Germantown (now PA) in 1732.

Three of our ancestors moved from Harrisburg, PA. shortly after the French and Indian War, up the Susquehannah River and about 125 miles north through the woods just south of the New York State line, three families of them, the MC INTOSH, RANDALL and CEASE families, with only one means of transportation -- an Indian travois (tra' voy). This consisted of a pole attached to the back pad and belly-band of a pony – a pole on each side with the rear end dragging on the ground. Across these poles two beams were attached from pole to pole, on which beams was constructed a crude platform carrying an iron kettle (barrel capacity), a spinning wheel, and a feather bed (prototype of our mattress).

On this conveyance rode (sic ?) my great ___ grandfather, (I never learned how many greats preceded the title) a six weeks old infant in the arms of his mother, who, as a concession to her recent maternity was carried thus. The other two women and balance of cortege walked – with a man with an ax clearing the way – 'swamping a trail' as it was more recently expressed. This ax-man was flanked on either side by another man shouldering a rifle on guard against hostile Indians. (Note: These Indians, the Mohawks, were incited by the British (our present friends ?? and recipients of our largesse) to massacre Americans, who at the time had no wealth to bestow and no delusions as to the propriety of doing as we of their progeny seem to have acquired.

Two of our ancestors, subsequent to that time, reportedly furnished the blood to paint the post – in the massacre on the present site of the town in New York named in commemoration of that occurrence ---- PAINTED POST.

I recall hearing my father (Sidney T. CEASE) – another restless type who lived while he breathed – tell of his father (Alexander) having received a letter from the old country – addressed only to Alexander CEASE, America . He received it after it had traveled – and been opened by mistake several times – over the United States. But it was received in time. Never knew the content, but it was evidently from Germany, containing some inquiry from a relative."

The Third American Generation

28. WILLIAM-³ TANNER, son of Magdalena⁻² MAC INTOSH (Alexander-¹) and Samuel TANNER, was born 4 February 1783 at Pine Plains, Dutchess County, NY. He was called " General " – but this researcher does not know why – it was not for any military service.

He married three times, first to Margaret STREVER ca 1805. She was the daughter of John Adam STREVER and Elizabeth STREVER, and was born 22 Jan 1785; died 15 July 1830, buried at Pine Plains.

His married second wife, Almyra/Almira CARD Finch, on ___ 1832. She was the daughter of ____ CARD and _____, and the widow of James FINCH (1789 – 1831-32). She was born 13 Oct 1791, and died 6 July 1844 (58-8-23) . She is buried at the Winchell Burying Ground, Amenia, NY. (Reference: " Burying Grounds of Sharon, Ct., Amenia & NE, NY ")

His third wife was Elizabeth (Betsey) DAVIS. They were married 15 July 1847 at Pine Plains, the Rev Joseph B. BREED, officiating. Elizabeth/Betsey was born 27 Dec 1799, died 8 Nov 1856 (56-10-13) and is buried at Pine Plains.

William-³ TANNER died 14 Jan 1867 at Ancram, Columbia County, NY and is buried with two of his wives at Pine Plains, NY (Reference: Gravestones of Dutchess County, NY, page 200)

Children of William-³ TANNER and Margaret STREVER:
Surname **TANNER**

+	**114. STREVER**	born 8/18 Aug 1806 Ancram, Columbia County, NY; died 10 Feb 1865 1 married Esther SILVERNAIL 20 Jan 1831 (she born 1 Nov 1801; died 28 Jan 1838) 2 married Elizabeth SHADIC/SHADICK 2 May 1844 (she born 31 Aug 1820, Col. Co.; died 11 Sep 1865 (45-11d) buried Evergreen Cemetery, Pine Plains, Dutchess, NY
+	**115. RACHEL**	born 22 Mar 1808 Ancram; died 8 Oct 1866 married Willis HOAG (resided near Boston Corners, NY) (he born 4 July 1805; died 8 Mar 1867)
+	**116. ELIZA**	born 24 Feb 1810, Ancram, NY; died ____ married Jonathan HEAD
+	**117. LAURA**	born 13 Dec 1812 Ancram, died 3 June 1865 married Adam SILVERNAIL ca 1833-34 resided Valatie, NY (he born 24 Apr 1812; died 25 Mar 1873) (he s/o John SILVERNAIL and Eve HOYSRADT)
	118. Mary Ann	born 8 Mar 1814 Ancram; died 26 Mar 1886 ; buried Pine Plains
+	**119. ELIZABETH** "Betsey "	born 17 July 1816 Ancram; died 15 Jan 1892 married John McArthur SMITH 16 Oct 1845 (he born ca 1817; died 16 Oct 1895) (he s/o Nicholas SMITH and Polly MC ARTHUR) (grandson of John Thiess SMITH, Jr. and Phebe WILSON)
	120. Samuel	born 6 Jan 1819 Ancram; died 30 June 1865; never married buried Evergreen Cemetery, Pine Plains, NY
	121. Emeline	born 13 Feb 1821 Ancram; died 29 Aug 1894; never married

The Third American Generation

Children of William-[3] TANNER and Margaret STREVER, continued:
Surname **TANNER**

+   **122. WILLIAM W.**   born 25 Nov 1822 Ancram; died 4 Oct 1881 (59 yr)
    1 married Hannah Elizabeth STREVER 9 Dec 1855
    (she born 1 Feb 1834; died 15/18 May 1864)
    (she dau/o Uldrick STREVER and Amanda KINNEY)
    2 married Amy E. WHEELER Wallace 3 June 1869
    (she born ca 1848; died 15 Feb 1913) resided Tanner's Station
    buried Evergreen Cemetery, Pine Plains, NY

Child of William-[3] TANNER and Myra CARD Finch:
Surname **TANNER**
    123. Reuben   born 10 Mar 1833 Ancram; died 11 Nov 1837   EOL
    buried Evergreen Cemetery, Pine Plains, NY

Ancestry of William-3 TANNER
William-[1] TANNER was born ca ___ in England, and came to America with two brothers. He first settled along the Susquehannah River and later resided at the " Clove", Dutchess County, NY.

He married Rachel DE LONG on 9 Jan 1740 at Fishkill, NY. She was the daughter of Jan DE LONG and Anna Magdalena WEISER, and was born ____, baptized Mar 1722; died ___. William-[1] TANNER died ca 1785. They were the parents of 4 sons: William-[2]; James-[2]; Reuben-[2] and Samuel-[2] born 4 Apr 1758, who married Magdalena-[2] MAC INTOSH. They were the parents of William-[3] TANNER (above)

William-[1] TANNER also had five daughters: Hannah who married ___ THOMPSON; Margaret who married ___ RADEL; Rachel who married Alexander-[2] MAC INTOSH; Martha who married ___ THOMAS; and Maribe(th) who married ____ THOMPSON.

The Commemorative Biographical Record for Dutchess County (NY) page 800, lists Samuel J. TANNER born ca 1845 and stating that " he belongs to one of the pioneer families of the county. His great grandfather having been one of the early settlers of the Town of Dover. It further states " the great grandfather, believed to be William TANNER – was a native of England, and that while serving in the British Army was captured by the Spaniards and would have starved to death had it not been for the kindness of the Spanish women."

30. ALEXANDER-[3] TANNER, brother of above, was born 20 Feb 1785 at Pine Plains, Dutchess County, NY. He had a twin sister Margaret.

He married Nancy E/C MERRITT on _____. She was the daughter of _____ MERRITT and _____, and was born 13 July 1786 ; died 19 Mar 1856. Alexander-[3] TANNER died 9 Aug 1841.

Children of Alexander-[3] TANNER and Nancy MERRITT:
Surname **TANNER**

+   **124. OLIVE EMELINE**   born ca 1811; died ____
    married Dr. Stephen PLATNER 10 Mar 1831 at the Reformed Church
                                   Claverack, NY

+   **125. SAMUEL A.**   born ca 1815 Copake, NY; died 19 Mar 1856
    married Maria-[5] ROCKEFELLER
    (she born 10 Sep 1829 Copake; died _____)
    (she dau/o William-[4] ROCKEFELLER and Charity MC DONALD)
    William-[4] ROCKFELLER s/o Diell/Teal-[3] ; William/Wilhelm-[2]; Johan Thiel -[1] ROCKEFELLER)

Reference: ROCKEFELLER Genealogy, published 1910, Vol 1-3.

32. JOHN-[3] TANNER, brother of above, was born 6 March 1788 at Pine Plains, Dutchess County, New York. His first marriage was to Olive MERRITT on __ ___ 1813. She was the daughter of _____ MERRITT and ____ of Stephentown, Rennsalaer County, NY, and was born ca 1787; died 11 Sep 1822.

He married second to Mrs. Christina FINGAR Mosher ca 1824 at Copake, NY. She was the daughter of Johannes FINGAR and Tysje DEKKER, and the widow of _____ MOSHER. She was born 21 Mar 1798; died 3 Apr 1870.

John-[3] TANNER shared a farm with his brother Alexander in the western part of Taghkanic . He later moved from the "lake" farm, leaving its operations to his daughter Nancy Alma and her husband Jeremiah SIMMONS. The farm was still in the family in 1937, his grandson Henry -5 TANNER was residing there. John-[3] TANNER died 29 Jan 1869 Taghkanic, Columbia County, NY

Children of John-[3] TANNER and Olive MERRITT:
Surname **TANNER**

	126. Un-named infant	born ca 1814-15; died young
+	**127. NANCY ALMA** 'Almy"	born 15 Mar 1816 Taghkanic, NY ; died there 2 Dec 1870 married Jeremiah SIMMONS (he born ca 1807; died 27 Aug 1888)
+	**128. SALLY ANN**	born 13 Oct 1817; died 17 Mar 1869 married James YORKER resided Copake, NY
	129. Rachel	born 14 Oct 1820; died 8 March 1865; never married

Children of John-[3] TANNER and Christina FINGAR Mosher:
Surname **TANNER**

	130. Olive E.	born 7 March 1824; died ____ married Socrates VALENTINE ca ___ (he of Auburn, Cayuga, NY) (he born 1823; died _____) a brick mason Child: George-[5] VALENTINE born ca ____
+	**131. JANE MARGARET**	born 7 Apr 1825; died _____ resided Hillsdale, NY married David SHULTS/SHULTIS/SHULTIES 15 Nov 1853
+	**132. AMBROSE**	born 27 Nov 1828; died 4 March 1905 (76) 1 married Jane Catherine SHADIC 12 Feb 1863 (she born _____; died 2 Nov 1873) 2 married Georgia Anna L. SILVERNAIL ca 1879 (she born 12 Nov 1849; died 25 Oct 1881) 3 married Locelia STREVER 17 Oct 1883 resided Copake, NY (she dau/o James M. STREVER and Loretta ____) (she born 25 Dec 1844; died ____ (still living 1920)
	133. William / John Wm.	born 21 Jan 1832; died Jan 1863; never married EOL
+	**134. ALEXANDER**	born 2 Oct 1833; married Vera Margaret LYALL
	135. James Monroe	born 30 June 1836; died young EOL
	136. Reuben C.	born 2 Apr 1837; died 20 June 1862; never married EOL
+	**137. CATHERINE MELINDA (Kate)**	born 12 Sep 1841 married Friend SIMONS resided Hillsdale, NY

24

The Third American Generation

33. MARY MAGDALENA-[3] TANNER, daughter of Rachel[-2] MAC INTOSH (Alexander[-1]) and Samuel TANNER, was born 2 Nov 1790 at Pine Plains, Dutchess County, NY.

She married William T. WOOLDRIDGE on ____18__ . He was the son of John WOOLDRIDGE and ____, and was born ca 1790, died 26 May 1872. He was a farmer. Mary Magdalena-[3] TANNER died 1 July 1864.

Children of Mary Magdalena-[3] TANNER and William T. WOOLDRIDGE:
Surname **WOOLDRIDGE**

+	**138. PHILO**	born 8 Feb 1816, NY; died 6 May 1891; a carpenter
		married Gertrude DYKEMAN ca ____
		(she born Feb 1827; died ____) resided Pine Plains, NY
	139. Clarissa	born 24 Oct 1817; died 2 Jul 1846; buried Bethel Cemetery, NY
		married Freeman P. SIBLEY
+	**140. HARRIET**	born 10 July 1820 NY; died 18 Oct 1870; resided Pine Plains
		married James MC CARRICK ca ____
		(he born ca 1815; died 2 June 1872)
	141. William	born ca 182_, NY; died ____
+	**142. MARY JANE**	born 12 Nov 1827; married Joel W. KELSEY
		(he born ca 1820 ME; died ____)

34. JAMES-[3] TANNER, brother of above, was born 12 January 1795 at Pine Plains, Dutchess County, NY. He was the twin brother of Reuben-[3] TANNER (# 35). He married first to Annis/Anna WELLS/WALES ca 1813-14. She was the daughter of _____ WELLS/WALES and ____, and was born ca _____ Scotland, died 11 May 1849 and is buried in Ancram Free Cemetery.

He married his second wife, Catharine/Kate BURGER ca ____. She was the daughter of _____ BURGER and ____, and was born ca 1791-2 NY; died ____. His third wife was Sally KIPP. James-[3] TANNER died 11 Feb 1877, and is buried at Ancram Free Cemetery, Columbia County, NY.

Children of James-[3] TANNER and Anna/Annis WELLS/WALES:
Surname **TANNER**

+	**143. JOHN J.**	born ca 1815-16; died 22 Sep 1896
		married Caroline HAWVER ca ____
		(she born ca 1815; died 1897) both buried Ancram Union Cemetery
	144. Mary Ann	born ca 1820 NY; died ____
		married George S. SNYDER 11 March 1836 at the Reformed Church
		Claverack, NY
+	**145. OLIVE EMELINE**	born ca 1824; married Reuben LOOMIS
		(he s/o John R. LOOMIS and Mary BELCHER) (he born ca 1818 NY
	146. Samuel	born ca 1826; died ____ ; never married EOL
+	**147. MORRIS**	born 19 Dec 1827; died ____
		married Lucinda Diane COLEPAUGH 23 Jan 1847
	148. Sarah	born ca ____ ; married Peter RUSH; resided Penn Yan, NY
		Child: Annis-[5] BUSH born ca ____
	149. William	born ca ____ ; died ____
+	**150. JAMES**	born ca 1832 ; died ____
		1 married Sarah HUMMEL ca ____
		2 married Rachel _____
	151. Eliza	born ca _ 1833 /34/; died ____; according to the 1850 Census
		she was living with Ambrose LOOMIS
	152. Annis	born 1836; died ____ ; married ____ KNICKERBOCKER
		Children: Eugene-[5] born ca ____ and Ida-[5] KNICKERBOCKER

35. REUBEN L-[3] TANNER, brother of above, was born 12 January 1795 at Pine Plains, Dutchess County, New York. He married Lydia RICHTER/REIGHTER on Wednesday 21 January 1824 at Dutchess County, NY. The marriage ceremony was performed by the Rev Mr. PRICE. Both the bride and groom resided at Northeast, Dutchess , County, NY. Lydia was the daughter of ____ RICHTER/REIGHTER and _____, and was born ca 1800 NY; died ____. Reuben-[3] TANNER died 3 May 1849.

Children of Reuben-[3] TANNER and Lydia RICHTER:
Surname **TANNER**

153. Mary	born ca _____, died _____	
	married William BROOKSBY of Hudson, NY	
	Child: William-[5] BROOKSBY born ca ____	
154. Caroline	born ca 1829-30 NY; married John TEAL no issue	EOL
	(he born ca 1809; died _____; a shoemaker) res. Hudson, Col., Co.	
155. William	born ca 1838 NY; died ____; never married	EOL

36. CLARISSA-[3] TANNER, sister of above, was born 16 January 1797 at Pine Plains, Dutchess County, New York. She married Adam A. STREVER, a farmer, ca 1819. He was the son of John Adam STREVER and Elizabeth STREVER, and was born 24 Nov 1793 at Pine Plains; died 14 July 1866 (72-7-20). Clarissa-[3] TANNER died 4 Dec 1877 (80-10-18). They are both buried at the Evergreen Cemetery, Pine Plains, N Y.

Children of Clarissa-[3] TANNER and Adam STREVER:
Surname **STREVER**

156. Rachel	born 1 Oct 1820 Ancram; died 2 Aug 1882; never married	EOL
+ **157. SYLVESTER**	born 29 March 1822 Ancram,NY; died 18 Jan 1902 (79-10-11)	
	1 married Phebe SHELDON (she born ca 1833; died 14 Feb 1870)	
	2 married Matilda J. SHELDON (she born 1834 ; died 24 Aug 1895)	
	buried Evergreen Cemetery, Pine Plains, NY	
158. Clara	born ca _____; died before 1850 NY	
159. Benjamin A.	born 19 June 1830 Ancram; died _____	
	married Amelia J. COLLIER 26 Dec 1855	
	Children: Frederick Henry-[5] born ca 1861; died 1945 and Rachel Tanner-[5] STREVER born 17 Nov 1865.	

37. ANTHONY-[3] TANNER, brother of above, was born 13 August 1799 at Pine Plains, Dutchess County, NY. He married first to Catherine SIMMONS on ___ at ____. She was the daughter of David SIMMONS (1772-1854) and Margaret VAN DEUSEN (1777-1849), and was born 30 Jan 1802; died 3 Feb 1834 (32yr. 4 da.), possibly from childbirth.. Anthony-3 TANNER married second to Mary Eliza SIMMONS Call. She was born ca 1798-99 NY; died _____. Anthony-[3] died 14 Jan 1877 and is buried at the Knickerbocker Ground # 101.

Children of Anthony-[3] TANNER and Catherine SIMMONS:
Surname **TANNER**

160. Sylvester (twin)	born 16 May 1828 NY; died 8 Nov 1844 (age 16)	EOL
161. Samuel (twin)	born 16 May 1828 NY; died 19 Feb 1830 (1-9-3)	EOL
162. Henry W.	born ca Feb 1834; died 7 Sep 1855 (age 21)	EOL

Children of Anthony-[3] TANNER and Mary SIMMONS Call:
Surname **TANNER**

163. Philo	born ca 1837 NY; married Rosie THOMPSON
	Child: Frances Cora-[5] TANNER born ca ___; married Robert SWART
164. Elizabeth/Eliza	born ca 1840; married Lawrence CROUSE
	Child : Julia-[5] CROUSE born ca 1867)

38. HENRY -³ TANNER, brother of above, was born 9 Nov 1801 at Pine Plains, Dutchess County, NY. His first marriage was to Eliza-⁷ HINSDALE on ____. She was the daughter of Whiting⁻⁶ HINSDALE and possibly Amy RIGGS, and was born ____; died before 1833. He married second to Catherine SNYDER Shadic(k) on ____. She was the daughter of William P. SNYDER and Barbara KLAPPER, and the widow of _____ SHADIC(K), and was born 9 Aug 1802/12 at _____, NY.

Child of Henry-³ TANNER and Eliza HINSDALE;
Surname **TANNER**

         165. Whiting Hinsdale   born ca 1831, NY; died ____
                                  married Catherine E. _____; (she born ca 1830; died ____)
                  Children: Louisa Adda⁻⁵ born ca 1860 and George H⁻⁵ TANNER born ca 1862

Children of Henry-³ TANNER and Catherine SNYDER:
Surname **TANNER**

+   **166. CLARISSA**   born ca 1833 NY; died _____; resided Taghkanic, NY
                                 married Henry FRISS 12 Oct 1853 at the Reformed Church
                                                      Claverack, New York
                                 (he s/o Jacob FRISS and Anna Maria STREVER)

         167. Sarah   born ca 1835 NY; died _____
                                 1 married Henry ____; 2 married Ephraim MILLER 26 Feb 1882
                                 (he s/o Samuel MILLER and Marie SHUFELT)

+   **168. PETER**   born ca 1838-39 NY; died _____
                                 married Ann MEYERS; resided family homestead Churchtown, NY

+   **169. HIRAM**   born ca 1840-41; died _____
                                 married Anna HOAG 19 Sep 1866 Reformed Church, Claverack
                                 (she born ca 1846; died ____)
                   Children: Delbert⁻⁵ born ca 1868 and Henry S⁻⁵ TANNER born ca 1871

+   **170. LOUISA/LOUISE**   born ca Nov 1841 NY; died bet. 1920-30
                                 married James Lawrence BASHFORD ca 1872

+   **171. STEPHEN H.**   born June 1848 NY; died ____
                                 married Anna/ Annie E. TEATOR resided Taghkanic, NY
                                 (she born June 1859; died ____)

39. SAMUEL S-³ TANNER, brother of above, was born 6 August 1804 at Dutchess County, New York. His first marriage was to Fannie STREVER on 16 Jan 1834. She was the daughter of _____ STREVER and _____, and was born 14 July 1807; died 9 Oct 1835 and is buried in the private Henry R. HOYSRADT Farm Cemetery, at Ancram, Columbia County, NY.

He married second to Mary Betsey/ Elizabeth LOWN on 17 Nov 1838 at _____. She was the daughter of _____ LOWN and ____, and was born 2 March 1814; died 30 Nov 1846 (32-8-28). She is buried at the Bethel Cemetery.
His third wife was Julia P. SHELDON. They married on 15 Nov 1847. She was the daughter of ____ SHELDON and ____, and was born ca 1824/26 NY; died _____. Samuel-³ TANNER, a farmer, died 7 Feb 1891.

Children of Samuel S-³ TANNER and Mary Betsey LOWN:
Surname **TANNER**

         172. William H.   born 22 Oct 1840; married Mary Ann MILLER Apr 1864
+   **173. FRANCES**   born 29 March 1842 NY; married Henry PALMER
+   **174. MARY**   born 28 March 1844 NY; died _____
                                 married Jonathan/John HEAD, Jr. 15 Mar 1875 (# 383)
                                 (he s/o Eliza-³ TANNER (# 116) and Jonathan HEAD)
                                 resided near Boston Corners, NY

Children of Samuel S-[3] TANNER and Mary Betsey LOWN:
Surname **TANNER**

175. Samuel J.	born 24 Oct 1845 NY; died ____	
	married Fannie E. VAN AUKEN 28 Nov 1894 (she of Poughkeepsie)	
	Child: Charles[6] TANNER born Nov 1895	

Children of Samuel S-[3] TANNER and Julia SHELDON:
Surname **TANNER**

+	**176. ELIZABETH**	born 4 Nov 1848 NY; died _____	
		married Samuel TITUS 17 Mar 1868; resided Stanford, NY	
	177. George	born 8 Nov 1851; died _____	
	178. Julia A.	born 22 July 1857 ; died _____; never married	EOL

40. MORRIS-[3] TANNER, brother of above, was born 6 Apr 1807 at Pine Plains, Dutchess County, NY. He married Sally Ann SNYDER on 24 November 1832 at the Reformed Church, Claverack, NY. She was the daughter of _____ SNYDER and ____, and was born Mar 1813 NY; died 1901. Morris-[3] TANNER, a boot and shoe maker, resided Taghkanic, and Claverack, Dutchess County, NY., and died 30 Dec 1877 at Churchtowm, Columbia County, NT.

Children of Morris-[3] TANNER and Sally Ann SNYDER:
Surname **TANNER**

+	**179. MARY ANN**	born 1 Jan 1834 NY; died 10 Mar 1875	
		married Jacob MILLER after 1860	
	180. Catherine	born ca 1837 NY; died _____	
	181. Washington	born Mar 1839 NY; died 1915; never married	EOL
	182. Peter M.	born 2 Dec 1840/41; died 1907	
		married Margaretha TANNER 17 Jan 1872 resided Claverack	
		(she dau/o Strever TANNER and Elizabeth SILVERNAIL)	
		(she born Dec 1834; died ____) (# 367)	
	183. Adaline	born ca 1843 NY; died ____	
+	**184. CHRISTINA**	born ca 1847 NY; died 1927	
		married Freeman B. MILLER	
		(he born 1844; died 1911)	
	185. William	born May 1850 NY; died 29 Jul 1901	
		1 married Marietta/Etta SILVERNAIL	
		(she dau/o Norman SILVERNAIL and Catherine CLARK)	
		(she born ca 1865; died _____)	
		2 married Charity FRISS 1886	
	186. Augusta	born ca 1853 Claverack, NY; died	
	187. Herbert	born ca 1856	

MACKINTOSH   MAC INTOSH   MC INTOSH

The Fourth American Generation

47. MARY-[4] CALDWELL, daughter of Claracy/ Clara-[3] MAC INTOSH (Simon-[2]; Alexander-[1]) and Samuel CALDWELL, was born __ ___ 1823 at _____ New York. She married James MC DONALD, a carpenter, on ___ 18__. He was the son of ____ MC DONALD and ____, and was born ca 1823 MN; died 28 May 1894. Mary-[4] died _____. They are buried at _____.

Children of Mary-[4] CALDWELL and James MC DONALD:
Surname **MC DONALD**

+	**188. MARY E.**	born 2 Oct 1849 Brooklyn, NY; died 2 June 1922
		married Horace N. SCOTT 14 Dec 1870 Canton, Bradford, PA.
		(he born 13 Sep 1837 Troy Twsp. PA; died 31 Dec 1916)
+	**189. GEORGE W.**	born June 1855 PA; died _____
		married Jane D. _____ ca 1880
	190. Samuel	born ca 1857; died ca 1893; never married EOL
	191. James	born ca 1859; died _____
+	**192. CLARA**	born __ ___ 1861, PA; died 13 Sep 1938 Queens Village, LI, NY
		married William Tyler-[5] STERLING 21 Apr 1887
		(he s/o Sarah Adeline-[4] MC INTOSH and Charles STERLING)
		(he born 2 Feb 1862; died 2 Feb 1955) (# 327)
	193. Anna	born ca 1863 PA.; died _____
	194. Willie	born ca 1868 PA., died _____

References: Addie WATTS Crawford; Sterling family records, Census records

50. RULUF CRANE-[4] MAC INTOSH, son of Jonathan-[3] MAC INTOSH (Simon-[2]; Alexander-[1]) and Anise CRAIN/CRANE, was born 23 Aug 1820 at _____, New York. He married Helen Theodosia MOREY on __ Feb 1847 at ____. She was the daughter of ____ MOREY and _____, and was born 1828 NY, died ____.

Ruluf C-[4] MAC INTOSH purchased land in Lake County, Illinois on 4 Feb 1846. It contained 80+ acres and was located in the 3rd PM Meridian, Township 46-N, Range 9-E, Section 9. At that time he was living in McHenry County, IL. Nothing further is known about his wife, but it is known that his daughter Amelia went to CA. at a later date, via the Isthmus of Panama.

Ruluf-[4] MAC INTOSH went to California in 1849 and originally settled in Woodbridge, San Joaquin County, just outside Lodi. Reportedly, he went West, leaving his wife, son and unborn daughter, to look for his father, Jonathan, and found him in Virginia City, NV. The 1880 Census stated that Jonathan-[3] owned a saloon in Virginia City, Storey, Nevada, and listed Ruluf-[4], a widower, as also keeping a saloon there. Ruluf-[4] died ca 1896 at Knights Landing, Stanislaw, CA.

Children of Ruluf-[4] MAC INTOSH and Helen MOREY:
Surname **MAC INTOSH**

+	**195. EDWIN ALBERT**	born 19 March 1848 IL
		married Mary E. ROBINSON 1 Dec 1887
		(she born Jan 1861 CA; died _____)
	196. Amelia J. (Julia)	born 21 Mar 1850 IL; died _____
		married Dr. W. B. PORTER Nov 1882
		(1900 resided CA with brother)(she listed as a widow)

52. GEORGE SIMON-⁴ MAC INTOSH, brother of above, was born 25 June 1823 at McGrawville, Cortland County, NY. He married first to Sarah Ann PATTERSON on 9 Nov 1859. She was the daughter of _____ PATTERSON and Anna CARPENTER, and was born 11 June 1832; died 1/3 Nov 1874.

George-⁴ MAC INTOSH married second to Addie PATTERSON on ____. It is not known whether she was a relative of his first wife, or the widow of a PATTERSON. She was born ____; died ca 1894. No issue from that union. George Simon-⁴ MAC INTOSH died 23 Oct 1884 at Olean, NY.

Children of George Simon -⁴ MAC INTOSH and Sarah PATTERSON:
Surname **MAC INTOSH**

	197. Un-named infant	born and died Aug 1860	
+	**198. WILLIAM P.**	born 21 Nov 1861; died _____ Memphis, TN	
		married Margaret C. LOUGHLIN 8 Jan 1885 Olean, NY	
	199. Georgia	born 25 Dec 1863; died Aug 1910; teacher Westfield, NJ	EOL
	200. Sara	born 28 Aug 1865; died _____; resided CA	
+	**201. ANNA BELLE**	born 6 Nov 1870 NY; died _____ NJ	
		married Dr. Frederick Adrian KINCH of NJ	
		(resided 267 E. Broad St., Westfield, NJ)	
	202. Frank	born 26 Oct 1874; died 25 July 1875 Olean, NY	EOL

53. MARIETTE / MARYETTE-⁴ MAC INTOSH, sister of above, was born 23 Sep 1824 at Cortland County, NY. She married Alexander CHASE on ____ at _____. He was the son of Orrin CHASE and Sophia DILLINGHAM and was born ca 1823 Great Valley, Cattaraugus, NY; died ____ MI.

They resided at Humphrey, Cattaraugus County, NY. Marriette-4 MAC INTOSH died there 1896.
On the 1860 Census, Marriette-⁴ had Edwin A-⁵ and Amelia J-⁵ children of Ruluf-⁴, residing with them.

Children of Mariette-⁴ MAC INTOSH and Alexander CHASE:
Surname **CHASE**

	203. Orrin H.	born __ ___ 1848; married Nancy _____
	(Child: Edwin-⁶ CHASE born ca 1869)	
+	**204. JONATHAN E.**	born Aug 1849; died 18 Aug 1920
		married Charlene/Cherlena M. BARNETT
		(she dau/o E. S. BARNETT and Sarah A ____)
		(she born May 1855 CT.; died _____)
+	**205. ADALINE M.**	born ca 1851; married John W. BIGGS
	206 Annis S.	born ca 1853
	207. Clara/Carrie B.	born ca 1857
+	**208. RULUF A.**	born 10 Mar 1859 NY; died 7 Feb 1949 Los Angeles, CA

54. EDWIN JONATHAN-⁴ MAC INTOSH, brother of above, was born 6 Nov 1826 at Homer, Cortland County, NY. He left home at the age of 17 (1842) and went to Ontario County, NY where he became a blacksmith. In 1857 he enlisted in the Army --- the 10th Infantry, and was discharged in 1858. He then went to Ohio and later to New Orleans, LA. where he enlisted in Company C. of the 4ᵗʰ Artillery. He spent a year in Florida and then returned back to New York State. In 1861 he went to Fort Sumter , and helped raise the first flag there. He was a commissary and quartermaster sergeant – holding that rank for 4 years. He was in Mexico during the War, stationed on the Rio Grande at Mere. He drew a pension and was discharged in 1864. Afterwards, he moved to California.

His was married to his first wife, Melancy D. MINOR, on 9 Feb 1862 at Woodbridge, CA. The ceremony was performed at the residence of J.M. BURT by the Rev Colin ANDERSON.. She was the daughter of _____ MINOR and _____, and was born 5 Jan 1835 South Lee, MA; died 24 July 1871at Woodbridge, CA.

probably in childbirth or as a result of it. His second wife was Lydia BLAKESLEE. They married July 1876. She was the daughter of_____ BLAKESLEE and ____, and was born ca 1838 NY; died ____. Edwin J-4 MAC INTOSH died of pneumonia on 19 April 1909 at Li, in the San Joaquin Valley of CA. He and his second wife are buried at The Masonic Cemetery at Woodbridge, CA. Note: Edwin Jonathan[4] MC INTOSH was a member of the CA State Assembly from 1880-81; and he was also a member of the Freemasons.

Children of Edwin Jonathan[-4] MAC INTOSH and Melancy D. MINOR:
Surname **MAC INTOSH**

209. Thomas B.	born Sep 1869 CA ; died 1931	
	married Katherine M./ Mary Katherine _____	
	(she born 1863 Canada, immigrated 1881; naturalized 1895)	
	Children: Ila U[-6] born Mar 1897, died 1925 ; and Josie [-6] MAC INTOSH born ____)	
210. Melancy A.	born 15 July 1871 CA; died 29 Dec 1945 San Francisco, CA	
	married _____ KENNEDY/ KENNEY	
	Children: Emma[-6] born ca 1900 and William[-6] KENNEDY?KENNEY born 1902	
	References: Stockton (CA) Daily Independent 26 Feb 1862 and 31 July 1871. Family data and Census info	

56. SILVERTUS DARWIN-[4] MC INTOSH, brother of above, was born 13 May 1831 at Homer, Cortland County, New York. He married Susan Cornelia PRATT on 5 Jan 1861 at ____, NY. She was the daughter of Rollin PRATT and Susan EVARTS, and was born Jan 1839; died Jan 1914. Silvertus[-4] MC INTOSH died 8 Jan 1886 at Allegany, Cattaraugus County, NY. (Note: One source has Silvertus middle name as DeForest and Susan Cornelia's surname as EVERETTS)

Silvertus MC INTOSH served aboard the US PAW PAW, a wooden center-wheel steamer originally named ST. CHARLES , and purchased by the US Navy at Chicago, IL 9 Apr 1863, then converted into a "tinclad" gunboat.. It was re-named the US PAW PAW 12 May 1863, also designated as gunboat # 31, with Acting Master Augustus THOMPSON in command.

The PAW PAW patrolled the upper Mississippi protecting Union communication and supply bases from guerilla attacks. Gen. William Tecumseh SHERMAN , in acknowledging the arrival of gunboats stated " Of course we will get along together elegantly, all I have (Lt. Cmdr. S L Phelps, senior Naval Officer on the Tenn. River) he can command, and I know the same feeling pervades every sailor's and soldier's heart. We are as one. " The joint effort solidified the Union's position and helped prepare for SHERMAN's march to the sea. The PAW PAW remained active until the end of the Civil War, and helped maintain control of the vast river system.

Children of Silvertus Darwin[-4] MC INTOSH and Susan Cornelia PRATT:
Surname **MC INTOSH**

	211. Salina G. (f)	born ca 1863 NY; died 1871
+	**212. ADDIE**	born 16 Oct 1864 NY; died 30 Oct 1935 Bradford Co., PA
	CORNELIA	married Myron D. JOHNSON 8 Dec 1883
		(he born 4 Apr 1864 NY; died 31 Dec 1916 Bradford, McKean, PA)
		(he s/o Stephen Titus JOHNSON and Achsah Eunice BEALS)
+	**213. ANNIS S.**	born 1 Mar 1867 Humphrey, Cattaraugus, NY; died 23 Aug 1948
		1 married John Allen PARKER 25 Jan 1885 Great Valley, NY
		(he born ca 1864; died 1897)
		2 married John R. COWAN ca 1905
		(he born ca 1867, died _____)
	214. John Edwin	born 10 Nov 1871; died 23 May 1913 Allegany, NY
		married Evelyn BRINK
+	**215. ELIZABETH**	born 6 Oct 1875; died 29 Oct 1960 Allegany, NY
	CLARA	married Edgar Hardin BURLINGAME ca 1891 / 92
+	**216. LILLIE FIDELIA**	born 7 Apr 1878; died 12 Mar 1930 Bradford Co., PA
	(Lily)	married Charles Henry FIELD, Jr. 23 Jan 1907 Allegany, NY
	217. Grace Urbana	born 19 May 1880; died 9 Oct 1963 Springville, NY
		married Stephen Darwin BARBER
		(he born 13 April 1879; died 5 Jan 1939 Olean, Cattaraugus, NY)
		(he s/o Lysander Leroy BARBER and Louise Adelphia RUSSELL)

Children of Silvertus[4] Darwin MC INTOSH and Susan Cornelia PRATT, continued:
Surname **MC INTOSH**

218. Judson Rollin	born 9 July 1882; died 12 April 1913; married Frances BARBER	
	(she dau/o Lysander Leroy BARBER and his 3rd wife Emma ADELL	
	(she born 31 Aug 1888; died Oct 1918 Olean, NY)	

Children: Cornelia-[6] born ca 1910; died 1988; Nelson E-[6] born 1911, died 1919; and John E-[6] MC INTOSH born ca 1913, died 25 Oct 1985.   These children were living with their aunt Grace Barber (**#217**) in 1920 at Cory Ward, Erie, PA

58. SARAH-[4] (Sally) MAC INTOSH, sister of above, was born 29 October 1834 at Cortland, County, NY. She married George REYNOLDS before 1857. He was the son of _____ REYNOLDS and _____, and was born Apr 1833 NY; died 1913. They resided (1880) Humphrey Town, Cattaraugus County, NY. Sarah-[4] MAC INTOSH died 1904.

Children of Sarah-[4] MAC INTOSH and George REYNOLDS:
Surname **REYNOLDS**   (all children born Cattaraugus County, NY)

219. George	born ca 1857	
+ **220. DENNIS G.**	born Oct 1859; died 1954; married Luna BELLAMY ca 1880	
221. Elmer E.	born Mar 1862; died _____	
	married May C. _____ 1899 (she born June 1880 Canada)	
	(resided Franklinville, Cattaraugus County, NY)	
	Children: Helen M-[6] born ca 1901 and Forland-[6] REYNOLDS born ca 1905 NY	
222. Alton	born ca 1864; died young	EOL
223. Rettie (f)	born ca 1868; died young	EOL
224. Jennie	born ca 1871; not on 1880 Census; possibly died young	EOL
+ **225. CORA B.**	born 26 Sep 1873 ; died _____	
	married Thomas G. MC WILLIAMS ca 1896; (he born 27 July 1872)	

59. WILLIAM ARTHUR-[4] MAC INTOSH, son of Henry-[3] MAC INTOSH (Simon-[2]; Alexander-[1]) and Mary Ann SMITH, was born 16 April 1817/18 at _____ Delaware County, New York. He married Catherine E. BURNSIDE on ___18__ at _____. She was the daughter of _____ BURNSIDE and _____, and was born ca 1822 Delaware Co., NY; died 29 July 1895. William-[4] MAC INTOSH, a farmer, died 16 Dec 1900 at Washington, DC. He and his wife are buried at Bloomville, Delaware Co., NY

Children of William A-[4] MAC INTOSH and Catherine BURNSIDE:
Surname **MAC INTOSH**

+ **226. JAMES H.**	born 4 Apr 1845 Del. Co., NY.; died 23 June 1926 Washington, DC
	married Lucy Amanda DALES 1870 (she from Kortright, Del., NY)
	(she born ca 1850 NY;(she dau/o Orrin DALES and Angeline _____)
+ **227. WILLIAM**	born 10 May 1850 Bloomville, NY; died 31 Oct 1939 NY
ARTHUR	married Sarah Eliza MC INTYRE /MC INTIRE Oct 1875
	(she born 27 Apr 1851; died 18 Sep 1939)
228. John Burnside	born 9 Dec 1856; died 15 Jan 1857; buried Bloomville, NY

60. EMELINE-[4] MAC INTOSH, sister of above, was born 7 Nov 1821 at Delaware County, NY. She married John BURNSIDE, brother of Catherine (above) , born 9 May 1816, died 17 May 1851. She married second to Francis FULLER, a widower. He was the son of _____ FULLER and _____, and was born 24 July 1827; died 31 July 1885 Bloomville, NY. (Francis FULLER married first to Elizabeth A._____, and had a son Stephen FULLER born ca May 1850) Emeline-[4] MAC INTOSH died 11 Dec 1893 at Bloomville, and is buried in the Bloomville Cemetery

MACKINTOSH   MAC INTOSH   MC INTOSH
The Fourth American Generation

Children of Emeline-[4] MAC INTOSH and John BURNSIDE:
Surname **BURNSIDE**

+	**229. MARY ANN**	born ca 1847 NY; died Apr 1928 ; buried Riverside Cemetery
		married John Eaton POWELL
		(he born ca 1843 NY; died 7 June 1925 (82))
		(he s/o John POWELL and Hettie ____)
	230. Un-named twins	born before 1851; died in infancy

62. CAROLINE-[4] MAC INTOSH, daughter of William-[3] MAC INTOSH (Simon-[2;] Alexander-[1]) and Elizabeth KIFF, was born 22 Aug 1821 at Kortright, Delaware County, NY. She married Lewis P. WILLIAMS on 3 Dec 1839 at ____. He was the son of David WILLIAMS ++ and Rachel HAYDEN, and was born 29 Jan 1816 PA; died 3 Nov 1885 PA. Caroline-[4] MAC INTOSH died 9 July 1858 at Canton Township, Bradford County, PA. She and her husband are buried at the cemetery in Alba, Bradford County, PA.
++ David WILLIAMS was born ca 1783 in Wales. It is reported that he came to America to avoid military service. He first resided in troy, PA (1812). His wife, Rachel HAYDEN was born ca 1790; died 29 Mar 1865. David WILLIAMS died 10 Feb 1849 at Alba, PA.

Children of Caroline-[4] MAC INTOSH and Lewis P. WILLIAMS:
Surname **WILLIAMS**

+	**231. MARY ELIZABETH**	born 6 Feb 1842 PA; died 2 Feb 1923 New Castle, IN
		married Gilbert MC NAUGHT
		(he born ca 1837 Granville, PA; died 1 Feb 1895 New Castle, IN)
+	**232. JANE H.**	born ca 1842 PA; died Mar 1883; married Erskine PACKARD
		(he born 1836 Wellsboro, PA; died ____)
+	**233. LUCY**	born ca 1844 PA.; married Clark MC MAHON
		(he born ca 1843 Williamsport, PA; died ____)
+	**234. GEORGE W.**	born 8 May 1847 PA; married Ellen Ann LILLEY 1 Nov 1871
+	**235. EDWIN C.**	born 13 July 1849 PA; died 17 Apr 1925 Canton, PA
		1 married Ella/Ellen WHITEHEAD
		(she born ca 1850; died before 1881)
		(she dau/o Jay WHITEHEAD +++ and Jane L. ____)
		2 married Elizabeth THORN(E) 13 Apr 1881 (she born 3 Sep 1859)
		(she dau/o Watson THORN(E) ++++and Susan APGAR)

Note: +++ Jay WHITEHEAD served as a Cpl. in Co K, 187th Regiment , PA Artillery during the Civil War
++++ Watson THORN(E) served as a Pvt. in the 3rd Regiment PA Heavy Artillery

	236. Charles M.	born Apr 1855 PA; died 7 Oct 1917; no issue EOL
		married Belle THORN(E) (sister of Elizabeth, above)
	237. Thomas	born ca 185_; died young EOL

References: History of the Northern Tier Counties , Colonial and Revolutionary Families, PA
Vol.7, page 399 – new series; Bradford County, PA patriots; Census and family data

63. SARAH JANE-[4] MAC INTOSH, sister of above, was born 23 January 1823 at Delaware County, NY. She married first to ____ TANNER on 16 Oct 1846. Reportedly there were no children of this marriage. Her second marriage was to Alonzo GREENO(UGH) on ____ 18__. He was the son of Emerson GREENO and Anna ____, and was born 28 June 1813; died 15 Mar 1850, and is buried at Alba, PA.

Child of Sarah Jane-[4] MAC INTOSH and Alonzo GREENO:
Surname **GREENOUGH**

	238. Milton	born ca 1849 Alba, PA; died 10 June 1850 Alba EOL

64. CHARLOTTE-[4] MAC INTOSH, sister of above, was born 16 Sep 1824 at Kortright, Delaware , County, NY. She married Daniel RANDALL on 8 Oct 1846. He was the son of Timothy RANDALL (Shubel) and Nancy WILSON, and was born 6 Feb 1823 Delaware County, NY; still living 1910 at

The Fourth American Generation

Canton, PA. Charlotte-[4] died 25 Oct 1881 PA. Daniel RANDALL married second to Amanda CASE ca Nov 1881 at Canton, Bradford Co., PA. She was born 18 June 1825, died 9 Oct 1901.

Children of Charlotte-[4] MAC INTOSH and Daniel RANDALL
Surname **RANDALL**

239. Nancy Elizabeth	born 28 May 1851; died 1917; buried Mott Cemetery, Leroy, PA		
	1 married Daniel McKean LILLEY+ 12 Oct 1870		
	(he s/o John LILLEYand 2nd wife Lemira MC KEAN)		
	(he born Dec 1843 died before 7 Oct 1905)		

Child: Carleton—[6] LILLEY born Nov 1872; married Lizzie ____
2 married Irvin WHITEHEAD 26 Sep 1907
Note + Daniel LILLEY served in G2 , PA Heavy Artillery during the Civil War

240. La Fayette D	born 26 June 1849 Armenia Twsp, PA; died 31 Mar 1916 EOL	
"Lafey"	married Electra MORGAN 1875	
	(she dau/o Samuel MORGAN and Maria SPENCER)	
	(she born July 1849 Tioga Co.,; died ____)	
+ **241. DANIEL W.**	born Dec 1854 PA; died 27 Dec 1941	
	married Kathryn/ Katherine " Kittie " MC KENZIE	
	(she dau/o William MC KENZIE and Catherine SCOTT)	
	(she born Aug 1861; died 1924)	
+ **242. GRACE JANE**	born 31 Jan 1860; died ca 1935; resided Clinton County, PA	
	married Dana Thomas AYRES 21 Feb 1877	
	(he born 16 Jan 1850; died Feb 1933)	

66. HARRIET-[4] MAC INTOSH, sister of above, was born 8 March 1827 at Kortright, Delaware County, NY. She married Lorenzo THOMAS, a farmer, on 24 Nov 1848. He was the son of Alvin THOMAS (s/o Jacob THOMAS and Susannah ROWLEY) and Amy HARDING (dau/o Samuel HARDING and Love MAYHEW), and was born 15 Jan 1827; died 25 Feb 1879. Harriet-4 died 1879 at Canton, PA. Lorenzo THOMAS lived most of his life in PA, but moved to Southern Kansas a few years before he died. His death occurred on 25 Aug 1879.

Children of Harriet-[4] MAC INTOSH and Lorenzo THOMAS:
Surname **THOMAS**

+ **243. WILLIAM**	born 15 Jan 1850 PA; died 12 April 1932		
PERCIVAL	1 married Lydia Helen WILLIAMS 18 Sept 1872		
	(she born 1 Nov 1848; died 1 May 1883) 2 married ____FREEMAN		
	(she dau/o George FREEMAN and Amelia ____)		
244. Alvin W.	born 21 Oct 1852 PA; died 18 May 1857 EOL		
+ **245. AMY ISABEL**	born 26 Jan 1854; died 5 Jan 1934		
	married Ordonio Lazelle FIELD 15 Sep 1874		
	(he s/o George FIELD ++ and Caroline Amelia FREEMAN)		
	(he born 21 Mar 1856; died 1936/37)		
246. Anna	born ca 1856; died _____		
+ **247. LEWIS**	born 30 June 1858 PA; died _____; resided Southport, PA.		
RANDALL	married Minerva OSTRANDER ca 1884		
	(she born 1 May 1857; died 24 Mar 1932)		
248. Frank H.	born 15 Dec 1860; died _____		
+ **249. SUSAN ETTIE**	born 28 Mar 1863; died 19 Oct 1906		
	married Homer E. TREAT (he born _____ Morris Run, PA)		
250, Esther	born ca 1864; died _____		
251. Thomas Lazelle	born 3 Apr 1872; died 11 Aug 1926; married Fannie PHILLIPS		

Children: Leah-[6]; Gertrude-[6;] Russell-[6]; and Flossy-[6] THOMAS

Note: ++ George FIELD, born Delhi, Delaware Co., NY 28 Aug 1828 at Delhi, Delaware County, NY, married Caroline Amelia FREEMAN. She was born ca 1832; died 1887. George was the son of Abiezer FIELD, Jr. and Hannah WILBUR, natives of Taunton, MA. Abiezer was born 31 Oct 1785, died 13 Apr 1858. George settled on Armenia Mountain in 1836. He was a Civil War veteran (Co. C, PA 7th Cavalry) and died 8 Apr 1919 Armenia, PA .He and Hannah had 9 children: Abizer, Christopher, Loretta, Calista, Phineas, Oritha, Adelaide, Oliver Dutton, and **Ordonio Lazelle FIELD (above).**

67. MICHAEL EDEN-[4] MC INTOSH, brother of above, was born 23 Dec 1830 at Kortright, Delaware County, NY. He married Martha Helen LONGLEY on 15 July 1854 at Tonawanda, New York. She was the daughter of John LONGLEY and ___, and was born 9 May 1838; died 1 Oct 1900 at Harbor Springs, MI. According to the 1870 Census, Michael-[4] worked in a sawmill. He died 19 Apr 1918 at Harbor Springs.

Children of Michael-[4] MAC INTOSH and Martha Helen LONGLEY:
Surname **MAC INTOSH**

	252. Lydia J.	born 23 Aug 1855 PA; died 1862 PA; buried Old Covert Cemetery Armenia Mountain	
+	**253. MARY CAROLINE**	born 9 May 1858 Tioga Co., PA; died 8 Aug 1920 married Sidney-[3] CEASE (# 112) 15 Sep 1875 Blossburg, PA	
	254. Ida May	born ca 1860 PA; died 28 May 1885; never married	EOL
	255. Lewis G.	born 6/7 Oct 1862 PA; died 2 Oct 1865 PA (gs)	EOL

Obituary for Michael-[4] MC INTOSH   1918
M.E. MC INTOSH, was born in Schoharie County. NY Dec 23 1830. One of eighteen children of William and Elizabeth MC INTOSH. He was married to Martha LONGLEY June 15 1854. Four children were born to this union. Lydia, Mary, Ida and Louis all having passed away but one, Mrs. Mary CEASE. He enlisted in the Civil War in 1862, serving until discharged. Came to Emmett Co., Michigan in 1877, settling where the CEASE farm now is until 1896. Then resided in Harbor Springs until the death of his wife in 1900. He leaves his daughter Mary, five grandchildren, fourteen great grandchildren, one brother Louis in Clarion and two sisters Lucy Crawford and Stella Howe in Pennsylvannia. He was a great Bible student and formed his own beliefs from what he read and saw (seen) for himself. His hope was that he might live to see the end of the present World War 1. Another pioneer and soldier has finished the fight to live. Being eighty seven years, three months and 17 days old. Funeral services were held Friday April 15 in the Stutsmanville M.E. Church, conducted by Rev Lieck of Harbor Springs. Burial beside his wife in Harbor Springs.

68. SUSAN-[4] MC INTOSH, sister of above, was born 13 March 1834 at Kortright, Delaware County, NY. She married John RANDALL on ___ 1853. John was the son of Timothy RANDALL (Shubel: Jeremiah) and Nancy WILSON, and was born ca 1832 NY; died 1871 Union Twnship, PA. Susan-[4] died 27 Nov 1888

Children of Susan-[4] MC INTOSH and John RANDALL:
Surname **RANDALL**

256. Clarence	born ca 1854, PA; died 12 Aug 1862 Tioga Co., PA	EOL
257. Stephen	born ca ____, PA	
258. Lulu	born ca ____,	
259. John Stephen	born 25 Mar 1862; died July 1916 Bernice, PA	
260. Susie Bell	born _____; died 1866	
261. Carl Lilley ++	born 8 Nov 1872; died 7 Oct 1953 PA	

++ This child was adopted by Daniel LILLEY and Nan RANDALL. He married Phoebe Elizabeth HOLCOMBE 18 May 1898. She was born 28 Jan 1876 Leroy , PA; died ___; buried Park Cemetery. Canton, Bradford, PA

71. ELIZA ANN-[4] MC INTOSH, sister of above, was born 8 May 1838, probably Amenia, PA. She married N. Byron CASE ca 1855/56. He was the son of Samuel CASE and Zeruah THOMAS, and was born 20 Feb 1832 Troy, Bradford, PA; died 6 Aug 1916 at Troy. A farmer, Byron and his wife lived and died on a farm near Alba, PA. They celebrated their golden wedding anniversary. Eliza-[4] died 2 May 1907.

Children of Eliza-[4] MC INTOSH and N. Byron CASE:
Surname **CASE**

262. Ada / Adah L.	born Apr 1857 Canton, PA; died before 1947

Children of Eliza-[4] MC INTOSH and N. Byron CASE, continued:
Surname **CASE**

	262. Ada, cont'd:	1 married Henry J. BALDWIN (he born 1850; died ____)
		(he poss. s/o Aaron BALDWIN and Sarah _____)

Child: Harry-[6] BALDWIN born Mar 1880; married Jessie BRYAN, divorced, no issue; EOL

		2 married Professor ____ THOMAS of CA.
+	**263. MILTON A.**	born 29 May 1859 PA; died 20 Feb 1937 Sayre, Bradford, PA
		1 married Eugenia THOMAS 25 Nov 1880 at Troy, PA
		2 married Minnie MAYNARD ca 1910
		married Lilly WILLIAMS Turner 2 Nov 1929 Williamsport, PA
+	**264. GRACE**	born ca 1866/67 Troy, PA; died ____
		married Charles RHOADES of Elmira, NY (he born ____; died 1939)
+	**265. NELSON W.**	born Apr 1871 Troy, PA; died ____
		married Eva J. HACKETT ca 1893; resided NH
	266. Samuel Shepherd	born ca 1876; died ____; married Addie M. _____; no issue EOL
	267. Charlotte	born Apr 1882 Troy, PA; died 1932 Elmira, NY
	(Lottie)	married Earl Clarke ROBY 24 Dec 1903 Alba, Bradford, PA

72. FERNANDO-[4] MAC INTOSH (Finand/ Finando), brother of above, was born 27 Aug 1840 at Armenia Township, Bradford County, PA. He married Rosalie Ellen/ Ellen Rosalie-[4] LYON of Ward, Tioga, PA. ca 1861/62. She was the daughter of James-[3] LYON (John-[2], Moses-[1]) and Calista FIELD (Abizer, Jr.; Abizer), and was born ca 1844 PA; died ca 1935. Fernando-[4] died 1918 at Niagara Falls, NY.

Children of Fernando-[4] MC INTOSH and Rosalie Ellen LYON:
Surname **MC INTOSH**

+	**268. WILLIS E./**	born 14 June 1863, Ward Twsp. PA; died 8 Jan 1911 Morris Run, PA
	WILLIAM E.	married Sarah MC GARRY ca 1895
		(she born Oct 1872 Morris Run, PA; died 23 Nov 1927 NY)
	269. Charles/ Charley	born 12 May 1865 PA; died 1932; never married EOL
	270. Cora D.	born 28 July 1870/73; died _____
		1 married Bert CULVER ca 1900

Child: Joel-[6] CULVER born 4 Apr 1901 PA; died____; married Leona ____; resided Niagara Falls, NY 1930

		2 married Lewis Joseph JUNK ca 1917 (as his 2nd wife)
		(he born Dec 1870 PA; died _____) resided Niagara Falls, NY
		(poss. s/o John JUNK and Margaret _____)

73. LEWIS H[4] MC INTOSH, brother of above, was born 20 June 1843 at Armenia Twsp., Bradford County, New York. He married Norminda SMITH ca 1865/66. She was born ca 1849, MI; died ____. They divorced and she married second to Richard ROCKWELL Lewis-[4] MC INTOSH married second to Catherine E. CARTRIGHT/CARTWRIGHT on 11 April 1886. She was born Saginaw, MI ca 1853; died before 1900. At the time of his second marriage he resided in Friends(hip) Township, Tioga County, PA. He married his third wife, Amanda MC CADE, ca 1900 at Harbor Springs, MI. She was born ca 1865 MI; died ____. They resided Clarion, MI where he was occupied as a "land looker". He died 1918 (age 75) at Clarion, MI.

Children of Lewis-[4] MC INTOSH and Norminda SMITH:
Surname **MC INTOSH**

	271. Nettie	born 1867 PA; died ____
+	**272. MAUDE**	born 17 June 1868 PA; died 18 Feb 1939
		married Charles Augustus BATTERSON at Troy, PA on _____
	273. Clarence	born Nov 1873 PA; died _____

MACKINTOSH   MAC INTOSH   MC INTOSH
The Fourth American Generation

74. ROSALTHEA AMANDA-⁴ MC INTOSH, sister of above, was born 13 May 1845 at Armenia Twsp., Bradford County, PA. She married Francis "Frank " CURE of Texas. He was the son of John Secore CURE and Cynthia ____, and was born 18 July 1837 PA; died 26 Apr 1919 Corpus Christi, TX. Rosalthea Amanda-⁴ MC INTOSH died 23 Oct 1926 Galveston, Nueces, TX.

Children of Rosalthea Amanda-⁴ MC INTOSH and Frank CURE:
Surname **CURE**

+	**274. ALVIN**	born ca 1862 PA; died ____
		married Martha Jane GUATNEY 17 May 1882 Labette, KS
		(she born 15 Feb 1867 IL; died 1 Nov 1936)
+	**275. ANDREW**	born Apr 1864 PA; died 1948 CA; married Rebecca SCHOLES
	JOHNSON	(she born 2 Nov 1878 TX, died 24 Sep 1963 Long Beach, CA)
	276. Gurden Felter	born 6 Jan 1866 PA; died 29 Nov 1941 Los Angeles, CA
	"Gurd"	married Hermina "Minnie" M. BRUNE

Child: Gertrude-⁶ CURE born ca 1892; died 1950

	277. John	born 11 June 1869 MO; died 12 Sep 1933 Bexar County, TX
		married Marnie V. ____ ca 1899 (she born ca 1877 OH ; died ____
	278. George	born ca 1872 KS; died _____
	279. Lizzie / Elizabeth	born ca 1874 /75 KS; married Samuel A. MAVERICK
+	**280. DELLA**	born 25 Dec 1876 KS; 1 married _____ WILKINS
		2 married Morris Alexander CROOKS ca 1900
		(he born ca 1867; died ca 1918)
		3 married George ALLISON before 1930
	281. Senora /Nora	born Feb 1879 Mt. Pleasant , Labette, KS; died Oct 1968 Paducah, KY
		married Thomas J. PRESTON ca 1910

Children: William-⁶ born ca 1902; Teddy-⁶ born ca 1904; Lucy-⁶ born ca 1907; Beatrice-⁶ born ca 1916; and Helen-⁶ PRESTON born ca 1919

	282. James A.	born June 1887 TX; died 17 Nov 1953 Houston, Harris Co., TX	
		(he clerk in an oil refinery)	
	283. Juanita	born Oct 1893 TX	284. Gladly born Feb 1896 TX

76. LUCY DELPHINE-⁴ MAC INTOSH, sister of above, was born 13 Aug 1848 /49 at Armenia Twsp., Bradford County, PA. She married Hugh-³ CRAWFORD +++ of Pittsburgh, PA on 17 Apr 1865 at Troy , Bradford County, PA. He was the son of William-² CRAWFORD (Hugh-¹) and Harriet STEWART/STUART. He was born 28 Nov 1840 at Emsworth, Allegheny County, PA, was a Civil War veteran serving in Company B, 4th PA Cavalry, and died 3 Aug 1915 at Canton, Bradford County, PA. Lucy Delphine-⁴ MAC INTOSH died 17 Oct 1922. They are buried at the Main Street Cemetery in Canton

Children of Lucy Delphine-⁴ MAC INTOSH and Hugh-³ CRAWFORD:
Surname **CRAWFORD**

+	**285. JOHN WILLIAM**	born 3 June 1867 Armenia, PA; died 1921 Blossburg, PA
		married Meda ANDRUS Nov 1889
		(she dau/o Cephas Elisha ANDRUS and Lucy BAILEY)
		(she born 14 Nov 1870, Canton, PA; died 4 Mar 1940)
+	**286. BYRON HUGH**	born 3 May 1869 Pittsburgh PA; died 1951 Canton, PA)
		married Adelaide/Addie WATTS 4 July 1888
		(she dau/o Robert T. WATTS and Jane BONNELL)
		(she born 4 July 1871; died 21 June 1960)
	287. Harriet Jane	born 21 Nov 1872 Blossburg, PA; died Feb 1936
		married Esbon Walter COLE 21 Nov 1891
		(he s/o WW COLE and Nettie _____)
		(he born 12 May 1870; died 1947) no issue EOL

37

Children of Lucy Delphine-[4] MC INTOSH and Hugh-[3] CRAWFORD, continued:
Surname **CRAWFORD**

288. Minnie	born ca 1874 Armenia, PA; died ca 1875	EOL
289. James	born 27 May 1876 (gs); died 13 April 1928	
	married Lillian MUFFLEYca 1911; divorced; she born June 1878 PA	
290. LENA BELLE	born __ March 1879 Fallbrook, Tioga, PA	
	married George W. FELIX 17 Feb 1895 Elmira, NY	
	divorced 1930; died 7 Jan 1941 Hornell, NY; buried Canton, PA	
291. Charles John	born 27 Aug 1884 Fallbrook, PA; died 1960 , buried Canton, PA	
	married Dora SCHAEFER March 1905 Elmira, NY	
	(she dau/o Henry SCHAEFER and Jennie TEMPLE)	
	(she born 4 Mar 1885; died Feb 1974 Canton, PA)	

+++ Ancestry of Hugh-[3] CRAWFORD (above)

The extreme ancestor of this ancient family of CRAWFORD, in Scotland, was Reginald. He was the youngest son of Allen, 4th Earl of Richmond. Margaret of Loundon, wife of Sir Reginald CRAWFORD , was the only daughter of James DE LONDOUN, feudal Lord of Loundon. (Burke's Peerage)

Hugh-[1] CRAWFORD, son of Samuel-[A] CRAWFORD, was born ca 1763 at "Swonkford", County Down, Ireland. He came to America in 1795 with his wife and baby son Hugh-[2]. His wife was Jane MC DOWELL, born County Down, Ireland ca 1762. She was the daughter of the Rev Robert MAC DOWELL, and a member of the Church of Glastry, Parish of Ballyhalbert.

Hugh-[1] CRAWFORD and his wife first settled in Carlisle, PA, living there a few years before moving to Allegheny County, PA. A deed to land there was recorded 20 Aug 1817 (Deeds and Records, recorded at Pittsburgh, Vol. 22, pages 505-506) Hugh-1 CRAWFORD and his wife are buried at Mt. Nebo Cemetery Presbyterian Churchyard. Hugh-1 died 21 Oct 1847, and his wife died 16 Sep 1850.

They had 6 children: 1. Hugh-[2] who came with them from Ireland and is believed to have died as an infant. **2. WILLIAM-[2] was born 20 July 1796 at Carlisle, PA and married Harriet STEWART/STUART in 1824**. She was the daughter of James STEWART and Catherine SCHAEFER. The third son was named Hugh also, and was born Apr 5 ,1800 at Carlisle, PA He married Sarah DAY. Their fourth child Polly-2 was born ca 1803 and married Arthur JOHNSON. Child # 5 was James-2, born 10 Apr 1805 art Carlisle and married Anna Jane CRAYTON. Their youngest son was Isaac, born 16 Dec 1807 and married first to Mary Ann RHINEHART, second ____. WILLIAM-[2] CRAWFORD and his wife Harriet had 12 children, including Hugh-3, (above) born 28 Nov 1840, who married Lucy Delphine-[4] MAC INTOSH.

77. ESTELLA-[4] (Stella) MAC INTOSH, sister of above, was born 21 October 1850 at Armenia Township, Bradford County, PA. She married James HOWE on 15 Nov 1868 at Troy, PA. He was a Civil War veteran, having served as a Pvt. in Company K, 138th PA Infantry, as well as Company L , 15th PA Cavalry. He was the son of John HOWE and Caroline ____, and was born 3 Apr 1843; died 8 May 1919 at Canton, PA. Estella-[4] died 15 April 1927 at Horseheads, NY. They are both buried at Canton, PA.

Children of Estella-[4] MAC INTOSH and James HOWE:
Surname **HOWE**

+	**292. THOMAS LORENZO**	born 19 Sep 1869 ; died 27 Jan 1944 Corning, NY
		married Mary DWYER 1894 FallBrook, PA
		(she born ca 1865 PA; died ____)
+	**293. FRANK EUGENE**	born 4 Nov 1873 Fallbrook, PA; died 13 May 1939
		married Jeanette (Nettie) WEBSTER 27 Sep 1899 Elmira, NY
	294. Charles Hugh	born ca 1878 PA; died _____; married Nellie F. ELTZ
		(she dau/o Jennie B ELTZ; she born July 1883 NY) EOL
+	**295. ADAH**	born ca 1881 PA; died _____; resided Horseheads, NY
		married Frank FULKERSON ca 1911
+	**296. LAZELL ERSTIN**	born 11 May 1884 PA; died Jan 1940; resided Elmira, NY
		married Cora HARRINGTON 20 June 1906 Elmira Heights, NY
	297. William	born ca 1891, NY; died ____; 1 married Minnie _____
		2 married Harriet _____ (she born 1899-1900 NY; died ____)

Children: Ernst-[6] born ca 1918 NY; and Willis-[6] HOWE born ca 1920 NY

80. HENRY-[4] MAC INTOSH, son of Matthias-[3] MAC INTOSH (Simon-[2], Alexander-[1]) and Sarah/ Sally LOCKWOOD, was born 18 Oct 1830 at Kortright, Delaware County, NY. He married Clara/Clarissa DOUGLAS on 23 Oct 18644 at Newburyport, MA. Clara was the daughter of ____ DOUGLAS and ____, and was born 31 Mar 1845 at Louisville, NY; died 26 September 1920 Canton , St. Lawrence County, NY. Henry-[4] MAC INTOSH died 13 April 1891 at Colton, St. Lawrence, NY, and is buried at Beech Plains.

Children of Henry-[4] MAC INTOSH and Clara DOUGLAS:
Surname **MAC INTOSH**

+	**298. ETTA ANGELINE** **"Ettie"**	born 11 Sep 1865 Cherry Flats, Tioga, PA married Chester A. CRANDALL 22 Oct 1886 (he born 14 Apr 1853; died 18 Oct 1915) died 5 Mar 1934 Auburn, Cayuga County, NY
+	**299. CLARA ELIZABETH** "Lizzie / Lixxie "	born 8 Dec 1866 Covington Township., Tioga, PA married Martin L. HEWITT 20 May 1885 (he s/o Hiram HEWITT and Mary WILLETT) (he born 10 June 1853; died 22 Oct 1919 Pierrepont, NY) died 13 March 1934 Pierrepont, St. Lawrence, NY
+	**300. GEORGE LEWIS**	born 17 Nov 1868 Covington, PA; died 14 Oct 1957 married Myrtle GRAVES 11 Oct 1893 Colton, NY (she born 12 Aug 1871 Marshfield, MO; died 8 May 1946) (she dau/o Joshua A. GRAVES and Hannah S. HOGLE)

82. FRANCES (Fanny) C -[4] MAC INTOSH, sister of above, was born 12 Feb 1834 at Kortright, Delaware County, NY. She married Charles E-[4] KIFF , a carpenter, on 5 Nov 1854 at ____, PA. He was the son of Erastus-[3] KIFF (Andrew-[2]; George-[1]) and _____, and was born ca 1833/34 at Delaware County, NY. . 'Fanny"-[4] MAC INTOSH died 24 Sep 1897 at Alba, Bradford Co., NY. They are both buried there.

Children of Frances/Fanny-[4] MAC INTOSH and Charles-[4] KIFF:
Surname **KIFF**

+	**301. ROWLAND P.**	born 11 Aug 1855 Bradford Co., Pa; died _____ married Cora MANDEVILLE 26 Apr 1882
	302. Melvin	born Oct 1857 Bradford Co., PA; married Ella FOX Sept 1886 Children: Alice-[6] (poss. Genevieve A.) born Mar 1893 and Harvey-[6] KIFF born May 1889
	303. Sigel	born ca 1863 Bradford Co., NY; died ____ married Matilda E.___ca 1891 (he a farmer, resided Athens, PA) EOL
+	**304. CLARA BELL**	born 24 Jul 1865 Bradford Co., PA; died 30 Mar 1964 Troy, PA married George Phelps FREEMAN, Jr. 24 Sep 1885 (he born 24 Sep 1858 Alba, PA; died 13 Nov 1926)

83. ANDREW-[4] MAC INTOSH, brother of above, was born 4 Sep 1836 at Delaware County, New York. He married Ida Ophelia JENNINGS on 2 May 1869 at Wellsboro, Tioga County, PA. She was the daughter of Jonathan JENNINGS and Caroline M. ELLENWOOD, and was born 5 Apr 1851 at Covington, PA; died 10 May 1927 at Elmira, Chemung Co.,, NY. Andrew-[4] MAC INTOSH died 20 Dec 1879 at Blossburg, PA.

Children of Andrew-[4] MAC INTOSH and Ida Ophelia JENNINGS:
Surname **MAC INTOSH**

+	**305. LEWIS THEODORE**	born 8 June 1870 West Covington, PA; died 29 Dec 1938 Elmira, NY married Carrie EDWARDS Oct 1904/05
	306. Carrie Mae	born 3 Jan 1872 West Covington, PA; died 1962 , no issue EOL married Harry Ellison COVENOY 22 Mar 1899 (he s/o Joseph COVENOY and Philena CAMPBELL) (he born 18 Nov 1873; died 10 April 1954)

Children of Andrew-[4] MAC INTOSH and Ida Ophelia Jennings, continued:
Surname **MAC INTOSH**

+	**307. THOMAS G.**	born 14 Dec 1874 West Covington, AP; died 22 Dec 1952 Blossburg married Nellie Ethel WATKINS (she born 9 July 1879; died 5 Aug 1958)
	308. Henry Erstine	born 6 May 1876 West Covington, PA; died _____ no issue EOL married Clara Doud YOUMANS 2 May 1911

86. LEWIS LOCKWOOD-[4] MAC INTOSH, brother of above, was born 12 Oct 1846 at Ward Township, Tioga County, PA. He married Rose/Rosa -[8] KLOCK +++ on 1 August 1872 at _____ PA. She was the daughter of Edwin-[7] KLOCK (Adam-[6;5;4;3]; Jacob-[2;] Hendrik-[1]) and his first wife, Mary PETRIE, and was born 30 June 1855 at Charleston Twsp, Tioga County, PA; died 17 May 1927 at Mansfield, PA. Lewis Lockwood-[4] MAC INTOSH died 2 Nov 1936 at Mansfield, PA.

Children of Lewis L-[4] MAC INTOSH and Rose/Rosa KLOCK:
Surname **MAC INTOSH**

	309. Sarah Ann (Sadie)	born 3 Nov 1876 Covington, PA ; died 1961/62 no issue EOL married Lyman Delos GOODSPEED 3 July 1893 (he s/o Arthur GOODSPEED and Mary FROST) (he born 8 Oct 1871; died 1932)
	310. Edwin Klock	born 26 Sep 1883 Covington, PA; died 1945 no issue EOL married Helen RUSSELL 12 June 1915 at Sharpstown, MD. (she born 1 July 1894; died _____)
+	**311. FREDERICK**	born 24 Sep 1890 W. Covington, PA; died 26 Nov 1977 Mansfield, PA married Clara TREAT 27 Mar 1916 Wellsboro, PA (she dau/o Sylvester TREAT and Sarah MILLER) (she born 28 Feb 1893 Chatham Twsp, PA; died 25 July 1975

Ancestry of Rose/Rosa-[8] KLOCK

Hendrick-[1] KLOCK came to this country from Hesse Kessle in Germany, to Camp Queensbury in 1710. His ancestors were Holland Dutch and their surname was VAN KLOCK .

Hendrick-[1] had 9 children including Colonel Jacob-[2] KLOCK who signed the Mohawk Valley Declaration of Independence on 4 July 1776. His son, Adam-[3] KLOCK, born 1732 married Caty SEEBER. Their son Adam-[4] , born 22 May 1751 , married Catherine STAURING; and died 10 Jan 1841. Adam-[5] born 22 Nov 1781, married Catherine SNYDER. Adam-[6] born 1800, married Nancy HART ca 1820. They were the parents of Edwin-[7], born 1833, who married first Mary PETRIE; and second Charlotte YOUMANS. Edwin-[7] and Mary PETRIE were the parents of Rose/Rosa-[8] who married Lewis-4 MAC INTOSH (above).

Lewis Lockwood-[4] MC INTOSH Obituary

Lewis L. MC INTOSH, 90, died Monday 2 Nov 1936 at the home of his daughter, Mrs. Sadie Goodspeed in Mansfield, PA. The son of Matthias and Sarah (LOCKWOOD) MC INTOSH , he was born 12 Oct 1846 on Armenia Mountain. In 1870 he married Miss Rosa KLOCK, who died 17 May 1927. For many years a farmer in Covington Township , he moved to Mansfield in 1917 , and until the death of Mrs. MC INTOSH resided on South Main Street. Since her death he had made his home with his daughter. He was a member of the Church of Christ, Covington. Surviving are his daughter, two sons Fred MC INTOSH of Covington Township and Edwin of Sharpstown, MD; and a granddaughter Miss Marion MC INTOSH of Covington. The funeral was held Thursday at 2 PM at the home of his daughter, the Rev David GRIFFITHS of the Baptist Church officiating. Burial was in Prospect Cemetery.

89. ABIGAIL WEEKS-[4] (Abbie) MAC INTOSH, daughter of Alexander-[3] MAC INTOSH (Simon-[2;] Alexander-[1)]) and Hannah GEROWE, was born 10 July 1832 Bloomville, Delaware County, NY. She married Perry H. HARDING, a painter, on 7 Oct 1852 at Canton, Bradford County, PA. He was the son of Dr. Theodore HARDING ++ and Rosalinda SOPER ++, and was born 29 Nov 1830 Bloomville, Delaware County, New York;; died 21 Dec 1884 at Canton, PA. Abigail-[4] MC INTOSH died 13 Jan 1888 at Elkland/ Canton, PA.

Children of Abigail Weeks-[4] MC INTOSH and Perry H. HARDING:
Surname **HARDING**

+	**312. CLARA HELEN**	born 9 Aug 1854 Canton, Bradford, PA
		1 married John Griffin PALMER 10 Apr 1877
		(he born 7 Apr 1854; died 29 July 1922)
		2 married William Thomas VAN RIPER of Vernon, NY 18 Jan 1896
		(he born 18 Jul 1841; died 24 Mar 1931 NJ)
		(he s/o Jacob VAN RIPER and Margaret DIPLEY)

Note: VAN RIPER enlisted in the Civil War as a member of the 9th NJ Co., on 20 Sep 1861; discharged 12 July 1865. He served under General BUTLER in the Army of the James

	313. Mary Emma	born 31 July 1858; died 7 March 1860 EOL
+	**314. CURTIS MERRITT**	born 27 June 1962 Bradford Co., PA; died 22 Aug 1935
		married Mina AYRES 19 Aug 1885
		(she born 28 June 1868; died _____)
		(she dau/o Alan AYRES and Lydia RANDALL)
+	**315. SARAH FRANCES**	born 7 July 1865 Bradford., PA; died 29/30 May 1917 Elkland, PA
		1 married John Walter HAMMOND 30 Sep 1886
		(he s/o John G. HAMMOND and Adeline _____)
		(he born 18 Oct 1866; died _____)
		2 married Clark BAILEY 11 Aug 1912 (he born ca 1849)
+	**316. LUNA BELL**	born 15 July 1870 Susquehanna, PA.
		1 married Byron Grant CORNELIUS ca 1896
		(he born 8 March 1868; died 23 Dec 1909; he was a Tanner)
		2 married Truman SAVEY 20 Sep 1917
		(he born 18 Jan 1870; died 28 Jan 1952)
		(he s/o Mathew SAVEY and Mary FERGUSON)

++ Dr. Theodore HARDING , the son of Samuel HARDING and Love MAYHEW, was born 8 Oct 1798 VT; died 31 Dec 1869. He married 5 June 1823 to Rosalinda SOPER. She was the daughter of Roger SOPER and Melinda ROSE, and was born 8 Jan 1802, died 1 Sept 1878. Roger SOPER (Levi) was born 23 Dec 1774; married Melinda ROSE Jan 1797, came from CT about 1800 and died 17 July 1857 at Columbia, Bradford, PA.. Melinda was born 15 Apr 1777 and died 28 Jan 1841.

Dr. Theodore HARDING was an " Eclective Physician " (a Botanic Physician) – he used native plants for medicinal purposes. He resided at Canton, Bradford County, PA., and was a recruiter during the Civil War.

Dr. Theodore HARDING and his wife were the parents of 8 children: Harriet born Sep 1824 Canton, PA; Marianne born 3 Aug 1826; PERRY H (above) born 29 Nov 1830; Cynthia born 30 July 1833; Melinda born 18 May 1836; Helen born 17 Dec 1838; Loretta born 10 July 1842 and Alice HARDING born 2 July 1847.

92. THEOPHILUS FLETCHER-[4] MAC INTOSH, son of George-[3] MAC INTOSH (Simon-[2]; Alexander-[1]) and Sarah/Sally JACQUISH, was born 30 Nov 1829 Kortright, Delaware County, New York. He was extensively reviewed in : The Leading Citizens of Delaware County, NY. The following are excerpts from that book:

" Theophilus F. MC INTOSH, editor and proprietor of the Delaware Republican, one of the leading papers of the county, has exercised a marked influence on the affairs of this section of New York, as a progressive, public-spirited citizen, having aided in guiding its political destiny as well as in promoting its interests materially, socially and morally."

" Theophilus F. MC INTOSH acquired his education in the district schools and the printing office, in the latter place gleaning a vast fund of general information. In Feb 1843, being then a sturdy lad of thirteen years, and thrown somewhat on his own resources, he came to the village of Delhi where he secured the position of "devil" in the Gazette printing office. " From 1843 to 1850, seven years, he worked for his room and board and a small allowance for clothes, becoming " well versed in the various duties of a newspaper office, and an expert in the art of printing."

He decided to get more education, and later entered the Express office as a compositor, remaining there for four years, also serving as the Assistant Postmaster of Delhi during that time. The succeeding 5 years were spent in Bloomville working at the Mirror. In 1858, the Rev C B SMYTH established a paper at Delhi, that was published in the office of the Mirror. Mr. MC INTOSH was engaged to do the typesetting , and the following May they purchased a press and material at Walton, later moving it to Delhi. This was the nucleus of the later Republican office. In the spring of 1860 Alvin STURTEVANT and Mr. MC INTOSH formed a partnership and started the Delaware Republican, issuing the first paper on 14 May 1860.

In January 1869 Mr. MC INTOSH became the sole proprietor of the Republican. " Mr. MC INTOSH was elected County Treasurer in 1869 for a term of three years, and served so satisfactorily that in 1872 he was re-elected for another three years." He also served on the Republican County Committee and was a delegate to six state conventions.

In 1858, Theophilus married Frances S. KEELER of Bloomville. She was the daughter of the Honorable Stephen H. KEELER and Betsey L. _____, as well as the granddaughter of the Honorable Martin KEELER, a former Sheriff and Judge of Delaware County, and one of the most prominent and influential men of his day. Frances was born 25 Sep 1833 and died 9 Dec 1896. Theophilus F-[4] MC INTOSH died 29 Oct 1901. He and his wife are buried at Woodland Cemetery, Delhi, NY.

Children of Theophilus F-[4] MC INTOSH and Frances KEELER;
Surname **MC INTOSH**

+	**317. ROBERT PERRY**	born 24 Mar 1859 Bloomville, NY; died ca 1937 Delhi, NY married Harriet Lamont JAMIESON/JAMISON 9 Feb 1897 (she dau/o Robert JAMIESON and Mary LAMONT of Hamden, NY) (she born 18 Feb 1863; died 1954)
+	**318. CHARLES KEELER**	born 25 Nov 1860 NY; died ca 1930) (1920 resided Syracuse, NY) married Nellie ROGERS
+	**319. HENRY MARTIN**	born 25 Sep 1863; died 1934 married Sarah Belle "Sadie " BURROUGHS (she born 25 Nov 1874 IA; died 2 Oct 1894) (she dau/o Samuel S. BURROUGHS and Amanda MACKEY)
+	**320. FRANCES/Fanny SUSAN**	born 3 June 1867; died 1932 married James Merton RONEY
+	**321. GEORGE WALTER**	born 1 March 1871; died 1949; married Rella MC GONAGLE ca 1895 (she born 30 Nov 1871 KY; died 20 April 1948 Jefferson, KY)
+	**322. FRANK EDWARD**	born 23 Aug 1879 NY ; died 17 Aug 1950 VT) married Fanny YENCER 1911 (she born 21 Aug 1877; died 14 Sep 1967 Burlington, VT 1962)

References: Family records; " First Families of America" Abridged Compendium by Frederick VICKERS, page 318; Rockwell and Keeler Genealogy, J. Boughton, 1903, page 454-55

95. SOPHRONIA-[4] MC INTOSH, sister of above, was born 23 May 1837 at Delaware County, NY. She married Joel B. CARPENTER, a carpenter, on 22 Jan 1867 at the Delhi (NY) Methodist Episcopal parsonage. He was the son of John L. CARPENTER and Juliette Ann E. ___, and was born 4 Jan 1844 NY; died 12 Oct 1893 (gs). Sophronia[4] MC INTOSH died 29 Sep 1898 at Delhi. They are buried at Woodland Cemetery there.

Children of Sophronia-[4] MC INTOSH and Joel B. CARPENTER:
Surname **CARPENTER**

	323. George M.	born Aug 1873 NY; died 1935 Walton, NY	no issue EOL
		married Eleanor PLACE Eells 11 Mar 1914 Walton, NY	
		(she dau/o Lewis B. PLACE and Mary O'BRIEN)	
		(she born 26 Sep 1862; died _____)(1 m. Wm. Hamilton EELLS)	
+	**324. CORA J.**	born Jan 1876 NY; died Jan 1957 Hancock, NY	
		married Charles ROGERS of Walton, NY	
	325. Fannie	born 2 Dec 1880; died 20 Sep 1884	EOL

96. OLIVE W-[4] MC INTOSH, sister of above, was born __ June 1839 at Delhi, Delaware County, NY. She married Reuben Henry DART on 20 Jan 1864 at ____. He was the son of David Mack DART and

Mary MONTGOMERY, and was born 1 May 1842 at Roxbury, Delaware County, NY; died ca 1920. Reuben and Olive-4 were divorced before 1897. On 18 Dec 1897, he married for a second time to Caroline Catherine SMITH and resided thereafter in IL. Olive W[4] died ca ____.

Children of Olive W-[4] MC INTOSH and Reuben Henry DART:
Surname **DART**
>   326. Mary E   born Feb 1867 NY; died after 1930   no issue   EOL
>   married George Wealy CRARY ca 1886 (he born Jan 1861 NY)
>   (he s/o Moses P. CRARY and Elizabeth Ann PRESTON)

98. SARAH ADELINE-[4] MC INTOSH, daughter of Simon-[3] MC INTOSH, Jr. (Simon-[2]; Alexander-[1]) and Esther SUTTON, was born 22 Feb 1833 at Delhi, Delaware County, NY. She was the twin sister of Mary Caroline-4 MC INTOSH.   She married Charles STERLING on 15 April 1856 at Troy, Bradford County, PA. , the Rev C. MC DOUGAL officiated. Charles STERLING was the son of Charles STERLING and Elizabeth TYLER, and was born 4 May 1827 Ellisburg, Jefferson County, NY; died 31 Dec 1899 at Canton, Bradford County, PA. Sarah Adeline[4] MC INTOSH died 14 Aug 1865 at Susquehanna Depot, Susquehanna County, PA. She and her husband are buried at Park Cemetery, Canton.

Child of Sarah Adeline-[4] MC INTOSH and Charles STERLING:
Surname **STERLING**
+   **327. WILLIAM**   born 2 Feb 1862 Susquehannah Depot, PA
>   **TYLER**   married Clara J-[5] MAC DONALD 21 April 1887 (# 192)
>   (she born ca 1861 PA; died 13 Sep 1938 Queens Village, LI, NY)
>   (she dau/o Mary-[4] CALDWELL (# 47) and James MC DONALD)
>   died 2 Feb 1955 Queens Village, LI, NY

99. MARY CAROLINE-[4] MC INTOSH, twin sister of above, was born 22 Feb 1833 at Delhi, Delaware County, NY. She married first to Henry L. GREENOUGH on __ ____ 1854. Henry was the son of Leonard GREENO(UGH) (Daniel) and Clarissa MANLEY of Rutland, VT., and was born 18 Dec 1821 VT; died 2 Mar 1868 PA. Her second marriage was to Charles A. DAY on ____. He was born ca 1823 NY; died 1894. She married third to Caleb CASE on 25 Dec 1894. He was born 16 Nov 1825, died 29 Jan 1915. Mary Caroline-[4] MC INTOSH died 17 Sep 1914 at _____.

Children of Mary Caroline-[4] MC INTOSH and Henry GREENO(UGH):
Surname **GREENO(UGH)**
+   **328. MERTON**   born 2 Jan 1856 East Troy, PA; died 25 May 1935 Sayre, PA
>   **EMERSON**   married Mary E. VAN HORN
>   (she born Sep 1862 PA; died _____)
>   (father born ____DE; mother born ____ PA)
+   **329. CLARENCE**   born 27 June 1857 East Troy, PA; died _____
>   **LACELL**   married Ida NEVIN
+   **330. CHARLES**   born 31 Aug 1865 East Troy, PA; died 29 June 1920 Sayre, PA
>   **HENRY**   married Wrexieville/Rexie CASE 3 Nov 1886 Troy, PA

101. ELIZABETH JANE-[4] MC INTOSH, sister of above, was born 28 Nov 1837 (gs) at Ward Township, Tioga County, PA. She married first to James H. WHITEHEAD on 24 May 185 _ at Elmira, NY. He   was the son of William WHITEHEAD (born 1800, NJ) and _____, and was born June 1832 PA; died during the Civil War on 21 March 1865. Unknown if his death was from a war injury or an illness. He is buried at the Becker Corners Cemetery, Fallbrook Road, Tioga County, PA.

She married second to Charles STERLING, the widower of her older sister Sarah Adeline[4] MC INTOSH.

MACKINTOSH   MAC INTOSH   MC INTOSH
The Fourth American Generation

They were married on 16 April 1867 at Susquehanna, PA. Charles STERLING was born 4 Apr/May 1827 at Ellisburg, Jefferson County, NY; died 31 Dec 1899 at Canton, PA. Elizabeth[-4] MC INTOSH died 19 May 1896 at Addison, Steuben County, NY, where she had gone for cancer surgery. She is buried with her second husband at Park Cemetery, Canton, PA.

Child of Elizabeth Jane-[4] MC INTOSH and James WHITEHEAD:
Surname **WHITEHEAD**

	331. Sterling Hall	born 8 Apr 1861; died 24 Dec 1864; Buried Becker Cemetery

Children of Elizabeth Jane-[4] MC INTOSH and Charles STERLING:
Surname **STERLING**

+	**332. FREDERICK**	born 10 July 1867 Alba, Canton Township, PA
	JAMES	married Nancy Mae WILLIAMS 1 Jan 1887
		(she dau/o Joseph WILLIAMS and Mary Anna KRIEGER)
		(she born 30 Oct 1868 Troy, PA; died 9 Sep 1945 Canton, PA)
		died 28 Jan 1927 Canton, PA.
	333. George Lee	born ca 1874 Canton, PA; died 5 Feb 1895 Elmira, Chemung, NY

Obituary for Charles STERLING

" Apr 4, 1827, in the Village of Ellisburg, Oswego County, New York, Charles STERLING was born. He was the second child of Charles and Elizabeth Tyler STERLING, and one of a family of 5: Martin, Charles Wallace, Mary and John. When 3 years of age his

parents moved to Alba, Pennsylvania. Here his mother soon died; whereupon the family was broken up, and Charles entered the home of Mrs. Easter (should be Esther) Armstrong, where he remained until he was 12 years old. The years from 12 to 21 he spent in Ohio with his older brother Martin T. STERLING. Then returning to Pennsylvania he settled in Susquehanna, where he learned the trade of a moulder, and worked for many years in the employment of the Erie Railroad.

July 2, 1857, Mr. STERLING was married to Sarah Adeline MAC INTOSH, and to them was born one son, William (Tyler) STERLING, now of 759 Park Place, Elmira (NY)

Sep 19 1864, Mr. STERLING enlisted in the service of the Union, entering Company M . 2nd PA Heavy Artillery, though serving with the 112th PA Volunteer Infantry, 18th A.C. His services consisted of scouting, skirmishing, guard and garrison duty, and detachment at Bermuda Hundred as support to Heavy Artillery Redoubt, about six weeks in the winter of '64-'65. Later he was ill for three months and was treated in quarters. he was honorably discharged at Harrisburg June 13, 1865.

Soon after leaving the Army– Aug 14, 1865 – Mrs. Sterling died. Thereupon Charles STERLING removed to Troy, NY where he was employed for some time in a large foundry, his position resting on the fact that he was an exceedingly skillful moulder.

Again he returned to Pennsylvania, drawn back to what had been the home of his boyhood days. He purchased a foundry in Alba, which he successfully conducted for several years. Later, though still living in Alba, he was employed in the foundry of Thompson & Kucher of Canton.

At Alba, April 15, 1866, Charles STERLING was married to Elizabeth Jane MAC INTOSH, who was born Nov 28, 1838 in Ward Tioga County, PA., daughter of Simon and Esther Sutton MAC INTOSH, and widow of James H. WHITEHEAD. Two sons have been born to them: Frederick J. who now lives upon the homestead; and George L., who died in Elmira Feb 5, 1895.

Leaving Alba in 1870, on account of his health, he settled on what was then called the MAC INTOSH farm, a mile northwest of Canton, and here he resided until his death Sunday Dec 31. Mrs. Sterling preceded him to the home beyond, having entered into rest May 19, 1896. Mr. STERLING leaves only one living relative, a nephew, save his two sons and their families.

He had held at various times, since moving to Canton, the office of assessor, judge, and inspector of elections and district register. For many years he had been an active member of Ingham Post, No. 91 of the G.A.R.

When about 30 years of age, he was converted, and united with the Methodist Episcopal Church of Susquehanna. Since 1870 he has been an honored member of the Methodist Church of this place, and for more than half of that time a member of the official board of the same.

For some years, his health has been failing; and friends have known these past weeks that the end must be near. He passed away on the evening of Sunday Dec 31, 1899, thus being at the time of his decease nearly 73 years of age. The funeral was held at the Methodist Episcopal Church last Wednesday afternoon. Old and full of days, though not what we would call and aged man – has

44

The Fourth American Generation

Charles STERLING laid him down for the last long sleep, leaving behind him an untarnished name, and the memory of a helpful, upright Christian character."

Note: His grandson Charles Lee-6 STERLING often remarked that his grandfather had died in the last hour of the last day of the last year of the century.

102. ELECTA ADELIA-[4] MC INTOSH, sister of above, was born 8 Oct 1841 at Ward Township, Tioga County, PA. She married Silas Newton DANN on 10 January 1866 at Granville, Mifflin County, PA. He was the son of Harvey DANN (25 Oct 1815 – 10 May 1900) and Azuba MC MULLEN , and was born 28 March 1839 at Greenfield, Luzerne County, PA; died 27 Feb 1894. Silas DANN , a farmer, went to Bradford County ca 1849, and resided at Canton, PA. Electa Adelia[4] MC INTOSH died 9 Jan 1929. She and her husband are buried at Canton, PA.

Children of Electa Adelia-[4] MC INTOSH and Silas Newton DANN:
Surname **DANN**

+	**334. STERLING**	born 10 Jan 1868 Canton, PA; died 7 Mar 1941
	JAMES	married Ethel Mae HAVENS 14 July 1891
	335. Edward Wardell	born 8 Mar 1874 Canton, PA; died 19 Jan 1905; never married EOL

104. GEORGE WASHINGTON-[4] MC INTOSH, brother of above, was born 8 Feb 1844 at Ward Twsp, Tioga County, PA. He served in Company G, 8th PA Volunteer Cavalry during the Civil War. He was wounded, captured and held by the Confederates on Belle Island. He married S. Louise/Louisa WISE on 15 Nov 1866 at Newberry, PA , the Rev FINNEY officiating. Louise/Louisa was the daughter of _____ WISE and _____, and was born Aug 1847; died 1934 (age 86) at Williamsport, PA. where they had resided for many years. George W-[4] MC INTOSH died _____.

Children of George Washington-[4] MC INTOSH and Louise/Louisa WISE:
Surname **MC INTOSH**

	336. Grace/Gracie	born Aug 1867 PA; died _____
		married William (Will) H. RICKART ca 1889 (he born Nov 1863 PA)
		Child: George-[6] RICKART born ca 1896 PA
	337. Howard	born ca 1869 PA; died _____; resided Conneant, OH
		married Julia EARLICH
		(she born ca 1882 NY; died _____)
		Children: George-[6] born ca 1913 OH; and Grace-[6] MC INTOSH born ca 1916 OH
	338. Charles	born Aug 1873 PA ; died _____
		married Pearl _____ ca 1898
		Note: 1900 resided Findlay City, Hancock, OH
	339. Elizabeth Ames	born Feb 1877; died _____ no issue EOL
	" Lizzie "	married Harry Parker KEYTE ca 1913; resided Williamsport, PA
		(he born 10 Jan 1874 PA; had 7 children from a 1st marriage)
	340. Julia Moyer	born Nov 1880 PA; died _____
		married Rev James Bannon SWOPE Jan 1930 (as his 2nd wife)
		(he s/o Godfrey SWOPE and Mary A _____)
		(he born Aug 1883 PA; died _____)
		Note: He was a Lutheran pastor in Chicago; and had 4 sons from a first marriage: Bowman, Frederic, Paul H. and Warren SWOPE
+	**341. HELEN LOUISE**	born Mar 1883 PA; died _____
		married John Theodore HAND of South Williamsport, PA
		(he s/o Charles HAND and Mary E _____ -)
		(he born Nov 1880 NJ; died
	342. George W., Jr.	born ca 1885; died _____;married Annie _____
		Child: Florence-[6] MC INTOSH born ca 1914
	343. Pearl May	born ca _____ 344. Sarah born Aug 1887 PA; had TB

The Fourth American Generation

106. CHARLES MELVIN-[4] MC INTOSH, brother of above, was born 20 May 1852 at Troy, Bradford County, PA. He married Emma MELLOR on ___ at _____. She was the daughter of ____ MELLOR and _____, and was born Aug 1860 England; died 23 March 1923 PA. She is buried at Park Cemetery, Canton, Bradford, PA. They had resided in Williamsport before their divorce. Charlie MC INTOSH died ____.

Children of Charles-[4] MC INTOSH and Emma MELLOR:
Surname **MC INTOSH**

+	**345. WILLIAM JOHN**	born 21 Aug 1888; died ca 1958 PA; resided Canton, PA
		married Eva MAC KNESS
		(she born 25 Mar 1897 England; died 4 Jan 1992 Canton, PA)
	346. Clifford A.	born 9 Feb 1890; died Sep 1960; married Luella L. WILSTON
		(she born 11 Aug 1906 Grover, PA; died 8 Nov 1982)
		(she dau/o Ephraim WILSTON and Anna June _____)
		buried Grover Cemetery, near. Canton, PA
	347. Hazel M.	born Oct 1892; died _____
		1 married Roy ELSTON (resided Elmira, NY 1913)
		2 married James BABCOCK (resided Buffalo, NY 1923)

Note: There was a 4th child, George, who died at an early age

108. JAMES LEROY-[4] CEASE, son of Julia-[3] MC INTOSH (Simon-[2]; Alexander-[1]) and Alexander H. CEASE, was born Dec 1841 at Armenia. PA. His parents were both born in New York.

He married Amanda -[6] MOORE on _____ 1865. She was the daughter of Israel-[5] MOORE (Samuel-[4];) and Harriet-[4] KIFF (James-[3] ; Andrew-[2]; George-[1]) . She was born July 1848 PA; died ____.

Leroy CEASE was a veteran of the Civil War, having served as a Pvt. with the 132nd PA Infantry from 11 Aug 1862 to 15 May 1863 (9mo 4da) . He was a farmer residing at Gillett, Bradford County, PA when he died on 16 March 1923 at Gillett, PA. Note: They were both still living according to the 1910 Census.

Children of Leroy-[4] CEASE and Amanda-[6] MOORE:
Surname **CEASE**

+	**348. CHARLES L.**	born March 1866 PA; died ___;
		married Gertrude WRIGHT ca 1890
		(she dau/o Merton WRIGHT and Angelina _____)
		(she born Apr 1871 PA; died _____)
+	349. Crayton G.	born Nov 1868 PA; died _____; resided Gillett, PA
		married Minnie L. CHASE 1891 (she dau/o Simeon CHASE)
	350. Lyle Snyder	born 6 Jan 1875 Bradford Co., PA; died _____
		married Emma _____ 1897 (she born ca 1880; died _____)

Children: Arthur-[6] born ca 1903; Lillian-[6] born ca 1904 and Helen K-[6] CEASE born ca 1917

	351. Harriet/Hattie	born after 1870; resided Elmira Chemung, NY
+	**352. LILLIAN** "Nellie "	born 21 May 1878 PA; died ____
		married Robert -[8] LANDON 31 Aug 1894
		(he s/o Merton-[7] LANDON and Augusta B. GOFF)
		(he born ca 1874; died 1916)

111. NELSON PRINCE-[4] CEASE, brother of above, was born __ Feb 1850 at ____ PA. He married Margaret " Mag " EATON on __ ___ 1870. She was the daughter of _____ EATON (born VT) and _____ (born PA), and was born May 1848 PA; died 1924 PA. Nelson -[4] CEASE , a sawyer by trade, died ca 1921. In 1900 they resided at Armenia, PA.

Children of Nelson Prince-[4] CEASE and " Mag " EATON:
Surname **CEASE**

+	**353. ROSABELLE**	born Dec 1872 Pa; died 25 Jan 1953 Leroy, PA
	"Belle"	married Frank WELCH (he s/o Horace WELCH and Mary ____)
		(he born Mar 1871; died ____)
+	**354. WILLARD**	born ca 1874 PA; died ca 1936
		married Edith MOORE
		(she dau/o George Dudley MOORE and Frances C. SMITH)
		(she born 22 May 1882; died 2 July 1948 Canton, PA)
+	**355. LUCY M.**	born May 1879 PA; died 1969
		married Delos-5 KIFF
		(he s/o John-[4] KIFF and Susan BASCOMB)
+	**356. ALEXANDER M.**	born Feb 1881 PA; died 1944+
	(Aleck)	1 married Martha Mary _____
		(she born ca 1873; died 1927)
	357. Un-named child	born _____; died before 1900
	358. Gerald Nelson	born 17 June 1890 PA; married Stella May WELLMAN
		(she dau/o Charles Alex WELLMAN and Alice Ann AKIE)
		(she born 31 Oct 1885; died Jan 1953)

112. SIDNEY THEOPHILUS-[4] CEASE, brother of above, was born 2 Nov 1854 at Bradford Co., PA. He married Mary Caroline-[5] MC INTOSH (# 253) on 15 Sep 1875 at Blossburg. PA. She was the daughter of Michael Eden-[4] MC INTOSH and Martha LONGLEY, and was born 8 May 1858 Tioga County, PA; died 8 Aug 1920 at Harbor Springs, MI. Sidney-[4] CEASE died 8 March 1914 of spinal cancer at Harbor Springs, MI. They are both buried at Lakeview Cemetery, Harbor Springs, MI.

Children of Sidney T.-[4] CEASE and Mary Caroline-[5] MC INTOSH:
Surname **CEASE**   (a double MC INTOSH line)

+	**359. HERMAN**	born 23 Dec 1876 Tioga Co., PA; died 27 Dec 1949 Chicago, IL
	THEOPHILUS	married Loda BRIGGS ca 1904
+	**360. FRED A.**	born 28 Apr 1879 Tioga Co., PA; died 5 June 1949 Harbor Springs, MI
		married Della JOHNSON
+	**361. JULIA ANN**	born 20 June 1883 Tioga, PA; died 29 Oct 1962 Windsor, Ont., Canada
		1 married John W. LANE 30 Aug 1904 – divorced
		2 married David WALSH 22 Nov 1910
	362. IDA MYRTLE	born 8 Sep 1886 Harbor Springs; died 19 Aug 1912 Harbor Springs
		married William GREGORY 12 Oct 1904
+	**363. CARL SIDNEY**	born 17 May 1891 Harbor Springs; died 7 Apr 1947 Harbor Springs
		married Sylvia BOETTGER ca 1914
	364. Earl Robert	born 28 Nov 1894; died 26 Feb 1895 Harbor Springs, MI EOL
+	**365. MILDRED IRENE**	born 9 Jun 1897 Harbor Springs; died 29 Nov 1988 MI
		married William BOETTGER 22 June 1915
	366. Martha Helen	born 24 Aug 1900 Harbor Springs, MI; died 3 May 1903 same place

References: Arlayne BOETTGER Lipchinsky, dau/o Mildred Irene CEASE; Harbor Springs, MI; personal knowledge

114. STREVER-[4] TANNER, son of William-[3] TANNER (Magdalena-[2] MAC INTOSH; Alexander-[1]) and Margaret STREVER, was born 18 July 1806 at Ancram, Columbia County, NY.

He married first to Esther SILVERNAIL on 20 Jan 1831 at ____. Witnesses at the marriage were William TANNER and Henrich HOYSRADT. They resided at Boston Corners, NY. Esther was the daughter of John/Johan SILVERNAIL and Eve HOYSRADT, and was born 31 Oct 1806; died in the childbirth of her daughter Esther, on 28 Jan 1838. (reference: Old Gravestones of Dutchess Co, Pine Plains cemetery)

Strever-[4] TANNER married second to Elizabeth SHADIC(K) on 2 May 1844. She was the daughter of Peter SHADIC(K)/SHADWICK/SCHADOWEK and Catherine SNYDER, and was born 31 Aug 1820 at Taghkanic, Columbia County, NY; died 11 Sep 1865 (45 yr 11 da). Strever-[4] TANNER, a farmer died 10 Feb 1865 (58-6-22) . They are both buried at Pine Plains.

Children of Strever-[4] TANNER and Esther SILVERNAIL:
Surname **TANNER**

	367. Margaretha	born 24 May 1833 Ancram; died _____	no issue	EOL
		married Peter M. TANNER 17 Jan 1872 (# 182)		
	368. Esther	born 28 Jan 1838 Ancram; died 13 Dec 1873; never married		EOL

Children of Strever-[4] TANNER and Elizabeth SHADIC(K):
Surname **TANNER**

	369. Catherine	born 6 Feb 1847 Ancram; died 7 June 1868; married Arthur MILLER
		Child: Strever-[6] MILLER born ca ____; died young
	370. Mary Ann	born 30 Aug 1848 Ancram; died 18 May 1876 EOL
+	**371. ELIZABETH**	born 27 Jul 1850 Ancram; died 12 Feb 1934 Earlham, Madison, IA
		married Milton Abram SMITH 16 Jan 1873 NY
		(he born 24 July 1850; died 8 Aug 1931)
+	**372. RACHEL**	born 30 May 1852 Ancram; died 11 May 1890
		married Warren VOSBURGH
		(he born ca 1841; died _____)
+	**373. WILLIAM B.**	born 27 May 1854 Ancram; died 1932; buried Pine Plains, Dutch. Co.
		married Lucy SMITH 23 Feb 1876
		(she dau/o Alvin SMITH and Phoebe BUTTS)
		(she born 23 Mar 1857; died 1920)
+	**374. LAURA**	born 13 May 1857 Ancram, NY; died 1890)
		married John VOSBURGH (he born ca 1855) (res. Ancram, NY)
		(he s/o Abram A. VOSBURGH and Catherine FELLER)
+	**375. PETER**	born 28 Aug 1858 Ancram; died ____; married Emma HAM

115. RACHEL-[4] TANNER, sister of above, was born 22 March 1808 at Ancram, Columbia County, New York. She married Willis HOAG on __ 18__. He was the son of Samuel HOAG, Sr. and Charlotte HEPBURN, and was born 4 July 1805; died 8 March 1867. Rachel-[4] TANNER died 8 Oct 1866. They are buried at Pine Plains, Dutchess County, New York. They resided North Copake, Columbia County, NY.

Children of Rachel-[4] TANNER and Willis HOAG:
Surname **HOAG**

	376. Margaret	born 20 Oct 1830; died 10 Aug 1872; never married	EOL
	377. Mary	born ca 1832 / 33; died 14 Sep 1891; never married	EOL
	378. Laura	born ca 1834 / 35; died 1908; never married	EOL
+	**379. JAMES**	born 30 May 1838; died 20 Nov 1874 (36-5-22)	
		married Ann/Annie SMITH 18 Sep 1867	
		(she dau/o Duncan SMITH and Nancy McARTHUR)	
	380. William	born 30 Apr 1844; died _____; never married	EOL
	381. Anna Catherine	born 9 Jan 1852; married Rev, James H. MITCHELL 10 June 1875	
		Children: Willis H-[6] born 10 June 1876 and Clarence W-[6] MITCHELL born 1 June 1879	

116. ELIZA-[4] TANNER, sister of above, was born 24 Feb 1810 at Ancram, Columbia County, NY. She married Jonathan HEAD on _____ at _____. He was the son of ____ HEAD and _____, and was born ca 1810, NY; died _____. Eliza-[4] TANNER died ca ____. They resided at Ancram.

The Fourth American Generation

Children of Eliza-[4] TANNER and Jonathan HEAD:

Surname **HEAD**

+	**382. WILLIAM**	born ca 1832; died 31 March 1899; married Laura MC ARTHUR
		resided Ancram Lead Mines, NY
+	**383. JONATHAN, JR.**	born ca 1835/36 NY; died ____
		married Mary [-4] TANNER (# 174)
		(she dau/o Samuel S-[3] TANNER (# 39) and Mary Betsey LOWN)
+	**384. MARY ANN**	born ca 1837, NY; died ____; married Thomas DYE
	385. Margaret	born ca 1839 NY; died ____
		1 married ____ LYONS; 2 married Perry BENJAMIN
	386. Eliza	born ca 1845 Ancram, NY; died ____ (dau Eliza MAGEE – no info)
		married Thomas (Tom) MAGEE/ MC GEE
	387. Elizabeth	born ca 1847 NY; died ____; no issue EOL
		married Ed SHELDON; resided Copake Iron Works, NY

117. LAURA-[4] TANNER, sister of above, was born 13 December 1812 at Ancram, Columbia County, New York. She married Adam SILVERNAIL ca 1833. Adam, the son of Johan/John SILVERNAIL and Eve HOYSRADT, was born 24 April 1812; died 25 March 1873. Laura-[4] TANNER died 3 June 1865. They resided Valatie, NY.

Children of Laura-[4] TANNER and Adam SILVERNAIL:

Surname **SILVERNAIL**

388. Peter	born 1837/38; died ____; he was a school teacher
	married Emily Caroline MAGEE 1863
	Children: twins Anna-[6] and Arthur-[6] born ca 1867; William-[6] SILVERNAIL born ca 1869
389. William H.	born May 1838; died ____; he was a lawyer
	1 married Mary L. SPEAR 1877
	(she dau/o Samuel SPEAR and Minerva G. ____)
	2 married May North STALEY 1896
390. Sarah E.	born ca 1841 NY
391. Margaret A.	born 9 Mar 1843 NY; dy 392. Laura born ca 1850/51 NY

119. ELIZABETH-[4] TANNER, sister of above, was born 17 July 1816 at Ancram, Columbia County, NY. She married John McArthur SMITH on 16 Oct 1845. John was the son of Nicholas SMITH (John Theiss SCHMIDT, Jr) and Polly MC ARTHUR, and was born ca 1817; died 16 Oct 1895. Elizabeth-[4] TANNER died ____.

Children of Elizabeth-[4] TANNER and John McArthur SMITH:

Surname **SMITH**

	393. Mary	born 11 Sep 1846; died ____; resided Millerton, NY
		married Charles COOK 23 Nov 1870
		Child: Anna/Annie-[7] COOK born 5 Oct 1877, married Martin PALMER – child: Russell C-[8] PALMER
	394. Sarah	born 10 July 1848; died ____ no issue EOL
		married Lewis M. HOYSRADT 18 Nov 1875
	395. William Nicholas	born 5 March 1851; died ____;
		1 married Alice M. HOLLAND 18 Nov 1874
		(she born ____; died 12 May 1890) Child: William-6 SMITH born ca ____
		2 married Annie POTTER 22 March 1893; resided Ancram
+	**396. WARD**	born 5 Aug 1853; died ____; resided Ancram Lead Mines
		married Elsie Adella TRIPP 27 Nov 1878 (she born ca 1858 NY)
		(she dau/o William H. TRIPP and Mary Etta RHODE)

122. WILLIAM W-[4] TANNER, brother of above, was born 25 November 1823 at Ancram, Columbia County, NY. He was a farmer. His first wife was Hannah Elizabeth STREVER. They married on ___ at ____. Hannah was the daughter of Uldrick STREVER and Amanda KINNEY, and was born 1 Feb 1834; died 15 May 1864. He married second to Amy E. WHEELER Wallace on ___. She was the daughter of ____ WHEELER and _____; and the widow of _____ WALLACE, and was born ca 1848; died 15 Feb 1913. William-[4] TANNER died 4 Oct 1881 (age 59) and is buried at Evergreen Cemetery, Pine Plains, NY. They resided at Ancram and Tanner's Station, New York.

Children of William W-[4] TANNER and Amy WHEELER Wallace:
Surname **TANNER**

397. Inez	born 4 May 1873; died ____	
	married Frank MILLIUS 5 Sep 1894	
398. Samuel	born 8 June 1875; died _____	
	married Rhoda WILTSIE ca 1896; divorced	
399. Ruth	born 28 Dec 1879; died ____	
400. La Fayette Tripp	born 18 July 1880; died _____	
	1 married Mary C. _____	
	2 married Rhoda WILTSIE Tanner (formerly wife of his brother)	
401. Nellmine M./Libby	born 20 Oct 1881; died _____	

124. OLIVE EMELINE-[4] TANNER, daughter of Alexander-[3] TANNER (Magdalena-[2] MAC INTOSH, Alexander-[1]) and Nancy MERRITT, was born ca 1811 at possibly Claverack, Columbia County, New York. She married Dr. Stephen PLATNER on 10 March 1831 at The Reformed Church of Claverack, NY. Alexander TANNER was a witness. (Marriage records of the Ref Ch of Claverack #2344) Dr. Stephen H. PLATNER was the son of Mark PLATNER and Annatje/Anna Nancy STRONG, and was born 8 Nov 1806 NY; died _____(possibly before 1870). Olive Emeline-[4] TANNER died ____. They resided at Copake, Columbia County, NY.

Children of Olive Emeline-[4] TANNER and Dr. Stephen PLATNER:
Surname **PLATNER**

402. Nancy	born ca 1832; died 18 Mar1852	(age 20)		EOL
403. Mary E.	born 1836; died 20 Dec 1857			EOL
404. Emily	born ca 1839; died 2 Aug 1853	(age 14)		EOL
+ **405. DELIA**	born ca 1846; died ____			
	married Henry D. MYERS			
406. Stephen	born and died before 1850			EOL
407. Angeline	born after 1850	408. Ida	born ca 1854	

125. SAMUEL A-[4] TANNER, son of Alexander-[3] TANNER (Magdalena-[2] MAC INTOSH; Alexander-[1]) and Nancy MERRITT, was born ca 1815 at _____, New York. He married Maria-[5] ROCKEFELLER +++ on ____ (before 1858). She was the daughter of William-[4] ROCKEFELLER and Charity MC DONALD, and was born 10 Sep 1829; died _____ (living 1900, residing with daughter Ida at Tyre, Seneca County, NY) Samuel A-[4] TANNER died _____.

Children of Samuel A-[4] TANNER and Maria-[5] ROCKEFELLER:
Surname **TANNER**

409. Palman	born ca 1858 Montezuma, NY; died 1860 same place	EOL
410. Ida M.	born May 1860; died ____	
	married Augustus J. UPHAM ca 1889	
	(he born ca 1861; still living 1930)	

Child: Wesley R-[6] UPHAM born 17 Nov 1896; married Loretta ___ ca 1921; had dau May-[7] born ca 1926

The Fourth American Generation

Ancestry of Maria-5 ROCKEFELLER
Reference: ROCKEFELLER Genealogy by Henry Oscar ROCKFELLER, MD, published by Knickerbocker 1910

Johan[-B] ROCKENFELLER, was born ca 1628; died 24 July 1702 Elscheid, Germany. His son Tonges[-A] ROCKENFELLER was born ca 1658; married Gertrude PAULI in Feldkirchen, Germeny and died in Elscheid on 18 July 1707.

Tonges[-A] ROCKENFELLER had 7 children – among them Johann[-1] Thiel/Diell ROCKEFELLER, born July 1695 at Elscheid, Germany. He married Anna Gertrude ALSDORF and died in Germantown, NY in 1769. Johan[-1] ROCKEFELLER came to America before 1735. He and Anna had 11 children. His 7 child was William[-2] ROCKEFELLER who was born 6 Oct 1737.

William[-2] ROCKEFELLER , who married Margaret BAHR and died 1786, was the father of Diell/TEAL[-3] ROCKEFELLER who was born _____; baptized 31 July 1779. Teal/DIELL[-3] married Helen WHEELER and resided at Copake, NY. They were the parents of William-4 who married Charity MC DONALD. He was born 28 Jan 1801; died ____. William[-4] and Charity MC DONALD had 14 children. Maria , was their the 6th child, and was born 10 Sep 1829 and married Samuel A-[4] TANNER(above)

127. NANCY ALMA-[4] (Almy) TANNER, daughter of John-[3] TANNER (Magdalena-[2] MAC INTOSH; Alexander-[1]) and Olive MERRITT, was born 15 March 1816 at Taghkanic, Columbia County, New York. She married Jeremiah SIMMONS ca 1833 . He was the son of David SIMMONS and Anna Margrieta "Margaret" VAN DEUSEN, and was born 3 July 1807; died 27 Aug 1888. Nancy-[4] TANNER died 2 Dec 1870 at Taghkanic, NY. They are buried in the West Copake Reformed Church Cemetery.

Child of Nancy Alma-[4] TANNER and Jeremiah SIMMONS:
Surname **SIMMONS**

	411. John	born 25 Apr 1836; died Feb 1888; resided Taghkanic, NY
	412. Margaret Ann	born ca 1839; married Myron SHULTS; died 3 Nov 1863 Pine Plains
		Child: Ellsworth-6 SHULTS born _____
+	**413. MARTIN**	born 12 May 1840 Dutchess Co.,NY; died 19 Feb 1888 Dutchess Co.
		married Ellen FITZGERALD 4 Mar 1868
		(she dau/o Michael FITZGERALD and Kate O'BRIEN)
		(she born 7 Apr 1850 Dutchess Co., NY; died 30 Aug 1890)
	414. Robert	born 15 June 1842; died 17 May 1888
		married Rosanna SHULTS (Child: Jay-6 SIMMONS born ca 1874)
	415. Mary Emma	born 20 Aug 1844; died _____
		married Luke D. WYMBS 21 Aug 1872; resided Glenham, NY
		Child: Ola-6 WYMBS born _____
	416. Anna Lucelia	born 28 May 1846; married Robert WOOD; died 9 Dec 1918
		Child: Robert-6 WOOD, Jr. born ca 1887
+	**417. JAMES**	born 11 Aug 1848; died Jan 1914 NJ
	MONROE	married Frances Minerva (Minnie) HANKHURST
	418. Ida (twin)	born 29 July 1851; married Walter John MILLER; died 4 Jan 1932
		Child: Ethel-6 MILLER born ca _____
+	**419. ADA** (twin)	born 29 July 1851; died 4 Jan 1931
		married Charles KELLERHOUSE ca 1873
	420. Lyman	born 10 Sep 1854; married Ophelia FRIESS no issue EOL
+	**421. ALMA MAE**	born 31 May 1856; married Frank INGLES; died 14 Oct 1918
	422. Norton	born 16 Aug 1858; died 1901

128. SALLY ANN-[4] TANNER, sister of above, was born ca 1820 at Taghkanic, Columbia County, New York. She married James YORKER on _____ at ____. He was the son of _____ YORKER and _____, and was born ca 1806; died _____. Sally Ann-[4] TANNER died ____.

Children of Sally Ann-[4] TANNER and James YORKER:
Surname **YORKER**

+	**423. EMILY/EMMA**	born Sep 1842 MA; died before 1874
		married Morton H. COMSTOCK 28 Dec 1861

Children of Sally Ann-[4] TANNER and James YORKER, continued:
Surname **YORKER**

+	**423. EMILY** , cont'd;	(he s/o Hugh COMSTOCK and Polly AVERY) (he born ca 1840 NY; died 2 Feb 1903)
+	**424. MARTHA ANNA**	born ca 1847-48 MA.; died _____
	(Ann)	married Morton H. COMSTOCK 4 Sep 1874 (as his 2nd wife)
	425. Ada	born ca 1854 MA 426. Jenny/ Geneva born Nov 1857 MA

131. JANE MARGARET-[4] TANNER, half sister of above, daughter of John-[3] TANNER (Magdalena-[2] MAC INTOSH; Alexander-[1]) and Christina FINGAR Mosher , was born ca _____ . She married David SHULTIS on _____ . He was the son of _____ SHULTIS and _____ , and was born _____ ; died _____ . Jane Margaret-[4] TANNER died _____ .

Children of Jane Margaret-[4] TANNER and David SHULTIS:
Surname **SHULTIS**

+	**427. EMMAGEN/**	born 31 Oct 1854 NY; died 1883
	EMOGENE	married John CONKLE ca 1877 (he born ca 1854; died 1916)
	428. Alexander Tanner	born 20 Apr 1856
		1 married Alice TREBILCOX Feb 1889; resided Hillsdale, NY
		2 married Minnie J. WILLIAMS no issue EOL
		(she dau/o Elijah WILLIAMS and _____) (she born ca 1876)
	429. Anna L.	born ca 1859; died 1859 EOL
	430. Emily C.	born 16 Apr 1861; died _____
		married Norman RONEY (he born ca 1857; died ____)
	431. Carrie	born 10 Nov 1864; died ____; married Frank SHULTIS ca 1882
		Children: Albert-[6] born ca 1887 and Mary-[6] SHULTIS born ca 1887
	432. Emma M./	born 26 Feb 1867 / 68 NY; died _____
	Minnie	married Charles M/W SHELDON ca 1883
		(he born Sep 1863 NY; died _____) resided Sayre, PA 1900-1930
		Children: Clarence-[6] born July 1885; Fred-[6] born Mar 1886; Anna-[6] born Nov 1888, married James L. LINEHAN (he born ca 1885 PA); and Georgia A.-[6] SHELDON born 1901

132. AMBROSE L-[4] TANNER, brother of above, was born __ Nov 1828 at Columbia County, NY. He married first to Jane Catherine SHADIC on ____ at ____ . She was the daughter of ____ SHADIC and _____ , and was born _____ ; died ____ . His second wife was Georgia Anna SILVERNAIL. She was the daughter of Henry SILVERNAIL and Dorothy CLARK, and was born 12 Nov 1849; died 25 Oct 1881.

His third wife was Locella STREVER. They married 15 Dec 1886. She was the daughter of ___ STREVER and ____ , and was born Dec 1844; died ____ . Ambrose L-[4] TANNER died 4 March 1905 (age 76) and is buried at the Reformed Church Cemetery in Copake, NY.

Children of Ambrose L-[4] TANNER and Jane SHADIC:
Surname **TANNER**

	433. John L.	born 20 Nov 1863; died _____
		married Carrie BUSH 8 Nov 1887 (she born Apr 1870 NY)
		Children: Abram-[6] born Mar 1890 and Mabel-[6] TANNER born Aug 1892
+	**434. BELLE**	born 10 Aug 1867; died ca 1919
		married John H. PELLS 15 Dec 1886
		(he born 16 May 1864; died 1930)
+	**435. HENRY S.**	born 24 Aug 1869; died _____
		married Libby MC INTYRE 11 Jan 1893
		(in 1937 he resided on the farm of John-[3] TANNER)

Children of Ambrose L-[4] TANNER and Jane SHADIC, continued:
Surname **TANNER**

+   **436. BLANCHE**   born 4 Oct 1873; died _____
                                                     married Harry CARLE of Maryland, ca 1892

Child of Ambrose L-[4] TANNER and Georgianna SILVERNAIL:
Surname **TANNER**

            437. Ambrose Jay   born 13 Sep 1880; died 26 Sep1881; buried Copake, NY   EOL

134. ALEXANDER-[4] TANNER, son of John-[3] TANNER (Magdalena-[2] MAC INTOSH; Alexander-[1])
and Christine FINGAR Mosher, was born ca 1834 at Copake, Columbia County, NY. He married Vera
Margaret LYALL on ___ at _____ . She was the daughter of the Rev William LYALL (Presbyterian
minister born Scotland) and Sarah A. _____ (born CT). Vera was born ca 1842 Ward 18, NY, NY; and
died _____ . Alexander-[4] TANNER died _____ .

Children of Alexander-[4] TANNER and Vera LYALL:
Surname **TANNER**

+   **438. GENEVIEVE**   born 24 Feb 1860; baptized 2 June 1860 W. Copake; died _____
                 Jennie   married Oliver COONS   no issue   EOL
+   **439. WILLIAM**   born 28 Aug 1863 NY; baptized 10 Oct 1863 Copake, NY
                 JOHN   married Rose Ruth ROWLEY
                                                     buried Hudson Cem.
+   **440. J. EDWARD LYALL** born ca 1878; died _____ ; married Margaret MESICK

137. CATHERINE MELINDA-[4] (Kate) TANNER, sister of above, was born Sep 1841 at Copake,
Columbia County, NY. She married Friend SIMONS on _____ at _____ . He was the son of ____SIMONS
and ____ , and was born Nov 1843 NY; died _____ . In 1880 , 1900 they resided at Hillsdale, Columbia,
NY. Catherine -[4] TANNER died _____ (before 1920).

Children of Catherine Melinda-[4] TANNER and Friend SIMONS:
Surname **SIMONS**

            441. Jay   born ca 1869 NY; died _____ ; married Joanna LUTZ
                             Child: Madaline-[6] SIMONS born _____
            442. Maude   born ca 1870; died _____
                                                    married Fred A. JORDAN 27 Nov 1890
                                                    (he s/o William JORDAN and Marion E _____)
                                                    (he born ca 1867; died _____)
            443. George   born Feb 1875; died _____ ; never married   EOL

138. PHILO-[4] WOOLDRIDGE, son of Mary Magdalena-[3] TANNER (Rachel-[2] MAC INTOSH,
Alexander-[1]) and William T. WOOLDRIDGE, was born 8 Feb 1816 at Dutchess County, New York. He
married Gertrude DYKEMAN on _____ at _____ . She was the daughter of _____ DYKEMAN (born
Germany) and ____ , and was born Feb 1827 NY; died _____ . Philo-[4] WOOLDRIDGE died 6 May 1891.
They resided at Pine Plains, Dutchess County, NY.

Children of Philo-[4] WOOLDRIDGE and Gertrude DYKEMAN:
Surname **WOOLDRIDGE**

            444. William   born 31 March 1848 Dutchess Co., died 6 May 1893
            445. Franklin Pierce (twin)born 18 Nov 1853 NY; died _____
+   **446. RUFUS**   (twin)   born 18 Nov 1853 NY; died _____
                 KING   married Anna JONES 23 Nov 1880
            447. Jacob P.   born 30 Sep 1862; died ____ ; married Annie L.___ ca 1895

The Fourth American Generation

140. HARRIET[-4] WOOLDRIDGE, sister of above, was born 10 July 1820 Dutchess County, New York. She married James MC CARRICK on ___ at ____. He was the son of ____ MC CARRICK and _____, and was born Feb 1815; died 2 June 1872 (57 yr 4 mo). Harriet[-4] died 18 Oct 1870 (50yr3mo)

Children of Harriet-[4] WOOLDRIDGE and James MC CARRICK:
Surname **MC CARRICK**

448. Robert	born ca 1842 NY; died ____ (living 1910); married Amy ____		

Children: Clarence-[6] born 1874; Howard-[6] born 1876 and Nellie-[6] MC CARRICK born ca 1878

Note: Robert MC CARRICK enlisted 18 Sep 1861 in the Civil War as a Pvt. In Company B, NY 80th Infantry Regiment, mustered out 1864. In 1906 was admitted to the US National Home for Disabled Veterans at Togus, Kennebec. ME. He asked to be discharged 11 July 1909 to the custody of his son Clarence of Malden, MA.

	449. Sylvester	born 2 Sep 1843 NY; died 7 March 1845 (1-6-5)	EOL
+	**450. EDWARD**	born ca 1845/ 46 NY; died _____	
		1 married Lovina _____ (she born ca 1851 CT; died _____)	
		2 married Adda _____ (she born ca 1866; died ____)	
	451. Mary	born ca 1848 NY; died _____	
	452. Margaret	born ca 1851 NY; died _____	
	453. Francis/William	born 14 Dec 1856 NY; died 16 June 1858 (1-10-2)	EOL
	454. Clarissa	born Oct 1859 CT; died 9 Jan 1876 (16yr3mo)	EOL
	455. Anna	born ca 1863 CT; died _____	

142. MARY JANE[-4] WOOLDRIDGE , sister of above, was born 12 Nov 1827 at Dutchess County, New York. She married Joel W. KELSEY ca ____. He was the son of ____ KELSEY and _____, and was born Dec 1819 ME; died ____ OH. In 1850 they resided in Toledo, Lucas County, Ohio where he was a lumber dealer. In 1870 resided in Washington, Lucas Co., OH, and later moved back to Toledo where he was a pork packer. Mary Jane-[4] WOOLDRIDGE died before 1900 OH.

Children of Mary Jane[-4] WOOLDRIDGE and Joel W. KELSEY:
Surname **KELSEY**

	456. Joseph R.	born Oct 1851 OH; married Mary B ____ ca 1882
		(she born June 1858 ; 1900 resided Omadi, Dakota, Nebraska)
+	**457. EDWARD W.**	born Apr 1855 OH; died 11 Sep 1917 Lucas County, OH
		married Elizabeth L. ____ (she born Dec 1864)
	458. Harry M.	born 13 Apr 1859 OH; married _____

Children: Florence-[6] born June 1887 and Eloise J-[6] KELSEY born Aug 1889

	459. John M.	born May 1862 OH; married Louise C. _____ (she born ca 1870 NJ)

143. JOHN J-[4] TANNER,, brother of above , was born __ __ 182_ at ____, New York. He married Caroline HAWVER on ___ at ____. She was the daughter of ____ HAWVER and ____, and was born ca 1815 Germany; died ca 1891. John J-[4] TANNER died ca 1897 and is buried at the Union Ancram Cemetery, Ancram, New York.

Children of John J-[4] TANNER and Caroline HAWVER:
Surname **TANNER**

	460. Margaret	born _____; died young	EOL
	461. Annis	born _____; died ____	
	462. Jane	born ca 1843; died young	EOL
+	**463. RUEY/RHEA**	born ca 1844; died ____	
		married Thomas SCUTT; (he s/o Grove SCUTT and _____)	
	464. Reuben	born ca 1845; died ____; resided Philmont, Columbia Co., NY	
		married Catherine BENGHER/BURGHER no issue EOL	

Children of John J-⁴ TANNER and Caroline HAWVER, continued:
Surname **TANNER**

465. Mary Ann	born ca 1847; died 1907: buried Union Ancram Cemetery		
	married Jake BANHOTEL after 1880		
	(Child: Jennie-6 BANHOTEL born ___; married Emory JOHNES; resided Ancram, NY		
466. Catherine	born _____; died young		EOL
467. Homer	born _____; died young		EOL
468. Eliza	born _____; died young		EOL
+ **469. JOHN J.**	born ____; died ____		
	married Margaret MAGELEY; resided Hudson, Columbia Co., NY		
470. Marilla	born _____; died ____ ; 1 married Charles COLE		
	Children: Charles W-⁶; Amelia E-⁶; Willie C-⁶ ; Ada B-⁶; and Eddie D-⁶ COLE		
	2 married William RIVENBURGH; resided Philmont, NY		
+ **471. JACOB H.**	born Aug 1859; died 25 Aug 1940 Ancram		
	married Minnie WILLIS of Hillsdale, NY (she born ca 1863; died __)		

145. OLIVE EMELINE-⁴ TANNER, sister of above, was born ca 1824 at Ancram, Columbia County, NY. She married Reuben LOOMIS. He was the son of _____ LOOMIS and ____, and was born 3 Dec 1817 NY; died _____. Olive Emeline-⁴ TANNER died _____.

Children of Olive Emeline-⁴ TANNER and Reuben LOOMIS:
Surname **LOOMIS**

472. James	born 7 July 1846 North East,NY; married Elizabeth HOYSRADT
	Children: Nina-⁶ born 10 Dec 1870, died 17 Dec 1871; and Mina⁶ LOOMIS born 27 Nov 1871, died 17 Dec 1871
473. Mary A.	born 22 May 1848/49 NY; died ____
474. William Henry	born 1851; died 1859
475. Martha Jane	born Sept 1860/61 NY ; died ____; married Harley BROWN
476. Ida	born Oct 1866 NY

147. MORRIS-⁴ TANNER, brother of above, was born 19 Dec 1827 at Ancram, Columbia County, New York. He married Lucinda Diantha COLEPAUGH 23 Jan 1847. She was the daughter of Andrus/ Andrew COLEPAUGH and Polly MIERS/MYERS, and was born ca 1827; died ca 1898. Morris-⁴ TANNER died 13 Feb 1899 and is buried at the Town Hill Cemetery, Salisbury, CT.

Children of Morris-⁴ TANNER and Lucinda Diantha COLEPAUGH:
Surname **TANNER**

477. James	born 6 Nov 1848		
+ **478. CHARLES A.**	born 1850 NY; died ___; married Augusta C. REEVES 10 July 1874		
479. Milton W. (twin)	born 30 Sep 1851 NY; died ____		
480. Wesley (twin)	born 30 Sep 1851 NY; died ____		
	married Christina RICHMOND 23 May 1883		
+ **481. ELIZABETH**	born 12 Aug 1853 NY; died ____		
	married Henry W. VOSBURGH 14 Jan 1875		
482. Lewis F.	born 10 Dec 1855 NY; died 1866		EOL
483. Anna	born 6 Dec 1858; died ____; married Norman KILMER 27 Dec 1875		
	(he born ca 1855 ; died _____)		
	Child: Ward-⁶ KILMER born ca 1878		
484. Willis W.	born 13 Sep 1860 NY; died ____		
485. William	born 5 Mar 1862; married Etta SILVERNAIL; resided CT		
	Child: Eva⁶ TANNER born 17 Aug 1886		
486. Alida	born 27 July 1863; died __; married Henry S. DARLING 22 Dec 1893		
487. Martha J.	born 17 Apr 1865; died 1866		EOL
488. Arthur	born 7 Nov 1867		

150. JAMES-[4] TANNER, brother of above, a lighthouse keeper, was born ca 1832 at _____, NY. He married first to Sarah HUMMEL on ____ at _____. She was the daughter of Peter HUMMEL and Mary A. _, and was born ____; died ___. His second wife was Rachel A. ____. She was born ca 1829; died _____. James -[4] TANNER , a lighthouse keeper, died possibly before 1870. Resided Saugerties, Ulster Co., NY

Children of James-[4] TANNER and _____:
Surname **TANNER**

489. William P.	born ca 1853	
490. Solomon M.	born July 1857 NY; died ____, a shoemaker	
"Sol"	married Lettie J. _____ 1887; resided Canton, St. Lawrence, NY	
	(she born ca 1860)	
491. Jane M.	born ca 1860	

157. SYLVESTER-[4] STREVER, son of Clarissa-[3] TANNER (Rachel-[2] MAC INTOSH; Alexander-[1]) and Adam STREVER, was born 29 March 1822 at Ancram, Columbia County, New York. He married first to Phebe SHELDON on ____ at ____. She was the daughter of _____ SHELDON and _____, and was born 8 Nov 1831; died 14 Feb 1870 (38-3-6) . His second marriage was to her sister , Matilda SHELDON. She was born ca 1833; died 24 August 1895 (age 62). In 1860 he was a resident of Gallatinville, Columbia County, NY. Sylvester-[4] was a farmer, and died 18 Jan 1902 (79yr10mo) and is buried at Evergreen Cemetery, Pine Plains, NY.

Children of Sylvester-[4] STREVER and Phebe SHELDON:
Surname **STREVER**

+	**492. CLARA /**	born ca 1851 NY; died ____ (living 1920 Livingston Co., NY)
	CLARACY	married Dr. Charles COLE of Pine Plains, Dutchess Co., NY
	493. Adam A.	born 27 Nov 1852 NY; died 13 Dec 1899 (47-1-17 gs)
	494. Samuel J.	born Nov 1854 NY; died _____
	495 Monroe	born 1856 NY; married Rose E. _____
	Children: Walter M.-[6] born ca 1899; and Monroe J.-[6] STREVER born 17 Oct 1908; died 29 June 2000 Dover, DE	
+	**496. SHELDON P.**	born ca 1859; died _____
		married Alice ENDERLIN ca 1898
		(she dau/o Adolph ENDERLIN (born Germany) and Mary _____)
		(she born May 1872; died _____)
	497. Lewis Sylvester	born ca 1863 NY; died 25 Oct 1900 (age 37) gs
	498. Frances B (f)	born ca 1867; baptized 3 July 1868
	499. Ulysses Grant	born July 1868; baptized 3 July 1868
		married Isabelle C. BALL ca 1895 no issue EOL
		(she dau/o _____ BALL and Sarah LANE) (she born Mar 1875)

166. CLARISSA-[4] TANNER, daughter of Henry-[3] TANNER (Rachel-[2] MAC INTOSH; Alexander-[1]) and Eliza HINSDALE, was born Nov 1836 at ____, NY. She married Henry FRISS , of Taghkanic, NY, on 12 Oct 1853 at The Reformed Church of Claverack, New York. (# 2775) . Their witness was Jacob FRISS. Henry was the son of Jacob FRISS and Anna Maria STREVER, and was born ca 1825 NY; died before 1900. Clarissa-[4] TANNER died 5 Sep ____. They resided Taghkanic, NY.

Children of Clarissa-[4] TANNER and Henry FRISS:
Surname **FRISS**

500. Henry S.	born ca 1856; married Jennie _____ (she born ca 1863; died before 1920		
Child: Roy-[6] FRISS born ca 1899 Claverack, NY			
501. William L.	born July 1857		
502. Peter M.	born ca 1860; married Nellie _____ 1892 ; no issue		
503 Elizabeth	born ca 1862	504. Edgar	born ca 1864

Children of Clarissa-[4] TANNER and Henry FRISS, continued:
Surname **FRISS**

    505. Frank   born ca Apr 1867; married Emma _____ (she born ca 1868; died ____)
                Children: Clarence A-[6] born 28 Jan 1894; Beulah-[6] born ca 1899 and Orrin L.-[6] FRISS born ca 1902
    506 Charles   born ca 1869/70
    507. Melvin   born ca 1871; married Idella _____(she born ca 1878; died before 1920)
            Children: Lauren-[6] born ca 1904; Lyle-[6] born ca 1906; Leland-[6] born ca 1908; LaVerne-[6] born
                  ca 1911; and H. Kenneth-[6] FRISS born ca 1913
+   **508. CLARISSA L.**   born July 1873; married Freeman HOTALING
    509. Jacob   born 9 Aug 1875; married Marjorie Bruce RAUGHT
            Children: Harvey-[6] born ca 1904; and James-[6] FRISS born ca 1917

169. HIRAM-[4] TANNER, half brother of above, son of Henry-[3] TANNER (Rachel-[2] MAC INTOSH; Alexander-[1]) and Catherine Snyder, was born ca 1840 at Taghkanic, Columbia County, NY. He married Anna Maria HOAG ca ___. She was the daughter of ___ HOAG and ___, and was born 1846; died _____.

Child of Hiram -[4] TANNER and Anna HOAG:
Surname **TANNER**
+   **510. ADELBERT**   born 19 Oct 1867 Taghkanic, NY; died _____
                     married Jurilla / Rilla FINKLE 21 Dec 1892
                     (she dau/o Abram FINKLE and Josephine COONS)
                     (she born 20 Dec 1874; died _____)

168. PETER-[4] TANNER, brother of above, was born July 1838 at Taghkanic, Columbia County, New York. He married Catherine Ann MEYERS on ____ at ____. She was the daughter of _____ MEYERS and _____, and was born March 1843; died _____. Peter-[4] TANNER died _____.

Children of Peter-[4] TANNER and Catherine A. MEYERS:
Surname **TANNER**
    511. Etta/ Ettie   born Nov 1864; married Horton BRYANT ca 1883
                    (he born Dec 1861; s/o Milton BRYANT and Lucinda _____)
    512. Kate / Katie   born Sep 1869; died _____
    513. Lawrence A.   born May 1879; died ____; married Fannie/Fanny May_____

170. LOUISA/LOUISE-[4] TANNER, sister of above, was born Nov 1841 at ____, New York. She married James Lawrence BASHFORD ca 1872 at Claverack, Columbia County, NY. He was the son of Byaly BASHFORD and Betsey SNYDER, and was born June 1838 NY; died before 1920. Louisa/Louise-[4] TANNER died before 1930 .

Children of Louisa-[4] TANNER and James Lawrence BASHFORD:
Surname **BASHFORD**
    514. Wilson   born 15 Nov 1881 NY; died _____
                  married Florence _____ (she born 1879/80 NY; died _____)
            Children: Ida L.[6] born ca 1903 NY; and Byaly[6] BASHFORD born ca 1906 NY

171. STEPHEN H-[4] TANNER, brother of above, was born June 1848 at ____, New York. He married Anna (Annie) E. TEATOR ca ____ at Taghkanic, Columbia County, NY. She was the daughter of _____ TEATOR and _____, and was born June 1859; died ____. Stephen H-[4] TANNER died ____.

Children of Stephen H-[4] TANNER and Annie TEATOR:
Surname **TANNER**
    515. Roy S.   born 11 Mar 1887; died ____; resided Claverack, Columbia Co., NY
                married Mae ROCKEFELLER 26 Aug 1914

Children of Stephen-[4] TANNER and Annie TEATOR, continued:
Surname **TANNER**

515. cont'd. (Roy S.)   (she dau/o James D. ROCKEFELLER and Margaret H. RACE)
                           (she born 5 Dec 1892 Copake, Col., NY; died _____)
              Children: Dorothy A.-[6] born ca 1917; Eleanor N.-[6] born ca 1919 and Beulah E-[6] TANNER born ca 1921
516. William H.   born Oct 1879 Taghkanic; died ____; married Lillie _____
                          (she born ca 1888; died _____) Child: John A-[6] TANNER born ca 1907

173. FRANCES (Fannie)-[4] TANNER, daughter of Samuel S-[3] TANNER (Rachel-[2] MAC INTOSH; Alexander-[1]) and his second wife Mary Betsey LOWN, was born 29 March 1842 _____, NY. She married Henry PALMER on ___ 1867 at ____. He was the son of Obediah PALMER and Catherine ____, and was born Feb 1840 NY; died _____. Fannie-[4] TANNER died ____.

Children of Fannie-[4] TANNER and Henry PALMER:
Surname **PALMER**

517. Henry, Jr.   born July 1884 NY; died _____

174. MARY-[4] TANNER (see Jonathan/John HEAD, Jr. (# 383)

176. ELIZABETH M-[4] TANNER, half sister of above, daughter of Samuel S-[4] TANNER and his third wife Julia SHELDON, was born Nov 1848 at Pine Plains, Dutchess County, NY. She married Samuel TITUS ca 1868 at ____. He was the son of John TITUS and Ann __, and was born May 1843 ; died _____.

Children of Elizabeth M-[4] TANNER and Samuel TITUS:
Surname **TITUS**

518. Julia A.   born 29 Sep 1870 Pine Plains; died _____
                          married Roscoe C. WRIGHT 21 Oct 1897;   (he born 9 Mar 1872)
519. Mary Elizabeth   born 19 Nov/Dec 1879; died _____

180. MARY ANN (Annie)-[4] TANNER, daughter of Morris-[3] TANNER (Rachel-[2] MAC INTOSH; Alexander-[1]) and Sally Ann SNYDER, was born ca 1835 at Columbia County, NY. She married Jacob MILLER on ____ at ____. He was the son of ____ MILLER and ____, and was born ca 1825 NY; died _____. Mary Ann-[4] TANNER died ____. They resided at Gallatin, Columbia County, NY.

Children of Mary Ann-[4] TANNER and Jacob MILLER:
Surname **MILLER**

520. Estella   born Nov 1859 Gallatin; died _____
521. Ada   born _____; married Victor SMITH
522. Carrie   born _____; married BURCH
523. Jennie   born ca ____
              Reference: TANNER Family Records

184. CHRISTINA-[4] TANNER, daughter of Morris-[3] TANNER (Rachel-[2] MAC INTOSH; Alexander-[1]) and Sally Ann SNYDER, was born ca 1847 NY. She married Freeman B.MILLER ca ____. He was the son of ____ MILLER and _____, and was born ca 1844; died ca 1911. Christina-[4] TANNER died ca 1927.

Children of Christina-4 TANNER and Freeman B. MILLER:
Surname **MILLER**

+   **524. JULIET/JULIETTE** born ca 1874 NY; died _____
                          married Edward (Ed) MACY ca _____
525. George T.   born ca 1880; married Mae L. VAN DEUSEN (she born ca 1881)
526. Luella/ Lulu   born ca 1882 NY

188. MARY E-[5] MC DONALD, daughter of Mary-[4] CALDWELL (Clara-[3] MC INTOSH; Simon-[2]; Alexander-[1]) and James MC DONALD, was born 2 Oct 1849 at Brooklyn, New York. She married Horace N. SCOTT, as his second wife, on 14 Dec 1870 at Canton, Bradford County, PA. He was the son of Zina/Zeriah L. SCOTT (Jonathan) and Jane Ann WARD (Eliphalet) and was born 13 Sep 1837 at Troy Township, Bradford, PA; died 31 Dec 1916 . (Horace was married first to Jane L.WELCH on 15 Oct 1866 Troy, PA. She was the daughter of Jefferson WELCH and Lucy Ann PALMER, and was born ca 1843 PA; died 24 Nov 1868. (Jane WELCH and Horace SCOTT had a child Grace May SCOTT born ca 1867, died 13 June 1869.) Horace SCOTT died 31 Dec 1916 Canton, PA. Mary-[5] MC DONALD died 2 June 1922 Canton, Bradford, PA. They are buried at Park Cemetery, Canton, PA.

Horace SCOTT served in the Civil War. He enlisted on 27 Aug 1861 (PA) in Company D, 106th Infantry Regiment as a Pvt. He was a wagonner. He participated in the battles of Gettysburg, Spotsylvannia Court House, VA; Cold Harbor, VA; Petersburg, VA , etc. He filed for invalid pension 6 Feb 1889 (Application # 688402) and his widow filed 6 Sep 1917 (# 1093171)

Children of Mary-[5] MC DONALD and Horace SCOTT:
Surname **SCOTT**   (all children born Canton, Bradford, PA)

527. George H.	born 29 Aug 1872 ; died 25 Feb 1888 Canton, PA		EOL
528 Eva Isabel	born 22 June 1875; died 1932		
	married Charles WITHEY 18 Dec 1894	no issue	EOL
	(he born 6 Mar 1876 PA; died _____)		
	(he s/o Samuel WITHEY and Lucy Ellen CAMP)		
529. Myra Maynard	born 29 May 1880; died 29 Mar 1882 Canton, PA		EOL
530. Edna Jane	born 20 May 1883 PA; died ____		
	married Lant COON ____; divorced	(he born Dec 1878 PA)	

Children: Lester S-[7] born 1903, and Luella M-[7] COON born ca 1908

+	**531. GUY WINFIELD**	born March 1885 PA; married Nellie May SMITH
	532. Ruby	born Jan 1890 PA; died _____; married Sam SMITH ca 1914

Children: Samuel-[7] born ca 1915 PA, and Ruby-[7] SMITH born ca 1919 PA

189. GEORGE H-[5] MC DONALD brother of above, was born June 1856 at possibly Brooklyn, New York. He married Mary E. ____ ca 1885 at Bradford County, PA. She was born Sept 1859; died ____. George -[5] MC DONALD died ____.

Children of George-[5] MC DONALD and Mary E. ____:
Surname **MC DONALD** (all born Bradford County, PA)

533. Marie L.	born June 1881; died _____
534. Harry L.	born Aug 1885; died _____
535. CLARA E.	born March 1888; died _____ ;married Robert Henry DEVINE
	(he born 14 Feb 1880 PA; died _____)
536. Herbert F.	born July 1895; died _____

192. CLARA-[5] MC DONALD   (see William Tyler-[5] STERLING # 327)

195. EDWIN ALBERT-[5] MC INTOSH, son of Ruluf C-[4] MAC INTOSH (Jonathan-[3]; Simon-[2]; Alexander-[1]) and Annis CRANE, was born 19 March 1848, IL. He married Mary E. ROBINSON on 1 Dec 1887 at _____. She was the daughter of _____ ROBINSON and _____, and was born ____; died ___.

Edwin Albert-[5] MC INTOSH died _____. Folk lore says that Edwin Albert -[5] MC INTOSH, went West , looking for his father, Ruluf-[4] MAC INTOSH, who left home when Edwin was a little boy and his sister had not yet been born. He found him in Virginia City, NV where he owned an operated a Saloon. Edwin -[5] MAC INTOSH took a job as a teamster, working for Fred "Borax" SMITH , driving 20 mule teams from Tonopah, Nevada across Death Valley to Boron, CA. (The museum in Boron verified this info) In 1887 he married Mary ROBINSON, and settled in Stockton, CA

He and his wife lost their house in the 1906 earthquake. Folk lore tells that Edwin's bed traveled across the bedroom, causing him to fall downstairs into the street. He got up and rushed to his place of employment on Battery Street and saved the company's records from being destroyed.

Child of Edwin Albert-[5] MC INTOSH and Mary ROBINSON:
Surname **MC INTOSH**

+	**537. FREDERICK**	born 24 June 1884 Napa, CA ; died 1938 (cancer)
	DRYDEN	married Flora R. HUDSON

198. WILLIAM P-[5] MC INTOSH, son of George Simon-[4] MC INTOSH (Jonathan-[3;] Simon-[2]; Alexander-[1]) and Sarah PATTERSON, was born 21 Nov 1861 at Cortland/ McGrawville, Cortland County, NY. He married Margaret C. LOUGHLIN on 8 Jan 1885 at Olean, New York. She was the daughter of _____ LOUGHLIN and _____, and was born Aug 1862 NY; died _____. They later resided in the 19th Ward of Memphis, Shelby County, TN. William P-[5] MC INTOSH died ____.

Children of William P-[5] MC INTOSH and Margaret LOUGHLIN:
Surname **MC INTOSH**

538.	Marie Frances	born 20 April 1886 NY; died _____; school teacher
539.	Florence C.	born Apr 1890 NY/PA; died _____
540.	George Simon	born 18 Jan 1892 NY/PA; died ___; married Julia W. __; she born GA. (student at Tennessee University, Knoxville, TN in 1916)
541.	Harold Francis	born 21 July 1893 WV; died _____
542.	Peter Loughlin	born 18 Dec 1899 OH ; died ____
543.	William P., Jr.	born 1 Dec 1901; died ____ married Mildred W. _____ (Child: Dorothy A-[7] MC INTOSH born ca 1928)

201. ANNA BELLE-[5] MC INTOSH, sister of above, was born 6 Nov 1870 at Cortland, NY. She married Dr. Frederick KINCH , of Westfield, NJ, on ____ 1896. Dr. KINCH was the son of Dr. Frederick A. KINCH and Harriet L. ___, and was born 30 Aug 1860 NJ; died ____.

Children of Anna Belle-[5] MC INTOSH and Dr. Frederick KINCH:
Surname **KINCH**

544.	Annabell(e)	born Dec 1899 NJ; died ____
545.	Frederick, Jr.	born 21 Oct 1901 Westfield, NJ; died June 1975 Summit, NJ.

204. JONATHAN E-[5] CHASE, son of Mariette-[4] MC INTOSH (Jonathan-[3]; Alexander-[2;1]) and Alexander CHASE, was born Aug 1849 at _____ Great Valley, Cattaraugus County, NY. He married Cherlena/Charlene Mary BARNETT ca 1873 at ____. She was the daughter of Edward S BARNETT and Sarah A. _____, and was born May 1855 CT; died ____. Jonathan-[6] CHASE died 18 Aug 1920.

Children of Jonathan-[6] CHASE and Charlene/ Cherlena BARNETT:
Surname **CHASE**   (all children born Nebraska)

546.	George B.	born Dec 1876 (listed on the 1878 Cass Co.,NE Census as a "nuisance")
547.	James E.	born Apr 1880; married Blanch W. _____

Children: Katherine-[8] born ca 1908, married G. McCALEB; and James, Jr.-[8] CHASE born 23 Aug 1912

Children of Jonathan-[5] CHASE and Charlene BARNETT, continued:
Surname **CHASE**

548. Jonathan Ballock	born 6 Mar 1883 died 29 June 1949 TX	
	married Emma Worrill KEY 1 Jan 1908 Columbus, GA	
	(she born 9 Nov 1887; died 4 Oct 1978)	

Children: Ann-[7] CHASE born ca ___; and Jonathon Ballock-[7] CHASE, Jr. born ca ____

549. Kittie B.	born Feb 1885
550. Frank M.	born Aug 1886
551. Nathan B.	born Nov 1888
	married Juliette C. _____ ca ____
	(she born ca 1890 Nebraska; died ____)

Children: (all born TX) Juliette-[7] born 1912; Nathan B-[7] Jr. born 1915;
and Jim C-[7] CHASE born 1921

205. ADALINE M-[5] CHASE, sister of above, was born ____ 1851 at Humphrey , Cattaraugus County, NY. She married John W. BIGGS ca ___. He was the son of John BIGGS (born England) and Charlotte _____ (she born ME/VT), and was born ca 1847 ___ Iowa, died ____. Adaline M-[5] CHASE died ____.

Children Of Adaline M-[5] CHASE and John W. BIGGS:
Surname **BIGGS**

552. Jessie A.	born Apr 1876 IL, died ___
	married Henry A. Purviance GOW , Sr. ca 1901
	(he born 30 July 1877 Fontanelle, Adair Co., IA; died _____
	(he s/o George Loudon GOW and Laura Belle PURVIANCE)

Children: Paul L-[7] born 12 Aug 1904 Greenfield IA.; Henry A P-[7], Jr. born ca 1905/06 IA. ,died 3 June 1929 San Diego, CA; and Margaret-[7] GOW born ca 1910

	553. Howard Alonzo	born 1879 Polk Co., IA; died _____
+	**554. GRACE EDNA**	born ca 1881 Madison Co., IA; died ca 1965 Ipswich, SD
		married Robert Morris KITCHELL 27 Nov 1901 Winterset, IA
		(he born 17 Feb 1878 IA; died Dec 1965 Ipswich, SD.
	555. William Charles	born 29 Dec 1883 Madison Co., IA; died ____
+	**556. ETHEL ANICE**	born ___ 1887 Madison Co., IA; died 1965
		married Robert S. ROBBINS
		(he born 9 Jan 1886 IL, died 16 Nov 1941 CA)

207. RULUF ARTHUR-[5] CHASE, brother of above, was born 10 March 1859 at Franklinville, NY. He married **Mary E.** ____ ca 18__ at ____.She was born ca 1859 at ____, IL.; died ____. Ruluf-[5] CHASE was a minister in the Methodist Episcopal Church, and moved about the country quite a bit. Each Census finds him in another state. Ruluf-[5] died 7 Feb 1949 at Los Angeles, CA. He had lived in NY, IL; IA; and CO before ending in CA.

Children of Ruluf-[5] CHASE and Mary E. _____:
Surname CHASE

557. Winnifred H M	born 1885 IA; died ____
558. Ruluf A.	born 5 Feb 1897 CO; died Jan 1981 CA

212. ADDIE CORNELIA -[5] MC INTOSH, daughter of Silvertus-[4] MC INTOSH (Jonathan-[3]; Simon-[2]; Alexander-[1]) and Susan Cornelia PRATT, and was born 16 Oct 1864 at Humphrey, Cattaraugus County, NY. She married Myron D. JOHNSON on 8 Dec 1883. He was the son of Stephen Titus JOHNSON and Achsah Eunice BEALS, and was born 4 Apr 1864; died 31 Dec 1916. Addie C-[5] MC INTOSH died 30 Oct 1935.

Children of Addie Cornelia-[5] MC INTOSH and Myron D. JOHNSON:
Surname **JOHNSON**   (all born Allegany, Cattaraugus, NY)

+	**559. SILVERTUS H.**	born 16 Oct 1886 NY; died 26 Dec 1952 Bradford, PA
		married Jennie GAHAGAN
		(she born 17 May 1888 Gahagan Station,PA; died 28 July 1970)
	560. Marion	born ca 1887; died young
	561 Bertha	born ca 1888; died 11 May 1892
	562. Frances	born Oct 1891 NY ; died 23 May 1892
	563 Fanny	born 1 June 1893; died same day
	564. Frank L.	born 11 July 1895 Allegany, NY; died 5 Oct 1977
		married Rae H. WILLIAMS (she born ca 1897; died 1972)
+	**565. MARGARET**	born 11 Oct 1898 PA; died Jan 1987 Meadville, PA
		married Ralph Homer WHITEMAN (he born 10 Mar 1895 PA)
	566. Ruth E.	born 24 Nov 1904 PA; died May 1984 Erie, PA
		1 married Clarence Leroy JONES: Child: Phyllis JONES born ca 1928
		2 married Harold N.WHITELING (born 6 May 1906 PA; died 1995

213. ANNIS-[5] MC INTOSH, sister of above, was born 1 March 1867 at Humphrey, Cattaraugus County, NY. She married John Allen PARKER on 25 Jan 1885 at Great Valley, Cattaraugus County, NY. He was the son of Allen PARKER and Sarah E. LOTT , and was born ca 1864; died 12 Jan 1897. She married 2nd to John R. COWAN ca 1905. He was born ca 1867 PA. Annis-[5] MC INTOSH died 23 Aug 1948.

Children of Annis-[5] MC INTOSH and John Allen PARKER:
Surname **PARKER**

	567. Fred A.	born Sept 1887 Olean, NY; died 10 Aug 1904
	568. Florence M.	born Oct 1888; died 6 Dec 1907; married _____ SWEENEY
+	**569. JOHN MORRIS**	born 31 Dec 1891 Olean, Cattaraugus Co., NY; died 17 Oct 1977 NY
		married Neva Evadna SAMPSON 18 Sep 1912
	570. Joseph Pratt	born ca 1895; died 1951

215. ELIZABETH CLARA-[5] MC INTOSH, sister of above, was born 6 October 1875 at Cattaraugus County, NY. She married Edgar Hardin BURLINGAME ca 1891/92. He was the son of Asa Francis BURLINGAME and Emeline PARKER, and was born 26 Jan 1868 Olean, Cattaraugus, NY; died there 14 February 1942. Elizabeth-[5] MC INTOSH died 29 Oct 1960 at Allegany, NY.

Children of Elizabeth Clara-[5] MC INTOSH and Edgar Hardin BURLINGAME:
Surname **BURLINGAME**   (all children born Cattaraugus County, NY)

571. Alice E.	born 10 June 1893; died 29 Dec 1982; unmarried	EOL
572. Arthur Fayette	born 22 Oct 1894; died Sept 1963; married Gertrude _____	
573. Elsie Marie	born 8 April 1896; died _____; unmarried	EOL
574. Ester	born June 1897; died ____;	
575. Edgar Hardin, Jr.	born 22 Feb 1899; died _____	
576. Laurence M.	born ca 1902; died 21 March 1969	
	married Lila M. HAUN (she born 22 Feb 1902; died 15 Mar 1992)	
	(she dau/o Andrew Nelson HAUN and Alice Emenetta NOYES)	
	Children: Oscar R-[7] born 1925; Lois Adele-[7] born ca 1926; died 2003;	
	and Clifford Ralph-[7] BURLINGAME born 21 Oct 1929; died 31 Aug1997	
577. Dorothea E.	born 23 Aug 1904; died 30 Aug 1943; unmarried	EOL
578. Raymond J.	born 7 Dec 1906; died 9 Aug 2000 Olean, NY	
579. Infant	born 1907; died 1907	EOL
580. Nellie F.	born ca 1909; died _____	
581. Anna P.	born 27 Sept 1910; died 27 Mar 1911	EOL

216. LILLIE FIDELIA-[5] (Lily) MC INTOSH, sister of above, was born 7 April 1878 at Cattaraugus County, NY. She married Charles Henry FIELD, Jr on 23 January 1907 at Alleghany Co., NY. He was the son of Charles Henry FIELD and Lucinda CULVER, and was born 16 July 1873; and died 16 July 1939 at Little Valley, Cattaraugus County, NY. Lillie-[5] MC INTOSH died 12 March 1930.

Children of Lillie Fidelia-[5] MC INTOSH and Charles FIELD, JR.:
Surname **FIELD**

582. dau	born ca 19__; no other info- possibly named Alice	
583. Howard Allen	born 15 July 1911; died 20 Dec 1987 Olean, NY	
584. Vernon E.	born 27 July 1916; died 7 March 2005 Allegany, NY	
	(served in the US Army in World War 2)	
585. Helen Lea	born 15 August 1918; died 7 July 1986 Spencerport, Cattaraugus, NY	
	married Earl Marcus BENNETT 14 Sept 1940	
	(he s/o Ralph Devere BENNETT and Viva Sophia CLAPP)	
	(he born 21 Dec 1917 Ischua, NY; died 4 May 1988 Spencerport, NY)	

220. DENNIS G-[5] REYNOLDS, son of Sarah/Sally-[4] MC INTOSH (Jonathan-[3]; Simon-[2]; Alexander-[1]) and George REYNOLDS, was born Oct 1857 at Cattaraugus County, NY. He married Luna BELLAMY ca 1880. She was the daughter of _____ BELLAMY and ____, and was born Oct 1861; died 1916. They resided Franklinville, Cattaraugus County, NY. Dennis-[5] REYNOLDS died ____.

Children of Dennis G-[5] REYNOLDS and Luna BELLAMY:
Surname **REYNOLDS**

+ **586. MYRTLE**	born ca 1881 NY; died ca 1925	
ELEANOR	married Floyd Harvey KLOCK ca 1905	
	(he born ca 13 Aug 1877 NY ; died 29 Nov 1926)	
587. Irving H.	born Dec 1890 NY; died ____	
588. Hazel E.	born Oct 1892 NY ; died Aug 1958; married Frank A. MILLER	
	(he born ca 1895; died ____)	
Child: Florence-[7] born ca 1917, died 2003		
589. Nellis Alton	born 5 Mar 1896 NY, died 10 Aug 1962 Stark, OH	
	married Isabelle C. ____ca 1922 (she born ca 1903, died ____)	

225. CORA B.-[5] REYNOLDS, sister of above, was born 26 Sep 1873 at Franklinville, Cattaraugus County, NY. She married Thomas G. MC WILLIAMS ca 1896. He was the son of Ransom MC WILLIAMS and Lavinia C. BRESIE, and was born 27 July 1872, died 8 Aug 1911 Hnsdale, Cattaraugus Co., NY. Cora B-[5] REYNOLDS died 1967.

Children of Cora B-[5] REYNOLDS and Thomas MC WILLIAMS:
Surname **MC WILLIAMS**

590. ETHA L.	born 10 Mar 1897 Franklinville, NY; died 20 Sep 1989	
	1 married George William SENEAR ca 191_	
	(he born 16 June 1874, died 8 Mar 1968)	
	(he s/o Henry B. SENEAR and Kate TORRELL)	
	2 married Clarence BANCROFT	
591. Venus Birdell (m)	born 29 Dec 1905; died Jan 1977 Buffalo, NY	
	married Anna I. MORANSKI (she born ca 1908)	
Children: 4 ch. including Vincent Birdell-[7] McWILLIAMS born 11 Mar 1927, died 29 June 1998 Buffalo, NY;		
and Genevieve-[7] McWILLIAMS born ca 1929		

226. JAMES H-[5] MC INTOSH, son of William-[4] MC INTOSH (Henry-[3]; Simon-[2]; Alexander-[1]) and Catherine BURNSIDE, was born 4 April 1845 at Bloomville, Delaware County, New York. He married

Lucy Amanda DALES of Kortright, Delaware County, NY, on ___ 1870. She was the daughter of Orrin DALES (Alexander) and Angeline KENYON, and was born ca 1850; died before 1920.

James-[4] MC INTOSH had a career in education – first serving as a teacher at Sylvania, PA; then later becoming the school commissioner for Delaware County. NY. Still later he moved to Washington, DC where he had a distinguished career in government service for 38 years prior to his retirement in 1925 .(1887-1925) He was the Assistant Chief of the Widows' Division, United States Pension office. He may have married a second time, and in 1920 was listed with a wife Catherine E., born ca 1851. He died 23 June 1926, and is buried in his hometown of Bloomville,.NY

Children of James H-[5] MC INTOSH and Lucy Amanda DALES:
Surname **MC INTOSH**

	592. Lulu May	born ca 1873 Sylvania, PA; died 13 Dec 1946; never married EOL
+	**593. KATE ANGELINE**	born 28 Jan 1880 NY; died 9 Sep 1923
		married Reverdy J. CLAGETT
	594. Anna Belle	born 23 Oct 1883 NY; died 1914; married Frank LINELL EOL

227. WILLIAM ARTHUR-[5] MC INTOSH, brother of above, was born 10 May 1850 at Bloomville, Delaware County, NY. He married Sarah Eliza MC INTYRE on __ 1875. She was the daughter of ____ MC INTYRE and ____, and was born April 1851 NY; died ca 1939. William-[5] MC INTOSH died 31 Oct 1939. They are buried in Riverside Cemetery, Bloomville, NY.

Children of William Arthur-[5] MC INTOSH and Sarah Elizabeth MC INTYRE:
Surname **MC INTOSH**

	595. Harry Arthur ++	born 31 May 1880 Bloomville; died 9 July 1962 Cooperstown, NY
		married Ada LILLIG of Dubuque, IA
		(she born ca 1877; died 21 Sep 1941) no issue EOL
+	**596. JESSIE SARAH**	born 24 Dec 1885 NY' died 7 Jan 1968 ; buried Riverside Cemetery
		married William BURKETT (he from Boulder City, NV)
	597. William Burnside	born 25 Feb 1888 NY; died 1958; never married EOL

++ Obituary for **Harry Arthur-[5] MC INTOSH** - published Delhi, NY 1962

----- " he died Bassett Hospital, Cooperstown, NY. He was born in Bloomville, NY. As a child he resided on farms in the vicinity of Bloomville and Delhi, then in the village of Delhi, NY. He was graduated from Delaware Academy in 1898 and taught school in the Sherwoods district before going to Iowa in 1900 where he remained 49 years. In Iowa he taught school and later entered business college. For a number of years he was employed by the Chicago, Milwaukee and St. Paul Railroad in the Dubuque area as Assistant to the Superintendent of Motive Power (the locomotives of the railroad collectively).

He was a staunch Democrat and was appointed Collector of Internal Revenue for the State of Iowa during Woodrow WILSONS' administration. Later he became a travelling auditor with the Iowa Power and Light Company – remaining there until his retirement. For the past 12 years (1950-62) he resided with his sister, Mrs. Jessie M. Burkett in Delhi, and she was his only surviving relative. Mr. MC INTOSH was a member of the Second Presbyterian Church and the Delhi Masonic fraternity. Burial will be in Riverside Cemetery, Bloomville, NY, where several generations of the family are buried. "

229. MARY ANN-[5] BURNSIDE, daughter of Emeline-[4] MAC INTOSH (Henry-[3]; Simon-[2]; Alexander-[1]) and John BURNSIDE, was born ___ 1847 at Bloomville, Delaware County, NY. She married John E. POWELL on ___ at ___. He was the son of John POWELL and Hettie/Hetty _____, and was born ca 1843 NY; died ___. He was a plumber and tinsmith, and also owned a hardware store in Bloomville. Mary Ann-[5] BURNSIDE died ca 1928.

Children of Mary Ann-[5] BURNSIDE and John POWELL:
Surname **POWELL**

+	**598. EUGENE M.**	born 18 Oct 1866 Roxbury, NY; died 16 Nov 1953 Delhi, NY
		married Cora A. BROWN 27 Oct 1892 Bloomville, NY
		(she born _____; died 16 Nov 1949) buried Riverside Cemetery

Children of Mary Ann-[5] BURNSIDE and John POWELL, continued:
Surname **POWELL**

599. William	born ca 1870/71 Delaware County, NY; died _____	
	married _____ AINSLIE no issue	EOL
600. Emma M.	born Aug 1879 Kortright, NY; died _____	
	buried Bloomville, NY never married	EOL

231. MARY ELIZABETH -[5] **WILLIAMS**, daughter of Caroline-[4] MAC INTOSH (William-[3]; Simon-[2]; Alexander-[1]) and Lewis P. WILLIAMS , was born 6 Feb 1841 at Troy, PA. She married Gilbert MC NAUGHT of Granville Bradford County, PA on ___ 18__. He was the son of John MC NAUGHT (born in Scotland) and Sally A. ____, and was born ca 1836; died 1 Feb 1895-96 at New Castle, IN. Mary Elizabeth-[5] WILLIAMS died there 2 Feb 1923. Gilbert MC NAUGHT served as a Pvt. in Company E, 13th PA Infantry Regiment briefly, and then in Company E, 50th Regiment of the NY Engineers until the end of the Civil War.

Children of Mary Elizabeth-[5] WILLIAMS and Gilbert MC NAUGHT:
Surname **MC NAUGHT**

601. Ida G.	born ca 1869 PA; died ____
	married Hoy BOCK 20 July 1904 Henry Co., IN; resided IN
	(he s/o William B. BOCK and Araminta S. ____)
	(he born ca June 1868 IN; died _____; was a bank teller)
602. Anna Henrietta	born Aug 1872 PA; married Walter S. WRIGHT 26 Oct 1896
	(he born ca 1871 PA; died _____)

Children: Harry[7] born July 1897; Grace[7] born ca 1903; and Doris[7] WRIGHT born ca 1905;   all born West Virginia ; 1910 resided Appleton, Clark, KS

603. John Gilbert	born 8/18 June 1874 PA; died 1932 Lake Co., FL
604. Arthur	born _____ PA; died _____

232. JANE H-[5] WILLIAMS, sister of above, was born 16 April 1842 at ___. She married Erskine PACKARD of Wellsboro, PA on _____. He married second ca 1885 to Luella J. KNAPP, and was the father of two sons by that marriage: Carl born 1888 and Frederick PACKARD born ___. Erskine was the son of William M. PACKARD and Dolly SPENCER, and was born 15 Mar 1836 ; died 18 Sep 1906, buried Alba, Bradford County, PA. Jane-[5] WILLIAMS died 20 March 1883.

Children of Jane-[5] WILLIAMS and Erskine PACKARD:
Surname **PACKARD**

+	**605. LEWIS**	born 6 Nov 1863; died 1931 PA
	ERSKINE	married Lenora/Nora DOBBINS ca 1887
+	**606. CAROLINE DELL**	born July 1867; died _____
		married Galen Guy AYRES 2 Nov 1887 (he from Alba, PA)

233. LUCY ADELAIDE-[5] WILLIAMS, sister of above, was born 20 March 1844 at Bradford County, PA. She married John Clark MC MAHAN ca 1865 at _____. He was the son of William Reed MC MAHAN and Sarah CLARK, and was born Nov 1842 , died 27 Oct 1904 Troy, PA. He served in the Civil War in D Company, 132nd PA Infantry. According to the Civil War Pension Index, he applied for invalid status on 28 Nov 1877, and his widow applied for benefits on 5 Dec 1904. They resided in Canton Township, Bradford County, PA. Lucy-[5] WILLIAMS died 28 May 1911.

Children of Lucy-[5] WILLIAMS and John Clark MC MAHAN:
Surname **MC MAHAN**

607. William	born ca 1867 PA; died _____
608. Anna	born ca 1868 PA; died ____

Children of Lucy-[5] WILIIAMS and John Clark MC MAHAN, continued:
Surname **MC MAHAN**

609. Alice E. born Oct 1874 PA; died 1951; married Isaac B Grange STEAD
(he born 19 Aug 1873/74 PA; died 12 Oct 1948 PA)
(he s/o Isaac B STEAD and Mary E. _____)
Children: Harold-[7] born Sep 1893 and Evelyn-[7] STEAD born ca 1902 PA

610. Walter born ____; died _____

234. GEORGE-[5] WASHINGTON WILLIAMS, brother of above, was born 8 May 1847 at Bradford County, PA. He married Ellen/Ella/Ellie Ann LILLEY on 1 Nov 1871 at _____, PA. She was born 3 Aug 1854 PA; died 3 Oct 1938. George -5 died 20 May 1925. They are buried at the Turner Cemetery.

Children of George-[5] WILLIAMS and Ellen LILLEY:
Surname **WILLIAMS**

+ **611. LILLEY BELLE** born 2 Oct 1876 PA; died 1953 Bradford Co., PA
1 married Charles Harpy TURNER 17 Dec 1896
(he born 28 Oct 1876; died 1 June 1920)
(he s/o Fred B. TURNER and Emeline A. _____)
2 married Milton A[-5] CASE 2 Nov 1929 (his 3rd marriage)
(he born ca 1857; died Feb 1937)

+ **612. CHARLES** born 19 Apr 1878 PA; died before 1947
  MC KEAN married Elsie KILBOURN 9 Jan 1901 (she born 9 July 1879 PA)

613. Arthur James born 6 Dec 1885/86 ; died 5 Dec 1912; married Mary BORELO

614. Carrie L. born 24 May 1888 PA; died 28 Feb 1928 , married Lynn ROCKWELL

235. EDWIN CHURCHILL-[5] WILLIAMS, brother of above, was born 13 July 1849 at ____, PA. He married first to Ellen/Ella WHITEHEAD ca___. She was the daughter of Jay WHITEHEAD and Jane L. ____, and was born ca 1850; died 1879, probably as a result of childbirth. His second marriage was to Elizabeth/Libby THORNE on 13 April 1881. She was the daughter of Watson THORNE and Susan APGAR, and was born 3 September 1859; died ca 1932. Edwin-[5] WILLIAMS died 17 Apr 1925 at Canton Township, Bradford County. PA.

Child of Edwin-[5] WILLIAMS and Ellen WHITEHEAD:
Surname **WILLIAMS**

+ **615. JENNIE** born Jan 1879 PA; died 23 Feb 1910 (in childbirth)
  CAROLINE married Archie KILBOURN

Children of Edwin-[5] WILLIAMS and Elizabeth THORN(E) :
Surname **WILLIAMS**

616. Lewis Paul born 30 Mar 1883; died 1 Mar 1908

+ **617. SAMUEL** born 17 Oct 1886/87 PA; died Dec 1918
  WATSON married Ella Caroline EGLI (she born ca 1893; died 1978)
  Child: Samuel Edwin-7 WILLIAMS born ca 1919; died 1981

+ **618. SETH EDWIN** born 6 Feb 1888 PA; died 1932
married Sarah NORTH (she born ca 1887; died ____)

619. Lloyd Ralph born 17/18 Sep 1901/02; died 30 Dec 1947 Sayre, PA
married Marion L. STORR Nov 1933
(she born 1909; died 1952) (Child: Jeanette-[7] WLLIAMS born ____)

240. DANIEL W. [-5] RANDALL, son of Charlotte-[4] MAC INTOSH (William-[3]; Simon-[2]; Alexander-[1]) and Daniel RANDALL, was born Dec 1854 PA. He married Kathryn/ Kate/ Kittie MC KENZIE ca 1878 at ____. She was the daughter of William MC KENZIE and Catherine SCOTT, and was born Aug 1861; died 1924. Daniel-[5] RANDALL died 27 Dec 1941.

Children of Daniel W-⁵ RANDALL and Kate MC KENZIE:
Surname **RANDALL**

	620. Lydia	born Dec 1879 PA
	621. Clare M.	born ca 1881 PA; died ____; married Mary WHIPPLE 16 Oct 1901
		(she dau/o Judson WHIPPLE and Helen A. MORSE)
		(she born ca 1882 PA; died ____)
	622. Josie	born July 1883 PA; died _____
+	**623. GERTRUDE**	born 2 July 1886 Union Twsp, Tioga,PA; died 25 May 1979
	JANE	married Benjamin Dean. LANDON 2 June 1909
+	**624. OLLIE DAN**	born 14 Apr 1889 Union Twsp., PA; died 18 Jan 1976 Burlington, PA.
		married Louise MIELKE buried East Canton Cemetery
		(she born 27 Dec 1900 E. Hampton, MA; died Oct 1969 Canton, PA)
+	**625. GEORGE**	born 11 Mar 1896 Canton, PA; died 3 Mar 1960 Dallas, TX
	WAYNE	married Edna Eloise/ Louise HUNT 27 Sep 1924 Williamsport, PA
		(she born 28 June 1889 Williamsport,PA; died 7 Feb 1942 same place)
		(she dau/o Harry Bruce Landon HUNT and Anna Laura MIDDLETON

242. GRACE-⁵ RANDALL, sister of above, was born 31 Jan 1860 at Troy PA. She married Dana Thomas AYRES, a blacksmith, Feb 1877. He was the son of Andrew AYRES, Jr. and Sarah/Sally DUNBAR, and was born 16 Jan 1850 Canton, PA; died 21 Feb 1933 Clinton County, PA. Grace-⁵ RANDALL died 16 Feb 1936.

Children of Grace-⁵ RANDALL and Dana Thomas AYRES:
Surname **AYRES**

+	**626. NANCY AMELIA**	born 28 May 1878 PA; died 6 Dec 1970
	(Nan)	married Paul I. FREEMAN (conductor on the steam RR)
		(he born 16 Oct 1874 Canton, PA; died 17 Aug 1948)
		(he s/o Henry Watson FREEMAN and Eliza H _____)
	627. Clara Evelyn	born Jan 1880 PA; died 30 May 1942
		married Evelyn PAINTON (owned Painton's Bakery, Elmira)
		(he born 1883; died 193_)
		(he s/o Gilmore PAINTON and Clara E. _____)
		Child: Clara-⁷ PAINTON born 16 Feb 1913; died 20 Mar 1993
	628. Helen Grace	born July 1885 PA; died _____
		married Guerdon Major PORTER (he born Sep 1878 PA; died _____
		(he s/o Albert Z. PORTER and Florence I. AYERS)
		Children: Madeline Alberta-⁷ born ca 1908, and Eustace-⁷ PORTER born 1913
+	**629. D. HOWARD**	born 30 Dec 1889 PA; died _____;
		married Julia A. SNYDER
	630. Alvin Dana	born 5 Apr 1897 PA; died 14 Nov 1955 ; foreman in coal mine
		married Ruby Elizabeth "Betsey " MULLEN ca 1917
		(she born 1 Oct 1897; died Feb 1991 Lock Haven, Clinton, PA)

243. WILLIAM PERCIVAL-⁵ THOMAS, son of Harriet-⁴ MC INTOSH (William-³; Simon-²; Alexander-¹) and Lorenzo THOMAS, was born 15 Jan 1850 PA. He married first to Lydia Helen WILLIAMS ca 1871 at ____. She was the daughter of Obadiah WILLIAMS and Hannah KEYES, and was born 1 Nov 1848 PA; died 1 May 1883. His second wife was possibly Grace FREEMAN, daughter of George FREEMAN and Amelia __. She was born Mar 1880; died _____. William P-⁵ THOMAS died March 1932

MACKINTOSH   MAC INTOSH   MC INTOSH
The Fifth American Generation

Children of William P-5 THOMAS and Lydia Helen WILLIAMS;
Surname **THOMAS**

631. Charles <u>Harry</u> born 23 Nov 1873; died 14 Dec 1937 Troy, PA
married Eva May KENNEDY 15 Mar/ May 1901
(she born ca 1878; died 25 Mar 1919)
Children: Lynn-7 (m) born 28 Aug 1910, and William Laurence-7 THOMAS born 19 Jan 1915 PA,
married Leah BELLIS Oct 1935

632. William Lewis born 11 Apr 1877 Troy, PA; died _____
married Rebecca WALKER 14 Feb 1914
(she born 4 Sep 1884; died ___) resided Baltimore, OH   EOL

633. Floyd born ca 1879; died at age 2 months

634. Edward C. born 12 Sep 1881; died ____; married Flora FLEMING 4 Mar 1907
(MASON) ++ (she born 17 Sep 1880; died May 1969 Elmira, NY)
++ He was adopted out at age 2 ½ to an Arthur MASON, his name was changed to MASON
Child: Laurence-7 MASON born 13 July 1910, married Dorothy DOLL 22 Oct 1935

245. AMY ISABEL-5 THOMAS, sister of above, was born 26 Jan 1854 at_____, PA. She married Ordonio <u>Lazelle</u> FIELD on 15 Sep 1874. He was the son of George FIELD and Caroline Amelia FREEMAN, and was born 21 March 1856; died 1936 /37. They resided at Armenia, Bradford County, PA. Amy Isabel-5 THOMAS died 5 Jan 1934 .

Children of Amy Isabel -5 THOMAS and O. Lazelle FIELD:
Surname **FIELD**

+ **635. HARRIET A.** born 12 Oct 1876; died 16 June 1928
"Hattie" married Marshall Jenkins THOMAS 15 Feb 1899
(he s/o Edward THOMAS and Rebecca NELSON)
(he born 5 Aug 1867 Nelson, PA; died 19 June 1961 Canton, PA)

636. George S. born 3 Aug 1878; died 13 Feb 1879   EOL

637. Evelyn J. born 13 Aug 1880 ; died _____ Sayre, PA   no issue   EOL
married Ray D. NEWELL 23 May 1925
(he born ca 1883, PA; died _____)

638. Freddie S. born 15 June 1885; died 24 Feb 1886   EOL

+ **639. HELEN** born Oct 1887; died 1947;
MILDRED 1 married Lyman Porter SHOEMAKER ca 1909
(he s/o Amasa F. SHOEMAKER and Ellen MILDRED)
(he born ca 1886; died 15 Sep 1910)
Child: Pauline-7 SHOEMAKER born 21 May 1910, married
2 married Harry E. BROOKS ca 1916; (Child: Margaret-7 BROOKS)

+ **640. THOMAS** born 25 Oct 1893 PA; died 13 July 1965
LAZELLE 1 married Isabel R. SUTTON 20 July 1914; divorced
(she born ca 1895; died _____)
Child: Robert L-7 FIELD born 21 Oct 1916 NY; died Jan 1978 Philadelphia, PA)
2 married Isabel Merrill HOYT   (she born 1898; died 1937)
3 married Velma Alice CHAPPELL

641. Luella Amy born 13 June 1898 Canton, PA; died 17 Dec 1982 (84)
married Irving L. HAWKINS 21 Dec 1922 no issue   EOL
(he born 1896; died 24 July 1971)

247. LEWIS RANDALL-5 THOMAS, brother of above, was born 30 June 1858 at Troy, Bradford Co., PA. He married Armetta <u>Minerva</u> OSTRANDER ca 1884/85 at Southport, PA. She was the daughter of Mathew OSTRANDER and Sarah Minerva WOODCOCK, and was born 1 May 1857 at Lymansville, Potter, PA; died 24 March 1932. Lewis Randall-5 THOMAS died 8 March 1948 at Keating, PA.

Child of Lewis R-[5] THOMAS and Minerva OSTRANDER:
Surname **THOMAS**

+ **642. MYRTLE**	born 12 Apr 1886; died May 1984 San Luis Obispo, CA	
GLENN	married Elmer Earl HOPPER 27 Sep 1909	
	(he born 22 Oct 1899; died 23 July 1976 San Luis Obispo, CA	
	(he s/o John HOPPER and Rosanna _____)	

643. Homer Lazelle   born 29 Sep 1887; died _____   Child: Billy E-[7] THOMAS born 20 Feb 1925
married Olga Marie NELSON 16 Nov 1918/ 22 Dec 1919
(he served in Co. C, 112 Infantry Regt; slightly wounded)

644. Edna Mae   born 15 Feb 1889; died ____
married Anton M. ANDERSON 7 Feb 1910 (he born 28 Sep 1887 Denmark)
(he served US Navy WW 1 aboard the USS JOUETT, a submarine destroyer)
Child: Thomas Albert-[7] ANDERSON born 16 Oct 1910

645. Almond   born 22 Sep 1890; died _____; married Edith CORY 10 Dec 1924 PA
(she born 31 Dec 1900; died 21 Feb 1982)
Children: Almond Cory-[7] born 16 Feb 1930; Gary Eugene-[7] born 3 Oct 1933; Richard Francis-[7]
born 23 Apr 1935; and Lewis Ronald-[7] THOMAS born 31 Oct 1936

646. Roy Ostrander   born 28 Nov 1892; died ___; married Hazel HANSEN 24 July 1920
(she born 23 Nov 1898; died ____)
(served in the US Navy during WW1, made 18 trips across the Atlantic on the captured
German transport ship,the USS Von Steuben
Children: Kenneth Leroy-[7] born 31 Mar 1921; and Donald Harold-[7] THOMAS born 6 July 1926

647. Claire McKinley   born 4 Nov 1896 ; married Hazel Jane MOWERY 27 Nov 1926
(she born 5 Dec 1899; died _____)
(served in the US Navy with his brother, on the same vessel)

648. Freddie   born 4 July 1898; died Oct 1898   EOL

649. Olive Belle   born 20 March 1900; died 24 Feb 1988 Oklahoma City, OK
married William J. SCHREIBER 20 June 1923
Children: Jack Harrison-[7] born 5 Dec 1925 and William Thomas-[7] SCHREIBER born 29 Sep 1927

650. Vera Alberta   born 30 Jan 1903; died Jan 1978 Fairview, Erie, PA
married Albert Anton HAUBER 14 Apr 1934
(he born 7 Nov 1906 PA; died Feb 1976 Erie, PA)
(he s/o Engelbert/Albert HAUBER and Crescentia "Cence" GEIGER)
Child: Marilyn Ann-[7] HAUBER born 22 Dec 1936;

249. SUSAN ETTIE-[5] THOMAS, sister of above, was born 28 March 1863 at ___ PA. She married
Homer E. TREAT ca 1882 at ____ . He was the son of Leroy TREAT and Roseanna J.___, and was born
Oct 1859 Morris Run, PA; died ____ . Susan Ettie-[5] THOMAS died 19 Oct 1906.

Children of Susan Ettie-[5] THOMAS and Homer TREAT:
Surname **TREAT**

651 Archie I.   born 26 Aug 1886
652. Howard Albert   born 28 Jan 1891 ; married Anna JORDAN
653. Ralph Homer   born 10 Mar 1898; married Mary _____   (she born ca 1898)
Children: Frances-[7] born ca 1921, and Irving-[7] TREAT born on 1925
654. Clyde   born 21 Apr 1904; died Jan 1986 Elmira, Chemung, NY

263. MILTON A-[5] CASE, son of Eliza-[4] MC INTOSH (William-[3]; Simon-[2]; Alexander-[1]) and N. Byron
-[4] CASE (Samuel-[3,2]; Phillip-[1]), was born 29 May 1859 at Troy, Bradford County, PA. He married
Eugenia E. THOMAS on 25 Nov 1880 at Troy, Bradford, PA. She was the daughter of Alexander Hamilton
THOMAS and Elizabeth BECKER, and was born 3 July 1858 at Bradford County, PA; died ca 1909 . He
married second to Minnie MAYNARD ca 1910 at ____ . She was born ca 1877; died 19 May 1923. He
married his third wife, Lilley WILLIAMS-[6] Turner, on 2 Nov 1929. She was the widow of Charles

TURNER, and the daughter of George-[5] WILLIAMS (Caroline-[4] MC INTOSH; William[3]; Simon-[2]; Alexander-[1]) and Ella Ann LILLEY, and was born 2 Oct 1876; died 1953, PA. Milton A-[5] CASE died 20 Feb 1937 at Sayre, Bradford County, PA.

Children of Milton A-[5] CASE and Eugenia THOMAS:
Surname **CASE**

+	**655. ELIZA A.**	born 29 Aug 1884 Troy, PA; died 1944 Troy
	(twin)	married Herman R. BOYER 24 Dec 1914 ; (he born 5 July 1885)
		(he s/o Samuel BOYER and Cecilia CRIST)
+	**656. ELIZABETH A.**	born 29 Aug 1884 Troy, PA; died 15 Sep 1966 Troy, PA
	(twin)	married Elwyn Phelps MC KEAN 25 Mar 1910 Towanda, PA
		(he born 12 June 1882; died 1955)
	657. Bertha	born 1 Jan 1886 Alba, PA; died 12 Oct 1918
+	**658. MEADE**	born 25 April 1889; died 15 June 1966 Troy, PA
	THOMAS	married Louise BROWNSON 12 Oct 1910

264. GRACE J.-[5] CASE, sister of above, was born ca 1867 at Troy, Bradford County, PA. She married Charles M. RHOADES ca 1886. He was born ca 1866 PA; and operated a bakery and grocery store. [5]

Children of Grace-[5] CASE and Charles M. RHOADES;
Surname **RHOADES**

659. Edna E./M	born ca 1888 PA; died ____;
	married Jerry C. BLAIR 21 Sept 1908 Welland, Ontario, Canada
	(he s/o Addison Dewitt. BLAIR (a lawyer) and Jennie E. MARSH)
	(he born June 1885 Elmira, NY; died ____)
	Children: Elizabeth born ____, died young; Jerry-[7] Jr. BLAIR born ca 1914 Elmira, NY
660. Byron N.	born ca 1894/5; died ___; married Irene WHEATON ca 1914; divorced (she born 21 Apr 1895)
661. Ada M.	born ca 1898 PA; died ____; married _____ COONEY
	Child: Frances-[7] COONEY born ca 1918
662. Charles Alfred	born 4 Dec 1909 PA; died 9 Apr 1993 Ulster, Bradford, PA.

265. NELSON W.-[5] CASE, brother of above, was born __ April 1871 at Troy, Bradford County, PA. He married Eva G. HACKETT ca 1893.She was the daughter of James M. HACKETT and Anna S. _____, and was born June 1873 ____, VT; died _____. Nelson W-[5] CASE died ____.

Children of Nelson W-[5] CASE and Eva HACKETT:
Surname **CASE**

+	**663. EDNA MAY**	born 15 Aug 1894 NH; died 14 May 1922 Concord, NH
		married John Fogg DREW 20 Oct 1917 Concord, Merrimack, NH
		(he s/o John Alva DREW. and Mary Jane RUNNELLS)
		(he born 10 Mar 1896 NH; died Jan 1972 Lincoln, Grafton, NH)
	664. Helen B.	born Mar 1896; died before 1930; married Arthur George LONG
		(he born 5 May 1891 VT; died Apr 1972 Concord, NH)
		Children: Edna B-[7] born ca 1915, married ____ CLEVELAND; and Robert M-[7] LONG born Feb 1919 NH
	665. Henry Nelson	born 13 June 1898 NH; died May 1967 Concord, Merrimack, NH
	666. Eva U.	born ca 1901 NH
	667. Jessie A.	born ca 1903 NH

267. CHARLOTTE A-[5] " Lottie " CASE, sister of above, was born April 1882 at Troy, Bradford, PA. She married Earl Clark ROBY 24 Dec 1903 at Alba, Bradford, PA. He was the son of _____ ROBY and Flora Adele CLARK, and was born ca 1886 PA; died _____. Charlotte-[5] CASE died ca 1931 Elmira, NY.

Children of Charlotte-[5] CASE and Earl Clark ROBY:
Surname **ROBY**

	668. Flora E.	born 23 Jul 1910 PA; died 9 Nov 1990 NY.
		married Raymond MADDOX ca 1932
		(he born 27 Mar 1909 NY; died 9 Dec 1984 FL)
		Child: George Raymond-[7] MADDOX born 25 Nov 1943; died 28 March 1994 FL
+	**669. SAMUEL NELSON**	born 25 Nov 1913 Troy, PA; died 1966 NY
		married Olga Ila WINKLER ca 1938
		(she born 27 Feb 1910; died 13 Aug 2009 Athens, PA)
		(she dau/o Samuel WINKLER and Mary KIR)
	670. Lillian	born ca 1925; died ca 1927

268. WILLIAM E-[5] MC INTOSH, son of Fernando-[4] MC INTOSH (William-[3]; Simon-[2]; Alexander-[1]) and Rose/Rosa LYON , was born 14 June 1863 at Ward Township, Bradford County, PA. He possibly married first to Agnes Catheryn ____ on ____ at ____. (Nothing more has been found about her other than a gravestone at the site of Willis/William MC INTOSH that states Catheryn 1871-1913).

He married second to Sarah MC GARRY ca 1895. She was the daughter of Bernard MC GARRY and Jane GILMORE (Edward), and was born Oct 1872 Morris Run, ____ Co., PA; died 23 Nov 1927 at New York City, NY., and is buried in the Calvary Cemetery there. William/Willis-[5] MC INTOSH died 8 Jan 1911 and is buried at the Arbon Cemetery, Blossburg, PA.

Children of William/Willis-[5] MC INTOSH and Sarah MC GARRY:
Surname **MC INTOSH**

	671. John	born 10 Apr 1897; died 18 July 1899 Morris Run, PA
		(buried Catholic Cemetery, Blossburg, PA)
+	**672. FRANCIS CURTIS**	born 30 July 1899 Morris Run; died 20 July 1977 Suffern, NY
		married Mildred Marie EMMS 14 Nov 1923 Blossburg, PA
		(she dau/o Herbert Charles EMMS and Sarah Eliza WARD)
		(she born 20 Oct 1903 Morris Run; died 13 July 1979 Suffern, NY)
	673. James Bernard	born 20 Sep 1902 Morris Run,; died 13 July 1972 Newark Valley, NY
		married Julia Louise HOSKINS ca 1939
		(she born 16 Aug 1909; died Jan 1980 Endicott, NY)

272. MAUDE-[5] (Nettie) MC INTOSH, daughter of Lewis H-[4] MC INTOSH (William-[3]; Simon-[2]; Alexander-[1]) and Norminda SMITH, was born Dec 1868 at _____, PA. She married A. Charles BATTERSON ca 1890. He was the son of ____ BATTERSON and Sarah J. PORTER, and was born June 1868 PA, died _____. Maude-[5] MC INTOSH died 18 Feb 1939 at Troy, Bradford, PA.

Children of Maude-[5] MC INTOSH and Charles BATTERSON:
Surname **BATTERSON**

	674. Lewis Earl	born 12 Apr 1895; died 22 Mar 1921 ; served in WW1 EOL
+	**675. JAMES LEON**	born 16 Oct 1896; died 1 Feb 1968 Troy, PA
		1 married Ruth Mildred MC KEE 3 June 1915 (divorced)
		(she dau/o Thomas Edward MC KEE and Edith H. GILBERT)
		2 married Elizabeth SCHUCMER of Troy, PA on ____
		(she born ca 1899; died 23 Feb 1938)

274. ALVIN-[5] CURE, son of Rosalthea-[4] MC INTOSH (William-[3]; Simon-[2]; Alexander-[1]) and Frank CURE, was born ca 1862 at ____, PA. He married Martha Jane GUATNEY on 17 May 1882 at Mt. Pleasant , Labette County, KS. She was the daughter of _____ GUATNEY and _____, and was born 15 Feb 1867 IL; died 1 Nov 1936. Alvin-[5] CURE died 17 May 1882 at Labette County, KS..

Children of Alvin-[5] CURE and Martha GUATNEY:
Surname **CURE**

	676. Frances	born 28 May 1884
+	**677. JOHN WILLIAM**	born 10 Dec 1888 KS; died 28 Sep 1924; married Jessie Edith NUNN
	678. Ida	born 4 Nov 1890 MO; 9 Oct 1965 OK
	679. Albert R.	born 3 Feb 1892 TX; died 6 Dec 1933
	680. Sarah	born 4 March 1895 TX; died 16 Apr 1935

275. ANDREW JOHNSON-[5] CURE, brother of above, was born 12 April 1864 at Canton, Bradford, PA. He married Rebecca SCHOLES ca 1902 .She was born the daughter of _____ SCHOLES and _____ MINOR, and was born 2 Nov 1878,TX; died 24 Sep 1963 Long Beach, CA. Andrew J-[5] CURE died 11 July 1948 Long Beach, CA .

Children of Andrew J-[5] CURE and Rebecca SCHOLES::
Surname **CURE**

681. Juanita <u>Ruth</u>	born 6 Oct 1902 TX; died 27 Feb 1980 Los Angeles, CA
	married Lynn H. BROWNE
	(he born 26 June 1898 Lawrence, KS; died 23 June 1969 los Angeles)
682. MILDRED I.	born 30 July 1904 TX; died 2000; married Verald Elton PAYNE
	(he born 7 Nov 1902 Elgin, IL; died 8 Feb 1974 Hemet, Riverside, CA
	(he s/o Charles B. PAYNE and Dora A. _____)
683. Andrew J. Jr.	born 5 Oct 1906 El Paso, TX; died 13 May 1954 Denver, CO
	married Gene M. _____ ca 1928
	Child: Richard Λ-[7] CURE born _____; served in the USAF
684. Ray Scholes	born ca 1912 TX; died _____; married Marjana _____
	Child: Andrew J-[7] CURE born ca 1930 Los Angeles, CA
685. Helen L.	born ca 1913 KS; died _____
686. Rhoda L.	born 18 Mar 1922 KS; died 12 Dec 1991 Lane County, OR
	(a concert pianist, she married Chester S. MAC PHERSON)
687. Gerald	born ca 1925

280. DELLA-[5] CURE, sister of above, was born 25 Dec 1876 KS. She married first to _____ WILKINS before 1893. Her second marriage was to Morris Alexander CROOKS ca 1900 TX. He was the son of Thomas Jefferson CROOKS and Winnie EDMUNDSON, and was born 1869 TX , died 18 Aug 1918 at Nueces County, TX. Her third husband was George ALLISON, a carpenter. He was born 1867 IL. They married after 1920 TX. Della-[5] died 1965 Lynwood, CA. Resided Corpus Christi, Nueces County, TX.

Children of Della-[5] CURE and Morris Alexander CROOKS:
Surname **CROOKS**

688. Virginia Countess	born 5 Dec 1906 OK ; died 11 Nov 1989 San Berrnardino, CA
	married Calvin LEWIS ca _____ Child: Billie Jean-7 LEWIS born ca 1923
689. Frank	born 16 Oct 1909 OK; died Nov 1979 George West, Live Oak, TX.
	married Eunice Ora Lee CUSTER
	(she dau/o Andrew Jackson CUSTER and Margie Lee SMITH)
	(she born 22 Apr 1911 TX; died 6 Mar 1988 TX)
690. Tom	born 27 June 1912 OK; died 30 Apr 1986 Long Beach, CA
	married Lacine " Betty " EVANS
	(she born 15 Mar 1913 OK; died 24 Feb 1994 Long Beach, CA)
	Children: Kathy-[7] born _____, and Marilyn-[7] CROOKS born ___
691. Nora Fay	born ca 1914 OK; died 17 Aug 1989 Salem, OR
	married Dan Allen SIMS
692. John <u>Potter</u>	born 23 July 1916 OK. ; died 2 Sep 1944 TX

The Fifth American Generation

285. JOHN WILLIAM[5] CRAWFORD, son of Lucy Delphine-[4] MC INTOSH (William-[3]; Simon-[2]; Alexander-[1]) and Hugh CRAWFORD II (William; Hugh-[1]) , was born 3 June 1867 at Armenia Township, Bradford County, PA. He married Meda ANDRUS on 2 Nov 1889 at Canton, Bradford, PA. She was the daughter of Cephas ANDRUS and Lucy BAILEY, and was born Nov 1870/72; died 4 March 1940 at Elmira, Chemun County, NY. John William-[5] CRAWFORD died ca 1921 and is buried at the Main Street Cemetery, Canton, PA.

Childen of John William-[5] CRAWFORD and Meda ANDRUS:
Surname **CRAWFORD**

	693. Hugh III	born 28 Sep 1891 Canton, PA; died 7 March 1925 +++++	
		married Florence BAKER 21 Dec 1911 no issue	EOL
		(she born 28 May 1893; died ____)	
+	**694. PEARL**	born 14 Aug 1894 Canton, PA; died 1922 Cleveland, OH	
		1 married Max SANFORD 24 Dec 1913	
		(he born ___; died ____; from New York City)	
		2 married _____ HINSHELWOOD	
	695. Gwendolyn C.	born 25 May 1898 Canton, PA; died 15 Aug 1967	EOL
		married W. Charles BARBER May 1928; resided Elmira, NY	
		(he was managing editor of the Elmira Advertiser)	

+++++   This article appeared in the Addison (NY) Advertiser on Thursday 12 March 1925

HUGH CRAWFORD SHOT DEAD IN DRUNKEN BRAWL AT VAN VLEETS
Dane Mc Chesney Admits Shooting and is Held at Bath Jail – Without Witnesses to Crime It Will Be Difficult to Disprove His Statement That Crawford Attempted to Assault Him With Stick of Wood

Hugh Crawford of Elmira, aged 35, was shot and killed instantly shortly after ten o'clock Saturday night as the result of a drunken brawl in the home of Dane McChesney, aged 48, at Van Vleets station, on the B&S railroad, seven miles south of Addison. Hugh Crawford, the murdered man, worked as an auto mechanic at the Chatfield Garage here several years ago. He was an overseas veteran and came here Friday afternoon from Elmira with his wife, who was formerly Miss Florence Baker, daughter of Mrs. Dell Baker of Elkland, PA.; formerly of Addison, started for Elkland by auto. The auto was unable to negotiate Addison Hill and the trip was abandoned. Mrs. Crawford was taken aboard another car enroute to Elkland.

About 7 o'clock Crawford put in an appearance at the home of McChesney. The two men started out together. They returned about ten o'clock according to Mrs. McChesney, who was formerly Miss Nellie Levi of Addison She says she did not hear any quarreling or shots fired. She stated that the first she knew of any trouble was about one o'clock Sunday morning. She got up and went to the kitchen seeing Crawford lying on the floor with blood oozing from a hole in his chest. Mrs. McChesney immediately went to the home of Mrs. Cora Harrau and asked Mrs. Harrau or some member of her family to come down to her house as there was a sick man down there.

" I Shot a Man Last Night" Mc Chesney Told Neighbors
However Mrs. Harrau did not pay any attention to the matter and did not go to the McChesney home. At 4:30 o'clock Sunday morning Mrs. McChesney went to the home of another neighbor, Silas Ripley. Owing to sickness in the family, Mrs. Ripley's mother, Mrs Barbara Bardwell was up at the time and answered the door. Mrs. McChesney asked if they would call a doctor for her as there was a man lying on her kitchen floor – bleeding from the mouth, but the neighbors did not consider the request seriously. Finally, at 9:30 o'clock Sunday morning, Mc Chesney himself went to the home of another neighbor, Wilber Bullock and said: " Come down to my place Wilber I shot a man last night." In explanation of the affair he told Mr.

Bullock that they were arguing during a drunken brawl and that he tried to get Crawford to leave his home, and also not to come back. Mr. Bullock did not consider Mc Chesney seriously, but went with him more to humor him than anything else, and when they got to the McChesney house, McChesney said he did not want to go into the house with Bullock. Mr. Bullock pushed open the kitchen door and found Crawford's body on the floor with a bullet wound through the chest and to heart. Mr. Bullock immediately sent for Constable Ray Dean and Justice of the Peace Darcy A. Rowley was notified .

He summoned Dr. Bernard Israel of Addison who performed the autopsy. There were two shots fired and were heard by Gerald Woodbeck, Elmer Harrau and William Woodbeck who were boiling sap not far from the McChesney home. This was about 10:30 Saturday night The weapon was a double barrel shotgun. The second shot is thought to have killed Crawford. Mc Chesney was placed under arrest by Undersheriff Hardenbrook and taken to Bath at 2:15 o'clock Sunday afternoon. The body of Crawford was removed to MacDowell's undertaking rooms and the following day shipped to Canton, PA for burial.

Woman's Unusual Act

Mrs. Mc Chesney, according to neighbors and others who were at the Mc Chesney home Sunday, acted most strangely. With Crawford's body on the floor in the middle of her kitchen, between the stove and the table, she cooked food for herself, stepping across the corpse to the table to eat. She did not seem much concerned over the shooting and stated that she would stick by Mc Chesney. Wilber F. Knapp of Bath, has been retained as the attorney for the defendant, and he has retained former Deputy Sheriff Hugh McChesney, a relative of the defendant, to investigate the circumstances surrounding the shooting.

Shot Cut Off Arteries Above the Heart

The shot severed the arteries leading from the heart to the lungs and the victim bled to death. The facts so far brought to light indicate that the two men were in an intoxicated condition. McChesney admits the shooting and declares he cannot remember how it happened . He is reported to have declared that he tried to get Crawford to leave the house but the latter refused to go. Neighbors say that the two men were seen to go away in an auto early in the evening and that both were intoxicated. They were alleged to have visited a road house between Freeman and Addison. At 9:30 o'clock Crawford ,alone in his car, ran off the road near the Greenfield barn in Freeman. He was headed toward Van Vleets.

Willis R. Perry of the Advertiser , was a schoolmate of young Crawford's father, mother , uncle and aunts in Canton, PA. Hugh Crawford, the elder, grandfather of the victim, built and operated a lumber and feed mill there, and died some years ago, followed more recently by his wife. His children were Byron, William, Harriet, and Lena Crawford. At the time Mr. Perry knew the family well. William, father of young Hugh, married Meda Andrus of Canton, was badly crippled by (an) accident and died after a long period of disability, since which time his widow has been residing in Elmira. The other members of the family, so far as known at this writing are in Canton, Williamsport and Hornell.

Murder Victim Buried

Steuben County authorities are of opinion that there were no circumstances leading up to the shooting except intoxication and a quarrel without reason. The two men were friends and had no differences , and it is believed that the trouble was the result of insane drunkenness.

At the jail McChesney is regarded as not a bad fellow, the Sheriff stated. He is a blacksmith by occupation and has been in no previous trouble. Both of the men had good reputations.

Mrs. Meda Crawford and Miss Gwendolyn Crawford, mother and sister, respectively of the unfortunate man, accompanied the body to Canton where it will be placed in the family plot in the cemetery there.The funeral was held Wednesday afternoon at 2 o'clock from the home of Byron Crawford, an uncle of the decedent.

286. BYRON HUGH-[5] CRAWFORD, brother of above, was born 3 May 1869 at Canton, Bradford County, PA.. He married Adelaide "Addie" WATTS on 4 July 188 at Canton. She was the daughter of _____ WATTS and Doris A. WRIGHT, and was born 21 June 1860 at Canton, PA; died ____. Byron Hugh-[5] CRAWFORD died 1 Nov 1951. They are both buried at Main Street Cemetery, Canton , PA.

Children of Byron Hugh-[5] CRAWFORD and Addie WATTS:
Surname **CRAWFORD**

+	**696. KATHLEEN LOUISE**	born 21 May 1889 Canton, PA; died before 1960 married Norvin Clark HOLMES 10 Sep 1910 (he s/o Samuel HOLMES and Ella CLARK) (he born 14 May 1886 Philadelphia, PA; died 5 Apr 1956)	
	697. Nellie Bly	born 9 Feb 1891 PA; died 30 Jan 1895 (4 yr) buried Main Street Cemetery, Canton PA.	EOL

290. LENA BELLE-[5] CRAWFORD, sister of above, was born 10 March 1879 at Fallbrook, Tioga County, PA. She married George Washington FELIX on 19 Feb 1895 at Elmira, Chemung County, NY. He was the son of Daniel G. FELIX and Mary Amanda MANDERBACH, and was born 26 Feb 1877; divorced ca 1930; died 9 March 1975 North Hornell, Steuben County, NY. Lena Belle-[5] CRAWFORD died 7 Jan 1941 (61-10) at Hornell, New York and is buried at the Rural Cemetery there.

Children of Lena Belle-[5] CRAWFORD and George W FELIX:
Surname **FELIX**

+	**698. ALVERDA MARIE**	born 27 June 1895 Canton, PA; died ca 1981 married Victor W. HANN 17 Apr 1916 (he from Hornell, NY)
+	**699. HARRIETT LUCILLE**	born 22 June 1897 Canton, PA; died 16 June 1980 Hornell, NY married John George HUBERT 17 Apr 1915 Anton, PA

292. THOMAS LORENZO-[5] HOWE, son of Estella Phebe-[4] (Stella) MC INTOSH (William-[3]; Simon-[2]; Alexander-[1]) and James HOWE, was born 19 Sept 1869 at FallBrook, Tioga County, PA. He married Mary Margaret DWYER ca 1894. She was the daughter of Patrick DWYER and Mary RYAN, and was born ca 1865/66 FallBrook; died _____. Thomas L-[5] HOWE died 27 Jan 1944 at Corning, Steuben, NY.

Note: on the 1900 Census (Corning, NY) it stated that she had had 3 children, but only one (James)was living at that time.

Children of Thomas Lorenzo-[5] HOWE and Mary DWYER:
Surname **HOWE**

+	**700. JAMES LESLIE**	born 16 Sep 1898 FallBrook, PA; died Mar 1975 Corning, NY married Anna M. PRENDERGAST (she born ca 1895 NY; died ____) (she dau/o _____ PRENDERGAST and _____)
+	**701. MARIE**	born ca 1901 NY; died 9 Apr 1962 Corning, NY married Edward L. BAVIS ca _____ Corning, NY
	702. John R.	born 17 March 1903 NY; died Sept 1975 Corning, NY

293. FRANK EUGENE-[5] HOWE, son of Estella-[4] MC INTOSH (William-[3]; Simon-[2]; Alexander-[1]) and James HOWE, was born 4 November 1873 at FallBrook, Tioga County, PA. He married Nettie Jeanette WEBSTER on 27 September 1899 at Elmira, NY. She was the daughter of Roswell Ives WEBSTER and Adaline/Addie/ Addlyn BUTTON, and was born 25 Aug 1880 PA, died 8 Feb 1946. Frank E-[5] HOWE died 13 May 1939.

Children of Frank E-[5] HOWE and Jeanette WEBSTER:
Surname **HOWE**

703. Clyde Fulton	born 22 Dec 1907 PA; died 5 Jan 1972 Pittsburgh, PA	
	1 married Edna E. ____ ca 1930	
	Note: She appears on the 1930 Census, and also in the 1938 Corning Directory, no other info)	
	2 married Ruth ALLEN June 1946	
	(she dau/o John Landrum ALLEN and Evalina _____)	
	(she born 1 Nov 1905; died 3 Jan 1972)	
704. Alberta Ada	born 14 April 1910 PA; died Oct 1985 NY, a beautician	
	married Anthony J. FRATARCANGELO ca 1939/40	
	(he born 22 Mar 1914; died 12 Oct 2007 NJ)	
705.. Jeanette/Jean A.	born 16 Oct 1916; died 15 Oct 1990 Corning, NY, a beautician	
	married J. Lloyd SUTHERLAND ca ___	
	(he born 22 Dec 1912 NY; died 26 June 2001 Corning, NY)	
	(he s/o Thurlow J. SUTHERLAND and Anna M. LANGENDORFER)	

295. ADA(H) M-[5] HOWE, daughter of Estella-[4] MC INTOSH (William-[3]; Simon-[2]; Alexander-[1]) and James HOWE, was born ca 1881 ____, PA. She married Frank Bowman FULKERSON ca 1911. He was the son of William O. FULKERSON and Katura _____, and was born 20 May 1886 at Liberty, Tioga County, PA; died _____ They resided at Horseheads and Elmira, NY. Ada(h)-[5] HOWE died _____.

Children of Ada(h)-[5] HOWE and Frank FULKERSON:
Surname **FULKERSON**

706. Nellie E.	born ca 1913/14 PA; died _____	
	missionary in So. America; graduate of Mansfield (PA) Normal School	
707. Estella	born ca 1916; married Robert (Bob) _____	

296. LAZELL ERSTIN-[5] HOWE, brother of above, was born 11 May 1884 at FallBrook, Tioga County, PA. He married Cora HARRINGTON ca ____. She was the daughter of Anson B. HARRINGTON and Alice HERMAN, and was born Jan 1889, PA; died _____. Lazell-[5] HOWE died 6/16/Jan 1940 at Corning, Steuben, NY after an extended illness.

Children of Lazell E-[5] HOWE and Cora HARRINGTON:
Surname **HOWE**

+	**708. LAZELL**	born 1/2 July 1907 Arnot, PA; died 27 Jan 1990 (SSDI)
	HARRINGTON	married Ida May TEACHMAN 25 Sep 1930
		(she dau/o Walter TEACHMAN and _____)
		(she born 21 Feb 1908 Farmington, Tioga, PA; died 22 Nov 1994)
+	**709. ALICE E.**	born 16 Nov 1909 NY; died 24 June 1995 Fort Worth, TX
		married Kenneth M. SNYDER ca 1930 (born 1910; died 1932)

298. ETTA (Ettie) ANGELINE-[5] MC INTOSH, daughter of Henry-[4] MC INTOSH (Matthias-[3]; Simon-[2]; Alexander-[1]) and Clara DOUGLAS, was born 11 Sep 1865 at Cherry Flats/ Covington, PA. She married Chester A. CRANDALL on 22 Oct 1886 at ____. He was the son of John CRANDALL and Lucy HOWARD and was born 14 April 1853 Pierrepont, St. Lawrence County, NY; died 18 Oct 1915 at Potsdam, NY. Etta Angeline-[5] MC INTOSH died 5 March 1934 at Auburn, Cayuga County, NY.

Children of Etta Angeline-[5] MC INTOSH and Chester CRANDALL;
Surname **CRANDALL**

+	**710. ADA LUCY**	born 22 July 1887 Pierrepont, NY; died 12 Aug 1960 Auburn, NY
		married Jessie/Jesse T. WAIT(E) 30 Dec 1912 Potsdam, NY
		(he born 7 Dec 1886; died 27 Feb 1963 Orlando, FL)

Children of Etta Angeline-⁵ MC INTOSH and Chester CRANDALL, continued:
Surname **CRANDALL**

711. Elizabeth	born 28 Jan 1889; died 30 Jan 1889; buried Beech Plains, NY	
712. Leon Ransom	born 1 June 1890 Pierrepont; died 1893	
713. Ruth Elizabeth	born 1 Sep 1894 Crary Mills, NY; died Dec 1975 Potsdam, NY	
714. Roy/Ray Harry	born 23 July 1897; died 22 Oct 1918 France (killed in WW 1)	

+ **715. STANLEY ORRIN** born 21 Jan 1902 Pierrepont; died 5 Mar 1956 Rochester, NY
married Dorothy CASTILLON 15 Apr 1925
(she born 4 Oct 1904; died 4 July 1954)

+ **716. MARION LOUISE** born 11 Apr 1903; died 1 Feb 1976 Edinburgh, TX
1 married Norman Kenneth SHEPARD 29 Nov 1924; divorced
(he born 4 Oct 1903; died before 1955)
2 married Arthur DE HOLLANDER 26 Nov 1955
(he born 23 Aug 1907; died 1 Feb 1960)

299. CLARA ELIZABETH-⁵ MC INTOSH, sister of above, was born 8 Dec 1866 at Covington Township, PA. She married Martin HEWITT on 20 May 1885. He was the son of Hiram HEWITT and Mary WILLETT, and was born 10 June 1853 at Pierrepont, St. Lawrence County, NY; died 22 Oct 1919. Clara-⁵ MC INTOSH died 13 March 1934.

Children of Clara-⁵ MC INTOSH and Martin HEWITT:
Surname **HEWITT**

+ **717. THERON WILBUR** born 19 Feb 1887 Pierrepont, NY; died 13 Sep 1949
married Mabel Captola GREEN (she b. 3 July 1892; died 3 July 1957)

718. Etta Jane	born 1 Jan 1901; died ____ 1901	EOL
719. Sanford Lewis	born 7 Sep 1905; died 22 Sep 1924 (19yr)	EOL

300. GEORGE LEWIS-⁵ MC INTOSH, brother of above, was born 17 Nov 1868 at Covington, PA. He married Myrtle GRAVES on 11 October 1893 at Colton, St. Lawrence County, NY. She was the daughter of Joshua GRAVES and Hannah S. HOGLE, and was born 12 Aug 1871 Marshfield, MO.; died 8 May 1946. George Lewis-⁵ MC INTOSH died 14 Oct 1957 at _____ .

Children of George Lewis-⁵ MC INTOSH and Myrtle GRAVES:
Surname **MC INTOSH**

+ **720. HENRY LEWIS** born 27 July 1893 Pierrepont, NY; died 9 Feb 1963
1 married Leah BROWN 27 Oct 1920
(she born _____; died 23 Feb 1922 in childbirth (baby also died)
2 married Erva PLUMB 12 May 1940
(she born 13 Dec 1909; died Oct 1971 Canton, St. Lawrence, NY)

721. Leland Victor (Lee) born 3 May 1896 Pierrepont; died 5 Feb 1952   no issue   EOL
married Geneva COOK 30 June 1931
(she born 1 Oct 1898 Hermon, NY; died Dec 1968 NY)

722. Agnes Fay   born 11 June 1899, died 29 Nov 1900   EOL

301. ROWLAND P.-⁵ KIFF, son of Fanny-⁴ MC INTOSH (Matthias-³; Simon-²; Alexander-¹) and Charles KIFF, was born 11 Aug 1855 at _____, PA. He married Cora E. MANDEVILLE on 26 April 1882. She was the daughter of Virgil Alonzo MANDEVILLE (Ira) and Millicent WILCOX (Joseph), and was born 1 Sept 1864 at Trucksville, Luzerne, PA.; died 1936 Canton, PA. Rowland -⁵ KIFF died before 1930.

Children of Rowland-⁵ KIFF and Cora MANDEVILLE:
Surname **KIFF**

723. Grover Charles   born 19 Jan 1883 nr. Canton, PA; died suddenly 9 Dec 1932 PA

304. CLARA BELL-[5] KIFF, sister of above, was born 24 July 1865 at ____, PA. She married George Phelps FREEMAN, Jr. on 24 Sep 1885. He was the son of George Phelps FREEMAN, Sr. and Emeline PALMER, and was born 24 Sep 1858; died 13 Nov 1926 at Alba, Bradford County, PA.

Children of Clara Bell-[5] KIFF and George FREEMAN, Jr.:
Surname **FREEMAN**

	724. Ivy/Iva Adell	born 22 Dec 1889; died 14 Feb 1980 Elmira, Chemung, NY
		married Ray MC NEAL 29 Jan 1912
		(he s/o Edward MC NEAL and Lovina _____)
		(he born 2 Sep 1889; died Feb 1921) resided Elmira, NY
+	**725. MYRTLE**	born 31 July 1887; died 5 July 1949 Alba, PA
	FRANCES	married Frank H. THOMAS 17 Aug 1909 (he from Alba, PA)
		(he s/o Alvin THOMAS and Ella DEWEY)
+	**726. FANNIE**	born 7 Dec 1895; died 8 May 1971 Towanda, PA)
	PEARL	married George A. GARD 13 Jan 1917 Towanda, PA
		(he s/o George B. GARD and Joanna POST)
		(he born 3 Mar 1892; died 1 Aug 1978)

305. LEWIS THEODORE-[5] MC INTOSH, son of Andrew-[4] MC INTOSH (Matthias-[3]; Simon-[2]; Alexander-[1]) and Ida Ophelia JENNINGS, was born 8 June 1870 at West Covington, PA. He married Carrie EDWARDS on __ 1904/05 . She was the daughter of George EDWARDS and Ida _____, and was born Nov 1878 NY; died ____. Lewis-[5] MC INTOSH died 29 Dec 1939 at ____, PA.

Children of Lewis Theodore-[5] MC INTOSH and Ida Ophelia JENNINGS:
Surname **MC INTOSH**

727. Raymond	born 19 Feb 1904; died Dec 1979 NY Child: Mary-[7] MC INTOSH born _____
	married Lonell B. JOHNSON ; resided Cayuta, NY
728. Clifford L.	born ca 1906; died 12 Mar 1956 (age 50)
"Tip"	married Gertrude _____; resided Horseheads, NY
	(she born 25 July 1909; died 19 Aug 2002 Lowman, Chemung, NY)
	Child: Donald E-[7] MC INTOSH born ____; married Lorraine REIDY
729. Ida Mae	born 10 May 1909; died 14 May 1989 Taft, Kern, CA
	married __ OSBORNE
	Child: Joyce-[7] OSBORNE born May 1938, married ____ OLIN
730. Milton E.	born ca 1908; died 2 April 1965; buried Horseheads,NY
"Ted"	married Myrtle ____
	Children: dau (no name ,married Howard BROWN; and Milton Louis-[7] MC INTOSH born ca 1932)
731. Gertrude	born ca 1913; died _____ ; married _____ GRUBER
	(he born 11 June 1912; died 26 Aug 1990)

307. THOMAS G-[5] MC INTOSH, brother of above, was born 14 Dec 1874 at West Covington, PA. He married Nellie Ethel WATKINS on ___ at ____PA. She was the daughter of Frank WATKINS and Grace M. ___, and was born Apr 1879; died _____. Thomas-[5] MC INTOSH died 22 Dec 1952 at Blossburg, PA.

Child of Thomas-[5] MC INTOSH and Nellie WATKINS:
Surname **MC INTOSH**

+	**732. RANDALL**	born 21 Aug 1911 PA; died 14 Dec 1998 Covington, PA
	THOMAS	married Julia Ann SPENCER (she born 25 Apr 1918; died 15 Jan 1981
		(she dau/o Lyman SPENCER and Eleanor/Elinor DINSMORE)

311. FREDERICK-[5] MC INTOSH, son of Lewis Lockwood-[4] MC INTOSH (Matthias-[3]; Simon-[2]; Alexander-[1]) and Rose KLOCK, was born 24 Nov 1890/91 at West Covington, PA. He married Clara

TREAT on 27 March 1916 at Wellsboro, PA. She was the daughter of Sylvester TREAT, Jr. and Sara Cloos MILLER, and was born 28 Feb 1893; died 25 July 1975. Frederick-[5] MC INTOSH died 26 Nov 1977 and is buried at Prospect Cemetery, Mansfield, PA.

Children of Frederick-[5] MC INTOSH and Clara TREAT:
Surname **MC INTOSH**

+	**733. MARIAN**	born 26 Sep 1917 Covington, PA; died 5 July 2003 Mansfield, PA	
		married Miles FENSTERMACHER 22 June 1941	
		(he born 29 May 1919; died 18 Sep 1965)	
	734. Harold Emmett	born 18 Aug 1919; died 22 May 1927 Mansfield, PA	EOL
	735. Lewis Frederick	born April 1934; died April 1934 (3 da)	EOL

312. CLARA HELEN-[5] HARDING, daughter of Abigail Weeks-[4] (Abbie) MC INTOSH (Alexander-[3]; Simon-[2]; Alexander-[1]) and Perry H. HARDING, was born 9 Aug 1854 at Canton, Bradford County, PA. She married first to John Griffin PALMER on 10 April 1877 at ____, PA. He was the son of _____ PALMER and ____, and was born 7 Apr 1854; died 29 July 1922. Her second marriage was to William VAN RIPER on 18 Jan 1896. He was from Verona, NY, and was born 1 Apr 1841, died _____. He served in the Civil War, enlisting in the 9th NJ Company on 20 Sept 1861, and discharged 12 July 1865, He served under General BUTLER in the Army of the James.

Child of Clara Helen-[5] HARDING and John PALMER:
Surname **PALMER**

+	**736. ALFRED EARL**	born 30 Jan 1882; died _____
		married Ann Jane KEELER 3 Sept 1904
		(she born 6 May 1879 Sligo Co., Ireland; died _____)

314. CURTIS MERRITT-[5] HARDING, brother of above, was born 27 June 1862 at Canton, Bradford County, PA. He married Mina L. AYRES 19 Aug 1885 at Canton, PA. She was the daughter of Edgar Allen AYRES and Lydia M. RANDALL, and was born 28 June 1866; died _____.Curtis M-[5] HARDING died 22 Aug 1935 Canton, PA. He was a graduate of Canton (PA) High School and Illinois Wesleyan University.

He was Superintendent of Schools at Wellsville, NY for a number of years. He was in charge of the public schools at Canton, PA for 9 years, President of the Bradford County School Directors Association for 3 years, and was elected to the PA. Legislature in 1920, 1924, and 1928 where he sponsored a number of educational bills.

Children of Curtis Merritt-[5] HARDING and Mina AYRES:
Surname **HARDING**

+	**737. MINA LEONE**	born 22 June 1888 Canton, PA; died 16 June 1966 Lancaster, PA
		married Michael Joseph MC NERNEY 22 June 1908
		(he born 27 Nov 1883; died 1949)
	738. Dorothy A.	born 28 Apr 1893 ; died Mar 1980 Bradford County, PA
		1 married Fred Stewart HARTMAN 9 Sept 1914
		(he son of Frederick B. HARTMAN and Marie Anna STERNER)
		(he born 6 May 1891; died _____)

Child: Stewart Harding-[7] HARTMAN born 25 Feb 1920; died 7 Sep 1995 Camp Hill, PA
Note: Mr. HARTMAN was the Executive Secretary of the Educational Dept. at the State Capitol in Harrisburg, PA

2 married Preston F. MARSHALL ca 1917 ++
(he born 23 June 1893; died 16 June 1966)

Child: Preston F-[7] MARSHALL born 2 Apr 1918 MA; died 10 Nov 2002 CA
++ Preston MARSHALL was a career Navy man. He was an officer, listed on the
1930 Census at San Diego as a Lt. Commander; served on the USS CASE

315. SARAH FRANCES-⁵ HARDING, sister of above, was born 7 July 1865 at Canton, Bradford, PA. She married first to John Walter HAMMOND on 30 Sep 1886. He was born 18 Oct 1866; died _____. Sarah married second to Clark BAILEY 11 Aug 1912. He was born ca 1849, died ____. Sarah Frances-⁵ HARDING died 29 May 1917.

Child of Sarah Frances-⁵ HARDING and John HAMMOND:
Surname **HAMMOND**

739. Mildred Genevieve   born 16 May 1889 Elmira, Chemung Co., NY; died June 1982 NV
                            1 married Jesse COTTINGHAM 5 June 1907
                            (he gs/o William COTTINGHAM Burnstown, MN)
                            (he born 12 Jan 1875 England; died 5 Aug 1951 MN)
            Children: Charlotte Frances-⁷ born 15 Sep 1911; Henry-⁷ COTTINGHAM
            born 12 Aug 1913, died 3 Dec 1995 Jacksonville, AL

                            2 married Elmer Thomas BUTLER 17 Nov 1920 NV
                            (he born 19 Nov 1892 MN; died 1937; an undertaker)
            Children: Benjamin Franklin-⁷ born 21 May 1922, died 16 June 1981 Seattle, WA;   Mildred Genevieve-⁷ born 26 Aug 1923, died 15 May 1924; and Beverly May-⁷ BUTLER born 5 Dec 1924

                            3 married Plato Stover STOUT (he born 1896, died 1966)
                            4 married Charles Sydney TREMEWAN 25 Jan 1947 NV
                            (he born 11 Aug 1881 NV; died Feb 1971)

316. LUNA BELL-⁵ HARDING, sister of above, was born 15 July 1870 at Susquehanna, PA. She married first to Byron Grant CORNELIUS ca 1896. He was the son of Joseph H. CORNELIUS and Elizabeth MC INTYRE, and was born 8 Mar 1868; died 23 Dec 1909. he was a foreman in a Tannery.   Her second marriage was to Truman SAVEY on 20 Sep 1917 at _____. He was the son of Mathew S. SAVEY and Mary ____, and was born Jan 1870 NY, died _____. 1930 they resided Nelson, Tioga, PA

Children of Luna Bell-⁵ HARDING and Byron Grant CORNELIUS:
Surname **CORNELIUS**

740. Charles Church   born 7 June 1898 ME, died May 1961; undertaker
741. Curtis Harding   born 7 July 1906 Elkland, PA; died July 1982 Tucson, AZ
                        married Mary Ellen WALKER 25 Dec 1930
                        (she d/o Daniel WALKER and Mary Ellen __)(she born 8 Feb 1908)

317. ROBERT PERRY-⁵ MC INTOSH, son of Theophilus Fletcher-⁴ MC INTOSH (George-³; Simon-²; Alexander-¹) and Frances KEELER, was born 24 March 1859 at Bloomville, Delaware County, NY. He married Harriet Lamont JAMIESON on 9 Feb 1897. She was the daughter of Robert JAMIESON and Mary LAMONT, and was born 18 Feb 1863; died __ 1954.

Robert-⁵ MC INTOSH succeeded his father, Theophilus, as Editor and publisher of the Delaware Republican, a newspaper published at Delhi, Delaware County, NY. He was an elder of the Presbyterian Church at Delhi and was a Freemason. Robert-⁵ MC INTOSH died __ ___ 1937. He and three preceding generations of the MAC INTOSH clan are buried in the Woodland Cemetery. His grandfather, George-3, purchased the plots.

Children of Robert Perry-⁵ MC INTOSH and Harriet Lamont JAMIESON:
Surname **MC INTOSH**

+   **742. ROBERT**   born 21 Feb 1898 Delhi, NY; died 14 Feb 1989 NY
      PERRY, Jr.   married Grace L. LEE ca 1934
                               (she born 8 Oct 1901 Newark, NY; died Nov 1973 NY)
743. Katherine Jamieson   born 22 Feb 1900 Delhi, NY; died _____; never married   EOL

Children of Robert Perry-5 MC INTOSH and Harriet JAMIESON, continued:
Surname **MC INTOSH**

+ **744. CHARLES** | born 18 Mar 1902 Delhi; died June 1976 Rochester, NY
married Gertrude PALMITER ca 1933
(she dau/o Harley E. PALMITER and Edna BULKLEY)
(she born 19 Feb 1902 Brookfield, NY; died Nov 1993 Rochester, NY

745. Helen Carol | born 28 July 1905 Delhi; died 2 Mar 1959; never married
graduate of Syracuse University – 1929

+ **746. FRANCES KEELER** | born 3 Nov 1908 Delhi; ;married Hugh Gilchrist DICK, PhD 1936
(he born 14 Dec 1909 NY; died 31 Dec 1971 Los Angeles, CA)
(he s/o Herbert DICK and Isabella _____)

318. CHARLES KEELER-5 MC INTOSH, brother of above, was born ca 1860 at Bloomville, Delaware County, NY. He married Nellie A. ROGERS of Syracuse, Onondaga County, NY. on ___ 1886. She was the daughter of _____ ROGERS and Augusta WRIGHT, and was born Jan 1869 NY; died _____. Charles-5 MC INTOSH worked many years for the Railway Mail Service , and died ca 1930 at Syracuse, NY.

Children of Charles Keeler-5 MC INTOSH and Nellie ROGERS:
Surname **MC INTOSH**

+ **747. WALTER PERRY** | born 14 June 1889 Delhi, NY; died 11 Nov 1872 (age 83)
married Mary Louise DURBIN 5 Oct 1912 Syracuse, NY

319. HENRY MARTIN-5 MC INTOSH, brother of above, was born ca 1863 Bloomville, Delaware County, NY. He married Sadie BURROUGHS ca _____. She was the daughter of Samuel BURROUGHS and Amanda M. _____, and was born Nov 1873 IA; died _____. They resided at Dexter, MO for many years and Henry died there ca 1934.

Children of Henry Martin-5 MC INTOSH and Sadie BURROUGHS / BURROWS:
Surname **MC INTOSH**

748. Grace M | born 2 Aug 1895 Dexter, MO; died Jan 1974 Dexter, Stoddard, MO
1 married Holger M. CHRISTENSEN 6 Jan 1917 Dexter , MO.
(he born ca 1896; died before 1920)
In 1920 Grace, a widow, worked as a nurse in the Bethesda Foundling Home (orphanage) in St. Louis, MO
2 married Cecil THOMASSON after 1936   no issue   EOL
(he born 6 Dec 1910; died Dec 1987 Dexter, MO.)

320. FRANCES (Fanny) M-5 MC INTOSH, sister of above, was born 3 June 1867 at Bloomville, Delaware County, NY. She married James Merton RONEY ca 1894. He was the son of Thomas RONEY born NY)and Mary A. _____ (born Ireland), and was born ca 1863 NY; died _____. They resided at Buffalo, NY. and later Ilion, NY., where Frances died ca 1932.

Children of Frances-5 MC INTOSH and James Merton RONEY:
Surname **RONEY**

749. Frances | born ca ____; died before 1912   EOL
750. George Fletcher | born 14 Feb 1896 NY; died 23 Apr 1970 Vista, San Diego, CA.
married Agnes C. ___ ca 1924 (she born ca 1896 Scotland)
Children: George M-7 born ca 1925 NY; and John J-7 RONEY born ca 1927/28 NY

321. GEORGE WALTER-5 MC INTOSH, son of Theophilus-4 MC INTOSH (George-3; Simon-2; Alexander-1) and Frances KEELER, was born 1 March 1871 at Delhi, Delaware County, NY. He married Rella MCGONAGLE ca 1895 at Louisville, Kentucky. She was the daughter of Henry C. MCGONAGLE and ___, and was born ca 1872 IN; died ____. George Walter-5 MC INTOSH died 13 Mar 1949.

Children of George Walter-[5] MC INTOSH and Rella MC GONAGLE:
Surname **MC INTOSH**

751. Mildred M. "Trixie " born 18 Aug 1901 Jefferson, KY; died 24 Mar 1972 Louisville, KY;
married Robert Edmister MORRISON 30 Apr 1940 Washington, DC
(he born 13 Sept 1890; died 20 Nov 1960)

752. Charlotte M.   born 7 Dec 1903 KY; died 13 May 1986 Louisville, KY
(Lottie)   married Mora Eugene HELM 17 Apr 1927   no issue   EOL
(he s/o Mora Alonzo HELM and Sara Rachel FLOWERS)
(he born 23 Dec 1898 KY; died 4 Feb 1961 KY)

+   **753. ROBERT**   born 31 Jan 1908 KY; died Sep 1977 Louisville, KY)
WALTER   married Edith HOBBS 4 June 1932 (she b. 3 Oct 1914; died May 1989

754. Frances   born 1 Feb 1910 Jefferson, KY; died 2 June 1913 Louisville, KY

322. FRANK EDWARD-[5] MC INTOSH, brother of above, was born 23 August 1879 at Delhi, Delaware County, NY. He married Fanny YENCER ca 1911. She was the daughter of Charles Volney YENCER and his second wife Martha Ann SHURTLIFF, and was born 21 Aug 1877; died 14 Sep 1967 Burlington, VT., Frank-5 MC INTOSH, who was President. of the Chittenden Co. (VT) Trust Co., President of the Adsit Coal Co., Managing Director of the General Ice Cream Corp, all of Burlington, died ___ 1950.

Child of Frank Edward-[5] MC INTOSH and Fannie YENSER/YENCER:
Surname **MC INTOSH**
+   **755. MERWIN**   born 21 Oct 1912 Delaware Co., NY; died 9 May 1991 Pinellas, FL
KEELER   married Margaret Rathburn ROYCE ca 1934 Burlington, VT
(she dau/o Frank Bertrand ROYCE and Flora RATHBURN)
(she born 24 Jan 1912 St. Albans VT; died 2 Dec 2001 FL)

324. CORA J-[5] CARPENTER, daughter of Sophronia-[4] MC INTOSH (George-[3]; Simon-[2]; Alexander-[1]) and Joel A. CARPENTER, was born ca January 1874 NY. She married Charles A. ROGERS of Walton, NY. He was born 18 Sep 1873 NY; died Nov 1965. Cora-5 died Jan 1957 at Hancock, Delaware , NY.

Child of Cora-[5] CARPENTER and Charles ROGERS:
Surname **ROGERS**
756. Anna Kathryn   born 28 Jan1907 NY; died 15 Dec 2000 Farmington, Stafford, NH
married BillingsWaldo CHAMBERLIN , PhD. 1940 +++
(he s/o Daniel CHAMBERLIN and Elizabeth _____)
(he born 13 Oct 1905; died 28 Jan 1986 Hanover, Grafton, NH)
Children: John-[7] born _____; and David-[7] CHAMBERLIN born ____

+++ WALDO CHAMBERLIN, Distinguished Educator and Statesman
(Excerpts from an article originating at Dartmouth College)
"Waldo CHAMBERLIN, for many years a professor of Government in the Graduate School of Arts and Sciences of NYU. In 1961 he moved to Dartmouth College, where he served for eight years as Dean of Summer Programs , and retired in 1971 as a professor of history. During World War II, CHAMBERLIN held posts in the US Department of State and other federal agencies, and at the end of the war he became a documents officer for the United Nations in its preparatory stages and first years. The United Nations remained one of his prime interests, and he studied, taught, and wrote about it until the end of his career." Professor CHAMBERLIN'S widow gave his papers and writings on the United Nations to Dartmouth College . They are in the Rauner Special Collections Library there .

327. WILLIAM TYLER-[5] STERLING, son of Sarah Adeline-[4] MC INTOSH (Simon,Jr.-[3]; Simon-[2]; Alexander-[1]) and Charles STERLING, was born 2 Feb 1862 at Susquehanna Depot, Susquehanna County, PA. He married Clara J/G-[5] MAC DONALD (# 192) on 21 April 1887 at ____ PA. She was the daughter of Mary-[4] CALDWELL (Clara-[3] MC INTOSH; Simon-[2]; Alexander-[1]) and James MAC DONALD, and was born ca 1861 at ____ PA; died 13 Sep 1938 Queens Village, Long Island, NY. William Tyler-[5] STERLING was associated with Standard Oil of New Jersey for many years, owning a considerable amount of stock, which supported his family in style for many more years. He died 2 Feb 1955, his 93rd birthday.

Children of William Tyler-[5] STERLING and Clara MAC DONALD:
Surname **STERLING**

	757. Sarah Adeline	born 20 Oct 1888, NY; died Aug 1972 Syracuse, NY
		married August Percival " Percy " LOEWE ca 1922; divorced ca 1924
		(he s/o Dietrich E. LOEWE and Christina__) (he born 26 Feb 1894 CT)
+	**758. MARGUERITE**	born 20 Oct 1899 NY; died Nov 1978 Syracuse, NY
	ESTHER	married Charles Harold TRELAWNY 21 Dec 192_
		(he s/o Charles A. TRELAWNY and Mary A.____ (born England)
		(he born 21 Dec 1885 Torquet, England; died Jan 1932 NY)
		(he immigrated to this country with his parents in 1892)

Reference: Naturalization Petition for Charles Harold TRELAWNY was # 26185; Admitted 2 Mar 1922 # 1409687 (Vol. 107)

328. MERTON EMERSON-[5] GREENOUGH, son of Mary Caroline-[4] MC INTOSH, (Simon, Jr.-[3]; Simon-[2]; Alexander-[1]) and Henry GREENOUGH, was born 2 January 1856 at East Troy, Bradford County, PA. He married Mary E. VAN HORN on ___ 1880. She was the daughter of ___ VAN HORN and _____, and was born Sep 1862 PA; died _____. Merton E-[5] GREENOUGH died 25 May 1935.

Children of Merton E-[5] GREENOUGH and Mary VAN HORN:
Surname **GREENOUGH**

	759. Henry, Jr.	born 7 June 1881 PA; died 29 Oct 1966 ;married Margaret SLADE
	760. Harry A.	born ca 1881 PA; died _____ no issue EOL
		married Clara REYNOLDS (she born ca 1880/81; died _____)

Note: Harry was in the US Railway Mail Service

+	**761. WILLIS**	born 29 July 1884 PA; died Oct 1966 Troy, PA
	BENJAMIN	married Nettie Hannah LEONARD
		(she born 12 Feb 1888 E. Troy, PA; died 1967)

329. CLARENCE LACELL-[5] GREENOUGH, brother of above, was born 27 June 1857 at East Troy, Bradford County, PA. He married Ida Ann NEVIN 20 Sept 1883 St. Paul, MN. She was the daughter of John NEVIN and Jerry D. __, and was born 1867 MN, died 24 Mar 1924. Clarence L-[5] died 1 Sep 1891.

Child of Clarence L-[5] GREENOUGH and Ida Ann NEVIN:
Surname **GREENOUGH**

	762. Clarence Douglas	born 16 July 1884 MN; died 14 Oct 1949
		married Lillian Goldie CHAPMAN 4 Mar 1902 St. Paul, MN
		(she dau/o George H. CHAPMAN and Ellen M.) (she born ca 1880 MN)

Children : Sybil-[7] born ca 1904 and Maxine Chapman-[7] GREENOUGH, born 11 Nov 1907; married 1926 to ____ ST. GERMAINE; died 3 Jan 1993 FL
Note: Douglas-[6] GREENOUGH was a switchman on the Omaha Railroad

330. CHARLES HENRY-[5] GREENOUGH, brother of above, was born 31 Aug 1865 at East Troy, Bradford County, PA. He married Wrexieville "Rexie" Eliza CASE on 3 Nov 1886 at Troy, PA. She was the daughter of Caleb CASE and Nancy SMITH , and was born 1 Nov 1864; died 8 June 1936. Charles Henry-[5] GREENOUGH died 29 June 1920 at Troy, PA., and is buried in Glenwood Cemetery.

Children of Charles H-[5] GREENOUGH and Rexie CASE:
Surname **GREENOUGH**

	763. Clarence Lee	born 8 June 1889 Troy, PA; died 8 Nov 1967 Bath, New York
		1 married Louise CRAWFORD ca 1911
		2 married Grace Rockwell LEGGETT Besley (dau/o Charles LEGGETT
		(she born 25 April 1889; died Nov 1984 Troy, PA)

Children of Charles-[5] GREENOUGH and Rexie Case, continued:
Surname **GREENOUGH**

+	**764. CALEB C.**	born 3 Jan 1893 Troy, PA; died 25 March 1987 Troy		
		married Gladys ALLYN 29 Aug 1923 PA		
		(she dau/o Arthur William ALLYN and Lillian Caroline "Lottie" PIATT)		
		(she born 3 July 1903 Leona ,PA; died 23 Jan 1993 East Troy, PA		
+	**765. HELEN**	born 9 Apr 1894 Troy; died _____		
	CAROLINE	married Charles <u>Tracy</u> METZGER 16 Sep 1916		
		(he born 24 Sep 1893; died 25 Aug 1963)		

Note: He owned the Troy (PA) Marble and Granite Company

	766. Monema A.	born 17 Sep 1895; died 12 Aug 1989	no issue	EOL
		married John N. KENYON 19 Apr 1929		
		(he born 27 Aug 1886; died 18 June 1962)		

Note: John N. KENYON had a degree from Columbia University, and was a consulting engineer. .

+	**767. PAIGE HENRY**	born 27 Feb 1897; died 30 Oct 1980 Elmira, Chemung, NY
		married Eula Marian KNOWLDEN 11 Oct 1926
		(she dau/o Harry KNOWLDEN and Marion Kirkwood INNES (Robert)
		(she born 12 Sep 1900 Granville Center, PA; died 7 Nov 1981)
+	**768. IDA MAE**	born 10 Sep 1898; died 28 Nov 1989
		married Howard Alfred DUNBAR 8 Sep 1920
		(he s/o Bert DUNBAR and Emma HEIDA)
		(he born 30 Oct 1895; died July 1933)
+	**769. PAUL E.**	born 31 July 1900; died 16 May 2000 Gillett, PA
		married Ina Russell TOMLINSON 1920
		(she dau/o Edward V. TOMLINSON and Isabelle M. HAVENS)
		(she born 6 Sept 1901 Troy, PA; died 12 Jan 1996)

332. FREDERICK JAMES-[5] STERLING, son of Elizabeth Jane-[4] MC INTOSH (Simon , Jr.-[3]; Simon-[2]; Alexander-[1]) and Charles STERLING was born 10 July 1867 at Alba, Bradford County, PA. He was the half-brother of William Tyler-[5] STERLING.(# 327)

On 1 January 1887 he married Nancy Mae WILLIAMS. She was the second of nine children of Joseph Henry WILLIAMS ++ and Mary Anna KRIEGER+++, and was born 30 Oct 1868 at Troy, Bradford County, PA; died 9 Sep 1945 at Canton, Bradford, PA.   Fred J. STERLING, a farmer , horticulturist, taxidermist, hunter and long time Health Officer for Canton, was a gentle man who died 28 Jan 1927 at Canton, PA. He and his wife are buried at Park Cemetery, Canton.

++ Joseph Henry WILLIAMS , was the s/o of Charles WILLIAMS and Eleanor HIGHBEE/HIGHBY, and
was born 16 Apr 1841 Troy, PA. Little or nothing is known of the years after his children were born – as he
"disappeared " leaving his wife and children for reasons unknown. In 1910 he was residing in Montrose,
Susquehanna, PA, was listed as a salesman of hardware, and single. Reportedly he moved on to Ohio, and folklore tells of his residing
in the Cincinnati area, and dying there. He may possibly have been indigent, as reports also state he was buried in a Potter's Field. (
Have not been able to locate a cemetery)

+++ Mary Anna KRIEGER, wife of Joseph Henry WILLIAMS, was the daughter of Jonathan KRIEGER and Nancy LANDIS, and
was born 27 Nov 1848 at Jackson, Lycoming, PA; and died ca 1924 in CA.

Children of Frederick James-[5] STERLING and Nancy Mae WILLIAMS
Surname **STERLING**

+	**770. MARY**	born 4 Feb 1888 Canton, PA; died 17 Mar 1974 Cranston, RI
	ELIZABETH	married Harry J. EY
		(he born ca 1880 NY; died ca 1946 RI)
		(he s/o August EY (born Prussia) and Ellen _____, born PA

Children of Frederick James-[5] STERLING and Nancy Mae WILLIAMS, continued:

Surname **STERLING**

+   **771. CHARLES**   born 19 Dec 1890 Canton, PA; died 6 March 1942 Syracuse, NY
     (Henry) **LEE**   married Hazel Frances-[9] DOTY 24 Mar 1921 Syracuse, NY
     (she dau/o John Christy-[8] DOTY, Jr.++ and Mary Matilda FRENCH)
     (she born 10 Dec 1898 Syracuse, NY; died 16 Jan 1971 Syracuse, NY
     (both buried North Syracuse Cemetery, North Syracuse, NY)

++ (John Christy-[7] DOTY; Britain-[6]; William-[5,4]; Jacob-[3]; Isaac-[2]; Edward -[1] of the MAYFLOWER)

     772. Ray Parsons Stuart   born 22 Jan 1895 Canton, PA; died 28 July 1913 Canton
     (died of Bright's disease ; single)   EOL

     773. Julia Mae   born 11 Jan 1912 Canton, PA; died 1 Mar 1986 Lakeland, FL.
     married Joseph RICKARD 18 Nov 1936 Canton, PA.   EOL
     (he born 30 Oct 1911 PA; died 19 Oct 2000 Canton, PA)
     (she joined DAR 1947 on the Simon-[2] MAC INTOSH line)

Note: Adopted 2 children – 1. George QUINN born 15 Feb 1948 PA; died ____; Sarah Jane ____ born 7 June 1952

334. STERLING JAMES-[5] DANN, son of Electa Adelia-[4] MC INTOSH (Simon, Jr-[3]; Simon-[2]; Alexander-[1]) and Silas Newton DANN, was born 10 Jan 1868 at Canton, Bradford County, PA. He married Ethel Mae HAVENS on 14 July 1891 at Canton. She was the daughter of _____ HAVENS and _____, and was born Dec 1866 PA; died 1926. Sterling James-[5] DANN died 7 Mar 1941 at Canton, PA. He and his wife are buried at Park Cemetery there.

Children of Sterling James-[5] DANN and Ethel Mae HAVENS:

Surname **DANN**

+   **774. ARTHUR B.**   born 15 June 1892; died Oct 1870
     married Margaret ENGLISH
     (she born 27 July 1891; died Apr 1972 Canton, PA)
     (she dau/o Harvey P. ENGLISH and Bertha M _____)

+   **775. DR. LELAND**   born 26 June 1894 PA ; died 15 Aug 1964 NY
     HAVENS   married Renee' F. _____ on _____ at _____ France
     (she born 11 Dec 1895 France; died 27 Mar 1968)

Note: He was a surgeon. He was with the State Dept. in Washington, DC until his retirement.
They are both buried in the Long Island National Cemetery

     776. Orpha/Ortha H.   born ca 1895; died 3 Apr 1935 Arkansas

     777. Donald Silas   born 20 June 1899 PA; died 1955; married Lynn HELM   EOL

+   **778. GRACE E.**   born 21 Mar 1901 PA; died 4 Sep 1970 Watkins Glen, NY
     married George WHITING 19 Jan 1924
     (he born 21 Apr 1900; died Nov 1967)

341. HELEN L.-[5] MC INTOSH, daughter of George Washington-[4] MC INTOSH (Simon, Jr-[3]; Simon-[2]; Alexander-[1]) and Louisa/Louise WISE, was born ca 1883 PA. She married Theodore John HAND, of South Williamsport, PA, on _____ at ____. He was the son of Charles H. HAND (born England) and Mary Elizabeth HUGHES (born England), and was born Nov 1880 NJ. died _____. Helen L-[5] MC INTOSH died _____. Resided South Williamsport, Lycoming County, PA.

133,135,137,139

Children of Helen L-[5] MC INTOSH and Theodore John HAND:

Surname **HAND**

     779. Emily Louise   born ca 1909 PA; died ____

     780. John William   born 5 May 1911 PA; died ___; married Marjorie Carol WINTER 1946
     (she born 6 Jan 1909 NJ; died 12 Oct 1993 Trenton, NJ)

     781. Grace Elizabeth   born ca 1914 PA; died _____

     782. George M.   born ca 1916 PA

     783. Charles   born ca 1921 PA

The Fifth American Generation

345. WILLIAM JOHN-[5] MC INTOSH, son of Charles Melvin-[4] MC INTOSH (Simon, Jr-[3]; Simon-[2]; Alexander-[1]) and Emma MELLOR, was born 21 Aug 1887 at Canton, PA. He married Eva MAC KNESS / MAC NESS / MAC INNES ca 1924 at ____. She was the daughter of ____ MAC KNESS and _____, and was born 25 Mar 1897; died 4 Jan 1992. William John-[5] MC INTOSH died ca 1958 at ____, PA.

Children of William John-[5] MC INTOSH and Emma MELLOR:
Surname **MC INTOSH**

+	**784. WILLIAM GEORGE**	born 13 Sept 1925 PA; died 1992 Canton, PA married Clara HURLBURT ca ____
	785. Clifford John	born 2 Nov 1926 PA; died 7 Aug 2000 Elkhart, IN 1 married Gay FLEMING ca ____; divorced 2 married Evelyn/Eva ROTH

Children : Clifford-[7] Jr. born 28 Oct 1957, and Susan-[7] MC INTOSH born 28 Jan 1969

348. CHARLES L-[5] CEASE, son of Leroy-[4] CEASE (Julia Ann-[3] MAC INTOSH; Simon-[2]; Alexander-[1]) and Amanda-[6] MOORE, was born Mar 1866 at Canton, Bradford County, PA. He married Gertrude WRIGHT on ___ 1889 at _____ PA. She was the daughter of Merton WRIGHT and Angeline _____, and was born Apr 1871 PA; died ____. Charles-[5] CEASE died ca 1924 at Canton, PA.

Children of Charles-[5] CEASE and Gertrude WRIGHT:
Surname **CEASE**

	786. Howard Archie	born 21 July 1890 PA; died Aug 1974 Spencerport, NY
	787. Doris	born __ July 1893/94; died _____
	788. Leroy / Roy J.	born Aug 1898 PA; died ____; married Irene D. _____
	789. Nellie	born ca 1904 PA; died _____
+	**790. EDWARD D.**	born 13 Mar 1905 PA; died 31 July 1984 Troy, PA married Ruth Eileen BACORN 1938 (she born ca 1917; died 2002)
	791. Carl/Carlyle	born ca 1906 PA; died ca 1912 PA
	792. Flossie/ Florence	born ca 1910 PA

352. LILLIAN (Nellie) -[5] CEASE, sister of above, was born 21 May 1877/78 at _____ PA. She married Robert B-[8] LANDON on 31 Aug 1894. He was the son of Merton C -[7] LANDON (Benjamin-[6] ++; Ezra-[5]; [4]; Laban-[3]; William-[2]; Daniel-[1]) and Augusta B. GOFF, and was born June 1874 Canton, Bradford County, PA, and died 1916. Lillian/Nellie-[5] CEASE died ____.

Children of Lillian-[5] CEASE and Robert -[8] LANDON:
Surname **LANDON**

+	**793. HAZEL F.**	born 15 Oct 1895 PA; died _____; married Edward E. RYAN
+	**794. LEWIS E.**	born 7 Dec 1898/99 PA; died married Marie MC CLURE 26 June 1925 Corning, NY (b. 1903 NY)

++ Note: Regarding the grandparents of Robert-[8] LANDON:

Benjamin-[6] LANDON was born ca 1824 at Canton, PA. His wife Mary A. BARROW, was born ca 1827 at Delhi, Delaware County, NY. When she was quite small, her parents moved to Union, Tioga County, PA. On 24 May 1846 she married Benjamin LANDON of East Canton, and resided there until 1874 when they moved to Canton . Mary A. (BARROW) Landon was a member of the Church of Christ for over 30 years and was an active worker . " She was one who tried all through life to make it lively and pleasant to all around her. The following poetry was attached to her will and bequest, which shows her full sentiments in every respect :"   (the preceding a partial comment in her obituary).

MACKINTOSH   MAC INTOSH   MC INTOSH
The Fifth American Generation

WHEN I AM DEAD

I would not have the rude and gaping crowd
Around me gather, and mid lamentation loud
Tell of my virtues, and with vain regret
Bemoan my loss, and leaving me forget.
But I would have the few of kindly heart
Who, when misfortunes came, so nobly did their part,
And oft by thoughtful deeds their love express –
These would I have, no more, no less.
When I am dead!

When I am dead,
I would not have the high and storied stone
Placed o'er my grave, and then be left alone:
But I would have some things I once did love,
Ere I did leave the joyous world above,
Placed o'er me. And each succeeding year
I'd have my friends renew them, and oft linger near,
With loving thoughts upon the dear one laid below,
And talk of times departed long ago, When I am dead!

When I am dead,
Forgive- Oh this I pray far more than all -
The anguish that I have caused, the deed
                          beyond recall.
Think kindly of me as I lie so still,
So poor a subject for an angered will;
Think of some generous deed, some good
                          word spoken,
Of hearts bound up I found all sad and
                          broken;
Think gently, when this last long rest is
                          mine,
And gaze upon my form with look benign,
When I am dead!

Franklin P. DALY, In Guardian

353. ROSA BELLE-[5] CEASE, daughter of Nelson-[4] CEASE (Julia Ann-[3] MC INTOSH, Simon-[2]; Alexander-[1]) and Margaret (Mag) EATON, was born Dec 1872 at Canton, Bradford County, PA. She married Frank P. WELCH on ___ at ___. He was the son of Horace WELCH and Mary E. WELCH, and was born Mar 1871 Canton, PA; died 17 Nov 1952 Leroy, PA. Rosa Belle-[5] CEASE died 25 Jan 1953.

Children of Rosa Belle-[5] CEASE and Frank P. WELCH
Surname **WELCH**

+	**795 . LEAH M.**	born July 1897 PA; died ca 1970
		married Milo Denton TILLOTSON ca 1923
		(he born 24 Oct 1898; died May 1969 Canton, PA)
	796. Marguerite	born 10 Oct 1902 Canton, PA; died June 1982 Canton no issue EOL
		married Russell FREEMAN ca 1922 (he born ca 1903 PA; died _____

354. WILLARD L-[5] CEASE, brother of above, was born ca 1874 at ____ PA. He married Edith MOORE on ____. She was the daughter of George Dudley MOORE and Frances/Frankie SMITH, and was born 22 May 1882 Armenia Township, Tioga, PA; died 2 July 1948 Canton, PA Willard-[5] CEASE died ca 1936.

Children of Willard-[5] CEASE and Edith MOORE:
Surname **CEASE**

+	**797. LYSLE WILLARD**	born 17 Oct 1903 PA; died Apr 1992 Virginia Beach, VA.
		married Alwyn Christina WYLE
		(she dau of Dr. Edwin Arthur WYLE and Alice Louise SMITH)
		(she born 27 Apr 1907 Argentina; died 15 Mar 2001 Virginia Beach)
	798. Frances	born 17 Sep 1904; died May 1987 PA.
		marred Joseph H. ZELL 1936 Dubois, PA no issue EOL
+	**799. NELSON DUDLEY**	born Sep 1909 PA; died _____
		1 married Beatrice _____ (she born _____; died 1944)
		2 married Cleo Wilma FULLER Leighton (wid /o Floyd E. LEIGHTON
		(she daau/o Clyde Wm. FULLER and Myrtle J. HOGABOOM)
		(she born 6 Dec 1920 Wheelerville, Sullivan Co., PA; died _____)

87

355. LUCY M-[5] CEASE, sister of above, was born ca 1880 at _____, PA. She married Delos E-5 KIFF, ca 1902/03 at _____. He was the son of John Mabie-[4] KIFF; (Erastus-[3]; Andrew-[2]; George-[1]) and Susan BASCOM/BASCOMB, and was born June 1873 PA; died 1944. Lucy M-[5] CEASE died ca 1969.

Children of Lucy M-[5] CEASE and Delos-[5] KIFF:
Surname **KIFF**

	800. Donald Herbert	born 20 Sep 1905 NY; died 19 Apr 1996 Elmira, NY
		married Ava Marie BEDFORD 24 Nov 1943
		(she born 16 Mar 1914; died 11 Oct 2002 Elmira, NY)
+	**801. HELEN L.**	born ca 1909 NY; died ca 1910 PA
		married James STRAUSS (he born ca 1910; died _____)
	802. John N.	born Apr 1922 PA; died 23 May 2010 Elmira, NY
		married Doris _____ (Child: Donald J-[5] CEASE born ca 1962)

356. ALEXANDER-[5] CEASE (Aleck), brother of above, was born Feb 1881 at _____ PA. He married first to Martha Mary _____ ca 1900. She was born ca 1873 PA; died ca 1927 Canton, PA. His second wife was Molly _____. (No other info on her; and no issue). Alexander -[5] CEASE was a sawyer and foreman in a woodworking plant in Canton, PA. He died ca 1944.

Child of Alexander-[5] CEASE and Martha _____:
Surname **CEASE**

803. Hilton	born ca 1901; died _____ no issue	EOL
	married Charlotte "Lettie" REXFORD (born Oct 1891; died 1973)
	(she dau/o Burton REXFORD and Clara D. BECKER)

359. HERMAN THEOPHILUS-[5] CEASE, son of Sidney T-[4] CEASE (Julia Ann-[3] MAC INTOSH; Simon-[2;] Alexander-[1]) and Mary Caroline-[5] MC INTOSH (Michael-[4]; William-[3]; Simon-[2]; Alexander-[1]), and was born 23/30 Dec 1876 Tioga County, PA. He married Loda May BRIGGS on 19 Dec 1904 at Emmett Co., Michigan. She was the daughter of Robert Cornell BRIGGS and Anna Lodesca FINNE, and was born 24 Aug 1885 WI; died 2 Jan 1956 CA. Herman-[5] died 27 Dec 1949 (stomach cancer) Chicago.

Children of Herman-[5] CEASE and Loda BRIGGS:
Surname **CEASE**

	804. Grace Irene	born 18 Oct 1906 Rhinelander, WI ; married Clarence S. BEYER
		died Jan 1970 Huntington Beach, CA
		Child: Lorraine June -[7] BEYER born ca 1934; died 2005
	805. Sidney Robert	born 14 Nov 1907 Rhinelander, WI; died 7 July 1921
		Note: He was killed by a playmate who was playing with a gun
+	**806. DORIS MAY**	born 21 Apr 1910 Rhinelander, WI; died 23 June 1958 (suicide)
		married Clinton A. JOHNSON
	807. Charles F.	born 2 Dec 1919 Rhinelander; died Mar 1969 Berwyn, Cook, IL

360. FRED A-[5] CEASE, brother of above, was born 28 Apr 1879 at Tioga County, PA. He married Della JOHNSON/JOHNSTON ca 1903. She was the daughter of _____ JOHNSON/JOHNSTON (born Canada) and _____ (born Canada), and was born ca 1881 MI; died 12 July 1943 Harbor Springs, MI. Fred-[5] CEASE died of stomach cancer on 5 June 1949 at Harbor Springs., MI.

Child of Fred-[5] CEASE and Della JOHNSON/JOHNSTON:
Surname **CEASE**

+	**808. LUTHER EARL**	born 10 July 1903 Harbor Springs,MI; died 1957 Harbor Springs
		married Beatrice Blossom DOVE ca _____ (cancer)
		(she dau/o Albert B. DOVE and Ina M _____) (she born 24 Oct 1904; died 1995)

361. JULIA M-[5] CEASE, sister of above, was born 20 June 1883 at Bradford County, PA. She married first to John W. LANE on 30 August 1904 at Center Township, Emmett Co., Michigan. He was the son of Samuel LANE and Elizabeth PATEN, and was born ca 1868; died ____. They were divorced ca 1908. She married second on 22 Nov 1910 to David WALSH at Emmett County, MI. He was the son of _____ WALSH and ____, and was born ca 1886 at Belfast, Ireland, and died 1955 at Windsor, Ontario, Canada. Julia-[5] CEASE died ____.

Child of Julia-[5] CEASE and John W. LANE:
Surname **LANE**
+   **809. ROBERT**   born ca 1907; died 24 Dec 1934 Windsor, Ontario, Canada (suicide)

Note: Robert used the name of his step-father (WALSH), although he was never legally adopted. He never married , but lived with a woman by the name of Phyllis Mary COOK. They had 2 sons. After Roberts' death she married a _____ RICHARD. She was born 6 June 1909; died 15 Dec 1988.

Children of Julia-[5] CEASE and David WALSH:
Surname **WALSH**
+   **810. HELEN**   born 16 Aug 1911; died ____; married Joseph DALPE 9 Sep 1933
       811. Isabel   born 26 Sep 1914; died 1972 Detroit, MI; never married
+   **812. GORDON**   born 8 Feb 1918 Blenheim, Ontario, CAN; died 20 Oct 1971 Detroit
                                    married Kathleen Frances LEAVER 16 May 1942
                                    (she born 11 May 1918 Windsor, ONT; died _____

362. IDA MYRTLE-[5] CEASE, sister of above, was born 8 Sep 1886 at Friendship Twsp, Emmett, Michigan. She married William W. GREGORY, of Readmond Twsp, MI on 12 Oct 1904. He was the son of William S. GREGORY +++ (born Canada) and Ella M. BAKER (born Canada), and was born 31 Aug 1881 MI, died 1953 Charlevoix, MI. Ida Myrtle-[5] CEASE died 19 Aug 1912 of rheumatoid arthritis at Hayes Twsp, Charlevoix County, MI.

Note: Part of her obituary read " Myrtle was loved by all who knew her and it can be truthfully said her home was one where love was the ruling power. She had been ill health the past 16 months and last Tuesday evening realizing the end was near she left a goodbye message for all her friends and peacefully passed into the arms of her Savior as a tired child rests its head on its mothers bosom. She finished her life's work in twenty-five years, eleven months and eighteen days ."

Note: William S. GREGORY (Jr.) was the son of William S. GREGORY, Sr and Eliza MC INTOSH (both born Canada) . Eliza MC INTOSH , born 1821, was the daughter of Lachlan MC INTOSH and Katie BRUNDAGE. William W. GREGORY married second to Edie ___ , and had 4 more children. Opal, Ruby, Harold and Winifred GREGORY.

Children of Ida Myrtle-[5] CEASE and William GREGORY:
Surname **GREGORY**
       813. Willis F.   born 30 Dec 1907; died Dec 1984 Charlevoix, MI
       814. Dorothy Nell   born ca 1908; died 22 Feb 1908   EOL
       815. Roland Fay   born ca 1909; died 3 July 1910   EOL
       816. Clifton E.   born 25 Apr 1911; died 10 July 1996 Charlevoix, MI
                                    married Amelia _____

363. CARL SIDNEY-[5] CEASE, brother of above, was born 17 May 1890/91 at Harbor Springs, MI. He married Sylvia Elizabeth Hannah BOETTGER on 19 Dec 1912. She was the daughter of John BOETTGER and Mary / Maria C GRAVEL/GRAUEL (both born Germany) , and was born 29 Dec 1894 Ayr, MI; died 22 Sep 1985 at Harbor Springs, MI. She was the sister of William BOETTGER who married Carl's sister Mildred-[5] CEASE (below) Carl-[5] CEASE died 7 Apr 1947 at Harbor Springs.

Children of Carl-[5] CEASE and Sylvia BOETTGER:
Surname **CEASE**

+	**817. LAWRENCE RICHARD**	born 11 July 1914 Harbor Springs; died 24 June 1986 Petoskey, MI married Betty Jean ROBINSON ca 1938 (she born 21 June 1922; died 6 June 1944 Petoskey, MI)
	818. Lenard William (Mike)	born 21 Apr 1916 Harbor Springs; died 20 Oct 1984 married Vivian Davis SCOTT ca 1945 (she born 6 June 1915; died Jan 1983 Petoskey, Emmett, MI
+	**819. NINA MAE**	born 30 Sep 1918 Harbor Springs; died 6 Nov 1998 MI married Byron Russell LIGHTFOOT 25 Jan 1936 (he s/o Edward E. LIGHTFOOT and Mabel GOODRICH) (he born 24 Jan 1913 Harbor Springs; died 10 Aug 1995)
	820. Herman Allen	born 25 June 1920, MI; died 5 Oct 1976 Little Traverse, Harbor Sprgs. married Joyce MOYER (she born 22 Aug 1932; died _____) Children: Herman-[7] born ___; Sylvia-[7] CEASE born ___; married Edward FISHER
	821. Clarence Sidney (twin)	born 15 June 1922; died 22 July 1979 Nicoma Park, OK married Marjorie Wilcox SINCLAIR ca 1950
	822. Mary E. (twin)	born 15 June 1922; died 2 May 2009 Petoskey, MI EOL
	823. Peggy Elnor	born 26 Feb 1936; married Albert BREMMEYR 7 July 1956 Children: Maria-[7] born ___; Mark-[7] born ___, and Monica L-[7] BREMMEYR born ___; married Phillip SMELT

365. MILDRED IRENE-[5] CEASE, sister of above, was born 9 June 1897 at Harbor Springs, MI. She married William Henry BOETTGER on 22 June 1915 at Harbor Springs. He was the son of John BOETTGER and Maria GRAVEL (GRAUEL) , and was born 31 March 1884; died 7 Nov 1957 at Ayr, Emmett County, Michigan. He is buried in the North Ayr Cemetery. Mildred-[5] CEASE died 29 Nov 1988 at Harbor Springs, Michigan.

Children of Mildred-[5] CEASE and William BOETTGER:
Surname **BOETTGER**

+	**824. JUANITA MARY**	born 12 Apr 1916 Ayr, MI; died 9 Oct 1993 Alanson, MI married William NEWSOME 6 Jan 1937 (he born 22 Aug 1916; died 8 Apr 2000 Alanson, MI)
+	**825. WILLIS EARL**	born 25 Dec 1917 Ayr, MI; died 23 Mar 1988 Anchorage, Alaska married LOUISE HERZIG 14 Nov 1941 Lewis County, MO. (she born 14 Nov 1920; died 3 Feb 2002 Anchorage, AK.
+	**826. ARLAYNE IRENE** "Punk"	born 29 Oct 1919 Ayr, MI; died 21 June 2008 Harbor Springs MI married Joseph LIPCHINSKY 29 Mar 1946 (he born 7 Dec 1917; died _____)
+	**827. RACHEL JANET** "Jan"	born 14 July 1922 Ayr, MI; died 22 Mar 1996 Marquette, MI married Weldon D. HART 2 Feb 1943 (he born 19 Nov 1921; died 3 July 2001 Marquette, MI)
+	**828. HELEN LOUISE**	born 17 Feb 1924 Ayr, MI; died 22 Mar 2002 Mason, OH married Benjamin BRAVARD ca 1943 (he born 13 Jan 1919 KY; died 18 Nov 1995 Hamilton, OH)
+	**829. ERSHEL LEONA**	born 4 Dec 1925 Ayr, MI; died 1 June 1981 Traverse City, MI married Richard LA COMBE 28 Dec 1945
+	**830. DERLA GALE**	born 23 Aug 1927 Ayr, MI; married Erwin SYDOW 3 Jan 1947 (he born 15 Aug 1927; died 23 May 2008 Phoenix, AZ)
+	**831. HERMA JEAN**	born 16 Sep 1929 Ayr, MI; married Philip A. ABRUNZO 17 Jan 1949 (he born 1922, NY)

Children of Mildred-[5] CEASE and William BOETTGER:
Surname **BOETTGER**

+	**832. ALYCE JOAN**	born 27 Jan 1932 Ayr, MI; 1 married Clarkson MOST ca 1950 (he born 8 May 1929; died 27 Mar 1962) 2 married George CONRAD 29 Dec 1973
+	**833. BOYD REX**	born 9 Dec 1933 Ayr, MI; married Mary GORZINSKI 16 Oct 1959
+	**834. STANLEY FRANK**	born 3 Dec 1934 Ayr, MI; died 13 Sep 1977 Traverse City, MI married Ruth AVERY ca 1961 ; divorced
+	**835. MAX GILBERT**	born 24 June 1936 Ayr. MI; married Mary Fay ULRICH 9 June 1958
+	**836. AVIS ANNE**	born 17 Sep 1938 Ayr, MI; 1 married Everett LAKE Aug 1955; div. 2 married James CAMPBELL
	837. Robert Gary	born 29 Jan 1940 Ayr, MI; died 26 Sep 1993 San Antonio, TX married Gisela KOEBERLEIN ca 1972 ; divorced 1984 (she born 10 Dec 1940 Vienna, Austria)

371. ELIZABETH-[5] TANNER, daughter of Strever-[4] TANNER (William-[3]; Magdalena-[2] MC INTOSH, Alexander-[1]) and Elizabeth SHADIC(K), was born 27 July 1850 at Ancram, Columbia Co., NY. She married Milton Abram-[5] SMITH (Abram-[4]; Andrew-[3]; John-[2]; Johan Theiss-[1]) on 16 Jan 1873 at Madison Co., IA. Milton-[5] SMITH was born 24 Jan 1850 at Ancram, Columbia Co., NY, and later went to Chicago, where he spent about 6 months working the Union Stockyards before going to Madison Co. IA. Milton-[5] died 8 Aug 1931 at Earlham, Madison Co., IA. Elizabeth-[5] TANNER died 12 Feb 1934.

Children of Elizabeth-[5] TANNER and Milton Abram-[5] SMITH:
Surname **SMITH**

+	**838. WILLIAM TANNER**	born 14 Jan 1874 Ancram Lead Mines; died 11 Nov 1964 Waverly, IA married Laura Maudelle ARNOLD 25 Mar 1913 Dexter, Iowa (she born 1 Mar 1877; died 2 May 1935)	
	839. Fred	born 28 May 1875 Ancramdale, NY; died 1 June 1932 Des Moines, IA married Rose Ann SLATTERY 20 Feb 1907 KS (she born 17 Mar 1878 LI, NY; died 27 Feb 1979 Earlham, IA) (she dau/o William SLATTERY and Jane MANGAN)	
+	**840. ASA**	born 12 Sep 1877 Earlham, IA; died 20 Dec 1958 Perry, Dallas, IA married Rosa June MC CLURE 16 Dec 1903 IA (she born 23 July 1885; died 13 Feb 1973) (buried Penn Center Cemetery, Earlham, Madison, IA)	
+	**841. CLARENCE**	born 11 Feb 1880 Earlham, IA; died 2 Apr 1956 Earlham married Delia Emma MC CLURE 2 Sep 1918 (she born 23 Nov 1889; died 27 Jan 1972)	
+	**842. CHESTER A.**	born 27 Jan 1882 Earlham; died 28 Jan 1957 Des Moines, IA married Maggie Susie PEARSON 8 Dec 1909 IA (she born 24 Oct 1888; died 29 Apr 1975)	
	843. Claudie	born 29 Mar 1884 Earlham; died 13 Mar 1885 Earlham, IA	EOL
+	**844. RAYMOND**	born 28 May 1886 Earlham, IA; died 4 June 1964 IA 1 married Martha Minerva DE VAULT 28 Feb 1912 (she born 2 Jan 1886; died 28 Feb 1913) 2 married Grace CADE 22 Aug 1917 (she born 26 Oct 1885; died 14 May 1933) 3 married Bertha Ellen ALEXANDER 21 Feb 1938 (she born 8 Dec 1892; died 20 May 1973)	
	845. Pearl Gladys	born 8 Sep 1888 Earlham, IA; died 13 Feb 1974 Earlham married Ralph R. PRICE 3 Oct 1931 (as his 2nd wife) (he born 1 July 1882; died 13 Dec 1935) no issue	EOL

372. RACHEL-[5] TANNER, sister of above, was born 30 May 1852 at Ancram, Columbia County, NY. She married Warren L. VOSBURGH ca 1872 at ____ . He was the son of Conrad I. VOSBURGH and Eliza/Angeline __ , and was born ca 1841; died _____ . Rachel-[5] TANNER died 11 May 1890 at _____ . They resided near Boston Corners, NY.

Children of Rachel-[5] TANNER and Warren VOSBURGH:
Surname **VOSBURGH**

	846. Eunice	born ca _____	
+	**847. EGBERT**	born 18 Oct 1874 NY; died ca 1945	
	TANNER	married Delia SILVERNAIL 24 Sep 1893 CT (she born ca 1876)	
	848. Conrad	born 6 Jan 1876 NY; died 21 Feb 1882	EOL
	849. Emmett	born 6 Sep 1877; died 2 Nov 1883	EOL
+	**850. ESTHER**	born 25 Aug 1879 ; died 1968	
		married Ward SILVERNAIL ca 1895-98	
		(he born ca 1858; died _____) (resided Copake, NY 1930)	
	851. Melvina	born 5 July 1883; died 3 Feb 1884	EOL
	852. Nettie	born Nov 1884; died ____	
	853. Laura	born ca 1889; died 1940 Child: Earl-[7] KLINE born ____	
		married Charles H. KLINE (he born ca 1887; died ca 1965)	
	854. Clarence Simmons	born 3 Dec 1891 ; died July 1973 Albany, NY; worked for NYCRR	
		married Augusta ARANOVE (she born ca 1895 Russia; died ____)	
	855. Lizzie	born July 1894	

373. WILLIAM B.-[5] TANNER, brother of above, was born 27 May 1854 at Ancram, Columbia County, NY. He married Lucy SMITH on 23 Feb 1876 at ____ . She was the daughter of Alvin SMITH and Phoebe BUTTS, and was born 22 Mar 1857; died ca 1920. William B-[5] TANNER died ca 1932 , and is buried at Pine Plains, Dutchess County, NY.

Children of William-[5] TANNER and Lucy SMITH:
Surname **TANNER**

856. Annie	born 3 July 1879	858. Fred	born 6 May 1885
857 George	born 4 Mar 1883	859. Irving	born ca _____

374. LAURA-[5] TANNER, sister of above, was born 13 May 1857 at Ancram, Columbia County, NY. She married John George VOSBURGH on ___ at ____ . He was the son of Abram A. VOSBURGH and Catherine FELLER, and was born ca 1854 NY; died 16 May 1923 at Pine Plains, Dutchess County, NY. Laura-[5] TANNER died 11 May 1890 Pine Plains, Dutchess Co., NY

Children of Laura-[5] TANNER and John VOSBURGH:
Surname **VOSBURGH**

+	**860. PETER**	born 13 Dec 1876 NY; died 30 Aug 1968 Stamford, CT		
	TANNER	1 married Maude L. HUSTED ca 1903		
		(she dau/o Frank B. HUSTED and Janice A. _____)		
		(she born ca 1887; died 1914)		
		2 married Lillian Margaret CODY (she born 22 June 1884; died 20 Nov 1934)		
	861. Emmett	born ca 1879; died 1879		
	862. Loda	born 1883; died 1894	863. Rachel	born ____

375. PETER-[5] TANNER, brother of above, was born 28 Aug 1858 at Ancram, Columbia County, NY. He married Emma HAMM Mar 1883 at ____ . She was the daughter of Peter HAMM and Mary L HALLOCK , and was born 24 April 1864 NY; died 21 June 1936 Sharon, CT. Peter-[5] TANNER died _____ .

The Fifth American Generation

Children of Peter-[5] TANNER and Emma HAMM:
Surname **TANNER**

864. Grant	born 31 Dec 1885 Ancram,NY; died 28 Apr 1945 Hartford, CT.	EOL
865. Percy	born 9 Jan 1898 CT.; died 13 Sep 1989 Hartford, CT.	
	married Elizabeth _____	

Children: Dorothy E-[7] born ca 1923 CT, and Richard-[7] TANNER born ca Feb 1926 CT.

379. JAMES-[5] HOAG, son of Rachel-[4] TANNER (William-[3]; Magdalena-[2] MAC INTOSH; Alexander-[1]) and Willis HOAG, was born 28/30 May 1838 at Ancramdale, Columbia County, New York. He married Ann/Annie SMITH on 18 Sep 1867. She was the daughter of Duncan SMITH and Nancy McARTHUR, and was born ca 1846 NY; died ca 1923. James-[5] HOAG died 20/22 Nov 1874.

Children of James-[5] HOAG and Ann SMITH:
Surname **HOAG**

866. Willis	born 28 Oct 1868 NY; died 1952; resided Ancramdale, NY
867. Asa	born 9 Aug 1870 NY;
	1 married Mattie A. WILLIAMS 9 Sep 1896
	(she born 25 June 1878; died 29 Mar 1898)
	(she dau/o John M. WILLIAMS and _____)
	2 married Ruth LOWN ca 1913 / 14
	(she born 30 Apr 1883 Ancram Lead Mines, NY; died 22 Apr 1965)
	(she dau/o William W. LOWN and Isabelle FINKLE)

Child: James-[7] HOAG born 27 Oct 1917; died 7 Aug 2008 Copake, NY

382. WILLIAM-[5] HEAD, son of Eliza-[4] TANNER (William-[3]; Magdalena-[2] MAC INTOSH; Alexander-[1]) and Jonathan HEAD, was born ca 1832 at Ancram, NY. He married Laura MC ARTHUR on ____ at ____. She was the daughter of _____ MC ARTHUR and _____, and was born ca 1832 NY, died ____. William-[5] HEAD died 31 Mar 1899 at _____.

Children of William-[5] HEAD and Laura MC ARTHUR:
Surname **HEAD**

868. Adam	born ca 1857	870. Lovett	born ca 1867
869. Samuel	born ca 1860	871. Sarah	born ca 1869

383. JONATHAN-[5] HEAD, Jr, , brother of above, was born 1835/36 at Ancram, Columbia County, New York. He married Mary-[4] TANNER (# 174) on ____ at ____ NY. She was the daughter of Samuel-[3] TANNER (Rachel-[2] MAC INTOSH, Alexander-1) and Mary Betsey LOWN, and was born 28 Mar 1844 .

Children of Jonathan-[5] HEAD, Jr. and Mary -[4] TANNER:
Surname **HEAD**

	872. John	born 22 Dec 1872; died ____	
+	**873. SAMUEL S.**	born 27 Nov 1876 Copake, NY; died Jan 1963	
		married Florence M. _____ (she born ca 1886 NY; died ____)	
	874. John Henry	born 1879	875. William born 1882; died _____

384. MARY ANN-[5] HEAD, sister of above, was born ca 1837 at Ancram, Columbia County, NY. She married George Thomas DYE on ____ at ____. He was the son of John DYE and Frances STANLEY, and was born ca 1824 England, died ____.

Children of Mary Ann-[5] HEAD and George Thomas DYE:
Surname **DYE**

876. Fred	born ca 1868; died _____; resided Copake Iron Works, NY

Children of Mary Ann-⁵ HEAD and GeorgeThomas DYE:
Surname **DYE**

+   **877. MADELINE E.**   born 30 Dec 1869; died _____; resided Pittsfield, MA
        married Austin E. WRIGHT 1 March 1890
        (he born Oct 1865; died 15 Sep 1944)
    878. Anna   born _____; died _____; resided Holyoke, MA
        1 married _____ LYONS; 2 married Perry L. BENJAMIN
        (he s/o N P BENJAMIN and Helen ____)   (he born ca 1866 NY)

396. WARD-⁵ SMITH, son of Elizabeth-⁴ TANNER (William-³; Magdalena-2 MAC INTOSH; Alexander-¹) and John McArthur SMITH, was born 5 Aug 1853 at Ancram, Columbia County, New York. He married Elsie Adelia TRIPP on 27 Mar 1878 at Ancram. She was the daughter of _____ TRIPP and _____, and was born 10 Apr 1858 Ancram; died _____. Ward-⁵ SMITH died 3 Aug 1917.

Children of Ward-⁵ SMITH and Elsie Adelia TRIPP:
Surname **SMITH**

    879. Allen C.   born 1 Sep 1883 Ancram Columbia, NY; died _____
        married Mary HOAG (she dau/o Samuel T. HOAG and Mary PLACE
        (she born 6 July 1887; died ____) Child: Sara A-7 SMITH born ca 1916

405. DELIA-⁵ PLATNER, daughter of Olive Emeline-⁴ TANNER (Alexander-³ TANNER; Magdalena-² MAC INTOSH; Alexander-¹) and Dr. Stephen PLATNER, was born ca 1846 at Copake, Columbia County, New York. She married Henry D. MYERS ca 1865 at ____. Delia-⁵ PLATNER died ____.

Children of Delia-⁵ PLATNER and Henry D. MYERS:
Surname **MYERS**

+   **880. HENRY D.**   born May 1866 NY; died ____
        married Ella S._____ ca 1887   (she born Mar 1867 NY; died ____)
    881. Luella   born ca 1868 NY; died _____

413. MARTIN-⁵ SIMMONS, son of Nancy Alma-⁴ (Almy) TANNER (John-³ TANNER (Magdalena-² MAC INTOSH, Alexander-¹) and Jeremiah SIMMONS (David) was born 12 May 1840 at Dutchess County, NY. He married Ellen FITZGERALD on 4 March 1868 at ____, NY. She was the daughter of Michael F. FITZGERALD and Kate O'BRIEN, and was born 7 Apr 1850 Dutchess Co., NY; died 30 Aug 1890 at Dutchess Co., NY. Martin-⁵ SIMMONS died 19 Feb 1888 at Dutchess County.

Children of Martin-⁵ SIMMONS and Ellen FITZGERALD:
Surname **SIMMONS**

+   **882. JAMES FINCH**   born 24 Sept 1869 Blue Store, Columbia Co., NY
    883. Margaret/Ellen   born 27 Oct 1873; died 30 Dec 1956; unmarried   EOL
    884. Franklin Cornelius   born 19 Feb 1875; died ____; married Ethel ____
    885. Walter John   born 3 Aug 1879; died 24 June 1949 Pittsfield, MA
        married Lena M. WENTWORTH ca ____ (she born May 1883)
        (she dau/o Charles E. WENTWORTH and Maria SARGENT)
        Children: Ralph W-7 born ca 1916, and Mildred S-7 SIMMONS born ca 1917
    886. Frederick Harry   born 28 Apr 1880; died Sep 1967 Columbia County, NY
    " Fred "   married Aura GARDINER ca 1909 (she born ca 1882)
        Child: Pauline-7 SIMMONS born ca 1909/10
    887. Alice Lucelia   born 15 March 1883; died _____; married George TAYLOR
    888. William Henry   born 14 July 1885; died ____; married Ruth COLLETTE
    889. Ernest Martin   born 16 July 1888; died 29 June 1971 Leavenworth, KS
        married Carrie YOAKUM   Child: Ernest M. Jr-7 born ca 1922 KS

417. JAMES MONROE-⁵ SIMMONS, brother of above, was born 11 Aug 1848 at Taghkanic, Columbia County, NY. He married Frances Minerva (Minnie) HANKHURST Wishart ca ____, as her 2ⁿᵈ husband.. She was the daughter of ___ HANKHURST and ____, and the widow of John WISHART, by whom she had 3 sons. She was born Oct 1859 NY; died ____.

Children of James Monroe-⁵ SIMMONS and Minnie HANKHURST:
Surname **SIMMONS**

	890. Florence	born April 1891 NJ
	891. Mabel M.	born Mar 1893 NJ
+	**892. LESTER NORTON**	born 31 Dec 1895 NJ; died 14 July 1977 Lake Worth, FL 1 married Hazel DOULL ca 1918 (she born ca 1896; died ca 1925) 2 married Bess WILLIAMS (she born 26 Nov 1897 IL, died 10 Aug 1980 FL)
	893. May K.	born Apr 1897 NJ
+	**894. HAROLD**	born 20 Apr 1900 NJ; died 23 March 1977 married Mildred LA POINTE

419. ADA FRANCES-⁵ SIMMONS, sister of above, was born 29 July 1851 Dutchess County, NY. She married Charles James KELLERHOUSE ca 1873 at ____. He was the son of Jonas K. KELLERHOUSE and Sarah / Sally MINK, and was born 26 Dec 1849 Gallatin, Columbia County, NY; died 19 Dec 1920. Ada-⁵ SIMMONS died 4 Jan 1931. They resided many years at Pine Plains, Dutchess County, NY.

Children of Ada-⁵ SIMMONS and Charles KELLERHOUSE:
Surname **KELLERHOUSE**

- 895. May /Mary Ellen — born Nov 1876; died ____; married Arthur W. MILLER
- 896. Iola — born !879; died _____; married Sampson Oliver HALEY 11 June 1908
- 897. Sarah/ Sadie C. — born Mar 1886; married _____ RIVENBURG
  - Child: Gladys E-⁷ RIVENBURG born ca 1911 NY
- 898. Charles James , Jr. — born Oct 1891 NY; died May 1971 Clinton Corners, Dutchess, NY
  married Goldie Kathryn COUSE 28 Sept 1910
  (she dau/o Daniel COUSE and Elizabeth _____)
  (she born 4 Sept 1893; died _____)
  - Child: Adeline-⁷ KELLERHOUSE born ca 1912; died _____)
- 899. Nellie — born July 1896 NY

421. ALMA M ⁵ SIMMONS, sister of above, was born 31 May 1856 at Dutchess County, NY. She married Frank INGLES ca 1875 at Dutchess Co., NY. He was the son of Peter INGLES and Catherine____, and was born Mar 1852 NY; died ____. Alma-⁵ SIMMONS died 14 Oct 1918

Children of Alma-⁵ SIMMONS and Frank INGLES:
Surname **INGLES**

900. Llllian/Lilly	born ca 1877	903 Edna S	born May 1890
901. Angela/Angie	born ca 1880	904. Evaline H.	born July 1893
902. Edward Joseph	born 7 Apr 1888		

423. EMILY ANN/ EMMA-⁵ YORKER, daughter of Sally Ann-⁴ TANNER (John-³; Magdalena-² MAC INTOSH; Alexander-¹) and James YORKER, was born ca 1843/44 at ____, NY. She married Morton Hugh-⁸ COMSTOCK on 28 Dec 1861. He was the son of Hugh-⁷ COMSTOCK and Polly AVERY, and was born 17 Feb 1840 Great Barrington, Berkshire, MA; died 2 Feb 1903. Emily-⁵ YORKER died before 1874.

++ Note: According to the " History and Genealogy of the COMSTOCK Family in America " , Family 1206 - Morton H-[8] COMSTOCK (# 4251) was descended from Hugh-[7]; Lancaster,[6]; [5]; Gideon-[4]; Samuel-[3]; Daniel-[2] and William-[1] COMSTOCK. They settled in Massachusetts.

Children of Emily/ Emma [5] YORKER and Morton H-[8] COMSTOCK:
Surname **COMSTOCK**

	905.Alice A.	born 6 June 1862	
	906. Morton J.	born 19 Nov 1863	
+	**907. RALPH J.**	born Oct 1864, married Annie L. _____ (she born ca Apr 1869)	
+	**908. WILLIAM HUGH**	born 3 July 1870,MA; died 19 Jan 1944 Great Barrier, MA	
		married Grace May BENNETT 5 June 1905	
		(she born 20 June 1880; died _____)	
		(she dau/o James Edwin/Edward BENNETT and Lucy _____)	
	909. Maude Ella	born 21 Sep 1872, never married	EOL

424. MARTHA ANNA-[5] (Ann) YORKER, sister of above was born ca 1847/48 at _____, NY. She married Morton H. COMSTOCK, as his 2nd wife, on 4 Sep 1874. He was previously married to her sister Emily Ann/ Emma-[5] YORKER, above.

Children of Martha Anna-[5] YORKER and Morton H. COMSTOCK:
Surname **COMSTOCK**

910. Harry Hugh	born ca 1876; died 15 Nov 1902; killed in a mill accident	
911. Flora May	born 3 Mar 1884, never married	EOL

427. EMMAGEN-[5] SHULTIS, daughter of Jane Margaret-[4] TANNER (John-[3]; Magdalena-[2] MAC INTOSH; Alexander-[1]) and David SHULTIS, was born 31 Oct 1854 at _____, NY. She married John CONKLE ca 1874. He was the son of _____ CONKLE (born England)and _____, and was born 1852/54; died 1916. Emmagen-[5] SHULTIS died ca 1883.

Children of Emmagen-[5] SHULTIS and John CONKLE:
Surname **CONKLE**

912. David T.	born 12 Aug 1878; married Elizabeth _____
913. Aura L.	born 7 Oct 1881

434. BELLE-[5] TANNER, daughter of Ambrose-[4] TANNER (John-[3]; Magdalena-[2] MAC INTOSH; Alexander-[1]) and Jane SHADIC(K), was born 10 Aug 1867. She married John PELLS on 15 Dec 1886. He was the son of Peter PELLS and Phebe A. LINK, and was born May 1864; died ____. Belle-[5] TANNER died ca 1919.

Child of Belle-[5] TANNER and John H. PELLS:
Surname **PELLS**

+	**914. FLORENCE B.**	born 10 July 1889; died _____
		married George L. MILLER (he s/o John H. MILLER and _____)
		(he born ca 1880 NY; died _____)
	915. John L.	born 9 Sep 1904; died Nov 1982 Hamilton, OH

435. HENRY S-[5] TANNER, brother of above, was born 24 Aug 1869 at Copake, Columbia County, New York. He married Elizabeth L. (Libby/Libbie) MC INTYRE ca 1892 at ____. She was the daughter of _____ MC INTYRE and _____, and was born Dec 1874; died ____. Henry S-[5] TANNER died _____.

The Fifth American Generation

Child of Henry S-[5] TANNER and Libby MC INTYRE:
Surname **TANNER**

916. Guy McIntyre   born 5 Oct 1893 Columbia Co., NY; died ____
married Bessie MERRIFIELD ca 1913
(she born Dec 1887; died _____) Child: Phillip-[7] TANNER born ca 1913 NY

436. BLANCHE-[5] **TANNER**, sister of above, was born 4 Oct 1873 at Copake, Columbia County, NY. She married Harry A. CARLE on ___ at ____. He was the son of Abram CARLE and Harriet ____, and was born ca 1872; died _____. Blanche-[5] TANNER died _____. 1880 resided Hudson, Columbia County, NY. He was a boat builder.

Children of Blanche-[5] TANNER and Harry A. CARLE:
Surname **CARLE**

+   **917. LLOYD**   born 23 Oct 1892 Columbia Co., NY; died 2 Jan 1969, MD
         AMBROSE   married Leona Alexandra MULLEN ca 1910
         (she born 18 July 1890; died 19 Jan 1971 MD)
918. Clifford Harry   born 16 Aug 1895; died Oct 1977 NY
919. Mildred B.   born ca 1905
920. Claribell   born ca 1913   921. Evelyn G.   born ca 1914

438. GENEVIEVE-[5] **(Jennie) TANNER** daughter of Alexander-[4] TANNER; John-[3]; Magdalena-[2] MAC INTOSH; Alexander-[1]) and Vera LYALL, was born 24 Feb 1860 at Copake, Columbia County, NY, and baptized 2 June 1860 at the West Copake Reformed Church. She married Oliver A. COONS ca 1867. He was the son of Alfred COONS and Julia ____, and was born Sep 1860; died _____.

Children of Genevieve-[5] TANNER and Oliver COONS:
Surname **COONS**

922. Myrtle E.   born Dec 1895; died _____; married Edward HAMM
         baptized 5 Sep 1896 St. Johns Dutch Reformed Church, Upper Red Hook
923. Mildred G.   born May 1898; died _____   (1930 unmarried, a domestic)

439. WILLIAM JOHN-[5] **TANNER**, brother of above, was born 28 Aug 1863 NY; baptized 10 Oct 1863 at West Copake Reformed Church. He married Rose Ruth ROWLEY ca 1891 at ___. She was the daughter of Nathan John ROWLEY and Mary Ann PULVER, and was born 8 Mar 1873 Ghent, Columbia Co., NY; died 29 Oct 1935 Canaan, Columbia, NY.. William-[5] TANNER died _____. They are buried at Hudson, Col. County, NY.

Children of William J[5] TANNER and Rose Ruth ROWLEY:
Surname **TANNER**   (children born Austerlitz, Columbia County, NY)

924. Vera Maria   born 17 Mar 1892 NY; died 24 Feb 1979 W. Stockbridge, MA
         married Charles Carel NADLER ca 1921
         (he born 7 Jan 1894 NY; died _____)
925. son – unnamed   born 1894; died 1894
926. Helen Rowley   born 8 Nov 1897 NY; died 15 May 1994 Wappingers Falls, NY
         married Frank F. NESTLER 2 July 1928   (a basketmaker)
         (he born 8 Jul 1892/3, died 26 Sep 1955 Wappingers Falls, NY)
         (he s/o Julius NESTLER and Augusta _____)
         Child: Bruce-[7] NESTLER born 9 May 1929 NY
927. Alexander Lyall   born 15 Apr 1900 NY; died 24 June 1979 Wappinger Falls, NY
         married Grace E. SHUFELT 16 Apr 1929 Columbia Co., NY
         (she dau/o Elbert SHUFELT and Mary Agnes BIDWELL)
         (she born 23 Mar 1905; died 20 Apr 1996 W. Greenbush, Col., NY)

Children of William John -5 TANNER and Rose ROWLEY, continued:
Surname **TANNER**

928. Ruth Dorothy	born 6 Aug 1902 NY; died 4 Nov 1992	
929. Irving Minot	born 9 Jan 1905 NY; died 25 Feb 1985 FL	
	married Dorothy May BENWAY (she born ca 1912, died 1980)	
930. Reuben William	born 22 May 1907 NY; died 15 Feb 1988	
	married Laura May SHUFELT (child: Wm. Reuben 1934-2000)	
	(she born 7 Mar 1908; died 5 July 1985 Columbia Co., NY)	
	(she sister of Grace E. SHUFELT, (above)	
931. Elsie/Elise Wilding	born 5 May 1909; died 26 June 1968 NY	
932. Frances Margaret	born 1 Aug 1911; died 8 Sept 1913	
933. Nathan John	born 22 Feb 1913; died Aug 1920	
934. Doris Elizabeth	born 21 Oct 1916; died 26 March 1978 Pittsfield, MA	

440. J. EDWARD LYALL-[5] TANNER, brother of above, was born 11 Sep 1877 at Copake, Columbia County, NY. He married Margaret MESICK ca 1905 at ____. She was the daughter of _____ MESICK and ____, and was born ca 1881 NY; died _____. Edward L-[5] TANNER , a bank teller, died _____.

Child of Edward Lyall-5 TANNER and Margaret MESICK:
Surname **TANNER**

935. J. Edward Lyall, Jr.   born ca 1907; died ____; never married   EOL

446. RUFUS KING-[5] WOOLDRIDGE, son of Philo-[4] WOOLDRIDGE (Mary Magdalena-[3] TANNER; Rachel-[2] MAC INTOSH, Alexander-[1]) and Gertrude DYKEMAN, was born 18 Nov 1853. He had a twin brother Franklin Pierce-[5] WOOLDRIDGE. Rufus-[5] married Anna JONES on 23 Nov 1880. She was the daughter of ___ JONES and ____, and was born ca ____. Rufus King-[5] WOOLDRIDGE died _____.

Children of Rufus-[5] WOOLDRIDGE and Anna JONES:
Surname **WOOLDRIDGE**

+	**936. HARRY F.**	born ca 1885 GA; died 13 May 1954 West Hartford, CT
		married Mary T/J. _____ (she born ca 1891 Canada)
+	**937. CLARENCE BUDD**	born 1 Jan 1886 Macon, GA; died _____
		married Mary Edna ____ ca 1916
	938. Jacob P.	born _____

Note: All three brothers owned Wooldridge Brothers Trucking Company, and contracted with the US Mail Service for delivery services.

450. EDWARD-[5] MC CARRICK, son of Harriet -[4] WOOLRIDGE (Mary Magdalena-[3] TANNER; Rachel-[2] MAC INTOSH; Alexander-[1]) and _____ MC CARRICK, was born ca 1846 NY. He married first to Lovina _____; she born ca 1851 CT; died __. His second wife was Adda _____. She was born ca 1866 ; died _____. Resided Salisbury, Litchfield, CT.

Child of Edward-[5] MC CARRICK and Lovina _____:
Surname **MC CARRICK**

939. Edward Reuben	born ca 1871/ 72 CT ; died ____
	married Edith M. FRENCH (Child: Mildred-7 MC CARRICK born ca 1909)
940. Harriet	born ca 1875 CT; died _____

Children of Edward -[5] MC CARRICK and Adda _____:
Surname **MC CARRICK**

941 Florence	born Dec 1889 CT	942. Gertrude A	born Feb 1891

457. EDWARD W.-[5] KELSEY, son of Mary Jane-[4] TANNER (John-[3]; Magdalena-[2] MAC INTOSH; Alexander-[1]) and Joel W. KELSEY, was born Apr 1855 OH. He married Elizabeth L. _____ ca 1884. She was the daughter of _____ and _____, and was born Dec 1864; died _____. Edward-[5] KELSEY died 11 Sep 1917 at Lucas County, OH. Resided Toledo, OH

Children of Edward-[5] KELSEY and Elizabeth L. _____:
Surname **KELSEY**
> 943. Edward W. Jr.   born Sep 1885 OH; he was an attorney; married Charlotte ?__ ca 1913
>> Children: Dwight E-[7] born ca 1917 OH, and Edward W-[7] KELSEY born ca 1922 OH
> 944. Lilian M.   born May 1890 OH

463. RUEY-[5] TANNER, daughter of John-[4] TANNER (James-[3]; Rachel-[2] MAC INTOSH; Alexander-[1]) and Caroline HAWVER, was born ca 1843/44 NY. She married Thomas SCUTT on ___ at ____. He was the son of Grove(nor) SCUTT , of West Taghkanic, NY and ____, and was born ca 1836 NY; died ____.

Children of Ruey-[5] TANNER and Thomas SCUTT:
Surname **SCUTT**

+	**945. GROVENOR**	born 7 July 1867 NY; died 4 Apr 1948 Ancram, Columbia County, NY married Ella M. SHOOK ca 1887
	946. William	born ca 1869 NY; died ____
	947. John	born ca 1874 NY; died ____
	948. Carrie	born ca 1875 NY
	949. Martha	born ca 1879 NY
	950. RICHARD	born 12 Nov 1886 NY; married Emily A. ____ (she born ca 1887 NY

469. JOHN J-[5] TANNER, brother of above, was born April 1854 NY. He married Margaret MAGELEY ca ____. They resided Hudson, Columbia County, NY. She was the daughter of _____ MAGELEY and _____, and was born May 1856, died _____. John J-[5] TANNER died _____.

Children of John J-[5] TANNER and Margaret MAGELEY:
Surname **TANNER**

951. Jessie	(m)	born 20 Oct 1874 Columbia Co., NY; died ____; married Grace RACE
952. Anna		born 1877; died ____; married Charles WEIR
953. Frederick		born 1879; died ____
954. John		born Sep 1882; died ____
955. Augusta	(f)	born Nov 1884; died ____
956. William/Willie		born June 1888; died ____ married Emma STOLP
957. Nina		born Aug 1890
958. Mabel		born Jan 1895
959. Ruth		born Jan 1897

471. JACOB-[5] TANNER, brother of above, was born May 1858/59 at _____, NY. He married Minnie WILLIS of Hillsdale, NY ca 1886. She was the daughter of Stillman H. WILLIS and Christina _____, and was born 7 Feb 1863; died 20 Feb 1946, Ancram, NY. Jacob-[5] TANNER died at Ancram , Columbia County, NY 25 Aug 1940.

Children of Jacob-[5] TANNER and Minnie WILLIS:
Surname **TANNER**
> 960. Cora   born Nov 1886
> 961. Myrtle   born Feb 1888

Children of Jacob-[5] TANNER and Minnie WILLIS:
Surname **TANNER**

962. Bethadra P.	born Nov 1889; married Myrtle BROWN ca _____	
	(she born ca 1887 NY; died _____)	
	(she dau/o George BROWN and Mary J. _____ (born Germany)	
	Child: Roy B-[7] TANNER born ca 1916 NY	
963. George R.	born Sep 1891; died 1 March 1923; married Luella MYERS	
964. Floyd Gardner	born 20 Feb 1894; died 1954	
965. Frank Willis	born 30 Nov 1895; married Emilie _____	
966. Dewey	born 6 Aug 1898; died Aug 1957	
967. Florence W.	born May 1900	
968. Charles	born 4 Oct 1903; died May 1980 Rochester, Monroe, NY	
969. Roy G.	born 4 Jan 1905; died 9 Nov 1991	
970. Virginia F.	born ca 1908	

478. CHARLES ANDREW-[5] TANNER, son of Morris-[4] TANNER (James-[3]; Rachel-[2] MC INTOSH; Alexander-[1]) and Diantha COLEPAUGH, was born 15 Aug 1847. He married Augusta C. REEVES on 10 July 1874 at _____. She was the daughter of _____ REEVES and _____, and was born5 Feb 1849, died 21 Mar 1917. Charles-[5] TANNER died 3 Apr 1908.

Children of Charles-[5] TANNER and Augusta C. REEVES:
Surname **TANNER**

+	**971. CHARLES WESLEY**	born 2 May 1875 Salisbury, CT; died 28 Mar 1956 E. Orange, NJ. married Margaret O'SHAUGHNESSY
	972. Louisa J.	born 19 Feb 1879 Salisbury, CT.; died _____
+	**973. WILLIAM . REEVES**	born 27 Aug 1882 Salisbury, CT; died 26 Dec 1929 Millerton, NY married Alice Bridget POLLARD

481. ELIZABETH G-[5] TANNER, sister of above, was born12 Aug 1853 at _____. She married Henry W. VOSBURGH on 14 Jan 1875 at ___. He was the son of Orvie VOSBURGH and Mary _____, and was born 9 June 1847, died 1 May 1892 Armenia, Dutchess, NY. Elizabeth-[5] TANNER died ____.

Children of Elizabeth-[5] TANNER and Henry VOSBURGH:
Surname **VOSBURGH**

974. Frank Arthur	born 16 Feb 1876 NY	975. James L.	born 10 Sep 1888

492. CLARISSA/ CLARA -[5] STREVER, daughter of Sylvester-[4] STREVER (Clarissa-[3] TANNER; Rachel-[2] MAC INTOSH; Alexander-[1]) and Phebe SHELDON, was born June 1851 at Dutchess Co.,, NY. She married Dr. Charles E. COLE, MD, of Pine Plains, Dutchess County, NY ca _____.

He was the son of Peter S. COLE, a Physician, and Catherine _____, and was born ca 1850, died before 1900. Clarissa T-[5] STREVER was a druggist, and died ca _____.

Child of Clara-[5] STREVER and Dr. Charles E. COLE:
Surname **COLE**

976. Harry S.	born Sept 1878 Pine Plains, NY; a druggist, died _____	
	married Mary _____ ca 1907 (she born ca 1879; died _____)	

496. SHELDON P-[5] STREVER, brother of above, was born ca 1859, probably at Gallatinville, NY. He married Alice May ENDERLIN ca 1898. She was the daughter of Adolph ENDERLIN (born GER) and Mary ____, and was born May 1872 NY; died _____. Sheldon-[5] STREVER died ____. In 1920 they resided at Rhinebeck, Dutchess County, NY.

Children of Sheldon-[5] STREVER and Alice ENDERLIN:
Surname **STREVER**

977. Charles Augustus	born 23 Jan 1899 NY; died Feb 1964 NY	
	married Marion DICKINSON	
	(she dau/o Van Wagner DICKINSON and Edith ____)	
978. Mary E.	born ca 1906	
979. Lewis G.	born ca 1911	

508. CLARISSA LOUISE/LOUISA -[5] **FRISS**, daughter of Clarissa-[4] TANNER (Henry-[3]; Rachel-[2] MAC INTOSH; Alexander-[1]) and Henry FRISS, was born ca 1872/73 at Taghkanic, Columbia, County, NY. She married Freeman HOTALING on ___ . He was born Apr 1876; died _____ . Clarissa-[5] died _____ .

Children of Clarissa-[5] FRISS and Freeman HOTALING:
Surname **HOTALING**

980. Frank	born 10 July 1900 NY; died Feb 1972
	married May VAN HOESEN ca 1919
	Children: Beulah-[7] born ca 1924; Lena-[7] born ca 1924; and Mildred-[7] born ca 1928
981. Gladys	born ca 1903 NY; died ____
982. Melvin	born ca _____ NY
983. Earl	born ca 1909 NY

510. ADELBERT-[5] **TANNER**, son of Sarah-[4] TANNER (Henry-[3]; Rachel-[2] MAC INTOSH; Alexander-[1]) and Henry S- TANNER , was born 19 Oct 1867 Taghkanic, Columbia County, NY. He married Jurilla / Rilla FINKLE on 21 Dec 1892 at ____ . She was the daughter of Abram FINKLE and Josephine COONS, and was born 20 Dec 1874 NY ; died _____ . Adelbert-[5] TANNER died _____ .

Children of Adelbert-[5] TANNER and Rilla FINKLE:
Surname **TANNER**

	984. Lemuel	born ca 1894; died ca 1895
+	**985. MINA J.**	born 29 Mar 1904; died May 1975 Livingston, Columbia Co., NY
		married Paul Edward HOFFMAN
		(he born 13 Dec 1894 NY; died 9 Apr 1976)
		(he s/o Clarence HOFFMAN and Mary ____ of Glencoe Mills, NY)

524. JULIET / JULIETTE- [5] **MILLER**, daughter of Christina-[4] TANNER (Morris-[3]; Rachel-[2] MAC INTOSH; Rachel-[1]) and Freeman B. MILLER, was born ca 1874 NY. She married Ed MACY ca ____ . He was the son of _____ MACY and ____ , and was born ____ , died ____ . Juliet-5 died ____ .

Child of Juliet-[5] MILLER and Ed MACY:
Surname **MACY**

+	**986. MARGARET**	born 30 May 1914 Hudson, Columbia Co., NY
	KATHRYN	married Leon SIGLER ca 1932
		(he s/o Ellsworth SIGLER and Minnie F. THORPE)
		(he born 18 Dec 1910 North East, Dutchess, NY; died 5 Apr 1966 Columbia, NY)

MACKINTOSH   MAC INTOSH   MC INTOSH

531. GUY WINFIELD-[6] SCOTT, son of Mary E-[5] MC DONALD (Mary-[4] CALDWELL; Clara-[3] MAC INTOSH; Simon-[2]; Alexander -[1]) and Horace SCOTT, was born 27 Mar 1885 at Canton, Bradford County, PA. He married Nellie May SMITH on ____ at ____. She was the daughter of ____ SMITH and ____, and was born 12 Jan 1893; died Feb 1986 Montgomery County, PA. Guy-[6] SCOTT died before 1930.

Child of Guy Winfield-[6] SCOTT and Nellie May SMITH:
Surname **SCOTT**

	987. Grace M.	born ca 1911 PA; died ____
	988. Merritt E.	born 19 June 1912 PA; died July 1977 Canton, PA
		married Katherine COMFORT 24 Sep 1936
		(she dau/o William T. COMFORT and Elisa Rebecca KINNEY)
		(she born 5 June 1914 PA; died 18 Nov 1996 Canton, PA)
		Child: Wayne-[8] SCOTT born ____
	989. William J.	born 13 Apr 1914 PA; died 27 July 1989
+	**990. NEVA**	born 27 Feb 1918 PA; died Nov 1993 Pasadena, CA
	CHARLOTTE	married Sigfrid E. SANDSTROM
		(he born 10 May 1924 Los Angeles, CA; died ____)
		(he s/o ____ SANDSTROM and ____ JOHNSON)
	991. Mary	born ca 1921 PA; died ____

535. CLARA-[6] MC DONALD, daughter of George-[5] MC DONALD (Mary-[4] CALDWELL; Clara-[3] MC INTOSH; Simon-[2]; Alexander-[1]) and Mary E.____, was born ca 1888 at ____ PA. She married Robert Henry DEVINE ca 1908 at ____ PA. He was the son of ____ DEVINE and ____, and was born 14 Feb 1880; died ____. Clara-[6] MC DONALD died ____.

Child of Clara-[6] MC DONALD and Robert DEVINE:
Surname **DEVINE**

992. Robert G.	born ca 1924 PA; died ____

537. FREDERICK DRYDEN-[6] MC INTOSH, son of Edwin Albert-[5] MC INTOSH (Ruluf C-[4]; Jonathan-[3]; Simon-[2]; Alexander-[1]) and Mary E. ROBINSON, was born 24 June 1884 Napa, CA. He married Flora R. HUDSON on ____ CA. She was the daughter of Fred HUDSON and Jane ____, and was born ca 1890 IL; died ___. Frederick-[6] MC INTOSH died ca 1938 of cancer. He was an electrician in a shipyard.

Children of Frederick-[6] MC INTOSH and Flora HUDSON:
Surname **MC INTOSH**

993. Thelma Elizabeth	born ca 1911 CA; died 2001
994. Dryden Hudson	born 15 June 1913 CA; died 7 Dec 1978 Marysville, Yuba, CA.
	Children: Dryden Frederick-[8] born 21 Apr 1937 and Kenneth Leland-[8] MC INTOSH born ca ___; and Gary Stephen-[8] MC INTOSH born ca 1949, married ____; had son Zane-[9] MC INTOSH born ca ____

554. GRACE EDNA-[6] BIGGS, daughter of Adaline M-[5] CHASE (Mariette-[4] MC INTOSH; Jonathan-[3]; Alexander-[2;1]) and John W. BIGGS, was born ca 1881 at Madison County, IA. She married Robert Morris

KITCHELL on 27 Nov 1901 at Winterset, IA. He was the son of Wesley Charles KITCHELL and Mary E. MORRIS, and was born 17 Feb/ Mar 1878 IA; died Dec 1965. Grace-[6] BIGGS died ca 1965 Ipswich, S D

Children of Grace Edna-[6] BIGGS and Robert Morris KITCHELL:
Surname **KITCHELL**

995. Helen	born ca 1905; married Roland Redmond/Redman COOPER
	(he born 26 June 1900 IA; died _____)
	(he s/o Edgar Lee COOPER and Eleanor McMILLAN)
+ **996. MORRIS LESTER**	born 24 Oct 1910; died 13 Nov 2008 Aberdeen, Brown Co., SD
	married Irene F. KRAFT 15 Nov 1942 Newcastle, WY.
	(she dau/o Leo B. KRAFT and Anna NIKOLAS)
	(she born 11 Feb 1918 Roscoe, SD; died 27 Jan 2006 Aberdeen, SD)
997. Mary Adaline	born 17 Aug 1913; died 6 May 1988 Flathead, MT
	married Henry Lee VEDRINE
	(he s/o Eugene H. VEDRINE and Hannah ____)
	(he born ca 1915 Whitefish, Flathead, MT; died 28 Jan 1984 MT)
998. Maxine	born 31 Aug 1915; died 7 Jan 2004 Willmar, MN
	married Floyd KASEL 18 Apr 1937 Ipswich, Edmunds, SD
999. Robert John	born ca 1921; married Gleva PETERSON
	(she dau/o Alfred PETERSON and Beulah ____)
	(she born ca 1928 Kent, Edmunds, SD; died _____)

556. ETHEL ANICE/ANNIS-[6] BIGGS, sister of above, was born ca 1887 at Madison County, IA. She married Robert Stevens ROBBINS ca ____. He was the son of Frank M. ROBBINS and Grace STEVENS, and was born 9 Jan 1886 IL; died 16 Nov 1941 CA. Ethel A-[6] BIGGS died ca 1965.

Children of Ethel A-[6] BIGGS and Robert S. ROBBINS:
Surname **ROBBINS**   (all children born San Diego, CA)

1000. Robert Stevens, Jr.	born 15 Feb 1912; died 1978
1001. William A.	born 30 Jan 1915; died Dec 1975
1002. Beatrice	born 27 Nov 1919; died _____

559. SILVERTUS H-[6] JOHNSON, son of Addie C-[5] MC INTOSH (Silvertus-[4]; Jonathan-[3]; Simon-[2]; Alexander-[1]) and Myron D. JOHNSON (Stephen T; Roswell), and was born 16 Oct 1886 at Humphrey, Cattaraugus County, NY. He married Jennie GAHAGAN on 19 May 1909. She was the daughter of John Spencer GAHAGAN (John M.) and Litholet Elizabeth LETTIE (George Henry, Jr; George Henry), and was born 17 May 1888 Gahagan Station, PA; died 28 July 1970 at Bradford, McKean, PA. Silvertus-[6] JOHNSON, Secretary-Treasurer and Purchasing Agent for the Bradford Motor Works, died 26 Dec 1952 at Bradford, McKean, PA. He and his wife are buried at Willowdale Cemetery, Bradford, PA.

Children of Silvertus-[6] JOHNSON and Jennie GAHAGAN:
Surname **JOHNSON**

1003. Marion Ruth	born 30 May 1910; died 8 Aug 1993 Lancaster, PA
	married Cecil B. HALLER 11 Nov 1932
	(he born 15 Jan 1908; died 6 July 1948 Bradford, PA)
	(he s/o Albert HALLER and Bessie WINTRINGHAM)
1004. Robert Leon	born 1 Dec 1914; died 19 July 2008 New Castle, Lawrence, PA
	married Betty Grace BALAZ 4 Apr 1942
	(she born 13 Jan 1917; died _____)
1005. William Kenneth	born 12 Jan 1921; married _____ FISCHER
1006. Joanne Elizabeth	born 9 July 1928; married Charles John MC INTYRE 2 Sep 1950
	(he born 15 Mar 1921; died _____)

565. MARGARET C.-[6] JOHNSON, sister of above, was born 11 Oct 1898 at Cattaraugus County, NY. She married Ralph Homer WHITEMAN 24 Dec 1919. He was the son of David Henry WHITEMAN and C. Mabel BROWN, and was born 10 Mar 1895, died 28 Oct 1980. Margaret[6] JOHNSON died Jan 1987 at Meadville, PA.

Children of Margaret[6] JOHNSON and Ralph WHITEMAN:
Surname **WHITEMAN**

	1007. Barbara May	born 15 Feb 1923
		married Robert PEIL
+	1008. **VIRGINIA**	born 23 Mar 1927; married Elmer Ray BUSCH
	LOUISA	(he born 6 July 1927; 30 Mar 2007 Ocala, FL)
		(he s/o Charles W. BUSCH and Hazel RAY)

569. JOHN MORRIS-[6] PARKER, son of Annis-[5] MC INTOSH (Silvertus-[4]; Jonathan-[3]; Simon-[2;] Alexander-[1]) and John Allen PARKER, was born 31 Dec 1891 at Olean, Cattaraugus County, NY. He married Neva Avadna SAMPSON on 18 Sept 1912 at ___ . She was the daughter of Clinton D.SAMPSON and Maud M. ____, and was born July 1896 Jones, Elk, PA; died 1957. John Morris-[6] PARKER died 17 Oct 1977 at Allegany, Cattaraugus County, NY.

Children of John M-[6] PARKER and Neva Avadna SAMPSON:
Surname **PARKER**

1009. Maxine Avadna	born 24 July 1915; died 24 Dec 1959
	married John F. MOORE 22 Apr 1931
1010. Richard Joseph	born 20 Feb 1917; died 8 June 1975 Bradford, PA
	married Kathalene Lucille MANWARING 22 May 1937 Bradford, PA
	(she born ca 1915; died 1995) divorced ca 1949

Children: Gerald Morris-[8] PARKER; and Richard Manwaring-[8] PARKER (1938-1989)

1011. Marjorie Eleanor	born 17 Aug 1918 PA; died 20 July 1982 Allegany, Cattaraugus, NY
	married Lawrence John FOSTER, Sr. 6 Dec 1945
	(he s/o Eugene Francis FOSTER and Irene Catherine LIPPERT)
	(he born 2 Jan 1922 Olean, NY; died 1 May 1981 Olean)

Children: 3 sons and 1 daughter (including Lawrence-[8] FOSTER, Jr.)

586. MYRTLE ELEANOR-[6] REYNOLDS, daughter of Dennis G-[5] REYNOLDS (Sarah/Sally-[4] MC INTOSH, Jonathan-[3]; Simon-[2]; Alexander-[1]) and Luna BELLAMY, was born ca 1881 NY. She married Floyd Harvey KLOCK before 1906. He was the son of Perry Ayers KLOCK and Nellie SKINNER, and was born 13 Aug 1877 NY; died 24 Nov 1926 NY. Myrtle-[6] REYNOLDS died ca 1925.

Children of Myrtle-[6] REYNOLDS and Floyd Harvey KLOCK:
Surname **KLOCK**

1012. Wilma Eleanor	born 2 Feb 1906; died 17 Feb 1959
	1 married Earl DAVIS (marriage annulled)
	2 married Harry J. BREWER 5 Dec 1936

Children: Helen Kay-8 born ca 1944; and Carol-8 BREWER born ca 1947

1013. Helen Lucile	born 16 Apr 1910/11; died 2000
	1 married Herbert REID

Child: William-8 REID born ca ____)

	2 married Leonard DINGLEDEY

590. ETHA L.-[6] MC WILLIAMS, daughter of Cora B-[5] REYNOLDS (Sarah/Sally-[4] MC INTOSH; Jonathan-[3]; Simon-[2]; Alexander-[1]) and Thomas G. MC WILLIAMS, was born 30 March 1897 at Franklin, Cattaraugus County, NY. She married first to George William SENEAR 24 January 1914 (age 16). He was the son of Henry SENEAR and Kate TORRELL, and was born 16 June 1874 Dearborn, MI; died 8

Mar 1968 Olean, Cattaraugus Co., NY. They divorced and she married second to Clarence ANCROFT.

Children of Etha L-[6] MC WILLIAMS and George SENEAR:
Surname **SENEAR**

	1014. Katherine/Catherine	born ca 1915/16
	1015. Robert J.	born 30 Nov 1917; died 15 May 2001
	1016. Geraldine J.	born 15 Nov 1919; died 26 Dec 2001 Spokane, WA.
	1017. DeLaura Mae /	born 27 Apr 1924; died 20 Jan 1995
	Laura	married John TETLAK 6 Sept 1948
		(he born ca 1914; died 1999) (6 children)
+	**1018. KENNETH E.**	born 26 May 1926; died 18 Jan 2011 Cattaraugus Co., NY
		Married Ruth D. CATELL (she born ca 1929; died 1987)
	1019. Rose	born ca 19__; married _____ FORRESTER
	1020. David J.	born 8 May 1930; living 2011

Children of Etha L.[6] MC WILLIAMS and Clarence BANCROFT:
Surname **BANCROFT**

	1021. June	born ca 193_; married _____ PERRY
++	1022. Franklin Clarence	born 25 March 1936 Troupsville, NY; died 31 Janusry 2004
		married Dorothy RODRIGUES of Peabody, MA

Children: Richard-[8] John-[8]; and Cynthia-[8] BANCROFT born____, married _____ ALLISON

	1023. Dorothea M.	born 10 June 1938; married _____ COLETTA

++ Obituary for Franklin C. BANCROFT
The Boston Herald 4 February 2004

Franklin C. BANCROFT of Peabody, former Boston fire lieutenant, died Sunday at his home after a brief illness. Born in Troupsville, NY, Mr. BANCROFT attended schools in Arkport, NY and would later move to Peabody (MA).   A Navy veteran of the Korean War, he served on the USS Coral Sea, and was a member of the Naval Reserve until 1962.

In 1964, Mr. BANCROFT joined the Boston Fire Dept. in East Boston with Engine 56 and retired as acting captain in 1997 after 34 years of service He was active in the South Congregational Church in Peabody and served as a deacon in the church.

Mr. BANCROFT was a member of the AFL-ClO, Local 718 in Boston, Florian Hall and the Salem YMCA.

He is survived by his wife, Dorothy (RODRIQUES) of Peabody, two sons, Richard of Melrose, and John of Peabody; a daughter Cynthia ALLISON OF Peabbody; a (half) brother David SENEAR of New York; three sisters, Rose Forrester, June Perry and Dorothea Coletta, all of NY; seven grandchildren and many nieces and nephews.

A funeral service will be held at 9:30 AM today at South Congregational Church, Peabody. Burial will be in Puritan Lawn Memorial Park, Peabody.

593. KATE ANGELINE-[6] **MC INTOSH**, daughter of James H-[5] MC INTOSH (William-[4]; Henry-[3]; Simon-[2]; Alexander-[1]) and Lucy Amanda DALES, was born 28 Jan 1880 at _____, Delaware County, NY She married Reverdy Johnson CLAGETT on 25 Jan 1899 at _____. He was the son of Thomas Weston CLAGETT and Mary Mackall BOWIE, and was born 25 Jan 1877 at Prince George's County, MD; died _____. Kate Angeline-[6] MC INTOSH died 9 Sep 1923 at _____.

Children of Kate Angeline-[6] MC INTOSH and Reverdy CLAGETT:
Surname **CLAGETT**

+	**1024. LUCY AMANDA**	born 25 May 1907; died July 1987 Evanston, IL	
		married Curtis F. PRANGLEY (of Washington, DC)	
		(he born 11 July 1905; died Oct 1976 IL)	
	1025. Reverdy, Jr.	born ca 1908; died 12 June 1950 never married	EOL

Note: He served in WW 2 as a Sgt. in the 881 NP CO CMP USAF, and is
buried at Arlington National Cemetery, VA. Section 12, Site 8100

596. JESSIE SARAH-[6] MC INTOSH, daughter of William Arthur-[5] MC INTOSH (William-[4]; Henry-[3]; Simon-[2]; Alexander-[1]) and Sarah May MC INTYRE, was born 24 Dec 1885 at Delaware County, NY. She married William R. BURKETT on ___ at ____. He was the son of _ BURKETT and _____, and was born ____; died ___. They resided at 15 Clinton Street, Delhi, NY, where Jessie Sarah-[6] died Jan 1968.

Child of Jessie-[6] MC INTOSH and William BURKETT:
Surname **BURKETT**

1026. William McIntosh	born ca 1914 NY; died 1932	never married	EOL

598. EUGENE M-[6] POWELL, son of Mary-[5] BURNSIDE (Emeline-[4] MC INTOSH; Henry-[3]; Simon-[2]; Alexander-[1]) and John E. POWELL, was born 18 Oct 1866 at Roxbury, Delaware County, NY. He married Cora A. BROWN on 27 Oct 1892 at Bloomville, Delaware County, NY. She was the daughter of John BROWN and Sarah N. ____, and was born ca 1864 NY; died 16 Nov 1949. Eugene-[6] POWELL died 16 Nov 1953. He and his wife are buried at Riverside Cemetery, Bloomville, NY. Mr. POWELL owned and operated a department store in Bloomville for 50 years, retiring in 1943. He was a member of the Bloomville Methodist Church and the Delhi (NY) Masonic Lodge.

Children of Eugene-[6] POWELL and Cora BROWN:
Surname **POWELL**

1027. Cora Gladys	born 21 Nov 1896 NY; died July 1984 Delhi, NY		
	married Milton H. HENDERSON	no issue	EOL
	(he born 6 July 1894; died May 1978)		
1028. Sarah M.	born ca 1899-1901; died _____	never married	EOL

605. LEWIS ERSKINE-[6] PACKARD, son of Jane-[5] WILLIAMS (Caroline-[4] MC INTOSH; William-[3]; Simon-[2]; Alexander-[1]) and Erskine PACKARD, was born ___ 1863 at ____ PA. He married first to _____ (unknown) . His second marriage was to Nora / Lenora I./ Nora DOBBINS on ____. She was the daughter of William S. DOBBINS and Sarah ____, and was born ca 1867; died 21 Aug 1947. Lewis E-[6] PACKARD died 1 Feb 1930. They are buried at Glenwood Cemetery, Troy, Bradford, PA.

Children of Lewis Erskine-[6] PACKARD and Nora DOBBINS:
Surname **PACKARD**

+ **1029. IRENE LUCY**	born 10 Dec 1893 PA; died 21 Feb 1988	
	married Ralph PACKARD of Granville, Summit, PA	
	(he s/o William B. PACKARD and Anna Margaret AYRES)	
	(he born 17 June 1890 PA; died Jan 1964)	
1030. Jennie May	born ca 1896 PA; died _____; married Earl H. SEELEY of Alba, PA	
	(he born ca 1896 Granville, Bradford, PA; died ____)	
1031. Howard	born ca _____ PA; died _____	

606. CAROLINE DELL-[6] " Carrie " PACKARD, sister of above, was born July 1867 at ____ PA. She married Galen Guy AYRES of Alba, Bradford County, PA on 2 Nov 1887 at ____ Bradford County. He was the son of John H. AYRES and Mary __, and was born March 1861 PA; died ___. Caroline-[6] PACKARD died _____.

Children of Caroline-[6] PACKARD and Galen Guy AYRES:
Surname **AYRES**

+ **1032. MABEL**	born Feb 1893 PA; married John E. WEATHERBEE	
	(he born 20 Jan 1891 PA; died Jan 1963 PA)	
1033. Lewis/Louis T.	born Dec 1897 PA; died _____	
+ **1034. FLORENCE MAY**	born 23 Dec 1907 Canton, PA; died 12 Dec 1977 Canton	
	married Arthur Howard GRACE (he s/o GRACE and Etta VAN DYKE)	

611. LILLEY BELLE[6] **WILLIAMS**, sister of above, was born 2 Oct 1876 at ____ Bradford County, PA. She married first to Charles Frederick (Harpy) TURNER on 17 Dec 1896. He was the son of Fred B. TURNER and Emeline A. ____, and was born 28 Oct 1875; died 1 June 1920. She married second to Milton A.-[5] CASE 2 Nov 1929. He was the son of Eliza[-4] MC INTOSH (William-[3]; Simon-[2]; Alexander-[1]) and Byron CASE, and was born ca 1858; died Feb 1937. He had two prior marriages. His first wife was Eugenia THOMAS with whom he had 4 children. Lilly Belle-[6] WILLIAMS died ca 1953, PA.

Children of Lilly Belle-[6] WILLIAMS and Charles TURNER:
Surname **TURNER**

	1035. Frank Soper	born 11 May 1898; died 20 May 1898	EOL
+	**1036. LEWIS MC KEAN**	born 1 July 1899 PA; married Bessie CONRAD 29 Nov 1921/22	
+	**1037. ERNEST (Val)**	born 29 Dec 1901 PA; died Mar 1969	
	INVALDA	married Helen Luella GREGORY 1 Sep 1923	
+	1038. Ellie Emma	born 1 Dec 1904 PA; (Child: Ellie Jean-[8] METZGER born 27 June 1929	
		married John Adam METZGER 22 Aug 1927	
	1039. Charles H.	born 10 Nov 1906; died 26 Nov 1906	EOL
	1040. Frederick James	born 20 July 1909 PA; died 22 Feb 1983 Burlington, Bradford. PA	

612. CHARLES MC KEAN (Mac)-[6] **WILLIAMS**, son of George-[5] WILLIAMS (Caroline[-4] MC INTOSH; William-[3]; Simon-[2;] Alexander[-1]) and Ellen Ann LILLEY, was born 19 Apr 1878 at ___ Bradford County, PA. He married Elsie Leda KILBOURN on 9 Jan 1901 Bradford County, PA. She was the daughter of Perry KILBOURN and Harriet NICHOLS, and was born 9 July 1879 Union, Tioga, PA; died 3 Oct 1938. Charles "Mac"-[6] WILLIAMS died before 1947. They are buried in the Turner Cemetery.

Children of Charles "Mac" -[6] WILLIAMS and Elsie KILBOURN:
Surname **WILLIAMS**

	1041. Helen Louise	born 31 Mar 1906 Union, PA; died 19 Nov 1992
		married Maynard SCHMELZLE 19 Sep 1928 (he of Liberty, PA)
		(he s/o George SCHMELZLE and Elizabeth WATKINS)
		(he born July 1907; died 1 Jan 1970)
	1042. Marion Margaret	born 18 Feb 1908 PA; died ____(living 2003)
		1 married Herbert JONES 2 Aug 19__ (he of Grover, PA)
		(he s/o John JONES and Harriet JACKSON)
		(he born 18 Feb 1898 PA; died ____)
		2 married _____ DONALDSON of Wellsboro, PA
	1043. Mildred Luella	born 21 Dec 1909 PA; died _____
		1 married _____ MASON; 2 married _____ BISHOP
+	**1044. DORIS LILLIAN**	born 12 Nov 1912 PA; died 21 Dec 2003 Miami, FL
		1 married Walter C. MASE of Gleason, PA on 21 Mar 1936
		(he s/o Harry F. MASE and Edna M. PARKER)
		(he born 12 June 1912 PA; died June 1971 PA)
		2 married Lester Erwin GROOVER ca ____
+	**1045. HARRIET**	born 4 May 1915 PA; died 22 Jan 2006 Naples, FL
	ELLIE	married Ralph Walter AUSTIN 18 May 1936
		(he born 1 May 1915; died 3 Aug 1982 Roaring Branch, PA)
	1046. Charles McKean, Jr.	born 20 June 1917 PA; married ___ MC ILWAIN of Leolyn, PA
	1047. Florence	born _____ PA; died _____; married Hamilton TODD

615. JENNIE CAROLINE[-6] **WILLIAMS**, daughter of Edwin C-[5] WILLIAMS (Caroline[-4] MC INTOSH; William-[3]; Simon-[2]; Alexander[-1]) and Ella WHITEHEAD, was born 6 Jan 1879 at ____, PA. She married Archie McKean KILBOURN on 18 Oct 1906. He was the son of Delos KILBOURN and Eva Delight WEST, and was born May 1878, died 27 Apr 193_. Jennie-[6] WILLIAMS died 23 Feb 1910..

Children of Jennie Caroline[-6] WILLIAMS and Archie McKean KILBOURN:
Surname **KILBOURN**

      1048. Edwin D.(twin)   born 23 Feb 1910 PA; died _____

      1049. Evelyn Elizabeth (twin) born 23 Feb 1910 PA; died June 1963
                            married Grant Willard SCHANBACHER   (1900-38)

617. SAMUEL WATSON[-6] WILLIAMS; half-brother of above, son of Edwin Churchill[-5] WILLIAMS (Caroline-[4] MC INTOSH; William-[3]; Simon-[2]; Alexander-[1]) and Elizabeth THORN(E), was born 17 Oct 1887 at Canton, Bradford, PA. He married Ella Caroline EGLI on ____ at ___. She was the daughter of Jacob EGLI and Nora ____, and was born 26 Sep 1893 Muncy, Lycoming, PA; died 26 Feb 1978 PA. Samuel-[6] WILLIAMS died 18 Dec 1918 at Bradford County, PA.

Children of Samuel[-6] WILLIAMS and Ella EGLI:
Surname **WILLIAMS**

      1050. Samuel Edwin   born 26 May 1919 Muncy, PA; died 11 May 1981 Canton, PA.
                            married Kathryn Alice FULKERSON
                            (she born 15 Aug 1917 PA; died 10 Jan 1997 Canton, PA)

618. SETH EDWIN[-6] WILLIAMS, brother of above, was born 6 Feb 1889 at Canton, PA. He married Sarah M. NORTH ca 1913. She was the daughter of ____ NORTH and ____, and was born ca 1887 PA; died _____ (her parents were born Germany) Seth-[6] WILLIAMS, a repairman on the Railroad, died ca 1932 at _____. In 1920 and 1930 they resided at Southport, Chemung County, NY.

Children of Seth[-6] WILLIAMS and Sarah NORTH:
Surname **WILLIAMS**

      1051. Dorothea E.   born Sept 1917 PA   1052. Lewis   born ca 1923 NY

623. GERTRUDE JANE[-6] RANDALL, daughter of Daniel-[5] RANDALL (Charlotte-[4] MC INTOSH; William-[3]; Simon-[2]; Alexander-[1]) and Kate MC KENZIE, was born 2 July 1886 Union, Tioga, PA. She married Benjamin Dean LANDON on 2 June 1909. He was the son of Clarence C. LANDON and Mary Adelle GRISWOLD, and was born 28 April 1881 Union, Tioga, PA; died 8 March 1950. Gertrude-[6] RANDALL died 25 May 1979.

Children of Gertrude[-6] RANDALL and Benjamin Dean LANDON:
Surname **LANDON**

      1053. Mae Kathryn   born 9 March 1910; died 19 Nov 1980; 1 married ____ DARROW
                    Child: Benjamin-[8] DARROW born ca ___ Canton, PA
                    2 married Robert L. FITCH ca 1950
          Children: LaVonne-[8] born ca ___,married Ralph BROWN and Sally-[8] FITCH born ca ____ , married Paul LOCKE
      1054. Myrtle Lucille   born 18 Aug 1912; died 12 Feb 1995
                            married Davis Eugene VAN DYKE 30 April 1932 Montour Falls, NY
                            (he born 14 July 1909 PA; died 15 Mar 2000 Troy, PA)
         Children: Nancy-[8] born ca ___ · Virginia Ann-[8] born ca ___ , married ____ ANGRADI; Lynne-[8] born ca ___,
        married ____ HERTEL; and Susan-[8] VAN DYKE born ca ___, married ____ SCHIESS
      1055. Roy Daniel   born 5 Aug 1917; died ____ Canton, PA
                            married Harriet Lorena WILLIAMS 28 June 1942 Canton, PA
                Children: Allyn R-[8] born ca ___; Kathy-[8] LANDON born ca _____
      1056. Charlotte   born 20 July 1919 North Union, PA; died 29 Jan 1987 Canton, PA
                            1 married Marvin W. STALKER
                            (he born 9 Apr 1915; died _____)
               Child: Paul-[8] STALKER born ca _____ (he resided Hammondsport, NY)
                    2 married Duane A. SHOEMAKER (he born 23 Mar 1919 PA; died 1977)

624. OLLIE DAN-[6] RANDALL, son of Daniel-[5] RANDALL (Charlotte-[4] MC INTOSH; William-[3]; Simon-[2]; Alexander-[1]) and Kate MC KENZIE, was born 14 Apr 1889 at Union Township, PA. He married Louise MIELKE ca ___. She was the daughter of Charles MIELKE (born Germany) and ____, and was born 27 Dec 1900 East Hampton, MA; died Oct 1969 Canton, PA. Ollie Dan-[6] RANDALL died 18 Jan 1976 at Burlington, PA. They are buried at the East Canton Cemetery.

Child of Ollie Dan-[6] RANDALL and Louise MIELKE:
Surname **RANDALL**

1057. Ollie David — born 13 May 1930 Canton, PA; married Beatrice C. WOODARD 18 Jan 1958 (she dau/o John D. WOODARD and Minnie RUDY) (she born 29 July 1929 Canton, PA ; died ____)
Children: Dean Leslie-[8] born ____, and Donald Albert-[8] RANDALL born ____

625. GEORGE WAYNE-[6] RANDALL, brother of above, was born 11 Mar 1896 at Canton, Bradford County, PA. He married Edna Eloise HUNT on 27 Sept 1924 at Williamsport, Bradford, PA. She was the daughter of Harry Bruce Landon HUNT and Anna Laura MIDDLETON, and was born 28 June 1889 at Williamsport, PA, and died there on 7 Feb 1942.
Note: Edna Louise HUNT had a son named Harold Paul HUNT, born 7 Nov 1908 Lycoming, PA.

Child of George Wayne-[6] RANDALL and Edna Eloise HUNT:
Surname **RANDALL**

+ **1058. KATHRYN ANN** born 29 Oct 1926; died 21 Jan 2009 Montoursville, Lycoming, PA married Clayton Larue STERNER after 1945 (he born 23 Apr 1926 PA; died 24 Oct 2004 Montoursville, PA)

626. NANCY AMELIA-[6] (Nan) AYRES / AYERS, daughter of Grace Jane-[5] RANDALL (Charlotte-[4] MC INTOSH; William-[3]; Simon-[2]; Alexander-[1]) and Dana Thomas AYRES/AYERS, was born 28 May 1878 at Bradford County, PA. She married Paul Ira FREEMAN 7 Jan 1895 at Alba, PA. He was the son of Henry Watson FREEMAN and Eliza H. ____, and was born 16 Oct 1874 Alba, PA; died 1948. In 1920 they resided at Watkins Glen, Schuyler County, NY where he was a conductor on the railroad. In 1930 their residence was in Elmira, Chemung County, NY. Nancy-[6] AYRES died 6 Dec 1970 Elmira,, NY.

Children of Nancy-[6] AYRES / AYERS and Paul Ira FREEMAN:
Surname **FREEMAN**

+ **1059. ROBERT AYRES /AYERS** born 9 Feb 1896 Canton, PA; died 16 Sep 1959 Elmira, Chemung, NY
1 married Eliza Mae AVERY 8 June 1914 (she born 8 Feb 1896; died 28 Sep 1928)
2 married Addah C. LARCOM

1060. Harold James — born 6 Feb 1897 Alba, PA; died 22 Nov 1918 Elmira, NY

1061. Pauline Eliza — born 28 July 1898 Elmira PA; died 18 Sep 1966 married Harold TITUS 4 June 1917 (he born 7 Sep 1895; died 16 Oct 1947)
Child: Nancy Ann-[8] TITUS born 29 Jun 1918, died 24 Aug 2001 Dardanelle, Arkansas married Norman STAGE ca ____, he born ca 1915

1062. Watson Dana — born 20 Sep / 3 Oct 1905 PA; died 4 Sep 1980 married Caroline Anna LaDOW 4 Aug 1923 Hammondsport, NY (she born 5 Sep 1901; died 3 June 1973) (she d/o Alphonso C. LaDOW and Cora Davis)
Children: dau born ____; married ____SOTHERDEN; son born ____, married ____REALS; son born ____, married ____ SMILEY; dau born ____, married JANSSEN; dau born ____, married ____ SMITH

+ **1063. LYNN CLIFFORD** born 23 Sep 1906 PA; died May 1979 married Mary Violet FAIRMAN 8 June 1927 (she born 1 Jan 1905)

629. D. HOWARD-⁶ AYRES / AYERS, brother of above, was born 30 Dec 1890 at Canton, Bradford County, **PA.** He married Julia A/J. SNYDER ca _____ . She was the daughter of _____ SNYDER and ____ , and was born ca 1892, PA. ; died ____ . D. Howard-⁶ AYRES died ____ .

Children of D. Howard ⁶ AYRES and Julia A. SNYDER;
Surname **AYRES**

1064. Marion G.	born ca 1912 PA	1067. Paul F.	born 21 Jan 1919, PA
1065. Florence P.	born 1914 PA		died 28 Nov 1994 , Elmira, NY
1066. Harvey D.	born 1916 PA	1068. Howard R.	born 1924 NY

635. HARRIET "Hattie"-⁶ FIELD, daughter of Amy Isabel-⁵ THOMAS (Harriet-⁴ MC INTOSH; William-³; Simon-²; Alexander-¹) and D. Lazelle FIELD, was born 12 Oct 1876 at Canton, Bradford, PA. She married Marshall Jenkins THOMAS on 15 Feb 1899. He was the son of Edward THOMAS and Rebecca NELSON, and was born 5 Aug 1867 PA; died 19 June 1961 Canton, PA. Harriet-⁶ FIELD died 16 June 1928 Canton, Bradford Co., PA.

Children of Harriet-⁶ FIELD and Marshall Jenkins THOMAS:
Surname **THOMAS**

+   **1069. EDWARD FIELD** born 15 Dec 1900 PA; died _____
                              married Martha WHERRY 10 Aug 1925
                              (she dau/o Samuel WHERRY and Mary FERRY)
                              (she born 3 Mar 1903; died 9 Mar 1987)

    1070. Hugh T.   born 24 Oct 1902 PA; died 26 Apr 1905   EOL
    1071. Lazelle F.   born 13 Dec 1903 PA; died June 1964
                              married Emma JENKINS 9 July 1924 ; divorced
                              (she dau/o Harvey JENKINS and __) (she born 25 Nov 1908)
              Children: twin daughters Marjorie-⁸ and Marie-⁸ THOMAS born 10 Nov 1924
    1072. Bruce A.   born 5 Dec 1906 PA; died 5 Dec 1993 Wellsville, Allegany, NY
                              married Mildred ELLIOTT 25 Jan 1930 (she from Mt. Morris, NY)
                              (she born 30 Sept 1901; died _____)
                    Child: Robert Bruce-⁸ THOMAS born 10 Aug 1933
    1073. J. Evalyn   born 10 Apr 1908 PA; died 7 Sep 1981 Binghamton NY ; teacher
+   **1074. ISABELLE**   born 10 Oct 1915 PA; died Nov 1988 Canton, PA
                              1 married Herman SCHOLTZ 27 Nov 1931 (he from Alba, PA)
                              (he born ca March 1912; died in World War 2)
                              2 married Carl H. KROTZER 31 Aug 1946 Philadelphia, PA.

639. HELEN MILDRED-⁶ FIELD, sister of above, was born Oct 1887 at Canton, Bradford County, PA. She married first to Porter Lyman SHOEMAKER of Granville, PA on ____ . He was the son of Amasa SHOEMAKER and Ella A. ____ , and was born Aug 1885 Troy, PA; died ca 1911. Her second husband was Harry E. BROOKS of Binghamton, NY. He was the son of ____ BROOKS and ____ , and was born ca 1890 Binghamton, NY; died ____ . They were married ca 1916.

Child of Helen-⁶ FIELD and Porter SHOEMAKER:
Surname **SHOEMAKER**
+   **1075. PAULINE**   born 21 May 1910 Troy, PA; died 25 May 1987
                              married Lynn J. MCONNELL 29 March 1934 (he born 5 Oct 1909)
Child of Helen-⁶ FIELD and Harry E. BROOKS:
Surname **BROOKS**
    1076. Margaret   born ca 1920; died ____ ; married _____ HOLES

642. MYRTLE GLEN-[6] THOMAS, daughter of Lewis Randall-[5] THOMAS (Harriet-[4] MC INTOSH; William-[3]; Simon-[2]; Alexander-[1]) and Minerva OSTRANDER, was born 12 Apr 1886 PA. She married Elmer Earl HOPPER on 27 Sep 1909. He was the son of John HOPPER and Rosanna____, and was born 22 Oct 1889 PA ; died 23 July 1975 San Luis Obispo, CA. He was a Free Methodist and held revival services. Myrtle Glen-[6] THOMAS died May 1984 at San Luis Obispo, CA.

Children of Myrtle Glen-[6] THOMAS and Elmer Earl HOPPER:
Surname **HOPPER**

1077. Robert Lewis	born 5 July 1910 PA; died 19 Jan 1982 Ventura, CA	
	married Pearl PENDERGAST 26 May 1934 (she born 16 Nov 1908)	
1078. Irma Marion	born 3 Dec 1911 PA; died 8 Feb 1993 CO ; divorced	
	married Donald Leroy MARTIN 24 Oct 1941 Las Vegas, NV	
	(he born 19 Oct 1917 MT; died 24 Nov 1997 San Diego, CA)	
	(buried Ft. Rosencrans National Cemetery, San Diego, CA)	
1079. Donald Vincent	born 3 Sep 1914 Los Angeles, CA; died 28 Jan 1986 Los Angeles	
	married Mildred Louise HANSEN	
	(she born 20 Aug 1908 AZ; died 20 Dec 1984 Long Beach, CA)	
1080. Edna Mae	born 10 Aug 1916 CA; died 13 Apr 2005 CA	
	married Francis E. JESPERSON	
	(he born 25 Feb 1917 CA; died 27 Jan 2004 CA)	
	(he s/o Christian JESPERSON and Jennie _____)	
1081. Betty Jean	born 15 Dec 1918 PA; died ____	
	married Oscar Edward BENJESTORF 1 Mar 1941 Atascadero, CA	
	(he born 7 May 1919 CA; died 16 July 1963 Los Angeles, CA)	
	(he s/o Alexander BENJESTORF and Goldie BUFFINGTON)	
+ **1082. MIRIAM LOUISE**	born 25 Nov 1923 PA; died 25 Sept 2010 San Luis Obispo, CA	
	1 married Gerald Woodrow DORMAN 29 June 1941 CA	
	(he born 30 Dec 1919 MO; died 19 Dec 1990 San Luis Obispo, CA)	
	2 married Howard Leonard IVERSEN	
	(he born 18 Mar 1912 Paso Robles, CA; died 31 May 2006)	

655. ELIZA A-[6] CASE, twin daughter of Milton A-[5] CASE (Eliza-[4] MC INTOSH; William-[3]; Simon-[2]; Alexander-[1]) and Eugenia THOMAS was born 29 Aug 1884 at Troy, Bradford County, PA. She married Herman Roy BOYER on 24 Dec 1914. He was the son of _____ BOYER and ____, and was born 5 July 1885; died 1961. Eliza-[6] CASE died ca 1944 at Troy.

Children of Eliza-[6] CASE and Herman BOYER:
Surname **BOYER**

1083. Alvin Samuel	born 3 April 1919 PA; 15 Aug 2011 Fresno, CA
1084. Nelson Wood	born 2 May 1925; died June 1966 PA; buried Alba, PA
	married Betty MINGOS ca 1950
1085. Evelyn E.	born 8 May/ Aug 1921 PA

656. ELIZABETH A-[6] CASE, twin sister of above , was born 29 Aug 1884 at Troy, Bradford County, PA. She married Elwyn Phelps MC KEAN on 25 Mar 1910 at North Towanda, Bradford, PA. He was the son of Isaac J. MC KEAN and Emma M. PHELPS, and was born 12 June 1882 PA; died 1955 at Troy, PA. Elizabeth-[6] CASE died 15 Sep 1966 at Troy, Bradford, PA. They resided at W. Burlington , Bradford, PA.

Children of Elizabeth-[6] CASE and Elwyn MC KEAN:
Surname **MC KEAN**

+ **1086. MILTON I.**	born 12 July 1911 PA; died May 1977 Springfield, MO
1087. Ralph Eugene	born 12 June 1912 PA; died Feb 1982 Ulster, Bradford, PA

Children of Elizabeth-[6] CASE and Elwyn MC KEAN, continued:
Surname **MC KEAN**

+   **1088. LYNN E. (m)**   born 29 Sep 1913 West Burlington, PA; died _____
                                  married Frances Mae TUTTLE 27 Nov 1936

    1089. May/ Mary Emma   born 27 July 1915 PA; died ____

    1090. Raymond L.   born 2 June 1920 Burlington, PA; died 7 Mar 1978 Troy, PA
                                    served in the US Army in World War 2

    1091. B. Phillips   born 7 March 1922; died 14 June 1926

    1092. Henry A   born 27 Sep 1925 PA; died 27 Dec 1999 Troy, Bradford, PA
                                    served as a PFC in the USA Army during the Korean War

    1093. Pauline E.   born 31 Oct 1926; died 23 June 2009 Troy, PA; she was an RN
          "Polly"   married Lee R. CLEVELAND, Jr. 23 July 1953
                         (he born 31 Aug 1925 Troy, PA; died _____)

658. MEADE THOMAS-[6] CASE, brother of above, was born 25 Apr 1890 at Troy, Bradford, PA. He married Louise H. BROWNSON on 26 Oct 1910 at ____. She was the daughter of Thomas E. BROWNSON and Clara <u>Belle</u> _____, and was born Jan 1888 at W. Burlington, Bradford, PA; died ____. Meade-[6] CASE died 15 June 1966 at Troy, PA.

Child of Meade Thomas-[6] CASE and Louise BROWNSON:
Surname **CASE**

+   **1094. THOMAS**   born 17 Mar 1912 PA; died 30 June 1994 Troy, PA.
           BYRON   married Sara WRISLEY 9 Sep 1939
                         (she born 15 July 1916; died 19 July 1999 Troy, PA)

663. EDNA MAY-[6] CASE, daughter of Nelson-[5] CASE (Eliza-[4] MC INTOSH; William-[3]; Simon-[2]; Alexander-[1]) and Eva HACKETT, was born 15 Aug 1894 at North Field, NH. She married John Fogg DREW, 20 Oct 1917 at Concord, NH. He was the son of John Alva DREW and Mary Jane RUNNELLS, and was born 10 Mar 1896 Concord, NH; died 24 Jan 1972 Windsor, VT. Edna May -[6] CASE died 14 May 1922, presumably in childbirth, at Concord, NH.. (Note) John DREW married twice more. His second wife was Mary Frances HAWKINS by whom he had 4 children. His third wife was Jeanette Evangeline WATTERSON by whom he had another three children.

Children of Edna-[6] CASE and John Fogg DREW.:
Surname **DREW**

    1095 Margaret   born ca 1921 NH   1096. Edna   born 14 May 1922 NH

669. SAMUEL NELSON-[6] ROBY, son of Charlotte-[5] CASE (Eliza-[4] MC INTOSH, William-[3], Simon-[2], Alexander-[1]) and Earl Clarke ROBY, was born 25 Nov 1913 at Troy, Bradford County, PA. He married Olga Ila WINKLER ca 1938. She was the daughter of Samuel WINKLER and Mary KIR, and was born 27 Feb 1910; died 13 Aug 2009 at Athens, PA. Samuel-[6] ROBY died 1966. Olga married second to Harrison RUTTY who died in 2001.

Children of Samuel Nelson-[6] ROBY and Olga WINKLER:
Surname **ROBY**

    1097. Kay   born ____; married Dale HURD; resided Schenectady, NY
                  Children: Dale-[8], Jr. and Timothy -[8] HURD

    1098. Nancy Doreen   born ____; married Paul CASSELBURY; res. NY

    1099. Jack   born ____; resided Cape Canaveral, FL

    1100. Donald   born ____; married Stephanie ___; res. Elmira Hts., NY
                  Children: Donald-[8] Jr.

    1101. Raymond   born ____; married Laurie ____; resided Brandon, FL

672. FRANCIS CURTIS-[6] MC INTOSH, son of William E-[5] MC INTOSH (Fernando-[4]; William-[3]; Simon-[2]; Alexander-[1]) and Sarah MC GARRY, was born 30 July 1899 at Morris Run, PA. He married Mildred Marie EMMS on 14 Nov 1923 at Blossburg, PA. She was the daughter of Herbert Charles EMMS and Sarah Eliza WARD, and was born 20 Oct 1903 Morris Run; died 13 July 1979 at Suffern, NY. Francis Curtis-[6] MAC INTOSH died 20 June 1977 at Suffern, NY. They are buried at Gate of Heaven Cemetery, Valhalla, New York.

Children of Francis Curtis-[6] MC INTOSH and Mildred EMMS:
Surname **MC INTOSH**

+	**1102. WILLIAM FRANCIS**	born 10 Oct 1935 New York, NY; died _____ married Miriam Blanche MC NALLY 21 Sep 1957 New York, NY. (she born 11 June 1938 Bronx, NY;)
+	**1103. DONALD CURTIS**	born 16 Nov 1928 New York, NY; died 28 May 1987 New York, NY 1 married Rosemary DUFFY ca ____ Syracuse, NY 2 married Virginia MC GUIGAN ca 1949 Detroit, MI. (she born 24 May 1933 New York, NY ;)

675. JAMES LEON-[6] BATTERSON, son of Maude-[5] MC INTOSH (Lewis-[4]; William-[3]; Simon-[2]; Alexander-[1]) and Charles BATTERSON, was born 16 Oct 1896. He married Ruth Mildred MC KEE on 3 June 1915. She was the daughter of Thomas Edward MC KEE and Helen GILBERT, and was born June 1897; died ____. They divorced ____. He married second to Elizabeth SCHUCMER of Troy, PA on ___ at ____. She was the daughter of ____ SCHUCMER and ____, and was born ca 1899; died 23 Feb 1938. James-[6] BATTERSON died 1 Feb 1968 at Troy, PA.

Child of James-[6] BATTERSON and Ruth MC KEE:
Surname **BATTERSON**

	1104. Willis Edward " Bill "	born 29 July 1916 Troy, PA; died 28 Mar 1989 Troy, PA. married Geraldine "Judy" SMITH 22 July 1936

Children: Lewis "Butch"-[8] born ___, married Bonnie____; and Beverly-[8] BATTERSON born ___, married Wm. SMITH

677. JOHN WILLIAM-[6] CURE, son of Alvin-[5] CURE (Rosalthea-[4] MC INTOSH; William-[3]; Simon-[2]: Alexander-[1]) and Martha Jane GUATNEY, was born 10 Dec 1888 at Labette County, KS. He married Jessie YOUNGER Roy ca 190_, as her second husband. She was the daughter of Charles YOUNGER and _____, was born 23 Jan 1883 MO; died 15 May 1966 at Galena, KS. She had previously been married to Charles ROY ca 1899 and had three children with him: Cleo ROY born Mar 1900, Lloyd ROY born ca 1902, and Ralph ROY born ca 1904. John William-[6] CURE died 28 Sep 1924 at Galena, Cherokee, KS.

Children of John William-[6] CURE and Jessie YOUNGER Roy:
Surname **CURE**

1105. Harold John	born 9 June 1908; died 15 Mar 1945 Cologne, Germany WW2
1106. Ferrell William	born 9 May 1910; died 12 Oct 1981
1107. Wanda Lee	born 28 Feb 1912; died 18 Sep 1981; married ? PIERSON; res. SD
1108. Herman Albert	born 15 Nov 1915 KS; died 17 Apr 1975
1109. Jamia Marcell	born ca 1918 KS; married _____ FAULKNER
1110. William " Billie"	born ca 1920
1111. Lorene Louise	born ca 1923; died 1998; married Lloyd LYERLA
1112. John Calvin	born ca 1924

682. MILDRED I-[6] CURE, daughter of Andrew Johnson-[5] CURE (Rosalthea-[4] MC INTOSH; William-[3]; Simon-[2]; Alexander-[1]) and Rebecca SCHOLES, was born 31 July 1904 TX. She married Verald Elton PAYNE on ____. He was the son of Charles B. PAYNE and Dora A. ____, and was born 7 Nov 1902 Elgin, IL; died 8 Feb 1974 Hemet, Riverside, CA. Mildred-[6] CURE died 28 Sep 2000 at Newhall, CA.

Children of Mildred I-⁶ CURE and Verald PAYNE:
Surname **PAYNE**

| 1113. Robert Sterling | born 10 Mar 1932 CA; died 27 Oct 2005 CA | Child: Daniel-⁸ PAYNE |

married Yolanda FIERROS (she born ca 1931; died 1996)

1114. Charles E. born _____ 1115. Douglas A. born _____

694. PEARL M-⁶ CRAWFORD, daughter of John-⁵ CRAWFORD (Lucy Delphine-4 MC INTOSH; William-3; Simon-2; Alexander-1) and Meda ANDRUS, was born 14 Aug 1894 at Canton, Bradford . She married first to Max SANFORD on 24 December 1913. He was born ____; died before 1920. Her second marriage was to _____ HINSHELWOOD 16 January 1921 OH. He was the son of _____ HINSHEL-WOOD and ____, and was born ____, died _____. Pearl-⁶ CRAWFORD died ca 1922 at Cleveland, Ohio.

Child of Pearl-⁶ CRAWFORD and _____ HINSHELWOOD:
Surname **HINSHELWOOD**

1116. Shirley Jean born 16 Jan 1921 OH; died 17 Mar 1986
1 married Clare R. BROWN 16 Nov 1963 Orange County, CA
2 married Loyal D. WOODRUFF 6 Jan 1974 Orange County, CA.
(he born ca 1926 ; died ____) divorced June 1975 Orange Co., CA.

696. KATHLEEN LOUISE-⁶ CRAWFORD, daughter of Byron Hugh-⁵ CRAWFORD (Lucy Delphine-^{4;} MC INTOSH, William-³; Simon-^{2;} Alexander-¹) and Addie WATTS, was born 21 May 1889 at Leolyn , PA. She married Norvin Clark HOLMES of Philadelphia, PA. on 10 Sep 1910. He was the son of Samuel HOLMES and Ella CLARK of Philadelphia, and was born 14 May 1886; died 5 Apr 1956 Roaring Branch, Lycoming County, PA. Kathleen-⁶ CRAWFORD died before 1960. She and her husband are buried in the family plot at Park Cemetery, Canton, Bradford, PA.

Children of Kathleen-⁶ CRAWFORD and Norvin HOLMES:
Surname **HOLMES**

1117. Norvin Clark , Jr. born 19 Aug 1911 Leolyn, PA; died 2 Mar 1979 Ft. Lauderdale, FL ; served as a Cpl. in the US Army in WW 2

+ **1118. RODMAN CRAWFORD** born 16 Sep 1914 Leolyn; died 29 Oct 1963 Sayre, PA
married Ethel KEAGLE 22 July 1933
(she born 12 Feb 1910; died 28 Jan 1986)

1119. Ella Jane Clark born 23 Dec 1915 Leolyn,PA; died _____ (living 2008 Palm Bay, FL
married ___FREY; resided Plantation, FL

1120. Crawford Clark born 4 June 1917; died 14 Oct 1950 Cedar Ledge, Bradford, PA
married Marie CAMPBELL

1121. Franklin Pierce born 4 June 1917; died 3 Mar 2008 (POW WW2)
married Mary E. MORRIS; resided Canton, PA
(she born _____; died 6 Oct 2005)

1122. Kenneth C. born _____ PA; died 4 June 1945 (WW2)
buried Park Cemetery 24 May 1949 EOL

1123. Edwin C. * born 3 Aug 1924 Leolyn,PA; died 22 Aug 1948 Leolyn,PA EOL

* Note: Newspaper reported : he " was killed instantly in a spectacular accident on Rt. 14 - 6 miles south of Canton (PA) . He was an interior decorator, had been employed in Atlanta, GA, and was visiting his parents in Leolyn ".

698. ALVERDA-⁶ FELIX, daughter of Lena Belle-⁵ CRAWFORD (Lucy Delphine-⁴ MC INTOSH; William-³; Simon-²; Alexander-¹) and George FELIX, was born 27 June 1895 at Canton, Bradford County, PA. She married Victor Warren HANN, of Hornell, Steuben County, NY, on 7 Apr 1917. He was the son of _____ HANN and ____, and was born 6 Nov 18991 Steuben County, NY; died ____.

Child of Alverda[6] FELIX and Victor HANN:
Surname **HANN**

> 1124. Berta/Bertha   born 27 Sep 1919 NY; died _____; married _____ O'BRIEN
> Children: Nancy -[8] born ca 1942 Hornell, NY; and Diane Elizabeth[8] O'BRIEN born July 1943 Hornell, NY

699. HARRIET[6] FELIX, sister of above, was born 22 June 1897 at Canton, Bradford County, NY. She married Jon George HUBERT , of Hornell, NY, on 17 Apr 1915. He was the son of Lorenz (Lawrence) HUBERT and Amelia A. SONNENBERG, and was born 8 Feb 1892 at Buffalo, Erie County. NY; died 3 Dec 1979 at North Hornell, Steuben County, NY. Harriet[6] FELIX died 16 June 1980.

Children of Harriet[6] FELIX and Jon HUBERT:
Surname **HUBERT**   (all children born Hornell, Steuben County, NY)

+	**1125. LUCILLE MARIE**	born 18 Jan 1916; died 27 May 2007 Houghton, Allegany, NY
		married Kenneth CROSTON 18 Jan 1934 Hornell ; divorced 1970
		(he s/o John W. CROSTON and Maude _____)
		(he born ca 1915; died 1978)
+	**1126. BETTY JUNE**	born 4 Sep 1921; died _____; divorced 1994
		married Norman K. WALKER 11 Oct 1947 Hornell, NY
+	**1127. HARRIETT JANE**	born 24 Mar 1925; died _____
		married Richard W. BRADLEY 9 Apr 1943 Atlanta, GA.
		(he born 25 July 1919; died 28 Dec 1996 Wellsville, Allegany, NY
+	**1128. ROSAMOND ANN**	born 29 Aug 1929 ; died _____
		married Jack G. ORDWAY 28 Sep 1948 Hornell, NY
		(he born ca 1927) (s/o Bertram J. ORDWAY and Elizabeth C. _____)

700. JAMES LESLIE-[6] HOWE, son of Thomas Lorenzo[5] HOWE (Estella[4] MC INTOSH; William-[3]; Simon-[2] Alexander-[1]) and Mary Margaret DWYER, was born 16 September 1898 at FallBrook, Tioga County, PA. He married Anna M. PRENDERGAST, ca _____. She was the daughter of _____ PRENDERGAST and _____, and was born 1895 NY; died _____ Corning, Chemung, NY. James L-[6] HOWE died March 1975 at Corning.

Children of James L-[6] HOWE and Anna M. PRENDERGAST:
Surname **HOWE**

1129. John D.	born ca 1921	1131. Harrison J.	born ca 1925
1130. Donald L.	born ca 1922	1132. Robert L.	born ca 1929

701. MARIE-[6] HOWE, sister of above, was born ca 1901, probably at FallBrook, Tioga County, PA. She married Edward L. BAVIS, as his second wife, on 16 Oct 1926 at Corning, NY. He was the son of William M. BAVIS and Theressa M. HEFFERNAN, and was born Jan 1886, died 30 Apr 1937. He was a railroad claims agent. His first marriage was to Irene WISER 5 Feb 1912. Marie-[6] HOWE died 9 April 1962 at Corning, Chemung, NY.

Children of Marie-[6] HOWE and Edward L. BAVIS:
Surname **BAVIS**

> 1133. Mary   born Sep 1929 NY; died _____
> 1134. Claire/Clare   born
> 1135. Ann Louise   born 15 July 1933; died 1 March 1989 Corning, NY

708. LAZELL HARRINGTON-[6] HOWE, son of Lazell Erstin-[5] HOWE (Estella[4] Mc INTOSH, William-[3], Simon-[2], Alexander-[1]) and Cora HARRINGTON, was born 2 July 1907 at Arnot, PA. He married Ida Mary TEACHMAN 25 Sept 1930 at _____. She was the daughter of Walter TEACHMAN and _____, and was born 21 Feb 1908 at Farmington, Tioga, PA; died _____. Lazell H-[6] HOWE died _____.

Children of Lazell H-[6] HOWE and Ida TEACHMAN:
Surname **HOWE**

1136. Joyce N.	born 27 Sep 1931, died ____, resided Penn Yan, NY
	married Robert DE MELLO
1137. **DONALD K.**	born 27 Feb 1935; died 28 Feb 2009
	married Marilyn SIMONDS ca 1959

709. ALICE E-[6] HOWE, sister of above, was born 16 Nov 1909 NY. She married Kenneth M. SNYDER ca 1930. He was the son of _____ SNYDER and ____, and was born ca 1909/10; died ca 1932. He was a news reporter for the Elmira Advertiser. Alice-[6] HOWE died 24 June 1995 Fort Worth, TX.

Children of Alice-[6] HOWE and Kenneth M. SNYDER:
Surname **SNYDER**

1138. Kenneth	born ca 1931 NY; died _____
1139. Richard	born ca 1932 NY; died _____

710. ADA LUCY[6] CRANDALL, daughter of Etta-[5] MC INTOSH (Henry-[4]; Matthias-[3]; Simon-[2]; Alexander-[1]) and Chester CRANDALL, was born 22 July 1887 at Pierrepont, St. Lawrence County, New York. She married Jesse T. WAIT(E) on 30 Dec 1912 at Potsdam, NY. He was the son of _____ WAIT(E) and _____, and was born 7 Dec 1886; died 27 Feb 1963 at Orlando, FL.

Ada Lucy-[6] CRANDALL died 12 Aug 1960 at Auburn, Cayuga County, NY.

Child of Ada Lucy-[6] CRANDALL and Jesse T. WAIT(E):
Surname **WAIT(E)**

1140. Ruth Elizabeth	born 24 Mar 1923 Auburn, NY; died 25 Dec 2002 Daytona Beach, FL
"Betty"	married Dr. D W BEARS 20 Jan 1945 Auburn, NY

Children: Jean-[8] born 16 Mar 1946; and Nancy-[8] BEARS born ____

715. STANLEY ORRIN[6] CRANDALL, brother of above, was born 21 Jan 1902 at Pierrepont, St. Lawrence County, NY. He married Dorothy CASTILLON on 15 Mar 1925. She was the daughter of Steven CASTILLON (born France) and Anna ____ (born Ireland) , and was born ca 1905 NY; died _____. Stanley Orrin-[6] CRANDALL died 5 Mar 1956 at _____.

Children of Stanley Orrin-[6] CRANDALL and Dorothy CASTILLON:
Surname **CRANDALL**

+ **1141. ANN ETTA**	born 22 Dec 1925 NY; died _____
	1 married Spiro Joseph PETERS 25 Feb 1951 Rochester, Monroe, NY
	Note: he was killed in the Korean War, lost over the Yalu River
	2 married William STEAR/SPEAR Oct 1954 (he born 16 Jan 1926)
+ **1142. ROBERT STEPHEN**	born 18 July 1927 Cranberry Lake, NY; died ____ 9 Oct 19__
	married Betty Ann WOLF 4 Sep 1948 Rochester, NY
	(she born 9 Oct 1927 NY; died 13 Sep 2007 Rochester, NY)
	(she dau/o Henry WOLF and Irene _____)

716. MARION LOUISE-[6] CRANDALL, sister of above, was born 11 Apr 1903 at Pierrepont, St. Lawrence County, NY. She married Norman Kenneth SHEPARD on 29 Nov 1924 at Skaneateles, Onondaga County, NY. He was the son of Norman J. SHEPARD and Inez _____, and was born 4 Oct 1903 Skaneateles, NY; died 27 Oct 1972 Corpus Christi, TX. They divorced ca ____. She married second to Arthur de HOLLANDER on 26 Nov 1955. He was the son of John J. de HOLLANDER and Elizabeth _____ (of Rochester, NY), and was born 24 Aug 1907, died Feb 1960. Marion Louise-[6] CRANDALL died 1 Feb 1976 Mc Callen, TX.

The Sixth American Generation

Children of Marion Louise-6 CRANDALL and Norman SHEPARD:
Surname **SHEPARD**

+	**1143. NORMA LOUISE**	born 16 Mar 1929 Skaneateles, NY; died _____ married William SCHULTZ 13 Nov 1947 Skaneateles (he born 31 Mar 1927 Auburn, NY; died ____)
+	**1144. DOROTHY JEAN**	born 13 Jan 1932 NY; died _____ married Selma A. DECKER 7 Aug 1948 Harlinger, TX (he born 22 Jan 1931; died 8 Nov 1992 Boca Raton, FL)

717. THERON WILBUR-6 HEWITT, son of Clara Elizabeth-5 MC INTOSH (Henry-4; Matthias-3 Simon-2; Alexander-1) and Martin HEWITT, was born 13 Feb 1887 at Colton, St. Lawrence County, NY. He married Mable/Mabel Captola GREEN on ____. She was the daughter of James A. GREEN and Captola M. NORMAN, and was born 3 July 1892; died 3 July 1957. Theron-6 HEWITT died 13 Sep 1949.

Children of Theron Wilbur-6 HEWITT and Mabel GREEN:
Surname **HEWITT**

+	**1145. GLENN HOWARD**	born 28 Aug 1913; died 15 Oct 1994 Potsdam, St. Lawrence, NY married Mabel VAUGHN ca 1933
+	**1146. FAY NELSON**	born 3 July 1915 NY; died 14 July 1995 Potsdam, NY married Bernice WHITCOMB 26 June 1954 (she born ca 1932; died 2000)
+	**1147. ALICE JUNE**	born 10 June 1920 NY; died 17 Mar 2005 Canton, NY married Ralph VAN BROCKLIN of Colton, NY

720. HENRY LEWIS-6 MC INTOSH, son of George Lewis-5 MC INTOSH (Henry-4; Matthias-3; Simon-2; Alexander-1) and Myrtle GRAVES, was born 27 July 1893 at ___, NY. He married 1st to Leah BROWN on 27 Oct 1920 at ____. She was born ____, and died during childbirth on 23 Feb 1922. Henry Lewis-6 MC INTOSH married 2nd to Erva PLUMB on 12 May 1940. She was the daughter of _____ PLUMB and _____, and was born 13 Dec 1909; died Oct 1971. Canton, St. Lawrence County, NY. Henry-6 MCIINTOSH died 9 Feb 1963 at ____, NY.

Children of Henry-6 MC INTOSH and Erva PLUMB:
Surname **MC INTOSH**

1148. Barbara Fay	born 25 May 1942; married Leon LA BRAKE 4 Sep 1959		
1149. Myrtle Ann	born 9 July 1943	1150. John Henry	born 6 Jan 1945

725. MYRTLE FRANCES-6 FREEMAN, daughter of Clara Bell-5 KIFF (Fanny-4 MC INTOSH; Matthias-3; Simon-2; Alexander-1) and George FREEMAN, was born 31 July 1887 at Alba, Bradford County, NY. She married Frank H. THOMAS , of Alba, on 17 Aug 1909. He was the son of _____ THOMAS and ____, and was born 17 July 1884 PA; died 10 Jan 1957. Myrtle Fances-6 died 5 July 1949.

Children of Myrtle Frances-6 FREEMAN and Frank THOMAS:
Surname **THOMAS**

1151. George Alvin	born 12 Aug 1910; died 19 Sep 1945 married Empsie WALKER 23 Jan 1933 (she born 23 Jan 1914) Child: Ronald Walker-8 THOMAS born 18 Apr 1937; married _____ Children of Ronald-8 : Greg-9; Jeff-9; Pam-9 and Mike-9 THOMAS
1152. Wayne Freeman	born 4 Sep 1913; died _____; married Helen MILLER EOL
1153. Francis Paul	born 29 Mar 1917 PA; died _____; married Ruth JAMES (she born 24 Nov 1920 NYC; died _____)

Children: James H-8 born ___, married Jane MEBUS, and Jane Ann-8 THOMAS born ____

726. FANNIE PEARL[-6] **FREEMAN**, sister of above, was born 7 Dec 1895 at ___ PA. She married George Albert GARD, of Towanda, PA, on 13 Jan 1917 at Williamsport, PA. He was the son of George B. GARD and Joanna POST, and was born 3 Mar 1892 PA; died 1 Aug 1978. Fannie Pearl[-6] FREEMAN died 8 May 1971 Wysox, PA.

Children of Fannie Pearl[-6] FREEMAN and George A. GARD:
Surname **GARD**

+	**1154. GEORGE EVERETT**	born 7 Nov 1918 Wysox Twsp, PA; died Feb 2003 Columbia, PA married Dorothy M. JOHNS 13 June 1942 Columbia, PA
+	**1155. WALTER FREEMAN**	born 26 Nov 1923 Wysox Twsp, PA; died 8 Feb 1977 Middletown, NY married Rose THOMSON 22 Nov 1950

732. RANDALL THOMAS[-6] **MC INTOSH**, son of Thomas[-5] MC INTOSH (Andrew[-4]; Matthias[-3]; Simon[-2]; Alexander[-1]) and Nelle WATKINS, was born 21 Aug 1911 at ___, PA. he married Julia Ann SPENCER on 25 Apr 1938 at ____, PA. She was the daughter of _____ SPENCER and ____, and was born 25 Apr 1918; died 15 Jan 1981, and is buried at Blossburg, PA. Randall T[-6] MC INTOSH died _____.

Children of Randall Thomas[-6] MC INTOSH and Julia Ann SPENCER:
Surname **MC INTOSH**

1156. Thomas Randall   born 18 Sep 1939 Blossburg, PA (married 5 times)
               married Susan LARSEN 23 June 1990;div; married Rebecca " Becky " Jackson
1157. James Lyman   born 25 Apr 1942 Blossburg, PA
               baptized 25 Aug 1962 at Canadian MC INTOSH reunion
               Children: John Patrick[-8] born___, married Karen Paige HELMS 13 Aug 1994; Michael[-8] born ___
1158. Richard Charles   born 1 Aug 1944, PA; baptized 25 Aug 1962 at Canadian reunion

733. MARIAN[-6] **MC INTOSH**, daughter of Frederick[-5] MC INTOSH (Lewis L[-4]; Matthias[-3]; Simon[-2]; Alexander[-1]) and Clara TREAT, was born 26 Sep 1917 at Blossburg, PA. She married Miles L. FENSTERMACHER, Jr. on 22 June 1941 at Mansfield, PA. He was the son of Miles FENSTERMACHER and ____, and was born 28 Apr 1915, died 18 Sep 1965. Marian[-6] died 5 July 2003 at Mansfield, PA.

Children of Marian[-6] MC INTOSH and Miles FENSTERMACHER, Jr.:
Surname **FENSTERMACHER**

+	**1159. PATSY/ PATRICIA**	born 12 Mar 1945 PA; 1 married Robert CALKINS 28 July 1966 Pottsgrove, PA; divorced 2 married John D. ACKLEY 18 Aug 1990
	1160. June	born 21 June 1946 Pottsgrove, PA Note: Enlisted in US Navy in May 1966 married Richard L TEAGUE; divorced no issue EOL
+	**1161. MILES L. III**	born 18 Apr 1948 Pottsgrove, PA. 1 married Nancy JONES ; div.; 2 married Michelle BURNS Dec 1984

736 ALFRED EARL[-6] **PALMER**, son of Clara Helen[-5] HARDING (Abigail Weeks[-4] MC INTOSH, Alexander[-3]; Simon[-2]; Alexander[-1]) and John Griffin PALMER, was born 30 Jan 1882, Bradford County, PA. He married Ann Jane KEELER on 3 Sep 1904. She was born 6 May 1879 at Sligo County, Ireland.

Child of Alfred[-6] PALMER and Ann Jane KEELER:
Surname **PALMER**

1162. Helen Jean   born 10 May 1909 Montclair, NJ
               married Clinton Hoffman HOUSEL 18 June 1932
               (he born 10 July 1907; died Apr 1984 Pennington, Mercer, NJ
               (he s/o Clinton Rittenhouse HOUSEL and Carrie HOFFMAN)
               Child: Clinton Palmer[-8] HOUSEL born 21 Feb 1936

737. MINA LEONE[6] HARDING, daughter of Curtis Merritt-[5] HARDING (Abigail-[4] Weeks MC INTOSH; Alexander-[3]; Simon-[2]; Alexander-[1]) and Mina AYRES, was born 22 June 1888 at Canton, PA. She married Michael Joseph MC NERNEY 22 June 1908 at ___. He was the son of John Joseph MC NERNEY and Catherine Celia FLANAGAN, and was born 27 Nov 1883; died 1949. Mina Leone-[6] died 16 June 1966 at Lancaster, PA. Buried Park Cemetery, Canton, PA. On the 1920 Census for Lancaster, Michael MC NERNEY was listed with the occupation as that of manager of a sand mine.

Children of Mina Leone-[6] HARDING and Michael J. MC NERNEY:
Surname **MC NERNEY**

1163. John Harding	born 27 July 1910/12; died 28 Sep 1918	EOL
1164. Mina Katherine	born 9 May 1914; died 28 Sep 2008 ; never married	EOL
1165. Michael Jr. "Mack"	born 20 June 1915 Honey Brook, PA; died Sept 1973 Bel Air, MD. married Frances Bernetta BURKHOLDER 25 June 1938 (she born 24 Apr 1908; died July 1978) (she of Honey Brook, PA) (she dau/o David Lee BURKHOLDER and Anna Moyer BOLL)	

Child: Patricia Kathleen-[8] MC NERNEY born 1941, died 1941

1166. Robert Edward	born 15 Oct 1922; died June 1945 Lancaster, PA
1167. James Francis ++	born 15 Apr 1928; died 16 Oct 2005 San Diego, CA. married Norma NEUMANN 30 May 1952 FL (she born ca 1931; died 2002)

Children: Steven -[8] and David-[8] MC NERNEY

++   **Obituary for James F. MC NERNEY**
James F. MC NERNEY,77, died October 16th (2005) in San Diego , CA. Born and raised in Lancaster (PA), he was a 1946 graduate of Lancaster Catholic High School. He was also a 1951 graduate of the US Naval Academy, and earned a Masters Degree in Aeronautical Engineering from MIT.   Jim and his late wife, Norma, were married for 50 years prior to her death in 2002. He is survived by his sister Mina K. MC NERNEY of Whiteville, NC; two sons, Steve of Ho Ho Kus, NJ, and David of Ramona, CA; 5 grandchildren, a nephew Michael J. MC NERNEY of Lancaster, and two nieces Eileen Steele of Lancaster and Maureen Donahue of Framingham, MA.. Jim spent 30 years in the US Navy, retiring with the rank of Captain. His last assignment was serving as military staff officer in the office of the Secretary of Defense. He then became project manager for the tomahawk cruise missile for General Dynamics Corporation and later formed the Military Avianics Division for TRW. Aviation was a life long passion, from building model airplanes to flying supersonic jets as a test pilot, to building his own radio controlled jet model airplanes.

742. ROBERT PERRY[6] MC INTOSH, JR. , son of Robert Perry-[5] MC INTOSH (Theophilus-[4]; George-[3]; Simon-[2]; Alexander-[1]) and Harriet JAMIESON, was born 21 Feb 1898 at Delhi, Delaware County, NY. He married Grace l. LEE of Newark, NY on ____ at ____. She was the daughter of ____ LEE and ____, and was born 8 Oct 1901; died Nov 1973. Robert Perry-[6] MC INTOSH died 14 Feb 1989.

Children of Robert Perry-[6] MC INTOSH, Jr. and Grace LEE:
Surname **MC INTOSH**

1168. Mary Louise	born 21 Sep 1935 Rome, NY married Joseph GLASS, Jr. ca 1960 (1967 resided Poultney, VT)
1169. Jeanette	born 8 Oct 1937 Rome, NY; married Albert SINNIGEN ca 1960

744. CHARLES LAMONT[6] MC INTOSH, brother of above, was born 18 Mar 1902 at Delhi, Delaware County, NY. He married Gertrude PALMITER ca 1933 at Rochester, Monroe County, NY. daughter of Harley E. PALMITER and Edna BULKLEY, and was born 19 Feb 1902 Brookfield, NY; died Nov 1993 Rochester, NY. Charles Lamont-[6] MC INTOSH died June 1976 at Rochester, NY.

Children of Charles Lamont-[6] MC INTOSH and Gertrude PALMITER:
Surname **MC INTOSH**

1170. Helen Claire	born 19 June 1935; married Thomas R. SCHRADER ca 1960 Rochester, NY
1171. Linda Jamieson	born 23 July 1939; married James D. HOWE ca 1967 Rochester, NY

746. FRANCES KEELER[-6] **MC INTOSH**, sister of above, was born ca 1908 at Delhi, Delaware County, NY. She married Hugh Gilchrist DICK, PhD of Delhi ca 1936. They were childhood sweethearts. He was the son of ____ DICK and _____, and was born at Whitehall, NY on 14 Sep 1909; died 31 Dec 1971 at Los Angeles , CA.

Hugh G. DICK., PhD received his BA from Union College in 1930, and his PhD from Cornell University, Ithaca, NY in 1937, the year in which he joined the faculty at UCLA. Hugh DICK was concerned from the beginning of his career with the relationship between science and literature.   "As a teacher, he won the affectionate admiration of distinguished doctoral students and beginning freshman alike by the gentle but precise guidance that he gave with contagious enthusiasm. ----
From 1960 -65 he was chairman of the Department of English, successfully implementing policies which brought that department to its position among the top twelve in the nation. ----- He was a member of the committee that in 1957 recommended the establishment of a school of library science at UCLA."   Quotations from an article written in 1975,In Memoriam of Hugh DICK, by Ada B. Nisbet, Lynn White, Jr. and James E. PHILLIPS

Child of Frances Keeler[-6] MC INTOSH and Hugh G. DICK:
Surname **DICK**
        1172. Robert McIntosh   born 12 Mar 1946 Los Angeles, CA

747. WALTER PERRY[-6] **MC INTOSH**, son of Charles Keeler[-5] MC INTOSH (Theophilus[-4]; George[-3]; Simon[-2;] Alexander[-1]) and Nelle ROGERS, was born 14 Jun 1889 at Delhi, Delaware County, NY. He married Mary Louise DURBIN on 5 Oct 1912 at Syracuse, Onondaga county, NY. She was the daughter of Frank I. DURBIN and Amelia DREYTHALER, and was born Oct 1891 Weedsport, Cayuga County, NY; died _____.   Walter[-6] MC INTOSH was a graduate of the Class of 1912, Syracuse University. He was an educator all of his life. He was an English teacher, later serving as a Vice-Principal at North High School, Syracuse, NY. Still later he became the Principal of Central High School, also in Syracuse. He died on 11 Nov 1972 , at the age of 83.

Children of Walter-[6] MC INTOSH and Mary Louise DURBIN:
Surname **MC INTOSH**

+	**1173. NORMA**	born 10 July 1913 Syracuse, NY; died 18 Oct 1969 Skaneateles, NY
		married Ralph HONSBERGER 1 Sep 1934
		(he born 4 Dec 1911; died 28 May 1991)
+	**1174. MARGERY**	born 10 Aug 1916 White Plains, NY; died _____
		married G. Frank DOLBEAR 3 May 1941 Syracuse, NY
		(he born 10 Aug 1914; died 15 Nov 1999 Syracuse, NY)

753. ROBERT WALTER[-6] **MC INTOSH**, son of George Walter[-5] MC INTOSH (Theophilus-[4]; George -[3]; Simon-[2]; Alexander[-1]) and Rella MC GONAGLE, was born 31 Jan 1908 at Louisville, KY. He married Edith HOBBS on 4 June 1932 at ____ KY.

Children of Robert-[6] MC INTOSH and Edith HOBBS:
Surname **MC INTOSH**
        1175. Patricia Jean   born ca 1934 ; 1 married Charles Thomas PATTON ca 1952
                Children: Denise Faye[-8] born ca 1953, married _____ HALL; and Jeffrie-[8] PATTON born ca 1958
        1176. Robert Dwight   born ca 1941; married Sandra Jean SCHNEIDER ca 1960

744. MERWIN KEELER[-6] **MC INTOSH**, son of Frank Edward-[5] MC INTOSH (Theophilus[-4], George[-3]; Simon-[2]; Alexander[-1]) and Fannie YENCER, was born 21 Oct 1912 at Delhi, Delaware county, NY. He married Margaret Rathburn ROYCE of Burlington, VT ca 1933. She was the daughter of Frank Bertrand ROYCE and Flora RATHBURN, and was born 24 Jan 1912; died ____ . Before retiring in 1959 to FL Merwin-6 ran the McIntosh Service Station in S. Burlington, VT. He died on 9 May 1991 at Pinellas, FL.

Children of Merwin Keeler-[6] MC INTOSH and Margaret ROYCE:
Surname **MC INTOSH**

1177. Frank Edward	born ca 1934; married _____	Child: Rob Roy-[8] MC INTOSH born ____
1178. James R.	born ca 1936; died ca 1959	never married EOL

758. MARGUERITE ESTHER-6 STERLING, daughter of William Tyler-5 STERLING (Sarah Adeline-4 MC INTOSH; Simon-3, Jr. ; Simon-2; Alexander-1) and Clara MC DONALD, was born 20 Oct 1899 at _____, PA. She married Charles Harold TRELAWNY of Torquet, England, on 21 Dec 1923 at New York, NY. He was born 21 Dec 1885 Torquet, England; died Jan 1932 at New York, NY. Marguerite-6 STERLING lived at Queens Village, LI, New York, moving to Syracuse, NY, where she died Nov 1978.

Children of Marguerite-6 STERLING and Charles TRELAWNY:
Surname **TRELAWNY**

	1179. Arthur William "Bill"	born 8 Dec 1924 PA; did 9 Dec 2005 Syracuse, NY married Jean LA MERANDE of Canada; divorced	EOL
+	**1180. ROBERT STERLING**	born 24 May 1926 PA; died_____ married Wilma BROWN of Syracuse, NY; divorced	
+	**1181. DR. GILBERT STERLING**	born 12 Nov 1929 NY; married Florence MULHOLLAND	

761. WILLIS BENJAMIN-6 GREENOUGH, son of Merton-5 GREENOUGH (Mary Caroline-4 MC INTOSH; Simon, Jr-3; Simon-2; Alexander-1) and Mary VAN HORN, was born 29 July 1884 Troy, Bradford County, PA. He married Nettie Hannah LEONARD ca 1913. She was the daughter of ____ LEONARD and ____, and was born 12 Feb 1888 East Troy, PA; died 1967. Willis-6 GREENOUGH died 9 Oct 1966 at Troy, PA.

Children of Willis-6 GREENOUGH and Nettie LEONARD:
Surname **GREENOUGH**

	1182. Merton Joseph	born 21 Feb 1918 Troy, Pa; died ____ married Ruth MAAG 9 Aug 1940 Washington, DC Children: Susan-8 born ____, and Amy-8 GREENOUGH born ____
+	**1183. JANET G.**	born 24 June 1919 Troy, PA; died 3 Feb 2003 Walter Reed Hospital married Angus C. GOODSON

764. CALEB C-6 GREENOUGH, son of Charles-5 GREENOUGH (Mary Caroline-4 MC INTOSH; Simon, Jr-3; Simon-2; Alexander-1) and Wrexieville CASE, was born 3 Jan 1893 at ____, PA. He married Gladys ALLYN on ____ at East Troy, PA. She was the daughter of Arthur ALLYN and Lottie ____, and was born 3 July 1903 Leona, PA; died 23 Jan 1993. Caleb C-6 GREENOUGH died 25 Mar 1987 E. Troy

Children of Caleb C-6 GREENOUGH and Gladys ALLYN:
Surname **GREENOUGH**

+	**1184. ROBERT HENRY**	born 18 Feb 1925 PA; died ____ married Shirley DUNBAR 14 Nov 1942 (she born 6 Oct 1925 PA)
+	**1185. DOROTHY**	born 27 Sep 1928 PA; died _____ married Edward AUSTIN 6 Apr 1948 Troy, PA (he born 30 May 1926 PA; died _____)
+	**1186. SHIRLEY**	born 12 Jan 1931 PA; died _____ married Milford KINSMAN 27 May 1950 (he born 28 Sep 1928 PA; died 2 July 2007 Troy ,PA) (he s/o Meredith KINSMAN and Myrtle _____)

765. HELEN CAROLINE-6 GREENOUGH, sister of above, was born 9 April 1894 at Troy, PA. She married Charles Tracey METZGER on 16 Sep 1916 at ___,PA. He was the son of William E. METZGER and Elinett MASOIR, and was born 24 Sep 1893 Blossburg, PA, died 25 Aug 1963. He was the owner of the Troy Marble and Granite Company, Troy, PA for many years. Helen C-6 GREENOUGH died ____.

Children of Helen[6] GREENOUGH and Tracy METZGER:
Surname **METZGER**

+   **1187. CHARLES LEE**   born 14 Apr 1922; died 24 Feb 2006 Elizabethtown, Lancaster, PA
                                         married Edith (Suzy) MERRICK 8 Mar 1947
                                         (she born 31 Dec 1920; died 24 Dec 2009)
          Note: Charles was a Mechanical Engineer, and traveled for his company to South Africa, Europe, Australia and Japan

+   **1188. PHILIP F.**   born 3 July 1925 PA; died 14 Feb 2004 Columbia Crossroads, PA
                                         1 married Anise SMITH 11 Aug 1956 (she born 9 May 1931)
                                         2 married Lorraine BAILEY York

767. PAIGE HENRY[6] GREENO(UGH), brother of above, was born 27 Feb 1897 at Troy, Bradford, PA. He married Eula Marian KNOWLDEN 11 Oct 1926. She was the daughter of Harry KNOWLDEN and Marion Kirkwood INNES, and was born 12 Sep 1900 ; died 7 Nov 1981 at Elmira, Chemung, NY. Paige[6] GREENO(UGH) died Oct 1980 at Elmira, Chemung, NY.

Child of Paige[6] GREENO(UGH) and Eula KNOWLDEN:
Surname **GREENO(UGH)**

      1189. Charles Henry   born 1 May 1939; NY;   married Edith HAINES 22 Sep 1962
              Children: Pamela[8] born 19 Sep 1963 and Debbie[8] GREENO(UGH) born Oct 1966

768. IDA MAE[6] GREENOUGH, sister of above, was born 10 Sep 1898 at Troy, Bradford, PA. She married Howard Alfred DUNBAR on 8 Sep 1920. He was the son of Burt DUNBAR and Emma HEIDA, and was born ca 1896, PA; died July 1933. Ida Mae-[6] GREENOUGH died 28 Nov 1989.

Children of Ida Mae-[6] GREENOUGH and Howard DUNBAR:
Surname **DUNBAR**

      1190. Beatrice Elaine   born 19 Aug 1923; died of polio on 11 Aug 1952
                         married Harry HAGER, Jr.   Child: Martin-[8] HAGER born 8 June 1951

769. PAUL ELDON-[6] GREENOUGH, brother of above, was born 31 July 1900 at Troy, Bradford, PA. He married Ina Russell TOMLINSON ca 1920. She was the daughter of V. Edward TOMLINSON and Isabell M. HAVENS, and was born 6 Sep 1901; died 12 Jan 1996. Paul E-[6] GREENOUGH died 16 May 2000 Resided Gillett, PA.

Paul-[6] GREENOUGH had a fascination for the railroad from the time he was a little boy, and when he was 18 he went to work for the Pennsylvannia Railroad. He worked at the Southport Yards in Elmira where he was a brakeman. He also traveled on trains that were taking coal from Elmira to Williamsport. When he first began they would haul 45-50 cars of coal to a train, later when the steam engines came into being, they could haul 85-90 cars. He had a second reason for loving the railroad, for that was where he met his future wife. She was riding the train to get to Meeker Business School in Elmira. They married in 1920 and he took her on a train ride to Niagara Falls. Their marriage lasted over 75 years.

Children of Paul Eldon-[6] GREENOUGH and Ina TOMLINSON:
Surname **GREENOUGH**

+   **1191. MARJORIE**   born 16 Oct 1921 PA; died 18 Dec 2007 Mansfield, Tioga, PA
                                     married Kirtland Peter CLARK
                                     (he born 28 Apr 1921 Covington, PA; died 13 Apr 2000 Mansfield)
                                     (he s/o William CLARK and Florence Esther BRUIELLY)
      1192. C. Edward   born 27 Nov 1923; 6 Mar 2000 (see KIFF section # 514)
                                     married De Lecia Mae DIX ca 1944/45; divorced
                                     (she dau/o Lewis Edward DIX and Hazel CONGDON)
                                     (she born 6 July 1922 Gillett, PA; died 3 Oct 2008 Cresswell, OR)
              Children : Dale-[8] born 11 Jan 1947 and Stephen-[8] GREENOUGH born 27 Aug 1949
      1193. Paul Eldon, Jr.   born 27/29 Jan 1928; married Helen RODGER 1 Aug 1954
              Child: Paul Gregg-[8] GREENOUGH born 14 Jan 1960

Children of Paul [6] GREENOUGH and Ina TOMLINSON, continued:
Surname **GREENOUGH**

1194. Donna Jean   born 30 Jan 1933; married William BEECHEY, Jr. 4 July 1952
Children: Danielle[8] born 17 July 1953 and Rodney[8] BEECHEY born 5 Sep 1957

770. MARY ELIZABETH[6] (Beth) STERLING, daughter of Frederick James[5] STERLING (Elizabeth [4] MC INTOSH; Simon, Jr[3]; Simon[2]; Alexander[1]) and Nancy Mae WILLIAMS, was born 4 Feb 1888 at Canton, Bradford County, PA. She married Harry Jacob EY ca 1908/09. He was the son of August EY (born Germany) and Lillian T._____ (born NY), and was born 19 Sep 1879 NY; died ca 1945/46 Cranston, RI. He operated a wholesale grocery business in Cranston. Mary Elizabeth-[6] STERLING died there on 17 March 1974.

Children of Mary Elizabeth-6 STERLING and Harry J. EY:
Surname **EY**

1195. Beatrice Elizabeth	born 5 Aug 1910; died Jan 1995 North Hampton, NH
	1 married Richard Grunwell AARON; divorced; no issue
	(he s/o James C. AARON and Helen GRUNWELL)
	(he born 6 Jan 1906 PA; died 5 Mar 1946 Alameda, CA)
	2 married Homer STODDARD no issue EOL
	(he born 9 Feb 1907 ; died Oct 1985 North Hampton, NH)
1196. Clifford Sterling	born 13 July 1917; died Feb 1976 Warwick, RI
	married Elizabeth SEATON ____ Providence, RI
	(she born 30 Apr 1922; died _____)

Children: Frederick Sterling-[8] EY born 31 Oct 1952 RI; Thomas Seaton-[8] EY born 3 July 1955 RI
Note: Frederick Sterling EY, MD at Pacific Oncology PC, Tualitin, Oregon

771. CHARLES LEE[6] STERLING, brother of above, was born 19 Dec 1890 at Canton, Bradford County, PA. He was born on the site of the original Simon MC INTOSH farm on Curran Mountain, outside of Canton, PA. When he was 11 or 12 years of age, his parents moved to a farm at 298 Troy Street, Canton. He attended schools there, graduating from Canton High School.

At age 19 or 20, he decided that he would like to travel cross country and experience " first-hand" this beautiful land from coast to coast and from top to bottom. He traveled, mostly by rail, to 44 of the then 48 states plus the Territory of Alaska. In that era, he was probably considered a "hobo".

He stopped at various places, and worked to earn enough money to continue his journey. After nearly two years, he had seen much of the country and so he decided that he would return East and begin his studies for the ministry. He entered Cazenovia Seminary (later Cazenovia College) located east of Syracuse, NY in Madison County. He was working his way through college, serving as a handyman, waiter etc. when our countries' involvement in World War 1 commenced. It was here, also, that he met his future wife, Hazel Frances DOTY. The day after War was declared he went to Syracuse, NY to enlist in the US Navy. (16 Apr 1917)

During his service "Lee" STERLING kept a diary of his experiences, including the torpedoing and sinking of his ship, the USS WESTOVER on 11 July 1918. Prior to service on the USS WESTOVER, he had made seven or eight trips across the Atlantic on the USS MONTANA. Those trips had been more or less uneventful, and there had been no encounters with German U-boats. On his first trip aboard the USS WESTOVER, a merchant ship which had been converted to a Navy escort vessel, things changed drastically.

124

On the 28th of June 1918, the WESTOVER experienced engine trouble, and had to stop in mid-ocean. The convoy, of which they were a member, slowed and waited for them a reasonable length of time, but informed the WESTOVER that the convoy needed to continue on, advising the Captain of the WESTOVER that he should turn around and head state-side. After an extended period of time, the repair of the main air pump was completed. At that time the ships' Captain decided that they would not head state-side, but continue on and catch up with the convoy.

On the 29th of June, he wrote in his diary, that. they were desperately trying to overtake the convoy. Again, on July 4th he wrote that they still had not been able to re-join the convoy. On that day also, they received an SOS from the USS WESTGATE, whose Captain stated the " they were being chased by a submarine". The Captain of the WESTOVER still insisted that they could make up the distance between themselves and their convoy. They seemed to be plagued with engine problems, but received no more news of submarine activity.

On the 11th of July 1918, their luck "ran out" and at approximately 7:30 AM the WESTOVER was hit mid ship with a torpedo from a German U-boat. Another followed shortly, and within an hour the WESTOVER was below the surface of the Atlantic.

Lee STERLING had just settled into his hammock, after working in the engine room all night. He was still fully dressed because of the fact that they were in a "battle zone" and needed to be ready for this type of event. He rushed to his battle station within seconds, as the word had already been given to abandon ship as soon as the main engines had been shut down.

The lifeboat that he was assigned to, had already been lowered before the engines were stopped, and it was drawn into the propeller, with all 11 crew members being killed. Fortunately, the rest of the crew members were able to survive the disaster. They drifted at sea, in an open lifeboat, for five days and four nights before they were rescued by an American destroyer, the USS CONNER.

Five days and four nights in an open life boat with little to eat or drink. Hot days and very cold nights, clothing wet all the time made it a severe ordeal on the men. When they were finally rescued, Lee STERLING, and the others, were suffering from exposure and literally unable to walk. This exposure caused Lee STERLING to suffer from rheumatoid arthritis the remainder of his life.

He was able to complete studies for the ministry at Syracuse University, and was ordained a Methodist minister in the Central New York Conference. He had to retire prematurely because his physical condition did not allow him to function as needed. His first church had been at Sterling, NY and he served as a pastor to the South Onondaga and Indian Reservation churches. He worked off and on at various other endeavors, as his health allowed and died on 6 Mar 1942 Syracuse, NY. He is buried next to his wife at North Syracuse, NY

He married Hazel Frances[9] DOTY on 21 March 1921 at Syracuse, NY. She was the daughter of John Christy[8] DOTY, Jr. (John Christy[7]; Britton[6]; William[5,4]; Jacob[3]; Isaac[2]; Edward[1] DOTY/DOTEN of the **MAYFLOWER**).

Children of Charles Lee[6] STERLING and Hazel Frances[9] DOTY:
Surname **STERLING**
+   1197.   **PAUL**   born 15 Apr 1922 Syracuse, NY;
           DE WITT   1 married Mildred G. BALCOM   May 1943 North Syracuse, NY
                            (she born 13 Sep 1924; died Jan 1991) divorced
                            (she dau/o Charles Alvin BALCOM and Leona Marcia LIGHTHALL)
                            2 married Josephine SHUBA 21 Aug 1946 Syracuse, NY
                            (she dau/o Lewis SHUBA and Stella SCHURICK) (born 21 Mar 1920)

Children of Charles Lee-[6] STERLING and Hazel Frances-[9] DOTY, continued:
Surname **STERLING**

+	**1198. FRANCES JEAN**	born 3 June 1927 Syracuse, NY; _____
		1 married George Dolbey DRISKO 31 Jan 1947 Syracuse, NY
		(he born 16 Nov 1917 Syracuse, NY; died 14 Jan 1994)
		(he s/o Henry William DRISKO and Leah Belle DOLBEY)
		2 married Paul Edward BOWKER 29 Mar 2003 NC

774. ARTHUR BURDELL-[6] DANN, son of Sterling James-[5] DANN (Electa Adelia-[4] MC INTOSH; Simon-[3], Jr.; Simon-[2]; Alexander-[1]) and Ethel HAVENS, was born 15 June 1892 at Canton, Bradford, PA. He married Margaret Johanna ENGLISH ca 1914. She was the daughter of Harvey Rufus ENGLISH and Bertha M. FERGU(N)SON, and was born July 1891 Granville, Bradford, PA; died Apr 1972 Canton, PA. Arthur B-[6] DANN died Oct 1970 at Canton, PA. In 1942 he worked at an Electrical Supply Co.

Children of Arthur B-[6] DANN and Margaret ENGLISH
Surname **DANN**

+	**1199. MARJORIE RUTH**	born 8 Mar 1915; died 9 May 2007; 1 married James John GALLO
		2 m. Leo H. LEWIS; 3 m. Edward Dow VAN DYNE 18 Oct 1958 NY
	1200. Betty Jane	born 27 Sep 1921; married _____ WAKEFIELD

775. LELAND-[6] DANN, brother of above, was born 26 June 1893 at Granby, NY. He married Renee' F. _____, in France after World War 1 . She was the daughter of _____ and _____, and was born 11 Dec 1895 (possibly France or Monaco); died 27 Mar 1968. Leland-[6] DANN was a Sgt. in the US Army during WW1 , and later served in the US Embassy until his retirement in ____. Leland-[6] DANN died Aug 1964 NY and is buried with his wife at the Long Island National Cemetery.

Child of Leland-[6] DANN and Renee' F. _____:
Surname **DANN**

1201. SONIA ETHEL	born 21 Oct 1922 France /Monaco; died 24 Oct 2007 Hudson, Pasco, FL
	1 married _____ BARR; 2 married Robert Harley CHRISTY

778. GRACE-[6] DANN, sister of above, was born 21 Mar 1901 at Canton, Bradford County, PA. She married George E. WHITING on 19 Jan 1924 at Canton, PA. he was the son of William WHITING and _____, and was born _____; died ____. Grace-[6] DANN died 4 Sep 1970 at Cortland, Cortland, NY. They divorced ca 1940 in Fl.

Children of Grace-[6] DANN and George WHITING:
Surname **WHITING**

+	**1202. GEORGE DANN**	born 5 Nov 1924 Canton, PA; died Feb 1986
		1 married Gwendolyn LAPE/LAPSE
		2 married Mila M. _____ (she born Nov 1948)
+	**1203. JAMES VINCENT**	born 19 May 1926 Canton, PA; died _____
		married Bernita M. BLANCHARD 20 Nov 1945
		(she born 31 Jan 1928; resided Solano Beach, CA)
		(she dau/o Oscar A. BLANCHARD and Elsie B. _____)
	1204. William Sterling	born 8 Oct 1932 Montour Falls, NY;
		married Ruth O'NEILL 18 Aug 1958 no issue EOL

784. WILLIAM GEORGE-[6] MC INTOSH, son of William John-[5] MC INTOSH (Charles-[4]; Simon-[3], Jr.; Simon-[2;] Alexander-[1]) and Eva MAC KNESS, was born 13 Sep 1925 at _____. He married Clara HURLBURT on ___ at ___. She was the daughter of _____ HURLBURT and _____, and was born ____, died ____. He was in the service during WW2. They resided Canton, Bradford, PA.

Child of William George[6] MC INTOSH and Eva MAC KNESS;
Surname **MC INTOSH**

    1205. Linda   born 12 Aug 1951 Canton, PA; died _____
                             married Roscoe BOWLING, Jr. 12 June 1971 Canton, PA.
                   Child: Dixie Michelle[8] BOWLING born 24 Jan 1976 Troy, PA

790. EDWARD D[6] CEASE, son of Charles[5] CEASE (Leroy[4]; Julia Ann[3] MC INTOSH; Simon[2]; Alexander[1]) and Gertrude WRIGHT, was born 13 Mar 1905 at Canton, PA. He married Ruth Eileen BACORN ca 1938 at ____. She was the daughter of Floyd Parker BACORN and Julia Elizabeth CHAPMAN, and was born ca 1917; died 15 Mar 2002. Edward D[6] CEASE died 31 July 1984 at Troy, PA.

Children of Edward[6] CEASE and Ruth BACORN:
Surname **CEASE**

    1206. Shirley   born _____ ; married David MANZER of Troy, PA
    1207. Julia /Judy   born _____ ; married Philip TAYLOR of Troy, PA
    1208. Ronald   born _____ ; died 1997   resided Clarks Summit, PA

793. HAZEL FLORENCE[6] LANDON-, daughter of Lillian[5] " Nellie " CEASE (Leroy[4]; Julia Ann[3] MC INTOSH; Simon[2]; Alexander[1]) and Robert LANDON, was born 15 Oct 1895 at ____ PA. She married Edward Eleazer RYAN on 25 Feb 1914 at ____. He was the son of _____ RYAN and _____, and was born 14 Mar 1888 PA; died 1964. Hazel[6] LANDON died Aug 1977.

Children of Hazel[6] LANDON and Edward RYAN:
Surname **RYAN**

+   **1209. WILLIAM**   born 5 Feb 1915; died _____ ; married Lucille HAMMOND
                              (she born ca 1918; died ____)
                              (she dau/o Ray HAMMOND and Nina H ____ of Elmira, NY)
    1210. Edward, Jr.   born 16 Aug 1917 ; died ____; married Rose RICE ca ____
                 Children: Edward[8] III born ____ , and Mary[8] RYAN born ____
+   **1211. LEWIS / LOUIS**   born 18 Nov 1918; died Oct 1983 Elmira, NY; married Cleo DECKER
    1212. Cleo M.   born 25 Jan 1921; died 10 Sep 1987 Elmira, NY   EOL
    1213. James   born 7 July 1925; died 10 July 1944; WW 2 Infantry – France

794. LEWIS / LOUIS[6] LANDON, brother of above, was born 7 Dec 1898 PA. He married Marie MC CLURE on 26 June 1925 at Corning, NY. She was the daughter of Adam MC CLURE and Mary ____, and was born ca 1903 NY. Lewis/Louis[6] LANDON, a civil engineer for Elmira, NY. He died Apr 1953 NY.

Children of Lewis[6] LANDON and Marie MC CLURE :
Surname **LANDON**

+   **1214. MARY LOU**   born 15 Oct 1924 NY; died 12 Nov 1982; married Ellis Frederic HAVENS
                              (he born 5 May 1924; died 17 Feb 1999 Elmira, NY)
                              (he s/o Carl Edward HAVENS and Esther Dean CRANDALL)
+   **1215. ROBERT**   born 10 July 1927, died May 1978 Corning, Steuben, NY
                              married Rita M. SCHIEFEN 7 Oct 1950 Elmira, NY
                              (she dau/o Carl SCHIEFEN and Mary Evelyn DUNN)
                              (she born 15 May 1929; died 27 Oct 2006 Horseheads, Chemung, NY
    1216. Nancy   born 14 Dec 1936

795. EMILY LEAH-[6] WELCH, daughter of Belle[5] CEASE (Nelson[4]; Julia[3] MC INTOSH; Simon[2]; Alexander[1]) and Frank Welch, was born ca 1897 at ____. She married Milo Denton TILLOTSON on ____ at _____. He was the son of Denton Morrell TILLOTSON and Arminda E. BELLOWS, and was born 24 Oct 1898 Canton, PA; died May 1969 Canton. Leah[6] WELCH died ca 1970.

Children of Emily Leah[6] WELCH and Milo TILLOTSON:
Surname **TILLOTSON**

1217. Beatrice Lowanda	born ca 1923; died 1994; 1 married _____ BROWN
	2 married Francis Edward PUTNAM (born 1917, died 1957)
1218. Marguerite L.	born ca 1926; died 1 Jan 2012
	married John D. CHAMPION; (he born ca 1924)
1219. Franklin R.	born ca 1924; married Madeline MOTT (living 2012)

797. LYSLE WILLARD[6] CEASE, son of Willard Lewis-[5] CEASE (Nelson-[4]; Julia Ann-[3] MC INTOSH; Simon-[2;] Alexander-[1]) and Edith MOORE, was born 17 Oct 1903 at Armenia Mountain, Canton, Bradford, PA. He graduated from the US Naval Academy, Annapolis, MD. with a rank of Ensign in the Class of 1926. He spent the next 30 years in the service of the US Navy, rising to the rank of Captain. When he retired from the Navy he went into Real Estate sales and spent another 16 years in that career at Napa, CA. In his later years he resided in Florida where he had horses and a 36' Chris Craft boat, which as he said " kept him busy and broke." Lysle -[6] CEASE married Alwyn Christina WYLE ca ____. She was the daughter of Dr. Edwin Arthur WYLE and Alice Louise SMITH, and was born 27 Apr 1927 in Buenos Aires, Argentina, died 15 Mar 2001. Her father was a clergyman , born in England, who traveled extensively and came to America from Canada in Aug 1920.   Lysle-[6] CEASE died 25 Apr 1992. He and his wife are buried at Arlington National Cemetery, Arlington, VA.

Children of Lysle Willard[6] CEASE and Alwyn Christina WYLE:
Surname **CEASE**

+	**1220. JACQUELINE ANN**	born ca 1930, married James Walter AILSTOCK, Jr. before 1950 1950 resided Beckley, WV; 1980 resided Virginia Beach,VA
+	**1221. STEPHEN W.**	born ca 1933; married _____
		Note: 1980 – held rank of Major in the USAF reserve, was a pilot for Pan American Airlines
+	**1222. DIANA BEECHING**	born 15 May 1936 Brooklyn, NY; married Christopher NICHOLSON (he born Mar 1929 NJ) 1980 resided Englewood, NJ

799. NELSON DUDLEY[6] CEASE, brother of above, was born 26 Sep 1909 at Bradford County, PA. He married first to Beatrice ____. (Nothing more known about her) His second wife was Cleo Wilma FULLER Leighton, and they were married on 21 July 1948 at ____. She was the daughter of Clyde William FULLER and Myrtle HOGABOOM, and was born ca 1921 PA; died ____. Her first husband was Floyd E. LEIGHTON. Nelson Dudley-[6] CEASE died 4 Dec 2000 at Canton, Bradford, PA.

Children of Nelson[6] CEASE and Beatrice ____:
Surname **CEASE**

1223. Norman   born _____   1224. Sharon   born ___; married Ed MC NETT

Child of Neslon[6] CEASE and Cleo Wilma FULLER:
Surname **CEASE**

1225. William A.   born _____; married Rosalie SCHANBACHER; res. Tulsa, OK

801. HELEN L[6] KIFF, daughter of Lucy M-[5] CEASE (Nelson-[4;] Julia Ann-[3] MC INTOSH; Simon-[2;] Alexander-[1]) and Delos E. KIFF, was born 31 July 1909 at Geneva, Ontario County, NY. She married James STRAUSS on ___ at ___. He was the son of Isaac E. STRAUSS and Fannie____, and was born 6 Jan 1908, died 26 June 1994 Horseheads, Chemung County, NY. Helen[6] KIFF died 28 Aug 1998 NY.

Children of Helen[6] KIFF and James STRAUSS:
Surname **STRAUSS**

1226. Richard	born poss. ca 1933	1228. Linda	born _____
1227. John M.	born ____	1229. Donna L.	born _____

806. DORIS MAY[6] **CEASE**, daughter of Herman Theophilus-[5] CEASE (Sidney-[4;] Julia Ann-[3] MC INTOSH; Simon-[2;] Alexander-[1]) and Loda BRIGGS, was born 21 April 1910 at Rhinelander, Wisconsin. She married Clinton A. JOHNSON ca 1927. He was the son of _____ JOHNSON and _____, and was born ca 1904 MN; died _____. Doris-[6] CEASE committed suicide on 23 June 1958.

Children of Doris-[6] CEASE and Clinton JOHNSON:
Surname **JOHNSON**

1230. Patricia	born 9 Dec 1929 IL; died _____
"Tricia"	married Wendell Robert KNUDSEN
	(he s/o Christian Frederick KNUDSEN and Edna Spra REED)
	(he born 3 Oct 1931; died 21 Oct 2009, MI)
1231. Norma	born _____; died 1988/89 (cancer)

797. LUTHER EARL [6] **CEASE**, son of Fred A-[5] CEASE (Sidney-[4;] Julia Ann-[3] MC INTOSH; Simon-[2;] Alexander-[1]) and Della JOHNSON, was born 10 July 1903 at Harbor Springs, Michigan. He married Beatrice Blossom DOVE on ___ at ____. She was the daughter of Albert DOVE and Ina M. ____, and was born 24 Oct 1904 at Emmett County, MI; died _____. Luther-[6] CEASE died ca 1957 from cancer. Beatrice married second to Lionel (Frenchie) BROSSEAU. She died 1995.

Children of Luther [6] CEASE and Beatrice DOVE:
Surname **CEASE**

+	**1232. BETTY JUNE**	born 4 Dec 1929 Harbor Springs, MI; 1 married Edward JOHNSEN (he born 1 Apr 1932 Hood River, OR; ____) 2 married John CHRISTIANSEN
+	**1233. LUTHER LLOYD**	born 12 Oct 1933 Harbor Springs; died 5 May 2005 Hood River OR married Bonnie June MAYS 1956 (she born 3 June 1932 Hood River) Note: He died from prostate cancer

809. ROBERT[6] **LANE (Walsh)**, son of Julia M-[5] CEASE (Sidney-[4;] Julia Ann-[3] MC INTOSH; Simon- [2;] Alexander-[1]) and John W. LANE, was born ca 1907 at ____. His mother and father were divorced when he was about a year old, and his step-father (David WALSH) wanted him to go by the name of WALSH, although he never legally adopted him. According to close relatives, his step-father abused him, which made him timid and insecure. He had a phobia/ aversion to marriage, although he lived for a number of years with a Phyllis Mary COOK, by whom he had two sons. After his death, she married a ____ RICHARD who legally adopted his sons. Robert LANE Walsh committed suicide by carbon monoxide poisoning on Christmas Eve (24 Dec 1934) at Windsor, Ontario, Canada.

Children of Robert-[6] LANE Walsh and Phyllis Mary COOK:
Surname **WALSH (later Richard)**

+	**1234. DONALD EUGENE**	born 26 Feb 1929 Ontario, Canada ; died ____ married Barbara Sue SEARLE 21 Oct 1950
+	**1235. ROBERT GEORGE**	born 22 Apr 1932 Ontario, Canada; died 25 July 1990 married Joan PATRICK

810. HELEN[6] **WALSH**, half-sister of above , daughter of Julia M-[5] CEASE (Sidney-[4;] Julia Ann-[3] MC INTOSH; Simon-[2;] Alexander-[1]) and David WALSH, was born 16 Aug 1911 Ontario, Canada. She married Joseph DALPE on 9 Dec 1933. He was the son of _____ DALPE and _____, and was born _____.

Child of Helen-[6] WALSH and Joseph DALPE:
Surname **DALPE**

+	**1236. THEODORE EUGENE**	born 10 Sep 1934; died 4 Apr 1963 Flint, MI. married Mary Ann LEWANDOWSKI Jan 1961; divorced

812. GORDON-6 **WALSH**, brother of above, was born 8 Feb 1918 at Blenheim, Ontario, Canada. He married Kathleen Frances LEAVER on 16 May 1942. She was the daughter of _____ LEAVER and ____, and was born 11 May 1918 Windsor, Ontario, Canada; died _____. Gordon-6 WALSH died 20 Oct 1971 at Detroit, Michigan.

Children of Gordon-6 WALSH and Kathleen Frances LEAVER:
Surname **WALSH**

+	**1237. MAUREEN ANN**	born 4 May 1945 Windsor, Ontario, Canada
		married William Edward STENBACK 26 Aug 1967
		(he born 29 Jan 1943 Detroit, MI;)
+	**1238. MARY LOU**	born 30 Apr 1948 Windsor, Ontario
		married Lawrence JACOB 26 July 1968; divorced
	1239. Robert Arthur	born 22 Mar 1954 Windsor, Ontario

817. LAWRENCE RICHARD-6 " **Bud** " **CEASE**, son of Carl-5 CEASE (Sidney-4; Julia Ann-3 MC INTOSH; Simon-2; Alexander-1) and Sylvia E. BOETTGER   , was born 11 July 1914 at Harbor Springs, Michigan. He married Betty June ROBINSON ca 1938. She was the daughter of _____ ROBINSON and ___, and was born 21 June 1922; died 1994. Lawrence-6 CEASE died 24 June 1986 at Resort, Emmett, MI

Children of Lawrence-6 CEASE and Betty ROBINSON:
Surname **CEASE**

	1240. David L.	born 3Oct 1938; died 19 May 1992; married Patty WARD
	1241. Ronald	born 17 May 1941; married Becky MARSHALL
+	**1242. KATHERINE DAWN**	born 25 Sep 1943; died 2000
		married Alton Leroy RADLE 8 Mar 1961(he born ca 1936; died 1999
	1243. Patricia	born _____; married Randy LAUER
	1244. Vicky	born 9 June 1955; married Wesley MC COY

Adopted son: Randall[8] Mc COY born 16 Oct 1959

819. NINA MAE-6 **CEASE**, sister of above, was born 30 Sep 1918 at Harbor Springs, Michigan. She married Byron Russell LIGHTFOOT on 25 Jan 1936. He was the son of Edward F. LIGHTFOOT and Mabel Edith GOODRICH, and was born 24 Jan 1913; died 10 Aug 1995 Harbor Springs. Nina Mae-6 CEASE died 6 Nov 1998 Harbor Springs, MI.

Children of Nina Mae-6 CEASE and Byron LIGHTFOOT:
Surname **LIGHTFOOT**

+	**1245. RHODA MAE**	born 18 Mar 1936 Emmett Co., MI
		1 married Robert J. FARRELL 11 Sep 1954 Harbor Springs, Mi
		(he born 5 May 1935 Charlevoix, MI)
		2 married Roger RITTER 30 Jan 1973
		(he s/o Willard T. RITTER and Isabelle A KNEIPER)
	1246. Leona Marie	born 20 Oct 1937; died same day
	1247. IMELDA JEAN	born 15 Feb 1939, Petoskey, MI.
		married Gerald Duane HOFBAUER 22 July 1957
		(he born 28 Sep 1935)
+	**1248. ALVIN LA RAY**	born 22 May 1941 Emmett Co., MI; died 21 Feb 2003 Harbor Springs
		married Susan Jane GARVER (she born 20 Mar 1943)
	1249. Marilyn Joyce	born 14 Oct 1943 Emmett Co., MI
		1 married Charles SCHLAPPI (he born 28 Dec 1943; died 5 Apr 1977
		2 married Robert TRUMAN 25 Mar/May 1983
		(he born 23 Aug 1947) (he had 3 children from a previous marriage)

824. JUANITA MARY-6 **BOETTGER**, daughter of Mildred Irene-5 CEASE (Sidney-4; Julia Ann-3 MC INTOSH; Simon-2; Alexander-1) and William Henry BOETTGER, was born 12 Apr 1916 Ayr, MI. She married William Alexander NEWSOME on 6 Jan 1937 at Levering, MI. He was the son of ___ NEWSOME and ____, and was born 22 Aug 1916 at Harbor Springs, MI; died 8 Apr 2000 at Alanson, MI. Juanita Mary-6 BOETTGER died 9 Oct 1993 at Harbor Springs, MI.

Children of Juanita Mary-6 BOETTGER and William NEWSOME:
Surname **NEWSOME**

	1250. Nelda Mae	born 5 May 1940 Petoskey, MI
		1 married George JONES 5 March 1976; divorced
		(he born 1 May 1936 Banner Elk, NC)
		2 married John HORNYAK 22 Feb 1985
	1251. William James	born 14 June 1941 Petoskey, MI
+	**1252. ARTHUR GEORGE**	born 18 Nov 1944 Cheboygan, MI
		married Tani DARLING 19 Dec 1964 (she born 10 Jan 1946)
	1253. Mary Lynn	born 18 July 1947 Cheboygan, MI
+	**1254. KENNETH EDWARD**	born 23 April 1952 Cheboygan, MI
		married Tina WINANS 24 Sep 1981 (she born 5 Sep 1962)
+	**1255. DENISE RENEE**	born 16 June 1958 Cheboygan, MI
		married Edward RHEW 13 Nov 1976 (as his 2nd wife)
		(he born 19 Dec 1953 Carp Lake, MI)

825. WILLIS EARL-6 **BOETTGER**, brother of above, was born 25 Dec 1917 at Ayr, Michigan. He married Louise HERZIG on 14 Nov 1941 at Monticello, Missouri. She was the daughter of Joseph HERZIG and Louise NAVROTRIL of Czechoslovakia., and was born 14 Nov 1920 in Glencoe, IL.; died _____. Willis-6 BOETTGER died 23 Mar 1988 at Spenard, Alaska.

Children of Willis-6 BOETTGER and Louise HERZIG:
Surname **BOETTGER**

	1256. Billie Joe	born 23 Feb 1943 Evanston, IL; died 20 Apr 1968 Anchorage, AK
	1257. Un-named boy	born 28 Oct 1945 Evanston, IL; stillborn
+	**1258. CAROL LEE**	born 2 Feb 1947 Evanston, IL.
		married James MURDOCK 17 Jan 1964
		(he born 13 Oct 1942 Detroit, MI)
+	1259. Patrick John	born 10 Nov 1949 Evanston, IL.
		married Judith ROSS 12 Sep 1973 (she born Aug 1948 Anchorage, AK

Child: Trisha-8 BOETTGER born 28 May 1976 Anchorage, AK

826. ARLAYNE IRENE-6 **BOETTGER**, sister of above, was born 29 Oct 1919 at Ayr, Emmett County, Michigan. She married Joseph Mitchell LIPCHINSKY on 29 March 1946 at Seattle, Washington. He was the son of Michael LIPCHINSKY and Mary REGULA, and was born 7 Dec 1917 at Mount Pleasant, PA; died _____ MI. Arlayne-6 BOETTGER died 21 June 2008 at Harbor Springs, MI.

Children of Arlayne-6 BOETTGER and Joseph LIPCHINSKY:
Surname **LIPCHINSKY**

+	**1260. CHERYL ARLAYNE**	born 1 Nov 1946 Seattle, WA; married David WILSON
		(he s/o Charles S. WILSON and Mary Mc CORMICK)
+	**1261. JOSEPH MITCHELL, Jr.**	born 7 May 1948 San Francisco, CA
		1 married Wanda Gail ODOM 27 May 1972 Escambia Co., FL
		divorced 16 May 1979
		2 married Jeanna Lurline CHILDERS 26 May 1979 FL.

Children of Arlayne-[6] BOETTGER and Joseph LIPCHINSKY, continued:
Surname **LIPCHINSKY**

1262. Charles	born 17 Nov 1951 Petoskey, MI; died 23 Feb 1978	
1263. Alinka Jan	born 29 Mar 1956 Bayonne, NJ;	
	1 married Robert SIMARD 2 Aug 1975	
	(he born 28 Sep 1954 Concord, NH; divorced 16 Mar 1979)	
	Child: Jason Barnard -[8] SIMARD born 5 Dec 1974 Pensacola, FL	
	2 married Richard Lee MINOR 11 Sep 1992 (he born 25 May 1944)	

827. RACHEL JANET-[6] BOETTGER, sister of above, was born 14 July 1922 at Ayr, Emmett, Michigan. She married Weldon Dale HART on 2 Feb 1943. He was the son of Victor HART and Emma L. ____, and was born 17 Nov 1921, died 3 July 2001 Marquette, MI. Rachel Janet-[6] BOETTGER died 22 Mar 1996 Marquette, MI. Weldon HART served as a Tec 5 in the US Army during World War 2.

Children of Rachel Janet-[6] BOETTGER and Weldon HART:
Surname **HART**

+	**1264. LANE VICTOR**	born 20 Oct 1946 Pontiac, MI
		married Susan Carol JACKSON 24 Feb 1968 Marquette, MI
		(she born 17 Mar 1947 Marquette, MI)
+	**1265. JANITH THERESA**	born 25 Feb 1952 Marquette
		married Dr. Samuel VASQUEZ 28 Mar 1982
		(he born 20 Nov 1944 Center, CO.)
	1266. Alicia	born 22 Sep 1960 Marquette
		married Thomas BROCHU 5 July 1985 San Diego, CA
		(he born 19 Aug 1949 Newark, NJ)

828. HELEN LOUISE-[6] BOETTGER, sister of above, was born 17 Feb 1924 at Ayr, Emmett, Michigan. She married Benjamin (Ben) F. BRAVARD ca 194_. He was the son of Omar BRAVARD and Grace ____ of Brooksville, Bracken, KY, and was born there 13 Jan 1919. Helen Louise-[6] BOETTGER died 22 Mar 2002 at Mason, Ohio.

Child of Helen Louise-[6] BOETTGER and Ben BRAVARD:
Surname **BRAVARD**

1267. Franklin Omar	born 22 July 1944 Bracken, KY	
	1 married Beverly _____; divorced; no issue	
	2 married Kathy Ann OSBORN, 14 Jul 1978 OH	
	3 married Chuckie KUPP ca 1985	

Note: Franklin adopted the daughter of his first wife. Her name was Amy Helena, born 3 Oct 1970 (not a McIntosh descendant)

829. ERSHEL LEONA-[6] BOETTGER, sister of above, was born 4 Dec 1925 at Ayr, Emmett, Michigan. She married Richard Armand LA COMBE on 28 Dec 1945 at __, MI. He was the son of Roy G.(Raoul) LA COMBE and Jeanne CASTANIER, and was born 31 Aug 1924 at Mackinaw, Emmet, MI; died 2 Mar 1991 Marquette, MI. Ershel-[6] BOETTGER died 1 June 1981 at Traverse City, MI.

Children of Ershel-[6] BOETTGER and Richard LA COMBE:
Surname **LA COMBE**

+	**1268. KATHERYN FAE**	born 20 June 1947 Cheboygan, MI
		married Ernest J. STOLPE 16 Aug 1966 (he born 4 Dec 1947)
+	**1269. DEBORAH SUZANNE**	born 30 Oct 1949 Cheboygan, MI
		married Dexter MC NAMARA 17 Mar 1978
		(he s/o Willard MC NAMARA and Violet LASLEY)
		(he born 3 Nov 1945)

Children of Ershel Leona-6 BOETTGER and Richard LA COMBE, continued:
Surname LA COMBE

	1270. Richard Brian	born 31 Aug 1952 Cheboygan, MI; died 7 Nov 1960 Carp Lake, MI
+	**1271. PATRICIA ANN**	born 19 Dec 1953 Cheboygan, MI
		1 married Wilford Dale DAVENPORT 9 Apr 1971; divorced Jan 1975
		2 married Ronald Allen GOONE 8 Jul 1977; divorced 31 May 1983
		3 married Calvin Edgar PELTZER, Jr. 23 Mar 1984
		(he s/o Calvin PELTZER, Sr. and Doris CAMPBELL)
	1272. Joseph Phillip	born 19 Nov 1957; died 22 Nov 1957 Petoskey, MI
	1273. Jeffry Lee	born 19 Nov 1957; died 21 Nov 1957 Petoskey, MI
+	**1274. MICHAEL VINCENT**	born 13 April 1959 Petoskey, MI; married Linda Marie BUSH 28 Dec 1981
		(she born 29 June 1962 Detroit, MI)
+	**1275. STEPHANIE K.** "Stacie"	born 29 June 1963 Petoskey, MI married Samuel Lee STAFFAN 29 Oct 1983
		(he s/o Jonathan STAFFAN and Sandra Lee CADWELL)

830. DERLA GALE-6 BOETTGER, sister of above, was born 23 Aug 1927 at Ayr, Emmett, Michigan. She married Erwin R. SYDOW on 3 Jan 1947. He was the son of Walter B. SYDOW and ____, and was born 15 Aug 1927 Brutus, MI.; died 23 May 2008 Phoenix, AZ. Derla Gale-6 BOETTGER died ____.

Note: Polk's Directory 1949 Petoskey, MI : Ad reads SYDOW, W B & Sons, Walter B., Morris J. and
Erwin R. Distributors of farm implements, International Trucks, Hudson motor cars sales and service. 411 Michigan

Children of Derla Gale-6 BOETTGER and Erwin SYDOW:
Surname **SYDOW**

+	**1276. DENNIS** "Denny"	born 10 Sep 1948 Petoskey, MI ; married Janet KLOSS (she born 2 Jan 1950 Petoskey, MI)
+	**1277. DANIEL ERWIN**	born 29 Apr 1952 Petoskey, MI; died 18 Oct 1980 Harbor Springs, MI married Cathy SCHAUM
		(she born 14 Oct 1954; she 2 married Ray JANKOVIAK)
		Child: Daniel Erwin-8 SYDOW, Jr. born 6 Mar 1977; died 22 Aug 1994 Readmond, MI
+	**1278. MICHAEL JOHN**	born 15 June 1955 Petoskey, MI; married Deborah HEINZ
+	**1279. MARTIN DALE**	born 15 Jan 1957 Petoskey, MI married Nada MITROVIC (she born 10 Dec 1958)

831. HERMA JEAN-6 BOETTGER, sister of above, was born 16 Sep 1929 at Ayr, Emmett, Michigan. married Philip Anthony ABRUNZO on 17 Jan 1949 at ____. He was the son of James ABRUNZO (born Italy) and Lana _____ (born Italy), and was born 26 Oct 1922 Elmira, NY.

Children of Herma Jean-6 BOETTGER and Philip ABRUNZO:
Surname **ABRUNZO**

+	**1280. JEAN IRENE**	born 21 Dec 1949 Elmira, Chemung, NY
		1 married John CASTRILLI 29 Jan 1972
		(he born ____ Bath, NY; died 21 Sep 1974)
		2 married Daniel Joseph CLARK, Sr. 15 Oct 1977
		(he born 27 May 1948, Sayre, PA)
	1281. James Patrick	born 24 Mar 1951 Elmira, NY
+	**1282. MARIA LUCIA**	born 12 Dec 1952 Elmira, NY married Kenneth M. HAGER 2 Aug 1975; (he born 23 Aug 1953)
	1283. William Joseph	born 21 Mar 1957 Elmira, NY

832. ALYCE JOAN-[6] BOETTGER, sister of above, was born 27 Jan 1932 at Ayr, Emmett, Michigan. She married Clarkson Cecil MOST 24 Apr 1950 at _____ . He was the son of Clark Findley MOST and Maria Martha LAYHER, and was born 8 May 1929, died 11 May 1962 Petoskey, MI. Alyce Joan[6] married second to George CONRAD on 29 Dec 1973. He was born 22 August 1931.

Children of Alyce Joan[6] BOETTGER and Clarkson MOST:
Surname **MOST**

+	**1284. CLARKSON CECIL, JR.**	born 20 May 1951 Petoskey, MI 1 married Debra Jean LOYER 25 June 1969 (she born 10 Nov 1953; divorced July 1974 2 married Diann RICHARDS 23 Aug 1974 (she born 22 Aug 1950; previously married)
	1285. Findley Mark	born 27 Aug 1952 Petoskey, MI married Peggy LAUGHBAUM _____; divorced
	1286. Matthew Brent	born 18 Dec 1956 Petoskey, MI; married Cheryl MESOCK
+	**1287. KATHLEEN MAERE**	born 11 Feb 1958, Petoskey, MI married Wesley LAUGHBAUM 2 Sep 1977; divorced (he born 7 Jul 1953)

833. BOYD REX[6] BOETTGER, brother of above, was born 9 Dec 1933 at Ayr, Emmett, Michigan. He married Mary A. GORZINSKI on 16 Oct 1959. She was the daughter of _____ GORZINSKI and _____, and was born 27 Oct 1936 at Kawkawlin, Michigan. Boyd[6] was a Bay City, MI fireman.

Children of Boyd Rex[6] BOETTGER and Mary GORZINSKI:
Surname **BOETTGER**

1288. William B	born 16 Jul 1960 Bay City, MI; fireman for Bay City, MI married Brenda Joyce HISTED 1 Aug 1981 (she born 17 Aug 1961 Bay City, MI)
1289. Joseph R.	born 9 Mar 1962 Bay City; married Dana Jo DENNEY 12 Nov 1982 (she born 10 Mar 1952 Mt. Pleasant. MI)
1290. Patricia M.	born 7 Aug 1964 Bay City married David HOLZSCHUH 12 Sep 1986 Ann Arbor, MI (he born 15 Feb 1960 Rapid City, SD)

834. STANLEY FRANK[6] BOETTGER, brother of above, was born 3 Dec 1934 at Ayr, Emmett, MI. He married Ruth AVERY ca _____. She was the daughter of _____ AVERY and _____, and was born 1 Nov 1940. They divorced ca _____. Stanley[6] BOETTGER died 13 Sep 1977 at Traverse City, MI.

Children of Stanley Frank[6] BOETTGER and Ruth AVERY:
Surname **BOETTGER**

1291. William Stanley	born 24 July 1962 Petoskey, MI married Elizabeth KENT 28 July 1987 (she born 26 Sep 1977 Traverse City) Child: Adam William-[8] BOETTGER born 12 May 1993 Detroit, MI
1292. Linda	born 26 June 1963 Petoskey, MI married Steven CATES 3 Mar 1989 Mt. Verde, FL (he born 31 Jan 1956) Child: Caleb Edward-[8] CATES born 20 Dec 1990 Kentwood, MI
1293. Karen Lynn	born 14 Jan 1966 Petoskey, MI; died 10 Apr 1966 Lake City, MI

835. MAX GILBERT-[6] BOETTGER, brother of above, was born 24 Jan 1936 at Ayr, Emmett, MI.. He married Fay ULRICH on 9 June 1956 at ____. She was the daughter of ____ ULRICH and _____, and was born 6 June 1938 at Petoskey, Michigan.

Children of Max-[6] BOETTGER and Mary ULRICH:
Surname **BOETTGER**

+	**1294. WILLIAM JAYE**	born 28 May 1957 Petoskey, MI
		1 married Deborah KALKOFEN ca _____, divorced; no issue
		2 married Nicole KRAUSE 27 July 1985; (she born 20 Sep 1966)
+	**1295. STEVEN CHARLES**	born 11 July 1958 Petoskey, MI
		1 married Jean WHITNEY; divorced (she born 14 July 1960)
		2 married Terese RIGGS (she born 2 Aug 1961)
	1296. Leon Rex	born 14 Apr 1961 Petoskey, MI
		married Ann Marie PUFFPAFF 17 Nov 1994
+	**1297. JACQUELYN KAY**	born 28 Sep 1963 Petoskey, MI
		1 married John Steven HALL/HULL; divorced (he born 19 Aug 1962)
		2 married Johnie DANIELS, Jr. 7 Sep 1992
		(he born 8 Jan 1960 Jacksonville, FL)
	1298. Max Gilbert (Jr)	born 28 Aug 1968 Petoskey, MI; marr Sandra KOLMAN 20 Jul 1993
		(she born 30 July 1971 Holland, MI)
	1299. Troy Crosby	born 18 Aug 1969 Petoskey, MI; died 5 July 1989 Clarksville, TN

836. AVIS ANNE-[6] BOETTGER, sister of above, was born 17 Sep 1938 at Ayr, Emmett, Michigan. She married first to Everett LAKE on – Aug 1955. He was the son of ___LAKE and ____, and was born 9 July 1935 at Tawas, MI. They divorced. She married second to James CAMPBELL on ____. He was the son of ___ CAMPBELL and___, and was born 23 Dec 1931 at Jackson, MI. 1990 they resided at Clark Lake, MI.

Children of Avis Anne-[6] BOETTGER and Everett LAKE:
Surname **LAKE**

	1300. Sheree Ann	born 12 Mar 1956 Petoskey, MI
		married David WILKINSON 18 May 1985
		(he born 15 Aug 1961 Jackson, MI)
+	**1301. TRINA PAMELA**	born 2 Nov 1958 Mason, MI
		1 married Robert TAYLOR ca May 1978; divorced
		2 married Kent KLEINSCHMIDT (he born 30 Feb 1958 Jackson, MI
	1302. Gretchen Lynn	born 14 Feb 1961 Jackson, MI
		1 married Ronald EVERS; divorced (he born 24 July 1960 Jackson)
		2 married David WITBECK July 1982 (he born 5 Dec 1961 SC)

838. WILLIAM TANNER-[6] SMITH, son of Elizabeth-[5] TANNER (Strever-[4]; William-[3]; Magdalena-[2] MAC INTOSH; Alexander-[1]) and Milton Abram SMITH, was born 14 Jan 1874 at Ancramdale, Columbia County, New York. He married Laura Maudelle ARNOLD on 26 Mar 1913 at Dexter, Dallas County, Iowa. She was the daughter of Jacob ARNOLD and Elizabeth ROW, and was born 1 Mar 1877 at Dexter ,IA; died 2 May 1935 at Des Moines, Polk County, Iowa. William Tanner-[6] SMITH died 11 Nov 1964 at Waverly, Bremer County, Iowa. He and his wife are buried at Dexter, Iowa.

Children of William Tanner-[6] SMITH and Laura M. ARNOLD;
Surname **SMITH**

+	**1303. HOWARD WILLIAM**	born 7 Mar 1914 Earlham, IA; died 8 Sep 1998 Bella Vista, AR
		married Shirley Kathleen BENNETT 14 sep 1945
+	**1304. HAROLD ARNOLD**	born 12 May 1915 Earlham, IA
		married Jennie PALS 17 Feb 1939

Children of William Tanner-[6] SMITH and Laura M. ARNOLD, continued:
Surname **SMITH**

+ **1305. ELIZABETH**   born 10 Mar 1920 Dexter, IA
   MARIE   married Cecil Carl BRANDENBURG 6 May 1949

840. ASA-[6] **SMITH**, brother of above, was born 12 Sep 1977 at Earlham, Madison County, Iowa. He married Rosa June MC CLURE on 16 Dec 1903 at Winterset, Madison County, Iowa. She was the daughter of James R V MC CLURE and Jemima M. PAISLEY, and was born 23 July 1885 Louisa County, Iowa; died 13 Feb 1973. Asa-[6] SMITH died 20 Dec 1958 at Perry, Dallas County, Iowa. He and his wife are buried at Penn Center, Madison County, Iowa.

Children of Asa-[6] SMITH and Rosa MC CLURE:
Surname **SMITH**

1306. Lucile Pauline	born 3 Jan 1905 Earlham; died 11 Jan 1905
1307. Gladys Emma	born 9 Apr 1908 IA; died Apr 1994 Earlham, Madison, IA
	1 married Wilford COUNTRYMAN 18 Dec 1932
	(he born 11 Jan 1899; died 24 July 1974)
	2 married Hugh WI(L)SON 24 Dec 1974 EOL

+ **1308. RAYMOND**   born 6 July 1911 Murray, Clark, IA; died 5 Sep 2002 Des Moines, IA
   VANATTA   married Pauline Rose ADDY 8 June 1932
                             (she born 29 Nov 1912; died 22 Apr 2008 IA)

+ **1309. HOMER**   born 2 May 1913 Earlham, IA; died 12 Feb 1999 Adel, Dallas, IA
   EDWARD   married Verna STONE 4 Nov 1938 Long Beach, CA; divorced
                             (she born 24 Dec 1908; died 23 Mar 1981)

+ **1310. MYRTLE**   born 22/27 Mar 1915 Winterset, Mad., IA; died 15 Dec 1996 Lehi, UT
   ELIZABETH   1 married John Donald FOX 29 Aug 1934 Adel, IA; divorced
                             (he s/o Carl Frederick FOX and Zeta MAGNEL)
                             2 married Edward Francis MC CORMICK

   1311. Lyle Clarence   born 28 Apr 1917 Madison, IA; died 18 Oct 1986 Council Bluffs, IA
                             1 married Mary Ann MEYER 15 May 1945
                             (she born 1 Jan 1918; died ___)
                             2 married Ruth HATCHER 20 Jan ____
                             (she born _____; died 13 Sep 1964) no issue   EOL

+ **1312. WILMA**   born 25 Feb 1925 Earlham, IA; died _____
   EILEEN   married Calvin Sherman MOORE, Jr. 28 Aug 1944
                             (he s/o Calvin Sherman MOORE and Leora THOMSON)
                             (he born 29 June 1917; died ___)
+ **1313. ILLA JUNE**   born 26 June 1928 Earlham, IA; died Feb 1991
                             married John Gerald DOLAN 27 May 1946
                             (he s/o Wilbur Thomas DOLAN and Mary Ann JAMES)
                             (he born 15 Sep 1925; died _____)

841. CLARENCE-[6] **SMITH**, brother of above, was born 11 Feb 1880 at Earlham, Madison County, Iowa. He married Della Emma MC CLURE on 2 Sep 1918. She was the daughter of James R V MC CLURE and Jemima PAISLEY, and was born 23 Nov 1889; died 27 Jan 1972 at Winterset, Madison County, Iowa. She was the sister of Rosa June MC CLURE who married Asa-[6] SMITH (above). Clarence-[6] SMITH died 2 Ape 1956 at Earlham, Iowa and is buried there.

Children of Clarence⁻⁶ SMITH and Della MC CLURE:
Surname **SMITH**   (all children born Earlham, Madison County, Iowa)

+ **1314. EDWIN ROBERT**   born 16 Feb 1922; died ___
married Doris Marjorie HADLEY 22 Aug 1943
(she dau/o Willard J. HADLEY and Delora Bernice COOK)
(she born 2 May 1924; died _____)

+ **1315. TWILA LEONE**   born 21 June 1923 ; died 7 Feb 2007 Des Moines, IA
1 married Charles Henry LEIGHTY 9 Oct 1942 (he born 5 Oct 1917)
(he s/o Earl Henry LEIGHTY and Mary Elizabeth BOOT)
2 married Robert Joseph EAGAN 22 June 1946   (divorced 1977)
(he s/o William F. EAGAN and Josephine SHERLOCK)
(he born 15 Jan 1915; died 7 Feb 2007 Des Moines, Polk, IA)

+ **1316. DORIS ROSA**   born 16 May 1926; died _____
married Francis RUTHERFORD 10 Dec 1946 ++
(he s/o Edward Francis RUTHERFORD and Naomi ____)
(he born 23 Mar 1921; died 3 Dec 1997 Churdan, Greene, IA)
++ Note: he served in the US Navy during WW2

842. CHESTER A⁻⁶ SMITH, brother of above, was born 27 Jan 1882 at Earlham, Madison, Iowa. He married Maggie Susannah (Susie) PEARSON on 8 Dec 1909 at Earlham, IA. She was the daughter of Samuel PEARSON and Emily Jane CECIL, and was born 24 Oct 1888 Union County, IA; died 29 Apr 1975 at Winterset, Madison County, IA. Chester⁻⁶ SMITH, a farmer, died 28 Jan 1957 at Des Moines.

Children of Chester A⁻⁶ SMITH and Susie PEARSON:
Surname **SMITH**   (all children born Earlham, Madison Co., IA)

1317. Lillie   born 1 July 1910 ; died 10 Sep 1910

+ **1318. CARL DONALD**   born 31 Jan 1912; died 21 Aug 1960 Des Moines, IA
married Naomi Ruth FOX 2 Sep 1934 (she born 30 May 1915)
(she dau/o William Harvey FOX and Flora Evelyn CUMMINS)

+ **1319. OPAL MAE**   born 1 May 1913; died 5 May 1995 Carlisle, IA
married Gail Levi NOLAND 30 Nov 1935
(he s/o Fred Alvard NOLAND and Nora Lucinda COOK)
(he born 30 May 1914; died 4 Dec 2006 Carlisle, Warren, IA)

+ **1320. DOROTHY JUNE**   born 15 Aug 1917; died 8 Apr 1985 Des Moines, IA
married Leonard ROUTH 28 Jan 1939 Ames, IA
(he s/o A L ROUTH and Ella CHRISTIAN)
(he born 31 Oct 1916; died 3 Mar 1996 Story City, Story, IA)

+ **1321. PAULINE ROSE**   born 28 Nov 1920; died 6 Oct 2010 Des Moines, IA.
married Carroll Fred NOLAND 10 Sep 1941
(he born 3 Sep 1915; died 28 Sep 2004 Adel, IA)

+ **1322. RUTH EILEEN**   born 30 Nov 1921; died 10 Mar 2003 Carlisle, IA
married Wayne NOLAND 2 June 1941 Albany, MO
(he born 13 Nov 1918; died 1 July 2001 Carlisle, IA)

+ **1323. LLOYD KENNETH**   born 22 May 1923; died 1 Jan 1997 Earlham, IA
married Carol Ione MC CARTHY 29 Sep 1945(she born 28 Sep 1926)
(she dau/o William Joseph MC CARTHY and Lura Almeda JACOBS

844. RAYMOND-⁶ SMITH , brother of above, was born 28 May 1886 at Earlham , Madison, Iowa. He married 1ˢᵗ to Martha Minerva DE VAULT on 28 Feb 1912. She was the daughter of ____ DE VAULT and ___ , and was born2 Jan 1886, died 28 Feb 1913. He married 2ⁿᵈ to Grace CADE on 22 Aug 1917. She was born 26 Oct 1885; died 14 May 1933. He married for the third time to Bertha Ellen ALEXANDER on 21

Feb 1938 at Des Moines, Polk, IA. She was the daughter of ___ ALEXANDER and ___, and was born 8 Dec 1892; died _____. Raymond[-6] SMITH died 4 June 1964 at Earlham, IA. He and his wives are buried at Penn Center Cemetery, Madison County, Iowa.

Child of Raymond-[6] SMITH and Martha Minerva DE VAULT:
Surname **SMITH**

+	**1324. MABLE OLIVE**	born 27 Feb 1913 Winterset, IA; died 9 Oct 2002 FL
		1 married Wilbur Lloyd SPEER 6 Nov 1932
		(he s/o Lloyd SPEER and Cara L. ____)
		(he born 4 Dec 1915; died 5 Oct 1961 Dexter, Dallas, IA)
		2 married George W. KING 5 Feb 1966
		(he born 23 Apr 1908; died 19 Oct 1969)
		3 married Howard SPRINGER (he born ca ____; died 25 Nov 1985
+	**1325. DALE EDWIN**	born 24 Nov 1918 Earlham, IA; died 17 Nov 2000 Houston, TX
		married Mary WOODS 4 Apr 1940 Nashua, Iowa
+	**1326. WILLARD CECIL**	born 13 Oct 1920 Earlham, IA; died 23 July 1994 Earlham, IA
		married Vina L. EMMONS 16 Nov 1942 Maryville, MO
		(she dau/o Layton E. EMMONS and Minnie P. _____)
		(she born 10 March 1923; had twin Sadie; died _____)

847. EGBERT TANNER[-6] **VOSBURGH**, son of Rachel-[5] TANNER (Strever-[4]: William[-3]; Magdalena-[2] MAC INTOSH ; Alexander-[1]) and Warren L. VOSBURGH, was born 18 Oct 1874 at Ancram, Columbia County, NY. He married Delia SILVERNAIL on 24 Sep 1893 CT. She was the daughter of John SILVERNAIL and Eliza ?, and was born ca 1876 NY; died _____. Egbert T[-6] VOSBURGH died ca 1945.

Children of Egbert-[6] VOSBURGH and Delia SILVERNAIL:
Surname **VOSBURGH**

+	**1327. ESTHER**	born ca 1895 CT; died _____
		married Charles ROBERTS, Jr.
		(he s/o Charles ROBERTS, Sr. and Abbie _____)
		(he born Oct 1881 Ancram, NY; died _____)
+	**1328. INA/ IVA L.**	born ca 1896 NY; died June 1983; married Avery John HAWVER
	1329. Wallace N.	born 5 Oct 1900 NY; died 11 Feb 1993 Hillsdale, NY
		married Myrtle BUSSETT

Children: Roslyn-[8] born ca 1925, and Evelyn-[8] VOSBURGH born ca 1928

850. ESTHER-[6] **MOLVINA VOSBURGH**, sister of above, was born May / Aug 1879 at Ancram, NY. She married Ward SILVERNAIL ca 1895. He was the son of Hiram Conrad SILVERNAIL and Amanda M. ____, and was born 2 Jan 1858; died 5 Jan 1952 Sharon, CT. Esther-[6] VOSBURGH died ____.

Children of Esther-[6] VOSBURGH and Ward SILVERNAIL:
Surname **SILVERNAIL**

+	**1330. WILLARD**	born 11 Sep 1897; died Oct 1964; married Rose M. GARRISON
	1331. Albert	born 9 Feb 1917 Copake, NY; died 15 Jan 1988 NY

860. PETER TANNER-[6] **VOSBURGH**, son of Laura-[5] TANNER (Strever-[4]; William[-3]; Magdalena-[2] MAC INTOSH; Alexander-[1]) and John VOSBURGH, was born 13 Dec 1876 at ____, NY. He married first to Maude L. HUSTED ca 1903. She was the daughter of Frank B. HUSTED and Janice A. ____, and was born ca 1887; died 1914. His second wife was Lillian Margaret CODY. They were married ca ____. She was the daughter of ____ and ____, and was born 22 June 1884; died 20 Nov 1934. Peter-[6] VOSBURGH , a brakeman and conductor on the railroad, died 30 Aug 1968 at Stamford, CT.

Children of Peter T-[6] VOSBURGH amd Maude L. HUSTED:
Surname **VOSBURGH**

1332. Harry	born ca 1906; died 1968	
1333. Frank T.	born ca 1908; died 12 Apr 1932	
1334. Maybel/Mabel	born ca 1909 ; died	
1335. Mildred L.	born 10 Mar 1912 NY; died Aug 1975 St Petersburg, FL	
	1 married Chauncey Edward CROWELL	
	(he born 29 Dec 1895; died June 1971 CT)	
	(he s/o Ernest Milton CROWELL and _____)	
	2 married Anthony M. CALKA (he born 12 Mar 1911; died 6 Aug 1979)	

873. SAMUEL S-[6] HEAD, son of Jonathan-[5] HEAD, Jr. (Eliza-[4] TANNER; William-[3;] Magdalena-[2] MAC INTOSH ; Alexander-[1]) and Mary-[4] TANNER (Samuel-[3;] Rachel-[2] MAC INTOSH; Alexander-[1]) was born 27 Nov 1876 at Copake, Columbia County, NY. He married Florence M _____ on --- at ____. She was born ca 1886 NY; died ____. Samuel-[6] HEAD died Jan 1963. 1920 resided Copake, NY

Children of Samuel-[6] HEAD and Florence M _____:
Surname **HEAD**

+	**1336. BESSIE**	born ca 1906 NY; married Clinton George BAINER ca 1926
		(he s/o Jacob BAINER and Ella SHAUGHNESSY)
		(he born 15 June 1896; died Jan 1978 Ancramdale, Col., NY)
	1337. Samuel J.	born 4 Oct 1907 NY; died 1973 Copake, Columbia, NY
	1338. Jesse A.	born 29 Dec 1909; died Nov 1984 Copake, NY
	1339. Myrtle	born 17 July 1913 NY; died 15 Aug 1993 Copake, NY
	1340. Hazel M.	born 12 Mar 1917 NY; died 24 Dec 1993 Copake, NY

877. MADELINE E-[6] DYE, daughter of Mary Ann-[5] HEAD (Eliza-[4] TANNER; William-[3]; Magdalena-[2] MAC INTOSH; Alexander-[1]) and George Thomas DYE, was born 30 Dec 1869 NY. She married Austin E. WRIGHT 1 March 1890. He was the son of Marquis L. WRIGHT and Orcelia/ Orselia MOODY, and was born Oct 1865; died 15 Sept 1944. Austin E. WRIGHT married second to Mabel B. WESTON. Madeline-[6] DYE died _____.

Children of Madeline-[6] DYE and Austin WRIGHT:
Surname **WRIGHT**

+	**1341. FREDERICK AUSTIN**	born 9 July 1892; died 1988
		married Valentine Bella MARCIL 26 June 1918 Holyoke, MA
		(she born 20 May 1893 Canada; died 1 Aug 1988 FL)
		(she dau/o Francois/Francis Xavier MARCIL and Celanire R. GINGRAS)

880. HENRY D-[6] MYERS, son of Delia-[5] PLATNER (Olive Emeline-[4] TANNER; Alexander-[3] TANNER; Magdalena-[2] MAC INTOSH; Alexander-[1]) and Henry D. MYERS, was born May 1866, NY. He married Ella S. _____ ca 1887 NY. She was the daughter of _____ , and was born March 1867 NY.

Children of Henry D-[6] MYERS and Ella S. _____:
Surname **MYERS**

1342. Edwin Dewey	born 17 Oct 1888 ; died _____; married and had at least 2 children	
1343. Frank Frederick	born 2 Jan 1891 NY; died Apr 1973 FL	
	married Alice H. _____ (she born ca 1899 NC)	
Children: Ethel Mae-[8] born ca 1920, and Frank F.-[8] Jr. born ca 1925 FL		
1344. Henry D., Jr.	born 6 Feb 1894; died June 1981 Albany, NY	
1345. Marvin T.	born 24 Aug 1899 NY; died Apr 1972 Albany, NY	

882. JAMES FINCH-[6] SIMMONS, son of Martin-[5] SIMMONS (Nancy Alma-[4] TANNER; John-[3]; Magdalena-[2] MAC INTOSH; Alexander-[1]) and Ellen FITZGERALD, was born 24 September 1869 at Blue Store, Columbia County, NY. He married Marybelle MAC FARLANE on 30 June 1903 at Pittsfield, MA. She was the daughter of Edward MAC FARLANE and Jennett (Jeanette) JACK, and was born 1 March 1874 at Thompsonville, CT; died 17 Nov 1947. James-[6] SIMMONS died 19 July 1958 at Pittsfield, MA where he had been a carpenter.

Children of James Finch-[6] SIMMONS and Marybelle MAC FARLANE:
Surname **SIMMONS**

1346. Ruth Elizabeth	born 23 May 1906; died ____	
	married John Sisson DINKEL 29 May 1932 Pittsfield, MA	
	Child: John Allen -* DINKEL born ca 1937 Columbus, OH	
1347. Marion Louise	born 9 May 1909; died 1992	
	married Lancelot WENHAM 22 July 1939	
1348. Mildred	born 26 Feb 1911; died 19 Sep 1911	EOL
+ **1349. EDWARD**	born 17 Feb 1914; died 28 Feb 1981 Pittsfield, MA	
MAC FARLANE	married Harriet Sarah COOPER Oct 1939 Albany, NY	
	(she dau/o Harley Hudson COOPER and Marion Craig TEABEAU)	
	(she born 23 Dec 1912; died 12 July 1982)	

892. LESTER NORTON-[6] SIMMONS , son of James Monroe-[5] SIMMONS (Nancy Alma-[4] TANNER; John-[3]; Magdalena-[2] MAC INTOSH; Alexander-[1]) and Frances Minerva " Minnie " HANKHURST, and was born 31 Dec 1895 NJ. He married 1st to Hazel DOULL ca 1918. She was the daughter of Percival " Percy " Charles DOULL (born England) and Nellie C. WOOD, and was born 31 Jan 1896; died 29 Oct 1925. He married 2nd to Bess WILLIAMS ca 1927. She was the daughter of Frank C. WILLIAMS and Maud ____, and was born 26 Nov 1897 IL; died 10 Aug 1980 FL. Lester Norton-[6] SIMMONS died 14 July 1977 Lake Worth, FL.

Children of Lester Norton-[6] SIMMONS and Hazel DOULL:
Surname **SIMMONS**

1350. Russell M.	born 13 April 1918 Bloomfield, NJ; died 1999
1351. Shirley M.	born 29 Nov 1919; died 13 Feb 2008
	married George P. SAWYER ca ____ (he born 6 Aug 1918 NJ) 5 ch.

Child of Lester Norton-[6] SIMMONS and Bess WILLIAMS:
Surname **SIMMONS**

1352. Jean	born ca 1928

894. HAROLD M.-[6] SIMMONS, brother of above, was born 20 April 1900 NJ. He married Mildred LA POINTE ca ____. She was the daughter of Alexander Pierre LAPOINTE and Marie HOGUE, and was born 11 Aug 1901 NY; died 25 Mar 2002 NJ . Harold-[6] SIMMONS died 14 July 1977 at Lake Worth, FL. Mildred LA POINTE married second to _____ SANDEMENICO.

Childrten of Harold-[6] SIMMONS and Mildred LAPOINTE:
Surname **SIMMONS**

+ **1353. ROBERT H.**	born 3 Mar 1924 NJ; died 12 Mar 2004 Manasquan, NJ.
	married Teresa SCHLECK (born ____; died 1998)
1354. William E.	born ca 1927; died ____ (living 2004 FL)
1355. Roger Wallace	born ca 1930 NJ; died 1999 FL

907. RALPH J.-[6] COMSTOCK, son of Emily/Emma-[5] YORKER (Sally Ann-[4] TANNER; John-[3]; Magdalena-[2] MAC INTOSH; Alexander-[1]) and Morton H-[8] COMSTOCK, was born ca 1865 MA. He married Annie L. ____ ca ___. She was born ca April 1869; died before 1930. They resided Norwalk, CT

Children of Ralph J-[6] COMSTOCK and Annie L. _____:
Surnmae **COMSTOCK**

1356. Alberta A.	born Jan 1895 Norwalk	1358. Lauretta/Loretta	born Oct 1899
1357. Ralph J.	born March 1897; died ____		

908. WILLIAM HUGH-[6] COMSTOCK, brother of above, was born 3 July 1870 MA. He married Grace May BENNETT on 5 June 1905. She was the daughter of Joseph Edwin/Edward BENNETT and Lucy ____, and was born 20 June 1880; died _____. William H-[6] COMSTOCK died 19 Jan 1944 at Great Barrington, MA.

Children of William H-[6] COMSTOCK and Grace May BENNETT:
Surname **COMSTOCK**   (all children born MA.)

1359. Harry William	born 14 Aug 1906; died 21 Sept 1996 W. Stockbridge, MA	EOL
1360. Dorothy E.	born ca 1907; poss died young	
1361. Grace Jeanette	born 9 June 1909	
1362. Alice Lucy	born 22 May 1911; died 7 Oct 1911	
1363. Harriet Bennett	born 27 Aug 1912	
1364. Marian Helena	born 7 Apr 1914	
1365. Lydia May	born 14 Mar 1916; died 13 Dec 1998 Housatonic, MA	
1366. Ruth Irene	born 18 Oct 1917; died 15 Apr 1971 MA.	
	married Peter D. DELMOLINO 27 Nov 1948	
	(he born 22 June 1917; died 25 June 1982 Great Barrington, MA)	
	(he s/o Steven DELMOLINO and Elizabeth ____)	
1367. Arthur Edwin	born 15 Feb 1919; died 6 May 1949 MA	
	married Radine A. HIGGINS (she born ca 1925)	

Child: Arthur Edwin-[8], COMSTOCK, Jr. born 13 Nov 1945

1368. Alfred Theodore	born 21 Aug 1921 MA; died 6 May 1999 Pittsfield, MA
	married Henrietta M. _____

914. FLORENCE B-[6] PELLS, daughter of Belle-[5] TANNER (Ambrose-[4]; John-[3]; Magdalena-[2] MAC INTOSH; Alexander-[1]) and John PELLS, was born 10 July 1889 at ____NY. She married George L. MILLER ca ___. He was the son of John H. MILLER and ____, and was born ca 1880 NY; died _____.

Children of Florence-[6] PELLS and George L. MILLER:
Surname **MILLER**

1369. Dorothy B.	born ca 1915	1371. George	born ca 1920
1370. Wilna / Wilma	born ca 1918	1372. John H.	born ca 1924

917. LLOYD AMBROSE-[6] CARLE, son of Blanch-[5] TANNER (Ambrose-[4]; John-[3]; Magdalena-[2] MAC INTOSH; Alexander-[1]) and Harry A. CARLE, was born 23 Oct 1892 at Hudson, Columbia County, NY. He married Leona Alexander MULLEN ca 1910. She was the daughter of Samuel Parkerson MULLEN (Samuel) and Mary Frances FRYE (David W) and was born 18 July 1890 Loudon, VA; died 19 Jan 1971, Prince Georges, MD. Lloyd-[6] CARLE, an auto mechanic, died 2 Jan 1969 Prince Georges, MD.

Children of Lloyd Ambrose-[6] CARLE and Leona MULLEN:
Surname **CARLE**

1373. Donald A.	born 12 Nov 1912; died 25 Jan 1993 MD
1374. Gordon D.	born ca 1914
1375. Marguerite Frances	born 12 July 1915 VA; died 1 Sep 1988 Fairfax, VA
	married Frank Harold HAHN 12 Aug 1950
	(he born 10 Jan 1897 IL, died 10 Apr 1972 Fairfax, VA)

Children: _____; and Clifford Harry-[8] HAHN born 9 May 1953, Washington, DC

Children of Lloyd Ambrose[-6] CARLE and Leona MULLEN, continued:
Surname **CARLE**

1376. Mildred C.	born ca 1917		
1377. Lloyd Allen	born 29 Dec 1917; died 17 June 1995 Ashtabula, OH		
	Note: He enlisted in the Army 30 Aug 1940 and served in the Infantry in World War 2		
1378. Clifford Harry	born ca 1920		
1379. Kenneth A.	born 29 June 1921 MD; died 20 Sep 1988 MD		
1380. William A.	born 6 Jan 1923 MD; died 11 Apr 1988 MD		
1381. Mary Easter/Esther	born ca 1924		
1382. Leona A.	born ca 1926	1383. S. Allen	born ca 1928

936. HARRY FRANKLIN[-6] **WOOLDRIDGE**, son of Rufus King-[5] WOOLDRIDGE (Philo-[4;] Mary Magdalena-[3] TANNER , Rachel-[2] MAC INTOSH, Alexander-[1]) and Anna JONES, was born 16 July 1884, GA. He married Mary J. ____ ca 1911. She was born ca 1891 Canada; died ____. Harry F-[6] WOOL-DRIDGE died 13 May 1954 at West Hartford, CT.

Children of Harry F-[6] WOOLDRIDGE and Mary J ____:
Surname **WOOLDRIDGE**

1384. Gertrude A.	born ca 1914 NY; died 25 June 2003 NJ.		
1385. Homer F.	born 1 Mar 1916 NY	1387. Elizabeth A.	born ca 1925 CT.
1386. Marie L.	born ca 1923 CT	1388. William R.	born ca 1928 CT

937. CLARENCE BUDD[-6] **WOOLDRIDGE**, brother of above, was born 1 Jan 1886 at Macon, Georgia. He married Mary Edna ____ ca 1916. She was born ca 1890 NY. They resided at West Hartford, CT.

Children of Clarence Budd-[6] WOOLDRIDGE and Mary Edna ____:
Surname **WOOLDRIDGE**

1389. Leila	born ca 1917 NY	
1390. Clarence B. Jr.	born 4 June 1920 CT; died 2 Dec 2009 FL.	
+ **1391. JOHN**	born 4 Jan 1928 CT; died 10 Apr 1995 CT.	
PHILO	1 married Virginia BARRETT Sept 1948; divorced 3 June 1975	
	(she born 3 Aug 1925; died 19 Feb 2009)	
	2 married Marie ____ May 1976; divorced 17 Jan 1978	

945. GROVENOR[-6] **SCUTT**, son of Ruey-[5] TANNER (John-[4]; James-[3]: Rachel-[2] MAC INTOSH; Alexander-[1]) and Thomas SCUTT, was born 7 July 1867 at Ancram, Columbia County, NY. He married Ella M. SHOOK ca 1888. She was the daughter of Jacob H. SHOOK and Phebe E ____ , and was born May 1870; died 1906 Ancram, NY. Grovenor-[6] SCUTT died 4 Apr 1948 at Ancram.

Children of Grovenor-[6] SCUTT and Ella SHOOK:
Surname **SCUTT**

1392. Caroline/ Carrie	born May 1893 NY; died ____	
1393. Helen Ruth	born 17 Jul 1903; died 22 Apr 1993 Livingston, Columbia, NY	
	married John Edward SIMMONS ca 1920	
	(he s/o Samuel S. SIMMONS and Kittie ____)	
	(he born Dec 1897; died ____)	
	Children: Samuel S-[8] born 8 Oct 1921, and Shirley May-[8] born 19 May/Aug 1923; and Dorothy M [8] SIMMONS born June 1925	
1394. Douglas	born ca 1906; died 1908	EOL

950. RICHARD[-6] **SCUTT**, brother of above, was born 12 Nov 1886 at Ancram, Columbia County, NY. He married Emily A ____ ca 19__. She was born ca 1889 NY; died ____. Richard -[6] SCUTT died ____.

Children of Richard-[6] SCUTT and Emily A. ____:
Surname **SCUTT**   (all children born Ancram, Columbia County, NY)

1395. Dorothy M.	born ca 1911		
1396. Vincent R.	born ca 1912; died 1925		
1397. Wesley I.	born ca 1915; died 1925	1400. Rosamond	born ca 1921
1398. Loretta C.	born ca 1916	1401. Gloria	born ca 1926
1399. Frances	born ca 1917	1402. Robert	born ca 1928

971. CHARLES WESLEY-[6] TANNER, son of Charles Andrew-[5] TANNER (Morris-[4]; James-[3]; Rachel-[2] MAC INTOSH; Alexander-[1]) and Augusta REEVES, was born 2 May 1875 at Salisbury, Litchfield, CT. He married Margaret O'SHAUGHNESSY ca ____ . She was born ____ , died ____ . Charles Wesley-[6] TANNER died 28 Mar 1956 at East Orange, NJ.

Children of Charles Wesley-[6] TANNER and Margaret O'SHAUGHNESSY:
Surname **TANNER**

1403. Frank	born ca 1901	1405. Margaret	born ca1914; died ca 1964
1404. Myrtle	born ca 1904	1406. William Charles	born ca 1919

973. WILLIAM REEVES-[6] TANNER, brother of above, was born 27 Aug 1882 Salisbury, Litchfield, CT. He married Alice Bridget POLLARD 2 Oct 1909 at Millerton, Dutchess County, NY. She was the daughter of James Patrick POLLARD and Margaret LAWLESS, and was born 30 Jan 1892 Dublin, Ireland; died 8 Nov 1983 Millerton, NY. William-[6] TANNER died 26 Dec 1929 Millerton, Dutchess, NY.

Children of William Reeves-[6] TANNER and Alice POLLARD:
Surname **TANNER**

1407. John Reeves	born ca 1911 CT; died 1971
1408. Marie	born 17 May 1913 CT; died 4 Nov1997; married Howard M. DENNIS
1409. Arthur Joseph	born 20 Sep 1914 CT.; died Aug 1987 Sharon , Litchfield, CT married Bertha MC CAULEY (she born ca 1918; died 1993)
1410. Charles S.	born 19 Apr 1916 CT; died 21 Apr 1975; married Elizabeth FOX
1411. Anna May	born 11 Oct 1917 NY; died 5 Dec 1921 Ancram, NY
1412. Richard Robert	born 20 Sep 1919 NY; married Ethel _____
1413. Chester Edward	born 27 Feb 1921 NY; died 27 Oct 2002 Canaan, CT
1414. George Allen	born 20 Apr 1922 NY; died 18 Jan 1964 West Point, NY married _____ BRENSLAWA
1415. Cecelia	born 26 June 1927; died 12 Dec 2004 SC married Lionel Arthur CLUFF (he born ca 1929; died 2005)

985. MINA J-[6] TANNER, daughter of Adelbert-[5] TANNER (Sarah-[4]; Henry-[3]; Rachel-[2] MAC INTOSH; Alexander-[1]) and RILLA FINKLE, was born 29 Mar 1904 at   , NY. She married Paul Edward HOFFMAN ca ____ . He was the son of Clarence HOFFMAN and Mary C. GARRISON of Glenco Mills, Columbia County, NY, and was born 13 Dec 1894, died 9 Apr 1976. He and his wife are buried at the Livinghston Reformed Cemetery, Livingston, NY. Mina-[6] TANNER died 1975.

Excerpted from the Columbia County (NY) WW1 Book , regarding Paul E. HOFFMAN:
" On Feb 22nd 1916, Hoffman enlisted in Company F, 10th Infantry, New York National Guard. On July 20th of the following year all national guard companies were federalized. Company F entrained for Fort Niagara on July 29th, 1917, received instructions in military tactics at the Fort for 3 months, and in October started for Camp Wadsworth in South Carolina. There Hoffman was assigned to Company F, 51st Pioneer Infantry , 4th Army Corps, with which unit he sailed for Brest in July 1918. Overseas he served on the Saint MIHIEL and Toul Sectors, taking part in the Saint Mihiel and Meuse-Argonne offensives. After the signing of the armistice he went into Germany with the Army of Occupation. Hoffman's return voyage to the United States was completed on July 3rd , 1919, and six days later he was honorably discharged from service ' **143**

Children of Mina J-[6] TANNER and Paul Edward HOFFMAN:
Surname **HOFFMAN**

1416 Evelyn	born ca 1922; died 1947
	married Arthur W. HOOD
	(he s/o Emery E. HOOD and Catherine _____)
	(he born 15 Jan 1918; died11 July 2001 Claverack, Columbia, NY)
1417. Pauline M.	born 7 Oct 1923; died ____
	married Earl E. RACE
	(he s/o Harold RACE and Gennie _____)
	(he born 12 Aug 1920 NY; died May 1975)

Children: Reginald-[8] born ca ____;married Susan; and Timothy Lee-[8] RACE born 19 Oct 1950, married _____, ch: Timothy, Jr. born 13 Oct 1977, died 16 Oct 1977

986. MARGARET KATHRYN-[6] MACY, daughter of Juliet-[5] MILLER (Christina-[4] TANNER; Morris-[3]; Rachel-[2] MAC INTOSH; Alexander-[1]) and Ed MACY, was born 30 May 1914 at Hudson, Columbia County, NY. She married Leon SIGLER 26 Sept 1932. He was the son of Ellsworth SIGLER and Minnie E. THORPE, and was born 18 Dec 1910 at NorthEast, Dutchess County, NY; died 5 April 1966 at Philmont, Columbia County, NY. Margaret K-[6] MACY died 2 Nov 1972 at Santa Clara, CA.

Children of Margaret-[6] MACY and Leon SIGLER:
Surname **SIGLER**

1418. Lowell Dale	born 27 Mar 1933 Hudson, NY; died 3 Feb 2009 Ghent, NY
1419. Norman L.	born 13 May 1934 ; died 6 July 2003 Hillsdale, Columbia, NY
	buried Mellenville Union Cemetery, NY

Child: Norman L-[8]. Jr. born 15 March 1963 Craryville, NY

	veteran of the US Army – served in Korea
1420. Adrian	born 25 Nov 1937; died 19 Feb 1968 in Vietnam
	married Elizabeth CANLER
1421. Rosalie	born ca 1939

990. NEVA CHARLOTTE-[7] SCOTT, daughter of Guy Winfield-[6] SCOTT (Mary E-[5] MAC DONALD; Mary-[4] CALDWELL; Clara-[3] MAC INTOSH; Simon-[2]; Alexander-[1]) and Nellie Mae SMITH, was born 27 Feb 1918 PA. She married Sigfrid F. SANDSTROM ca ____ . He was the son of _____ SANDSTROM and _____ JOHNSON, and was born 10 May 1924 Los Angeles, CA; died ____ . Neva-[7] SCOTT died Nov 1993 CA. 1960 resided Modesto, CA.

Children of Neva Charlotte-[7] SCOTT and Sigfrid SANDSTROM:
Surname **SANDSTROM**

1422. Stephen Paul	born 10 April 1951 CA; married Gayle Nevada HOLLIDAY 22 Aug 1970 NV
1423. David Jonathan	born 2 Nov 1952 Los Angeles, CA; died 18 Sept 1972 (killed in car crash)
1424. Deborah A.	born 10 Oct 1953 CA; married Brent Albert TACKETT 12 Aug 1972; divorced June 1976 (he born 20 July 1954 CA;) (he s/o _____ TACKETT and _____ MASHIER)
1425. Timothy Mark	born 30 March 1955; married Deborah S. MC KEE
1426. Donald	born (poss) 20 Sept 1962 CA.

996. MORRIS LESTER-[7] KITCHELL, son of Grace Edna-[6] BIGGS (Adaline M-[5] CHASE; Mariette-[4] MC INTOSH; Jonathan-[3]; Alexaner-[2,1]) and Robert Morris KITCHELL (CharlesWesley; John), was born 24 Oct 1910 at Ipswich, Edmunds County, SD. He married Irene KRAFT on 15 Nov 1942 at ___, SD. She was the daughter of Leo B. KRAFT and Anna NICKOLAS, and was born 11 Feb 1918; died 27 Jan 2006 at Aberdeen County, SD. Morris Lester-[7] died there on 13 Nov 2008.

Children of Morris Lester-[7] KITCHELL and Irene KRAFT:
Surname **KITCHELL**

1427. Thomas	born	; married Jean ____ ; resided Boise, ID
1428. Kathy	born	; married Frank NAKASE of Trabuco, CA
1429. Sherie	born	; married Leo VOJTA; resided Mobridge, SD

1008. VIRGINIA LOUISA-[7] WHITEMAN, daughter of Margaret C-[6] JOHNSON (Addie C-[5] MC INTOSH; Silvertus-[4]; Jonathan-[3]; Simon-[2]; Alexander-[1]) and Ralph Homer WHITEMAN, and was born 23 March 1927, died ____ . She married Elmer Ray BUSCH on 2 Aug 1947 at Oil City, PA. He was the son of Charles BUSCH and Hazel RAY, and was born 6 July 1927 Meadville, PA, died 30 Mar 2007 Ocala FL.

Children of Virginia Louise-[7] WHITEMAN and Elmer Ray BUSCH:
Surname **BUSCH**

1430. David P.	born ____	; married Julia _____
1431. Karen L.	born ____	; married Philip HENDERSON
1432. Gwendolyn M.	born ____	; married Phillip LATESSA
1433. Jeffrey A.	born ____	; married Laura _____

1024. LUCY AMANDA-[7] CLAGETT daughter of Kate Angeline-[6] MC INTOSH; James H-[5]; William-[4]; Henry-[3]; Simon-[2]; Alexander-[1]) and Reverdy CLAGETT, was born ca 1907 PA. She married Curtis F. PRANGLEY, of Washington, DC., on 1 Sept 1931. He was the son of Arthur George PRANGLEY and Blanche Irene DRAPER, and was born 11 July 1905 Washington, DC; died Oct 1976 Evanston, Cook, IL. Lucy Amanda-[7] CLAGETT died 31 July 1987, Cook County, IL.

Children of Lucy Amanda-[7] CLAGETT and Curtis PRANGLEY:
Surname **PRANGLEY**

1434. Lucy Amanda	born ca ____; died 31 July 1987 Cooks County, IL	
1435. Curtis F., Jr.	born 25 Aug 1932; died 5 Jan 1997 Evanston, IL	
	married _____ CHRISTENSEN	
1436. Christopher	born 7 Nov 1938; died same day	

1029. IRENE LUCY-[7] PACKARD, daughter of Lewis Erskine-[6] PACKARD (Jane-[5] WILLIAMS; Caroline-[4] MC INTOSH; William-[3]; Simon-[2]; Alexander-[1]) and Lenora/ Nora DOBBINS, and was born 10 Dec 1893 at ___, PA. She married Ralph Howard PACKARD on ___ at ___. He was the son of William B. PACKARD and Anna MARGARET AYRES, and was born 17 June 1890; died Jan 1964. Irene Lucy-[7] PACKARD died 21 Feb 1988.

Children of Irene Lucy-[7] PACKARD and Ralph Howard PACKARD:
Surname **PACKARD**

1437. Grace Lenora	born 2 Nov 1914; died 7 Apr 1991 La Porte, Sullivan, PA
	married Elmer E. FULLER, Jr. ca 1945 (he born 1920, died 1994)
	Child: Richard-[9] FULLER born ca ___
1438. Donald Ralph	born 19 Nov 1916; died 7 Sep 2009 Canton, PA
	married Louise CRANDELL 11 Mar 1939
	Children: Richard P-[9] and Marilyn Ballard-[9] PACKARD born ____
1439. Helen Muriel	born ca 1919; died___, 1 married ____ FLEMING
	Child: Peter-[9] FLEMING born ____
	2 married _____ BROWN (Child: Willard BROWN born ____)
1440. Anna Margaret	born ca 1921; died _____; married _____ KITTNER
1441. Rhea Emma	born ca 1922; died _____;
1442. Lewis Jerome	born 1 July 1926; died 30 Apr 2012
1443. Robert Arthur	born 18 Jan 1929

1032. MABEL LUCY-[7] AYRES, daughter of Caroline-[6] PACKARD (Jane-[5] WILLIAMS; Caroline-[4] MC INTOSH; William-[3]; Simon-[2]; Alexander-[1]) and Galen Guy AYRES, was born 10 Feb 1893 at Canton , PA. She married John Edgar WETHERBEE, of Alba, PA., ca 1914. He was the son of Otis WETHERBEE Mary L. ____, and was born 20 Jan 1891 Canton; died June 1963. Mabel-[7] AYRES died 5 June 1991.

Children of Mabel L-[7] AYRES and John WETHERBEE:
Surname **WETHERBEE**

1444. Maxwell B.	born ca 1919, PA; died 2002
1445. Janice Marie	born 10 June 1921, Alba, PA; died 19 Dec 1991 Wellsboro, PA
	married Miles MERRITT 11 Aug 1941
	(he s/o Mark M. MERRITT and Bessie G. KITTLE)
	(he born 2 Apr 1914; died 4 Apr 1978 Granville Summit, Brad., PA)

1034. FLORENCE MAY-[7] AYRES, sister of above, was born 23 Dec 1907 Canton, Bradford, PA. She married Arthur Howard GRACE on ____ at ____. He was the son of Howard E. GRACE and Henrietta VAN DYKE, and was born 26 Jan 1907 Springfield, Bradford Co., PA.; died Apr 1973 Canton, PA. Florence-[7] AYRES died 23 Dec 1977 at Canton, Bradford, PA.

Children of Florence May-[7] AYRES and Arthur Howard GRACE:
Surname **GRACE**

1446. Mary Lou	born ca 1932 Canton, PA; died _____
	1 married Alvin THOMAS 3 Sep 1950
	(he s/o Harry A. THOMAS and Bernice BERRY)
	(he born 30 June 1929 Troy, PA; died _____)
	2 married _____ PAPASON ; resided Alameda, CA
1447. Betty G.	born ca 1945; died 25 Feb 2004 Covington, PA
	married William CRANE ca 1954;

Children: Surname **CRANE**   Teresa-[9] born ___; married William YOUNG of Indiana, PA
Matthew -[9] born ___; married Barbara ____ of MO;   Robert[9] born ____; married Stephanie ___ of NC
Karen-[9] born ___; married Duane HARVEY of Mansfield, PA

1448. Helen Mary	born ca 1938 Canton, PA; married Robert RAINEY

1036. LEWIS MC KEAN-[7] TURNER, son of Lilly Belle-[6] WILLIAMS (George-[5]; Caroline-[4] MAC INTOSH; William-[3;] Simon-[2]; Alexander-[1]) and Charles Harpy TURNER, was born 1 July 1899 at Canton, Bradford, PA. He married Bessie CONRAD on 29 Nov 1922 PA. She was born ca 1899 PA

Children of Lewis-[7] TURNER and Bessie CONRAD:
Surname **TURNER**

1449. Howard William	born 5 Oct 1926, Montoursville, PA; died there 19 Jan 1982
	married Emma May EVANS
	(she dau/o Ruben EVANS and Grace COMPTON)
1450. Martin Frederick	born 23 May 1930 PA; died Apr 1976

1037. ERNEST INVALDA " Val "-[7] TURNER, brother of above, was born 29 Dec 1901 PA. He married Helen L. GREGORY on 21 Sep 1923 at ____. She was the daughter of Forest M. GREGORY and Etta/Ettie M. EVERY(Benjamin), and was born 27 Dec 1903; died May 1977 PA. Ernest died Mar 1969.

Children of Ernest Invalda-[7] TURNER and Helen GREGORY:
Surname **TURNER**

1451. James Ernest	born 8 July 1924; d. Aug 1973	1453. Helen Louise born 30 June 1927
1452. Ellie Marie	born 18 Oct 1925	1454. Robert Louis born 19 Jan 1936

1044. DORIS LILLIAN-[7] WILLIAMS, daughter of Charles McKean-[6] WILLIAMS (George-[5]; Caroline-[4] MAC INTOSH; William-[3]; Simon-[2;] Alexander-[1]) and Elsie Mead KILBOURN, was born 12 Nov 1912 at Leolyn, Tioga County, PA. She married 1st to Walter C. MASE , of Roaring Branch, PA, on 21 Mar 1936. He was the son of Harry F. MASE and Edna M. PARKER, and was born 12 June 1912 PA; died June 1971 PA. Doris married 2nd to Lester Erwin GROOVER ca____. He was the son of Thomas D. GROOVER and Evangeline ROWLEY, and was born 15 Jan 1911; died 22 Dec 1991 FL. Doris-[7] died 21 Dec. 2003 at Miami, FL.

Children of Doris-[7] WILLIAMS and Walter MASE:
Surname **MASE**

1455. Kenneth Jerome	born 8 Oct 1937 PA;
	married Camilla Gail GATTON ca 1963; resided Coral Gables, FL
1456. Richard D.	born 29 Aug 1940 PA; married Sylvia ____; resided Montoursville, PA

Children: Lynn-[9]; Marsha-9 and Michelle-[9] MASE

1045. HARRIET ELLIE-[7] WILLIAMS, sister of above, was born 4 May 1915 at ____, PA. She married Ralph Walter AUSTIN on 18 May 1936. He was the son of Leroy G. AUSTIN and Blanch TEBO, and was born 1 May 1915; died 3 Aug 1982 Roaring Branch, PA. She was a retired teacher from the Canton, PA area, and died 22 Jan 2006 at Naples FL.

Children of Harriet[7] WILLIAMS and Ralph Walter AUSTIN:
Surname **AUSTIN**

	1457. Donna Jean	born 23 Sep 1938 PA; died 1975
		married W. Alan MATSON
+	**1458. LEON GERALD**	born 2 July 1944, PA; 1 married Phyllis ISAACS
		2 married Cathy _____ Naples, FL
	1459. Barbara Eileen	born 23 Sep 1947 PA; married Larry STEINRUCK of Williamsport

1058. KATHRYN ANN[7] RANDALL, daughter of George Wayne[6] RANDALL (Daniel W-[5]; Charlotte -[4] MC INTOSH: William[-3]; Simon-[2;] Alexander[-1]) and Edna Eloise HUNT, was born 29 Oct 1926 PA. She married Clayton Larue STERNER ca _____ (after 1945). He was the son of John Clarence STERNER and Mildred ENGLISH, and was born 23 Apr 1926 PA, died 24 Oct 2004 at Montoursville, Lycoming, PA. He served as a Private in the US Air Corps in WW 2. Kathryn Ann[7] died 21 Jan 2009 at Montoursville, PA.

Children of Kathryn Ann[7] RANDALL and Clayton Larue STERNER:
Surname **STERNER**

1460. Kathy Louise	born _____; married _____ HARKEY
1461. Michael Francis	born 20 Dec 1949 PA;
1462. Kenneth Larue	born 1 June 1951 Williamsport, PA; died 10 Feb 1990
	married Rebecca WALKER
1463. Gerald Lee	born _____

1059. ROBERT AYRES[7] FREEMAN, son of Nancy Amelia[6] AYRES (Grace-[5] RANDALL; Charlotte-[4] MC INTOSH; William-[3]; Simon-[2;] Alexander-[1]) and Paul I. FREEMAN, was born 9 Feb 1896 at Canton, Bradford County, PA. He married Eiza Mae AVERY on 8 June 1914 at ___. She was the daughter of Albert AVERY and Bertha G. KEENEY, and was born 8 Feb 1896; died 28 Sep 1928. (possibly childbirth)

He married second to Addah C. LARCOM 17 Jan 1930 at Bath, NY. She was the daughter of Otis U. LARCOM and Jennie ____, and was born 30 June 1907; died 28 Dec 1995. Robert -[7] FREEMAN died 16 Sep 1959 at Elmira, Chemung County, NY.

Children of Robert Ayres[7] FREEMAN and Eliza AVERY:
Surname **FREEMAN**

1464. Helen Elizabeth	born ca 1915
1465. Robert Avery	born 7 Oct 1916; died 17 Nov 2007 San Jose, CA
1466. Richard James	born 3 Oct 1919; died 10 July 1997 Bradenton, Manatee, FL
1467. William Albert	born 25 July 1921; died May 1985
1468. Ruth	born ca 1925
1469. Paul Charles	born ca 1928; died 1928

Children of Robert Ayers-[7] FREEMAN and Addah C. LARCOM:
Surname **FREEMAN**

1470. son	born ca ___
1471. Harold Eugene	born 1 Sept 1932; died 9 July 2005 Elmira, NY
	1 married ____ A'HEARN; 2 married ____ BOWMAN
	3 married ____ FLUMAN
1472. dau	born ca _____

1063. LYNN CLIFFORD[7] FREEMAN, brother of above, was born 23 Sep 1906 at Canton, PA. He married Mary Violet FAIRMAN 8 June 1927. She was the daughter of Lloyd Jackson FAIRMAN and Emma Isabel GREEN, and was born 1 Jan 1905, died 25 Jan 2002. Lynn-[7] FREEMAN died May 1979 PA.

Children of Lynn Clifford[7] FREEMAN and Mary Violet FAIRMAN:
Surname **FREEMAN**

1473. Paul L.	born _____	
1474. Claire	born _____; married Sherman Virgil ROBERTS; divorced	
	(he born 15 Aug 1921 AL; died _____)	

Children: Marie[9] born, Mildred[9] born ___, and Robert[9] ROBERTS born ____

1475. Russell Dean   born _____

1069. EDWARD FIELD[7] THOMAS, son of Harriet[6] FIELD (Amy Isabel[5] THOMAS; Harriet[4] MAC INTOSH, William[3]; Simon[2]; Alexander[1]) and Marshall Jenkins THOMAS, was born 11 Dec 1899 at Canton, PA. He married Martha WHERRY ca Aug 1930 at _____PA. She was the daughter of Samuel WHERRY and Mary FERRY, and was born 3 Mar 1903; died 9 Mar 1987. Edward -[7] THOMAS died ___.

Children of Edward[7] THOMAS and Martha WHERRY:
Surname **THOMAS**

1476. Samuel Dee	born 15 Aug 1930; resided Blossburg, PA
1477. Edward Wherry	born 21 July 1932; resided Dover, NJ
1478. Jennifer	born _____; married Thomas MC GRAW; resided Miami, FL.

1074. ISABEL A.[7] THOMAS, sister of above, was born 10 Oct 1915 at Bradford County, PA. She married first to Herman SCHOLTZ, Jr. of Alba, Bradford, PA on 27 Nov 1931 at _____. He was the son of Herman SCHOLTZ, Sr. , and _____, and was born 7 March 1912, died in WW2. She married a second time on 31 Aug 1946 to Carl H. KROTZER at Philadelphia, PA. He was the son of Miles S. KROTZER and Deronda C. _____, and was born 28 Sep 1903; died July 1983 Canton, PA.. Isabel[7] THOMAS died Nov 1988 Canton, PA.

Children of Isabel[7] THOMAS and Herman SCHOLTZ:
Surname **SCHOLTZ**

1479. Marshall Edward	born 25 Apr 1932	1480. John	born 27 Sep 1938

1075. PAULINE-[7] SHOEMAKER, daughter of Helen[6] FIELD (Isabel[5] THOMAS; Harriet[4] MC INTOSH; William[3]; Simon[2]; Alexander[1]) and Porter SHOEMAKER, was born 21 May 1910 at _____, PA. She married Lynn (Lyndon) R. MC CONNELL on 29 Mar 1934. He was the son of _____ MC CONNELL and _____, and was born ca 1911 PA; died 30 Dec 1974. Pauline-[7] SHOEMAKER died 25 May 1987 at Canton, Bradford County, PA.

Children of Pauline-[7] SHOEMAKER and "Lynn" MC CONNELL;
Surname **MC CONNELL**

1481. Linda Lou	born ca 1936 PA;
	married Charles MILLER; resided Wilmington, DE
1482. Lynne	born July 1938; died Jan 1981 Wellsboro, PA
1483. David L.	born ca 1941
1484. Thomas	born ca _____; resided Canton, PA

1082. MIRIAM LOUISE-[7] HOPPER, daughter of Myrtle Glen[6] THOMAS (Lewis R.[5] ; Harriet[4] MC INTOSH; William[3]; Simon[2]; Alexander[1]) and Elmer Earl HOPPER, was born 25 Nov 1923 PA. She married first to Gerald Woodrow DORMAN ca _____. He was the son of _____ DORMAN and _____, and was born 30 Dec 1919 MO; died 19 Dec 1990 San Luis Obispo, CA.

She married second to Howard Leonard IVERSEN ca ___. He was born 18 March 1912, CA; died 31 May 2006. Miriam L-[7] HOPPER died 25 Sept 2010 San Luis Obispo, CA.

Children of Miriam-[7] HOPPER and Gerald W. DORMAN:
Surname **DORMAN**

1485. Gerald Wayne	born 15 Feb 1943 San Luis Obispo, CA
	married Penny J. NEEDHAM 26 June 1965 CA.
	(she born ca 1948;)
1486. Dianna L.	born 14 Aug 1946 CA.
	married David L. BABB 25 June 1966 San Luis Obispo, CA.
	(he born ca 1942 ;)

1086. MILTON I.-[7] MC KEAN, son of Elizabeth-[6] CASE (Milton A-[5]; Eliza-[4] MC INTOSH; William-[3]; Simon-[2]; Alexander-[1]) and Elwyn MC KEAN, was born 12 July 1911 PA. He married Alice J. TUTTLE ca 1939. She was the daughter of Clay TUTTLE and Frances ____, and was born 17 Dec 1917 Burlington, PA; died 23 June 2005 Marionville, MO. Milton-[7] MCKEAN died 17 May 1977 at Springfield, MO. He was a retired Mechanical Engineer

Children of Milton-[7] MC KEAN and Alice J. TUTTLE:
Surname **MC KEAN**

1487. Douglas M.	born ca _____; married Shirley _____; resided Springfield, MO.
1488. Robert B.	born ca _____; died
1489. Bonnie Ann	born ca 1943; 1 married _____ GOLDIN
	2 married Kent Paul " Kip " VETTER 30 Sept 1979 Lawrence , MO.
1490. Alan C.	born 19 Nov 1948; married Barbara ____; resided Middle Grove, NY
1491. Susan	born ca _____; 1 married _____ WITT
	2 married Tom BURTON; resided Springfield, MO

1088. LYNN E-[7] MC KEAN, brother of above, was born 29 Sept 1913 PA. He married Frances Mae TUTTLE, sister of Alice (above) on 27 Nov 1936 PA. She was born 14 Feb 1916; died 25 Oct 2004 at Troy, Pa. Lynn-7 MC KEAN died 24 Feb 1980 at Ulster, Bradford, PA.

Children of Lynn-[7] MC KEAN and Frances TUTTLE:
Surname **MC KEAN**

1492. James A.	born ca 1939 ;
	married Alice _____ ca ____, resided Ulster, NY
	Children: Jesse-8 born ca ____, married Sherry ____; and Elaine-[8] MC KEAN who married _____ SPENCER
1493. Margaret	born ca ___,
	married Gary E. CRANMER; resided Towanda, PA
	Children: Kyle-[8] born ca ____; and Heather-[8] CRANMER born ca ___ who married Brian MANCHESTER

1094. THOMAS BYRON-[7] CASE, son of Meade Thomas-[6] CASE (Milton-[5]; Eliza-[4] MC INTOSH; William-[3]; Simon-[2]; Alexander-[1]) and Louise BROWNSON, was born 17 Mar 1912 at, Bradford, PA. He married Sara WRISLEY on 9 Sep 1939 at ____. She was the daughter of Theodore WRISLEY and Mary BOURNE , and was born 15 July 1916 at West Burlington, Bradford, PA; died 19 July 1999 Portsmouth, NH. Thomas Byron-[7] CASE died 30 July 1994 at Troy. They are buried at Glenwood Cemetery, Troy, PA.

Children of Thomas Byron-[7] CASE and Sara WRISLEY:
Surname **CASE**

1494. Mary Louise	born 24 May 1942; married John WHEELER of Lee, NH
1495. Audrey Lucille	born 25 Oct 1943
	1 married ___ MEYLERT; 2 married ____ SCHANBACHER
1496. Eleanor Jean	born 15 July 1946;
1497. Janet Marie	born 25 Aug 1950; married Tom BERBINO Scotia, NY

1099. PAULINE E. (Polly)-[7] MC KEAN, daughter of Elizabeth-[6] CASE (Milton A-[5]; Elizabeth-[4] MC INTOSH; William-[3]; Simon-[2]; Alexander-[1]) and Elwyn MC KEAN, was born 31 Oct 1926. She married Lee R. CLEVELAND, Jr. on 23 July 1953. He was the son of Lee CLEVELAND and ____, and was born 31 Aug 1925 Troy, PA; died ____. "Polly "-[7] McKEAN died 23 Jan 2009 at Troy, PA.

Children of Pauline (Polly) -[7] MC KEAN and Lee CLEVELAND, Jr:
Surname **CLEVELAND**
1498. Gail	born ____; married Scott JACKSON ; resided Harrisburg, PA
1499. Lisa	born ____; married Steven FELDMAN ; resided Columbus OH.
1500. Sandra	born ____; married Kenneth VOEGTLEN; (he born 21 Mar 1967)

1102. WILLIAM <u>FRANCIS</u>-[7] MC INTOSH, son of Francis-[6] MC INTOSH (William E-[5]; Fernando-[4]; William-[3] MAC INTOSH; Simon-[2]; Alexander-[1]) and Mildred EMMS, was born 10 Oct 1935 at Woman's Hospital, New York City, NY. He married Miriam Blanche MC NALLY on 21 Sep 1957 at Mt. Washington Presbyterian Church, New York, NY. She was the daughter of _____ MC NALLY and ___, and was born 11 June 1938 at Royal Hospital, Bronx, NY.

Children of William <u>Francis</u>-[7] MC INTOSH and Miriam MC NALLY:
Surname **MC INTOSH**
1501. Donna Lea	born 23 July 1959 Columbia Presbyterian Hospital, NY, NY married George Anthony FREDERICKS 24 Oct 1981 NY, NY (he born 20 Mar 1958 NY, NY)
1502. William Donald	born 31 Jan 1962 Columbia Presbyterian Hospital, NY, NY

Note: This couple also adopted a child , Adam WILSON born 21 Oct 1964; married Dawn Marie NASH

1103. DONALD CURTIS-[7] MC INTOSH, brother of above, was born 16 Nov 1928 at New York, NY. He married first to Rosemary DUFFY in Childrens Court, Syracuse, Onondaga, NY. She was the daughter of _____ DUFFY and ____, and was born ____. Possibly this marriage ended in divorce. He married second to Virginia (MC)GUIGAN ca 1949 at Detroit, MI. She was the daughter of James (MC) GUIGAN and ____, and was born 24 May 1933 at New York, NY. Donald Curtis-[7] MC INTOSH died 28 May 1987 at NY, NY. He is buried at the Gate of Heaven Cemetery, Valhalla, NY. Virginia married second to Angelo BARTOLOTTA.

Children of Donald Curtis-[7] MC INTOSH and Virginia (MC) GUIGAN:
Surname **MC INTOSH**   (all children born St. Elizabeth's Hospital, NY, NY
1503 Ronald Francis	born 17 Aug 1950; died 1 July 1956	EOL
+ **1504. JAMES DENNIS**	born 9 Oct 1951; 1 married Fawn Renee COLBERT 2 married Gloria KARMASHIAN at Albany, NY	
1505. Gary Richard	born 2 Mar 1953	
1506. Cathy Ann	born 11 Mar 1958 married Michael C. SAVINO 17 Mar 1984 Livingston, NJ	

Children: Michael-[9] born ____, and Nicholas-[9] SAVINO born ca ____

1118. RODMAN CRAWFORD-[7] HOLMES, son of Kathleen Louise-[6] CRAWFORD (Byron-[5]; Lucy Delphine-[4] MC INTOSH; William-[3]; Simon-[2]; Alexander-[1]) and Norvin HOLMES, was born 16 Sep 1916 at Canton, Bradford, PA. He married Ethel Floy KEAGLE on 22 July 1933 at Hornell, NY. She was the daughter of Ulysses " Grant" Simpson KEAGLE and Ida May MASE, and was born 12 Feb 1910 Union, Tioga, PA; died 28 Jan 1986 at Canton, PA. Rodman-[7] HOLMES died 29 Oct 1963 at Canton, PA.

Children of Rodman-[7] HOLMES and Ethel KEAGLE:
Surname **HOLMES**
1507. Janice	born 26 Apr 1934 PA; married Michael DIEFFENBACH 25 Mar 1961

Children of Rodman-[7] HOLMES and Ethel KEAGLE, continued:
Surname **HOLMES**

1508. Rodman, Jr.	born 8 Oct 1937 PA
1509. Robert B.	born 6 Oct 1940; died 9 July 2002; married Dorothy _____ ca ____
1510. Norvin G.	born _____; married Donna _____
1511. Kathleen L.	born 8 Feb 1951; married Garry L. BAUMUNK (born 27 Mar 1954)

1125. LUCILE MARIE-[7] HUBERT, daughter of Harriet-[6] FELIX (Lena Belle-[5] CRAWFORD; Lucy Delphine-[4] MC INTOSH; William-[3]; Simon-[2]; Alexander-[1]) and Jon (John George) HUBERT, was born 18 Jan 1916 at Hornell, Steuben County, NY. She married Kenneth L. CROSTON on 18 Jan 1934 at Hornell. he was the son of John W. CROSTON and Maude ____, and was born 9 Jan 1915; died Jan 1978, Clifton, NJ. Lucile Marie-[7] HUBERT died 27 May 2007 Houghton, Allegany County, NY.

Children of Lucile Marie-[7] HUBERT and Kenneth CROSTON:
Surname **CROSTON**   (all children born Hornell, Steuben County, NY)

1512. John Leman	born 7 Aug 1934 (Vietnam Vet)
" Jack "	married Carolyn RAISH 16 Jan 1954

Children: Cynthia Ann-[9] born 19 Dec 1955, married Michael S. SUGG 19 May 1990 Greenville, NC;
and Cheryl-[9] CROSTON born ca 1958 Hornell, NY

1513. Neal Kenneth	born 17 June 1937; died 1985; married Martha EMORY ca 1955

Children: Jill-[9] born ___, married Warren TAPP; Christopher-[9] born ca 1965;
and Gregory-[9] CROSTON born 1967, died 1971

1514. Elaine Harriet	born 6 Apr 1946 ; married Michael COLE

Children: Jonathan-[9] born ___, and Aaron-[9] COLE born ____

1515. Terry	born _____; adopted out to a family by the name of TINGUELY

1126. BETTY JUNE-[7] HUBERT, sister of above, was born 4 Sep 1921 at Hornell, Steuben County, NY. She married Norman K. WALKER on 11 Oct 1947. He was the son of _____ WALKER and ____, and was born _____; died ____. Betty June-[7] HUBERT was a school nurse, and died _____.

Child of Betty June-[7] HUBERT and Norman K. WALKER:
Surname **WALKER**

1516. Marguerite Kay	born 19 Nov 1950 Geneva, Ontario, NY
	married Arden Duane WELLINGTON 1 Apr 1972; divorced 1994
	(he s/o Grant Ulysses WELLINGTON and Wilma BOYLAN)
	(he born 1 Aug 1949 Hornell, NY)

Children: Bonnie Kay-[9] born 29 Oct 1980 Johnson City, NY, and Brian Duane-[9] WELLINGTON born 12 May 1983 Johnson City

1127. HARRIET JANE-[7] HUBERT, sister of above, was born 24 Mar 1925 at North Hornell, Steuben County, NY. She married Richard West BRADLEY on 9 Apr 1943 at Atlanta, GA. He was the son of _____ (adopted by the Bradley family as an infant), and was born 1919 Chicago, IL; died 27 Dec 1996 at Wellsville, Allegany County, NY. Harriet-[7] HUBERT died _____.

Children of Harriet-[7] HUBERT and Richard BRADLEY:
Surname **BRADLEY**

1517. Richard Hubert	born ca 1945; married _____; divorced no issue
1518. Thomas Booth	born ca 1947
1519. Jeffrey Justin	born 14 July 1950 (Vietnam Vet – US Navy)
	married Terressa Jane STALEY 29 Sep 1973 Wellsville, NY

Children: Sarah-[9] born 1980; Rebecca-[9] born ___, and Justin-[9] BRADLEY born ___

1520. Carol Anne	born 1962 Wellsville, NY
	married John Edward FULMER 28 June 1986 ; divorced no issue

1128. ROSAMOND ANN[-7] **HUBERT**, sister of above, was born 29 Aug 1929 at North Hornell, Steuben County, NY. She married Jack ORDWAY, son of Bertram J. ORDWAY, on 26 Sep 1948 at Hornell, NY.

Children of Rosamond[-7] HUBERT and Jack ORDWAY:
Surname **ORDWAY**

1521. Kari Elizabeth	born ca 1953 Hornell, NY; 1 married Timothy KELLEY; divorced	
	2 married Lee MIFFLIN 14 Aug 1992 at Bath, Steuben, NY	
1522. Bradley	born 14 Feb 1959 Hornell, NY	
	married Mary KELLEY ca 1978 Canisteo, Steuben, NY	

Children: Joshua-[9] born 1978, Aubrey-[9] born ___, and Braelyn-[9] ORDWAY born ca ____

1141. ANNA ETTA-[7] **CRANDALL**, daughter of Stanley Orrin[-6] CRANDALL (Etta[-5] MC INTOSH; Henry[-4]; Matthias[-3] Simon[-2]; Alexander[-1]) and Dorothy CASTILLON, was born 22 Dec 1925. She married first to Spiro Joseph PETERS +++ on 25 Feb 1951. He was born 8 June 1925 at Buffalo, NY; died 13 Sep 1952. Anna Etta-7 CRANDALL married second to William STEAR on __ Oct 1954. He was the son of William Leo STEAR and Anna ARNOLD, and was born 16 Jan 1926 Rochester, Monroe County, NY; died 24 Apr 1994. Anna Etta-[7] CRANDALL died _____.

++ Spiro PETERS was a 1st Lieutenant in the US Air Force. during the Korean War. He was a crew member of a B-29 Superfortress Bomber with the 371st Bomber Wing based at Kadena Air Base, Okinawa. On Sep 13, 1952, while making a bomb run on the Suiho Hydroelectric Plant, his aircraft was hit by anti-aircraft fire. He was listed as missing in action and was presumed dead on 28 Feb 1954. Lt. PETERS was awarded the Air Medal, the Purple Heart, the United Nations Service Medal, the National Defense Service Medal and the Korean War Service Medal.

Children of Anna Etta-[7] CRANDALL and William STEAR:
Surname **STEAR**

1523. Carolyn	born 10 Nov 1955; died 25 Sep 1957		
1524. Ellen Amy	born 19 June 1958	1526. Robert Lawrence	born 27 Feb 1962
1525. William Lee	born 20 Feb 1960	1527. Martha Susan	born 23 Dec 1963

1142. ROBERT STEPHEN[-7] **CRANDALL**, brother of above, was born 18 July 1927. He married Betty WOLF on 4 Sep 1948 at Rochester, Monroe County, NY. She was the daughter of Henry WOLF and Irene _____, and was born 9 Oct 1927, died 13 Sep 2007 at Rochester, NY.

Children of Robert Stephen[-7] CRANDALL and Betty WOLF:
Surname **CRANDALL**

1528. Karen Ann	born 13 Dec 1949	1530. Barbara Jean	born 26 Jan 1954
1529. Susan Ruth	born 12 July 1952	1531. Robert Stephen, Jr.	born 6 Sep 1958

1143. NORMA LOUISE[-7] **SHEPARD**, daughter of Mary Louise[-6] CRANDALL (Etta[-5] MC INTOSH; Henry-[4]; Matthias[-3]; Simon[-2]; Alexander[-1]) and Norman SHEPARD, was born 16 Mar 1929 at Skaneateles, Onondaga County, NY. She married William SCHULTZ on 13 Nov 1947. He was the son of _____ SCHULTZ and ____, and was born 31 Mar 1927 Auburn, Cayuga County, NY; died _____.

Children of Norma LOUISE[-7] SHEPARD and William SCHULTZ.
Surname **SCHULTZ**

1532. William Eric	born1 May 1948	1535. Darryl Anne	born 22 Nov 1952
1533. Mary Christine	born 28 June 1950	1536. David Alan	born 25 July 1955
1534. Jeffery Mark	born 4 Dec 1951		

1144. DOROTHY JEAN[-7] **SHEPARD**, sister of above, was born 13 Jan 1932 at _____, NY. She married Selma Alexander DECKER, Jr. on 7 Aug 1948 at Harlinger, TX. He was the son of Selma Alexander DECKER, Sr. and Winnie Blanch VAUGHAN, and was born 14 Oct 1928 TX; died _____.

Children of Dorothy Jean[-7] SHEPARD and Selma A. DECKER, Jr.:
Surname **DECKER**

 1537. Kathleen Alice   born 18 Mar 1951 Cameron, TX
                           1 married Douglas Loren FALTINSON on 19 June 1971 TX
                           Child: Anna Marie-[9] FALTINSON born 3 Apr 1977 Wichita, TX
                           2 married (poss.) John M. GANNAWAY on 7 Apr 1984 TX
 1538. Lisbeth Jean   born 18 July 1953   Cameron County, TX

1145. GLENN HOWARD-[7] HEWITT, son of Theron Wilbur[-6] HEWITT (Clara[-5] MC INTOSH; Henry-[4]; Matthias[-3]; Simon[-2]; Alexander-[1]) and Mabel Captola GREEN , was born 28 Aug 1913 St. Lawrence County, NY. He married Mabel R. VAUGHN on _____ 1933 at ____. She was the daughter of _____ VAUGHN and _____, and was born 2 May 1912 NY; died 25 Jan 1998 at Potsdam, NY. Glenn Howard[-7] HEWITT died 15 Oct 1994 at Potsdam, NY.

Children of Glenn[-7] HEWITT and Mabel VAUGHN:
Surname **HEWITT**

 1539. June   born 31 May 1934 NY; married Howard MARSCHAT, Jr.
                          (he born 9 Mar 1936; died 13 June 2003 Canton, St. Lawrence, NY)
                          (he s/o Howard MARSCHAT, Sr. and _____)
 1540. Richard D.   born 6 Aug 1936 NY; died 7 June 2009 Palm Harbor, Pinellas, FL
 1541. Charlotte   born 16 Apr 1939; married Ralph GRANGER ca 1957
 1542. Sharon   born 5 Dec 1945
 1543. Diana (twin)   born 27 June 1949   1544. Donna (twin)   born 27 June 1949

1146. FAY NELSON-[7] HEWITT, brother of above, was born 3 July 1915 at ___, St. Lawrence. NY. He married Bernice WHITCOMB on 26 June 1954 at ____. She was the daughter of ____ WHITCOMB and _____, and was born ca 1932 NY; died 2001. Fay Nelson[-7] HEWITT died 14 July 1995.

Children of Fay Nelson[-7] HEWITT and Bernice WHITCOMB:
Surname **HEWITT**

 1545 Terry   born _____   1547. Toni Lee   born _____
 1546. Theron Russell   born ca 1957 St. Lawrence Co., NY; died _____ Buffalo, NY

1147. ALICE JUNE-[7] HEWITT, sister of above, was born 10 June 1920 at ____, St. Lawrence County, NY. She married Ralph VAN BROCKLIN of Colton, St. Lawrence County, NY. on _____. He was the son of Erskine VAN BROCKLIN and Louise MC DONALD, and was born 25 July 1914, died 24 Feb 1992 at Canton, St. Lawrence, NY. Alice June[-7] HEWITT died 17 Mar 2005 Canton, NY

Children of Alice June[-7] HEWITT and Ralph VAN BROCKLIN:
Surname **VAN BROCKLIN**

 1548. Fay Ralph   born 29 July 1937 NY;   married Barbara WADLEIGH 15 Aug 1959
 1549. Marthena   born 4 Apr 1939; married Albert WHITCOMB
 1550. Norma June   born 14 Aug 1941
 1551. Ronald Theron   born 2 Jan 1946; married Alice Elaine ALLEN June 1984
                          (she dau/o Stanley ALLEN and Vina Julia WALKER)
                          Child: Karen Louise-[9] VAN BROCKLIN born ____
 1552. Meribeth   born _____   1553. Arnold   born _____

1154. GEORGE EVERETT-[7] GARD, son of Fannie Pearl[-6] FREEMAN (Clara[-5] KIFF; Fanny-[4] MC INTOSH; Matthias[-3]; Simon[-2]; Alexander-[1]) and George Alvin GARD, was born 7 Nov 1918 at Wysox Township, PA. He married Dorothy M. JOHNS on 13 June 1942 at Columbia, PA. She was the daughter of Thomas JOHNS and Alice ____, and was born 8 Dec 1918 PA, died ____. George Everett-[7] GARD died Feb 2003 Columbia, Lancaster, PA

Children of George $^{-7}$ GARD and Dorothy JOHNS:
Surname **GARD**

1554. Barbara Sue	born 15 June 1946 Lancaster; married Philip L. KOHL 30 Oct 1971
1555. George Johns	born 27 June 1949 Lancaster, PA
	married Molly A. HARTENSTEIN 2 Oct 1987
1556. Linda Kay	born 28 Dec 1953 Lancaster, PA.

1155. WALTER FREEMAN^{-7} **GARD**, brother of above, was born 26 Nov 1922 at Wysox Township, PA. He married Rose THOMSON 22 Nov 1950. Walter F^{-7} GARD died 8 Feb 1977 at Middletown, NY

Child of Walter-^{7}GARD and Rose THOMSON:
Surname **GARD**

1557. Mark Freeman   born 8 Dec 1961 Middletown, NY

1159. PATRICIA / PATSY^{-7} **FENSTERMACHER**, daughter of Marian^{-6} MC INTOSH (Frederick^{-5}; Lewis L^{-4}; Matthias^{-3}; Simon^{-2}; Alexander^{-1}) and Miles L. FENSTERMACHER, Jr., was born 12 Mar 1945 at Pottsgrove, PA. She married first to Robert W. CALKINS on 28 July 1966 at East Chillisquaque Township, Pottsgrove, PA. He was the son of _____ CALKINS and ___, and was born ca 1943 Covington, PA. They divorced before 1990. She married second to John D. ACKLEY on 18 Aug 1990.

Children of Patsy^{-7} FENSTERMACHER and Robert CALKINS;
Surname **CALKINS**

1558. Danielle LaRae	born 3 Feb 1967
1559. Robert W., Jr.	born 13 Mar 1968 Troy, PA; married Tammy WILSON 21 Jan 1989

1161. MILES L^{-7} **FENSTERMACHER, III**, brother of above, was born 18 Apr 1948 at Pottsgrove, PA. He married first to Nancy JONES on ___ at ___. She was the daughter of ___ JONES and ____, and was born ___. They were divorced, and he married second to Michelle BURNS Dec 1984.

Children of Miles^{-7} FENSTERMACHER and Nancy JONES:
Surname **FENSTERMACHER**

1560. Miles L. IV	born 5 May 1971
1561. Wayne Asher	born 26 May 1975

Children of Miles^{-7} FENSTERMACHER and Michelle BURNS:
Surname **FENSTERMACHER**

1562. Samantha Jo	born 21 June 1985
1563. Meagan Rae	born 19 Jan 1987

1173. NORMA L^{-7} **MC INTOSH**, daughter of Walter Perry-^{6} MC INTOSH (Charles K^{-5}; Theophilus^{-4}; George^{-3}; Simon^{-2}; Alexander^{-1}) and Mary Louise DURBIN, was born 10 July 1913 at Syracuse, Onondaga, New York. She married Ralph Edward HONSBERGER on 1 Sep 1934 at Skaneateles, NY. He was the son of Orin Edwin HONSBERGER and Louise Elizabeth SCHOPP, and was born 4 Dec 1911 Buffalo, NY; died 28 May 1991 (age 79) He was the General Manager of the Mead Company, Syracuse Division, retiring in 1977. Norma^{-7} MC INTOSH died suddenly on 18 Oct 1969 while attending a social function at the Skaneateles Country Club. Ralph married second to Mary COCHRAN.

Children of Norma^{-7} MC INTOSH and Ralph HONSBERGER:
Surname **HONSBERGER**

+ **1564. GRETCHEN**	born 5 June 1937 Syracuse, NY
LOUISE	1 married John Albert DAWSON, Jr. ca ____; divorced
	2 married Robert J. REILLY resided Brookline, MA 2002
	(he born 1 Feb 1932 Westfield, MA; died 9 Apr 2004 MA)

Children of Norma-[7] MC INTOSH and Ralph HONSBERGER, continued:
Surname **HONSBERGER**
+   **1565. KAREN E.**   born 9 Sep 1942 Syracuse, NY
     married William EDGAR 10 July 19___ Skaneateles, NY

1174. MARGERY E[7] **MC INTOSH**, sister of above, was born 10 Aug 1916 at White Plains, NY. She married G. (George) Franklin DOLBEAR on 3 May 1941 at ____. He was the adopted son of Frederick Lloyd DOLBEAR and Marietta FLINT, and was born 10 Aug 1914; died 15 Nov 1999 at Syracuse, NY. His birth parents are unknown,, but his wife told this researcher that his birth surname was CAMPBELL.

Children of Margery-[7] MC INTOSH and G. Frank DOLBEAR:
Surname **DOLBEAR**
     1566. John Flint   born 11 July 1942 Syracuse, NY; never married
+   **1567. ROBERT BRUCE** born 29 Oct 1946 Syracuse, NY
     married Carol Ann ELMER ca _____; divorced
     1568. David Franklin   born 31 Jan 1948;   married Kathryn OSBORNE ca ____; divorced

1180. ROBERT STERLING[7] **TRELAWNY**, son of Marguerite Esther-[7] STERLING (William Tyler-[5]; Sarah Adeline-[4] MC INTOSH; Simon,Jr-[3]; Simon -[2]; Alexander-[1]) and Charles Harold TRELAWNY, was born 28 May 1926 at _____. He married Wilma BROWN of Syracuse, NY, on ____. She was the daughter of ____ BROWN and ____, and was born ____. They divorced ca ____.

Children of Robert S-[7] TRELAWNY and Wilma BROWN:
Surname **TRELAWNY**
     1569. Susan Marie   born 5 Oct 1951   1571. John Ralph   born 28 June 1953
     1570. Jeannie Roberts   born 28 June 1953

1181. DR. GILBERT STERLING[7] **TRELAWNY, BS, MS and PhD**, brother of above, was born 12 Nov 1929 at __, PA. He married Florence Ann MULHOLLAND 19 Nov 1950. She was the daughter of Edward MULHOLLAND and Sarah BRESLIN and was born 9 Jan 1932, died 22 Sep 2009 at Strasburg, VA. Dr. TRELAWNY was on the faculty of James Madison University at Harrisonburg, VA. He was a Microbiologist and retired as Professor Emeritus of the Biology Dept. of James Madison University.

Children of Gilbert S-[7] TRELAWNY and Florence MULHOLLAND:
Surname **TRELAWNY**
     1572. Edward Charles   born 17 Nov 1958, married Sheila ____
          Children: Dillon T-[9], William S-[9], and John E.-[9] TRELAWNY
     1573. Janice Ann   born 5 Sep 1960, died before 2009
     married James RATTENBURY
     1574. James   born _____

1183. JANICE E[7] **GREENOUGH**, daughter of Willis Benjamin-[6] GREENOUGH (Merton-[5]; Mary Caroline-[4] MC INTOSH; Simon, Jr-[3;] Simon-[2]; Alexander-[1]) and Nettie Hannah LEONARD, was born 24 June 1919 at Troy, Bradford County, PA. She married Angus C. GOODSON on ____ (before 1950). He was the son of Billie GOODSON and Mary/ Ella ____, and was born 10 July 1919 Allendale, SC ; died 13 Nov 2009 at Sterling, Loudon, VA. Janet-[7] GREENOUGH died 3 Feb 2003 at Walter Reed Medical Center. They are both buried at Arlington National Cemetery, VA.

An article in the Syracuse (NY) Herald Journal 8 Feb 1959 read as follows:
Major Angus C. GOODSON, who is being transferred to headquarters USAF in Washington, DC, was presented with the Air Force Commendation Medal for his distinguished service while at Rome (NY) Air Materiel area. The presentation was made by General Clyde H. MITCHELL.   The award reads in part " During his assignment, Major GOODSON demonstrated keen initiative, aggressiveness and high professional ability in the formulation of the communications-electronics obsolescence program, development

of the maintenance electronic support concept of the operation , and the integration of complex electronic equipment into the systems concept. " Major GOODSON had previously served at Griffis (Air Force Base, Rome NY) from 1942 – 45as a signal officer. He also served in India, Japan and Denmark. He retired from the service with a rank of Lt. Colonel.

Children of Janet[7] GREENOUGH and Angus GOODSON:
Surname **GOODSON**

1575. Angus II	born Sept 1950 NY; married Mary _____	
1576. Suzanne	born 9 May 1952 CA.; married James Edward DARNES (he born ca 1949; died 29 Jan 2012 Sterling, VA) (he s/o Horace E. DARNES and Clara A. _____)	
	Child: Grant Galbraith-[9] DARNES born ca ____	
1577. Signe	born ca 1954 Denmark; married Rick FORESTER	
1578. Patricia Ann	born 1 Oct 1956; married Andy DODSON	

1184. ROBERT HENRY[7] GREENOUGH, son of Caleb C[6] GREENOUGH (Charles[5;] Mary Caroline[4] MC INTOSH; Simon,Jr[3] ; Simon[2;] Alexander[1]) and Gladys ALLYN, was born 18 Feb 1925 at East Tory, Bradford, PA. He married Shirley B. DUNBAR on 14 Nov 1942 at Troy, PA. She was the daughter of Frank DUNBAR and Lena ___, and was born 6 Oct 1925, died 27 Feb 2009 Columbia Cross Roads, Bradford, PA. Robert[6] GREENOUGH died ___ .

Children of Robert H-[6] GREENOUGH and Shirley DUNBAR:
Surname **GREENOUGH**

+	**1579. ROBERT HENRY II**	born 30 Aug 1946 married Shirley COMFORT Jan 1965
	1580. Timothy Leonard	born 5 Feb 1949; married Kathy HALL
	1581. Brad Lee (twin)	born and died July 1952 1581. Brent Lee (twin)born and died July 1952
+	**1582. DEBBIE**	born 24 Aug 1953 1 married Gary NICHOLS ca ____; divorced 2 married James GUINAN June 1990
	1583. Vickie	born 7 Sep 1957

1185. DOROTHY[7] GREENOUGH, sister of above, was born 27 Sep 1927 at East Troy, PA. She married Edward AUSTIN on 6 Apr 1948 at Troy, PA. He was the son of Clarence J. AUSTIN and Emma ___, and was born 20 May 1926 PA.

Children of Dorothy[7] GREENOUGH and Edward AUSTIN:
Surname **AUSTIN**

1584. Larue	born 29 Sep 1947		
1585. Larry	born 18 Jan 1949; died 17 June 1965		
1586. Wesley	born 18 July 1950	1589. Nadine Sue	born 9 Jan 1959
1587. Ronald	born 21 Mar 1952	1590. Julia Ann	born 13 Mar 1963
1588. Cindy Lou	born 12 Dec 1957		

1186. SHIRLEY[7] GREENOUGH, sister of above, was born 12 Jan 1931 at East Troy, PA. She married Milford KINSMAN on 27 May 1950 at ____ PA. He was the son of Meredith KINSMAN and Myrtle ____, and was born 28 Sep 1928 PA; died 2 July 2007 PA.

Children of Shirley-[7] GREENOUGH and Milford KINSMAN:
Surname **KINSMAN**

+	**1591. PAMELA MAE**	born 30 Mar 1951; married _____ HASELTINE 15 May 1971 PA
+	**1592. PATRICIA**	born 22 Apr 1952; married Leon WEITZ 23 Apr 1977 East Troy, PA
+	**1593. GLEN M.**	born 20 Aug 1953; married Dorothy _____ 5 Apr 1980
+	**1594. KIM C.** (m.)	born 15 Aug 1956; married Dorothy CLARK 6 Oct 1979

Children of Shirley-[7] GREENOUGH and Milford KINSMAN, continued:
Surname **KINSMAN**

+   **1595. PENNY LOU**   born 11 Aug 1959
                                    married Douglas WALBORN 25 Apr 1981 (he born 24 Aug 1957)
+   **1596. PEARL**   born 20 Sep 1960 ; married Gerard SIMONIS 19 Oct 1985

1187. CHARLES LEE-[7] METZGER, Sr., son of Helen C[7] GREENOUGH (Charles.-[5]; Mary Caroline[4] MC INTOSH; Simon, Jr[3]; Simon[2]; Alexander[1]) and Tracey METZGER, was born 14 Apr 1922 _____, PA. He married Edith Ann " Suzzy" MERRICK on 8 Mar 1947. She was the daughter of Harold L. MERRICK and Helen BOOKER, and was born 21 Dec 1920 Wilmington, DE, died 24 Dec 2009 Elizabethtown PA. Charles Lee-7 METZGER died 24 Feb 2006 at Elizabethtown, PA.   Charles Lee-[7] METZGER received a BS from Drexel University (1947) he was a veteran of the US Army, having served with the 10th Air Service Squadron.

Children of Charles -[7] METGER, Sr. and Edith MERRICK:
Surname **METZGER**

        1597. Charles Lee, Jr.   born 27 May 1949; married Shirley C._____
                Children: Christopher J.-[9] born ca 1985, married Heidi ____ and Charles L-III -[9]METZGER
        1598. Helen M.   born 27 June 1951; married Ricke ZUMSTEG
                Child: Eric-9 ZUMSTEG born ___, married Liza ____

1188. PHILIP[7] F METZGER, brother of above, was born 2/3 July 1925 at ____, PA. He married Anise SMITH on 11 Aug 1956 at ___. She was the daughter of ___ SMITH and ____, and was born 9 May 1931. Philip[7] died 14 Feb at Columbia CrossRoads, Bradford, PA.

Children of Phillip-7 METZGER and Anise SMITH;
Surname **METZGER**

        1599. Denise   born 29 Apr 1959   1600. Yolanda   born 21 Nov 1961/63

1191. MARJORIE[7] GREENOUGH, daughter of Paul E[6] GREENOUGH (Charles[5]; Mary Caroline[4] MC INTOSH: Simon[3] Jr.; Simon[2]; Alexander[1]) and Ina TOMLINSON, was born 16 Oct 1921 at ____PA. She married Kirtland Peter CLARK on at ____. He was the son of William O. CLARK and Florence Esther BRUIELLY, and was born 28 Apr 1921 PA, died 13 Apr 2000 Mansfield, Tioga, PA. He was a US Navy veteran of WW 2, and is buried at the Oakwood Cemetery, Mansfield, PA. Marjorie[7] GREENOUGH died ca 2008.

Children of Marjorie-[7] GREENOUGH and Kirtland CLARK:
Surname **CLARK**

        1601. Gwendolyn   born __ June 19__ ; married David KING ca 1964
        1602. Monema   born 29 Jul 19__
        1603. Kirtland, Jr.   born 13 Aug 1944; married _____ Jan 1966
        1604. David   born 24 Aug 1946 ; married Janet _____ 3 June 1965

1197. PAUL DEWITT-[7] STERLING, son of Charles Lee[6] STERLING (Frederick James-[5]; Elizabeth Jane-[4] MC INTOSH; Simon[3], Jr.; Simon[2]; Alexander[1]) and Hazel Frances-[9] DOTY, was born 15 Apr 1922 at Syracuse, Onondaga County, NY. He married first to Mildred G. BALCOM on __ May 1943. She was the daughter of Charles Alvin BALCOM (20 Dec 1895 – Apr 1985 Oswego Co., NY) and Leona Marcia LIGHTHALL of Pulaski, Oswego County, NY, and was born 13 Sep 1924, died Jan 1991. They divorced, and she married second in 1956 to Walter MERRIAM who was killed in an automobile accident (18 Jan 1957, and tthird to ___ DAWLEY. Paul-[7] STERLING married second to Josephine-[2] SHUBA on 21 Aug 1946 at Syracuse, NY. She was the daughter of Lewis SHUBA and Stella SCHURICK, who were immigrants, and was born 21 Mar 1920 NY. Note: Paul and Jo celebrated their 66th wedding anniversary 21 Aug 2012.

158

Child of Paul D-[7] STERLING and Mildred BALCOM:
Surname **STERLING**

+   **1605. CONSTANCE**   **born 8 Jan 1944 Syracuse, NY; 1 married _____RIDGEWAY**
         LOUISE   (he s/o Myron RIDGEWAY and Marie HALE)
                            2 married Donald ROBERTS 2 Apr 1970
                            (he s/o George William ROBERTS and Lillian Johanna KLEVER)

Children of Paul D-[7] STERLING and Josephine SHUBA:
Surname **STERLING**

       1606. Paul DeWitt, Jr..   born 28 Oct 1947 Syracuse, NY
       1607. Phillip David   born 10 July 1953 Syracuse, NY
                             married Sharon Mae MARVIN 11 Sep 1982 Baldwinsville, NY
            (she dau/o Howard MARVIN, Jr. and Florence Mae MERRIWEATHER)
                             (she born 12 Oct 1950 NY;   )

+   **1608. ROBERT**   born 28 Aug 1954 Syracuse, NY
         EDWARD   married Carol Ruth KIRSCHENBAUM 23 Dec 1977 No. Syracuse
                             (she dau/o Charles KIRSCHENBAUM and Virginia YEACKEL)
                             (she born 25 Aug 1954)

1198. FRANCES JEAN-[7] STERLING, sister of above, was born 3 June 1927 at Syracuse, Onondaga County, New York. She graduated from North Syracuse High School , Class of 1944. She did her undergraduate and graduate studies at Syracuse University, studying Fashion Design and then Interior Design. She free lanced for many years in the Interior Design field. Later she began genealogical research, having one book published in 1993, another in 2001. She joined the DAR on the MC INTOSH line.

She married first to George Dolbey DRISKO on 31 Jan 1947 at Syracuse, NY. He was the son of Henry William DRISKO and Leah Belle DOLBEY, and was born 16 Nov 1917 Syracuse, NY; died 14 Jan 1994 at North Syracuse, NY. She married second to Paul Edward BOWKER on 29 Mar 2003 at Cary, NC. He was the son of Howard Edward BOWKER and Dorothy Mae McKINNEY, and was born 14 May 1926.

Children of Frances Jean-[7] STERLING and George Dolbey DRISKO:
Surname **DRISKO**

       1609. Linda Lee   born 11 June 1951 Syracuse, NY
                             graduated Wells College, Aurora, NY 1973 (Bio-Psych major)
                             1 married Charles John HICKOK 15 May 1976 Wells College Chapel
                             divorced 1990
                             2 married John Michael HURLEY 11 June 1994 North Syracuse, NY
                             (he s/o James Tully HURLEY and Teresa DONABELLA)
                             (he born 9 Dec 1950)
       1610. Charles Eric   born 27 July 1953 Syracuse, NY;   divorced 1984
         C. Eric   married Patricia A. TEMPLE 17 Mar 1979 North Syracuse, NY
                             graduated Auburn Community College – degree in Police Science

+   **1611. DANA**   born 29 July 1958 Syracuse, NY
         STERLING   married Jennifer Lynn REYNOLDS 17 Sep 1983
                             (she dau/o John Francis H. REYNOLDS and Patricia DAIR Brennan)
                             (she born 23 Apr 1961)
                             graduated Cornell University, Class of 1980 Major in Finance

1199. MARJORIE-[7] DANN, daughter of Arthur-[6] DANN (Sterling James-[5]; Adelia-[4] MC INTOSH, Simon-[3] Jr., Simon-[2]; Alexander-[1]) and Margaret ENGLISH, was born 8 Mar 1916 at ___,PA. She married first to James J. GALLO on ____. There are no known children of that union. She married second to Leo LEWIS before 1934, and her third marriage was to Edward Dow VAN DYNE 18 Oct 1958, Elmira, NY Marjorie-[7] DANN died 9 May 2007 Canton, Bradford, PA

Children of Marjorie-[7] DANN and Leo LEWIS:
Surname **LEWIS**

1612. Arthur Lee	born 22 July 1934; died 1968
1613. Stephanie	born 5 Nov 1938

Children of Marjorie-[7] DANN and ____ VAN DYNE:
Surname **VAN DYNE**

1614. Lynne Laird	born 21 Jan 1942; died 1977
1615. Donald Gary	born 11 Dec 1943/44; died 1983

1201. SONIA-[7] DANN, daughter of Leland[6] DANN (Sterling[5]; Adelia-[4] MC INTOSH; Simon[3], Jr., Simon[2]; Alexander[1]) and Renee' F. ____, was born 21 Oct 1922 France. She married first to ____ BARR on ____ at ____. He was the son of ____ BARR and ___, and was born ___; died ____. her second marriage was to Robert Harley CHRISTY on ___ at ____. He was the son of ____ CHRISTY and ____, and was born 16 Oct 1922; died 21 Dec 1986 Volusia FL. Sonia-[7] DANN died 24 Oct 2007 at Hudson, FL Sonia-[7] DANN enlisted in the Womans Army Corps on 19 Nov 1943 at Rochester, Monroe, NY.

Child of Sonia-[7] DANN and ____ BARR:
Surname **BARR**

1616. Donald	born ca ____

Children of Sonia-[7] DANN and Robert Harley CHRISTY:
Surname **CHRISTY**

1617. Roberta	born ___	1619. Willard	born ____
1618. Annette	born ____		

1202. GEORGE DANN-[7] WHITING, son of Grace[6] DANN (Sterling[5]; Adelia-[4] MC INTOSH; Simon[3] Jr.; Simon[2]; Alexander[1]) and George WHITING, was born 5 Nov 1924 at Canton, Bradford County, PA. He married first to Gwendolyn LAPE/LAPSE on ___ at ___. She was the daughter of ____ LAPE/LAPSE , and was born 19 Dec 1933; died 22 Apr 2006 Aurora, CO. They divorced July 1969. He married second to Mila ____ on ___ at ___. George-[7] WHITING died 11 Feb 1986.

Children of George-7 WHITING and Mila ____:
Surname **WHITING**

1620. Ernest Florentino	born 2 Nov 1982	1621. George Anthony	born 30 Aug 1986

1203. JAMES VINCENT-[7] WHITING, brother of above, was born 19 May 1926 at Canton, Bradford County, NY. He married Bernita BLANCHARD on 20 Nov 1945 at Reading Center, New York. She was the daughter of Oscar BLANCHARD and Elsie ____, and was born Jan 1928 at Watkins Glen, Schuyler County, NY. They resided at Solano Beach, CA.

Children of James Vincent-[7] WHITING and Bernita BLANCHARD:
Surname **WHITING**

+	**1622. JAMES STUART**	born 12 Jan 1947 married Patricia HAVENS	(she born 31 Dec 1946)
+	**1623. DONNA JO**	born 15 Oct 1948; married Harry ORLYK	(he born 8 Jan 1948)
	1624. John Robert	born 20 Aug 1952	
+	**1625. ANDREA LYNN**	born 10 Sep 1961 1626. David Blanchard	born 13 Mar 1963

1209. WILLIAM ARCHIE-[7] RYAN, son of Hazel Florence-[6] LANDON (Lillian-[5] CEASE; Leroy[4]; Julia-[3] MC INTOSH; Simon[2]; Alexander-[1]) and Edward Eleazer RYAN, was born 5 Feb 1915 at Elmira, Chemung, NY. He married Lucille DeEtta HAMMOND on 15 Apr 1939 NY. She was the daughter of Ray Friese HAMMOND and Nina Phidelia BERRY, and was born 4 Feb 1918 Elmira, NY; died 22 June 2007 at Oregon, Ogle, IL. They divorced Jan 1972. William A[7] RYAN died 30 May 1984 at Bath, Steuben County, NY.

Children of William-[7] RYAN and Lucille HAMMOND:
Surname **RYAN**

1627. Robert	born _____	1629. James	born _____
1628. Shirley	born _____	1630. Bonnie	born _____

1211. LEWIS / LOUIS R.-[7] RYAN, brother of above, was born 18 Nov 1919 at Elmira, Chemung, NY. He married Cleo Mae DECKER on ___ at ____. She was the daughter of Carl DECKER and Blanch ____, and was born 25 Jan 1921; died 10 Sept 1987 Elmira, NY.

Children of Lewis-7 RYAN and Cleo DECKER:
Surname **RYAN**

1631. Linda	born ____	1633. Kathy	born ____
1632. Lou	born ____		

1214. MARY LOU-[7] LANDON, daughter of Lewis/Louis-[6] LANDON (Lillian-[5] CEASE; Leroy-[4]; Julia-[3] MC INTOSH; Simon-[2]; Alexander -[1]) and Marie Mc CLURE, was born 15 Oct 1924 at ____ PA. She married Ellis Frederick " Gunner " HAVENS on ___ at ____. He was the son of Carl Edward HAVENS and Esther Dean CRANDELL, and was born 5 May 1924; died 17 Feb 1999 Elmira, NY. Mary Lou-[7] LANDON died 12 Nov 1982. Ellis married 2nd Margaret ____ O'HARA.

Children of Mary Lou-[7] LANDON and Ellis HAVENS:
Surname **HAVENS**

1634. JoAnn	born ____, married Robert GANCE; resided Sinking Spring, PA
1635. Maureen	born ____, married Robert CARMODY; resided Wilmington, NC
1636. Kim (m)	born ____, married Jeri _____ ; resided Wilmington, NC

 1215. ROBERT T-[7] LANDON, brother of above, was born 10 July 1927 at ____ PA. He married Rita M. SCHIEFEN on 7 Oct 1950 at Elmira, Chemung County, NY. She was the daughter of Carl Francis SCHIEFEN and Mary Evelyn. DUNN, and was born 15 May 1929; died 27 Oct 2006 at Horseheads, Chemung, NY. Robert-[7] LANDON died May 1978 at Corning, Steuben, NY.

Children of Robert-[7] LANDON and Rita SCHIEFEN:
Surname **LANDON**

1637. Eileen	born 27 Feb 1952; died 25 April 1993
1638. Thomas L.	born 9 Aug 1953; died 26 Feb 1997 Elmira, NY
1639. Susan F.	born _____; married _____ JOHNSON
	Children: Joshua-9 born ca ___, and Margo-9 JOHNSON born ca ___
1640. Mary K.	born _____; married Walter MELVILLE
	Children: Amy-9 born ca ___, Stephanie 9 born ca ___, and Alex-9 MELVILLE born ca _____

1220. JACQUELINE-[7] CEASE, daughter of Lysle W-[6] CEASE (Willard-[5]; Nelson-[4]; Julia Ann -[3] MC INTOSH; Simon-[2]; Alexander-[1]) and Alwyn Christina WYLE, and was born 23 June 1930 Bremerton, WA. She married James Walter AILSTOCK, Jr. ++ on ___ at ____ (before 1950). He was the son of James Walter AILSTOCK, Jr. and Garnette Roveda WHITE, and was born 6 May 1924 VA; died 24 March 1980 Virginia Beach, VA. Jacqueline-[7] CEASE died 19 April 1999 at Virginia Beach, VA.

++ Note: James Walter AILSTOCK, Jr. served as a Lt..in the US Army during WW2,
He served 38 months in the Pacific., 18 of those on Okinawa

Children of Jacqueline-[7] CEASE and J. W. AILSTOCK, Jr.:
Surname **AILSTOCK**

1641. Robin	born _____		
1642. Rebecca	born 1 Jan 1956. married Samuel F. ESLEECK		
1643. Gerry/Ginny	born _____	1644. John Christopher	born 4 Sep 1961

Children of Jacqueline-7 CEASE and J. W. AILSTOCK, Jr., continued:
Surname **AILSTOCK**

    1645. Dr.Lysle Kennedy   born 15 Mar 1965; Radiology and Nuclear medicine
    1646. James W III   born ____   1647. Joy   born _____

1221. STEPHEN W.-7 CEASE, brother of above,was born 4 Dec 1933 at ___, PA_. In 1950 he was a student at The Valley Forge Military Academy in Wayne, PA. In 1980 he was a pilot for Pan American Airlines, and resided in Portland, Oregon. He married first to _____; and married second to Mary LEWTON 5 Apr 1975 Multnomah, OR

Children of Stephen-7 CEASE and __?__:
Surname **CEASE**

    1648. Lysle Willard III   born 28 Apr 1957   1650. Stephanie   born _____
    1649. Colin McFarquar   born 10 Aug 1959

1198. DIANA BEECHING-7 CEASE, sister of above, was born 15 May 1936 at ___. She married Christopher Willard NICHOLSON on __ at ___. He was the son of ____ NICHOLSON and ____, and was born Mar 1929; died ____. In 1980 they resided at Englewood, NJ.

Children of Diana B-7 CEASE and Christopher NICHOLSON:
Surname **NICHOLSON**

    1651. dau   born ____   1653. dau   born ____
    1652. dau   born _____   1654. Christopher Willard born 3 Aug 1957

1232. BETTY JUNE-7 CEASE, daughter of Luther-6 CEASE (Fred-5; Sidney-4; Julia-3 MC INTOSH; Simon-2; Alexander-1) and Beatrice DOVE, was born 4 Dec 1929 at Harbor Springs, Emmett, MI. She married Edward JOHNSEN on ___. He was the son of ____ JOHNSEN and ____, and was born 1 Apr 1932 at Hood River, OR. She married second to John Ross " Jack " CHRISTIANSEN on ___ at ___. He was the son of Ephraim Merlin CHRISTENSEN and Ida Hortense CEDARLUND, and was born 17 Feb 1937, died 13 Dec 2008 Salem, OR. Resided Salem, OR

Children of Betty June-7 CEASE and Edward JOHNSEN:
Surname **JOHNSEN**

    1655. Christine Louise   born 2 Oct 1952 Corvallis, OR
    1656. Julie Ann   born 6 Nov 1954 Helens, OR; died 27 Dec 1980   EOL
    1657. Michael David   born 17 Dec 1956 Portland, OR; died 25 Jan 2005 Portland, OR
    1658. Daniel James   born 21 June 1958 Portland, OR

Children of Betty June-7 CEASE and John CHRISTENSEN:
Surname **CHRISTIANSEN**

    1659. Greg   born ca ____   1661. Vickie   born ca _____
    1660. Dan   born ca _____

1233. LUTHER LLOYD-7 CEASE, brother of above, was born 12 Oct 1933 at Harbor Springs, Emmett, MI. He married Bonnie June MAYS on 15 June 1956 at Hood River, OR. She was the daughter of ___ MAYS and ____, and was born 3 June 1932 at Hood River. Luther-7 CEASE died there 3 Mar 2005.

Children of Luther Lloyd-7 CEASE and Bonnie MAYS:
Surname **CEASE**

    1662. Terri Lou   born 30 July 1958 Colorado Springs, CO
                         married Daniel " Danny " MAY   Child: Nicholas -9 MAY born ____
    1663. Roxann Renee   born 15 Sep 1960 Hood River; 2 married Michael Lee COCHRAN 2001
    1664. Sean Michael   born 10 Sep 1970 Hood River, OR

Note: There are three more grandchildren of Luther-[7] CEASE – children of Roxann and her first husband Scott DELEPINE. They were married 23 June 1979 at Hood River. Their children are: Nicole-[9] Ashley-[9] and Tyler-[9] DELEPINE

1234. DONALD EUGENE-[7] WALSH / Richard , son of Robert-[6] LANE/WALSH (Julia-[5] CEASE; Sidney-[4;] Julia Ann-[3] MC INTOSH, Simon-[2]; Alexander-[1]) and Phyllis COOK, was born 26 Feb 1929 at Windsor, Ontario, Canada.   He married Barbara Sue SEARLE on 21 Oct 1950 at Ontario, Canada.

Children of Donald Eugene-[7] WALSH/RICHARD and Barbara SEARLE:
Surname **RICHARD**
+   **1665. JAN MARIE**   born 23 Feb 1952, married Dennis SIDORSKI 25 May 1974
        1666. Donald Christopher born 11 Apr 1955   1667. Joseph John   born 27 May 1957

1235. ROBERT GEORGE-[7] WALSH/ RICHARD, brother of above, was born 22 Apr 1932 at Windsor, Ontario, Canada. He married Joan PATRICK on ____ at ____.

Children of Robert-[7] WALSH/RICHARD and Joan Patrick:
Surname **RICHARD**
        1668. Robert Steven   born ____   1669. Randall   born ____

1236. THEODORE EUGENE-[7] DALPE, son of Helen-[6] WALSH (Julia-[5] CEASE; Sidney-[4;] Julia-[3] MC INTOSH; Simon-[2]; Alexander-[1]) and Joseph J. DALPE, was born 10 Sep 1934 at Detroit, MI. He married Mary Ann LEWANDOWSKI Jan 1961. She was the daughter of Francis Boniface LEWANDOWSKI and Helen ____, and was born ca 1938 MI. Theodore-[7] DALPE died 4 Apr 1963 at Flint, MI. His widow married 2nd to John ZIMMERMAN on 7 Sep 1965, and had the children' names changed to ZIMMERMAN.

Children of Theodore-[7] DALPE and Mary Ann LEWANDOWSKI:
Surname **DALPE / ZIMMERMAN**
        1670. David   born July 1961 Bloomington, IN
        1671. Ann Marie   born July 1963 Flint, Michigan

1237. MAUREEN ANNE-[7] WALSH, daughter of Gordon-[6] WALSH (Julia-[5] CEASE; Sidney-[4]; Julia Ann-[3] MC INTOSH; Simon-[2]; Alexander-[1]) and Kathleen Frances LEAVER, was born 4 May 1945 at Windsor, Ontario, Canada. She married William Edward STENBACK on 26 Aug 1967. He was the son of ____ STENBACK and ____, and was born 29 Jan 1943 Detroit, Michigan.

Children of Maureen-7 WALSH and William STENBACK:
Surname **STENBACK**
        1672. Julia Anne   born 30 July 1970
        1673. Kate Marie   born 2 Sep 1972

1238. MARY LOU-[7] WALSH, sister of above, was born 30 Apr 1948 at Windsor, Ontario, Canada. She married Lawrence JACOB on 26 July 1968. They divorced 1984.

Children Mary Lou-[7] WALSH and Lawrence JACOB·
Surname **JACOB**
        1674. Jesse Gordon   born 9 Nov 1974
        1675. Leah Michelle   born 5 June 1976

1242. KATHERINE DAWN-[7] CEASE, daughter of Lawrence-[6] CEASE (Carl-[5] Sidney-[4]; Julia Ann-[3] MC INTOSH, Simon-[2]; Alexander-[1]) and Sylvia BOETTGER, was born 25 Sep 1943 at Harbor Springs, MI. She married Alton Leroy RADLE on 8 Mar 1961. he was the son of Ralph E. RADLE and Honora V. ____, and was born 17 Aug 1936; died 5 March 1999. Katherine-[7] CEASE died 2000.

Children of Katherine Dawn-[7] CEASE and Alton RADLE:
Surname **RADLE**

1676. Alton Leroy, Jr.	born 8 Mar 1961			
1677. David Michael	born 28 Mar 1962	1679. Teresa Marie	born ____	
1678. Lawrence Richard	born ____	1680. Heather Jean	born 6 June 1973	

1245. RHODA MAE [7] **LIGHTFOOT**, daughter of Nina Mae-[6] CEASE (Carl Sidney-[5;] Sidney-[4]; Julia-[3] MC INTOSH; Simon-[2]; Alexander-[1]) and Byron Russell LIGHTFOOT, was born 18 Mar 1936 at Harbor Springs, Emmett County, MI. She married first to Robert J. FARRELL on 11 Sep 1954 at Harbor Springs. he was the son of ____ FARRELL and ____, and was born 5 May 1935 at Charlevoix, MI. They divorced and she married second to Roger RITTER on 30 Jan 1973. He was the son of Willard T. RITTER and Isabelle KNEIPER, and was born ____.

Children of Rhoda Mae-[7] LIGHTFOOT and Robert FARRELL:
Surname **FARRELL**

1681. Lissa Lynn	born 21 Mar 1955 Grand Rapids, MI
	married Douglas DOWNER divorced no issue
+ **1682. PATRICIA MAE**	born 27 May 1957 Traverse City, MI
	married Steven DORN 21 Apr 1984
1683. Michael John	born 27 May 1957 Traverse City, MI
	married Lydia KURTZEL 13 Oct 1990 (she born 15 Dec 1958)

Child: Elizabeth Marie-[9] FARRELL born 7 Apr 1991 Traverse City, MI

1684. Jeffery	born 19 Jan 1961 Traverse City, MI single 1995

1247. IMELDA L[7] **LIGHTFOOT**, sister of above, was born 15 Feb 1939 at Petoskey, Emmett Co., MI. She married Gerald Duane HOFBAUER on 22 July 1957. he was the son of ____ HOFBAUER and ___, and was born ____.

Children of Imelda-[7] LIGHTFOOT and Gerald HOFBAUER:
Surname **HOFBAUER**   (all children born Petoskey, MI

+ **1685. SUSAN ANN**	born 6 Aug 1958
	married Timothy Mark MAXWELL 27 Sep 1984
+ **1686. GRIF GERALD**	born 27 Aug 1959
	married Waynet STRADLING (she born 14 May 1961)
1687. Linda Lynn	born 6 Sep 1961; married Wayne MAYO 25 Sep 1983 divorced

Child: Tabitha Ann-9 MAYO born 13 July 1986 Tampa, FL

+ **1688. JAMES BYRON**	born 13 Aug 1963
	married Faith GREGORY 21 May 1988 (she born 10 Mar 1964)
+ **1689. THAD THOMAS**	born 21 July 1966
	married Sharon LONG (she born 22 May 1966)

1248. ALVIN[7] **LIGHTFOOT**, brother of above, was born 22 May 1941 at Emmett County, MI. he married Susan Jane GARVER on ___ at ____. She was the daughter of ___ GARVER and ____, and was born ___.

Children of Alvin-[7] LIGHTFOOT and Susan GARVER:
Surname **LIGHTFOOT**

+ **1690. AMY ELIZABETH**	born 19 July 1963 Huachua, AZ
	married Matthew CARTER 11 June 1983 (he born 6 Feb 1964)
1691. Betsey Lee	born 5 May 1965 Petoskey, MI
	married Anthony O'BERG 10 May 1989 (he born 13 Sep 1965)

Child: Jacob Anthony-[9] O'BERG born 5 Apr 1993 Petoskey, MI

Children of Alvin -[7] LIGHTFOOT and Susan GARVER, continued:
Surname **LIGHTFOOT**

>1692. Karen Ann   born 17 Oct 1967 Petoskey, MI
>   married Matthew DELNICK   (he born 27 Mar 1969)
>>Child: Emily Taylor-[9] DELNICK born 19 Aug 1993 Seattle, WA
>
>1693. Nancy Susan   born 9 Nov 1970 Petoskey, MI
>   married _____
>>Child: Trisha Susan-[9] ____ born 7 Apr 1992 Petoskey, MI

1249. MARILYN JOYCE[7] **LIGHTFOOT**, sister of above, was born 14 Oct 1943 at Emmett County, MI. She married first to Charles R. SCHLAPPI on ___ at ___. He was the son of ____ SCHLAPPI and ____, and was born 28 Dec 1943; died 5 Apr 1977. She married second on 25 Mar/May 1983 to Robert TRUMAN. He was the son of ___ TRUMAN and ____, and was born 23 Aug 1947. He had 3 children from a prior marriage: Angela born Oct 1969, Scott born 6 Aug 1970, and Brent TRUMAN born 21 May 1972.

Children of Marilyn Joyce-[7] LIGHTFOOT and Charles SCHLAPPI:
Surname **SCHLAPPI**   (all children born Petoskey, Emmett, MI)

>+   **1694. RUSSELL**   born 2 July 1963
>   **FORREST**   married Susan Joan STANDISH 21 May 1983 (she born 27 May 1962)
>+   **1695. KATHLEEN JOY** born 30 Jul 1964; married Kevin SADDISON Aug 1983
>+   **1696. ERIC CHARLES** born 16 July 1965
>   married Christi BODEN 15 Sep 1990   (she born 9 Jan 1972)
>   1697. Alan Wade   born 7 Apr 1969
>   married DeAnna K. TROYER 21 Sep 1990 (she born 12 Mar 1969)
>>Child: Charles Eli-[9] SCHLAPPI born 12 Mar 1993 Petoskey, MI)

1252. ARTHUR GEORGE[7] **NEWSOME**, son of Juanita Mary[6] BOETTGER (Mildred Irene[5]: Sidney[4;] Julia Ann[3] MC INTOSH; Simon[2] Alexander[1]) and William Alexander NEWSOME, was born 18 Nov 1944 at Cheyboygan, Michigan. He married Tani DARLING on 19 Dec 1964. She was the daughter of ____ DARLING and ____, and was born 10 Jan 1946.

Children of Arthur-[7] NEWSOME and Tani DARLING:
Surname **NEWSOME**

>1698. Arthur James   born 11 Oct 1966 Hancock, MI
>   married Gwendolyn Lou SMITH 30 Dec 1993
>1699. Paula Sue   born 4 Apr 1968 IL.;   married Ronald Edward LEPPER 2 Oct 1990
>>Children: Corey Raymond-[9] born 15 Nov 1991 Austin, TX and Jenna Lee-[9] LEPPER born 15 Nov 1993 Tucson, AZ
>1700. Carla Kay   born 1 Sep 1970 IL

1254. KENNETH EDWARD[7] **NEWSOME**, brother of above, was born 23 Apr 1952 at Cheyboygan, Michigan. He married Tina WINANS on 24 Sep 1981. She was the daughter of ____ WINANS and _____, and was born 5 Sep 1962.

Children of Kenneth Edward-[7] NEWSOME and Tina WINANS:
Surname **NEWSOME**

>1701. Kendra Lee   born 10 Apr 1982 Petoskey, MI
>1702. Timothy James   born 21 Oct 1983 Petoskey, MI
>1703. Whitney Noel   born 31 Dec 1987 Petoskey, MI

1255. DENISE RENEE[7] **NEWSOME**, sister of above, was born 16 June 1958 at Cheyboygan, MI. She married Edward RHEW on 13 Nov 1976. He was the son of ____ RHEW and ___, and was born 19 Dec 1953 at Carp Lake, Michigan.

Child of Denise Renee-[7] NEWSOME and Edward RHEW:
Surname **RHEW**
        1704. Jamie Lynn   born 27 Dec 1976 Petoskey, MI

1258. CAROL LEE-[7] BOETTGER, daughter of Willis Earl-[6] BOETTGER (Mildred-[5] ; Sidney-[4]; Julia Ann-[3] MC INTOSH; Simon-[2]; Alexander-[1]) and Louise HERZIG, was born 2 Feb 1947 at Evanston, IL. She married James MURDCK on 17 Jan 1964. He was the son of _____ MURDOCK and ____, and was born 13 Oct 1942 Detroit, MI. Carol Lee-[7] BOETTGER died Jan 1982 at Anchorage, AK.

Children of Carol Lee-[7] BOETTGER and James MURDOCK:
Surname **MURDOCK**
+   **1705. KENNETH**   born 14 Sep 1964 Anchorage, AK
       ALLEN   married Mary SIEVERS 30 Sep 1982 (she born 15 Dec 1965 MI)
+   **1706. HELEN**   born 26 Feb 1966 Anchorage, AK
                            married Randal K. IGOU   (he born 1 Jan 1958 Blythe, CA)

1260. CHERYL ALAYNE-[7] LIPCHINSKY, daughter of Arlayne Irene-[6] BOETTGER (Mildred Irene-[5] CEASE; Sidney-[4,] Julia Ann-[3] MC INTOSH; Simon-[2]; Alexander-[1]) and Joseph Mitchell LIPCHINSKY, was born 1 Nov 1946 at Seattle, WA. She married David Benjamin WILSON on 22 Dec 1974 at Denver, CO. he was the son of ____ WILSON and ____, and was born 5 Sep 1944 at Chicago, IL.

Children of Cheryl Alayne-[7] LIPCHINSKY and David WILSON:
Surname **WILSON**
        1707. Brian Benjamin   born 9 June 1978 Denver, CO
        1708. Grant Joseph   born 7 Aug 1979 Everett, WA.

1261. JOSEPH MITCHELL-[7] LIPCHINSKY, brother of above, was born 7 May 1948 at Vallejo, CA. He married first to Wanda Gail ODOM on 27 May 1972 at Escambia Co., FL. They divorced 16 May 1979. On 26 May 1979 he married second to Jeanne Lurline CHILDERS at Pensacola, FL. She was the daughter of ____ CHILDERS and ____, and was born 2 Nov 1959 at Pensacola, FL.

Children of Joseph Mitchell-[7] LIPCHINSKY and Jeanne CHILDERS:
Surname **LIPCHINSKY**   (all children born Pensacola, FL)
        1709. Mandy Marie   born 22 Dec 1979   1711. Max Madison   born 2 May 1982
        1710. Jamie Leigh   born 12 Dec 1980

1264. LANE VICTOR-[7] HART, son of Rachel Janet-[6] BOETTGER (Mildred Irene-[5] CEASE; Sidney-[4]; Julia Ann-[3] MC INTOSH; Simon-[2]; Alexander-[1]) and was born 20 Oct 1946 at Pontiac, MI. He married Susan Carol JACKSON on 24 Feb 1968 at Marquette, MI. She was the daughter of ____ JACKSON and ____, and was born 17 Mar 1947 at Marquette, MI.

Child of Lane Victor-[7] HART and Susan JACKSON:
Surname **HART**
        1712. Alana Sue   born 31 Mar 1969, Marquette, MI

1265. JANITH TERESA-[7] HART, sister of above, was born 25 Feb 1952 at Marquette, MI. She married Dr. Samuel T. VASQUEZ on 28 Mar 1982 San Diego, CA.. He was the son of ____ VASQUEZ and ____, and was born 20 Nov 1944 at Center, Colorado.

Children of Janith Teresa-[7] HART and Dr. Samuel T. VASQUEZ:
Surname **VASQUEZ**   (all children born San Diego, CA)
        1713. Samuel Joseph   born 3 Apr 1984   1714. Zanetta Joy   born 7 Sep 1985

Children of Janith Teresa-[7] HART and Dr. Samuel VASQUEZ, continued:
Surname **VASQUEZ**
> 1715. Melody Christina   born 17 Nov 1986
> 1716. Jonathon David   born 8 Dec 1988   1717. Unknown name   born ____

1268. KATHERYN FAE-[7] **LA COMBE,** daughter of Ershel Leona-[6] BOETTGER (Mildred Irene-[5] CEASE: Sidney-[4]; Julia Ann-[3] MC INTOSH; Simon-[2]; Alexander-[1]) and Richard Armand LA COMBE, was born 20 June 1947 at Cheboygan, MI. She married Ernest J. STOLPE on 16 Aug 1966. He was the son of ____ STOLPE and ____, and was born 4 Dec 1947.

Children of Katheryn Fae-[7] LA COMBE and Ernest STOLPE:
Surname **STOLPE**
> 1718. Valerie Dee   born 18 June 1968   1719. David Ernest   born 14 Jan 1970

1269. DEBORAH SUZANNE-[7] **LA COMBE,** sister of above, was born 30 Oct 1949 at Cheboygan, MI. She married Dexter MC NAMARA on 17 Mar 1978. He was the son of Willard MC NAMARA and Viola LASLEY, and was born 3 Nov 1945. He was married previously and had a son, William Marsh MC NAMARA born 17 Mar 1968.

Children of Deborah-[7] LA COMBE and Dexter MC NAMARA:
Surname **MC NAMARA**
> 1720. Derek Richard   born 2 Feb 1983 Petoskey, MI
> 1721. Shane Patrick   born 7 Apr 1987 Warren, MI.

1271. PATRICIA ANN-[7] **LA COMBE,** sister of above, was born 19 Dec 1953 at Cheboygan, MI. She married first to Wilford Dale DAVENPORT on 9 Apr 1971. They divorced Jan 1975. She married second to Ronald Allen GOONE on 8 July 1977. They were divorced 31 May 1983. Her third husband was Calvin Edgar PELTZER. They were married on 23 Mar 1984. He was the son of Calvin PELTZER,Sr. and Doris CAMPBELL , and was born 28 June 1942 at Baltimore, MD.

Child of Patricia-[7] LA COMBE and Wilford DAVENPORT:
Surname **DAVENPORT**
> 1722. Kerensa Kae   born 20 Aug 1972 Springfield, IL
Child of Patricia-7 LA COMBE and Ronald GOONE:
Surname **GOONE**
> 1723. Jeremy Allen   born 19 Aug 1976 Fallon, NV

1274. MICHAEL VINCENT-[7] **LA COMBE,** brother of above, was born 13 Apr 1959 at Petoskey, MI. He married Linda Marie BUSH on 28 Dec 1981. She was the daughter of ____ BUSH and ____, and was born 29 June 1962 at Detroit, MI.

Children of Michael-[7] LA COMBE and Linda BUSH:
Surname **LA COMBE**   (children born Bremen, IN)
> 1724. Justin Michael   born 12 Apr 1985; stillborn   1725. Kristy Maria   born 4 Mar 1986

1275. STEPHANIE K-[7] **LA COMBE,** sister of above, was born 29 June 1963 at Petoskey, MI. She married Samuel Lee STAFFAN on 29 Oct 1983. He was the son of Jonathan STAFFAN and Sandra Lee CADWELL, and was born 25 July 1963 at Cheboygan, MI.

Children of Stephanie-[7] LA COMBE and Samuel STAFFAN:
Surname **STAFFAN**   (born McDill AFB, Tampa, FL)
> 1726. Tania Marie   born 22 Mar 1984   1727. Samuel L., Jr.   born 27 Feb 1986

1276. DENNIS-[7] SYDOW, son of Derla Gale-[6] BOETTGER (Mildred Irene[-5] CEASE; Sidney[-4]; Julia[-3] MC INTOSH; Simon[-2]; Alexander[-1]) and Erwin SYDOW, was born 10 Sep 1948 at Petoskey, MI. He married Janet KLOSS on ____. She was the daughter of ____ KLOSS and ____, and was born 2 Jan 1950.

Children of Dennis-[7] SYDOW and Janet KLOSS:
Surname **SYDOW**   (all children born Petoskey, MI)
    1728. David Walter   born 30 Aug 1970; married Tammy Marie SPIERLING 13 July 1991
    1729. Angela Marie   born 10 Jan 1972   1730. Julia Anne   born 24 Apr 1981

1277. DANIEL ERWIN-[7] SYDOW, brother of above, was born 29 Apr 1952 at Petoskey, MI. He married Cathy SCHAUM on ____. She was the daughter of ____ SCHAUM and ____, and was born 14 June 1954. Daniel -7 SYDOW died 18 Oct 1980 at Harbor Springs, Emmett County, MI. Cathy SCHAUM Sydow married second to Ray JANKOVIAK ca 1984.

Children of Dennis-[7] SYDOW and Cathy SCHAUM:
Surname **SYDOW**
    1731. Christopher Robin   born 26 Jan 1974 Petoskey, MI
    1732. Daniel Erwin, Jr.   born 6 Mar 1977; died 22 Aug 1994 automobile accident

1278. MICHAEL JOHN-[7] SYDOW, brother of above, was born 15 June 1955 at Petoskey, MI. He married Deborah HEINZ on ____. She was born 13 Dec 1953 at Harbor Springs, MI.

Children of Michael-[7] SYDOW and Deborah HEINZ:
Surname **SYDOW**
    1733. Jaime Kristen   born 28 July 1977 Biddeford, Maine
    1734. Marcus Jeremy   born 1 Sep 1979 Rochester, Monroe, NY
    1735. Jessica Renee   born 28 May 1982 Rochester, NY

1279. MARTIN DALE-[7] SYDOW, brother of above, was born 15 Jan 1957 at Petoskey, MI. He married Nada MITROVIC on ____. She was the daughter of __ MITROVIC and ____, and was born 10 Dec 1958.

Child of Martin-[7] SYDOW and Nada MITROVIC:
Surname **SYDOW**
    1736. Anna Marie   born 18 Aug 1980 Cherry Point, NC

1280. JEAN IRENE-[7] ABRUNZO, daughter of Herma Jean-[6] BOETTGER (Mildred Irene[-5] CEASE; Sidney[-4]; Julia Ann[-3] MC INTOSH; Simon-[2]; Alexander[-1]) and Philip Anthony ABRUNZO, was born 21 Dec 1949 at Elmira, Chemung County, NY. She married first to John CASTRILLI on 29 Jan 1972. He was the son of ____ CASTRILLI and ___, and was born 13 May 1943 at Bath, Steuben County, NY., died 21 Sep 1974. There was no issue from that marriage. She married second to Daniel Joseph CLARK, Jr. on 15 Oct 1977. He was the son of ____ CLARK and ____, and was born 27 May 1948 at Sayre, PA.

Child of Herma Jean-[7] ABRUNZO and Daniel CLARK:
Surname **CLARK**
    1737. Daniel Joseph   born 1 Oct 1979 Sayre, PA.

1282. MARIA LUCIA-[7] ABRUNZO, sister of above, was born 12 Dec 1952 at Elmira, Chemung, NY. She married Kenneth M. HAGER on 2 Aug 1975. He was born 23 Aug 1953 at Elmira, NY.

Children of Maria Lucia-[7] ABRUNZO and Kenneth HAGER:
Surname **HAGER** (both born Chemung County, NY)
    1738. Andrew Martin   born 10 Jan 1978   1739. Jessica Maria   born 25 Apr 1980

1284. CLARKSON CECIL-[7] MOST, Jr., son of Alyce Joan-[6] BOETTGER (Mildred Irene-[5] CEASE ; Sidney-[4]; Julia Ann-[3] MC INTOSH; Simon-[2]; Alexander-[1]) and Clarkson Cecil MOST , was born 20 May 1951 at Petoskey, MI. He married first to Debra LOYER on 25 June 1969. She was the daughter of ____ LOYER and ____, and was born 10 Nov 1953. They divorced July 1974. His second wife was Diann RICHARDS. They married on 23 Aug 1974. She was the daughter of _____ RICHARDS and ____, and was born 22 Aug 1950. Diann had a daughter by a previous marriage, by the name of Brenda ____, born 10 Nov 1969. Clarkson-[7] MOST adopted her.

Children of Clarkson-[7] MOST, Jr. and Debra LOYER:
Surname **MOST** (both born Petoskey, MI)

1740. Sabrina Marie	born 14 Nov 1969	1741. Tanya Jean	born 8 Feb 1971

Child of Clarkson-[7] MOST, Jr. and Diann RICHARDS:
Surname **MOST**

1742. Trevor Clarkson   born 18 Jan 1976

1287. KATHELEEN MAERE-[7] MOST, sister of above, was born 11 Feb 1958 at Petoskey, MI. She married Wesley LAUGHBAUM on 2 Sep 1977. He was the son of ____ LAUGHBAUM and ____, and was born 7 July 1953. They divorced.

Child of Katheleen-[7] MOST and Wesley LAUGHBAUM:
Surname **LAUGHBAUM**

1743. Erika Jone   born 22 Mar 1979 Petoskey, MI

1294. WILLIAM JAYE-[7] BOETTGER, son of Max Gilbert-[6] BOETTGER (Mildred Irene-[5] CEASE; Sidney-[4]; Julia Ann-[3] MC INTOSH; Simon-[2]; Alexander-[1]) and Mary Fay ULRICH, was born 28 May 1957 at Petoskey, MI. He married first to Deborah KALKOFEN on ____. She was the daughter of _____ KALKOFEN and ____, and was born ____. They divorced, no issue. He married second to Nicole KRAUSE on 27 July 1985. She was born 20 Sep 1966.

Children of William-[7] BOETTGER and Nicole KRAUSE:
Surname **BOETTGER** (all born Petoskey, MI)

1744. Sarah Lynn   born 18 Mar 1985
1745. Ashley Marie   born 3 Feb 1986
1746. Elizabeth Jaye   born 27 June 1987

1295. STEVEN CHARLES-[7] BOETTGER, brother of above, was born 11 July 1958 at Petoskey, MI. He married first to Jean WHITNEY on ____. She was the daughter of _____ WHITNEY and ____, and was born ____. They divorced and he married second to Terese RIGGS on ____. She was born 2 Aug 1961.

Child of Steven-[7] BOETTGER and Jean WHITNEY:
Surname **BOETTGER**

1747. Steven Charles, Jr.   born 30 June 1975 Petoskey, MI

Children of Steven-7 BOETTGER and Terese RIGGS:
Surname **BOETTGER** (born Houston, TX)

1748. Tanya Marie	born 7 Feb 1982	1749. Nicole Lynn	born 30 June 1983

1297. JACQUELYN KAY-[7] BOETTGER, sister of above, was born 28 Sep 1963 at Petoskey, MI. She married John Steven HULL on ____. He was the son of ____ HULL and ____, and was born 2 Aug 1962.

Children of Jacquelyn-[7] BOETTGER and John HULL:
Surname **HULL** (born Petoskey, MI)

1750. John Steven	born 19 Aug 1981	1751. Autumn Elyse	born 31 Dec 1982

The Seventh American Generation

1301. TRINA PAMELA[-7] **LAKE**, daughter of Avis Anne[-6] BOETTGER (Mildred Irene[-5] CEASE; Sidney[-4]; Julia Ann[-3] MC INTOSH; Simon[-2]; Alexander[-1]) and Everett Lake, was born 2 Nov 1958 at Mason, MI. She married Robert TAYLOR ca May 1978 at Valpariso, IN. He was the son of ____ TAYLOR and ____, and was born ____. They divorced and she married second to Kent KLEINSCHMIDT on ____. He was the son of KLEINSCHMIDT and _____, and was born 30 Feb 1958 at Jackson, MI.

Child of Trina[-7] BOETTGER and Robert TAYLOR:
Surname **TAYLOR**
>   1752. Socha Ann   born 4 Sep 1978 Valpariso, Indiana

1303. HOWARD WILLIAM[-7] **SMITH**, son of William Tanner[-6] SMITH (Elizabeth[-5] TANNER; Strever-[-4]; William[-3]; Magdalena[-2] MAC INTOSH; Alexander[-1]) and Laura Maudelle ARNOLD, was born 7 Mar 1914 at Earlham, Madison County, Iowa. He married Shirley Kathleen BENNETT on 14 Sep 1945 at Boone, IA. She was the daughter of Robert BENNETT and Marian BARGER, and was born 14 Jan 1917 at Boone, IA, died 16 Jan 2008 at Fort Collins, Larimer, CO. Howard William-[7] SMITH died 8 Sep 1998 Bella Vista, Benton, Arkansas.

Children of Howard[-7] SMITH and Shirley BENNETT:
Surname **SMITH**

+	**1753. KATHLEEN**	born 12 Oct 1947 Des Moines, IA
	JOYCE	married Rex Donald FILER 13 June 1970
+	**1754. PHILIP**	born 4 Nov 1949 Des Moines, IA
	HOWARD	married Barbara June HULTMAN 28 Aug 1971
+	**1755. DAVID ROBERT**	born 16 Feb 1954 Oelwein, IA;
		married Pamela Jo WOESTE 9 Aug 1986

1304. HAROLD ARNOLD[-7] **SMITH**, brother of above, was born 12 May 1915 at Earlham, Madison County, IA. He married Jennie PALS on 17 Feb 1939 at Belmond, Wright County, IA. She was the daughter of Richard "Dick" D. PALS and Reka LOATS, and was born 20 Sep 1915, died 25 Nov 1982 at Belmond, IA.

Children of Harold A-[7] SMITH and Jennie PALS:
Surname **SMITH**   (all children born at Belmond, Iowa)

+	**1756. ROBERT**	born 1 Feb 1940
	WILLIAM	married Carolyn Kay MC CAFFERY 27 Dec 1963
+	**1757. JIM WARREN**	born 1 Sep 1944; married Judy Ann WOLTERS 10 Oct 1964
+	**1758. BRUCE**	born 25 Oct 1949
	HAROLD	married Patricia ANGEL 11 May 1974
	1759. Judy Kay	born 27 May 1954; married Jon KLINK 24 May 1980 Chicago, IL
		(he s/o Joseph KLINK and Bernice Irene OTTO)
		(he born 5 May 1941 Rockford, IA)

1305. ELIZABETH MARIE[-7] **SMITH**, sister of above, was born 10 Mar 1920 at Dexter, Iowa. She married Cecil Carl BRANDENBURG on 6 May 1949 at Nashua, Iowa. He was the son of Theodore John BRANDENBURG and Minnie Ida MANSKE, and was born 22 May 1922 at Sheldon, ND.

Children of Elizabeth[-7] SMITH and Cecil Carl BRANDENBURG:
Surname **BRANDENBURG**   (all children born at Des Moines, Iowa)

+	**1760. LINDA SUE**	born 15 Aug 1951; married William Michael REESE 29 Aug 1970
+	**1761. NANCY ANN**	born 2 June 1953
		married Robert LYDICK 16 Dec 1978 Alexandria, VA
+	**1762. DONNA KAY**	born 23 Jan 1955; married Joseph NIZZI 25 Sep 1976 W. Des Moines

The Seventh American Generation

1308. RAYMOND VANATTA[7] **SMITH**, son of Asa[6] SMITH (Elizabeth[5] TANNER; Strever[4]; William[3]; Magdalena[2] MAC INTOSH; Alexander[1]) and Rosa June MC CLURE, was born 6 July 1911 at Murray, Clark County, Iowa. He married Pauline Rose ADDY on 6 June 1931 at DeSoto, Dallas County, Iowa. She was the daughter of Ray Franklin ADDY and Lena Clara BERNAU, and was born 29 Nov 1912 at DeSoto, IA; died 22 Apr 2008 at Des Moines, Polk, IA. Raymond V[7] SMITH died 5 Sep 2002 at Des Moines.

Children of Raymond-[7] SMITH and Pauline ADDY:
Surname **SMITH**   (all children born Earlham, IA)
+   **1763. BETTY LOUISE** born 29 Sep 1932
                                    1 married Kenneth ARCHER 20 Aug 1950; divorced
                                    2 married Raymond GORDON ca 1952
+   **1764. KIETH / KEITH** born 16 Aug 1937; died 23 Mar 1985 Des Moines, IA
                  RAYMOND   married Sheryl Ann TIMONS Nov 1954
                                    (she born 5 Apr 1938)
+   **1765. GENE VANATTA** born 16 Nov 1939; married Nancy Louise KEENER 21 Oct 19__

1309. HOMER EDWARD[7] **SMITH**, brother of above, was born 2 May 1913 at Earlham, Madison County, Iowa. He married Verna Stafford STONE on 4 Nov 1938 at Long Beach, CA. She was the daughter of Spencer Elmore STONE and Lena May STAFFORD, and was born 27 Nov 1912 Portland, OR; died 2 Sept 2008 (age 95). They were divorced. Homer[7] SMITH married 2nd to Mae Mildred CONLEY on 22 Aug 1969 AT Dexter, Dallas, IA. died 12 Feb 1999 at Adel, Dallas, Iowa.

Children of Homer E-[7] SMITH and Verna STONE:
Surname **SMITH**
+   **1766. RICHARD**   born 7 Mar 1940 Long Beach, CA
                  CRAIG   1 married Judy Marlene PAULLIN 26 July 1959; divorced
                              2 married Elizabeth Louise AVITT 24 Sep 1965
                              (she born 26 Feb 1938)
+   **1767. HOMER**   born 23 June 1944 Washington, DC
                  EDWARD, Jr. 1 married June Elizabeth HATFIELD 22 Oct 1965
                              (she born 16 Mar 19__)
                              2 married Judy Faye WINSTONE 14 May 1975 TX
                              (she born 14 Feb 1949)

1310. MYRTLE ELIZABETH[7] **SMITH**, sister of above, was born 22 Mar 1915 at Winterset, Madison Co., Iowa. She married first to John Donald FOX on 29 Aug 1934 at Adel, Dallas, Iowa. He was the son of Carl Frederick FOX and Zeta MAGNEL/ MAGARREL, and was born 21 Dec 1912 at Rouleau, Saskatchewan Province, Canada. They divorced, and she married second to Edward Francis MC CORMICK on 20 May 1937. He was born 23 Jan 1914, died 1974. Myrtle[7] died 15 Dec 1996 Lehi, Utah.

Children of Myrtle-[7] SMITH and John FOX:
Surname **FOX**
         1768. Carl Donald   born 24 Feb 1935 Dexter, Dallas, IA; married Pauline GROTTE
+   1769. **DALE EDWARD** born 17 Nov 1936 Des Moines, Polk, IA
                              married Anna Ruth WILLARD 16 Jan 1957 Landrum, SC
Children of Myrtle-[7] SMITH and Edward MC CORMICK:
Surname **MC CORMICK**
+   **1770. ROY ASA**   born 13 July 1938 Dexter, Dallas, IA; married Yvonne WEBB
+   **1771. BILLIE WAYNE** born 7 July 1952; married Pauline _____
+   **1772. DAVID ALLEN** born 16 Sep 1954 Gary, Lake, IN
                              1 married Twila HADDOCK ____; divorced; 2 married Kay _____
         1773. Gary Lee   born _____ 1956 Irving, TX

The Seventh American Generation

1312. WILMA EILEEN-⁷ SMITH, sister of above, was born 25 Feb 1925 at Earlham, Madison County, Iowa. She married first to Calvin Sherman MOORE, Jr. on 28 Aug 1944 at Galveston, TX. He was the son of Calvin MOORE , Sr. and Leora THOMSON, and was born 29 June 1917 at Lewis, Cass County, Iowa; died 23 Mar 1966 at Dexter, Dallas, Iowa. Her second marriage was to John " Jack " Arthur WILLIAMS on 6 Aug 1966. He was the son of Edward WILLIAMS and Rillia GOLDMAN, and was born 11 May 1904 at Waba(s)h, IL; died 10 Mar 1999 at Stuart, Guthrie, IA.

Children of Wilma-⁷ SMITH and Calvin MOORE, Jr.:
Surname **MOORE**

+	**1774 SHERMAN DEE**	born 2 Nov 1945 Dexter, IA
		1 married Caren Coy BROWN 29 Oct 1965 Idaho Falls, ID
		(she born 6 Oct 1947; they divorced)
		2 married Pamela LIBIS 22 July 1977 Lake Tahoe, CA
		(she born 4 Apr 1951)
+	**1775. MICKEY LEE**	born 1 Apr 1947 Dexter, IA
		married Pillar POSADA 31 Dec 1976
		(she born 6 June 1955 at Bogota, Colombia, SA)
+	**1776. ANDREW JAY**	born 6 Jan 1949 Dexter, IA
	(twin)	1 married Deborah KO ____; divorced – no issue
		2 married Cathy ANDERSON 12 Jan 1974 Las Vegas, NV
		(she born 29 Aug 1959)
		(she dau/o Andrew ANDERSON and Betty ____)
+	**1777. ANTHONY JEROME**	born 6 Jan 1949 Dexter, IA
		married Tracey Lu MARTEN 24 June 1972
	(twin)	(she born 6 Feb 1953)
		(she dau/o Francis MARTEN and Lulu Belle ____)
+	**1778. SAMUEL CALVIN**	born 6 June 1952 Dexter, IA
		married Rachel SNOWDEN 19 Aug 1979 Des Moines, IA
		(she born 6 Feb 1953)
		(she dau/o Kernneth SNOWDEN and Alice ____)

1313. ILLA JUNE-⁷ SMITH, sister of above, was born 26 June 1928 Earlham, Madison, Iowa. She married John Gerald DOLAN on 27 May 1946 at Dexter, Dallas, Iowa. He was the son of Wilbur Thomas DOLAN and Mary Ann JAMES, and was born 15 Sep 1925; died ____. Illa June-⁷ died 31 Dec 1990 at Granger, Dallas County, Iowa.

Children of Illa June-⁷ SMITH and John Gerald DOLAN:
Surname **DOLAN**

+	**1779. LAWRENCE DAVID**	born 28 July 1946 Dallas Co., IA
		1 married Roberta BUCKHOLZ 14 Aug 1965 ; divorced
		2 married Jackie _____; divorced; 3 married Jennie _____
+	**1780. JOSEPH CRAIG**	born 15 Oct 1947 Dallas Co., IA; died 23 Mar 1973 Perry, IA
		married Gladys Virginia ROBERTS 29 Oct 1966
		(she born 10 Dec 1946)
		(she dau/o Willard ROBERTS and Grace BROWN)
+	**1781. JAMES ROBERT**	born 12 Dec 1949 Perry, Dallas Co., IA
		married Cristy BOYENS Nov 1967
+	**1782. VINCENT THOMAS**	born 1 Nov 1951 Perry, Dallas, IA
		1 married Becky MAXWELL ____; divorced -- no issue
		2 married Tresa _____ ; divorced – no issue
		3 married Katheryn Kay BRUDER (she born 23 Apr 1957)

1314. EDWIN ROBERT[-7] **SMITH**, son of Clarence[-6] SMITH (Elizabeth[-5] TANNER; Strever[-4]; William-[-3]; Magdalena[-2] MAC INTOSH; Alexander[-1]) and Della MC CLURE, was born 16 Feb 1922 at Earlham, Madison County, Iowa. He married Doris Marjorie HADLEY on 22 Aug 1943 at Earlham, Madison, IA. She was the daughter of Willard J. HADLEY and Delora Bernice COOK, and was born 2 May 1924 Earlham, Madison, IA.

Children of Edwin Robert[-7] SMITH and Doris HADLEY:
Surname **SMITH**   (all children born Dexter, Dallas, Iowa)

+	**1783. SHARON ELAINE**	born 30 Oct 1946
		married Donald Dean JONES 5 Sep 1970 Earlham, Madison, IA
		(he born 16 Jan 1944 Creston, Union, IA)
		(he s/o Alvah JONES and Louise _____)
+	**1784. BARBARA JEAN**	born 15 Dec 1947
		married Darwin Forest SNOOK, Jr. 6 July 1968
		(he born 16 July 1946)
		(he s/o Darwin SNOOK, Sr. and Lucille JELSMA)
+	**1785. EDWIN HOWARD**	born 25 June 1950
		married Connie Joann THRAILKILL 26 Aug 1972
		(she born 4 Mar 1954)
		(she dau/o Wayne Edward THRAILKILL and Ardith GENTRY)

1315. TWILA LEONE-[7] **SMITH**, sister of above, was born 21 June 1923 At Earlham , Madison County, IA. Her first marriage was to Charles H. LEIGHTY on 9 Oct 1942. He was the son of Earl Henry LEIGHTY and Elizabeth BOOT, and was born 5 Oct 1916 at Dexter, Iowa; died 6 July 1943.(He served in the US Air Corps in WW2; unknown if he was killed in the War) She married second to Robert Joseph EAGAN on 22 June 1946. He was the son of William F. EAGAN and Josephine SHERLOCK , and was born 15/26 Jan 1915 at Emmetsburg, Palo County, IA; died 6 Apr 1999 at Des Moines, IA. Twila Leone[-7] died 7 Feb 2007 at Des Moines, IA.

Child of Twila Leone[-7] SMITH and Charles LEIGHTY:
Surname **LEIGHTY** (later adopted by **EAGAN** and changed name)

+	**1786. RICHARD CHARLES**	born 26 Nov 1943 Downy, CA
		married Gloria CHROUP (she born 5 May 1943 Charles City, IA)
		(she dau/o Leon CHROUP and Adoline VENZ)

Children of Twila Leone[-7] SMITH and Robert EAGAN:
Surname **EAGAN**

+	**1787. KATHLEEN ANN**	born 23 Apr 1947 Spencer City, IA
		married Frank MC KIM 1966 (he born 20 Apr 1947)
		(he s/o Fred MC KIM and Leta HEATHMAN)
+	**1788. JEAN FRANCES**	born 2 Oct 1949 Emmetsburg, IA
		married James ZDRAZIL Apr 1968 Pocahontas, IA
		(he born 13 June 1948)
		(he s/o James ZDRAZIL and Marcella HRONEK)
+	**1789. PATRICK JOSEPH**	born 17 Dec 1951 Des Moines, IA
		married Susan WITT Jan 1973 San Antonio, TX
		(she born 4 Oct 1953)
		(she dau/o Marvin WITT and Mary STURDIVANT)
+	**1790. MARY JANE**	born 5 July 1955 Dubuque, IA
		married Michael REELITZ July 1974 Des Moines
		(he born 5 July 1950)
		(he s/o Carl REELITZ and Florence GROAT)

Children of Twila Leone-[7] SMITH and Robert EAGAN, continued:
Surname **EAGAN**

1791. Michael Robert	born 8 Nov 1957 Emmetsburg, IA	
	married Judy TRIPLETT Higgens; divorced --- no issue	
1792. Pamela Josephine	born 17 Nov 1961 Emmetsburg, IA	

1316. DORIS ROSA-[7] **SMITH**, sister of above, was born 16 May 1926 at Earlham , Madison County, IA. She married Francis Edward RUTHERFORD on 10 Dec 1946 at Earlham. he was the son of Edward Francis RUTHERFORD and Naomi V. JOHNSON, and was born 23 Mar 1921; died 3 Dec 1997 at Churdan, Greene County, IA. He was a veteran of WW2 (MM 1 , US NAVY) and is buried at St. Patrick's Cemetery there. Doris Rosa-[7] SMITH died ____ .

Children of Doris Rosa-[7] SMITH and Francis RUTHERFORD:
Surname **RUTHERFORD**

1793. Anna Marie	born 4 Feb 1950 Fort Dodge, IA	
	married Steve(n) HEMERLING 8 May 19__	
+	**1794. DOROTHY JEAN**	born 17 Jan 1952 Fort Dodge, IA
		married Thomas WHITVER 23 Apr 1982 Jefferson, IA
1795. Kenneth Edward	born 27 Jan 1954 Jefferson, IA	
1796. Joyce Rose	born 5 Aug 1956 Jefferson, IA	
+	**1797. LARRY DEAN**	born 19 Sep 1957 Jefferson, IA
		married Laura HERTAGE 15 Sep 1981
		(she born 14 Jan 19__) (she dau/o Gordon HERTAGE and _____)
1798. Linda Kaye	born 30 May 1960 Jefferson, IA	
	married Steve(n) RINGGENBURG 30 May 1985 Churdan, IA	

Note: He had 2 children from a previous marriage: Wesley born 4 July 1977 and Matthew born 28 Dec 1979

1318. CARL DO)NALD-[7] **SMITH**, son of Chester-[6] SMITH (Elizabeth-[5] TANNER; Strever-[4;] William-[3;] Magdalena-[2] MAC INTOSH; Alexander-[1]) and Maggie Susannah PEARSON, was born 31 Jan 1912 at Earlham, Madison, Iowa. He married Naomi Ruth FOX on 2 Sep 1934. She was the daughter of William Harvey FOX and Flora Evelyn CUMMINS, and was born 30 May 1915 Adel, Dallas, IA; died _____ . Carl Donald -[7] SMITH died 21 Aug 1960 at Des Moines, IA.

Children of Carl Donald-[7] SMITH and Naomi FOX:
Surname **SMITH**

+	**1799. RONALD HARVEY**	born 2 Apr 1940 Des Moines, IA
		1 married Tina M. TODD 27 Jan 1962; divorced Jan 1973
		2 married Diane L. CIPOLLA 6 Jul 1973
+	**1800. CARLA CORINNE**	born 22 Sep 1945 Des Moines, IA
		1 married Ronald HAWBAKER 21 June 1963; divorced Mar 1969
		2 married Ronald Leroy MYERS 11 Apr 1969

1319. OPAL MAE-[7] **SMITH**, sister of above, was born 1 May 1913 at Earlham, Madison County, Iowa. She married Gail Levi NOLAND on 30 Nov 1935 at Guthrie Center, Guthrie County, Iowa. He was the son of Fred Alvard NOLAND and Nora Lucinda COOK, and was born 30 May 1914 at Spirit Lake, Dickinson County, IA; died 4 Dec 2006 at Carlisle, Warren County, IA. Opal-[7] SMITH died 5 May 1995 at Carlisle.

Children of Opal-[7] SMITH and Gail NOLAND:
Surname **NOLAND**

+	**1801. MARY JANE**	born 31 Oct 1937 Perry, IA
		1 married Edgar GUSTAFSON Mar 1961; divorced
		2 married Gordon RUE 1976

Children of Opal-7 SMITH and Gail NOLAND, continued:
Surname **NOLAND**

+ **1802. LUCINDA SUE** born 31 Mar 1940 Des Moines, IA
married Richard Duane DRAPER 7 June 1959

+ **1803. ROSALIND
EILEEN** born 1 Sep 1941 Des Moines, IA
1 married Larry RICHMOND 21 Dec 1960; divorced
2 married Lawrence Lester LAGERQUIST

+ **1804. ALVARD A.** born 2 Mar 1945 Des Moines, IA
married Arlene _____ 25 Nov 1966 Hawaii

+ **1805. ROBERTA
GAIL** born 3 Dec 1949 Des Moines, IA
married Richard John GRAY 23 Sep 1968

1320. DOROTHY JUNE-7 **SMITH**, sister of above, was born 15 Aug 1917 at Earlham, Madison County, Iowa. She married Leonard A. ROUTH on 28 Jan 1939 at Ames, Story County, IA. He was the son of Arlen " Arlie " L. ROUTH and Ella CHRISTIAN, and was born 31 Oct 1916 at Hamilton County, IA; died 3 Mar 1996 at Story City, Story, IA. Dorothy June-7 SMITH died 8 Apr 1985 at Des Moines, Polk, IA. She is buried at the Ames Municipal Cemetery, Story County, IA.

Children of Dorothy June-7 SMITH and Leonard ROUTH:
Surname **ROUTH**

1806. Chester Arlen born 14 Aug 1944 Des Moines, IA
married Ann BISHOP 14 Aug 1963 Ames, Iowa

+ **1807. KATHLEEN
ANN** born 1 June 1953 Ames, iowa
married Kenneth MISKELL 7 Nov 1978
(he s/o Kermit MISKELL and Wilma TURNER)

1321. PAULINE ROSE-7 **SMITH**, sister of above, was born 28 Nov 1920 at Earlham, Madison County, IA. She married Carroll Fred NOLAND on 10 Sep 1941. he was the son of Fred Alvard NOLAND and Nora Lucinda COOK, and was born 30 Sep 1915 at Spirit Lake , Dickson County, IA; died 28 Sep 2004 Adel, Dallas, IA. He was the brother of Gail NOLAND (above) who married Opal-7 SMITH. He served in the US Army (Tec 4) during WW2 and is buried at Bear Creek Cemetery, Dexter, IA. Pauline-7 SMITH died 6 October 2010 at Des Moines, IA..

Children of Pauline Rose-7 SMITH and Carroll NOLAND:
Surname **NOLAND**

+ **1808. JOSEPH
LLOYD** born 5 Aug 1943 Des Moines, IA
married Linda SAMS 29 Aug 196_ Des Moines, IA
(she dau/o Wilbur SAMS and Doris OVERTON

+ **1809. JAMES
CARROLL** born 27 Mar 1946 Des Moines, IA
1 married Susan _____ ; divorced
2 married Maura PEGLAR; divorced; 3rd Linda MURKEN

+ **1810. DONALD
EDWIN** born 12 Jan 1950 Des Moines, IA
married Marlene O'BRIEN 4 Dec 1971 Georgetown, IA

1322. RUTH ELLEN-7 **SMITH**, sister of above, was born 30 Nov 1921 at Earlham, Madison County, Iowa. She married Wayne Barnett NOLAND on 2 June 1941 at Albany, Gentry County, Iowa. He was the son of Fred Alvard NOLAND and Lucinda COOK, and was born 13 Nov 1918 at Spirit Lake, IA; died 1 July 2001 at Carlisle, Warren County, IA. Ruth Ellen-7 SMITH died 10 Mar 2003 at Carlisle Warren, IA.
Note: It is interesting to take note of the fact that 3 NOLAND brothers married 3 SMITH sisters)

Children of Ruth Ellen-[7] SMITH and Wayne NOLAND:
Surname **NOLAND**

+	**1811. BARBARA JO**	born 13 Mar 1942 Des Moines, IA
		married FOREST OVERTON Aug 1958 Indianola, IA
		(he born 28 Jul 1940)
+	**1812. ALICE MARIE**	born 12 Oct 1943 Des Moines, IA (he born 24 Dec 1941)
		married John CAMPBELL Aug 1960 Des Moines, IA; divorced 1984
+	**1813. LARRY FRED**	born 28 Feb 1951 Des Moines, IA
	(twin)	married Kathleen HIGGINS 14 Aug 1971 St. Ignace, MI
		(she born 10 Apr 1952)
+	**1814. GARY CHESTER**	born 28 Feb 1951 Des Moines, IA
	(twin)	1 married Shelley NELSON 13 Aug 1970 Middle River Friends Church, Warren County, Iowa.; divorced – no issue
		2 married Diane SHEETS 24 Feb 1977 – divorced

1323. LLOYD KENNETH-[7] **SMITH**, brother of above, was born 22 May 1923 at Earlham, Madison County, IA. He married Carol Ione MC CARTHY on 29 Sep 1945 at Des Moines, Iowa. She was the daughter of William Joseph MC CARTHY and Lura Almeda JACOBS, and was born 28 Sep 1926 Des Moines, IA; died _____. Lloyd Kenneth-[7] SMITH died 1 Jan 1997 at Earlham, IA.

Children of Lloyd-7 SMITH and Carol MC CARTHY:
Surname **SMITH**

+	**1815. WILLIAM LLOYD**	born 18 Sep 1946 Earlham, IA
		married Susan Ethel SCAR 4 Dec 1970 Dexter, IA
		(she born 19 Nov 1952)
		(she dau/o Leonard C. SCAR and Dorothy AURAND)
+	**1816. LINDA SUE**	born 18 Feb 1948 Earlham, IA
		married Stephen Victor STRONG 23 May 1966 Winterset, IA
		(he born 8 May 1945) (he s/o Arthur STRONG and Hattie _____)
	1817. Robert Carl	born 16 July 1949 Earlham, IA
		died 7 Feb 1970 Viet Nam
		buried Penn Center Cemetery, Madison County, Iowa
+	**1818. MICHAEL THOMAS**	born 1 June 1953 Winterset, Madison, IA
		1 married Michelle Rae MILLER 27 Jan 1973 Earlham, IA
		(she born 5 July 1955)
		(she dau/o Dr. Leo Francis MILLER and Carole SMITH)
+	**1819. DIANA LOUISE**	born 14 Nov 1957 Winterset, Madison, IA
		married Dwayne Dean SCAR 5 Mar 1976 Dexter, IA
		(he born 17 Aug 1956)
		(he s/o Norman SCAR and Catherine TEGALS)
	1820. Daniel Wayne	born 30 Mar 1960 Winterset, IA
+	**1821. MARK ALAN**	born 11 July 1967 Winterset, Madison, IA
		married Kelli A. MILLER 4 Mar 1989 Waterloo, Black Hawk Co., IA
		(she4 dau/o Harold MILLER and Judy _____)

1324. MABLE OLIVE-[7] **SMITH**, daughter of Raymond Vanatta-[6] SMITH (Elizabeth-[5] TANNER; Strever-[4]; William-[3]; Magdalena-[2] MAC INTOSH; Alexander-[1]) and Martha DE VAULT, was born 27 Feb 1913 Winterset, Madison County, IA. She married first to Wilbur Lloyd SPEER on 6 Nov 1932 at Earlham, IA. He was the son of Lloyd SPEER and Cora I. MARSTON, and was born 4 Dec 1915, died 5 Oct 1961 at Dexter, IA. He is buried at Penn Center Cemetery.

She married second to George W. KING on 5 Feb 1966. He was the son of ____ KING and ____, and was born ____, died 19 Oct 1969 at Des Moines, Polk County, IA. He is buried at St. Patrick's Cemetery, Cummings, Warren, IA. Her third husband was Howard SPRINGER. They married on ____. He was the son of ____ SPRINGER and ____, and was born ____, died 25 Nov 1985 at Des Moines, Polk , IA. He is buried at the Memorial Park Cemetery, Galesburg, IL.

Child of Mable[-7] SMITH and Wilbur SPEER:
Surname **SPEER**

+	**1822. MARTHA LOUISE**	born 31 Aug 1934 Dexter, Dallas, IA married James Maurice CLINE ca _____ ; divorced 1963 (he born 7 Oct 1930) (he s/o George CLINE and Dorothy DOWNS)

1325. DALE EDWIN[-7] SMITH, half brother of above, son of Raymond[-6] SMITH (Elizabeth[-5] TANNER; Strever[-4]; William[-3]; Magdalena-[2] MAC INTOSH ; Alexander-[1]) and Grace CADE, was born 24 Nov 1918 at Earlham, Madison County, IA. He married Mary WOODS on 4 Apr 1940 at Nashua, Chickasaw County, IA. She was the daughter of Austin WOODS and Eva ALEXANDER, and was born 4 May 1917 Winterset, IA; died ____. Dale [-7] SMITH died 17 Nov 2000 at Houston, Harris County, TX.

Children of Dale[-7] SMITH and Mary WOODS:
Surname **SMITH**

	1823. Marilyn	born 25 Nov 1942 Des Moines, IA 1 married Paul BRANDT 13 Aug 1963 Madison Co., IA; divorced 2 married Richard BUTLER ca _____ ; divorced 3 married Joseph LATTIN ca _____ ; divorced; 4 married Paul EATON
+	**1824. JAMES RAY**	born 10 Apr 1944 Des Moines 1 married Jean Ann PERCY 29 Mar 1968 Winterset, IA; divorced 2 married Linda Faye APPLEGATE 2 Aug 1986

1326. WILLARD CECIL[-7] SMITH, brother of above, was born 13 Oct 1920 at Earlham, Madison County, IA. He married Vina EMMONS on 16 Nov 1942 at Maryville, Nodaway County, MO. She was the daughter of Latin EMMONS and Minnie Pearl THORNBURG, and was born 10 Mar 1923 Earlham, IA, died _____. Willard-[7] SMITH died 23 July 1994 Earlham, IA.

Children of Willard [-7] SMITH and Vina EMMONS:
Surname **SMITH**   (all children born at Earlham, Madison County, Iowa)

+	**1825. JOYCE**	born 27 June 1944 1 married Roger Eugene NELSON ca ____ (he born 3 Nov 1946; died 8/12 Oct 1971 Tempe, AZ) (he s/o Robert Edward NELSON and Gladys Irene ALLIE) 2 married Larry G. EGEMO 3 Mar 1973 Earlham, IA (he born 26 July 1946; _____) (he s/o Truman Melborne EGEMO and Ruby ULSTAD)
	1826. Sandra Jean	born 4 Feb 1947 Earlham, IA; died 1 July 1947 Earlham
+	**1827. CONNIE LEE**	born 4 Sep 1948 married Paul Russell BARTLETT 3 Nov 1968 (he born 14 June 1946; _____) (he s/o John BARTLETT and Gladys Sophia FURNESS)
+	**1828. RICHARD DEAN**	born 24 May 1951; died 26 Oct 1972 Winterset, Madison, IA married Sheila TAYLOR 15 Aug 1970 Earlham, IA (she dau/o Henry M. TAYLOR and Edna _____)

1327. ESTHER[-7] **VOSBURGH**, daughter of Egbert Tanner[-6] VOSBURGH (Rachel[-5]; Strever[-4]; William-[3]; Magdalena[-2] MAC INTOSH; Alexander[-1]) and Delia SILVERNAIL, was born ca 1895, CT. She married Charles ROBERTS, Jr. on ____. He was the son of Charles ROBERTS, Sr. and ___, and was born Oct 1881 at Ancram, Columbia County, NY, died ____. Esther[-7] VOSBURGH died ____. They resided Copake, Columbia, NY.

Children of Esther-[7] VOSBURGH and Charles ROBERTS, Jr.:
Surname **ROBERTS**

1829. Helen	born ca 1913	
1830. Hazel	born ca 1914	
1831. Hattie / Hettie	born ca 1916	
1832. Harold	born 11 Nov 1919; died June 1977 Hillsdale, NY	

1328. INA[-7] **VOSBURGH**, sister of above, was born ca 1895 CT. She married Avery John HAWVER on ____ at ____. He was the son of William E. HAWVER and Georgianna _____, and was born 1 Dec 1899 NY; died _____. Ina-[7] VOSBURGH died June 1983.

Children of Ina-[7] VOSBURGH and Avery John HAWVER:
Surname **HAWVER**

1833. Lloyd H.	born 27 Feb 1920; died 7 July 2000 Miami, FL.
1834. Laura	born 1920
1835. FLOYD EDWARD	born 13 May 1923; died 2 June 1966 Prosser, WA married Pauline June HEILMAN (she born 4 June 1932; died 13 Dec 2003 WA)
1836. Francis	born ca 1924
1837. Clifton J.	born ca 1925; died 29 Mar 1994 Canaan, CT
1838. Carl H.	born 15 Dec 1926; died 22 Dec 2006 Groveland, FL

1330. WILLARD[-7] **SILVERNAIL**, son of Esther-[6] VOSBURGH (Rachel[-5] TANNER ; Strever[-4]; William[-3]; Magdalena[-2] MAC INTOSH; Alexander[-1)] and Ward SILVERNAIL, was born 11 Sep 1897 at Copake, NY. He married Rose GARRISON on ___ at ____. She was the daughter of William GARRISON and Emma _____, and was born 4 Aug 1896 Copake, died Oct 1968 Copake. Willard[-7] SILVERNAIL died 1 Oct 1964.

Children of Willard-[7] SILVERNAIL and Rose GARRISON:
Surname **SILVERNAIL**

	1839. Emily May	born 1 Sep 1917 Copake; died 31 Mar 1972 Hudson, NY married Arthur H. MIDDLEBROOK (he born ca 1915; died ca 1996)
	1840. Wallace C.	born ca 1919
+	**1841. EVELYN LOUISE**	born ca 1922; died 1972 married Clifton CONKLIN (he born 28 May 1915; died 1 May 1987)

1336 . BESSIE[-7] **HEAD**, daughter of Samuel-[6] HEAD (Jonathan [-5] Jr; Elizabeth[-4] TANNER; William[-3]; Magdalena[-2] MAC INTOSH; Alexander[-1]) and Florence M. ___, was born ca 1906, NY. She married Clinton George BAINER ca 1926. He was the son of Jacob BAINER and Ella SHAUGHNESSY, and was born 15 June 1896, died Jan 1978 at Ancramdale, Columbia County, NY. Bessie[-7] HEAD died ____.

Children of Bessie[7] HEAD and Clinton G. BAINER:
Surname **BAINER**

1842. Dorothy E.	born ca 1926; married Harry BALL 29 Dec 1946 (he born 10 June 1919; died 24 July 1982)

Children of Bessie-[7] HEAD and Clinton G. BAINER, continued:
Surname **BAINER**

1843. Geraldine O.	born 10 Mar 1928 NY
1844. Elizabeth Ann	born 30 Apr 1941
1845. Katherine	born 8 Mar 1944; resided Ancram, Craryville, NY

1341. FREDERICK AUSTIN-[7] WRIGHT, son of Madeline-[6] DYE (Mary Ann-[5] HEAD; Eliza-[4] TANNER; William-[3]; Magdalena-[2] MAC INTOSH; Alexander-[1]) Austin E. WRIGHT, was born 9 July 1892. He married Valentine Bella MARCIL on 26 June 1918 at Holyoke, MA. She was the daughter of Francois / Francis Xavier MARCIL and Celanire R. GINGRAS, and was born 20 May 1893 Canada, died 1 Aug 1988 FL.

Children of Frederick Austin-[7] WRIGHT and Valentine MARCIL:
Surname **WRIGHT**

1846. Constance Dorothy	born ca 1921; died 1951
1847. Shirley Madeline	born 7 Mar 1922; died 24 Feb 2007
	1 married Charles Lester MC QUILLAN 23 Aug 1941, divorced 1945
	(he s/o Charles L. MC QUILLAN and Ellen Helen LA COE)
	(he born 28 Apr 1920; died 13 May 1994 W. Springfield, MA)
	2 married Irving Eugene MEDE ca ____
	(he born ca 1914; died 2010)

Child: dau ____ born ca ____; married ____ VAUTIER
Child: Taylor -[9] VAUTIER born ca 1995

1350. EDWARD MC FARLANE-[7] SIMMONS, son of James Finch-[6] SIMMONS (Martin-[5]; Nancy Alma-[4] TANNER; John-[3]; Magdalena-[2] MAC INTOSH, Alexander-[1]) and _____, was born 17 Feb 1914. He married Harriet Sarah COOPER 28 Oct 1939. She was the daughter of Harley Hudson COOPER and Marian Craig TEABEAU, and was born 23 Dec 1912; died 12 July 1982. Edward M.-[7] SIMMONS died 28 Feb 1981 at Albany, NY

Children of Edward-[7] SIMMONS and Marian COOPER:
Surname **SIMMONS**

1848. Robert Cooper	born 3 May 1940 Pittsfield, MA; died 28 Nov 2000 Springdale, OH
	married Judith Ann KUSS 17 Sept 1960
	(she dau/o Rudolph Gerhart KUSS and Elizabeth Ann KULLMAN)
	(she born 12 Apr 1943 Milwaukee, WI; died 10 Jan 2010 Springdale, OH)

Children: son born ca ____; dau born ca ____

1849. dau	born ca 194____	1850. dau	born ca 194____

1354. ROBERT HAROLD-[7] SIMMONS, son of Harold M-[6] SIMMONS (James Monroe-[5]; Nancy Alma-[4] TANNER; John-[3]; Magdalena-[2] MAC INTOSH; Alexander-[1]) and Mildred LA POINTE, was born 2 March 1924 NJ. He married Teresa Marie SCHLECK 17 July 1946 NJ. She was the daughter of Anton Joseph SCHLECK and Anna Mary ENGEL, and was born 2 Nov 1923 NJ; died 12 Aug 1998 NJ. Robert H.-[7] SIMMONS died 12 March 2004 Manasaquan, NJ.

Children of Robert-[7] SIMMONS and Teresa Marie SCHLECK:
Surname **SIMMONS**

1851. Carol J.	born 28 Jan 1948 NJ; married Randy MAC CANICO, Jr.; resided NJ
	(he born 8 May 1947 NJ;)

Children: Randy-[9] III; Michael-[9]; Mark-[9]; and Melanie-[9] MAC CANICO

1852. Robert J.	born 14 Mar 1949; married Perla Lahica ____; resided NJ.

Children of Robert H-[7] SIMMONS and Teresa SCHLECK, continued:
Surname **SIMMONS**

1853. Joanne Christine	born 7 Jan 1951 NJ.; married Mike CASEY; resided AZ
1854. Mary Ellen	born ca 1952/53; married John MESSINA; resided FL
1855. Thomas Arthur	born 7 Sept 1954; married Beth ____; resided AZ
1856. Nancy Beth	born 19 Feb 1956; married Chris BRAIS; resided Walpole, MA
1857. Janet Louise	born 16 Feb 1957; married Mick DARCY; resided AZ
1858. Lorraine Grace	born 1 Apr 1958; married Craig ANDRES; resided NJ
	(he born 1 Sept 1955; _____)

Children: Brian-[9] and Jackie-[9] ANDRES

1391. JOHN PHILO-[7] WOOLDRIDGE, son of Clarence Budd-[6] WOOLDRIDGE (Rufus King-[5]; Philo-[4]; Mary Magdalena TANNER-[3]; Magdalena-[2] MAC INTOSH; Alexander-[1]) and Mary Edna _____, was born 4 Jan 1928 CT. He married first to Virginia BARRETT ca Sept 1948. She was the daughter of Edward H. BARRETT and Minora C. _____, and was born 3 Aug 1925; died 19 Feb 2009. They divorced on 3 June 1975. He married second to Marie _____ ca May 1976. Marie was born Jan 1943. They divorced on 17 Jan 1978. His first wife , Virginia, married second to a Waldron C. BEEKLEY.

Children of John Philo-[7] WOOLDRIDGE and Virginia BARRETT:
Surname **WOOLDRIDGE**

1859. Candace	born _____
1860. John P. Jr.	born _____
1861. Dane B.	born ____; married Diana ____; children: Kara and Jake
1862. Jeanne	born ____

180

1458. LEON GERALD^{-8} AUSTIN, son of Harriet^{-7} WILLIAMS (Charles^{-6}; George-^{5}; Caroline^{-4} MC INTOSH; William^{-3}; Simon^{-2}; Alexander^{-1}) and Ralph AUSTIN, was born 2 July 1944 PA. He married Phyllis ISAACS on ___ at ___ . She was the daughter of _____ ISAACS and ____, and was born ___ . They reside Canton, Bradford County, PA .

Children of Leon Gerald^{-8} AUSTIN and Phyllis ISAACS:
Surname **AUSTIN**

1863. Deborah Kay	born _____	; married Mark Allen MC DILL 9 Jan 1988
1864. Judy	born _____	; married Philip WERKHEISER
1865. Lou Ann	born _____	; married Rodney ITLE; res. Pasadena, CA

1504. JAMES DENNIS^{-8} MC INTOSH, son of Donald Curtis^{-7} MC INTOSH (Francis Curtis^{-6}; William E^{-5}; Fernando^{-4}; William^{-3}; Simon-^{2}; Alexander^{-1}) and Virginia GUIGAN, was born 9 Oct 1952. He married first to Fawn Renee COLBERT. They divorced and he married second to Gloria KARMASHIAN on _____ at Albany, NY

Children of James Dennis^{-8} MC INTOSH and _____:
Surname **MC INTOSH**

1866. Justin   born 8 May 1980; married _____
       Child: Jaden-^{10} MC INTOSH born 23 Aug 1998

1564. GRETCHEN^{-8} HONSBERGER, daughter of Norma-^{7} MC INTOSH (Walter-^{6}; Charles-^{5}; Theophilus-^{4}; George-^{3}; Simon-^{2}; Alexander-^{1}) and Ralph HONSBERGER, and was born 5 June 1936 at Syracuse, Onondaga, NY. She married first to a John DAWSON ca ____ . They divorced and she married second to Robert REILLY.

Children of Gretchen^{-8} HONSBERGER and John DAWSON:
Surname **DAWSON**

1867. Jane   born ca _____   1868. Paul   born ca _____

1565. KAREN $^{-8}$ HONSBERGER, sister of above, was born 9 September 1942 at Syracuse, Onondaga, NY. She married William EDGAR on 10 July 19__ at Skaneateles, NY. In 1991 they were residing in Maine.

Children of Karen^{-8} HONSBERGER and William EDGAR:
Surname **EDGAR**

1869. Amy   born ca _____   1871. Caroline   born ca _____
1870. William   born ca _____

1567. ROBERT BRUCE^{-8} DOLBEAR, son of Margery^{-7} MC INTOSH (Walter-^{6}; Charles-^{5}; Theophilus-^{4}; George-^{3}; Simon-^{2}; Alexander-^{1}) and G. Franklin DOLBEAR, was born 2 October 1946 at __, NY. He married Carol Ann ELMER on __ 197_. They were divorced. He married 2nd Penpan _____.

Child of Robert^{-8} DOLBEAR and Carol ELMER:
Surname **DOLBEAR**

1872. Owen Douglas   born 25 Oct 1973/8

1579. ROBERT HENRY-[8] GREENOUGH, son of Robert Henry-[7] GREENOUGH (Caleb-[6]; Charles-[5]; Mary Caroline-[4] MC INTOSH; Simon, Jr-[3]; Simon-[2;] Alexander-[1]) and Shirley DUNBAR, and was born 30 Aug 1946 at ____ PA. He married Shirley COMFORT Jan 1965. She as the daughter of _____ COMFORT and _____ and was born _____.

Children of Robert H-[8] GREENOUGH and Shirley COMFORT:
Surname **GREENOUGH**

      1873. Robert Henry III   born ____   1874. Nancy   born ____

1582. DEBBIE-[8] GREENOUGH, sister of above, was born 24 Aug 953 at _____, PA. She married first to Gary NICHOLS on _____ at ____. They divorced, and she married second to James (Jim) GUINAN on __ June 990 at ____.

Children of Debbie-[8] GREENOUGH and Gary NICHOLS:
Surname **NICHOLS**
1875. Lance   born _____   1876. Mark   born _____

1591. PAMELA MAE-[8] KINSMAN, daughter of Shirley-[7] GREENOUGH (Caleb-[6;] Charles-[5]; Mary Caroline-[4] MC INTOSH; Simon-[3], Jr; Simon-[2]; Alexander-[1]) and Milford KINSMAN, was born 20 March 1951 at East Troy, PA. She married _____ HASELTINE on 15 May 1971 at ___, PA.

Children of Pamela-[8] KINSMAN and _____ HASELTINE:
Surname **HASELTINE**
      1877. Melissa   born 30 Aug 1976   1878. Jeremy   born 4 June 1979

1592. PATRICIA-[8] KINSMAN, sister of above, was born was born 22 April 1952 at East Troy, PA. She married Leon WEITZ on 23 April 1977 at East Troy, PA.

Children of Patricia-[8] KINSMAN and Leon WEITZ:
Surname **WEITZ**
      1879. Lori Lee   born 28 Sept 1979   1881. Patricia Lee   born 25 Oct 1983
      1880. Virginia (Ginger)   born 19 Aug 1981

1593. GLEN-[8] KINSMAN, brother of above, was born 20 Aug 1953 at East Troy, PA. He married Dorothy _____ on 5 April 1980.

Children of Glen-[8] KINSMAN and Dorothy _____:
Surname **KINSMAN**
      1882. Katie Hope   born 13 Aug 1980 PA   1883. Ryan Glen   born Sep 1981 PA

1594. KIM-[8] KINSMAN, sister of above, was born 15 Aug 1956 at East Troy, PA. He married Dorothy CLARK on 6 Oct 1979 at ____,PA. She was born 16 July 57 at __, PA.

Children of Kim-[8] KINSMAN and Dorothy Clark:
Surname **KINSMAN**
      1884. Chelsea Marie   born 25 Feb 1983 PA
      1885.. Angela Irene   born 15 Feb 1986 PA
      1886. Leslie Owen   born 15 Apr 1990 PA

1595. PENNY LOU-[8] KINSMAN, sister of above, was born 11 Aug 1959 at East Troy, PA. She married Douglas WALBORN on 25 April 1981. He was born 24 Aug 1957 PA.

Children of Penny Lou[8] KINSMAN and Douglas WALBORN:
Surname **WALBORN**

1887. Lienne	born 10 Dec 1981 PA
1888. Christopher Caleb	born 23 June 1983 A
1889. Amber Ashley	born 29 June 1989 PA

1596. PEARL[8] KINSMAN, sister of above, was born 20 Sep 1960 at East Troy, PA. She married Gerald SIMONIS on 19 Oct 1985.

Children of Pearl[8] KINSMAN and Gerald SIMONIS:
Surname **SIMONIS**

1890. Jacob Richard	born 20 May 1986 PA
1891. Gordon Milford	born 19 April 1989 PA

1605. CONSTANCE LOUISE " Connie" [8] STERLING, daughter of Paul D[7] STERLING (Charles[6], Frederick J-[5]; Elizabeth Jane-[4] MAC INTOSH; Simon, Jr[3]; Simon-[2;] Alexander[-1]) and Mildred G. BALCOM, was born 8 Jan 1944 at Syracuse, Onondaga County, NY. Her parents divorced and she was raised by her maternal grandparents (Charles and Leona BALCOM) in Pulaski, Oswego County, NY. She married first to Steven RIDGEWAY ca 1962. He was the son of Myron RIDGEWAY and Marie HALE, and was born ca ____. They divorced and she married second to Donald ROBERTS ***on 2 Apr 1970. He was the son of George William ROBERTS and Lillian Johanna KLEVER, and was born _____. They resided at 4361 Forestbrook Dr, Liverpool, Onondaga, NY (Tel. # 315/ 622-3042)

*** Donald ROBERTS was previously married and had a daughter Laura Lee ROBERTS, who was born 9 May 1959. She married _____ GARGER, and had two children. Laura and her husband are both attorneys.

Children of Constance [8] STERLING and Steven RIDGEWAY:
Surname **RIDGEWAY**
(adopted by Mr. ROBERTS and **names changed to ROBERTS**

1892. Marcia Marie	born 6 May 1963
	married Steven RUGGIERO 13 July 1991
Child:	Amanda Lucia-[10] RUGGIERO born 17 Dec 2002
1893. Jeffrey Aries	born 3 Apr 1965
	married _____, divorced; resided San Diego, CA
	Children: Sidney-[10] (f) born 1987, and Shannon[10] ROBERTS born _____
1894. Susan Lynn	born 19 Mar 1966
	married Lexi Mikos KARSAY; divorced Jan 2010, resided AZ
	Children: Alexander Roy-[10] born 19 May 1998, and Zachary Charles-[10] KARSAY born 19 Apr 2001

Child of Constance-[8] STERLING and Donald ROBERTS:
Surname **ROBERTS**

1895. Christopher David   born 8 Feb 1978; married Mariana HALUK 4 July 2008

1608. ROBERT EDWARD[8] STERLING, half brother of above, son of Paul[7] STERLING and his second wife Josephine SHUBA, was born 28 Aug 1954 at Syracuse, Onondaga County, NY. He married Carol Ruth KIRSCHENBAUM on 3 Dec 1977 at the North Syracuse (NY) Baptist Church. She was the daughter of Charles Warren KIRSCHENBAUM, Jr. and Virginia Faith YEACKEL, and was born 25 Aug 1954.

Children of Robert Edward[8] STERLING and Carol KIRSCHENBAUM:
Surname **STERLING**

1896. Christopher Charles	born 4 Oct 1985 Rochester, Monroe, NY
1897. Emily Elizabeth	born 30 Sep 1988 Rochester, NY
	graduated from Wells College, Aurora, NY 2010

1611. DANA STERLING[-8] **DRISKO,** son of Frances Jean[-7] STERLING (Charles Lee-[6]; Frederick James[-5]; Elizabeth Jane[-4] MC INTOSH; Simon[-3], Jr; Simon[-2]; Alexander[-1]) and George Dolbey DRISKO, was born 29 July 1958 at Syracuse, Onondaga County, NY. He graduated from Cornell University 1980. He married Jennifer Lynn REYNOLDS on 17 Sep 1983 at Andrews Memorial Methodist Church, North Syracuse, MY. She was the daughter of John Francis Hanson REYNOLDS and Patricia DAIR Brennan Reynolds, and was born 23 April 1961 Syracuse, NY.

Children of Dana Sterling[-8] DRISKO and Jennifer REYNOLDS:
Surname **DRISKO**

    1898. Zachory John   born 25 March 1987 Syracuse, NY
       "Zack"   baptized June 1987 Andrews Memorial Methodist Church
                 graduated cum laude from University of North Carolina Wilmington Dec 2008
    1899. Maximilian Dair   born 10 May 1991 Syracuse, NY
       "Max"   baptized 25 Aug 1991 Andrews Memorial Methodist Church

1622. JAMES STUART[-8] **WHITING,** son of James Vincent[7] WHITING (Grace[-6] DANN; Sterling[5]; Adelia[-4] MC INTOSH; Simon[3],Jr; Smon[-2]; Alexander[-1]) and Bernita BLANCHARD, was born 12 Jan 1947 at ___. He married Patricia HAVENS on ____. She was born 31 Dec 1946.

Chidren of James-[8] WHITING and Patricia HAVENS:
Surname **WHITING**

    1900. James Maxwell   born 5 July 1975   1901. Sara Elizabeth   born ca _____

1623. DONNA JO[-8] **WHITING,** sister of above, was born 5 Oct 1948 at _____. She married Harry ORLYK on _____. He was born 8 Jan 1948.

Children of Donna Jo[-8] WHITING and Harry ORLYK:
Surname **ORLYK**

1902. Tessa Wren	born 15 June 1976	1904. Rachel	born 5 Mar 1982
1903. Joseph	born 16 Jan 1980	1905. Herron Ruth	born 4 Aug 1986

1625. ANDREA LYNN[-8] **WHITING,** sister of above, was born 10 September 1961 at ____, She was unmarried and the surnames for her children are not known to this researcher.

Children of Andrea Lynn[-8] WHITING and _____:
Surname Unknown (possibly WHITING)

    1906. Michael Paul   born 24 July 1979   1907. Nicole Lisette   born 23 June 1987

1665. JAN MARIE[-8] **WALSH-RICHARD,** daughter of Donald Eugene-[7] WALSH-RICHARD (Robert[-6] WALSH; Julia M[-5] CEASE; Sidney[-4]; Julia Ann-[3] MC INTOSH; Simon[-2]; Alexander-[1]) and Barbara Sue SEARLE, was born 23 Feb 1952 at Windsor, Ontario, Canada. She married Dennis SIDORSKI on 25 May 1974.

Children of Jan Marie-[8] WALSH-RICHARD and Dennis SIDORSKI:
Surname **SIDORSKI**

1908. Nathan	born 22 Mar 1975	1911. Jessie Lynor	born 28 Dec 1981
1909. Mathew James	born 10 Feb 1977	1912. Dennis	born 28 Sep 1983
1910. Andrew Christopher	born 22 Aug 1978		

1682. PATRICIA MAE[-8] **FARRELL,** daughter of Rhoda Mae-[7] LIGHTFOOT (Nina Mae-[6] CEASE; Carl Sidney-[5]; Sidney[4]; Julia-[3] MC INTOSH; Simon[-2]; Alexander[-1]) and Robert FARRELL, was born 27 May 1957 at Traverse City, MI. She married Steven DORN on 21 Apr 1984.

Children of Patricia Mae-8 FARRELL and Steven DORN:
Surname **DORN**
>   1913. Robert Hunter   born 14 Jan 1985 Madison, WI
>   1914. Schuyler Byron   born 11 Aug 1991

1685. SUSAN ANN-8 HOFBAUER, daughter of Imelda-7 LIGHTFOOT (Nina Mae-6 CEASE; Carl Sidney-5; Sidney-4; Julia-3 MC INTOSH; Simon-2; Alexander-1) and Gerald HOFBAUER, was born 6 Aug 1958 at Petoskey, MI. She married Timothy Mark MAXWELL on 27 Sep 1984.

Children of Susan Ann-8 HOFBAUER and Timothy MAXWELL:
Surname **MAXWELL**
>   1915. Kelsey Lynn   born 31 Dec 1984   1917. Mabel T.   born 15 Mar 1990
>   1916. Whitney Marie   born 25 May 1987

1686. GRIF GERALD-8 HOFBAUER, brother of above, was born 27 Aug 1959 at Petoskey, MI. He married Waynet STRADLING, ca ___. She was born 14 May 1961.

Children of Grif Gerald-8 HOFBAUER and Waynet STRADLING:
Surname **HOFBAUER**
>   1918. Jessica Jean   born 4 Jan 1983   1920. Joshua Grif Gerald   born 24 Mar 1989
>   1919. Wendee Mae   born 29 Mar 1986

1688. JAMES BYRON-8 HOPFBAUER, brother of above, was born 13 Aug 1963 at Petoskey, MI. He married Faith GREGORY on 21 May 1988. She was born 10 Mar 1964.

Children of James-8 HOFBAUER and Faith GREGORY:
Surname **HOFBAUER**
>   1921. Jordan James   born 7 Aug 1987   1922. Shane Douglas   born 9 Feb 1992

1689. THAD THOMAS-8 HOFBAUER, brother of above, was born 21 July 966 at Petoskey, MI. He married Sharon LONG on ___. She was born 22 May 1966.

Children of Thad-8 HOFBAUER and Sharon LONG:
Surname **HOFBAUER**
>   1923. Samantha   born 18 Sept 1988   1924. Jennifer Rose   born 19 Oct 1990

1690. AMY-8 LIGHTFOOT, daughter of Alvin-7 LIGHTFOOT (Nina-6 CEASE; Carl Sidney-5; Sidney-4; Julia-3 MC INTOSH; Simon-2; Alexander-1) and Susan GARVER, was born 19 July 1963 at Huachua, AZ. She married Matthew CARTER on 11 June 1983. He was born 6 Feb 1964.

Children of Amy-8 LIGHTFOOT and Matthew CARTER
Surname **CARTER**
>   1925. Allison Elizabeth   born 20 Aug 1989   1926. Mattthew Corey   born 22 July 1993

1694. RUSSELL FORREST-8 SCHLAPPI, son of Marilyn-7 LIGHTFOOT (Nina Mae-6 CEASE; Carl Sidney5; Sidney-4; Julia Ann-3 MC INTOSH; Simon-2; Alexander-1) and ___ SCHLAPPI, was born 2 July 1963 Petoskey, MI. He married Susan Joan STANDISH on 21 May 1983. She was born 27 May 1962.

Children of Russell-8 SCHLAPPI and Susan STANDISH:
Surname **SCHLAPPI**
>   1927. Christopher Charles born 11 Feb 1985   1928. Unknown   born ca _____

1695. KATHLEEN JOY-8 **SCHLAPPI**, sister of above, was born 30 July 1964 at Petoskey, MI. She married Kevin SADDISON in Aug 1983.

Children of Kathleen-8 SCHLAPPI and Kevin SADDISON:
Surname **SADDISON**

1929. Shari Lynn	born 16 Oct/Nov 1985	1931. Karl Michael	born 7 Dec 1990
1930. Raymond Charles	born 4 Mar 1987		

1696. ERIC CHARLES-8 **SCHLAPPI**. brother of above , was born 16 July 1965 at Petoskey, MI. He married Christi BODEN on 15 Sep 1990. She was born 12 Mar 1969.

Children of Eric-8 SCHLAPPI and Christi BODEN:
Surname **SCHLAPPI**

1932. Stephanie Ruth	born 25 May 1990	1934. Alexandria Foster	born 20 Feb 1994
1933. Michelle Nicole	born 21 Sep 1992		

1705. KENNETH-8 **MURDOCK,** son of Carol Lee-7 BOETTGER (Willis-6; Mildred-5 CEASE; Sidney-4; Julia-3 MC INTOSH; Simon-2; Alexander-1) and James MURDOCK, was born14 Sept 1964 at Anchorage, Alaska. He married Mary SIEVERS on 30 Sept 1982. She was born 15 Dec 1965 at ____, MI.

Children of Kenneth8 MURDOCK and Mary SIEVERS:
Surname **MURDOCK**   (children born Kenai, Alaska)

1935. John James	born 23 Oct 1983	1936. Dorian Kam	born 24 Aug 1989

1706. HELEN-8 **MURDOCK**, sister of above, was born 26 Feb 1986 at Anchorage, Alasks. She married Randall K. IGOU on ____. He was born Jan 1958 at Blythe, CA.

Children of Helen-8 MURDOCK and Randall IGOU:
Surname **IGOU**   (children all born at Kenai, Alaska)

1937. Michael James	born 26 Aug 1984	1939. Carol Jean	born 3 Feb 1988
1938. Timothy	born 26 Mar 1986	1940. Randall	born 10 Feb 1990

1753. KATHLEEN JOYCE-8 **SMITH,** daughter of Howard William-7 SMITH (William Tanner-6; Elizabeth-5 TANNER; Strever-4; William-3; Magdalena-2 MAC INTOSH; Alexander-1) and Shirley Kathleen BENNETT, was born 12 Oct 1947 at Des Moines, Polk County, IA. She married Rex Donald FILER on 13 June 1970 at Jewel, Hamilton County, IA. Rex FILER was the son of Amos FILER and Violet LENIG, and was born 28 Nov 1946 at Sioux City, IA.

Children of Kathleen Joyce-8 SMITH and Rex FILER:
Surname **FILER**

1941. Brock Amos	born 10 Jan 1974 Council Bluffs, IA
1942. Darrin James	born 20 Nov 1975 Marshalltown, IA

1754. PHILIP HOWARD-8 **SMITH**, brother of above, was born4 Nov 949 at Des Moines, Polk, Ia. He married Barbara June HULTMAN on 28 Aug 1971 at Belle Plain, IA. She was the daughter of Russell Eugene HULTMAN and June Harriett MC LENNAN, and was born 16 June 950 at Des Moines, IA.

Children of Philip Howard-8 SMITH and Barbara June HULTMAN:
Surname **SMITH**   (1st 2 children born DesMoines, IA; # 3 and # 4 born Salina, KS)

1943. Matthew Philip	born 17 Apr 1975	1945. Allison Barbara	born 16 July 1980
1944. Eric Russell	born 25 Mar 1978	1946. Mark Robert	born 19 Dec 1983

1755. DAVID ROBERT[8] **SMITH**, brother of above, was born 16 Feb 1954 at Oelwein, Fayette County, IA. He married Pamela Jo WOESTE on 9 Aug 1986 at Ames, Story County, IA. She was the daughter of Leland Neil WOESTE and Joyce Virginia HARTBECK, and was born 1 Nov 1952 at Manchester, Delaware County, IA.

Child of David Robert[8] SMITH and Pamela WOESTE:
Surname **SMITH**
       1947. Michael David   born 23 Sep 1988 Ames, IA

1756. ROBERT WILLIAM[8] **SMITH**, son of Harold Arnold[7] SMITH (William T[6]; Elizabeth[5] TANNER; Strever[4]; William[3]; Magdalena[2] MAC INTOSH; Alexander[1]) and Jennie PALS , was born 1 Feb 1940 at Belmond, Wright County, Iowa. He married Carolyn Kay MC CAFFERY on 27 Dec 1963 at Belmond, Iowa. She was the daughter of Robert MC CAFFERY and Ella SCHNUETTGER, and was born 27 Mar 1943 at Anilla, Iowa.

Children of Robert W[8] SMITH and Carolyn MC CAFFERY:
Surname **SMITH**   (all children born Belmond, Wright County, Iowa)
       1948. Kimberly Kay   born 29 Aug 1966
       1949. Steven Robert   born 7 Oct 1968
       1950. Roy William   born 5 Apr 1971
       1951. Michael Lee   born 19 Jan 1973, died 9 Apr 1973
       1952. Kerri D'Lynn   born 16 July 1974
       1953 . Brandon Lee   born 4 Sep 1975   1954. Bryan Anthony   born 15 Dec 1978

1757. JIM WARREN[8] **SMITH**, brother of above, was born 1 Sep 1944 at Belmond, Wright County, IA. He married Judy Ann WOLTERS on 10 October 1964 a Goodell, Wright County, IA. She was the daughter of Clarence WOLTERS and Gladys BOECK, and was born 9 July 1946.

Children of Jim Warren[8] SMITH and Judy WOLTERS:
Surname **SMITH**
       1955. Dee Ann   born 1 March 1966 Belmond, IA
                           married Vance Randall SPALDING 25 Aug 1990 Bonners Ferry, ID
       1956. Debra Ann   born 24 July 1967 Belmond, IA

1758. BRUCE HAROLD[8] **SMITH**, brother of above, was born 25 Oct 1949 at Belmond, Wright County, Iowa. He married Patricia ANGEL on 11 May 1974 at Nashua, Chickasaw County, Iowa. She was the daughter of Jess ANGEL and Verna LOVE, and was born 22 June 1951 at Mason City, Iowa.

Children of Bruce H[8] SMITH and Patricia ANGEL:
Surname **SMITH**
       1957. MacKenzie Sue   born 3 Dec 1977 Mason City, IA
       1958. Baron Michael   born 28 Apr 1980 Mason City, IA

1760. LINDA SUE[8] **BRANDENBURG**, daughter of Elizabeth Marie[7] SMITH (William T[6]; Elizabeth[5] TANNER; Strever[4]; William[3]; Magdalena[2] MAC INTOSH, Alexander[1]) and Carl BRANDENBURG, was born 15 Aug 1851 at Des Moines, Polk County, Iowa, She married William Michael REESE on 29 Aug 1970 at Des Moines. He was the son of Charles William REESE and Pauline Marie BROWN, and was born 25 May 1950 at Des Moines, IA.

Child of Linda Sue[8] BRANDENBURG and William REESE:
Surname **REESE**
       1959. James William   born 13 Dec 1972 Des Moines, IA

1761. NANCY ANN[8] **BRANDENBURG**, sister of above, was born 2 June 1953 at Des Moines, IA. She married Robert LYDICK on 16 Dec 1978 at Alexandria, VA. He was the son of Allen Raymond LYDICK and Jerri Wescott TOMPKINS, and was born 27 May 1947 at Jamaica, Long Island, NY

Children of Nancy[8] BRANDENBURG and Robert LYDICK:
Surname **LYDICK**

1960. Jerri Elizabeth	born 8 Aug 1988 Panama City Beach, FL	
1961. Laura Ann	born 16 Jan 1992 Panama City Beach, FL	

1762. DONNA KAY[8] **BRANDENBURG**, sister of above, was born 23 January 1955 at Des Moines, IA. She married Joseph NIZZI on 25 Sept _____ at Des Moines. He was the son of Remo NIZZI and Muriel SCHLABAUGH, and was born 18 Nov 1955.

Children of Donna[8] BRANDENBURG and Joseph NIZZI:
Surname **NIZZI** (all children born Des Moines, IA)

1962. Nickolas James	born 8 June 1978	1964. Sarah R.	born 25 Oct 1989
1963. Tracy Marie	born 30 June 1982		

1763. BETTY LOUISE[8] **SMITH**, daughter of Raymond Vanatta[7] SMITH (Asa[6]; Elizabeth[5] TANNER; Strever[4]; William[3]; Magdalena[2] MAC INTOSH; Alexander[1]) and Pauline ADDY, was born 29 Sep 1932 Earlham, Madison County, Iowa. She married first to Kenneth ARCHER on 20 Aug 1950. They divorced, and she married second to Raymond GORDON ca 1952.

Child of Betty[8] SMITH and Kenneth ARCHER:
Surname **ARCHER**

+	**1965. DEBORAH**	born 4 Apr 1951 Des Moines, IA.
		married David Loren BAYSINGER ca 1970; divorced

Children of Betty[8] SMITH and Raymond GORDON:
Surname **GORDON**

	1966. Jeffery Rae	born 2 Dec 1953 Des Moines
+	**1967. THERESA RAE**	born 5 Aug 1955 Des Moines; married Lynn WEINKAUF
	1968. Kathryn Rae	born _____ 1958 Des Moines; married David GROOM

1764. KIETH RAYMOND[8] **SMITH**, brother of above, was born 16 August 1937 at Earlham, Madison County, Iowa. He married Sheryl Ann TIMMONS on __ November 1954. She was the daughter of _____ TIMMONS and _____, and was born 5 Apr 1938 at Des Moines. Kieth[8] SMITH died 23 March 1985 at Des Moines, IA. And is buried at the Highland Memory Gardens in Des Moines.

Children of Kieth[8] SMITH and Sheryl TIMMONS:
Surname **SMITH**

+	**1969. DENISE**	born 11 Feb 1955 Des Moines, IA
	ROCHELLE	married Robert BRUCE 1 June 1974
+	**1970. CONNIE JEAN**	born 14 Oct 1956 Des Moines, IA
		married Gary LOFSTEDT 14 Oct 1980 Ames , IA
	1971. Sandra Suzanne	born 1 Jan 1958 Des Moine
	1972. Lori Diane	born 8 Mar 1961 Des Moine
		married Kevin BENNING 30 Aug 1980

1765. GENE VANATTA[8] **SMITH**, brother of above, was born 16 November 1939 Earlham, Madison County, Iowa. He married Nancy Louise KEENER on 21 Oct 195_.

Children of Gene[8] SMITH and Nancy KEENER:
Surname **SMITH**

	1973. Gene V.	born Aug 1960 Polk County, IA.
		married Cindy M. _____ 21 Oct 19__
		(she born 26 Feb 1962 Anacartic, WA)
+	**1974. GREGORY V.**	born 14 July 1962 Polk Co., IA
		married Wendy L. ANTHONY 26 Dec 1981
		(she dau Robert ANTHONY and Kay ____)
		she born 13 Aug 1957 Ponco City, OK)

1766. RICHARD CRAIG[8] **SMITH**, son of Homer Edward-[7] SMITH (Asa-[6]; Elizabeth-[5] TANNER; Strever-[4]; William-[3]; Magdalena-[2] MAC INTOSH; Alexander-[1]) and Verna STONE, was born 7 March 1940 at Long Beach, CA. He married first to Judy Marlene PAULLIN on 26 July 1959 at Des Moines, IA. They adopted four children++. They divorced and he married second to Elizabeth Louise AVITT on 24 Sep 1965 at Des Moines, IA. She was born 26 Feb 1938 at Newton, Jasper County, Iowa.

Children of Richard[8] SMITH and Elizabeth AVITT:
Surname **SMITH**

1975. David Paul	born 3 Jan 1967 Seattle, King Co., WA.
1976. Derek Dean	born 18 Oct 1968 Seattle, WA

> NOTE: The four adopted children of the first marriage are listed here
> for information only. They are not included in the MC INTOSH lineage
> Adopted surname of **SMITH**

1.	Michael Ward	born 24 Dec 1959; marrid Anita Louise JONES
2.	Craig Allen	born 2 May 1961; married Cynthia CADY
3.	Julia Ann	born 23 Aug 1962; married David Edwin BRINK
4.	Linda Luese	born 0 Nov 1962; married Greg Allen PEDERSON

1767. HOMER EDWARD[8] **SMITH, JR,** brother of above, was born 23 June 1944 at Washington, DC. He married first to June Elizabeth HATFIELD on 22 October 1965 at Marysville, Nodway County, MO. She was born 16 March 19__ at Des Moines, IA.

His second marriage was to Judy Faye WINSTONE McPherson on 14 May 1975 at Humble, TX. She was the daughter of _____ WINSTONE and _____, and was born 14 Feb 1949 at Chickasha, Grady County, Texas. She was married previously to _____ MC PHERSON and had two children from that union. They were Dewey Raymond MC PHERSON born 12 Jan 1968 OK, and Clinton Bell MC PHERSON born 26 Feb 1971 OK.

Children of Homer[8] SMITH and June HATFIELD:
Surname **SMITH**

1977. Brian Carl	born 10 May 1966 Des Moines, IA
1978. Laura Ann	born 5 Dec 1967 Mason City, IA

1769. DALE EDWARD[8] **FOX,** son of Myrtle Elizabeth [7] SMITH (Asa [6]; Elizabeth [5] TANNER; Strever [4]; William-[3]; Magdalena-[2] MAC INTOSH; Alexander-[1]) and John FOX, was born 17 Nov 1936 at Des Moines, Polk County, Iowa. He married Anna Ruth WILLARD on 16 January 1957 at Landrum, South Carolina.

Children of Dale-[8] FOX and Anna WILLARD:
Surname **FOX**

1979. Wanda Kay	born ____	1980. Edward	born ____

189

The Eighth American Generation

1770. ROY ASA^{-8} MC CORMICK, half-bother of above, son of Myrtle Elizabeth^{-7} SMITH (Asa^{-6}; Elizabeth-^{5} TANNER; Strever^{-4}; William^{-3}; Magdalena-^{2} MAC INTOSH; Alexander^{-1}) and Edward MC CORMICK, was born 13 July 1938 at Dexter, Dallas County, Iowa. He married Yvonne K. WEBB ca 1940. She was the daughter of Donald E. WEBB and Verena M. _____.

Child of Roy Asa^{-8} MC CORMICK and Yvonne WEBB:
Surname **MC CORMICK**
      1981. Teresa Gail   born _____

1771. BILLIE WAYNE^{-8} MC CORMICK, brother of above, was born 7 July 1952 at _____. He married Pauline _____ on ____.

Children of Billie^{-8} MC CORMICK and Pauline _____:
Surname **MC CORMICK**
      1982. Rebrandia   born _____   1984. Frank   born ____
      1983. Steven   born _____   1985. Tracy   born ____

1772. DAVID ALLEN^{-8} MC CORMICK, brother of above, was born 16 September 1954 at Gary, Lake County, Indiana. He married first to Twila HADDOCK ca 19____. They divorced and his second wife was Kay _____.

Child of David^{-8} MC CORMICK and Twila HADDCK:
Surname **MC CORMICK**
      1986. Mary Laden   born ca 1974

1774. SHERMAN DEE^{-8} MOORE, son of Wilma Eileen-^{7} SMITH (Asa-^{6}; Elizabeth-^{5} TANNER; Strever^{-4}; William^{-3}; Magdalena-^{2} MAC INTOSH; Alexander^{-1}) and Calvin Sherman MOORE, Jr., was born 2 Nov 1945 at Dexter, Dallas County, Iowa. His first marriage was to Caren Coy BROWN on 29 October 1965 at Idaho Falls, Bonneville County, Idaho. She was born 6 Oct 1947. They divorced ca ____.

His second marriage was to Pamela LIBIS on 22 July 1977 at South Lake Tahoe, CA. She was born 4 April 1951 Los Angeles, CA.

Children of Sherman^{-8} MOORE and Caren BROWN:
Surname **MOORE**
      1987. Katrina Lee   born 8 July 1970 Mountain View, CA.
      1988. Shanon Dyane   born 6 March 1972 San Jose, CA.

1775. MICKEY LEE^{-8} MOORE, brother of above, was born 1 April 1947 at Dexter, Dallas County, Iowa. He married Pilar POSADA on 31 December 1976 at Dexter, IA. She was the daughter of _____ POSADA and ____, and was born 6 June 1955 at Bogota, Colombia, South America.

Child of Mickey^{-8} MOORE and Pillar POSADA:
Surname **MOORE**
      1989. Oliver Calvin   born 0 June 1984 Roseville, CA.

1776. ANDREW JAY^{-8} MOORE, brother of above, twin of # 1781 below, was born 6 Jan 1949 at Dexter, Dallas County, Iowa. He married first to Deborah KO on ___. She was born 1 Sept 1956 at Philadelphia, PA. They divorced. There was no issue from that union.
His second marriage was to Cathy ANDERSON on 12 January 1974 at Las Vegas, Clark County, Nevada. She was the daughter of Andrew ANDERSON and Betty ___, and was born 29 August 1959 at Hawthorne, CA.

Children of Andrew[8] MOORE and Cathy ANDERSON:
Surname **MOORE**

1990. Asa Justin	born 30 Oct 1974 Trustin, CA	
1991. Tara Elizabeth	born 8 Aug 1977 Greenfield, Adair, Iowa	

1777. ANTHONY JEROME[8] MOORE, twin brother of above, was born 6 Jan 1949 at Dexter, Iowa. He married Tracey Lu MARTEN on 24 June 1972 at Pittsville, Wood County, Wisconsin. She was the daughter of Francis MARTEN and Lillie Belle _____, and was born 6 Feb 1953 at Wisconsin Rapids, Wood County, Wisconsin.

Children of Anthony[8] MOORE and Tracey MARTEN:
Surname **MOORE**

1992. Aaron Jason	born 18 April 1974 Iowa City, IA
1993. Shawn Ryan	born 22 Dec 1976 Des Moines, IA
1994. Travis Brandon	born 8 June 1981 Lacrosse, Wisconsin

1778. SAMUEL CALVIN[8] MOORE, brother of above, was born 6 June 1952 at Dexter, Iowa. He married Rachel SNOWDEN on 19 August 1979 at Des Moines, Polk County, Iowa. She was the daughter of Kenneth Chase SNOWDEN and Alice May CLARK, and was born 6 February 1953 at Colfax, Jasper County, Iowa.

Child of Samuel[8] MOORE and Rachel SNOWDEN:
Surname **MOORE**

1995. Natasha Leann	born 2 Dec 1981 Sunnyvale, CA.

1779. LAWRENCE DAVID-[8] DOLAN, son of Illa June-[7] SMITH (Asa-[6]; Elizabeth-[5] TANNER; Strever-[4]; William-3; Magdalena-[2] MAC INTOSH, Alexander-[1]) and John DOLAN, was born 28 July 1946 at Dallas County, Iowa. He married first to Roberta BUCKHOLZ on 14 August 1965. They divorced before 1968. His second marriage was to Jackie _____ ca ___. They were also divorced and he married third to Jennie _____.

Child of Lawrence-[8] DOLAN and Roberta BUCKHOLZ:
Surname **DOLAN**   (all children born Perry, IA)

1996. Paula	born 1 March 1967 Perry, Dallas County, IA		

Children of Lawrence-[8] DOLAN and Jackie ____:
Surname **DOLAN**

1997. Jeff	born 5 April 1968	1998. Bryant	born 11 Nov 1972

Children of Lawrence-[8] DOLAN and Jennie _____:
Surname **DOLAN**

1999. Michael	born 9 August 1973	2000. Matthew	born 22 Feb 1975

1780. JOSEPH CRAIG-[8] DOLAN, brother of above, was born 15 Oct 1947 at Dallas County, Iowa. He married Gladys Virginia ROBERTS on 29 October 1966 at Dallas County, IA. She was the daughter of Willard ROBERTS and Grace BROWN and was born 10 December 1946 at Cabool, Texas County, MO..

Children of Joseph-[8] DOLAN and Gladys ROBERTS:
Surname **DOLAN**

2001. Joseph Craig, Jr.	born Aug 1968 Perry, Dallas, IA
2002. Susan Marie	born 25 Nov 1970 Des Moines, Polk, IA

1781 JAMES ROBERT-[8] DOLAN, brother of above, was born 12 December 1949 at Perry, Dallas County, Iowa. He married Cristy BOYENS on __ November 1967.

MACKINTOSH   MAC INTOSH   MC INTOSH
The Eighth American Generation

Children of James[8] DOLAN and Cristy BOYENS:
Surname **DOLAN**   (children born Perry, Dallas County, Iowa)
    2003. Jennifer   born 15 May 1968   2004. Jason   born 11 Aug 1973

1782. VINCENT THOMAS[8] DOLAN, brother of above, was born 1 November 1951 at Perry, Dallas County, Iowa. He married first to Becky MAXWELL. They divorced without issue. His second wife was Tresa ____. They also divorced without issue. His third marriage was to Katheryn Kay BRUDER ca _____. She was the daughter of _____ BRUDER and ____, and was born 23 April 1957.

Children of Vincent[8] DOLAN and Katheryn BRUDER:
Surname **DOLAN**   (children born Jefferson, Greene Co., IL)
    2005. Shauna   born 9 Aug 1974   2006. Janelle   born 3 Sep 197_

1783. SHARON ELAINE[8] SMITH, daughter of Edwin Robert[7] SMITH (Clarence[6]; Elizabeth[5] TANNER; Strever[4]; William[3]; Magdalena[2] MAC INTOSH, Alexander[1]) and Doris HADLEY, was born 30 October 1946 at Dexter, Dallas County, Iowa. She married Donald Dean JONES on 5 September 1970 at Earlham, Madison County, Iowa. He was the son of Alva JONES and Louise ____, and was born 16 Jan 1944 at Creston, Union County, Iowa.

Children of Sharon[8] SMITH and Donald JONES:
Surname **JONES**
    2007. Kurt Allen   born 4 Nov 1973 Monroe, Greene County, IA
    2008. Gregory Scott   born 26 June 197_ Monroe, IA

1784. BARBARA JEAN[8] SMITH, sister of above, was born 15 December 1947 at Dexter, Dallas County, Iowa. She married Darwin Forest SNOOK, Jr. on 6 July 1968 at Earlham, Madison County, IA. He was the son of Darwin Forest SNOOK, Sr. and Lucille JELSMA, and was born 6 Jul 1946 at Leon, Decatur County, IA.

Children of Barbara[8] SMITH and Darwin SNOOK, Jr.:
Surname **SNOOK**
    2009. Brant Aron   born 28 Dec 1968 Dexter, IA
    2010. Michelle Lynn   born 22 Feb 1972 Corydon, Wayne, IA

1785. EDWIN HOWARD[8] SMITH, brother of above, was born25 June 1950 at Dexter, Dallas County, Iowa. He married Connie Joann THRAILKILL on 26 August 1972 at Earlham, IA. She was the daughter of Edward THRAILKILL and Ardith GENTRY, and was born 4 March 1954 at Earlham, Iowa.

Children of Edwin[8] SMITH and Connie THRAILKILL:
Surname **SMITH**
    2011. Cory Edward   born 15 Oct 1976 Sioux City, Iowa
    2012. Kieth A.   born 3 Oct 1978 Charles, MO.

1786. RICHARD CHARLES[8] LEIGHTY/ Eagan, son of Twila[7] SMITH (Clarence[6]; Elizabeth[5] TANNER; Strever[4]; William[3]; Magdalena[2] MAC INTOSH; Alexander[1]) and Charles LEIGHTY, was born 26 November 1943 at Downy, CA. He later changed his name to EAGAN – the surname of his step-father. He married Gloria CHROUP ca 19__. She was the daughter of Leon CHROUP and Adoline VENZ, and was born 5 May 1943 at Charles City, Iowa.

Child of Richard[8] LEIGHTY/ EAGAN and Gloria CHROUP:
Surname **EAGAN**
    2013. Brian Richard   born 11 Nov 1976 Elk Grove, Cook County, IL

1787. KATHLEEN ANN-8 EAGAN, half sister of above, daughter of Twila-7 SMITH (Clarence-6; Elizabeth-5 TANNER; Strever-4; William-3; Magdalena-2 MAC INTOSH; Alexander-1) and Robert EAGAN, was born 23 April 1947 at Spencer City, Iowa. She married Frank MC KIM ca 1966. He was the son of Fred MC KIM and Leta HEATHMAN, and was born 20 April 1947 at Emmetsburg, Palo Alto, IA

Children of Kathleen-8 EAGAN and Frank MC KIM:
Surname **MC KIM**
2014. Michelle Ann   born 7 Oct 1967 Emmetsburg, IA
2015. Scott Michael   born 6 Feb 1970 Fort Dodge, IA
2016. Matthew John   born 13 Sept 1973 Humboldt, IA

1788. JEAN FRANCES-8 EAGAN, sister of above, was born 2 October 1949 at Emmetsburg, Iowa. She married James ZDRAZIL on __ April 1968 at Pocahontas, Iowa. He was the son of James ZDRAZII and Marcella HRONEK, and was born 13 June 1948 at Pocahontas, Iowa.

Children of Jean-8 EAGAN and James ZDRAZIL:
Surname **ZDRAZIL**
2017. Angela Janine   born 3 Aug 1968 Lynwood , CA.
2018. Travis James   born 7 March 1970 Bellflower, CA

1789. PATRICK JOSEPH-8 EAGAN, brother of above, was born 17 December 1951 at Des Moines, Polk County, Iowa. He married Susan WITT on __ January 1973 at San Antonio, Texas. She was the daughter of Marvin WITT and Mary STURDIVANDT, and was born 4 October 1953 at Fort Leavenworth, KS

Child of Patrick-8 EAGAN and Susan WITT:
Surname **EAGAN**
2019. Kiel Patrick   born 29 Aug 1986 San Antonio, Texas

1790. MARY JANE-8 EAGAN, sister of above, was born 5 July 1955at Dubuque, Iowa. She married Michael REELITZ July 974 at Des moines, Iowa. He was the son of Carl REELITZ and Florence GROAT, and was born 5 July 1950 at Des Moines, Iowa.

Children of Mary-8 EAGAN and Michael REELITZ:
Surname **REELITZ**   (all children born Des Moines, Iowa)
2020. Meredith Leigh   born 4 July 1877   2022. Thomas Michael   born 21 Aug 1984
2021. Kathleen Ann   born 23 Jan 1981

1794. DOROTHY JEAN-8 RUTHERFORD, daughter of Doris Rosa-7 SMITH (Clarence-6; Elizabeth-5 TANNER; Strever-4; William-3 Magdalena-2 MAC INTOSH; Alexander-1; and Francis RUTHERFORD, was born 4 February 1950 at Fort Dodge, Webster County, Iowa. She married Thomas WHITVER on 23 April 1982 at Jefferson, Greene County, IA. He was married previously and had 2 children, Jane and Tracy.

Children of Dorothy-8 RUTHERFORD and Thomas WHITVER:
Surname **WHITVER**
2023. Allison   born 28 June 1985 Jefferson, IA
2024. Jason   born 4 April 1988 Jefferson, IA

1797. LARRY DEAN-8 RUTHERFORD, brother of above, was born 19 September 1957 at Jefferson, Greene County, Iowa. He married Laura HERTAGE on 15 September 1981 at Churdan, Greene County, IA. She was the daughter of Gordon HERTAGE and ____, and was born 14 January 19__.

Children of Larry-[8] RUTHERFORD and Laura HERTAGE:
Surname **RUTHERFORD**

2025.	Eric Allen	born 4 March 1982 Lake City, Calhoun, Iowa
2026.	Evan	born 2 Jan 1983 Fort Dodge, Webster County, Iowa

1799. RONALD HARVEY-[8] SMITH, son of Donald-[7] SMITH (Chester-[6;] Elizabeth-[5] TANNER: Strever-[4;] William-[3]; Magdalena-[2] MAC INTOSH; Alexander-[1]) and Naomi FOX, was born 2 April 1940 at Des Moines, Polk County, Iowa. He married 1st to Tina M. TODD on 27 January 1962. They were divorced Jan 1973. There was no issue from that marriage. He married 2nd to Diane L. CIPPOLLA on 6 July 1973.

Children of Ronald-[8] SMITH and Diane CIPOLLA:
Surname **SMITH**

2027.	Shane Jonathan	born 26 March 1979 Monroe, MI
2028.	Courtney Dominique	born 6 March 1986 Monroe, MI

1800. CARLA CORINNE-[8] SMITH, sister of above, was born 22 September 1945 at Des Moines, Polk County, Iowa. She married first to Ronald HAWBAKER on 21 June 1963 at Adel, Dallas County, Iowa. They were divorced March 1969. Her second marriage was to Ronald Leroy MYERS on 11 April 1969. Ronald MYERS was born ca ____ at Omaha, Douglas County, Nebraska.

Children of Carla[8] SMITH and Ronald HAWBAKER:
Surname **HAWBAKER/ MYERS** (adopted 1970 by Ronald MYERS)

+	**2029. TODD CARL**	born 27 March 1964 Des Moines, Iowa
		married Un-KYONG ca ____ Korea
	2030. Trevor Dean	born 2 July 1967 Des Moines

Child of Carla[8] SMITH and Ronald MYERS:
Surname **MYERS**

2031.	Tara Kristine	born 7 May 1970 Des Moine, Iowa

1801. MARY JANE-[8] NOLAND, daughter of Opal Mae-[7] SMITH (Chester-[6]; Elizabeth-[5] TANNER; Strever-[4;] William-[3]; Magdalena-[2] MAC INTOSH; Alexander-[1]) and Gail NOLAND, was born 31 October 1937 at Perry, Dallas County, Iowa. She married first to Edgar GUSTAFSON on __ March 1961. Other information unknown.

Children of Mary-[8] NOLAND and Edgar GUASTAFSON:
Surname **GUSTAFSON**

2032.	Tressa Ann	born 5 Oct 1961 Alexander, Douglas, MN
2033.	David Wayne	born 27 Dec 1963 Shakopee, MN

1802. LUCINDA SUE-[8] NOLAND, sister of above, was born 31 March 1940 at Des Moines, Polk County, Iowa. She married Richard Duane DRAPER on 7 June 1959 at Des Moines. He was born 30 Dec 1933 at Pacific Junction, Mills County, IA.; died 19 Aug 2011.

Children of Lucinda -[8] NOLAND and Richard DRAPER:
Surname **DRAPER**

+	**2034. DEBRA LYNN**	born 31 March 1960 Des Moines, IA
		married John Martin TEW 27 May 1978
+	**2035. RANDEL**	born 17 February 1962 Des Moines, IA
		married Melissa SPARKS
	2036. Roxanna May (twin)	born 2/22 September 1971 Des Moines
	2037. Roxanna Sue (twin)	born 2/22 September 1971 Des Moines

1803. ROSALIND EILEEN-[8] NOLAND, sister of above, was born 1 September 1941 at Des Moines, Polk County, Iowa. She married first on 21 December _____ to Larry RICHMOND. They divorced and she married 2nd to Lawrence Lester LAGERQUIST on ____.

Children of Rosalind-[8] NOLAND and Larry RICHMOND:
Surname **RICHMOND**

2038. Kirsten Eileen	born 10 May 1962 Oskaloosa, Mahaska County, Iowa
2039. Circe Eileen	born 16 June 1964 Mesa, Maricopa County, AZ
2040. Dierdre Eileen	born July 1965 Mesa, AZ

Child of Rosalind-[8] NOLAND and Lawrence LAGERQUIST:
Surname **LAGERQUIST**

2041. Desiree Eileen	born 29 January 1971 Seaside, Clatsop County, Oregon

1804. ALVARD A-[8] NOLAND, brother of above, was born 2 March 1945 at Des Moines, Polk County, Iowa. He married Arlene ____ on 25 November 1966 at ____, Hawaii.

Children of Alvard-[8] NOLAND and Arlene _____:
Surname **NOLAND**

2042. Michael Dwayne	born 7 June 1967	2043. Joshua Allen	born 26 April 1974

1805. ROBERTA GAIL-[8] NOLAND, sister of above, was born 3 December 1949 at Des Moines, Iowa. She married Richard John GRAY on 23 September 1968. They divorced after 1974.

Children of Roberta-[8] NOLAND and Richard GRAY:
Surname **GRAY**

2044. Christina Marie	born 7 Jan 1970 Robbinsdale, MN
2045. Richard John	born 13 July 1971 Pensacola, FL
2046. Peter Harris	born 3 April ___ Quantico, VA

1807. KATHERINE ANN-[8] ROUTH, daughter of Dorothy June[7] SMITH (Chester-[6]; Elizabeth-[5] TANNER; Strever-[4]; William-[3]; Magdalena-[2] MAC INTOSH; Alexander-[1]) and Leonard ROUTH, was born 1 June 1953 at Ames, Story County, Iowa. She married Kenneth MISKELL on 7 November 1978 at Story City, Story County, Iowa. He was the son of Kermit MISKELL and Wilma TURNER.

Children of Katherine-[8] ROUTH and Kenneth MISKELL:
Surname **MISKELL**   (both children born at Ames, Iowa)

2047. Bruce Aran	born 9 January 1980	2048. Heather Marie	born 25 Oct 1982

1808. JOSEPH LLOYD-[8] NOLAND, son of Pauline Rose-[7] SMITH (Chester-[6;] Elizabeth-[5] TANNER; Strever-[4]; William-[3]; Magdalena-[2] MAC INTOSH; Alexander-[1]) and Carroll NOLAND, was born 5 August 1943 at Des Moines, Polk County, Iowa. He married Linda SAMS on 29 August 196_ at Des Moines. She was the daughter of Wilbur SAMS and Doris OVERTON, and was born 21 June 19__, IA.

Children of Joseph-[8] NOLAND and Linda SAMS:
Surname **NOLAND**   (both children born at Des Moines, IA)

2049. Joseph Lloyd, Jr.	born 27 May 1986	2050. Julie Linn	born 26 June 1968

1809. JAMES CARROLL-[8] NOLAND, brother of above, was born 27 March 1946 at Des Moines, Iowa. He married first to Susan ____ on ____. They divorced in less than a year, and he married second to Maura PEGLAR. They also divorced.

Children of James[8] NOLAND and Maura PEGLAR:
Surname **NOLAND**
  2051. Benjamin George born 1 February 1971 Iowa City, Johnson County, Iowa
  2052. Samuel James born 7 June 1974 Iowa City; died 20 Sept 1974
  2053. Maggie Amanda born 27 January 1976 Iowa City, IA

1810. DONALD EDWIN[8] NOLAND, brother of above, was born 2 January 1950 at Des Moines, Polk, Iowa. He married Marlene O'BRIEN on 4 December 1971 at Georgetown, Monroe County, Iowa.

Children of Donald[8] NOLAND and Marlene O'BRIEN:
Surname **NOLAND** (all children born Des Moines, Iowa)
  2054. Kara Renee born 15 Oct 1973
  2055. Daniel Edward born 14 June 1977 2056. Kaleen Marie born 13 Sep 1983

1811. BARBARA JO[8] NOLAND, daughter of Ruth Ellen[7] SMITH (Chester[6]; Elizabeth[5] TANNER; Strever[4]; William[3]; Magdalena[2] MAC INTOSH; Alexander[1]) and Wayne NOLAND, was born 13 March 1942 at Des Moines, Polk County, Iowa. She married Forest OVERTON ca August 1958 at Indianola, Warren County, Iowa. He was the son of ___ OVERTON and ____, and was born 28 July 1940.

Children of Barbara[8] NOLAND and Forest OVERTON:
Surname **OVERTON**
+ **2057. PENNY** born 27 March 1959 Iowa City, IA
  SUSANNA married Roger CURRY 4 August 1979 Des Moines, IA
    (he born 14 Augsut 1960)
+ **2058. SCOTT WAYNE** born 18 March 1960/61 Des Moines
    married Laura VIRDEN 2 Oct 1980/81 Carlisle, Warren County, IA
+ **2059. ROBIN RUTH** born 30 October 1962 Des Moines, IA
    married Leonard CURRY 21 June 1979 Des Moines
  2060. Lorna Kay born 16 Aug 1962 Iowa City, IA

1812. ALICE MARIE[8] NOLAND, sister of above, was born 12 October 1943 at Des Moines, Polk County, Iowa. She married John CAMPBELL on __ August 1960 at Des Moines, IA. He was the son of ____ CAMPBELL and ___, and was born 24 December 1941. They divorced in August 1984.

Children of Alice[8] NOLAND and John CAMPBELL:
Surname **CAMPBELL**
  2061. Jerry Lee born 15 Jan 1961 Des Moines
    married Tereva (Terry) Denise VANDER POL at Red Rock Lake,
      Fifield Park, Marion, Iowa.
  2062. Crystal Marie born 15 February 1963 Des Moines
    married Rod STOUDE 11 Dec 1983 at Sandyville, Iowa
  2063. Brett Alan (twin) born 21 October 1965 DesMoines
  2064. Brian Eric (twin) born 2 Oct 1965 Des Moines

1813. LARRY FRED[8] NOLAND, brother of above, was born 28 February 1951 at Des Moines, Polk County, IOWA. He was the twin brother of # 1818 Gary Chester[8] NOLAND (below). He married Kathleen HIGGINS on 14 Aug 1971 at St. Ignace, Mackinac County, Michigan. She was the daughter of ____ HIGGINS and ___, and was born 10 April 1952.

Child of Larry[8] NOLAND and Kathleen HIGGINS:
Surname **NOLAND**
  2065. Kimberly Ann born 27 April 1975 Des Moines, IA

1814. GARY CHESTER[-8] **NOLAND,** twin brother of above, was born 28 February 1951 at Des Moines, Iowa. He married first to Shelley NELSON on 13 August 1970 at Middle River Friends Church, Warren County, Iowa. After a brief they divorced. There were no children from that marriage. He married second to Diane SHEETS on 24 February 1977 at Middle River Friends Church. They also divorced.

Children of Gary[-8] NOLAND and Diane SHEETS:
Surname **NOLAND**

2066. Michael Duane	born 16 December 1978 Des Moines, IA
2067. Robert Alan	born 11 October 1980 Des Moines

1815. WILLIAM LLOYD[-8] **SMITH,** son of Lloyd-[7] SMITH (Chester[-6]; Elizabeth-[5] TANNER; Strever[-4]; William-[3]; Magdalena-[2] MAC INTOSH; Alexander[-1]) and Carol MC CARTHY, was born 8 September 1946 at Earlham, Madison County, Iowa. He married Susan Ethel SCAR on 4 December 1970 at Dexter, Dallas County, Iowa. She was the daughter of Leonard C. SCAR and Dorothy AURAND, and was born 19 November 1952 at Des Moines, Iowa.

Children of William[-8] SMITH and Susan Ethel SCAR:
Surname **SMITH**

2068. Christine Lee	born 25 June 1971 Winterset, Madison, Iowa
2069. Bradley William	born 5 March 1975 Des Moines, IA

1816. LINDA SUE-[8] **SMITH,** sister of above, was born 18 February 1948 Earlham, Madison County, Iowa. She married Stephen Victor STRONG on 23 May 1966 at Winterset, Madison County, Iowa. He was the son of Arthur STRONG and Hattie ____, and was born 8 May 1945.

Children of Linda-[8] SMITH and Stephen STRONG:
Surname **STRONG**

	2070. Scott Arthur	born 20 December 1966 Anamosa, Jones County, IA
+	**2071 . JEFFREY**	born 30 January 1970 Anamosa, IA
	LLOYD	married Rebecca SHOEMAKER 30 January 1989
	2072. Gregory Stephen	born 31 December 1975 Des Moines, IA

1818. MICHAEL THOMAS[-8] **SMITH,** brother of above, was born 1 June 1953 at Winterset, Madison County, Iowa. He married first to Michelle Rae MILLER on 27 January 1973 at Earlham, Madison County, IA. She was the daughter of Francis MILLER and Caroline SMITH, and was born 5 July 1955. They divorced. He did not re-marry, but resided with a Mary ROONEY, fathering a set of twins who went by their mothers' name of ROONEY.

Children of Michael-[8] SMITH and Michelle MILLER:
Surname **SMITH**   (both children born Des Moines, IA)

2073. Jamie Thomas	born 23 April 1973	2074. Benjamin Drew born 4 October 1975

Children of Michael-[8] SMITH and Mary ROONEY:
Surname **ROONEY**

2075. Patrick Timothy	born 10 March 1989	2076. Katherine Jean born 10 March 1989

1819. DIANA LOUISE[-8] **SMITH,** sister of above, was born 14 November 1957 at Winterset, Madison County, Iowa. She married Dwayne Dean SCAR on 5 March 1976 at Dexter, Dallas County, Iowa. He was the son of Norman SCAR and Catherine TEGALS, and was born 17 August 1956.

Children of Diana-[8] SMITH and Dwayne SCAR:
Surname **SCAR** (children born Winterset, Iowa)

2077. Kandi Michelle	born 22 Dec 1977	2078. Nicholas James born 16 Aug 1979

1821. MARK ALAN-8 SMITH, brother of above, was born 11 July 1967 at Winterset, Madison County, Iowa. He married Kelli A. MILLER on 4 March 1989 at Waterloo, Black Hawk County, Iowa. She was the daughter of Harold MILLER and Judy _____, and was born _____.

Child of Mark-8 SMITH and Kelli MILLER:
Surnaame **SMITH**
>   2079. Katherine August   born 8 September 1989

1822. MARTHA LOUISE-8 SPEER, daughter of Mable Olive-7 SMITH (Raymond-6; Elizabeth-5 TANNER; Strever-4; William-3; Magdalena-2 MAC INTOSH; Alexander-1) and Wilbur SPEER, was born 31 August 1931 at Dexter, Dallas County, Iowa. She married James Maurice CLINE before 1955. He was the son of George CLINE and Dorothy DOWNS, and was born 7 October 1930. They divorced in 1963. (Note: thye adopted a child Catherine Marie who was born 23 Aug 1961 Des Moines, Iowa .

Children of Martha-8 SPEER and James CLINE:
Surname **CLINE**

+	**2080. JAMES PATRICK**	born 23 Dec 1955 Dexter, Iowa married Stacy Lynne EICKHORN 1 September 1979 Des Moines (she born 4 September 1957 Polk County, IA)
+	**2081. MICHAEL ALLEN**	born 8 August 1957 at Des Moines, IA married Rebecca Jane PARKS 11 November 1978 at Centerville, IA

1824. JAMES RAY-8 SMITH, son of Dale Edwin-7 SMITH (Raymond-6; Elizabeth-5 TANNER; Strever-4; William-3; Magdalena-2 MAC INTOSH; Alexander-1) and Mary WOODS, was born 10 April 1944 at Des Moines, Polk County, Iowa. He married first to Jean Ann PERCY on 29 March 1968 at Winterset, Madison County, Iowa. They divorced and he married second to Linda Faye APPLEGATE on 2 August 1986. (They had a child – name, dates and sex unknown)

Children of James-8 SMITH and JEAN PERCY:
Surname **SMITH**   (both children born Des Moines, IA)
>   2082. Angela Lea   born 8 Sept 1969   2083. Matthew Edward   born 23 Feb 1973

1825. JOYCE-8 SMITH, daughter of Willard Cecil-7 SMITH (Raymond-6; Elizabeth-5 TANNER; Strever-4; William-3; Magdalena-2 MAC INTOSH; Alexander-1) and Vina EMMONS, was born 27 June 1944 at Earlham, Madison County, Iowa.

Her first husband was Roger Eugene NELSON, who was born 3 Nov 1946; died 12 October 1971 at Tempe. AZ. He was the son of Robert Edward NELSON and Gladys Irene ALLIE.

Joyce married second to Larry G.EGEMO on 3 March 1973 at Earlham, Madison County, Iowa. He was the son of Truman Melborne EGEMO and Ruby ULSTAD, and was born 26 July 1946 at Story City, Story County, Iowa.

Children of Joyce-8 SMITH and Larry EGEMO:
Surname **EGEMO**   (both children born at Story City, IA)
>   2084. Beth Ann   born 15 Sept 1976; married Brad HANDLY
>   2085. Martin Dean   born 22 June 1979

1827. CONNIE LEE -8 SMITH, sister of above, was born 4 September 1948 at Earlham, Madison County, IA. She married Paul Russell BARTLETT on 3 November 1968' He was the son of John BARTLETT and Gladys Sophia FURNESS, and was born 14 June 1946.

The Eighth American Generation

Children of Connie Lee-[8] SMITH and Paul BARTLETT:
Surname **BARTLETT**

    2086. Joseph Paul   born 9 November 1975 Story City, IA
    2087. Timothy Lee   born 21 September 1984 Des Moines, IA

1828. RICHARD DEAN[8] SMITH, brother of above, was born 24 May 1951 at Earlham, Iowa. He married Sheila TAYLOR on 15 August 1970 at Earlham, Madison County, Iowa. She was the daughter of Henry M. TAYLOR and Edna ___, and was born ____. Richard Dean-[8] SMITH died 26 October 1972 at Winterset, Madison County, Iowa.

Child of Richard Dean-[8] SMITH and Sheila Taylor:
Surname **SMITH**

    2088. Richard Shawn   born 21 October 1972; died same day

1835. FLOYD EDWARD-[8] HAWVER, son of Ina/Iva L-[7] VOSBURGH (Egbert Tanner-[6] VOSBURGH; Rachel-[5] TANNER; Strever-[4]; William-[3;] Magdalena-[2] MAC INTOSH; Alexander-[1]) and Avery John HAWVER , was born 13 May 1923 at Copake, Columbia County, NY. He married Pauline June HEILMAN ca ____. She was the daughter of Casmer Paul HEILMAN and Dorothy Celesta HIXSON, and was born 4 June 1932 at Toppenish, Yakima County, WA; died 13 Dec 2000 at Yakima, WA. Floyd-[8] HAWVER died 2 June 1966 at Prosser, Benton County, Washington.

Children of Floyd-[8] HAWVER and Pauline HEILMAN:
Surname **HAWVER**

    2089. Linda   born ____; died 11 November 2009; married Donald GREENWOOD
          Children: Surname GREENWOOD: Charity[10], Donald[10] and Jennifer[10]
    2090. Elsie R.   born ____; married Bill MITCHELL
          Children: Surname MITCHELL: Barry[10], Billy[10] and Robert[10]
    2091. Wayne Leroy   born ____
                     married Kit M. Lou KEEZER
                     (she dau/o Harvey KEEZER and Hazel June HYSOM)
          Child: Surname HAWVER: Benjamin Matthew[10]
    2092. Vernon Dean   born 27 May 1954; died 25 Dec 1954

1841. EVELYN LOUISE-[8] SILVERNAIL, daughter of Willard-[7] SILVERNAIL (Esther-[6]; Rachel-[5] TANNER; Strever-[4]; William-[3]; Magdalena-[2] MAC INTOSH; Alexander-[1]) and Rose M. GARRISON, was born ca 1922 NY. She married Clifton CONKLIN ca ____. He was the son of Clarence CONKLIN and Gussie LASHER, and was born 28 May 1915; died 1 May 1987. Evelyn Louise-[8] SILVERNAIL died ca 1972.

Children of Evelyn-[8] SILVERNAIL and Clifton CONKLIN:
Surname **CONKLIN**

    2093. Larry Walter   born 26 February 1943; died 19 December 1996 NY
                      married Edwina Louise BAIRD
                      (she born 11 June 1962)
          Child: Clifton-[10] CONKLIN, Jr. born ____

MACKINTOSH   MAC INTOSH   MC INTOSH

1965. DEBORAH-⁹ ARCHER, daughter of Betty Louise-⁸ SMITH (Raymond Vanatta-⁷; Asa-⁶; Elizabeth-⁵ TANNER; Strever-⁴; William-³; Magdalena-² MAC INTOSH; Alexander-¹) and Kenneth ARCHER, was born4 April 1951 at Des Moines, Polk County, Iowa. She married David Loren BAYSINGER on __ ___ 1970. They divorced.

Children of Deborah-⁹ ARCHER and David BAYSINGER:
Surname **BAYSINGER**
    2094. Jennifer Lynn   born 7 May 1973 Des Moines, IA
    2095. Amy   born ____   2096. Kristi   born ____

1967. THERESA RAE-⁹ GORDON, half sister of above, and daughter of Betty Louise-⁸ SMITH and Raymond GORDEN, was born 5 August 1955 at Des Moi8nes, Iowa. She married Lynn WEINKAUF .__.

Children of Theresa-⁹ GORDON and Lynn WEINKAUF
Surname **WEINKAUF**
    2097. Cassandra   born ____
    2098. Wyatt   born ____   2099. Craig   born _____

1969. DENISE ROCHELLE-⁹ SMITH, daughter of Kieth Raymond-⁸ SMITH (Raymond Vanatta-⁷; Asa-⁶; Elizabeth-⁵ TANNER; Strever-⁴; William-³; Magdalena-² MAC INTOSH; Alexander-¹) and Sheryl Ann TIMONS, was born 1 February 1955 at Des Moines, Polk County, Iowa.. She married Robert BRUCE on 1 June 1974.

Children of Denise-⁹ SMITH and Robert BRUCE:
Surname **BRUCE**
    2100. Lynsey   born ____   2101. Ko_ten   born

1970. CONNIE JEAN-⁹ SMITH, sister of above, was born 14 October 1956 at Des Moines, Iowa. She married Gary LOFSTEDT on 14 October 1980 at Ames, Iowa.

Children of Connie-⁹ SMITH and Gary LOFSTEDT:
Surname **LOFSTEDT**
    2102. Alyce Anne   born 5 April 1981 Ames, IA
    2103. Kyle   born ____

1974. GREGORY V-⁹ SMITH, son of Gene Vanatta-⁸ SMITH (Raymond Vanatta-⁷; Asa-⁶; Elizabeth-⁵ TANNER; Strever-⁴; William-³; Magdalena-² MAC INTOSH; Alexander-¹) and Nancy KEENER, was born 14 July 1962 at Polk County, Iowa. He married Wendy J. ANTHONY on 26 December 1981. She was the daughter of Robert ANTHONY and Kay ____, and was born 11 August 1957 at Ponce City, Oklahoma.

Children of Gregory-⁹ SMITH and Wendy ANTHONY:
Surname **SMITH**
    2104. Justin J.   born 7 July 1984 Sacramento, CA
    2105.Trenton Robert   born ca 1989; died Oct 1989 UK; buried Pona City, OK

2029. TODD CARL-⁹ MYERS, son of Carla-⁸ SMITH (Carl-⁷; Chester-⁶; Elizabeth-⁵ TANNER; Strever-⁴; William-³; Magdalena-² MAC INTOSH; Alexander-¹) and Ronald HAWBAKER, was born 27 March 1964 at Des Moines, Iowa. He was adopted by his step-father,_____ MYERS, and his name was changed to MYERS. He married Un-KYONG of Korea on _____.

Child of Todd Carl-⁹ MYERS and Un-KYONG:
Surname **MYERS**
    2106. Trisha Ann   born 8 February 1985 Camp Hood, Texas

2034. DEBRA LYNN-⁹ DRAPER, daughter of Lucinda-⁸ NOLAND (Opal Mae-⁷ SMITH; Chester-⁶; Elizabeth-⁵ TANNER; Strever-⁴; William-³; Magdalena-² MAC INTOSH; Alexander-¹) and Richard DRAPER, was born 31 March 1960 at Des Moines, Polk County, Iowa. She married John Martin TEW on 27 May 1978.

Children of Debra-⁹ DRAPER and John TEW:
Surname **TEW**
    2107. Gregory Alan   born ca 1978 Des Moines
    2108. Heather Allison   born ca 1980 Des Moines

2035. RANDEL DUANE-⁹ DRAPER, brother of above, was born 17 February 1962 at Des Mones, Iowa. He married Melissa SPARKS ca ____.

Child of Randel-⁹ DRAPER and Melissa SPARKS
Surname **DRAPER**
    2109. Jarod Duane   born ca 1981

2057. PENNY SUSANNA-⁹ OVERTON, daughter of Barbara Jo-⁸ NOLAND (Ruth Ellen-⁷ SMITH; Chester-⁶; Elizabeth-⁵ TANNER; Strever-⁴; William-³; Magdalena-² MAC INTOSH; Alexander-¹) and Forest OVERTON, was born 27 March 1959 at Iowa City, Iowa. She married Roger CURRY on 4 August 1979 at Des Moines, Iowa.

Children of Penny-⁹ OVERTON and Roger CURRY:
Surname **CURRY**
    2110. Brian Anthony   born 25 April 1982 Des Moines, IA.
    2111. Adam Benjamin born 3 May 1983 Des Moines

2058. SCOTT WAYNE-⁹ OVERTON, brother of above, was born 18 March 1960/61 at Des Moines, Iowa. He married Laura VIRDEN on 2 October 1980 at Carlisle, Warren County, Iowa.

Children of Scott-⁹ OVERTON and Laura VIRDEN
Surname **OVERTON**
    2112. Tanner J. Scott   born 12 Aug 1981 Des Moines, IA
    2113. Tyler Nicholas T. born 9 July 1983 Des Moines

2059. ROBIN RUTH-⁹ OVERTON, sister of above, was born 30 October 1962 at Des Moins, Iowa. She married Leonard CURRY on 21 June 1979 at Des Moines.

Children of Robin-⁹ OVERTON and Leonard CURRY:
Surname **CURRY**
    2114. Kandi Jo   born 20 August 198_ Des Moines
    2115. Daniel   born 29 Dec 1983

The Ninth American Generation

2071. JEFFREY LLOYD-[9] STRONG, son of Linda-[8] Smith (Lloyd-[7]; Chester-[6]; Elizabeth-[5] TANNER; Strever-[4]; William-[3]; Magdalena-[2] MAC INTOSH; Alexander-[1]) and Stephen STRONG, was born January 1970 at Anamosa, Iowa. He married Rebecca SHOEMAKER on 30 January 1989.

Child of Jeffrey-[9] STRONG and Rebecca SHOEMAKER:
Surname **STRONG**
>   2116. Chadwick Jeffrey   born 11 July 1989 at Omaha, Nebraska

2080. JAMES PATRICK-[9] CLINE, son of Martha Louise-[8] SPEER (Mable Olive-[7] SMITH; Raymond-[6]; Elizabeth-[5] TANNER; Strever-[4]; William-[3]; Magdalena-[2] MAC INTOSH; Alexander-[1]) and James M. CLINE, was born 23 December 1955 at Dexter, Dallas County Iowa. He married Stacy Lynne EICKHORN on 1 September 1979 at Des Moines, Ia. She was born 4 September 1957 at Polk County, Iowa. They adopted a Korean child. She was born 2 Dec 1982 in Korea. They named her Hannah.

Child of James-[9] CLINE and Stacy EICKHORN:
Surname **CLINE**
>   2117. Adam Patrick   born 13 July 1981 Des Moines, Ia.

2081. MICHAEL ALLEN-[9] CLINE, brother oof above, was born 8 August 1957 at Des Moines, IA. He married Rebecca Jane PARKS ON 11 November 1978 at Centerville, Apanoose County, Iowa. She was the daughter of Dr. Gene PARKS, DO and Jane ___, and was born ca ____.

Children of Michael-[9] CLINE and Rebecca PARKS:
Surname **CLINE**
>   2118. Megan Elizabeth   born 13 May 1979 Des Moines, IA
>   2119. Shannon Louise   born 30 May 1982 Des Moines

Miscellaneous and Un-Attached American Records

Delaware County, NY

MC INTOSH, Harry W.	born 2 Dec 1912	parents Ira L. McINTOSH and Lillian NESBITT married "Betty" SCUTT
_____, William C.	born 9 Oct 1939	parents Harry McINTOSH and Betty SCUTT married Joyce LEWIS
_____, Howard J.	born 27 July 1900	parents Ira L. MCINTOSH and Lillian NESBITT married Hortense MILLS 11 Nov 1941
_____, Ira L.	born 29 Mar 1874	parents John McINTOSH and Sarah GOLDSMITH married Lillian NESBITT
NESBITT, Lillian	born 23 March 1877	parents William NESBITT and Maryetta LYON married Ira L. McINTOSH 11 Oct 1899
HEALY, Effie M.	born 28 Nov 1900	parents Thomas HEALY and Ellen SIMPSON married Howard J. McINTOSH 6 Dec 1920
SCUTT, J. Elizabeth	born 27 Mar 1917	parents Charles SCUTT and Mary SEIPLE married Harry W. McINTOSH
MC INTOSH, Rebecca Jean	born 20 May 1966	died 27 Aug 1966 parents Robert James McINTOSH and Beverly Jean JONES
_____, Richard Lonnie	born 27 June 1939	died 3 Oct 1976 parents Richard McINTOSH and Janice GAYLORD
_____, Walter H.	born 12 Apr 1880	died 18 Aug 1951 parents John McINTOSH and Sarah M. GOLDSMITH 1m. Margaret LAMBRECHT 2m. Sarah RUSSELL Sanford
_____, Sarah	born ca 1847	parents John McINTOSH and Nancy _____

Marriage Records Delaware County, NY

MC INTOSH, Alexander RD	married Ethelyn E. FRANCISCO 14 Oct 1924
_____, Anna B	married Albert SITZER 5 Mar 1918
_____, Elmer	married Addie WHITE 19 Apr 1912
_____, Henrietta	married Fred G. MAYHAM 8 Sept 1908
_____, Howard J.	married Effie HEALY 6 Dec 1920
_____, Reed L.	married Jennie SCHOVILLE 5 Nov 1919
_____, Walter H.	married Sarah M. SANFORD 3 Sep 1918

205

209

210

211

212

213

214

216

219

220

221

223

227

229

235

KIFF

KIFF
The First American Generation

1. GEORGE[1] **KIFF,** a sea captain and the immigrant, came to America at an early date. The exact time and place have not been documented. He and his wife, who remains unknown, were aboard a vessel which, according to folklore, was captured at sea and all of the crew, except one, were killed. It is not clear how they arrived on North American shores, but Newfoundland or Boston are two possibilities. The History of Delaware County, NY states that it was Newfoundland.

The spelling of this surname has been questioned by some researchers, thinking that it may have been KEEFE or O'KEEFE, since they were reportedly of Irish lineage. That question has no answer, to my knowledge. Many of the immigrants coming to America in the 1700's, and later, were illiterate. Their names were spelled phonetically by someone else. There were KIFF's in England, and since people moved between Ireland, England and Scotland, it is difficult to pinpoint their origin.

Genealogy is not an exact science, in fact it is not science at all. It is an organized search for data, so we accept the church records, the Census records, the folklore and the stories told by descendants over generations, and start from there.

It has been related that George KIFF's wife died " soon after their arrival ," leaving their two sons with her brother. The name of the brother and the place are still mysteries, but it has been told that Andrew-[2] KIFF did not share the views of his brother and uncle, and after being punished for fighting with his brother, he ran away from home at the age of 14 to join the Continental Army.

Children of George[1] KIFF and _____ :
Surname **KIFF**

+ **2. ANDREW**   born ca 1759(GS); died 6 June 1825 Bloomville, NY
                                   married Mary MABIE (Marie JUNTEAU) ca 1784 Westchester
                                                        County, New York

                                   (she was the adopted daughter of the MABIE family)
                                   (she born ca 1753 (gs) Arcadia (Nova Scotia, Canada)
                                   (she died 4 Apr 1835 (gs) Bloomville, Delaware, NY
                                   both buried Riverside Cemetery, Bloomville, NY

   3. George   born ca 17___   (no other info)

KIFF

2. ANDREW[-2] **KIFF**, son of George-[1] KIFF and _____, was born ca 1759 (gravestone inscription) at Newfoundland, or possibly Boston. Place is uncertain.

Andrew[-2] KIFF is reported to have joined the Continental Army at age 14. The Army at that time was camped out near Boston, MA. He participated in the Siege of Boston (April 1775- March 1776) and the Battle of Long Island (August 1776). He was a Private, and served in the Second Regiment of Westchester County, NY under Colonel Thomas THOMAS. He was drafted from Col. THOMAS' Regiment into Captain Richard SACKETT's Regiment of Col. LUDDINGTON's Regiment of the New York Militia.

After his service in the War, he married Mary MABIE, the adopted daughter of ____ MABIE and ____ca 1784. According to " tradition," Mary was born Marie JUNTEAU, of Acadian (Nova Scotia) parents . It is said that the MABIE family " found her on 10 September 1755 when the English drove the Acadians from their settlement". She was a small child at the time. According to her gravestone, she died 4 April 1835, in her 72nd year , which would make her born ca 1753. Andrew-[2] KIFF died 6 June 1827 at Bloomville, Delaware County, NY. He and his wife are buried at Riverside Cemetery there.

Children of Andrew-[2] KIFF and Mary MABIE:
Surname **KIFF**

+ **4. HANNAH** born 17 Aug 1785 Bloomville; died 20 June 1867 Bloomville
married Abraham COAN Dec 1819
(he s/o _____ COAN and _____) (War of 1812 veteran)
(he born 7 Jan 1792; died 11 Jan 1875 Bloomville, NY)

+ **5. JAMES** born 1787 Bloomville; died 6 July 1858 Bloomville, NY
married Elizabeth-[7] " Betty " MUNGER
(she dau/o Benjamin-[6] MUNGER +++++and _____) see below
(she born 22 Feb 1783 Dutchess Co.,; died 8 Mar 1880 Bloomville

+ **6. DR. WILLIAM** born 22 May 1790 Bloomville; died ca 1886 Tioga Point, PA
married Jane WALKER 9 July 1829 Tioga Point, Bradford, PA
(she dau/o _____ WALKER and _____)
(she born 10 Aug 1812 PA; died 1875)

+ **7. JEMIMA** born ca 1791 Bloomville; died 17 Jan 1868 Tioga County, PA
married William COVERT
(he s/o John COVERT and _____)
(he born 1791-2 Delaware Co., NY; died 1851 Tioga Co., PA

+ **8. PHOEBE** born 11 April 1792 Bloomville; died 11 June 1872 Armenia Twsp, PA
married John-[2] LYON 11 June 1812
(he s/o Moses-[1] LYON and Diadama BANKS)
(he born 29 Sep 1788; died 10 Dec 1853)

+ **9. LYMAN** born 13 May 1793 Bloomville; died 8 June 1876 Covington, Tioga, PA
married Mary L. CLEMONS
(she dau/o _____ CLEMONS and _____)
(she born ca 1791, NY; died _____

+ **10. ANDREW (Jr)** born ca 1796/97 NY; died 21 Mar 1888 PA
married Rebecca WARDELL ca 1830 Delaware Co., NY
(she dau/o Palmer WARDELL and Rebecca _____)
(she born 27 April 1807 NY; died 16 Nov 1898 Bradford Co., PA)

Children of Andrew[-2] KIFF and Mary MABIE, continued:
Surname **KIFF**

+	**11. PETER**	born ca 1800-01 Delaware Co., NY; died _____
		1 married Abigail Jemima-[2] LYON ca 1824 Bloomville, NY
		(she dau/o Moses[-1] LYON and Diadama BANKS)
		(she born 23 July 1803; died 24 May 1853 (gs)
		2 married Harriet H. _____
		(she born ca 1817 Westchester Co., NY; died ____)
+	**12. ELIZABETH**	born 20 July 1802; died 13 Dec 1879 Armenia Twsp., PA)
		married William[3] MAC INTOSH 23 March 1820
		(he born 22 July 1796; died 14 Jan 1879)
		(buried Old COVERT Cemetery, Armenia Mtn., PA
+	**13. ERASTUS**	born ca 1804 Bloomville, NY ; died 1887 MI
		married Sarah (Sally, Sary) PALMER
		(she dau/o _____ PALMER and _____)
		(she born ca 1803 Delaware Co., NY; died 1852 Tioga Co., PA)
		(buried Kniffin Cemetery, Armenia Mountain, PA)

History of Delaware County, NY (page 236)
Town of Kortright
W W MUNSELL (1797-1880)

"Andrew KIFF stood picket and helped to guard WASHINGTON'S camp during the Revolutionary War. His courage and fidelity were tested by the General himself, who, in disguise, attempted to pass the lines where young KIFF was stationed. Failing to scare or bribe the young man the general returned to the camp. In the morning KIFF was sent to appear at the General's headquarters. He was frightened. He feared something dreadful was about to befall him, but, to his surprise and satisfaction, the General received him kindly, and gave him a nice present of money for his conduct the previous night. He entered the Army when he was but 17 years old. He came from Newfoundland and was of Irish descent. "

Abstract of Wills of Delaware County, NY From Sept 1796 –December 1833
Original Wills at the Surrogate's Office, Delhi, NY
Will of Andrew KIFF of Kortright, Delaware County, New York , dated 25 May 1825

*In the name of God Amen, I **Andrew KIFF** of the Town of Kortright, County*
of Delaware, State of New York, being weak in body, but of sound mind
and memory, thanks to the Almighty God for the same, Do make public
and declare this my last will and testament in manner and
form following . First it is my will that all my just and lawful
Debts shall be paid. Also I give and divide unto my sons, Andrew KIFF
and Peter KIFF and to their heirs and assigns forever, the Grist Mill together
with one acre of land to accommodate such Mill. Also all the priviledges
of cutting ditches from the Delaware River to such Mill through
my land and supporting the same. Also I give and bequeath to my
Wife Mary one third of my Real Estate during her natural life in lieu of
Her dower. Said one third to be equally divided among my six sons
James KIFF Simon KIFF, Wm. KIFF Andrew KIFF Jr. Peter KIFF and
Erastus KIFF to be equally divided among them and to their heirs
And assigns forever – Also I give and bequeath unto Four Daughters
Hannah Coan, Phebe Lyon, Jemima Covert and Elizabeth McIntosh
Two hundred dollars such to be paid by my six sons, in eight equal
annual payments , Interest after it becomes due if not paid – the said

Andrew KIFF Will, continued:

> *two hundred dollars, to each of my daughters to be a lien on my Said Real*
> *Estate, as a mortgage until paid, also I give and bequeath unto my wife*
> *Mary, all of my household furniture of every description, to be deposed of*
> *At her Decease as she thinks proper, I also give unto said wife the old*
> *Brown Mare, I also give and bequeath unto my six sons all my personal*

> *Property to be equally divided among them after my debts are paid.*
> *Also it is my will that whereas I have paid for my son William certain*
> *Sums of Money since he was twenty one years of age, that the amount*
> *Of the same shall be deducted from his share of the land, and of my*
> *Said Son Wm. Should turn out land for his share or pay. It shall*
> *Be equally divided among my six sons – also it is my will that whereas*
> *I and Aaron Gregory have signed notes to the amount of three hundred*
> *And twenty five dollars with my son James for a certain piece or*
> *Parcel of land called the Munger flat and whereas I have paid the*
> *First installment myself and I am holden for the Remainder, it is my*
> *Will that the same amounts shall be deducted from his share of land*
> *Unless he will relinquish his title to said land in favor of my six*
> *Sons, also it is my will and I appoint and empower Nehemiah*
> *Gregory, Esq., John McDonald and John Lyon to make*
> *A division or partition of the third of my Real Estate bequeathed*
> *To my wife Mary, and also of the Real Estate divided to my six*
> *Sons, I also hereby appoint and empower Nehemiah Gregory, Esq.*
> *John McDonald, Sr. Esq,, and John Lyon Execcutors of this my*
> *last will and Testament, hereby revoking and canceling*
> *all other wills and Testaments by me heretofore made*
> In witness whereof I have here unto set my hand and seal
> ***This thirty first day of May in the year of our Lord one thousand***
> ***Eight hundred and twenty five.***
> *Signed Sealed Published and Declared by the testator to*
> *Be his last will and testament in presence of Us, who at the*

> *Request of the Testator subscribed our names as subscribing*
> *Witnesses in presence of the Testator.*
> *Signed Andrew Kiff (his mark X)*
> *Witnesses: Aaron Gregory, R.Wandby, and Jonathan Burdick*
> *State of New York, Delaware Countyy*
> This will was probated on 31 January 1827

Facts about Benjamin-[5] MUNGER (Samuel-[4]; Joseph-[3]; Samuel-[2]; Nicholas-[1])
Extracted from the MUNGER Book 1639-1914, compiled by J B MUNGER 1894-191
Pages 51-52

" At the breaking out of the Revolution he (Benjamin MUNGER) joined the American Army, leaving his wife and children in possession of his farm near Brooklyn, with an old man, a cripple, to stay with them. When New York fell into the hands of the British, the patriot families suffered severely at the hands of the Tories or "cow boys" as they were called. Some of these "cow boys" came to the (MUNGER) farm, took the horses, and with a halter hanged the old cripple almost to the death, to compel him to reveal where money was hid. This they did twice but failed each time. They then went into the house, and with the same halter, whipped grand-mother MUNGER, until she gave up all of her money and valuables. Grand-father came home shortly after this and because of the persecutions was compelled to sellout to the Tories for a trifling sum, and took his wife and children to Dutchess Co (NY).

In 1783, (he) bought land in Rumbout Precinct, Dutchess Co. NY, of John MUNGER of the same place. (probably John was his brother). He later in life removed to Fishkill, and from thence to Bloomville, Delaware Co., NY in the company of his son John M. in 1802."

"Other records secured are as follows: " Benjamin MUNGER enlisted 26 April 1758, age 28 from Long Island: trade Cord Wainder. Volunteer Capt. Nathan HYATT's Co; 5'8", grey eyes , complexion dark."

" Benjamin MUNGER, Dutchess County Militia, 2nd Regiment, Capt. BROWN. Land Bounty Rights " (NY in the Revolution, Page 240)

5. JAMES-³ KIFF, son of Andrew⁻² KIFF (George-¹) and Mary MABIE, was born ca 1787 at Bloomville, Delaware County, New York. He served in the War of 1812, and was occupied most of his life as a farmer.

He married Elizabeth⁻⁶ (Betsey) MUNGER on 5 September 1807. She was the daughter of Benjamin-⁵ MUNGER and ____, and was born ca 1783 Dutchess County, New York. According to MUNSELL'S book (published 1880) Elizabeth Kiff was still living , at the age of 97. She died 8 March 1880 Bloomville, NY.

James⁻³ KIFF died 6 July 1858 at Bloomville, NY. He and his wife are buried there at Riverside Cemetery.

Children of James-³ KIFF and Elizabeth-⁶ MUNGER:
Surname **KIFF**

+	**14. HANNAH**	born 25 August 1808; died 27 Sept 1881 PA
		married John S. BECKER 1 May 1830
		(he s/o John BECKER and Elizabeth MITCHELL)
		(he born 16 Nov 1806; died 5 April 1888 PA)
		buried Becker Corners Cemetery, Tioga Co., PA
	15. Andrew	born ca 1810-11 NY; died _____ (living 1880)
		poss. married Anna DUMOND
		(she sister of Jacob DUMOND (below))
		(she born 1809 NY; died after 1870, before 1880)
+	**16. HARRIET**	born 22 May 1818; died 31 March 1888 PA
		married Jacob Yaple DUMOND
		(he s/o Jacobus/James " Cobe" DUMOND and Jane Anne YAPLE)
		(he born Aug 1814 NY; died)
+	**17. JAMES DEWITT**	born ca 1826-27 Delaware Co., NY; died _____
		married Elizabeth Ann (Betsey) MC NAUGHT
		(she dau/o John MC NAUGHT and Isabella SCOTT)
		(she born 11 April 1835 NY; died ca 1925 NY)
	18. Melissa/ Millicent	born ca 1828 Delaware Co., NY; died _____

6. DR. WILLIAM-³ KIFF, brother of above, was born 22 May 1790 at Bloomville, Delaware County, NY. He married Jane B-³ WALKER on 9 July 1829 at Tioga Point, Bradford, PA, where he was a Physician. She was the daughter of Samuel⁻² WALKER (George⁻¹) and Sally SCHOONOVER, and was born 13 Aug 1813 Nichols, NY; died 15 July 1875 at Athens, PA.. Dr. William-³ KIFF died 10 Aug 1886 Athens, PA. They are both buried in the Tioga Point Cemetery, Athens, PA.   Reference: History of Waverly, NY Page 309

Children of Dr. William⁻³ KIFF and Jane WALKER:
Surname **KIFF**

	19. William Percival	born 16 Sept 1831 Athens, PA; died 13 Jan 1833; buried Tioga Point Cemetery
+	**20. HORACE**	born 20 Apr 1832 Athens, PA; died 1906 Athens, PA
	AGARD	married Louisa DRAKE 8 March 1854 Athens, PA
		(she dau/o John Lasell DRAKE and Betsey JOHNSON)
		(she born 3 Feb1834 VT.; died _____)
	21. Frances Jane	born 8 Feb 1834 Athens, PA; died ca 1917
		married Delos O. HANCOCK 15 Oct 1857 Athens, PA (a Lawyer)
		(he s/o Nathan HANCOCK and Anna _____)
		(he born 1 Oct 1821; died 19 Apr 1883 Owego, NY))

KIFF
The Third American Generation

Children of Dr. William-³ KIFF and Jane WALKER, continued:
Surname **KIFF**

22. Isabel   born 30 Nov 1835 Athens, PA; died Aug 1854; buried Tioga Point Cemetery
Reference: Old Tioga Point (PA) and Athens , Early Physicians Page 57-71; History of Waverly, NY, Page 305-09

Dr. William³ KIFF
" April 25, 1825, a stranger on horseback drew up at the door of SATTERLEE's
Tavern. Being questioned, he gave his name as Dr. William KIFF
on his way to Virginia to practice his profession. Dr. HOUSTON had just
left town, and Dr. HOPKINS was disliked by some few people. Here was
a good opening for a young physician, and Mr. SATTERLEE urged the young
man to stay, and so he did. Dr. KIFF was of Irish descent; his parents
came to America previous to the Revolution, in which his father took
part. They settled in this vicinity, but were driven out by the Indians,
and finally made a new home in Bloomville, Delaware County, N.Y.,
where William was **born May 22, 1790**. He served through the War of
1812 under Captain PENFIELD. When mustered out at New York City he
returned to his old home and studied medicine under Dr. CLARK. At
Tioga Point he very soon acquired an extensive practice and wore himself
out in hard country practice, riding hither and thither on his little
horse Lightfoot, who could pick her way even across a ford in the night.
He was an active and upright Mason, at his death one of the oldest members
of the fraternity in the state, being 96 years old.   July 9, 1829,
he married Jane WALKER and had four children. William d. young;
Horace, a well-known citizen, Frances (Mrs. Hancock), and Isabel,
who died 1854. His first house near the Old Exchange was burned, the
later one is still occupied by his daughter. "

7. **JEMIMA-³ KIFF,** sister of above, was born ca 1791 at Bloomville, Delaware County, NY. She married William
COVERT ca ____. He was the son of _____ COVERT and _____, and was born ca 1791-92, NY; died
ca 1851 Tioga County, PA He went from Delaware County to Armenia, PA about 1837. Jemima-³ KIFF died
17 January 1868 at Armenia, PA and is buried at the Old Covert Cemetery, McIntosh Hollow, PA.

Children of Jemima-³ KIFF and William COVERT:
Surname **COVERT**

+   **23. HARRY**   born September 1816 NY; died _____
                              married Oritha FIELD ca ____
                              (she dau/o Abiezer FIELD and Hannah WILBUR)
                              (she born 4 June 1814; died 18 July 1882) (68y-1m-14 da)gs
+   **24. DIANA/ DIANTHA**   born ca 1820 NY; died ca 1889
                              married Simon CONGDON before 1840
                              (he s/o Christopher Columbus CONGDON and Eunice May SQUIRES)
                              (he born ca 1807 NY; died 1903 Bradford, PA)
    25. Amanda Ann   born 13 March 1824 NY; died 8 Sept 1856 PA (32y-5m-26 da) gs
+   **26 ERASTUS R.**   born ca 1827-28 NY; died 17 June 1872 PA)
                              married Delight Delia CASE ca 1851
                              (she dau/o Philander CASE and Elizabeth GRANTIER)
                              (she born 6 June 1832 PA; died 15 Mar 1900)
                              (she married 2nd to George WING)
    27. Elizabeth/Eliza   born ca 1828-29 NY; died April 1865 PA; single   EOL
+   **28. ESTHER**   born ca 1832-34 NY; died 23 June 1885 PA)
                              married J. William KINCH
                              (he s/o John KINCH and ____)
                              (he born 7 Dec 1838; died 21 Nov 1894)
References: 1850 Census Armenia, PA; Gravestone Records Armenia Mountain, PA;
    29. Malvina   born ca 1835-36 NY; died 1 April 1899; single   EOL
Note: Resided w her sister Diana / Diantha Congdon in 1870

The Third American Generation

8. PHEBE-³ KIFF, sister of above, was born 1 April 1792 at Bloomville, Delaware, New York. She married John⁻² LYON on 11 June 1812. He was the son of Moses⁻¹ LYON and Diadama BANKS. (Moses⁻¹ was a Revolutionary War veteran) John⁻² LYON was born 29 September 1788 at Delaware County, NY; died 10 December 1853 at Franklin, Delaware, NY. They moved to Tioga County, PA. According to the 1850 Federal Census he was a farmer residing at Armenia Township, but returned to New York. Phebe⁻³ KIFF died 11 June 1872.

Children of Phebe ³ KIFF and John⁻² LYON:
Surname **LYON**

+	**30. WILLIAM R.**	born 7 January 1813 NY; died 1883 Ward, Tioga, PA
		married Rachel SCOUTEN/SCOUTON 8 Nov 1836
		(she listed on 1880 Census as Insane (melancholia)
		(she born ca 1818-20 Morrisanna, NY; died 1895 Ward, Tioga, PA)
+	**31. JAMES**	born 13 April 1815 NY; died 17 June 1885
		married Calista FIELD 10 Sept 1837
		(she dau/o Abiezer FIELD and Hannah WILBUR)
		(she born 30 April 1815; died 3 Dec 1901 Bradford Co., PA)
	32. Diadama	born 5 Feb 1817 Bloomville, NY; died _____)
		married Levi W. KIFF 5 Sep 1850
		(he s/o _____ KIFF and _____)
		(he born ca 1823; died 15 Oct 1893) res. Franklinville, Delaware, NY

Child: Melville O-⁵ KIFF born ca 1857 NY

	33. Andrew	born 30 November 1818 NY; died _____
		married Angelina HOYT Sept 1844
		(she dau/o _____ HOYT and _____)
+	**34. MARY**	born 20 Oct 1820 NY; died _____ IL
		married Rev. Festus Portius CLEVELAND 3 August 1840 Armenia, Brad., PA
		(he s/o Josiah Francis CLEVELAND and Lucy BRYAN)
		(he born 12 July 1817 Masonville,, Delaware, NY; died _____ IL)
+	**35. SARAH ELIZABETH**	born 25 Oct 1822 NY; died 17 Feb 1907 Ward, Tioga, PA)
		married Daniel HAGAR 24 Dec 1841 PA.
		(he s/o Jonas HAGAR (born VT) and _____)
		(he born 20 Sept 1820 Pike, Bradford, PA; died 22 June 1882 Ward, PA)
+	**36. NANCY THERESA**	born 17 March 1825 Bloomville, NY; died _____
		married Dr. John E. CLEVELAND 20 Nov 1850
		(he s/o Josiah CLEVELAND and Lucy BRYAN)
		(he born 4 Aug 1829; died _____)
	37. John Marcus	born 20 Sept 1827 NY; died 7 Aug 1830 Homer, Cortland, NY EOL
+	**38. HARRIET J.**	born 19 July 1829 NY; died _____
		married Seymour E. SMITH 1 Jan 1846 (he born ca 1823 NY)
	39. Electa A.	born 24 Dec 1831-2 Homer, NY; died _____
		married Marcus H. MALLORY 18 June 1857 Delaware Co., NY
		(he s/o Adna MALLORY and Angeline HANFORD)
		(he born ca 1833-34 NY; died _____)

Children: James-⁵ born ca 1858, and Flora H-⁵ MALLORY born ca 1864-65, died 1925

+	**40. MASON LEROY**	born 20 Feb 1834 Troy, PA; died 20 June 1908 Los Angeles, CA
		married Hannah Lawrence SCHIEFFELIN/ SHEFLIN 29 Jun 1857 Tioga, PA
		(she born 6 March 1840 Charleston, Tioga, PA; died 20 Feb 1935 Los Angeles, CA)

9. LYMAN-³ WILLIAM KIFF, brother of above, was born ca 1788, possibly at Westchester County, NY. He married Mary L. CLEMONS ca ____. She was the daughter of _____ CLEMONS and _____, and was born ca 1791, NY; died _____. Lyman-³ KIFF died 6 June 1876 at Covington Township, Tioga County, PA. The 1850 Federal Census had them residing at Armenia Township, Bradford, PA.

Children of Lyman[-3] KIFF and Mary CLEMONS:
Surname **KIFF**

+	**41. HARRIET**	born ca 1807-08 NY; died 12 April 1882 Blossburg, Tioga, PA
		married Jerome Henry PUTNAM 21 June 1830 Kortright, Delaware, NY
		(he s/o Thomas PUTNAM and Rosamund ROUNSEVELL)
		(he born ca 1807-08 Windsor, VT; died 1 Dec 1870 Wellsboro, PA
+	**42. SAMUEL**	born ca 1813, NY; died ____
	CLEMONS	married Susan H. KENYON 27 Feb 1833 Kortright, Delaware, NY
		(she dau/o James KENYON and Susannah PALMER)
	43. Lyman	born ca 1818 NY; died ___; residing with sister Mary (below) in 1870
+	**44. MARY L.**	born ca 1825 NY; died ___; single on the 1850 Census
		married Colburn CLEMONS ca _____

Note: A Joanna KIFF, born ca 1842, NY resided with this family in 1850.

10. ANDREW[-3] **KIFF**, brother of above, was born ca 1796-97 at Kortright, Delaware County, New York.
He married Rebecca WARDELL ca 1830. She was the daughter of Palmer WARDELL and Rebecca ____, and was
born 27 April 1807 NY; died 16 Nov 1898 Bradford County, PA. Andrew and his wife removed from New York
State sometime after 1850 (resided at Kortright, NY 1850 Census) They lived at the CASE Settlement, which was
near Troy, Bradford, PA. Andrew[-3] died 21 March 1888 Bradford County, PA.

Children of Andrew-[3] KIFF and Rebecca WARDELL:
Surname **KIFF**

+	**45. RICHARD D.**	born 2 Nov 1830 Delaware Co., NY; died ____, buried Woodland Cemetery
	WADLY/WARDELL	married Calista RITCHMEYER 30 June 1858 Gilboa, NY
		(she dau/o Martinus RITCHMEYER and Elizabeth RUSS)
		(she born 3 Nov 1826 Gilboa, Schoharie, NY; died _____
	46. Electa	born ca 1831 Delaware Co., NY; died 23 Nov 1894 Springfield, PA
		married Edwin BLAKESLEE 17 Sept 1871; as his second wife
		(he s/o Gervase BLAKESLEE and Polly GUERNSEY)
		(he born ca 1820 Harpersonville, NY; died 6 Nov 1884)
		(he 1 married Cythera HARKNESS; she died 1869
	47. Juliette	born 1 Sept 1833 Delaware Co., NY; died 3 Jan 1907 Sylvania, Bradford, PA
		married Seth PECK 7 Nov 1855
		(he s/o Peleg PECK and Lydia C. HUNTER)
		(he born 17 Apr 1829 PA; died 3 March 1869 Sylvania, Bradford, PA)

Child: Hibbard Floyd-[5] PECK born 13 Mar 1860 PA.; died 1893; a tinsmith

+	**48. HELEN**	born 3 Jan 1836 NY; died 13 March 1870 Topeka, KS)
	AUGUSTA	married Adrial Hebard CASE 1 Nov 1854 Sylvania Boro, PA
		(he s/o Elihu CASE and Charlotte PALMER)
		(he born 19 Dec 1828; died 7 Dec 1908 Topeka, KS)
+	**49. ISABELLA**	born ca 1839-40; died _____; married Edward L. STRAIT
		(he s/o Isaac Burton STRAIT and Maria BENSON)
		(he born Feb 1838 PA; died _____)
+	**50. WILLIAM M.**	born 8 Sept 1842 Delaware Co., NY; died 8 Dec 1889 Bradford Co., PA
		married Harriet / Hattie M. CASE
		(she dau/o Timothy CASE and Delia COWELL)
		(she born ca 1848-51 PA; died ____)
	51. Charles Stanley	born ca 1845 Delaware Co., NY; died ___; married Della Inez CASE ca 1873
		(she dau/o Nathan P. CASE and Sarah Maria CODDINGTON)
		(she born 14 Aug 1847 Bradford Co., PA; died 1899)

Children: Maude-[5] born ____; and Sadie-[5] KIFF born ____

	52. DeFrancey	born 17 Feb 1849 Delaware Co. NY; died 8 Jan 1862; buried Sylvania Cemetery

The Third American Generation

11. PETER[3] KIFF, brother of above, was born ca 1800-01 at Kortright, Delaware County, New York. He married first to Abigail Jemima-[2] LYON on ____. She was the daughter of Moses-[1] LYON and Diadama BANKS, and was born 23 July 1803; died 24 May 1853.

His second wife was Harriet H. _____. They married ca 185_. She was born ca 1817 at Westchester County, NY. According to the 1850 Federal Census, and the 1855 State Census for Kortright, he was a farmer, with real estate valued at $4000. Peter-[3] KIFF died ____.

Children of Peter-[3] KIFF and Abigail Jemima LYON.
Surname **KIFF**

53. S. Adelia	born ca 1825 NY; died _____	
	married Henry States BUTTS 4 Dec 1850 Bloomville, NY	
	(he s/o _____ BUTTS and _____)	
	(he born ca 1822; died _____)	
	Children: Ella-[5] born ca 1853; Virgilia-[5] born ca 1855; and Monta B-[5] BUTTS born ca 1858 Barton, Tioga, PA	

	54. Electa	born 10 June 1826; died 31 May 1827 (11m,21da)	
+	**55. HIRAM M.**	born ca 1828-29 Bloomville, NY; died 13 Feb 1885 NY	
		married Clarissa PECK 9 Jan 1856 Kortright, NY	
		(she dau/o_____ PECK and _____)	
		(she born ca 1830; died 27 Sep 1867 Roxbury, Delaware, NY)	
	56. Madby	born ca 1831 Delaware Co., NY; died _____	
		(1850 – was a teamster)	
	57 Susan Jane	born 3 Feb 1832; died 12 Jan 1843 (gs) buried Bloomville, NY	EOL
	58. Benjamin B.	born ca 1834-35 Delaware Co., NY; died _____	
		married Elizabeth _____ after 1860	
		(music dealer, farmer)	
	59. M. Percival	born ca 1837 Delaware Co., NY; died _____	EOL
		(1860 single, music dealer)	
+	**60. FRANCES ESTELLA**	born 10 Feb 1839 Kortright; died 28 April 1896 Hudson , Lenawee, Michigan	
		married Daniel Lee FRISBEE 10 Feb 1864 Delhi, NY	
		(he s/o Erastus FRISBEE and Elizabeth LEE)	
		(he born 19 Apr 1840 Delhi; died 28 Apr 1896)	
	61. Mary D.	born ca 1841 Delaware Co., NY	
		(1860 resided with her brother Hiram, above)	
	62. Charles E.	born 3 June 1843; died 12 Aug 1845 (2y,2m,9da) Bloomville, NY	EOL

Child of Peter-[3] KIFF and Harriet _____:
Surname **KIFF**

63. Harriet A.	born ca 1857, NY; died _____

12. ELIZABETH[3] KIFF, sister of above, was born 20 July 1802 at Kortright, Delaware, NY. She married William-[3] MAC INTOSH (Simon-[2], Alexander-[1]) on 22 March 1820 in Delaware County, New York. They had 18 children, some of whom died young. The further account of this family and future generations is in the MACKINTOSH, MAC INTOSH, MC INTOSH section of this book

13. ERASTUS[3] KIFF, brother of above, was born ca 1803-04 at Kortright, Delaware County, NY. He married Sarah (Sally, Sary) PALMER ca ____. She was the daughter of _____ PALMER and _____, and was born ca 1803 NY; died _____PA. They resided Armenia Mountain, Tioga, PA and are buried there at the KNIFFEN Cemetery. Erastus-[3] KIFF died ____.

Children of Erastus-[3] KIFF and Sarah PALMER:
Surname **KIFF**

+   **64. JOHN MABIE**   born 17 Oct 1823 Kortright, NY; died 1872 PA; buried Becker Corners
married Susan BASCOM(B) 25 Oct 1854
(she dau/o Joseph BASCOM(B) and Amaretta GRACE
(she born ca 1834 PA; died 11 Oct 1915) buried Troy, PA

+   **65. ANN ELIZA**   born ca 1824-25 NY; died _____
married Ambrose MURRAY

+   **66. HARRIET**   born ca 1827-28; died _____
married Israel MOORE
(he s/o ____ MOORE and _____)
(he born ___ Muncy, PA; died _____)

+   **67. LUCY**   born August 1830 NY; died 14 Feb 1914
married Daniel COSPER
(he s/o Peter COSPER and _____)
(he born 3 Oct 1828; died 13 March 1912)

+   **68. CHARLES E.**   born May 1832 NY; died 1910, buried Alba, PA Cemetery)
1 married Fanny C-[4] MAC INTOSH 5 Nov 1854
(she dau/o Matthias-[3] MAC INTOSH and Sally LOCKWOOD)
(see MAC INTOSH section for descendants)
2 married Polly Rowena BOYCE Murray/ McIlwain
(she born 3 Aug 1850; died 4 Jan 1938)

   69. Horace   born 17 Feb 1837 Bloomville, NY; died _____
1 married Olive BLAKEMAN
(she dau/o Asahel BLAKEMAN and Mary Ann _____)
(she born ca 1846 PA; died _____)
2 married Dell RITTENHOUSE
(she dau/o James RITTENHOUSE and Cassandra CONGDON)

+   **70. HELEN M.**   born Nov 1845 PA; died _____
married Warren W. WHITMAN
(he s/o Dr. Newberry WHITMAN and Josephine GRACE)
(he born Feb 1843 PA; died 1925)

14. HANNAH[-4] **KIFF,** daughter of James[-3] KIFF (Andrew-[2;] George-[1]) and Elizabeth/ Betsey MUNGER, was born 25 August 1808 at Kortright, Delaware County, New York. She married John S. BECKER on 1 May 180 at Andes, Delaware County, NY. He was the son of John BECKER and Elizabeth MITCHELL, of Ulster County, NY, and was born 16 Nov 1806 in Delaware County, NY ; died 5 April 1888. According to the 1880 Census for Armenia, PA, they were residing with their son Dewitt BECKER. Hannah[-4] KIFF died 22 Sept 1881.

Children of Hannah[-4] KIFF and John S. BECKER:
Surname **BECKER**

+	**71. ELIZABETH A.**	born ca 1831-32; died 21 Sept 1917 Bradford, PA
		married Alexander Hamilton THOMAS 1850
		(he s/o Alvin W. THOMAS and Amy HARDING)
		(he born 9 Sept 1829; died 15 Mar 1909)
	72. WILLIAM	born 24 Jan 1833; died Aug 1917
	HENRY	married Margaret MILLER Jan 1866
		(she dau/o Philip MILLER and _____)
		(she born 13 May 1848; died 12 Dec 1924)
+	**73. JAMES DEWITT**	born ca 1835 NY; died 1910 PA, buried Alba Cemetery
		married Sarah E. BOVIER 24 Aug 1865
		(she dau/o Solomon N. BOVIER and Elmira Amanda EDSALL)
		(she born 22 Oct 1841 Granville, PA; died 1915)

16. HARRIET[-4] **KIFF,** sister of above, was born 22 May 1818 at Delaware County, New York. She married Jacob Yaple DUMOND ca ____. He was the son of Jacobus/James DUMOND and Jane Anne YAPLE, and was born __ August 1814 NY; died _____ (living 1900) The DUMONDS settled in Armenia, PA ca 1839. Harriet[-4] KIFF died 31 March 1888. Jacob DUMOND married second, ca 1890, to Millie KIFF.

Children of Harriet[-4] KIFF and Jacob DUMOND:
Surname **DUMOND**

	74. James Kiff	born 28 Sept 1841; died 16 June 1864 (22y,9m,20 da) EOL
		buried Beckers Corners Cemetery, Armenia Mountain, PA
	75. Jane	born 4 March 1843 Armenia, Tioga, PA; died 15 Oct 1872 (29y 7m 11da)
		married Samuel KENDRICK/KENDREICK
+	**76. WILLIAM**	born 2 Nov 1845-46 PA; died 28 Feb 1913
	EUGENE	1 married Leila/Lelia PRATT 20 Oct 1880 Mainesburg, PA
		(she dau/o Asa PRATT and Mary Ann HARDING)
		(she born 31 Mar 1850; died 2 Apr 1896)
		2 married Elizabeth C. DOUGLAS ca 1898
		(she born ca 1855; died 28 Mar 1936 Canton, PA)
	77. Imogene	born ca 1847; died _____; married William BARBER
	78. John Harry/Henry	born 16 Jan 1848; died 26 June 1865 (en route home from the Civil War)
		buried Beckers Corners Cemetery
	79. Hamilton T	born 15 Feb 1850 ; died _____; 1880-1910 res. Charleston, Otsego, NY
		1920 resided NH, widowed
	80. Clarence D. (twin)	born 3 Apr 1856; died 8 Oct 1856; buried Beckers Corners Cemetery EOL
	81. Florence Edna (twin)	born 3 Apr 1856; died ca 1937 Troy, Bradford, PA
		married Albert MORGAN ca 1880; he was a lawyer
		(he born Sept 1856; died _____

Child: Harry A-[6] MORGAN born Jan 1884, married Ethel Mae HOLLAND (born ca 1889 NJ)(dau Dorothy Olive born ca 1913)

KIFF
The Fourth American Generation

17. JAMES <u>DEWITT</u>-4 KIFF, brother of above, was born ca 1826-27 at _____, Delaware County, New York. He married Elizabeth Ann MC NAUGHT ca 18 __. She was the daughter of John MC NAUGHT and Isabella SCOTT, and was born 11 April 1835 at Hobart, Delaware County, NY; died 1925 at Oneonta, Otsego, New York. According to the 1880 Federal Census Dewitt KIFF was a cooper, residing at that time in Kortright, Delaware County, NY.

Children of James Dewitt-4 KIFF and Elizabeth MC NAUGHT:
Surname **KIFF**

	82. Ella T.	born ca 1860 Delaware Co., NY; died _____
+	**83. JAMES LEONARD**	born Nov 1861-65 Delaware Co., NY; died _____
		married Susan L. CRAIG ca 1895 (she dau/o Robert CRAIG and Louise _)
		(she born ca 1870-72; died before 1920)

20. HORACE AGARD-4 KIFF, son of Dr. William-3 KIFF (Andrew-2; George-1) and Jane WALKER, was born 30 April 1832 at Tioga Point, PA. He married Louisa DRAKE 9 March 1854. She was the daughter of John Lasell DRAKE and Betsey JOHNSON, and was born 3 Feb 1834 Bennington, VT; died ___ Athens, PA. Horace Agard-4 KIFF died ca 1906 at Athens, PA.

Children of Horace Agard-4 KIFF and Louisa DRAKE:
Surname **KIFF**

84. Frances <u>Isabell</u>	born 7 Oct 1861 Athens, Tioga, PA; bapt 26 Nov 1865 Trinity Episcopal Church
(Frannie Bell)	Athens, PA ; died 29 June 1888 (possibly due to childbirth)
	married George H. NORTHRUP 24 Sept 1884 Athens, PA
	(he born 24 Apr 1856; died ca 1908)
	Children: Leah-6 born 13 Nov 1886, and Anna-6 NORTHRUP born 9 Mar 1888, died 12 Aug 1888
85. Sarah	born 8 May 1871 Tioga Point; died 2 July 1871 Tioga Point EOL

23. HARRY-4 COVERT, son of Jemima-3 KIFF (Andrew-2; George-1) and William COVERT, was born Sept 1816 at _____, NY. He married Oritha-2 FIELD _____. She was the daughter of Abiezer-1 FIELD and Hannah WILBUR, and was born 4 June 1814; died 18 July 1881 (68y 1m 14da) . She was a sister of Calista FIELD who married John LYON. Harry-4 COVERT died _____.

Children of Harry-4 COVERT and Oritha-2 FIELD:
Surname **COVERT**

+	**86. HENRY D.**	born 11 April 1839 Armenia, PA; died _____
		married Candace BURMAN 22 April 1866 Armenia, Bradford, PA
		(she dau/o Rev. Joel BURMAN and Betsey _____)
		(she born ca 1848 Sullivan, Tioga, PA; died ca 1919)
		1895 resided at Covert, PA (Civil War veteran)
+	**87 GEORGE L.**	born 22 July 1842 Ward Twsp. PA; died _____
		married Mary J. MERRIAM 8 Jan 1883 Corning, NY
		(she dau/o Albert MERRIAM and Harriet SMILEY)
		(she born 8 July 1853 Ashland, NY; died _____)
+	**88. EDWIN G.**	born ca 1850 PA; died _____; married Josephine BERMAN
		(she born ca 1853; died _____)
	89. Frances L.	born 20 Jan 1859 Bradford Co., PA; died 3 May 1939 Waynesburg, OH
		married Arthur Burton YOUMANS 27 Oct 1877
		(he s/o Nathan YOUMANS and Hannah Margaret VAN VLECK)
		(he born 3 Sept 1853 NY; died 5 Jan 1933 Waynesburg, OH)

24. DIANA/DIANTHA-4 COVERT, sister of above, was born ca 1820 NY. She married Simon CONGDON before 1840. He was the son of Christopher Columbus CONGDON and Eunice Mary SQUIRES, and was born ca

1807 NY; died 1903 Bradford County, PA. Diana/Diantha-[4] COVERT died ca 1889. 1850 resided Elba, Genesee, NY; 1870 resided Troy, Bradford, PA.

Children of Diana/Diantha-[4] COVERT and Simon CONGDON:
Surname **CONGDON**

90. Sylvia	born ca 1840 NY; died 1918	
91. Helen/Ellen	born ca 1842 PA; died 1867	EOL
+ **92. TYLER**	born ca 1846 PA; died ____; Civil War veteran	
	married Elizabeth (Libbie) RATHBUN	
	(she dau/o _____ RATHBUN and _____)	
	(she born ____; died _____)	
+ **93. VICTORIA**	born Sept 1848 NY; died 1880	
	married George RATHBUN ca 1872	
	(he s/o Allen RATHBUN and Ruth Eliza GATES)	
	(he born July 1842 Chenango County, NY; died _____)	
+ **94. SCHUYLER CHARLES**	born 9 Aug 1850 NY; died 1929	
	married Mary Elizabeth KINCH	
	(she born Feb 1850-51 NY; died 1923 Oneonta, NY)	
	(she dau/o Thomas KINCH and Sarah Jane CEASE)	
95. Peter	born ca 1852; died 1860	EOL
96. Porter	born ca 1854; died 1930	
	married Sarah C. _____ 1879 Barrington, Yates, NY	
	(she born April 1854 NY; died _____)	
	Child: Ella M-[6] CONGDON born ca 1902; died July 1891 MA	
+ **97. BURDETTE**	born ca 1855 Troy, PA; died ____ Elmira, NY (living 1920)	
	married Kate/ Catherine O'SHEA ca 1878	
	(she born ca 1862 NY; died _____(living 1920)	
+ **98. EDWIN EDGAR**	born April 1857 PA; died 1930; married Ella RUGGLES ca 1879	
	(she dau/o _____ RUGGLES and Malissa _____)	
	(she born July 1857; died _____)	
99. Ida	born ca 1859 PA; died 1880	EOL
100. Ellsworth	born ca 1862 PA; died ____	
	resided with his sister Victoria in 1880	
101. Abraham <u>Lincoln</u>	born ca 1864 PA; died ____	
	1 married Ida _____ ca 1886	
	2 married Anne MADIGAN ca 1890	
	Children: Paul-[6] born ca 1891 , and Karl-[6] CONGDON born ca 1892	

26. ERASTUS [4] **COVERT**, brother of above, was born ca 1827-28 at _____ Delaware County, New York. He married Delight Delia CASE ca 1851. She was the daughter of _____ CASE and ____, and was born ca 1833, PA.; died _____. Erastus-[4] COVERT died 17 June 1872 (age 44) at Ward Township., PA and is buried there at the MC INTOSH / COVERT Cemetery.

Children of Erastus-[4] COVERT and Delight CASE:
Surname **COVERT**

102. Ellen	born ca 1856-57 PA; died _____	
+ **103. MILTON**	born ca 1858 PA; died _____ IL.	
	married Sarah Elizabeth FISH ca 1875	
	(she born ca 1856-57 PA; died _____ IL)	
104 Clara	born ca 1860 PA; died _____	
105. William	born ca 1863 PA; died _____	
106. Sarah	born ca 1866 PA; died _____	107. Mary born ca 1868 PA; died _____

28. ESTHER[-4] COVERT, sister of above , was born ca 1832-34 at _____, Delaware County, New York. She married J. William KINCH ca ____. He was the son of John KINCH and _____, and was born7 Dec 1838; died 21 Nov 1894 (55y11m6da). Esther[-4] COVERT died 23 June 1885. She and her husband are buried at the Old Covert Cemetery, McIntosh Hollow, PA.

Children of Esther-[4] COVERT and William KINCH:
Surname **KINCH**

+	**108. IDA S.**		born Nov 1860; died 1932 , buried Alba Cemetery, PA	
			married Freeman W. BAILEY ca 1885	
			(he s/o Warren BAILEY and Rachael AVERY)	
			(he born Mar 1861 Alba, PA; died 2 Sept 1938 Canton, Bradford, PA)	
	109. John William		born ca 1864; died 1933 no issue	EOL
			married Lilly/Lillie M[-4] BECKER (# 232)	
			(she dau/o James Dewitt-[3] BECKER and Sarah BOVIER)	
			(she born 30 Aug 1866; died 10 Mar 1945)	
	110. Susie E.		born 28 Sep 1866 PA; died 6 May 1872 (5y10m8da)	EOL
			buried Old Covert Cemetery, McIntosh Hollow, PA	
	111. daughter	(twin)	born 15 Oct 1868; died 25 Oct 1870 (2y10da)	EOL
	112. George	(twin)	born 15 Oct 1868; died May 1931 Troy, Bradford, PA	
			1 married Grace S. FIELD 1887 (she born Feb 1867; died ____)	

Children: Frederick-[6] born Aug 1888, and Harry-[6] KINCH born Jan 1893
2 married Henrietta VAN DYKE Grace

30. WILLIAM R[-4] LYON, son of Phebe-[3] KIFF (Andrew-[2]; George-[1]) and John-[2] LYON (Moses-[1]), was born 7 January/June 1813 at Bloomville, Delaware County, NY. He married Rachel SCOUTEN on 8 Nov 1836 at ____. She was the daughter of _____ SCOUTEN and ____, and was born ca 1820 Morrisanna, NY; died _____. William-[4] LYON was still living in 1891.

Children of William R-[4]. LYON and Rachel SCOUTEN:
Surname **LYON**

+	**113. MELISSA**	born ca 1838 Union City, Tioga, PA; died 1904
	ADELAIDE	married David BEARDSLEY ca 1856 (he born ca 1825)
+	**114. STANLEY**	born ca 1840 PA; died 1910 PA.; married Laura Ann MORGAN ca ____
	WILLIAM	(she dau/o Dewitt/Dwight MORGAN and Clarinda WOOD
		(she born 29 July 1854 Armenia, PA; died 20 Aug 1942)
		(she married 2nd to Colson STONE
+	**115. FESTUS**	born ca 1842 PA ; died 19 Apr 1902
	WATSON	married Virginia " Jennie" ____ ca 186_
	116. Seth	born ca 1845 PA ; died
	117. Ruloff E.	born ca 1846 PA; died 3 Dec 1910

Note: Served in the Civil War: enlisted in the 50th Engineers on13 Feb 1864 at Candor, NY, mustered out 13 June 1865 at Fort Barry, VA. He is buried at Jefferson Barracks National Cemetery, MO.

31. JAMES[-4] LYON, brother of above, was born 13 April 1815 at Bloomville, Delaware County, NY. He married Calista-[2] FIELD on 10 September 1837 PA. . She was the daughter of Abiezer-[1] FIELD and Hannah WILBUR, and was born 3/30 April 1815; died 31 December 1901. James-[4] LYON died 17 June 1885. They are buried at the Old Covert Cemetery, McIntosh Hollow, PA.

Children of James-[4] LYON and Calista Field:
Surname **LYON**

+	**118. CHARLES**	born July 1838 PA; died 1910; married Polly L. COWAN ca 1863
	THEODORE	(she born Sept 1842 PA; died _____)

Children of James⁻⁴ LYON and Calista FIELD, continued:
Surname **LYON**

	119. Ellen Rosalie	born ca 1844-45 PA; died _____
+	**120. JOHN H.**	born June 1846 PA ; died 13 July 1922 Hampton, VA.
		married Rosanna _____ ca 1869 (she born March 1852; died _____)
	121. Nancy J.	born ca 1849-50 PA; died 1935 PA
		married Zachary COWAN ca _____ (he born ca 1848; died 1917)
+	**122. HIRAM**	born 2 Feb1853 PA; died Dec 1927
		married Fanny/Fannie M. DEWEY 1 Jan 1877
		(she dau/o Walter DEWEY and Cynthia WELCH) (she born Oct 1860 PA)
	123. Estella	born ca 1854 PA; died _____

34. MARY ROWENA⁻⁴ LYON, sister of above, was born 20 Oct 1820 at Bloomville, Delaware County, NY. She married the Reverend Festus Portius CLEVELAND*** on 3 August 1840 at Armenia, Bradford County, PA. He was the son of Josiah Douglas CLEVELAND and Lucy BRYAN, and was born 12 July 1817 at Masonville, Delaware County, NY; died ca ___ at _____ IL. Mary⁻⁴ LYON died _____ IL. The Rev. Festus CLEVELAND was the brother of Dr. John Emory CLEVELAND who married her sister Nancy⁻⁴ LYON (# 36). He died 4 June 1900.

Children of Mary⁻⁴ LYON and Festus CLEVELAND:
Surname **CLEVELAND**

+	**124. CELESTIA ANTOINETTE**	born 15 Nov 1841 Troy Bradford, PA; died _____
		married William Benson OWEN 22 Jan 1861 Ottawa, LaSalle, IL.
		(he was born 24 Jan 1826 Winchester, Clark, KY; died _____)
	125. Lucy Jane	born 28 June 1843 Masonville, NY; died _____
		married Charles Ezra SIMMONS 14 May 1866 Rockford, IL
		(he born 25 Dec 1845 Lake County, IL; died _____)

Child: Howard -⁶ Lisle SIMMONS born 22 Feb 1874 Chicago, IL

	126. Charles Benson	born 4 Feb 1845 Masonville, NY; died _____
		married Theodocia Backus GARRISON 15 Oct 1867 Rockford, IL
		(she born 6 April 1842 Newark, NJ; died _____)

Child: Edith Grace⁻⁶ CLEVELAND born 30 April 1897 Chicago, IL; died ____

****	**127. JOSIAH FRANCIS**	born 18 June 1847 Masonville, NY; died 4 Jan 1928
		1 married Electa Garrison PRICE 2 Nov 1869 Newark, NJ
		(she born 2 Oct 1847 Newark, NJ; died 29 Jan 1872 Newark)
		2 married Mary Elizabeth FRISBEE 25 Sep 1873 Chicago, Cook, IL
		(she born 20 May 1845 Little Falls, Herkimer, NY; died 8 May 1901
		(she dau/o Augustus FRISBEE and Hannah LACKLORE)

**** Note: " Josiah F. CLEVELAND, assistant land commissioner of the Chicago & Northwestern Railroad Co, Chicago, IL was born at Masonville, Delaware County, NY in 1847. He came to Illinois with his father Festus P. CLEVELAND, who was a clergyman in the Methodist Episcopal church. The subject of this sketch,, about 1867 began business life as a clerk in the mercantile business at Rockford, IL. Two years later he went to New York City, where he was employed as a book-keeper. In 1870 he came to Chicago, and was employed in an abstract office until after the great fire in 1871, when he went to Newark, NJ. Returning to Chicago in April 1872, he was employed in a real estate office, and in October of that year was appointed book-keeper and cashier of the Howe Sewing Machine Company. In April 1880, he was appointed chief clerk of the land office of the Chicago & Northwestern Railroad Company , to accept which he resigned the position with the Howe Sewing Machine Company. On May 1, 1882, he was appointed to the office of assistant land commissioner." Reference: History of Early Chicago by Albert D. HAGER , Page 787. *** Note: Festus Portius CLEVELAND, above, was a cousin of President Grover CLEVELAND

+	**128. FESTUS WANDBY**	born 19 Nov 1849 Masonville, NY; died 1926
		married Edith Clementine WILLIAMS 24 Nov 1875 Chicago, IL
		(she born 12 Oct 1853 Columbia, WI; died _____)

Children of Mary[-4] LYON and Festus CLEVELAND, continued:
Surname **CLEVELAND**

129. Phebe Isabella	born 2 Jan 1853 Masonville, NY; died _____)	
	married Milo Hutchinson ASPINWALL 20 Mar 1872 Joliet, IL	
	(he born 27 Jan 1849; died ____)	

Child: Mabel Florence-[6] ASPINWALL born 24 March 1874 Chicago, IL

130. William Seymour	born 4 Oct 1855 New Lenox, IL; died 6 April 1857 Wilmington, IL	EOL
131. Mary Durham	born 5 Nov 1859 Kankakee, IL; died 21 Feb 1860 Kankakee	EOL
132. John Durham	born 4 Aug 1861 Ottawa, LaSalle, IL; died _____	
	married Bertha Lucille CRAIG 21 Feb 1888 Cook County, IL	

Children: Antoinette-[6] born 9 Dec 1888 IL, died Nov 1960 IL; and Mary-[6] CLEVELAND born Jan 1890 IL; neither one ever married EOL

133. Alson Sherman	born 24 Aug 1864 Waukegan, IL; died 22 March 1870 Freeport, IL	EOL

35. SARAH ELIZABETH [-4] **LYON**, sister of above, was born 25 Oct 1822 at Bloomville, Delaware County, New York. She married Daniel[-3] HAGAR on 24 December 1841 at ____,PA. He was the son of Jonas[-2] HAGAR and Mary CURTIS, and was born 20 September 1820 at Pike, Bradford County, PA; died 22 June 1882 Armenia Twsp. Tioga County, PA. Sarah[-4] LYON died 17 Feb 1907 at Ward, Tioga, PA.

Children of Sarah[-4] LYON and Daniel HAGAR:
Surname **HAGAR**

	134. Della	born ca 1842 Union, Tioga, PA; died ca 1844 Union, PA	EOL
+	**135. LOIS OPHELIA**	born 18 Nov 1845 Tioga Co., PA; died ca 1917 Kane, McKean, PA	
		1 married Lewis GETSINGER ca 1865	
		(he s/o Anthony GETSINGER and Elizabeth _____)	
		(he born ca 1832 NJ; died Feb 1875 PA)	
		2 married William Franklin DAVIDS 8 Nov 1877 Pittsburgh, PA	
		(he born 3 June 1851/52 NY; died 5 Jan 1928 Akron, OH)	
+	**136. EMMA A.**	born 21 Jan 1848 Tioga Co., PA; died _____	
		married George H. MASON ca ____	
+	**137. EVALINA**	born 20 July 1850 Tioga Co., PA; died ___	
	LAVENCIE	married George J. BATEMAN ca _____ (he from Wyoming)	
	138. John Martin (twin)	born ca 1852; died ca 1853 Tioga Co., PA	EOL
	139 Jonas Marcus (twin)	born ca 1852; died ca 1853 Tioga Co., PA	EOL
+	**140. ROSA BELLE**	born 15 July 1855 Tioga Co., PA; died 30 March 1940 Canton, Pa	
		married Wilson Charles HILL ca 1874	
		(he s/o Osburn Hill and _____)	
		(he born March 1851; died 30 Dec 1930)	
+	**141. JOHN LYON**	born 28 Sept 1857 Ward, Tioga, PA; died 1923; buried Mansfield, PA	
		married Sarah Millard SHAW 4 July 1878	
		(she dau/o Daniel Merrill SHAW and Jane SEAMAN)	
		(she born 11 March 1855 Sullivan Twsp, PA; died ____)	
+	142. James W.	born 6 Dec 1861 Tioga Co., PA; died 16 Jan 1934 Canton, Bradford, PA	
		married Hannah Eva SHERMAN 12 July 1887 Towanda, PA	
		(she dau/o Leander SHERMAN and _____)	
		(she born 6 Aug 1863 PA; died 3 Sept 1945 Canton, PA)	
		(buried Park Cemetery, Canton, Bradford, PA)	

Children: Mabel S-[6] born 6 July 1889; died 12 May 1912 Canton, PA and Willard Sherman-[6] HAGAR born 22 Nov 1891; died Sept 1969 Camp Hill, PA

+	**143. FLORA**	born 6 Dec 1863 Tioga Co., PA; died _____
		married James T. CORNISH, a tinsmith, on ___ 1881
		(he born Jan 1857 England; died _____ PA)

36. NANCY THERESA **LYON**, sister of above, was born 17 March 1825 at Bloomville, Delaware County, New York. She married Dr. John Emory CLEVELAND on 25 Nov 1850 at Franklin, Delaware County, New York. He was the son of Josiah Douglas CLEVELAND and Lucy BRYAN, and was born 4 August 1829; died 6 Dec 1913. He was a graduate of the PA Medical College, Philadelphia, PA, and Gettysburg College 1861

Children of Nancy⁻⁴ LYON and Dr. John CLEVELAND:
Surname **CLEVELAND**

	144. Adele Virginia	born 31 April 1853; died ca 1921 (single)	EOL
+	**145. EMERSON JOHN**	born 7 July 1856; died ca 1922	
		married Jennie Florence ELLIOT 16 July 1884	

38. HARRIET⁻⁴ **LYON,** sister of above, was born 19 July 1829 at Bloomville, NY. She married Seymour E. SMITH on 1 June 1846 at ____ NY. He was the son of Bernice SMITH and Emily ___, and was born ca 1823 NY; died before 1892. He was a stone mason, and later worked as a clerk in a customs house. Harriet⁻⁴ LYON died between 1925-30. They resided Masonville, Delaware County, NY.

Children of Harriet⁻⁴ LYON and Seymour SMITH:
Surname **SMITH**

	146. Harriet A.	born ca 1853 NY; died _____
	147. Ruth E.	born ca 1856 NY; died _____
	148. John B.	born ca 1857 NY; died ca ____
	149. Miles S.	born Dec 1859/ Jan 1860; NY; died ca 1910 Binghamton, NY
		married Florence / Flora E. BROOKS ca _____
		(she born ca 1860 Smithville Flats, Chenango, NY; died 1954 Binghamton)
		(she dau/o Langdon Warren BROOKS and Harriet Mildred THORNTON)

Children: Grace Adell⁻⁶ born ca 1881, and Mattie Louise⁻⁶ SMITH born ca 1883 NY

+	**150. VANCE MARQUIS**	born Sept 1862 NY; died _____
		married Ida M. ____ (she born Nov 1865 NY; died ____)
	151. Alicia E.	born Feb 1867 NY; died _____
		married William Morgan JONES ca 1894
		(he born Aug 1857 Wales; died _____)

Child: Merwin G⁻⁶ JONES born 12 May 1895, NY; died _____)

40. MASON LEROY⁻⁴ **LYON**, brother of above, was born 20 February 1834 at Troy, Bradford, PA. He married Hannah Lawrence SCHIEFFELIN on 29 June 1857 at Knoxville, Tioga County, PA. She was the daughter of Jacob SCHIEFFELIN and Elizabeth CHAPMAN, and was born 6 March 1840 at Charleston, Tioga County, PA; died 20 February 1935 at Los Angeles, CA. Mason Leroy⁻⁴ LYON died 20 June 1908 at Los Angeles, CA. He died of tetanus (blood poisoning) one week after having stepped on a rusty nail while helping his son-in-law, Ira RUBENDALL, building contractor, and 13 months after moving to Los Angeles for retirement.

Children of Mason Leroy⁻⁴ LYON and Hannah SCHIEFFELIN:
Surname **LYON**

	152. William	born ca 1858 PA; died before 30 Aug 1860	EOL
	153.Cora Emma	born 24 June 1860; died 18 June 1939 Los Angeles, CA	
		1 married Lorenzo Perley DEARBORN 1 March 1888 Chicago, Cook, IL	
		2 married Edward HERR ca ____; divorced before 1900	
		3 married Grant BRITTEN before 1935	
+	**154. FRANK LEROY**	born 6 Oct 1863 PA; died 2 April 1914; married Mary CAHILL ca _____	
+	**155. SAMUEL MASON**	born 19 March 1868 Susquehanna, PA; died 18 Jan 1946 Los Angeles, CA	
		married Wilhelmina (Minnie) Christina SCHROEDER 17 July 1890, IL	
		(she born 6 Oct 1870 Freeport, IL; died 31 Dec 1949 Los Angeles, CA)	

Children of Mason Leroy [-4] LYON and Hannah SCHIEFFLIN, continued:
Surname **LYON**

	156. Charlotte Stewart	born 7 April 1871 PA; died 9 Feb 1954 Los Angeles, CA
	"Lottie" (twin)	1 married Steven MOORE ca ____ Stephenson Co., IL
		2 married Ira O. RUBENDALL ca 1905 IL (he born ca 1879 IL; died ____)
+	**157. WILLIAM**	born 7 April 1871 PA; died 7 July 1941 Los Angeles, CA
	FESTUS (twin)	married Mabelle O'KANE ca ____

41. HARRIET[-4] **KIFF**, daughter of Lyman[-3] KIFF (Andrew[-2]; George[-1]) and Mary CLEMONS, was born ca 1807-08 NY. She married Jerome Henry PUTNAM 21 June 1830 at Kortright, Delaware County, NY. He was the son of Thomas PUTNAM (Mayflower descendant) and Rosamund ROUNSEVELL, and was born ca 1809 at Windsor, Vermont; died 1 Dec. 1870 at Wellsboro, Tioga County, PA. Harriet-[4] KIFF died 12 April 1882 at Blossburg, Tioga, PA.

Children of Harriet[-4] KIFF and Jerome PUTNAM:
Surname **PUTNAM**

+	**158. HARRIET R.**	born 6 March 1831 Delaware Co., NY; died 1892
		married Lewis MILLS ca ____
	159. Mary	born ca 1833 Delaware Co., NY; died ____
+	**160. JEROME HENRY**	born 19 Sept 1837 Delaware Co., NY; died ____; married Elizabeth ____
	161. Thomas	born ca 1838 NY; died 1850 Blossburg, Tioga , PA
	162. Lyman	born ca 1843 Blossburg, PA; died ____
+	**163. VIALL A.**	born July 1845 Blossburg, Tioga, PA; died ____
		married Bertha BURGIN ca 18__
		(she dau/o ____ BURGIN and ____)(she born 12 Oct 1856 Switzerland)
	164. Francis / Frank	born ca 1847 PA 165. Fanny A. born Aug 1850 PA

42. SAMUEL CLEMONS[-4] **KIFF**, brother of above, was born ca 1813 at Kortright, Delaware County, NY. He married Susan H. KENYON on 27 February 1833 at Kortright. She as the daughter of James KENYON and Susannah PALMER, and was born 16 May 1811 Davenport, Delaware, NY died ____.

Children of Samuel[-4] KIFF and Susan KENYON:
Surname **KIFF**

	166. Susan Harriet	born ca 1834 PA; died 1915; buried Park Cemetery, Canton, PA
	167. James L.	born ca 1836 PA; died ____
		married Mariah L DOWD 1867 (she born ca 1838; died 1910)
	168. Lyman William	born Feb 1839 PA; died 1912
		married Melvina D. TOWNSEND ca 1864 (she born ca 1844; died ____)
		(she dau/o Claudius TOWNSEND and Marsha / Marcia EGGLESTON)
		Children: Effie S-[6] born ca 1865 and Frank[-6] KIFF born ca 1873
	169. Frances Isabel	born ca 1840 PA; died ____
+	**170. DAVID K.**	born July 1848 PA; died 22 Jan 1909
		married Clara Delilah GOODSELL ca 1871
		(she dau/o George GOODSELL and Olive HENDRICK)
		(she born 5 Aug 1854 NY; died 20 May 1935)
+	**171. PHOEBE**	born Feb 1851 PA; died 1909
		married Thomas Wilson PATCHEN 23 Feb 1877 Covington, PA
	172. Thomas	born ca 1853 PA; died
	173. Edgar Ferris	born ca 1854; died ____; harness maker
		married Phoebe M. JAQUISH ca 188_ (she born June 1862 PA)
		(she dau/o Horace S. JAQUISH and Mary A. ____)
		Child: Harry B-[6] KIFF born Nov 1888; married Minnie ____)

44. MARY L⁻⁴ KIFF, sister of above, was born ca 1825 at Delaware County, New York. She married Colburn CLEMONS ca _____. He was the son of _____ CLEMONS and _____, and was born ca 1800 CT; died _____. Mary L⁻⁴ KIFF died _____.

Children of Mary L⁻⁴ KIFF and Colburn CLEMONS:
Surname **CLEMONS**

> 174. Diana Madora   born ca 1863; died ca 1947
> married Edward A. WARTER(S) (he born ca 1865; died 1948)
> Child: Harry Oliver ⁻⁶ WARTER(S) born 19 Jan 1888 PA; died 23 Sept 1969; married Ethel Blanche WELLS 1908

45. RICHARD D. WADBY⁻⁴ KIFF, son of Andrew⁻³ KIFF (Andrew⁻², George⁻¹) and Rebecca WARDELL, and was born 22 Nov 1829 at Delaware Count, NY. He married Calista RITCHMEYER on 30 June 1858 at Gilboa, Schoharie County, New York. She was the daughter of Martinus RITCHMEYER and Elizabeth RUSS, and was born 3 Nov 1826 Gilboa, NY; died 16 Nov 1898. Richard D W⁻⁴ KIFF died _____, and is buried at Woodland Cemetery, Delhi, Delaware County, NY

Children of Richard D W⁻⁴ KIFF and Calista RITCHMEYER:
Surname **KIFF**

> 175. Charles Everett   born 18 April 1862 Kortright, NY; died before 1952
> married Mabel GILFILLAN 28 Oct 1891 New York City
> (she dau/o James GILFILLAN and Joanna Estelle THOMAS)
> (she born 26 Jan 1867 DC, died 20 July 1952)
>
> 176. May Louise   born July 1866 Delaware Co., NY; died _____
> married William GEMMEL
> (he born Apr 1863 Syracuse, NY; died _____)
> Children: Katherine⁻⁶ born Feb 1891 and Richard B⁻⁶ GEMMEL born July 1893

48. HELEN AUGUSTA⁻⁴ KIFF, daughter of Andrew⁻³ KIFF (Andrew⁻²; George⁻¹) and Rebecca WARDELL, was born 3 Jan 1836 at Delaware County, NY. She married Adrial Hebard CASE on 1 Nov 1854 at Sylvania Boro, PA. He was the son of Elihu CASE and Charlotte PALMER, and was born 19 Dec 1828; died 7 Dec 1908 at Topeka, Kansas. Helen Augusta-⁴ KIFF died 13 March 1870 at Topeka, Kansas.

Child of Helen Augusta⁻⁴ KIFF and Adrial Hebard CASE:
Surname **CASE**

> +   **177. DANIEL**   born 10 Feb 1864 Leavenworth, KS; died 11 July 1946 Hawaii
>   **HEBARD**   married Kathryn May MERRIAM 2 Sep 1890 Oberlin, OH

49. ISABELLA -4 KIFF, sister of above, was born ca 1839-40 NY. She married Edward L. STRAIT ca _____. He was the son of Isaac Burton STRAIT and Maria BENSON, and was born Feb 1838 PA; died _____.

Children of Isabella-⁴ KIFF and Edward STRAIT:
Surname **STRAIT**

> 178. Emma   born Jan 1867 KS; died _____
> 179. Laura   born Mar 1872 KS; died 24 July 1959 Riverside, CA
> 180. Augusta Di Francos   born 4 July 1878 KA; died 31 May 1969 Medford, OR
> married William Edward HENSON ca _____
> (he born 1875 TN; died 1956)
> Children: Mary Isabell-⁶ born ca 1911/12 CA; and Ruth Frances-⁶ HENSON born 25 Dec 1913 CA; died Feb 2008 OR; married Kermit Aikman CARROLL , son of Seth Oliver CARROLL and Rachel Grace AIKMAN, and was born 3 Oct 1908 IN; did 27 Nov 1989 Medford, OR

50. WILLIAM M⁻⁴ KIFF, brother of above, was born 8 September 1842 at Delaware County, NY. He married Harriet Melissa (Hattie) CASE ca 1866 at Troy, Bradford County, PA.. She was the daughter of Timothy N. CASE and Delia COWELL, and was born 5 April 1848 at Troy, Bradford, PA; died 15 Oct 1900 at Eldredsville, Sullivan County, PA. William⁻⁴ KIFF died 8 Dec 1889 Bradford County, PA., and is buried at the Sylvania Cemetery. Hattie CASE married 2ⁿᵈ to Burton Kingsbury LUTHER (as his third wife).

Children of William M⁻⁴ KIFF and Hattie CASE:
Surname **KIFF**

	181. Frank A.	born 12 Sep 1868 Mansfield, PA; died 10 May 1960 W. Burlington, PA	
		married Susie KNIGHTS 4 July 1891 at Troy, PA.	
		(she dau/o Allen KNIGHTS and Sarah STAGE)	
		(she born July 1867; died 31 Mar 1941 Sayre, PA)	
+	**182. CORA BELL**	born 24 Jan 1870 Bradford Co., PA; died 1953	
		married Jesse CHILSON ca 1898	
		(he s/o Harry L. CHILSON and Lydia Elizabeth VARGASON)	
		(he born Aug 1867 PA; died May 1941)	
	183. Frederick	born 22 Nov 1875; died 31 Aug 1876	EOL
+	**184. RUTH E.**	born 15 April 1881 Sylvania, PA; died ____	
		married Ernest Munro BESLEY 28 April 1896 Elmira, NY	
		(he s/o George N. BESLEY and Charlotte J. MUNRO)	
		(he born 28 Oct 1876 Austinville, PA; died 26 Dec 1962 Bainbridge, NY	
	185. JENNIE A /H	born 26 June 1885 PA; died 1956 PA	
		married Thomas Bell HULSLANDER 14 Oct 1902	
		(he s/o Charles Bell HULSLANDER and Jeanette FERGUSON)	
		(he born 2 Sept 1876 Tioga Co., PA; died 21 Jan 1959 Sullivan, Tioga, PA)	
	186. Blanche L.	born Oct 1889 PA ; died ____ ; married Joel E. SHEIVE of Sidney, NY 1910	

55. HIRAM M⁻⁴ KIFF, son of Peter⁻³ KIFF (Andrew⁻²; George-¹) and Abigail Jemima LYON, was born ca 1828 at ____ Delaware County, NY. He married Clarissa PECK 9 Jan 1856 at Kortright, Delaware County, NY. She was the daughter of David Woolsey PECK and Clarissa FERRIS, and was born ca 1830, died 26 September 1867. Hiram-⁴ KIFF died 13 February 1885 Delaware County, NY.

Children of Hiram M⁻⁴ KIFF and Clarissa PECK:
Surname **KIFF**

+	**187. ARTHUR DAVID**	born 10 April 1860 Delaware Co., NY; died 1 Jan 1949
		married Jennie A. RYER ca ____
		(she born 1 Jan 1860; died 1 Jan 1930 Delaware County, NY
	188. Levi	born ca 1862 Delaware Co., NY; died ca 1893 Delaware Co., NY
		married Jennie Polly ____ (she born ca 1862; died 1930)
	189. William Lincoln	born 26 June 1866 Delaware Co., NY; died 10 September 1955 NY
		1 married Fannie E. VERMILYA
		(she born ca 1867; died 1894 Delaware Co., NY)
		2 married Ann FAULKNER 29 Oct 1895
		(she dau/o Morris FAULKNER and Catherine ____)
		(she born 15 Jan 1871; died 18 Nov 1958 Accord, Delaware Co., NY)

Child: Fannie-⁶ KIFF born ca 1902; died 1998, married Edward DAVENPORT)

60. FRANCES ESTELLA⁻⁴ KIFF, sister of above, was born 10 February 1839 at Kortright, Delaware County, NY. She married Daniel Lee-⁹ FRISBEE son of Erastus-⁸ FRISBEE (Daniel-⁷, Gideon-⁶, Philip-⁵, Gideon-⁴; Edward-³; John-²; Edward-¹) and Elizabeth LEE on 10 February 1864 at Delhi. He was born 19 April 1840 at Delhi, Delaware, NY; died 28 April 1896 Hudson, Lenawee, Michigan. Frances E⁻⁴ KIFF died the same day. They both died from smallpox.   Reference: FRISBEE /FRISBIE Genealogy, Tenth Generation, Page 561

Children of Frances Estella[-4] KIFF and Daniel Lee[-9] FRISBEE:
Surname **FRISBEE**

	190. Frank Kiff	born 6 May 1866 Delhi, NY; died 20 April 1884 Oneonta, Otsego, NY EOL
+	**191. EMORY**	born 17 Nov 1868 Hamden, NY; died 5 June 1946 Kortright, NY
	PERCIVAL	married Lena Belle FORSYTH on 23 Jan 1895 at Franklin, Delaware, NY
		(she dau/o George FORSYTH and Mary Elizabeth LLOYD)
		(she born 16 Dec 1871 Sidney, Delaware, NY; died _____)
+ ***	**192. CLARENCE KIFF**	born 22 March 1873 Hamden, Del. NY; died 29 Nov 1948 Beacon, Dutch, NY
		married Kate Louise TOMLINSON 28 Sept 1903 Milford, CT

*** Clarence Kiff[5] FRISBEE, above, was adopted, after his parents death from smallpox, by Lewis BUSH of Walton, NY .Lewis BUSH and his wife Elizabeth were childless. They adopted him before 1880 and his name was changed to BUSH. He and Kate TOMLINSON divorced and according to the 1920 Federal Census, he was a patient at the Mattewan State Hospital. His descendants have the surname BUSH

64. JOHN MABIE[-4] KIFF, son of Erastus[-3] KIFF (Andrew[-2]; George[-1]) and Sarah PALMER, was born 17 Oct 1823 at Kortright, Delaware County, New York. He married Susan/Susannah BASCOM(B) on 25 October 1854 at ____, PA. She was the daughter of Joseph Bascom(b) and Amaretta GRACE, and was born13 January 1834, PA; died 11 Oct 1915. She was one of the first school teachers at Ward Township, Tioga County, PA. In 1850 she and her husband resided at Armenia, PA. John[-4] KIFF died ca 187_ at Ward, PA, and is buried at the Becker Corners Cemetery, Fallbrook Road, Tioga County, PA.

Children of John M[-4] KIFF and Susan/Susannah BASCOM(B):
Surname **KIFF**

	193. Amaretta	born ca 1856-57 PA; died ca 1910 (she was a school teacher)
	"Mettie"	married John ROLISON/ROLOSON no issue EOL
	194. Jennie J.	born 7 Jan 1858 Tioga Co., PA; died 17 Dec 1912; buried Becker Corners
		married Charles GREEN ca ____
		(he born 18 Oct 1846; died 29 Dec 1912)
	195. William	born 1861; died 15 Jan 1944
	196. Burton Harrison	born 13 June 1863 PA; died ____ PA no issue EOL
		1 married Jennie B. WOODIN (she born 16 Dec 1867; died 26 Feb 1914 PA)
		(she dau/o Allen WOODIN and Elsie TAYLOR)
		2 married Mrs. Myrtle Wolcott ca 1886;
+	**197. FRANKLIN**	born 24 July 1866 Ward Twsp. Tioga, PA; died Oct 1964 Waterloo, Seneca, NY
	CLAYTON	1 married Jennie L. WORDEN
	"Frank"	(she dau/o _____ WORDEN and _____)
		(she born 2 Apr 1872 Seneca Falls, NY; died 1932 NY)
		2 married Hannah W. TYMAN ca 1936
	198. George R.	born ca 1871-72 PA; died ca 1952 EOL
		married Clara RICKON / RICKEN no issue EOL
+	**199. DELOS E.**	born ca 1873-74; died 27 March 1944; married Lucy-[5] CEASE
		(she dau/o Nelson-[4] CEASE and Margaret EATON)
		(she born ca 1880 Morris Run, PA; died 1969)

65. ANN ELIZA[-4] KIFF, sister of above, was born ca 1824-25 at Kortright, Delaware County, NY. She married Ambrose MURRAY ca 18__. He was the son of Ambrose MURRAY and Harriet AVERY of Troy, Bradford County, PA., and was born ca 1815 NY; died ____.Ann Eliza[-4] KIFF died ____.

Children of Ann Eliza^{-4} KIFF and Ambrose MURRAY, Jr.:
Surname **MURRAY**

+	**200. LUMAN**	born April 1848 PA; died _____
		married Mary DICKINSON 22 Sept 1868 (she born ca 1850 PA; died _____)
+	**201. EDSON ALLEN**	born ca 1849; died 4 July 1876
		married Polly Rowena BOYCE ca ____
		(she dau/o William BOYCE and his 2nd wife Lydia M. WARD)
		(she born 3 Aug 1850 Bradford Co., PA; died ____)
		(she married 2nd Milton MC ILWAIN)(she married 3rd Charles KIFF (# 68)
	202. George	born ca 1851 PA; died ____; married Jane SPENCER
	203. Helen	born ____; died young EOL
	204. Harriet	born ca 1856 PA; died ____; married William DRESHER EOL
+	**205. HELEN**	born Nov 1865 PA; died _____
		married Fred H. JENNER ca 1883 (he born April 1860 PA; died _____)
	206. Frank	born ca 18 __; died age 18 EOL

66. HARRIET^{-4} KIFF, sister of above, was born ca 1827-28 at Kortright, Delaware County, NY. She married Israel MOORE ca ____. He was the son of ____ MOORE and ___, and was born ca 1820 Muncy, PA; died _____. Harriet-^{4} KIFF died ____.

Children of Harriet-^{4} KIFF and Israel MOORE:
Surname **MOORE**

+	**207. AMANDA**	born ca 1849 PA; died ____
		married Leroy CEASE ca _____
		(he s/o Alexander CEASE and Julia-3 MC INTOSH)
		(he born ca 1842, PA; died _____) a Civil War veteran
	208. Mary M.	born ca 1850-51 PA; died 1912; married Jacob THOMAS
	209. Walter	born 16 Dec 1853 PA; died 6 Feb 1938
		1 married Adorna UPHAM (1 daughter, no further info)
+	**210. GEORGE DUDLEY**	born 6 Nov 1855 Armenia, PA; died 30 March 1939 Armenia)
		married Frances " Frankie" Elizabeth SMITH 8 Oct 1874
		(she dau/o _____ SMITH and _____)
		(she born ca 1853; died 31 March 1928 Canton, PA)

67. LUCY^{-4} KIFF, sister of above, was born August 1831 at Kortright, Delaware, NY. She married Daniel COSPER ca 1857. He was the son of Peter COSPER and Anna BRITTON of Armenia, PA, and was born 3 October 1828; died 13 March 1912. Lucy^{-4} KIFF died 14 February 1914. They are buried at Alba, PA.

Children of Lucy^{-4} KIFF and Daniel COSPER:
Surname **COSPER**

+	**211. ADELL " Dell " EMMA**	born 4 Feb 1860; died 25 April 1926 Canton, Bradford, PA
		married Charles Lewis FREEMAN ca 1879
		(he born 13 May 1860 ; died 18 Jan 1934 PA)
	212. Walter	born ca 1861; died ca 1863 EOL
+	**213. SHEPARD S.**	born 1 August 1864 Canton, PA; died 30 March 1923 Alba, Bradford, PA
		married Jennie Mae SLINGERLAND
		(she born May 1867 Troy, PA; died 12 Nov 1957 Alba, PA)
		(she married 2nd to _____ CONDERMAN) Reference: Obituary
+	**214. FLORENCE JANE**	born 1867; died 1966
		married Willard H. DUNBAR 18 Sept 1890
		(he s/o Alvin T. DUNBAR and Isabella D. ____)
		(he born ca 1863; died _____)

Children of Lucy-[4] KIFF and Daniel COSPER, continued:
Surname **COSPER**

215. Helen May	born June 1870 ; died 1945; buried Alba Cemetery, Alba, PA
	married Perry Dwight FREEMAN ca 1892
	(he s/o Henry Watson FREEMAN and Belle DOUGLAS)
	(he born 9 March 1867; died 2 March 1946 Alba, PA)

Child: Eloise-[6] FREEMAN born Feb 1896 Canton, PA

68. CHARLES E[4] KIFF, brother of above, was born ca 1834 at Kortright, Delaware County, New York. He married Fanny C-[4] MAC INTOSH, daughter of Matthias-[3] MAC INTOSH (Simon-[2]; Alexander-[1]) on 5 November 1854. She was born 12 February 1834 NY; died 24 September 1897 at Alba, Bradford County, PA. He married 2nd to Polly Rowena BOYCE Cosper McIlwain , as her 3rd husband. Charles E. KIFF died ca 1910.

Children of Charles -[4] KIFF and Fanny C-[4] MAC INTOSH:
Surname **KIFF**

216. Rowland P.	born 11 Aug 1855 PA; died 1926 PA; buried Park Cemetery, Canton, PA
	married Cora Elizabeth MANDEVILLE 26 April 1882
	(she dau/o Byron W. MANDEVILLE and Mary E. BAIN)
	(she born 27 March 1864 NY; died 1936 PA)

Child: Grover Charles-[6] KIFF born 19 Jan 1883 PA; died 9 Dec 1932 (single)

+ **217. JAMES MELVIN**	born ca 1857-58; died _____
	married Ella FOX ca 1888
	(she dau/o Harvey F. FOX and Martha _____)
	(she born Sept 1866 PA; died _____)(living 1920)

218. Siegel O.	born ca 1863; died 1941 no issue EOL
	married Mertie / Myrtie / Matilda E. FOSS 20 June 1890
	(she dau/o George H. FOSS and Nancy BOTHWELL)
	(she born ca 1866; died _____)

+ **219. CLARA BELL**	born 24 July 1865; died 30 March 1946 Troy, PA ; buried Alba, PA)
	1 married George Phelps FREEMAN, Jr. 24 Sept 1885
	(he s/o George Phelps FREEMAN and Emoline PALMER)
	(he born 24 Sept 1858; died 13 Nov 1926)
	2 married Edward TOMLINSON

70. HELEN[4] KIFF, sister of above, was born Nov 1845 Kortright, Delaware, NY. She married Warren Willington WHITMAN ca ___. He was the son of Dr. Newberry WHITMAN, MD. and Josephine GRACE, and was born Feb 1843; died 1925. Warren WHITMAN served in the Civil WAR (noted in Vol III, page 69; US Soldiers of the Civil War) Helen-[4] KIFF died ____. In 1930 Helen-[4] KIFF was living with her daughter Josie in Springvale, Emmett County, Michigan.

Children of Helen-[4] KIFF and Warren WHITMAN:
Surname **WHITMAN**

220. Maggie	born 1871 PA; married _____HASSETT

Child: Mabel M-[6] HASSETT born ca 1907 MI; living with aunt ,Josie-5 D. PEARSON , in 1920

221. Josephine D.	born ca 1876 PA; died _____
" Josie "	married Martin James PEARSON before 1920 MI (as his 2nd wife)
	(he s/o James PEARSON and Esther Jane DE MARAY)
	(he born April 1864 Canada; immigrated to US 1874; naturalized 1880)
222. Grace Isabella	born 14 Sept 1885 MI; married _____ SMITH

KIFF

71. ELIZABETH A-[5] BECKER, daughter of Hannah-[4] KIFF (James-[3]; Andrew-[2]; George-[1]) and John S. BECKER, was born ca 1831-32 at Delhi, Delaware County, New York. She married Alexander Hamilton THOMAS on 4 February 1850 at Troy, PA. He was the son of Alvin W. THOMAS (Jacob) ++ and Amy HARDING, and was born 9 Sept 1829 PA; died 15 March 1901, PA. Elizabeth-[5] BECKER died 21 September 1917 at Bradford County, PA, and is buried at Alba, Bradford County, PA.

Note: Jacob THOMAS , born ca ___NH, moved in 1808 to Troy Twsp. PA and lived on a farm there until his death in 1841. He married Susannah ROWLEY, daughter of Dr. Reuben ROWLEY(a Revolutionary War soldier). Their children were Zeruah (Mrs. Samuel Case); ALVIN W.(above); Samuel; Hiram; Chester; Allen; Lucy M.(Mrs. Dummer LILLEY); and Jacob.

Children of Elizabeth-[5] BECKER and Alexander THOMAS:
Surname **THOMAS**

+	**223. ADOLPHUS E.**	born 9 Sept 1852 PA; died 21 Feb 1920
		married Marian BLAKEMAN ca _____
		(she dau/o Asel BLAKEMAN and Mary Ann LEWIS)
		(she born ca 1859 PA, died ca 1952, buried Alba, PA)
+	**224. BOLIVAR P.**	born 11 April 1854 PA; died 19 Nov 1912 PA; buried Alba, PA
		married Julia A. WILLIAMS
		(she dau/o Obediah WILLIAMS and Hannah KEYES)
		(she born 1 March 1853; died 24 March 1934; buried Beech Flats, PA)
	225. Henry	born 25 April 1856, PA; died 7 Jan 1935 no issue EOL
		married Helen E. BLAKEMAN 31 Jan 1878
		(she born 28 March 1857; died 28 March 1923)
+	**226. EUGENIA**	born 3 July 1858 PA; died ca 1909
		married Milton A. CASE 25 Nov 1880 Troy, Bradford, PA
		(he s/o Byron CASE and Eliza-4 MC INTOSH)
		(he born May 1858 Troy, PA; died ca 1937)
+	**227. ALVIN**	born 28 June 1860 PA; died 23 Jan 1939
		1 married Ella F. DEWEY ca _____
		(she dau/o George H. DEWEY and Sarah LOOMIS)
		(she born May 1861; died 3 May 1901)
		2 married Mary NEWELL 13 June 1906
+	**228. MEADE**	born 30 Oct 1866 PA; died 15 June 1945 Troy, Bradford, PA
		married Elizabeth " Lizzie " NEWELL
		(she dau/o Albert NEWELL and Olive Sophia SHERMAN)
		(she born 1871; died 1 Sept 1959 Sayre, PA)

72. WILLIAM HENRY-[5] BECKER, brother of above, was born 24 January 1833 at ____, Delaware County, NY. He married Harriet B. MILLER on 2 January 1866 at _____, PA. She was the daughter of Philip MILLER and _____, and was born 13 May 1848, PA; died 12 December 1924. William-[5] BECKER died August 1917.

Children of William-[5] BECKER and Harriet MILLER:
Surname **BECKER**

	229. Roland	born ca 1867; died 1928, buried Alba (PA) Cemetery
		married Julia Etta / Emma SMITH
		(she born ca 1872; did 14 Nov 1955 Staunton, VA)
	230. Lloyd/Floyd	born 16 May 1869; died 15 Feb 1897 Troy, Bradford, PA
+	**231. HIRAM MILLER**	born Nov 1870; died ____
		married Edna SMITH ca 1894 (she from Alba, PA)

73. JAMES <u>DEWITT</u>[-5] BECKER, brother of above, was born ca 1835 at ____, Delaware County, NY. He married Sarah E. BOVIER on 24 August 1865. She was the daughter of Solomon N. BOVIER and Elmira Amanda EDSALL, and was born 22 Oct 1842 PA; died 1915. Dewitt[-5] BECKER died ca 1910 and is buried at Alba, Bradford County, PA. In 1880 this family resided at Armenia, Tioga, PA.

Children of James <u>Dewitt</u>-[5] BECKER and Sarah BOVIER:
Surname **BECKER**

232. Lilly / Lillie	born 30 Aug 1866 Granville Ctr., PA; died 10 March 1945 Canton, PA		
	married John William-[4] KINCH (# 109)	buried Alba (PA) Cemetery	
+ **233. CLAUDE H.**	born May 1868 PA; died _____		
	married Minnie J. FIELD 1890-91		
	(she dau/o George FIELD and Caroline Amelia FREEMAN)		
	(she born June 1869; died _____)		
234. Eva	born July 1879 PA; died 1962; buried Windfall Cemetery		EOL
	married Archie Eugene PACKARD 2 April 1901 Alba, PA		
	(he s/o Winfield S. PACKARD and Elma FAULKNER)		
	(he born ca 1874; died 1959)		
235. Alta	born May 1883 PA; died _____		
	married Claude PACKARD ca ___ (he born 24 Oct 1880; died _____)		

Children: Fern Pearl-[7] PACKARD born 4 Sep 1903, married R. Carroll VANNOY, and died 3 May 1985 Towanda, PA.; and Dorothea-[7] PACKARD born Mar 1919 PA; died _____

76. WILLIAM EUGENE-[5] **DUMOND**, son of Harriet-[4] KIFF (James-[3]; Andrew-[2]; George-[1]) and Jacob Yaple DUMOND, was born 12 November 1845 at Armenia, Tioga, PA. He married first to Leila PRATT on 20 October 1880 at Mainesburg, PA. She was the daughter of Asa PRATT, Jr. and Mary Anne HARDING, and was born 31 March 1850; died 2 April 1896. His second marriage was to Elizabeth C. DOUGLAS ca 1898. She was born March 1855, and died 28 March 1936 at Canton, Bradford, PA. She is buried at the Beckers Corners Cemetery, Armenia Mtn, PA. William-[5] DUMOND died 28 July 1913.

Children of William-[5] DUMOND and Leila PRATT;
Surname **DUMOND**

+ **236. PERRY**	born 25 Feb 1882 PA; died _____	
EUGENE	married Edith Eliza MASON 29 Nov 1906	
	(she dau/o George Henry MASON and Addie Virginia DEWEY)	
	(she born 9 May 1891; died 1950 Edinsburg, PA)	
237. Minnie	born 24/27 August 1887-88; died 26 Feb 1902	EOL
238. Imogene	born _____; died _____; married William BARBER	

Child of William-[5] DUMOND and Elizabeth DOUGLAS :
Surname **DUMOND**

239. Ethel	born ca 1900 PA; died ____

83. JAMES LEONARD-[5] **KIFF**, son of James D-[4] KIFF (James-[3]; Andrew-[2]; George-[1]) and Elizabeth MC NAUGHT, was born November 1865 at ____ Delaware County, New York. He married Susan (Susie) CRAIG ca 1895. She was the daughter of Robert CRAIG and Louise____, and was born Nov 1870-73; died 6 July 1965. James Leonard-[5] KIFF died _____.

Children of James Leonard-[5] KIFF and Susan CRAIG:
Surname **KIFF**

240. Ralph Leonard	born 19 April 1897; died Sep 1974 Kingston, NY.; was a trainman
	married Eva May TAYLOR ca 1924 (she born 1902; died 1968)

Children: Gloria E-[7] born 1925 and Ralph J-[7] KIFF born 26 June 1928 NY

Children of James L-[5] KIFF and Susan (Susie) CRAIG, continued:
Surname **KIFF**

241. Walter Robert	born 11 June 1898 NY; died ____; was a painter	
242. Marshall	born ca 1904; died 1910 Sidney, NY	
243. Carlton	born 23 Feb 1907; died Aug 1984 Unadilla, NY	

86. HENRY D-[5] COVERT, son of Harry-[4] COVERT (Jemima-[3] KIFF; Andrew-[2]; George-[1]) and Oritha FIELD, was born 11 April 1839 at Armenia, Tioga County, PA. He married Candace A. BURMAN on 22 April 1866 at Armenia. She was the daughter of the Rev. Joel BURMAN and _____ SQUIRES, and was born ca ____, died 1919. Henry was a Civil War veteran, having served a Corporal in Co. C, 80th Regiment, 11th PA Cavalry. (Ref. History of PA, Vol. 1861-65) They resided at Covert, PA., and Henry-[5] COVERT died there on 21 April 1922. They are buried at the Covert Cemetery, Armenia Twsp. PA.

Children of Henry-[5] COVERT and Candace BURMAN:
Surname **COVERT**

244. William H.	born ca 1868; died ____, single	EOL
245. Bessie R.	born ca 1876; died _____	

87. GEORGE L-[5] COVERT, brother of above, was born 22 July 1842 at Ward Township, Tioga County, PA. He married Mary J. MERRIAM on 8 January 1884 at Corning, Steuben County, NY. She was the daughter of Albert MERRIAM and Harriet SMILEY, and was born 8 July 1854 at Ashland, NY; died ca 1900 at Armenia, PA. George-[5] COVERT died ca 1900 .

Children of George L-[5] COVERT and Mary J. MERRIAM:
Surname **COVERT**

+	246. Harriet S.	born 1 March 1884 PA; died _____
	"Hattie"	married Cola Walter-[6] LYON 26 March 1902 (#300)
		(he s/o Hiram-[5] LYON (# 122) and Fanny DEWEY)
		(he born 23 Nov 1880 PA; died 1937) (he was an attorney)
		(resided Orchard Park, Erie County, NY)
	247. Harry Albert	born Jan 1885 PA; died _____; a book-keeper
		married Jessie A. _____ ca 19__

Child: Eleanor-[7] COVERT born ca 1912 NY

Note: George L. COVERT enlisted in the Civil War on 12 Sept 1861 in Company C, 7th PA. Cavalry. He was taken prisoner at Gallatin, TN on 2 August 1862. After four months he was exchanged, and re-joined his Company at Nashville, TN. On 28 November 1863, he re-enlisted at Huntsville, AL as a veteran volunteer. On 20 June 1864 he was wounded in a battle near Kennesaw Mountain, GA .He was shot through the left lung and left wrist and 5 Sept 1865 was honorably discharged from the service. He studied to become a teacher at the (PA) State Normal School. In 1885 he built the first store in Armenia Twsp., and carried on a mercantile business for two years. In the meantime he circulated a petition for a Post Office at Covert, PA, which was established in July 1886. He was appointed Postmaster 8 July 1886, and later resigned so that O.D. FIELD could have the position.   Reference: History of Bradford County, page 748.

88. EDWIN G-[5] COVERT, brother of above, was born May 1848 PA. He married Josephine BERMAN ca ____. She was the daughter of __ BERMAN and ____, and was born ca 1853; died __. Edwin G-[5] COVERT died ____.

Children of Edwin-[5] COVERT and Josephine BERMAN:
Surname **COVERT**

248. Daisy	born May 1875; died _____	
	married Ceba D. WOOD ca 1895	
	(he s/o Frank H. WOOD and Lydia BAILEY	
	(he born July 1867 Columbia, Bradford, PA; died 9 Feb 1938)	

Child: Edwin F-[7] WOOD born 14 Oct 1893

249. Ada	born Oct 1884	

92. TYLER-5 CONGDON, son of Diana / Diantha-[4] COVERT (Jemima-[3] KIFF; Andrew-[2]; George-[1]) and Simon CONGDON, was born ca 1846 at _____, PA. He married Ruth Elizabeth " Lizzie " RATHBUN ca 1868. She was the daughter of _____ RATHBUN and _____, and was born ___; died ____. Tyler-[5] CONGDON served in the Civil War as a Pvt. In Co. K, of the 161st N Y Infantry Regiment from Jan 1864 to Dec 1865. Tyler-[5] died 1880.

Children of Tyler-[5] CONGDON and Ruth Elizabeth RATHBUN:
Surname **CONGDON**

250. Blanche W.	born ca 1869 NY; died _____; married Edward L. HYLER (he born ca 1873 MO; died _____) 1910 res. MO
251. Claude H.	born ca 1872 NY ; died before 1924 married Erma/Emma L. VANCE 30 Mar 1917 MO. (she may have been married previously to a _____ BOOKS) (she dau/o Millard Fillmore VANCE and Anna Louise COE) (she born Dec 1885 OH; died _____)

Children : poss. Walter V.-[7] born ca 1910 (listed as his step-son on the 1920 Census , but went by the name of CONGDON and Claude Herbert -[7] VANCE born 2 Mar 1921 MO; died 27 July ___ Cincinnati, OH

93. VICTORIA E-[5] CONGDON, daughter of Diana / Diantha-[4] COVERT (Jemima-[3] KIFF; Andrew-[2]; George-[1]) and Simon CONGDON , was born Sept 1848 ____, New York, She married George RATHBUN ca 1872. He was the son of Allen RATHBUN and Ruth Eliza GATES , and was born July 1842 at ___, Chenango County, NY, died _____. Victoria-[5] CONGDON died ca 1880.

Children of Victoria-[5] CONGDON and George RATHBUN:
Surname **RATHBUN**

252. Maude	born April 1884, Kansas City, MO; died _____
253. Allen M.	born Dec 1885 Kansas City, MO; died _____ 1 married Marion M. GLADDEN; 2 married Cassie E. HURLEY

94. SCHUYLER CHARLES-[5] CONGDON, brother of above, was born 9 Aug 1849-50. He married Mary Elizabeth KINCH ca ____. She was the daughter of Thomas KINCH and Sarah Jane CEASE, and was born Feb 1850-51 Meredith, Delaware, NY; died 1923 at Oneonta, NY. Schuyler-[5] CONGDON died 1929.

Children of Schuyler-[5] CONGDON and Mary Elizabeth KINCH:
Surname **CONGDON**

	254. Metta	born 2 June 1871 Troy, PA; died _____; married ____ HUDSON
	255. Helen	born 2 Feb 1873 Burlingame, KS; died ____ married Henry BRADLEY ca 1893 (he born ca 1862 Otsego Co., NY)
		Child: Leon-[7] BRADLEY born ca 1898 Otsego County, NY
+	**256. CLARENCE HERBERT**	born 20 Dec 1874 Burlingame, KS; died 24 Oct 1957 Oneonta, Otsego, NY married Arian MAPLES 20 July 1898 Oneonta, NY (she born 11 Oct 1877 Hartwick, NY; died _____)
	257. Dora	born 14 Nov 1876 Burlingame, KS; died _____
	258. James Tilden	born April 1879 Westford , NY; died 4 Dec 1955 Kern, CA
	259. Tyler	born 18 Sept 1880 Maryland, Otsego, NY; died 27 March 1952 NY 1 married Bessie BROWNELL ca 1904 Otsego County, NY (she born ca 1877; died 1906)
		Child: Eloise-[7] CONGDON born ca 1905; died 1990 2 married Minnie Belle HUYCK (she born ca 1876; died 1946)
	260. Mary Louise	born 2 Dec 1883 NY; died ____;
	261. Leland John	born June 1887 NY; died 12 April 1945 married Ethel B. SOUTHERN
		Child: Mattie E-[7] CONGDON born ca 1905 NY
	262. Schuyler Ellsworth	born 1 Dec 1895 NY; died 1 Feb 1897 NY EOL

97. BURDETTE[5] **CONGDON,** brother of above, was born ca 1855 PA. he married Kate/ Catherine O'SHEA ca ____. She was the daughter of ____ O'SHEA and ____, and was born ca 1862 NY; died ____According to the 1920 Federal Census for Elmira, Chemung Co., NY , they were both still living 1920).

Children of Burdette-[5] CONGDON and Kate O'SHEA:
Surname **CONGDON**

263. Claude	born ca 1879; died 1899	
264. Bennie	born ca 1880; died 1885	
265. Gertrude	born ca 1882; died ____	
266. Burdette Lloyd	born 19 Sept 1884 NY; died ____ he was a Lt. in the Elmira (NY) Fire Dept.	
	married Elizabeth D. ____ca ____	

Children: E. Rita-[7] born ca 1915 NY; and Joseph L-[7] CONGDON born ca 1917/18

98. EDWIN EDGAR[5] **CONGDON,** brother of above, was born April 1857 South Creek Twsp, Bradford County, PA. He married Ella RUGGLES ca 1879. She was the daughter of ____ RUGGLES and Melissa ____; and was born July 1857, died ____. Edwin Edgar-[5] CONGDON died 1930.

Children of Edwin Edgar-[5] CONGDON and Ella RUGGLES:
Surname **CONGDON**

267. Earl H.	born 26 Sept 1880 PA; died June 1971 St. Charles, MO.
	1 married Mamie D. SAWDEY ca 1902
	(she born ca 1883; died 1956)

Children: Edgar Fayette-[7] born ca 1906; died 1990; and Eloise-[7] CONGDON born ca 1914; died 1929

	2 married Evelyn CHAUNCEY (she born 1896; died 1989)
268. Lynn	born 14 August 1884 So. Creek Twsp, Bradford Co., PA
	married Belle Voorhees OLDROYD ca 1914

Child: Edith Belle-[7] CONGDON born ca 1915-16 Gillett, PA

269. Ray	born July 1885 PA; died ____
+ **270. BERT JAMES**	born March 1888 PA; died 1974
	married Edna ____ (she born ca 1888; died ____)
271. Blanche	born January 1895 Bradford Co., PA; died ___
	married A. Raymond DOUGLAS ca 1921

Children: James H-[7] born ca 1922 and Lynn R-[7] DOUGLAS born ca 1926

+ **272. HAZEL**	born 27 Sept 1897/ 98; died July 1980 Elmira, NY
	married Lewis Edward DIX ca 1921
	(he born 6 Nov 1895 Tioga, PA; died 14 Dec 1971 Elmira, Chenango, NY)
	(he s/o Charles E. DIX and Dora M. ____)

103. MILTON D[5] **COVERT,** son of Erastus[4] COVERT (Jemima-[3] KIFF; Andrew[2]; George[1]) and Delight Delia CASE, and was born ca 1858 PA; died ____, IL. He married Sarah Elizabeth FISH ca 1875. She was the daughter of ____ FISH and ____, and was born ca 1857 PA; died ____.

Children of Milton-[5] COVERT and Delight Delia CASE:
Surname **COVERT**

273. Bertha	born April 1879 PA; died ____; married Joseph BRADLEY
	(he born May 1878 England; died ____)

Children: Richard-[7] and Robert-[7] BRADLEY (twins) born ca 1904 NY

+ **274. CHARLES . MONROE**	born 26 Jan 1883 Bradford, Co., PA; died June 1957 married Harriet Frances SEARS
275. Josephine	born ca 1890 IL; died ____
+ **276. HARRY W.**	born 22 Feb 1894 IL; married Cora SHIPE ; died Oct 1965
277. Myrtle	born ca 1897 IL; died ____

Children of Milton-⁵ COVERT and Delight Delia CASE, continued:
Surname **COVERT**

      278. Herbert " Bertie "   born 1 April 1906 IL; died Aug 1974
                            married Sara / Sadie B._____ ca ___ ; (she born ca 1911 IL; died _____)
                    Child: Herbert-⁷ COVERT, Jr. born ca 1930 IL

108. IDA S-⁵ KINCH, daughter of Esther-⁴ COVERT (Jemima-³ KIFF; Andrew-²; George-¹) and William KINCH, was born November 1860 at _____Delaware County, NY. She married Freeman W. BAILEY ca 1885 Canton, Bradford, PA. PA. He was the son of Warren BAILEY and Rachael AVERY, and was born March 1861 PA; died Sept 1938 at Canton, PA. Ida S-⁵ KINCH died ca 1932 , They are buried at Alba Cemetery, Bradford, PA

Children of Ida S-⁵ KINCH and Freeman BAILEY:
Surname **BAILEY**

+   **279. HERBERT LEE**   born 11 Aug 1886 PA; died July 1967 Canton, PA
                            married Eva J. MC GUINNIS ca _____; (she born Feb 1892; died 1971)

+   **280. ESTHER G.**   born October 1894 PA; died October 1971 Cleveland, OH
                            married Martin Wiltsie RODIER ca ____
                            (he s/o Albert E. RODIER and Naomi VALE)
                            (he born 26 June 1891 PA; died 1944 PA)

114. STANLEY WILLIAM-⁵ LYON, brother of above, was born ca 1840 PA; died ca 1910. He married Laura MORGAN ca ____. She was the daughter of Dewitt / Dwight MORGAN and Clarinda WOOD ***, and was born 29 July 1854; died 20 Aug 1942. She married second to Colson STONE.

Children of Stanley William-⁵ LYON and Laura MORGAN:
Surname **LYON**

      281. Lewis D.   born 15 Dec 1873 Bradford Co., PA; died 13 Jan 1964 Rochester, Monroe, NY
+   **282. WALTER E.**   born 14 Jan 1881 Towanda, Bradford, PA; died 31 July 1959 Eagles Mere, PA
                          married Irene Montgomery RILEY 11 July 1934
                          (she born 3 Dec 1880; died 7 Nov 1967 Eagles Mere, PA) (Ref. Obituary)
      283. Ralph   born 1885 PA; died _____

*** Dwight MORGAN was born 8 June 1816; died 3 August 1888. His wife, Clarinda WOOD was born 15 April 1829; died 10 Sept 1888. They are buried at the Beckers Corners Cemetery, Tioga County, PA

115. FESTUS WATSON-⁵ LYON, brother of above, was born ca 1842 PA. He married Virginia " Jennie " ____ ca _____. She was born ca 1849 PA; died ____. Festus W., LYON enlisted in the Civil War, and served as a Private in Company D, 132ⁿᵈ PA. Infantry from 13 Aug 1862 until 29 May 1862. He died 19 April 1902 and is buried at Woodlawn National Cemetery, Elmira, NY.

Children of Festus Watson-⁵ LYON and Jennie _____:
Surname **LYON**

284. Stanley	born ca 1867 PA	287. Guy	born May 1876 PA
285. Willie	born ca 1870 PA	288. Nellie	born May 1879 PA
286. Robert	born ca 1872 PA	289. Lulu	born Aug 1882 PA

118. CHARLES THEODORE-⁵ LYON, son of James-⁴ LYON (Jemima-³ KIFF; Andrew-² : George-¹) and Calista FIELD, was born July 1838 at _____, PA. He married Polly Lorinda COWAN ca 1863 at ____. She was the daughter of _____ COWAN and _____, and was born Sept 1842 ; died ____.

According to the Federal Census they had 6 children, but this researcher has only found 4 of them.

KIFF
The Fifth American Generation

Children of Charles T.-5 LYON and Polly Lorinda COWAN:
Surname **LYON**

290. Nellie E.   born ca 1869 PA; died ____; married William B. NICOL ca 1900
Child: Genevieve E-7 NICOL born ca 1902 Buffalo, Erie County, NY

291. Herbert D / O.   born ca 1873 PA; died ____; married Susan M. _____ ca 1898
(she born ca 1877 NY; died _____)

292. Emery John   born April 1882 PA; died ____; he a glass cutter in Elmira, Chemung, NY 1910
married Lina M. _____ ca 19__
Child: Randolph-7 LYON born ca 1908 NY

293. Claude Charles   born 12 May 1885; died 22 Oct 1966 Troy, Bradford, PA.
married Louise Lydia KANT ca 19__ (resided Wisconsin)
(she born 3 Dec 1898 ; died 20 Feb 1988 Troy, PA)
(she dau/o Frederick William KANT and Pauline SCHOSCHNICK)

120. JOHN H-5 LYON, brother of above, was born June 1846 at _____, PA. He married Rosanna NEWELL ca 1869. She was born March 1852 MD; died _____ PA. John H-5 LYON, a Pvt. In Co. K, 50th New York Engineers during the Civil War, died 13 July 1922 at the US National Home for Disabled Veterans in Hampton, VA.

Children of John H-5 LYON and Rosanna NEWELL:
Surname **LYON**

+ **294. RHODA BELL**   born 1 April 1870; died 25 Aug 1950 Sayre. PA
married Thomas Leroy KINCH ca 1887
(he s/o Thomas KINCH and Sarah Jane CEASE)
(he born May 1860 Westford, Otsego, NY; died 8 June 1942 Troy, PA)

+ **295. LAYTON ROMAIN**   born 29 May 1873 PA; died 26 Aug 1952
married Lillie May SHERMAN 3 June 1894 Armenia, PA
(she born 17 Jan 1870 Troy, PA; died 5 Mar 1952 Troy, PA)
(she dau/o Simeon Leonard SHERMAN and Emma Josephine FIELD)

296. Harry Leonard   born 18 Nov 1876 Tioga, PA; died ____
married Mary ECKROYD ca ____
Children: Richard E-7 born ca 1916, and James M-7 LYON born ca 1917-18 PA)

297. Caroline C.   born June 1881 PA; died ____

298. Mason Leon   born 11 Nov 1884; died 16 April 1960
married Mabel A. PATTERSON ; (she born ca 1889; died 1978)
Child: Marian-7 LYON born July1909; died 1968

122. HIRAM-5 LYON, brother of above, was born 22 April 1853 PA. He married Fanny M. DEWEY on 1 January 1877 at _____. She was the daughter of Walter DEWEY and Cynthia WELCH, and was born 5 November 1860; died _____. Hiram-5 LYON died 8 Dec 1927.

Children of Hiram-5 LYON and Fanny DEWEY:
Surname **LYON**

+ **299. EDWARD ROY**   born 3 May 1878 PA ; died _____
married Helen CLARK 23 Nov 1910 (she dau/o ____ CLARK and _____)
(she born 12 June 1886; died _____)

+ **300. COLA WALTER**   born 23 Nov 1880; died 1937; he was an attorney
married Harriet -6 COVERT 26 March 1902 (#246)
(she dau/o George L.5 COVERT and Mary J. MERRIAM)
(she born 1 March 1883; died _____) resided Orchard Park, NY

301. Maude   born 30 Sept 1886; died _____unmarried; English teacher   EOL

302. Bessie   born 21 Sep 1888; died ____; married Burke Edmund CAREY 7 April 1936
(he s/o Joseph CAREY and Lavina TRASK)
(he born 7 April 1886 Fox, Sullivan, PA; died July 1970 Troy, PA)

124. CELESTIA ANTOINETTE[-5] CLEVELAND, daughter of Mary[-4] LYON (Phebe[-3] KIFF; Andrew[-2]; George-[1]) and Festus CLEVELAND, was born 15 Nov 1841 at Troy, Bradford, PA. She married William Benson OWEN on 22 January 1861. He was the son of Francis OWEN (born KY) and Elizabeth ____, and was born 24 January 1826 Winchester, Clark, KY; died ___ (before 1910). Celestia-[5] CLEVELAND died ____

Children of Celestia-[5] CLEVELAND and William Benson OWEN:
Surname **OWEN**   (all children born Frankfort, Will Co., Illinois)
    303. Marie Antoinette   born 24 April 1862; died 29 Dec 1894 Chicago, IL
                                     married David PALMER 14 Aug 1888 Mokena, IL
                                     (he born 7 Jan 1860 Vandalia, IL; died _____)
                                     (he s/o David PALMER and Katherine HICKEY)
        Children: Marguerite-[7] born 17 June 1889 Chicago; and Antoinette-[7] PALMER born 16 June 1890 Chicago, IL
    304. Cora Lincoln   born 8 Nov 1864
    305. Frances Belle   born 15 Oct 1866
    306. Grace Evaline   born 16 Aug 1870
    307. James William   born 22 March 1872; died Oct 1966 IL.
                                     married Alice Belle STORM ca _____   (she born ca 1875 IL)
        Child: Eunice-[7] OWEN born ca 1902 IL
+   **308. WILLARD**   born 16 March 1874 ; died 31 Jan 1928 Frankfurt, IL
        CLINTON   married Alice RAHM (she born ca 1877; died ____)
    309. Festus Edward   born 3 Dec 1877; died _____ (taught at the University of So. Calif.)
                                     married Daisy Ida ANDREWS 6 July 1904 Idaho
                                     (she born 16 Oct 1878; died 12 Nov 1948)
        Children: Wright E-[7] born 2 Mar 1913 CA, died Dec 1967; and Mary J-[7] OWEN born ca 1918
+   **310. ARTHUR**   born 23 March 1881 IL; died 30 Aug 1930
        CLEVELAND   married Evelyn Isabelle HAMMOND 2 June 1905
                                     (she born 19 Sep 1881 IL; died 20 Nov 1920)

127. JOSIAH FRANCIS[-5] CLEVELAND, brother of above, was born 18 June 1847 at Masonville, Delaware County, New York. He married first to Electa Garrison PRICE 2 Nov 1869 at Newark, Union County, New Jersey. She was the daughter of ___ PRICE and ____, and was born 2 Oct 1847 Newark, NJ; died 29 Jan 1872 Newark, NJ. He married 2nd to Mary Elizabeth FRISBEE on 25 Sept 1873 at Chicago, IL. She was the daughter of Augustus FRISBIE / FRISBEE and Hannah LACKLORE, and was born 20 May 1845 Little Falls, Herkimer, NY; died 8 May 1901. Josiah-[5] CLEVELAND died ____.

Child of Josiah-[5] CLEVELAND and Electa PRICE:
Surname **CLEVELAND**
    311. Festus Arthur   born 18 Feb 1871 Waukegan, IL; died 8 Feb 1880 Chicago, IL   EOL

Children of Josiah-[5] CLEVELAND and Mary Elizabeth FRISBEE:
Surname **CLEVELAND**
+   **312. AUGUSTUS**   born 19 Sept 1874 Chicago, Cook, IL; died
        FRISBEE   married Neira HATCHER ca 1899 (she born Jan 1878 OH)
    313. Eva May   born 22 June 1877 Chicago; died ____

+   **314. JOSIAH**   born 31 July 1882 Oak Park, IL; died 11 Oct 1948 Dallas, TX
        JUDSON   married Grace E. CARR   (she born Oct 1880 IL; died 1968)
                      (she dau/o Robert F. CARR and Emily Ann SMICK)

128. FESTUS WANDBY[-5] CLEVELAND, brother of above, was born 19 November 1849 at Masonville, NY. He married Edith Clementine WILLIAMS on 24 November 1875 at Chicago, IL. She was the daughter of ____ WILLIAMS and Elizabeth K.. ____, and was born 12 Oct 1853 Masonville, NY died ____. Festus-[5] died _____.

Children of Festus- W-⁵ CLEVELAND and Edith WILLIAMS:
Surname **CLEVELAND:**

	315. Winifred	born Sept 1876 IL; died 1965; married poss. Albert Alanson LANE
+	**316. PAUL**	born 24 Dec 1878 Oak Park, IL; died ____
	WILLIAMS	married Mary L. SPRING 4 Dec 1910

(she dau/o Sylvester O. SPRING and Anna F. ____)
(she born ca 1880 IL; died ____) (Child: Cynthia-⁷ CLEVELAND born ca 1919 IL)
Reference: Herringshaw's Blue Book of Biography, Page 102; Genealogy of the Cleveland & Cleaveland Families, CT. 1889

	317. Gertrude Isabel	born 14 July 1886 IL; died July 1887 IL.
		married Hayworth Perley BEARD ca ____

(he s/o George Anderson BEARD and Millie Blanche HAYWORTH)
(he born 24 Jan 1895 Vigo Co., Indiana; died 28 Feb 1945 Cook Co., IL)

135. LOIS OPHELIA-⁵ HAGAR, daughter of Sarah-⁴ LYON (Phebe-³ KIFF; Andrew-²; George-¹) and Daniel HAGAR, was born 8 November 1845 at Canton, Bradford County, PA. She married first to Louis Neipling GETSINGER (as his 2ⁿᵈ wife) ca 1865. He was the son of Anthony GETSINGER and Elizabeth ____, and was born ca 1832 NJ; died Feb 1875. Louis GETSINGER was married 1ˢᵗ to Sylpha ____ (born ca 1843 PA ; died before 1865)

From his 1ˢᵗ marriage, Louis GETSINGER had two daughters – Janette born ca 1858 NJ; and Mary E. born 3 Mar 1860 NJ. In 1860 he resided at Maurice River Twsp. Cumberland County, New Jersey. Lois-⁵ HAGAR married second to William Franklin DAVIDS on 8 November 1877 at Pittsburgh, PA. He was the son of ____ DAVIDS, and was born 3 June 1852 Redwood, NY; died 5 Jan 1928 at Akron, Ohio. Lois-⁵ HAGAR died ca 1917 at Kane Borough , McKean, PA.

Children of Lois Ophelia-⁵ HAGAR and Louis GETSINGER:
Surname **GETSINGER**   (listed as **DAVIDS** on the 1880 Census for Pittsburgh, PA)

	318. Josephine	born 9 July 1865 PA; died ____; (found no info on her after 1880)	
+	**319. RUTH ANN**	born 3/9 Jan 1869 PA; died 25 April 1922	
		married William Orlando TISDALL	+
	320. LOUIS	born 4 March 1870 PA; died 16 April 1946 Staunton, VA.	
	CHESSROWN	married Kathryn A. FABER 30 June 1898 PA	
		(she dau/o Louis Charles FABER and Marian G. SCHILLING)	
		(she born 17 Sep 1866 PA; died 3 Sep 1940 PA)	
	321. Kate / Catherine	born 12 Jan 1873; died ____	

Note: According to the PA. Soldier's Orphan's School, North Union, Fayette Co., PA (page 316) the four GETSINGER children (above) were placed there, ca March/ Apr 1875, after their father had died. They were still residing there when the 1880 Census was taken.

Children of Lois Ophelia-⁵ HAGAR and William Franklin DAVIDS:
Surname **DAVIDS**

	322. Ettie	born ca 1878-79 Pittsburgh PA; died 1900	EOL
	323. Jesse	born April 1880 PA; died 1900	EOL
+	**324. SAMUEL**	born April 1882 PA; died ____	
	PENN	married Cora WISE ca 1903; divorced ____ (she born Nov 1881 NY)	
		(she dau/o William WISE and Nancy Miranda CARRIER)	
	325. William F. Jr.	born 12 May 1883 PA; died ____ ; married Minnie May ____	
+	**326. ROBERT**	born 6 March 1887 PA; died June 1965 MD; he was a Clergyman	
	BREWSTER	married Isabell ____ ca 1906 (she born ca 1881 England)	
+	**327. CHARLES**	born 28 Jan 1889 OH; died Apr 1967 OH	
	PEARCE	married Julia Lucy KLINK 4 May 1912	

136. EMMA AMELIA[-5] **HAGAR** , sister of above, was born 21 January 1848 at Bradford County, PA. She married George Henry MASON ca ____ . He was the son of George MASON and _____, and was born ca 1839; died ____ .

Children of Emma[-5] HAGAR and George H. MASON
Surname **MASON**

328. Laura Emma	born June 1869; died ____	
	married Augustus Morris OWEN (as his 2nd wife) Aug 1895	
	(he born Sept 1843; died before 9 Jan 1893) (Civil War veteran)	
329. Daniel J.	born Dec 1872; died ____ ; married Jesse ____ resided Elmira, NY	
	Child: Helen C-[7] MASON born Sept 1899 NY	
330. Henry <u>Forrest</u>	born 3 July 1877 PA; married Rachel A. _____	
331. Archie B.	born ca 1882 PA; died ____ ; married Mary B. ____	
	Children: Harold E-[7] born ca 1905 PA; and Florence M-[7] MASON born ca 1915 NY	

137. EVALINA LAVENCIE-[5] **HAGAR,** sister of above, was born 20 July 1850 at Troy, Bradford County, PA. She married George Park BATEMAN 29 July 1867 at ____ , PA. He was the son of George B. BATEMAN and Eliza SAUNDERS, and was born 21 Jan 1845 Pontypool, Monmouthshire, Wales; died 2 April 1916 Sheridan, Wyoming. Evalina-[5] HAGAR died 1 April 1929.

Children of Evalina Lavencie-[5] HAGAR and George " Park " BATEMAN:
Surname **BATEMAN**

332. George Ellsworth	born 14 Jan 1869 OH; died 4 Dec 1940 WY; married Ella Ann GREENE	
	Children: Eva-[7] born ca 1890 and Ellsworth-[7] BATEMAN born ca 1893	
333. Frank Daniel	born 23 Nov 1870; died 6 Sept 1872	EOL
334. Burton Emery	born 28 Dec 1872 Wisconsico, PA; died 12 April 1960 Sheridan, WY	
	married Eva Jane KENLY 1897 Weston, WY(she born ca 1877)	
335. Daniel Merritt	born 20 Sept 1874; died 26 July 1954, resided Washington	
	married Minnie Mae LOEHR	
+ **336. ANDREW**	born 20 Aug 1876 McIntyre, PA; died 4 Dec 1970 Blossburg, PA	
PARKER "PARK"	married Martha EDDINGS 14 Feb 1901	
	(she born 22 Sept 1881; died Oct 1975 Blossburg, PA)	
337. Sadie Eliza	born 29 Aug 1880; died 26 Sept 1881	EOL
338. Weldon Roy	born 1 April 1882; died 1 June 1958 Kent, WA	
339. Cora Ann	born 18 Jan 1884 PA; died 4 Sept 1884 PA	EOL
+ **340. MARTHA**	born 2 Feb 1885; died 1 Jan 1977 WA.	
PEARL	married Hugh Bruno OELKE; (he born 6 Sept 1876 Germany)	
341. Flora Jennie	born 9 Aug1888 IA; died 1 Jan1919 WY	
342. Arthur Willard	born 6 Feb 1892 NE; died 29 April 1924 WY	
	married Ethel Pearl BECKELSHYMER	
	Children: Maurice-[7] born 1913, died 1998, and Ellsworth Willard-[7] BATEMAN born ca 1915,died 1985	
+ **343. LULA BELLE**	born 29 April 1893 NE; died 23 July 1970 WA	
	married Dee Eanos GARRETT	

140. ROSA BELLE-[5] **HAGAR,** sister of above, was born 15 July 1855 at Bradford County, PA. She married Wilson Charles HILL 11 Jan 1874, PA. He was the son of Osborn M. HILL and Harriette E. BARRETT, and was born 4 March 1851; died 30 Dec 1930. Rosa Belle-[5] HAGAR died 30 March 1940. They are buried at Windfall Cemetery, Canton, PA

Children of Rosa Belle-[5] HAGAR and Wilson HILL:
Surname **HILL**

344. Edith	born ca ____ Ward, Tioga, PA	

Children of Rosa Belle-5 HAGAR and Wilson Charles HILL, continued:
Surname **HILL**

345. Charles Arthur	born 13 August 1875 Ward, PA; died 13 Dec 1954 Canton, Bradford, PA married Grace J. SEGAR /SEGUR	

Children: Ada B-[7] born ca 1899 and Arthur C-[7] HILL born ca 1903 PA

+ **346. EDNA IVA** born 8 May 1882 Ward, PA; died 5 Nov 1958 Canton, PA
married Henry Rothland WILCOX 10 Jan 1900
(he born 19 May 1857 Troy, PA; died 9 Nov 1948 Sayre, PA)

347. James Lowell born 20 Oct 1884 Ward, PA; died 29 Aug 1963 Troy, Bradford, PA
married Sarah Ida BURLINGAME 19 Sept 1906
(she born 10 Dec 1886 East Smithfield, PA; died 5 Dec 1970 Cape May, NJ)

Children: Ida Burdella-[7] born ca 1908, died 1991; and Wilson-[7] HILL born ca 1912 PA

348. Hollis Emery born 12 March 1891 Ward, Pa; died 2 Sept 1956 Canton, Bradford, PA
married Helen Myra SMITH 28 August 1915 Sayre, Bradford, PA
(she born 8 Jan 1897; died 5 Nov 1962 Canton, PA)

140. JOHN LYON-[5] HAGAR, brother of above, was born 28 September 1857 Ward, Tioga County, PA. He married Sarah Millard SHAW on 4 July 1878, PA. She was the daughter of Daniel Merrill SHAW and Jane SEAMAN, and was born 11 March 1855 at Sullivan Twsp, PA; died 1929. John Lyon-[5] HAGAR died 1923.

Children of John L-[5] HAGAR and Sarah SHAW:
Surname **HAGAR**

+ **349. CLAUDE** born 30 May 1879 Tioga, PA; died 1952 Mansfield, PA
 LYLE married Jennie Ethel BLY 1 Jan 1906
(she born 30 Oct 1881 PA; died 1959 Mansfield, PA)
(she dau/o Edgar Milton BLY and Vina Lucy LUCE)

350. Ora May born 28 April 1882 PA; died 1 July 1938 Mansfield, PA EOL
married Norman Jay BLY 14 Feb 1906; (he brother of Jennie BLY above)
(he born 1878; died 4 March 1957 Mansfield PA)

351. Sarah Jane born 21 Dec 1883 Tioga Co., PA; died 14 Dec 1930; unmarried EOL

352. Freeman Stanley born 20 Feb 1886 Tioga Co., PA; died 6 May 1916

143. FLORA D-[5] HAGAR, sister of above, was born 20 December1863 at _____ Tioga County, PA. She married James T. CORNISH, a tinsmith, ca _____. He was the s/o Alonzo CORNISH and Gladys N. _____, and was born 7 June 1857 at _____, England; died ____.

Children of Flora-[5] HAGAR and James T. CORNISH:
Surname **CORNISH**

353. William born 12 March 1881; died ___; married Lida L. _____ before 1918

Children: Glenn -[7] born ca 1903; and Gladys N-[7] CORNISH

354. Lulu G. born April 1883 PA; married Ira Harvey CRAYTON ca 1901
(he born ca 1874; died 1944)

Children: Lester-[7] born ca 1905 MA; and Willard-[7] CRAYTON born ca 1915 MA

**** 355. Grube Burdette born 19 Aug 1890 Punxautawney, PA; died 2 Jan 1950 Portland, Maine
married Susan Maria COLBY 23 June 1909 NH.
(she born 11 April 1889 NH; died 13 Jan 1963 Maine)

Children: Laura Elaine-[7] born 25 July 1910 NH, died 26 Nov 1910 NH; and Eleanor Marion-[7] CORNISH born 13 Nov 1920 York, ME

356. Ella V. born Aug 1892-93

Note: on the 1910 Census, it states there were 6 children born to this family, with only four living.

**** Grube Burdette CORNISH , was a Methodist minister. In 1909 he, and his wife, went to the Ozarks where he was a circuit rider preacher for the Methodist Episcopal Church. In those days, churches could not support a full-time preacher. One preacher served several churches, having to ride horseback to conduct services each Sabbath day, thus they became known as "circuit riders ". He was a pastor at numerous churches in Maine over his career. During WW 1 he served as a Chaplain, assigned overseas to the 5th Division, Trains and Headquarters from Feb 1918 to July 1919. In 1920 he joined the Maine National Guard, 103rd Infantry and served as a Chaplain there until 1935. He is listed in the Roster of Maine in the Military Service of the US and Allies in World War 1917-1919.

145. EMERSON JOHN-5 CLEVELAND, son of Nancy-4 LYON (Jemima-3 KIFF; Andrew-2; George-1) and Dr. John Emory CLEVELAND, was born 7 July 1856 at Masonville, Delaware County, NY. He married Jennie Florence ELLIOTT on 16 July 1884 at Canton, Bradford Co., PA. She was the daughter of Francis ELLIOTT and Elizabeth W. DAVIES, and was born Oct 1859 Canton, PA. Emerson-5 CLEVELAND, an attorney, died ca 1922.

Children of Emerson-5 CLEVELAND and Jennie ELLIOTT:
Surname **CLEVELAND**

357. Florence Jean	born 3 May 1885 Canton, PA; died ____
	married Dr. Tracy Beadle STURDEVANT 26 Oct 1912
	(he s/o Lewis Jones STURDEVANT and Harriet " Hattie" ROBERTS)
	(he born 8 Feb 1886; died 27 Dec 1955) (he was a dental surgeon)
358. Eloise Virginia	born 19 Feb 1887 Canton, PA; died _____

150. VANCE MARQUIS-5 SMITH, son of Harriet-4 LYON (Phebe-3 KIFF; Andrew-2, George-1) and Seymour SMITH, was born Sep 1862 at ____, NY. He married Ida M.____ ca 1884. She was the daughter of ____ and ____, and was born Nov 1865 NY; died ____. Vance-5 SMITH, a stock broker in Boston, died _____.

Children of Vance Marquis-5 SMITH and Ida M. _____
Surname **SMITH**

+	**359. HAROLD TAYLOR NIVEN**	born 15 Nov 1889 Brooklyn, NY; died Dec 1975 Brockton, MA married Ruth E. HARRIS ca _____ (she born ca 1891 MA; died _____)
	360. Marquis Seymour	born 13 Nov 1891 Springfield, MA; died _____ married Edith B. ____ ca 1916 (she born ca 1893 MA; died ____)

Children: Patricia C-7 born ca 1918; Constance V-7 born ca 1919; and Robert L-7 SMITH born 30 July 1920

154. FRANK LEROY-5 LYON, son of Mason Leroy-4 LYON (Phebe-3 KIFF; Andrew-2; George-1) and Hannah SCHIEFFELIN, was born 6 October 1863 at Bradford County, PA. He married Mary CAHILL ca ____. She was the daughter of ____ CAHILL and ____, and was born ____, died 30 Aug 1946. Frank-5 LYON died 2 April 1914.

Children of Frank Leroy-5 LYON and Mary CAHILL;
Surname **LYON**

+	**361. LOTTA STATIA**	born 21 July 1891 IL; died March 1988; married George Spencer LYMAN
+	**362. PAUL LEROY**	born 29 July 1893; died 6 March 1953 IL; married Cecile PRANTLE

155. SAMUEL MASON-5 LYON, brother of above, was born 19 March 1868 at Susquehanna, PA. He married Wilhelmina " Minnie " Christina SCHROEDER on 17 July 1890 at Freeport, Stephenson, IL. She was the daughter of _____ SCHROEDER and _____, and was born 6 October 1870 Freeport, IL; died 31 Dec 1949 at Los Angeles, CA. Samuel-5 LYON died 18 January 1946 at Los Angeles, CA

Children of Samuel-5 LYON and Minnie SCHROEDER:
Surname **LYON**

+	**363. LEROY MASON**	born 8 Feb 1891 Rockford, IL; died 31 Aug 1986 Freeport, IL
		1 married Orelda Grace REEDER 10 March 1910 Freeport, IL
		(she born 5 Feb 1894 Freeport, IL; died 18 Dec 1986 Freeport, IL)
		2 married Della GIBBON 19 Oct 1937 La Porte, Indiana
		(she born 18 Aug 1894; died 23 Dec 1984 Freeport, IL)

Children of Samuel-[5] LYON and Minnie SCHROEDER, continued:
Surname **LYON**

+ **364. RUTH**   born 8 Aug 1893 Freeport , IL; died 9 March 1974 Freeport, IL
      VICTORIA   married Guy Harry MYERS 22 Dec 1915 Freeport, IL
          (he born ca 1893 Sterling ,IL; died ca 1928 Texarkana, Bowie, TX)

+ **365. EDYTHE**   born 10 March 1895 WI; died 7 Aug 1988 WI
      HENRIETTA   married Elmer G. SOMMER 17 Jan 1919 Waukegan, Lake , IL
          (he born 9 Oct 1897 Milwaukee, W ; died 11 Aug 1992 Venice, FL)

+ **366. CARL DEWEY**   born 21 April 1898,Polo, IL; died 6 Aug 1968 Jasper, Arkansas

          married Hilda Frederica Maria SCHULTZ 16 Oct 1920 La Porte, Indiana
          (she dau/o William SCHULTZ and _____)
          (she born 16 Apr 1898 La Porte, IN; died 10 Dec 1954 Freeport, IL

367. Mary Louise   born 4 July 1901 IL; died October 1980 Savanna, IL
          married Alfred A. JUNG (he born ca 1893 IL)

368. Helen Marjorie   born 15 Feb 1904 IL; died 27 Dec 1979 Great Lakes, IL
          married Gordon D. KENDALL
          (he born 13 April 1901 IL; died 21 Sept 1977 Ventura, CA)
              Child: Nancy Lou-[7] KENDALL born ca 1939

369. Lois Dorothy   born 29 Oct 1905 IL; died Dec 1979 Burbank, CA
          1 married Ted C. MILLER; 2 married Clarence NELSON
          3 married Harry MARSDEN

+ **370. DONALD**   born 14 Feb 1908 Freeport, IL; died _____
      EDWARD   married Helen Elizabeth VAN DEEST 15 June 1929 Redding, CA
          (she born 22 Nov 1910 Freeport, IL; died 21 April 1974 West Allis, WI.

157. WILLIAM FESTUS-[5] **LYON,** brother of above, was born 7 April 1871 ____, PA. He married Mabelle O'KANE ca ____. She was the daughter of _____ O'KANE and ____, and was born ca 1877; died Oct 1938 at Los Angeles, Ca. William-[5] LYON died 7 July 1941 at Los Angeles CA.

Children of William Festus-[5] LYON and Mabelle O'KANE:
Surname **LYON**

371. William Joseph   born 24 June 1913; died ____
372. Jeanette   born 22 Dec 1919; died ____
          married John Wilson SHERWOOD 25 Feb 1941
          (he s/o Joseph Richard SHERWOOD and Josephine Antoinette ARNOLD)
          (he born 10 Oct 1912 Cook Co., IL; died 12 Apr 1995 FL)

158. HARRIET-[5] **PUTNAM,** daughter of Harriet-[4] KIFF (Lyman-[3]; Andrew-[2]; George-[1]) and Jerome Henry PUTNAM, was born 6 March 1831 Delaware County, NY. She married Lewis W. MILLS ca ____. He was the son of Levi MILLS and Mary RIKELDIFER, and was born ca 1831 PA; died ____. Harriet-[5] PUTNAM died ca 1892.

Child of Harriet-[5] PUTNAM and Lewis MILLS:
Surname **MILLS**

+ **373. JEANETTE**   born ca 1853 PA; died ca 1892
          married John S. DIETRICH (born ca 1831; died ca 1892)
374. Martin   born ca 1858 PA; died ____
          married Bella _____ ca 1884 (she born ca 1862 PA)
375. Artie (f)   born ca 1860 PA   376. George W.   born ca 1878 PA

The Fifth American Generation

160. JEROME HENRY[-5] **PUTNAM, Jr.** ,brother of above, was born ca 1837 NY. He married Elizabeth _____ ca 185_. She was born ca 1840 PA; died ___ . Jerome H-[5] PUTNAM died ____ .

Children of Jerome H-[5] PUTNAM, Jr. and Elizabeth ____ :
Surname **PUTNAM**

377. William	born ca 1861 PA; died _____		
378. Abraham	born ca 1865 PA; died _____; married Addie ____; he was a coal miner		
379. Ida	born ca 1868 PA	381. Jessie	born ca 1872 PA
380. Grace	born ca 1870 PA	382. Flora	born ca 1875 PA

163. VIALL A[-5] **PUTNAM,** brother of above, was born July 1845 at _____ . He married Bertha BURGIN ca 1888. She was the daughter of John Jacob BURGIN and Jacobea RUDIN, and was born 10 Oct 1855 Switzerland; died 8 Mar 1928. Viall-[5] PUTNAM died ____ . According to the 1900 Census they resided at Wellsboro, PA. Viall-[5] PUTNAM was a Private in Company G, 58th PA Infantry Regiment during the Civil War , having enlisted on 20 Feb 1862. Reference: History of PA Volunteers 1861-65

Children of Viall-[5] PUTNAM and Bertha BURGIN:
Surname **PUTNAM**

383. Nadine	born Feb 1890 IN	384. Minnie H.	born Oct 1892 IN
385. Allen Jerome	born 6 Aug 1893 PA; died 19 June 1953 Big Flats, Chemung, NY		
	married Catherine ABBOTT (she born ca 1899; died ____)		

Child: Abbott-[7] PUTNAM born ca 1920; died 2008

170. DAVID K[-5] **KIFF,** son of Samuel[-4] KIFF (Lyman[-3]; Andrew-[2;] George-1) and Susan KENYON, was born July 1848, PA. He married Clara Delilah GOODSELL ca 1871. She was the daughter of George GOODSELL and Olive HENDRICK, and was born 5 Aug 1854 NY; died 20 May 1935. David-[5] KIFF died 22 Jan 1909. David KIFF was in business with his son Arthur (KIFF & Son) in Corning, NY. City Directory described their shop as having bicycles, sundries and a repair shop .

Children of DAVID-[5] KIFF and Clara GOODSELL:
Surname **KIFF**

386. Archer	born ca 1873; died 1873
387. Arthur L.	born 13 April 1874; died 13 Aug 1947
	married Nellie M. _____ (she born ca 1877)

Child: Frank B.-[7] KIFF born 5 Dec 1900 NY; died Jan 1980 NY; married Virginia ____

388. May B.	born Jan 1882; died _____
389. Lelia / Lola	born Dec 1888 NY ; married George H. GRIMER (he born ca 1882)

Child: Lelia-[7] GRIMER born ca 1916 NY

171. PHEBE[-5] **KIFF,** sister of above, was born ca 1852 _____ , PA. She married Thomas Wilson PATCHEN before 1878. He was the son of Ira PATCHEN and Christiana PUTNAM, and was born 5 April 1852; died 25 Dec 1912. Phebe-[5] KIFF died ca 1909.

Children of Phebe-[5] KIFF and Thomas Wilson PATCHEN:
Surname **PATCHEN**   (all children born Covington, Tioga, PA)

	390. Lulu/Lula Inez	born 19 Mar 1878 PA ; died ____; married Harry E. WHEELER 24 Dec 1902
+	**391. FRANCES**	born 7 Dec 1879 PA; died 2 May 1963 NC
	ISABELLE	married Charles Henry WERLINE 30 July 1902
+	**392. PURLEY IRA**	born 15 Aug 1881 PA died 10 Jan 1958 Toledo, OH
		married Nellie Ada STONE

Children of Phebe-5 KIFF and Thomas Wil;son PATCHEN, continued
Surname **PATCHEN**

+	**393. MELVINA**	born 20 Jan 1884 PA; died 8 April 1927	
	BLANCHE " Vina "	married Jesse Rumsey FORD	
	394. Porter Putnam	born 18 April 1886 PA; died 10 Feb 1898	EOL
	395. Laura Belle	born 27 Aug 1892 PA; died 7 Dec 1893	EOL

177. DANIEL HEBARD-5 CASE, son of Helen Augusta-4 KIFF (ANDREW-3;2; George-1) and Adrial Hebard CASE, was born19 Feb 1864 at Leavenworth, KS. He married Kathryn May MERRIAM 2 Sept 1890 in Oberlin, Ohio. She was the daughter of _____ MERRIAM and ____, and was born 16 June 1867 LaGrange, Ohio; died 1 Jan 1952 Honolulu, HI. Daniel H-5 CASE was a general practice Attorney at Law. He died 11 July 1946 Hawaii.

Children of Daniel H-5 CASE and Kathryn MERRIAM:
Surname **CASE**

396. Adrial Hebard	born 20 Nov 1892 KS; died 16 May 1966 HI	
	married Elizabeth MC CONNELL	
	Children: 3 sons, including William Bradford-7 CASE born 30 Aug 1922 HI, died 22 Jan 1997 HI	
397. Cleo Anita.	born 13 July 1896 Topeka, KS; died 28 Dec 1976 Honolulu, HI	
398. Laura Althea	born 6 Mar 1902 HI; died _____; a teacher	

182. CORA BELLE-5 KIFF, daughter of William M-4 KIFF (Andrew-3; Andrew-2; George-1) and Harriet Melissa) CASE, and was born 24 Jan 1870, PA. She married Jesse CHILSON ca 1891. He was the son of Harry L. CHIL-SON and Lydia Elizabeth VARGASON, and was born Aug 1867 PA; died May 1941. Cora -5 KIFF died ca 1953.

Children of Cora Belle-5 KIFF and Jesse CHILSON:
Surname **CHILSON**

399. Maude Ruth	born 7 Oct 1899 PA	400. Mildred	born 6 Dec 1903 PA
401. Alfred E.	born 15 Feb 1902; died Feb 1974 Towanda, Bradford, PA		

184. RUTH EVANGELINE -5 KIFF, sister of above, was born 15 April 1880-81 Sylvania, Bradford County, PA. She married Ernest Monroe BESLEY on 28 April 1896 at Elmira, Chemung County, New York. He was the son of George N. BESLEY and Charlotte Jane MONROE, and was born 20 October 1876 at Austinville, Bradford County, PA; died 26 December 1962. Ruth E-5 KIFF died ca 1977.

Children of Ruth E-5 KIFF and Ernest M. BESLEY:

Surname **BESLEY**	(all children born Austinville, Bradford, PA)		
	402. Lynn William	born 28 Jan 1897 PA; died 16 Feb 1897 Austinville, PA	EOL
+	**403. PAULINE ETTIE**	born 26 April 1899-1900 PA; died 20 Feb 1960	
		married James Leon WHEELER	
+	**404. KENNETH NELSON**	born 25 July 1901 Austinville, PA; died ____	
		married Irene Mildred MYERS 27May 1922 Elmira, NY	
		(she dau/o Charles Henry MYERS and Elizabeth KRISTOF)	
		(she born 2 Sept 1903 NY; died _____)	
+	**405. LAWRENCE LAVERNE**	born 6 March 1904 PA; died ____	
		married Edna May WILSON 24 Nov 1926 Elmira, NY	
		(she dau/o John WILSON and Emma HALL)	
		(she born 28 May 1905 Gillett, Bradford, PA; died ____)	
	406. Dorothy Ruth	born ca 1908; died 2 Aug 1994; no issue	EOL
		1 married Theodore RUFF 26 Oct 1928 Waverly, NY; divorced	
		2 married George William HEIDEN 28 July 1946/47	
		(he s/o Herman W. HEIDEN and Anne Elizabeth MARTIN))	
		(he born 21 March 1914 Pittsford, NY; died 21 Oct 2000 Afton, Chenango, NY	

KIFF
The Fifth American Generation

Children of Ruth E-5 KIFF and Ernest M. BESLEY, continued:
Surname **BESLEY**

+   **407. LILLIAN JUNE**   born 25 June 1919 PA; died 10 April 2007 Bainbridge, Chenango, NY
                   married Arthur J. BOUVIER 8 March 1941 Sidney, NY
                   (he s/o Alfred BOUVIER and Eva WOOD)
                   (he born 5 July 1916 Malone, NY; died 30 June 2002 Norwich, NY)

185. JENNIE A /H-5 KIFF, sister of above, was born 26 June 1885 at Sylvania, Bradford County, PA. She married Thomas Bell HULSLANDER on 4 Oct 1902. He was the son of Charles Bell HULSLANDER and Jeanette FER-GUSON, and was born 2 Sept 1876 Sullivan, Tioga, PA; died 21 Jan 1959 Sullivan, PA. Jennie-5 KIFF died 1956.

Children of Jennie-5 KIFF and Thomas HULSLANDER:
Surname **HULSLANDER**

408. Inez Jeanette	born 25 Oct 1906 PA; died May 1986 Troy, PA.
	married George Franklin MUNRO 13 June 1929
409. Ernest J.	born ca 1907 PA: died ____ (on 1920 Census, no info after that)
410. Charles Bell	born 17 May 1909 PA; died 15 Feb 1963 Tioga, PA
	married Fern K. WILCOX (she born 28 Mar 1910 PA; died 1 May 1995 CA)
	(she dau/o James Lorenzo WILCOX and Maude Ann FOUST/FAUST)

187. ARTHUR DAVID-5 KIFF, son of Hiram M-4 KIFF (Peter-3; Andrew-2; George-1) and Clarissa PECK, was born 10 April 1860 at Delaware County, NY. He married Jennie A. RYER 16 Jan 1889. She was the daughter of ____ RYER and ___, and was born ca 1860 NY; died ca 1930 Delaware County, NY. Arthur D-5 KIFF died 30 Jan 1949 at Ashokan , NY

Children of Arthur David-5 KIFF and Jennie RYER:
Surname **KIFF**

411. Marcy William	born 10 Dec 1891 NY; died 26 Jan 1962 Los Angeles, CA
+ **412. JOEL METCALF**	born 17 Oct 1892 Hobart, NY; died Mar 1972 Kingston, Ulster, NY
	married Ester M. RODMAN ca 1917
	(she dau/o Frank RODMAN and Mary WALLACE)
	(she born ca 1896; died before 1946)
413. William H.	born 14 April 1896 NY; died _____
414. Merritt A.	born 2 June 1899 NY; died Dec 1986 Kingston, Ulster, NY
415. Mary E.	born 28 Nov 1903 NY; died 14 Aug 1993 Shokan , Ulster, NY
	married Floyd Edward MERRIHEW 30 April 1921 Roxbury, NY
	(he s/o Virgil R. MERRIHEW and Louella HESLEY)
	(he born 22 Nov 1891 NY; died Nov 1964 NY)

Child: Joyce Evelyn [7] MERRIHEW born 19 Jan 1927 NY; died 16 Dec 2000 Ft. Myers, FL.; married Robert Davey MOORE 27 Mar 1948 Brooklyn, NY. He s/o Frank MOORE and Kate DAVEY of Brooklyn, NY. He was born 26 Oct 1925 NY

191. EMORY PERCIVAL-5 FRISBEE, son of Frances Estella-4 KIFF (Peter-3; Andrew-2; George-1) and Daniel Lee FRISBEE, was born 17 November 1868 at Hamden, Delaware, NY. He married Lena Belle FORSYTHE 23 January 1895 at Franklin, Delaware County, NY. She was the daughter of George FORSYTHE and Mary Elizabeth LLOYD, and was born 16 December 1871 at Sidney Delaware, NY; died ____. Emory-5 FRISBEE died 5 June 1946 at Kortright, Delaware, NY.

Children of Emory-5 FRISBEE and Lena FORSYTHE:
Surname **FRISBEE**

+ **416. MILES PERCIVAL**	born 23 May 1897 Sidney, NY; died 15 Aug 1994 Tampa, FL
	married Ruth Anita HALLOCK 26 Dec 1937
	(she born 26 Sept 1908; died 11 May 1979 Tampa, FL)

280

Children of Emory -[5] FRISBEE and Lena FORSYTHE, continued:
Surname **FRISBEE**

	417. Leonard Dewey	born 3 Nov 1898 Sidney, NY; died 10 Feb 1927 Houston, TX	
	418. Florence Isabel	born 16 July 1900 Sidney, NY; died 23 Aug 1967 South Bend, Indiana	
		1 married Wilbur A. CORNELL 30 Dec 1920	

Child: Mildred Rozilla -[7] CORNELL Haines born 19 Sept 1922 Oneonta, Otsego, NY

2 married Louis B. HAINES 8 May 1931

+ **419. ERNEST FORSYTHE** born 5 Sept 1902 Kortright, Delaware, NY; died 1 Aug 1965 Oneonta, NY
married Doris E. WHITNEY 9 Nov 1940
(she dau/o ____ WHITNEY and Vesta J. MILLER)
(she born ca 1922 NY; died ____)

+ **420. RUTH LOUISE** born 3 June 1905 Kortright, NY; died 14 Dec 2002 Delhi, Delaware, NY
1 married Rolfe A. MILLER 1 Jan 1925
2 married Harold C. CAMPBELL 2 August 1937
3 married Burr C. HARDENBURGH 7 Sept 1957

421. Eulena Margaret born 15 December 1906 Kortright, NY; died 10 Feb 2003 Oneonta, NY
married Ralph H. TURNER 31 Aug 1929

Child: Evelyn Edith-[7] TURNER born 9 Jan 1933 Oneonta, Otsego, NY; married David SULLIVAN

+ **422. HUGH MIDDLETON** born 8 Oct 1908 Kortright, NY; died 28 Dec 1990 Sherburne, Chenango, NY
married Jean Adelia SHELLEY 6 Jan 1950 Kortright, NY
(she born 8 Aug 1930 Bloomville, NY; died 8 Feb 2012)

192. CLARENCE KIFF[-5] **FRISBEE Bush,** brother of above, was born 22 March 1873 at Hamden, Delaware County, NY. He was adopted by Lewis and Elizabeth BUSH of Walton, Delaware County, NY after his parents died. He married Kate Louise TOMLINSON on 28 Sept 1903 at Milford, New Haven, CT. She was the daughter of Charles A.TOMLINSON and Lucia E. ____, and was born ca 1873, died ____. They divorced. Clarence-[5] FRISBEE / Bush died 29 November 1948 at Beacon, Dutchess, NY.

Children of Clarence-[5] FRISBEE Bush:
Surname **BUSH**

	423. Lucie	born ca 1905; died ca 1906	EOL
	424. Dr. Milton T.	born 16 May 1908 MA; died 18 May 1984 TN; married Elaine SANDERS	
	425. Joan Elizabeth	born 3 Feb 1909 Natick, MA; died 24 Aug 2000 MA	
		married Herbert R. DANIELS 30 Sept 1933	
		(he born 15 March 1906 MA; died 13 July 1996 Dennis, Barnstable, MA)	

Child: Peter Raleigh-[7] DANIELS born 18 Sept 1950; married Donna KOLIKOF 7 June 1973

197. FRANKLIN "Frank" CLAYTON[-5] **KIFF,** son of John Mabie-[4] KIFF (Erastus-[3]; Andrew-[2]; George-[1]) and Susannah BASCOM(B), was born 24 July 1866 at Ward Township, Tioga, PA. He married first to Jennie S. WORDEN on 29 Dec 1897.. She was the daughter of ____ WORDEN and ____, and was born 2 April 1871-72 at Seneca Falls, Seneca County, NY; died 1932. "Frank" married second to Hannah W. TYMAN ca 1936. Frank-[5] is buried at Maple Grove Cemetery, Waterloo, New York.

Children of Franklin Clayton-[5] KIFF and Jennie WORDEN:
Surname **KIFF**

+ **426. MILDRED AMARILLUS** born 31 Dec 1899 Alba Mountain, Bradford, PA; died ____ Waterloo, NY
married George Leslie ACOR ca ____
(he born 28 Jan 1902 Muncy, Lycoming Co.,PA; died Aug 1966 Seneca Lake
(he s/o Harry Boyd ACOR and Catherine Elizabeth " Libbie" LAHR

427. Myrtle Susanna born 7 Sep 1902, Alba, Bradford, PA; died 23 Oct 1976 Waterloo, Seneca, NY
married William M. DAEFFLER 23 August 1941
(he born 17 January 1894; died 1976)

KIFF
The Fifth American Generation

Children of Franklin Clayton-5 KIFF and Jennie WORDEN, continued:
Surname **KIFF**

+   **428. GERTRUDE**   born 23 April 1905 Troy, Bradford, PA; died 19 Dec 1994 Penn Yan, Yates, NY
           LAURA   married John Leonard VAN HOESEN 24 July 1926
                         (he s/o Frank D. VAN HOESEN and Jennie Catherine DECKER)
                         (he born 28 July 1902 East Taghkanic, NY; died 3 Feb 1978 Waterloo, NY)

199. DELOS E[-5] **KIFF,** brother of above, was born ca 1873-74 at Tioga County, PA. He married Lucy May[-5] CEASE (Nelson[-4]; Julia-[3] MC INTOSH; Simon-[2]; Alexander-[1]) ca ___ . She was born 1879-80 at Morris Run, PA; died 1969. Delos[-5] KIFF died 27 March 1944 at Canton, PA. . They are buried at Park Cemetery, Canton, PA
Children of Delos[-5] KIFF and Lucy CEASE:
Surname **KIFF**

    429. Donald Herbert   born 20 Sept 1905 Leroy, NY; died 19 Apr 1996 Elmira, Chemung, NY
                         married Ava Marie BEDFORD 24 Nov 1941
                         (she born 16 March 1914 Forks Twsp, Sullivan, PA; died 11 Oct 2002 Elmira)
                         (she dau/o Bruce BEDFORD and Jennie MCCARTY)   EOL

+   **430. HELEN L.**   born 31 July1909; died 28 Aug 1998 Elmira, Chemung, NY
                         married James STRAUSS after 1930
                         (he born 6 Jan 1908 PA; died 26 June 1994 Horseheads, Chemung, NY

    431. John N.   born 15 April 1922; died 23 May 2010 Elmira, Chemung, NY
                         married Doris _____   Child: Donald J-7 KIFF born ca 1962

200. LUMAN-[5] **MURRAY,** son of Ann Eliza[-4] KIFF (Erastus[-3]; Andrew-[2]; George[-1]) and Ambrose MURRAY, Jr. was born April 1848 at Troy, Bradford, PA. He married Mary A. DICKINSON 22 September 1868. She was born June 1851, PA; died ____. Luman-[5] MURRAY served in Company F 11th PA Cavalry Regiment (108th Volunteers) in the Civil War from 3 May 1864 - 27 June 1865. He was a prisoner of war for 10 months. In 1883 he acquired 160 acres of land in Michigan, under the Homestead Act of 1862. He died ____ in Michigan..

Children of Luman-[5] MURRAY and Mary DICKINSON:
Surname **MURRAY**

    432. Minnie Bell   born ca 1870 PA; died _____
    433. Allen G.   born Jan 1873 PA; died ____   434. Musie (?)   born ca 1874 PA
                      married Louise _____   435. Claude   born ca 1877 PA
             Child: John A-[7] MURRAY born ca 1906 M I   436. Jennie   born June 1879 MI

201. EDSON ALLEN-[5] **MURRAY,** brother of above, was born ca 1849 Troy, Bradford, PA. He married Polly Rowena BOYCE ca 1866. She was the daughter of William BOYCE and Lydia M. WARD , and was born 3 August 1850; died 4 January 1938 Alba, Bradford, PA. Edson-[5] MURRAY enlisted in the Civil War 2 Feb 1864, in the same company and unit as his older brother Luman. He died 4 July 1876. Polly married 2nd to Milton MC ILWAIN, and 3rd to Charles E. KIFF (# 68)

Child of Edson-[5] MURRAY and Polly BOYCE:
Surname **MURRAY**

+   **437. HORACE**   born ca 1867 PA; died 20 July 1936 Alba, PA
                         married Alice PACKARD 19 Sept 1889 Canton, Bradford, PA
                         (she dau/o Joel PACKARD and Abigail REYNOLDS)
                         (she born ca 1875; died 3 Jan 1929 Alba, PA, buried Alba Cemetery)

205. HELEN-[5] **MURRAY,** sister of above, as born Nov 1865 Bradford County, PA. She married Fred H. JENNER ca 1883. He was the son of ____ JENNER and ____, and was born April 1860 PA; died ____NY.

Children of Helen-5 MURRAY and Fred JENNER:
Surname **JENNER**

    438. Harry E.   born 29 May 1885 PA; died June 1974 Seneca Falls, Seneca, NY
                          married Edith G. ____

            Children: Dorothy G-7 born ca 1914 and Barbara-7 Jenner born ca 1922 NY

+   **439. FRANK**   born 18 August 1887 PA; died Dec 1977 Canandaigua, Ontario, NY
        MURRAY   married Elizabeth ____ ;(she born 21 June 1886 NY; died Oct 1974 Geneva, NY

207. AMANDA-5 MOORE, daughter of Harriet-4 KIFF (Erastus-3; Andrew-2; George-1) and Israel MOORE, was born ca 1849 at ____, PA. She married Leroy J-4 CEASE (Julia Ann-3 MC INTOSH, Simon-2, Alexander-1) ca _____. He was born ca 1842; died 16 Mar 1923 PA. He served in the Civil War from 11 Aug 1862-24 May 1863 as a Pvt. In Co. C, 132nd Regt., PA Volunteers. (information from Project # 18078-27798 conducted by the Commonwealth of PA, Dept. of Military Affairs 1938-41; PA Veterans Burial Cards 1777-1999). Amanda-5 MOORE died ____.

Children of Amanda-5 MOORE and Leroy-4 CEASE:
Surname **CEASE**

+   **440. CHARLES L.**   born March 1866 PA; died ____; a blacksmith at Canton, PA
                          married Gertrude WRIGHT ca 1889 Canton, PA
                          (she dau/o Merton WRIGHT and Angeline ___) (she born ca 1869 PA)

    441. L. Snyder   born 6 Jan 1875 PA; married Emma _____; resided Gillett, PA
                          (she born ca 1881 PA; died ____)

            Child: Helen-7 CEASE born ca 1917

    442. Crayton G.   born Nov 1868 PA; died ____   EOL
                          married Minnie L. CHASE ca 1890-91 (she born May 1870 PA; died ___)

    443. Harriet "Hattie "   born ca 187_ PA; died ____, resided Elmira or Wainright, NY
    444. Lillian " Nellie "   born May 1877 PA; died _____
                          married Robert LANDON   (he s/o Merton LANDON and _____)
                          (he born June 1874 PA; died ____)

            Children: Hazel F-7 born ca 1895 PA, and Lewis E-7 LANDON born ca Dec 1898 PA

210. GEORGE DUDLEY-5 MOORE, brother of above, as born 6 November 1855 at ___, PA. He married Frances C " Frankie " SMITH ca ____. She was the daughter of _____ SMITH and ____, and was born ca 1853 PA; died 31 March 1928 PA. George Dudley-5 MOORE died 30 March 1939 Armenia Twsp, PA. They are buried at Park Cemetery, Canton, Bradford, PA.

Children of George Dudley-5 MOORE and Frances SMITH:
Surname **MOORE**   See MAC INTOSH – MC INTOSH Section for future generations

+   **445. OWEN L.**   born 25 Aug 1877 PA; died 29 July 1948 Canton, PA
                          married Nina May INGERICK
                          (she dau/o George INGERICK and Minnie IVES)
                          (she born 20 Dec 1880; died 2 Oct 1950, buried Turner Cemetery, Grover, PA

| **116. EDITH**   born 22 May 1882 Armenia Twsp, PA; died 2 July 1948 Canton, PA
                          married Willard L.-5 CEASE ca ___
                          (he s/o Nelson-4 CEASE and Margaret " Mag " EATON)
                          (he born 1 June 1874 Bradford Co., Pa; died 1936)

211. ADELL EMMA-5 " Dell " " Della " COSPER, daughter of Lucy-4 KIFF (Erastus-3; Andrew-2; George-1) and Daniel COSPER, was born 4 February 1860 at __, PA. She married Charles Lewis FREEMAN 12 Feb 1879. He was the son of Horace Dwight FREEMAN (Erastus) and Sylvia /Silva Case PALMER (Russell), and was born 13 May 1860; died 18 June 1934 Elmira, Chemung, NY. Dell-5 COSPER died 25 April 1926 at Canton, PA

Children of Adell[-5] COSPER and Charles FREEMAN:
Surname **FREEMAN**   (all children born Canton, Bradford, PA)

	447. Earl W.	born 3 March 1880; died 1894	EOL
+	**448. HARRY LEE**	born 9 Aug 1881; died 27 March 1929; married Pearl H. _____ ca ___	

449. Florence Lucy   born 8 Oct 1884; died 6 May 1917
                         married John Leland MC CONNELL (he born ca 1880 Ireland)
            Children: Francis Leland[-7] born 10 April 1908 Alba, PA, and Linden Ray[-7] MC CONNELL born 5 Oct 1909 Alba, PA

450. Silva Adell   born 28 Feb 1886; died 2 Sep 1971
451. Arthur Dwight   born 25 April 1888; died 13 Jan 1931; married Susie E. FREEMAN ca 1910
                         (she born ca 1883 PA; died 1910)
452. Daniel Otto.   born 13 Dec 1890; died 12 Sept 1975; married Marion I. PACKARD
                         (she born 19 Oct 1890 PA; died 22 Sept 1989 Canton, PA)
                         (she dau/o Winfield PACKARD and Alma FAULKNER)
            Child: C. Haldine[-7] FREEMAN born 19 March 1912 Canton, PA; died 1980; married Eloise M. CASE
            Nov 1936. She dau/o Carl Schutz CASE and Effie M. ___; and was born ca 1914 Canton, PA
453. Helen May   born Oct 1897; died 5 May 1989
454. Eliza Antoinette   born 1 Sept 1895; died 17 June 1989;
                         married Earl Wilbur LEONARD 21 Dec 1891
                         (he s/o Sumner A. LEONARD and Helen S. _____)
455. Theron E.   born 30 March 1897; died 4 Feb 1970; res. Troy PA
456. Lloyd Liston   born 27 Dec 1899; died 13 Dec 1969
                         married Leila Winifred SHADDUCK ca 1926 (she born ca 1911; died 1999)
457. Mamie Permelia   born 9 March 1901; died _____; res. Blossburg, PA; married ____ WHITE
458. Stuart Shepard   born 22 May 1905; died 24 May 1913   EOL

213. SHEPARD SILAS[-5] COSPER, brother of above, was born August 1864 at Canton, Bradford, PA. He married Jennie Mae SLINGERLAND ca ____. She was the daughter of David SLINGERLAND and Betsey ___ of Troy, PA., and was born 1 May 1867; died 12 Nov 1957 Alba, PA. Shepard[-5] COSPER died 30 March 1923. She married 2nd to ___ CONDERMAN, which was confirmed in her brothers' obituary.

Children of Shepard[-5] COSPER and Jennie Mae SLINGERLAND:
Surname **COSPER**

459. Lucy B.   born Feb1890 PA; died ____; married _____ MILLER ca _____
            Children: Charlotte M[-7] born ca 1915 PA, and Alice P[-7] MILLER born ca 1917 PA
460. Daniel Ray   born 6 July 1894 PA; died July 1984 Montour Falls, NY
                         married Marguerite CONVERSE ca 1915
                         (she dau/o Joseph CONVERSE and Mamie O'BRIEN
                         (she born ca 1896; died Jan 1966 Elmira, NY)
            Child: Donald J[-7] COSPER born Feb 1929
461. Herman S.   born 25 May 1903; died 9 Feb 1993 Indiana, PA
                         married Viola L. SHANK ca ___
                         (she dau/o Daniel W. SHANK and Elizabeth JENKINS)
                         (she born 15 March 1903; died June 1973 Williamsport, PA)
                         Resided Bloomsburg, Columbia County, PA
462. Otto I.   born 11 Feb 1908 PA; died April 1982 Danville, PA
                         married Leora LEGGETT ca ____ (she born ca 1908 PA)
                         (she dau/o Charles W. LEGGETT and Mary V. BENSON)

214. FLORENCE JANE [-5] COSPER, sister of above, was born April 1867 at Canton, Bradford County, PA. She married Willard Henry DUNBAR on 18 September 1890 at Canton, PA. He was the son of Alvin T. DUNBAR and Isabella D. ___, and was born Feb 1862 PA; died 1955. Florence[-5] COSPER died ca 1966.

Children of Florence[5] COSPER and Willard DUNBAR:

Surname **DUNBAR**   (all children born Canton, Bradford, PA)
  463. Elvira   born ca 1896; died ____
  464. Ivan Cosper   born 18 Dec 1899; died 1996
           married Keitha L. CORL ca ____; probably divorced
           (she dau/o Lucious H. CORL and Mary Marietta CRANDALL)
           (she born ca 1901 NY; died _____   (she 2 married James R. KELLY)
        Child: Donald-[7] DUNBAR born ca 1920 PA
  465. Clifford Lee   born 22 Oct / 25 Aug 1902; died 10 Sept 1974 Troy Pa.
  466. Percy M.   born 17 June 1906 ; died May 1974 Owego, NY
           married Kathryn M _____; 1930 resided Bloomfield, NJ
  457. Helen Adell   born ca 1908; died 1996

217. JAMES MELVIN[5] **KIFF**, son of Charles[-4] KIFF (Erastus[-3]; Andrew[-2]; George[-1]) and Fanny C[-4] MAC INTOSH (Matthias[-3]; Simon[-2]; Alexander-[1]), was born ca 1857-58 at Canton, Bradford County, PA. He married Ella FOX ca 1888. She was the daughter of Harvey F. FOX and Martha ____, and was born Sept 1866 Williamsport, Lycoming County, PA; died _____. James Melvin[-5] KIFF died ____.

Children of James Melvin-5 KIFF and Ella FOX:

Surname **KIFF**
  468. Alice Genevieve   born ca 1893 Alba, PA; died Dec 1968 FL
           married Stanley Colby BEAGLE 27 June 1914 +++
           (he s/o Loren Beagle and Estella BLANCHARD)
           (he born 6 Jan 1866 Otsego, NY; died May 1969 Ft. Lauderdale, FL)
       Child: John-[7] BEAGLE born ca 1920; died ____; was a Sgt.in the NY State Police at Albany
  469. Harvey   born ca 1899; died before 1910   EOL

+++ Article in the Dunkirk (NY) Evening News 30 June 1938   **21 Years a Cop – Never an Arrest**
Promotion of Sergeant Major Stanley BEAGLE , who has the longest service record in the state police, but who has never made an arrest, was announced today. After July 1, BEAGLE will be executive officer with headquarters in the capitol. In his 21 years with the troopers, Beagle explained, he has always been assigned to headquarters and has " never had the opportunity to arrest anyone". The post was created by the 1938 Legislature.

219. CLARA BELL[-5] **KIFF,** sister of above, was born 24 July 1865 PA. She married George Phelps FREEMAN, Jr. on 24 September 1885. He was the son of George Phelps FREEMAN, Sr. and Emoline PALMER, and was born 24 Sept 1858; died 13 Nov 1926 Alba, Bradford, PA. She married 2nd to Edward TOMLINSON. Clara Bell[-5] KIFF died 30 March 1946.

Children of Clara Bell[-5] KIFF and George FREEMAN, Jr.:

Surname **FREEMAN**
+ **470. MYRTLE**   born 31 July 1887 Alba, PA; died 5 July 1949 Troy, PA
   FRANCES   married Frank Hamilton-7 THOMAS (# 480)
           (he s/o Alvin. THOMAS and his 1st wife Ella F. DEWEY)
           (he born Sept 1884 PA; died 10 Jan 1957, buried Alba, PA)
+ **471. IVA ADELL**   born 22 Dec 1889 PA, died 11 Feb 1980, resided Elmira NY
           married Ray MC NEAL / MC NEILL 29 Jan 1912
           (he s/o Edward MC NEAL and Lovina ____)
           (he born 2 Sept 1889; died Feb 1921)
  472. FANNIE   born 7 Dec 1895 Troy, PA; died 8 May 1972 Towanda, PA
   PEARL   married George Albert GARD ca 1916
           (he s/o George Burgess GARD and Joanna POST)
           (he born 3 Mar 1892; died Aug 1978 Towanda , Bradford, PA)

KIFF

223. ADOLPHUS E.[-6] THOMAS, son of Elizabeth A.[-5] BECKER (Hannah-[4] KIFF; James-[3]; Andrew-[2]; George-[1]) and Alexander Hamilton THOMAS, was born September 1852 at Troy, Bradford, PA. He married Marian BLAKEMAN ca 1879. She was the daughter of Asel BLAKEMAN and Mary Ann LEWIS, and was born March 1859; died 1952. Adolphus-[6] THOMAS died 21 February 1920. They are buried at Alba, PA.

Child of Adolphus-[6] THOMAS and Marian BLAKEMAN:
Surname **THOMAS**

+	**473. LEON SHELDON**	born 24 Dec 1881 Canton, PA; died 23 Oct 1947 Alba, PA
		married Maude PACKARD 27 Nov 1903
		(she dau/o Winfield S. PACKARD and Alma FAULKNER)
		(she born 24 Oct 1880; died _____)

224. BOLIVAR[-6] THOMAS, brother of above, was born 1 April 1854 Bradford County, PA. He married Julia A. WILLIAMS on 17 Feb 1875. She was the daughter of Obediah WILLIAMS and Hannah KEYES , and was born 1 March 1853; died 24 /25 March 1934.and is buried at Beech Flats Cemetery. Bolivar-[6] THOMAS died 19 Nov 1922 and is buried at the Alba Cemetery, Alba, Bradford, PA.

Child of Bolivar-[6] THOMAS and Julia WILIAMS:
Surname **THOMAS**

474. Mae	born 3 July 1884; died _____; no issue EOL	
	married John W. MC KEE 8 June 1910	
	(he born 13 Sept 1881 PA; died _____)	

226. EUGENIA[-6] THOMAS, sister of above, was born 3 July 1858 Bradford County, PA. She married Milton A. CASE 25 Nov 1880. He was the son of Byron CASE and Eliza-[4] MC INTOSH (William-[3]; Simon-[2]; Alexander-[1]), and was born 29 May 1858 PA; died 20 Feb 1937. Eugenia-[6] THOMAS died ca 1909.

Children of Eugenia-[6] THOMAS and Milton A. CASE:
Surname **CASE**

+	475. Eliza A. (twin)	born 29 Aug 1884; died ca 1944 Troy, Bradford, PA
		married Herman R. BOYER 24 Dec 1914
		(he born 5 July 1885; died 1961)
		(he s/o Samuel BOYER and Cecelia CRIST)
+	476. Elizabeth A. (twin)	born 29 Aug 1884 Troy, PA; died _____
		married Elwyn MC KEAN 25 March 1910
		(he born ca 1882; died 1955)
	477. Bertha E.	born 1 Jan 1886 PA; died 12 Oct 1918
	478. Meade T.	born 25 April 1889; died 11 June 1966 Troy, PA
		married Louise BROWNSON 12 Oct. 1910
		(she was born 21 Jan 1883; died _____)

Child: Thomas B-[8] CASE born 17 March 1912 PA

227. ALVIN[-6] THOMAS, brother of above, was born 28 June 1860 at Bradford County, PA. He married first to Ella F. DEWEY on 18 January 1880. She was the daughter of George H. DEWEY and Sarah LOOMIS, and was born 3 May 1861; died 24 Nov 1903 Leroy, PA. He married his second wife, Mary NEWELL, on 13 June 1906. She was the daughter of Carlos S. NEWELL and Celestia DANN, and was born 16 /26 Nov 1876 at Troy, Bradford, PA; died 4 Sept 1961 at Troy, PA. Alvin-[6] THOMAS died 23 January 1939 Bradford County, PA. He was a farmer and a breeder of short horn cattle.

Children of Alvin-6 THOMAS and (1st wife) Ella F. DEWEY:
Surname **THOMAS**

+	**479. ORA LOUISE**	born 29 Nov 1880 /81 Bradford Co., PA; died 9 Nov 1953 Sayre, PA
		married Matthew Knickerbocker HOLCOMB 23 Oct 1900 Leroy, PA
		(born 15 July 1880 PA; died 4 Jan 1976 Gillett, Bradford, PA)
		buried Gillett (PA) Cemetery
+	**480. FRANK HAMILTON**	born 17 July 1884 Alba, PA; died 10 Jan 1957 Troy, Bradford, PA
		married Myrtle Frances-6 FREEMAN 17 Aug 1909 (# 470)
		(she dau/o George P. FREEMAN and Clara Belle-5 KIFF)
		(she born 31 July 1887 Alba, PA; died _____)
	481. Sarah	born 31 Jan 1892 Bradford Co., PA; died ____
		1 married Ross Gordon WILLIAMS (as his 2nd wife) 28 Nov 1936
		2 married Herman T. CHAAPEL ca ____
		(he s/o Lee Dayton CHAAPEL and Mary STEINHELPER)
		(he born 1 May 1896; died 11 Sept 1978)
	482. Eva Frances	born 13 May 1894 Bradford Co., PA; died _____
		married Guy Ezra RICHMOND 27 Feb 1911
		(he s/o Ruel RICHMOND and Rose BRISTOL)
		(he born 11 May 1892 PA; died April 1976 Pine Valley, Chemung, NY)
+	**483. HARRY ALVIN**	born 28 Jan 1897 Bradford Co., PA; died 1979 Alba, PA
		married Bernice BERRY ca 1924
		(she dau/o Edgar BERRY and Alice DOTY)
		(she born 25 April 1901 PA; died 1980)

Children of Alvin-6 THOMAS and (his 2nd wife) Mary NEWELL:
Surname **THOMAS**

+	**484. RAYMOND CARLOS**	born 24 Oct 1907 Troy, PA; died 23 Jan 1988 Burlington, Brad., PA
		married Mildred M. NENNINGER 4 April 1931
		(she dau/o Charles A. NENNINGER and Virginia ____)
		(she born 25 April 1911; died 1939)
+	**485. WILLIAM ALONZO**	born 12 Sept 1910 Bradford Co., PA; died _____
		married Vadys REESER 1 June 1935 Alba, PA
		(she dau/o Archie REESER and _____)
	486. Carlton Newell	born 24 July 1912 Bradford Co., PA; died 3 Nov 1995 Troy, PA
		married Doris _____

228. MEADE-6 THOMAS, brother of above, was born 30 October 1866 at Bradford County, PA. He married Elizabeth B. " Lizzie " NEWELL on 15 January 1890, PA. She was the daughter of Albert NEWELL and Olive Sophia SHERMAN, and was born 10 February 1871 PA; died 1 Sept 1959. Meade-6 THOMAS died 15 June 1945. They are buried at Alba Cemetery, Bradford County, PA.

Children of Meade-6 THOMAS and Elizabeth NEWELL:
Surname **THOMAS**

+	**487. ALBERT H.**	born 16 March 1894 PA; died 7 May 1981
		married Ruth A. WARREN 12 Feb 1913
		(she dau/o Lamarr WARREN and (1st wife) Nellie P. BUNYAN
		(she born 16 May 1894 PA; died 27 Feb 1987)
		(buried Crown Hill Memorial Park,, New Hartford, NY)
	488. Sherman Meade	born 5 Oct 1898 PA; died 13 Oct 1974 Troy, Bradford, PA
		married Florence SCOTT 14 May 1919
		(she dau/o Alvin SCOTT and Eva WILLIAMS)
		(she born 14 Sept 1897 PA; died _____) no issue EOL

229. ROLAND⁻⁶ **BECKER,** son of William Henry⁻⁵ BECKER (Hannah-⁴ KIFF; James⁻³; Andrew²; George⁻¹) and Harriet MILLER, was born December 1866 PA. He married Julia Etta/Emma SMITH ca 1890. She was the daughter of _____ SMITH and ____, and was born June 1868; died 14 Nov 1955 Staunton, VA. Roland⁻⁶ BECKER died 1928, and is buried at Alba Cemetery, Alba, PA.

Children of Roland⁻⁶ BECKER and Julia SMITH:
Surname **BECKER**

489. Mary E.	born ca 1901 PA; died _____	
490. Harriet M.	born ca 1904 PA; died _____; resided Staunton, VA	
	married J. C. RUTHERFORD	
+ **491. CHARLES M.**	born 15 Nov 1905 Blossburg, PA; died 6 Feb 1974 Millerton, Tioga, PA	
	married Benita MERRITT ca _____	
	(she dau/o Mark M. MERRITT and Bessie G. KITTLE)	
	(she born 7 Dec 1907 Granville, PA; died April 1984 Millerton, Tioga, PA)	

231. HIRAM MILLER ⁻⁶ **BECKER,** brother of above, was born November 1870 at ___ PA. He married Edna Eliza SMITH of Alba, PA ca 1894. She was the daughter of Theodore SMITH and Flora L. FREEMAN, and was born July 1875; died ____. Hiram Miller⁻⁶ BECKER died ____.

Children of Hiram Miller ⁻⁶ BECKER and Edna SMITH:
Surname **BECKER**

492. Dorothy	born March 1895; died _____
	married Vernon MC CARROLL of Utah ca 19____
493. Theodore Henry	born 22 July 1900 Alba, PA; died Feb 1964 Bethesda, MA
	married Sarah Madge JORDAN Sept 1929
	(she born 14 Oct 1901; died 4 Nov 1994)
	(she dau/o William JORDAN and Cora SMITH)
494. Kenneth Miller	born 20 March 1904; died April 1987 Watsontown, Northumberland, PA
	married Florence Williams DART 22 Apr 1930 Wellsboro, Tioga, PA
	(she born 4 Nov 1901 Wellsboro, PA; died 28 Nov 1993 Watsontown, PA
495. Janet F.	born ca 1908; died 1909

233. CLAUDE H ⁻⁶ **BECKER,** son of James Dewitt⁻⁵ BECKER (Hannah-⁴ KIFF, James⁻³; Andrew⁻²; George-¹) and Sarah BOVIER, was born May 1868 Armenia, PA. He married Minnie J. FIELD 26 March 1891. She was the daughter of George FIELD and Caroline Amelia FREEMAN, and was born June 1869 PA; died _____. Claude H⁻⁶ BECKER died ____.

Children of Claude-⁶ BECKER and Minnie FIELD:
Surname **BECKER**

496. Ralph F.	born Jan 1892; died before 1910	
497. John D. " Jack "	born 2 April 1893 PA; died July 1964 PA (single 1930)	EOL
498. Winifred A.	born 22 July 1897; died 25 Feb 1981 Forksville, Sullivan, PA	
	1 married Robert ROSE March 1943; divorced	
	2 married Ralph William GRIFFIN 13 May 1943 Towanda, PA	
499. Margaret	born ca 1907; died _____	

236. PERRY EUGENE ⁻⁶ **DUMOND,** son of William Eugene⁻⁵ DUMOND (Harriet⁻⁴ KIFF; James ³; Andrew⁻²; George-¹) and Leila Maria PRATT, was born 25 February 1882 PA. He married Edith Eliza MASON on 29 November 1906 PA. She was the daughter of George Henry MASON and Addie Virginia DEWEY, and was born 9 May 1891 PA; died 1950 Edinsburg, PA. Perry Eugene⁻⁶ DUMOND died ca 1951.

Children of Perry[-6] DUMOND and Edith MASON:
Surname **DUMOND**

+   **500. EUGENE**   born 24 April 1908 PA; died 22 Oct 1988 Billings, MT
           HENRY   married Margaret DUNWORTH 8 July 1929
                          (she born 26 April 1910; died 18 Feb 1997 Billings, MT)

     501. Lillian Elnora   born 4 June 1912; died ____

     502. Harold Hamilton   born 23 Jan 1915 PA; died ____
                          married Bernice BRADFORD 16 Feb 1934
                          (she born ca 1916 PA; dau/o George R. BRADFORD and Edith ____)
                 Child: Robert Wayne-[8] DUMOND born 9 July 1935

     503. Clyde Hollis   born 11/19 Nov 1916 PA; died Oct 1979 Towanda, PA
                          married Eva Catherine RUPERT   (she born ca 1920; died 1989)
                          (she dau/o Joseph Frederick RUPERT and Rose Marie SUNDERLIN)
         Children: 2 sons, no info; dau born ca , m. ____ AXBERG; dau born ca ___, m. ____ PATTERSON; dau born ca ___, m.____ MC CARRON; dau born ca ___, m. ___PETERSON

     504. George Edward   born 22 Feb 1919 PA; died 15 July 1995 Franklinville, Cattaraugus, NY

     505. Richard Mason   born 30 May 1923 PA; died 21 March 1981 Lewiston, PA
                          married Mareda Mae BOOSE   (she born 1925 PA ; died 6 March 1965)
                          (she dau/o Clarence William BOOSE and Blanch M. ____)
               Children: 4 daughters and 3 sons, no further info

     506. Clarence Arthur   born 19 June 1926 PA; died 21 Dec 1987 State College, PA
                          served in the US Navy during WW 2 (AOM 2nd Class)
                          buried Lewiston, Mifflin Co., PA

     507. Dorothy Margaret   born 12 Aug 1928 PA   508. Edith Geraldine   born 26 July 1932 PA

256. CLARENCE HERBERT[-6] **CONGDON,** son of Schuyler-[5] CONGDON (Diantha-[4] COVERT; Jemima-[3] KIFF; Andrew-[2]; Geprge-[1]) and Mary Elizabeth KINCH, was born 20 May / December 1874 at Burlingame, KS. He married Arian MAPLES 20 July 1898 Oneonta, Otsego, NY. She was the daughter of Melvin MAPLES and Hannah ____, and was born 11 Oct 1877 Hartwick, NY; died 16 Feb 1967 Oneonta, Otsego, NY. Clarence-[6] CONGDON died 24 Oct 1957 Oneonta, Otsego, NY.

Children of Clarence-[6] CONGDON and Arian MAPLES:
Surname **CONGDON**

+   **509. HELEN**   born 21 March / April 1899 Oneonta, NY; died 21 Dec 1987 Hartwick, NY
           HANNAH   married George Bernard BENEDICT 21 March 1922
                          (he born 27 Apr 1898 Concepcion, Chile; died 6 Nov 1991 Syracuse, NY)

     510. Maud Belle   born ca 1903; died 1988

     511. Gladys   born 28 Sept 1906; died 7 Aug 1999 New Berlin, Chenango, NY
                          married Theodore MONTHIE
                          (he s/o Herman MONTHIE and Paulena C. LORENZ)
                          (he born 14 Aug 1907; died 5 Sept 1958 Kinderhook, Columbia, NY)

270. BERT JAMES[-6] **CONGDON,** son of Edwin Edgar-[5] CONGDON (Diantha-[4] COVERT; Jemima-[3] KIFF; Andrew-[2]; George-[1]) and Ella RUGGLES, was born March 1888 PA. He married first to Edna L. QUAIL / QUEAL ca 1910. She was the daughter of James QUAIL/ QUEAL and Mary J. TICKNER, and was born Feb 1887 Wells, Bradford, PA; died 1925. He married 2nd to Louise E. TEARS ca 1928. She was the daughter of Adelbert TEARS and Nellie QUAIL / QUEAL, and was born ca 1903; died 1969. Bert James-[6] CONGDON died March 1974 Gillett, Bradford, PA.

Children of Bert James-[6] CONGDON and Edna QUAIL / QUEAL :
Surname **CONGDON**

     512. Bernice   born ca 1909 PA; died ____

     513. Edgar   born ca 1915 PA; died ____   514. Maria   born ca 1916 PA

Children of Bert James-⁶ CONGDON and Edna QUAIL/QUEAL, continued:
Surname **CONGDON**

515. Pauline Hazel.	born 29 Mar 1917 Gillett, PA; died 29 May 2004 Cayuta, Schuyler, NY
	married Lamar William " Bert " AVERY
	(he born 12 Dec 1915 Lockwood, Tioga, PA; died 7 June 2004
	(he s/o Mark John Longwell AVERY and Hilda NEWBERRY)

Children: 3 sons and 3 daus, including Larry Congdon-⁸ AVERY born ca 1939; died 2002

272. HAZEL EMMA-⁶ CONGDON, sister of above, was born 27 Sept 1897 PA. She married Lewis Edward DIX before 1920. He was the son of Charles E. DIX and Dora M ____, and was born 6 Nov 1895 Tioga, PA; died 14 Dec 1971 Elmira, Chemung, NY. Hazel-⁶ CONGDON died July 1980. Reference: Hazel and Lewis obituaries)

Children of Hazel-⁶ CONGDON and Lewis E. DIX:
Surname **DIX**   (all children born at Wells, Bradford County, PA)

516. DeLecia Mae	born 6 July 1922; died 3 Oct 2008 Creswell, OR
	married C. Edward-⁷ GREENOUGH ca 1944-45; divorced ca 1959/60
	(he MC INTOSH line # 1192)

Children: Dale E-⁸ " Happy " born11 Jan 1947, married Janet ___, resided Creswell, OR. and
Stephen-⁸ " Steve " GREENOUGH born 27 Aug 1949 , married Judy ___; resided Colville, WA

517. Edgar LaRue	born 25 Mar 1925; died 8 June 2000 FL
518. Dr. Donald M.	born ca 1927; died _____; resided Horseheads, NY
519. Rosalyn	born ca 1929; married Charles MARK; resided Atlanta, GA

274. CHARLES MONROE-⁶ COVERT, son of Milton-⁵ COVERT (Erastus-⁴ COVERT; Jemima-³ KIFF; Andrew-²; George-¹) and Delight Delia CASE, was born 26 January 1883 at Bradford County, PA. He married Harriet Frances SEARS ca 1903. She was the daughter of George W. SEARS and Martha Ellen WOOD, and was born 1 June 1882 Elgin, IL; died 5 March 1945 Rockford, IL. Charles M-⁶ COVERT died June 1957.

Children of Charles-⁶ COVERT and Harriet Frances SEARS:
Surname **COVERT**

520. Milton S.	born 3 Nov 1906 IL; died ____	524. Ida May	born ca 1919 NY
	married Ruby G. ____	525. Robert V.	born ca 1923 IL

Child: Barbara-⁸ COVERT born ca 1929 IL

521. Esther Harriet	born 22 May 1908 Woodstock, IL; died 3 Jul 1980 Santa Clara, CA
	married Corbin Brad MUNSON
	(he born 7 Sept 1903 IA; died 1 Mar 1983 Santa Clara, CA
	(he s/o _____ MUNSON and _____ DUNHAM)

Child: Ruth E-⁸ MUNSON born ca 1933 IL

522. Byrd Frances	born Mar 1910 IL; died 1988 Rockford, IL
	married Kenneth W. STENGER July 1943 Great Falls, Montana
	(he born ca 1906 IL; died 31 Mar 1999 Rockford, IL)
	(he s/o Charles Ernest STENGER and Eva Laverne KUNTZELMAN)
523. Charles M., Jr.	born ca 1917 NY; died ____

276. HARRY MILTON-⁶ COVERT, brother of above, as born 22 February 1894 at Algonquin, IL. He married Cora J. SHIPE ca ____. She was the daughter of William A. SHIPE and Hattie L. ___, and was born ca 1900/01 Algonquin, IL; died ___-. Harry Milton-⁶ COVERT died Oct 1965.

Children of Harry Milton-⁶ COVERT and Cora J. SHIPE:
Surname **COVERT**

526. Harry, Jr.	born ca 1920 IL; died ____
527. Walter W.	born ca 1922 IL; died ____
528. Kenneth R.	born 11 July 1923 IL; died July 1981 IL

Children of Harry Milton-[6] COVERT and Cora J. SHIPE, continued:
Surname **COVERT**

529. Calvin C.	born 24 Nov 1924 IL; died 1 Dec 1994		
530. Sarah H.	born ca 1929 IL	531. Lyle	born ca 1935

279. HERBERT LEE-[6] BAILEY, son of Ida S-[5] KINCH (Esther-[4] COVERT; Jemima-[3] KIFF; Andrew-[2]; George-[1]) and Freeman BAILEY, was born 11 Aug 1886 PA. He married Eva J. MC GUINNIS ca ____. She was the daughter of ____ MC GUINNIS and ____, and was born Feb 1892 Le Roy, Bradford, PA; died 1971. Herbert-[6] BAILEY died July 1967 Canton, Bradford, PA. They are buried at Alba Cemetery, Bradford Co., PA

Children of Herbert Lee-[6] BAILEY and Eva MC GUINNIS:
Surname **BAILEY**

532. Donald Herbert	born 10 May 1913 Canton, PA; died 9 Oct 1990 Elmira, NY
	married Marsleah C. MILLER
	4 children, including Carl D-[8] BAILEY born Sept 1936; died 1987 SC
533. Frances I.	born 31 July 1915 PA; died 10 Sept 2007 Syracuse, Onondaga, NY
	married _____ KOSMER
534. Galen F.	born 2 June 1919 PA; died 2 June 2005 Towanda, PA
	1 married _____ before 1944
	Child: Rodney N-[8] BAILEY born 31 March 1944 Williamsport, PA
	2 married Beulah MURPHY 4 June 1948 (reference: Obit)
	(she dau/o Howard E. MURPHY and Faith C. HORTON)
	(she born 19 Jan 1923 Binghamton, NY; died 16 Nov 1993 Towanda, PA)
	Children: Gary F-[8] born 5 Apr 1952 PA; and Cheryl K-[8] BAILEY born 15 Oct 1957 PA
535. Irene M.	born 4 Jan 1927; died 18 Oct 2010 Brethren Village, Lancaster, PA EOL

280. ESTHER G-[6] BAILEY, sister of above, was born 6 October 1894 PA. She married Martin Wiltsie RODIER ca ____. He was the son of Albert E. RODIER and Naomi VALE, and was born 26 June 1891 PA; died 4 Nov 1944 DeKalb, GA. Esther G-[6] BAILEY died October 1971/73 at Cleveland, OH.

Children of Esther G-[6] BAILEY and Martin RODIER:
Surname **RODIER**

536. Naomi V.	born ca 1912 PA; died _____
537. Esther Claire	born 1916 NJ; died May 1984 Manchester, NH
	married Thomas Russell BURNS, Jr.
	(he s/o Thomas R. BURNS, Sr. and Mary HARRINGTON)
	(he born 16 Oct 1910 Manchester, NH; died 26 July 1983 Manchester, NH)
	Child: Thomas Russell-[8] BURNS III born ____
538. Martin Wiltse, Jr	born ca 1918; died 13 April 2000 Yellowstone, Montana

282. WALTER E-[6] LYON, son of Stanley William-[5] LYON (William-[4]; Jemima-[3] KIFF; Andrew-[2]; George-[1]) and Laura MORGAN, was born 14 January 1881 Towanda, Bradford, PA. He married Irene Montgomery RILEY ca 1909. She was the daughter of John B. RILEY and Helena MONTGOMERY, and was born 3 Dec 1880; died 7 Nov 1967 Eagles Mere, PA. Walter-[6] LYON died 31 July 1959 Eagles Mere, Sullivan County, PA.

Child of Walter-[6] LYON and Irene RILEY:
Surname **LYON**

539. Elwyn Stanley	born 25 May 1909; died 9 Oct 2007 Eagles Mere, Sullivan Co., PA_
"Whitey"	married Esther Jane JONES 11 July 1934
	(she born 23 June 1909 Canton, PA; died 7 Jan 2002 Eagles Mere , PA.
	(he served in the US Coast Guard and the US Navy during WW 2)
	Child: Raymond M-[8] LYON born ca 1939; married Florence M. ____

KIFF
The Sixth American Generation

294. RHODA BELL⁶ LYON, daughter of John-⁵ LYON (James-⁴; Jemima-³ KIFF; Andrew-²; George-¹) and Rosanna NEWELL, was born 1 April 1870 at Troy, Bradford, PA. She married Thomas Leroy KINCH ca 1887 PA. He was the son of Thomas KINCH and Sarah Jane CEASE, and was born May 1860 Westford, Otsego, NY; died 8 June 1942 Troy, PA. Rhoda Bell-⁶ LYON died 25 Aug 1950 Sayre, PA

Children of Rhoda Bell-⁶ LYON and Thomas L. KINCH:
Surname **KINCH**

540. Rosa	born July 1891 PA; died 1946
541. Arian Eloise	born 16 Dec 1899 PA; died 11 Sept 1972 Troy, PA
542. Leon Thomas	born 15 July 1901 ; died May 1972 Troy, PA; married Gladys ___ ca 1929
543. Karl Layton	born 31 May 1904; died 915 Troy, PA

295. LAYTON ROMAIN-⁶ LYON, son of John H-⁵ LYON (James-⁴; Jemima-³ KIFF; Andrew-²; George-¹) and Rosanna NEWELL, was born 29 May 1873 PA. He married Lillie May SHERMAN ca 1894 / 5. She was the daughter of Simeon Leonard SHERMAN and Emma Josephine FIELD, and was born 17 Jan 1870 Troy, PA; died 5 March 1952 Troy, PA. . Layton-⁶ LYON died 26 Aug 1952.

Children of Layton-⁶ LYON and Lillie May SHERMAN:
Surname **LYON**

+ **544. EMMA AGNES**	born 3 Aug 1895 Ward, PA; died 12 May 1992 Burlington, PA married Walter Byron EVERTS 12 April 1915 (he born 13 Mar 1897 Springfield, PA; died 10 Nov 1947 Sayre, PA)
545. Leone / Leona	born 28 Jan 1903 PA; died Oct 1976 Tioga, PA married Hilton Maynard ROCKWELL ca ___ (he born 19 Oct 1894 Burlington, PA; died 13 Aug 1954 Sayre, PA) (he s/o Wesley Alfred ROCKWELL and Wilma Geraldine HALL) Children: 2 sons and 1 dau Irene-⁸ROCKWELL born ca ___; married Joseph RULA
546. J. Raymond	born ca 1905 PA; died _____; married Gladys _____ Child: Homer R-⁸ LYON born 19 Dec 1929 Troy, PA

299. EDWARD ROY-⁶ LYON, son of Hiram-⁵ LYON (James-⁴; Jemima-³ KIFF; Andrew-²; George-¹) and Fanny DEWEY, was born 3 May 1878 PA. He married Helen CLARK 23 Nov 1910. She was the daughter of _____ CLARK and ___, and was born 12 June 1886; died ____. Edward Roy-⁶ LYON died _____.

Children of Edward Roy-⁶ LYON and Helen CLARK:
Surname **LYON**

547. Marjorie L.	born 15 Oct 1911 PA; died Oct 1994 Towanda, Bradford, PA married Glenn Philip VITE ca 1930 (he born 2 March 1910; died June 1983 Towanda, PA) (he s/o Irving Howard VITE and Jennie C. _____) Children: Robert Glenn-⁸ born ca 1931, and Betty June-⁸ VITE born 28 Nov 1934
548. Dorothy L.	born 31 Dec 1913 Armenia Mtn., PA; died 3 Apr 2009 Horseheads, NY married Clarence HOYT 28 Oct 1950 Children: Midge-⁸born, married ___HARTMAN, and Janet⁸HOYT born ___ married John TIGHE (Ref: Dorothy Hoyt obit)
549. Robert	born 3 Aug 1916 PA; died _____
550. Edward, Jr.	born 3 Feb 1921; died _____
551. Stuart	born 28 Aug 1924

300. COLA WALTER -⁶ LYON, brother of above, was born November 1880 PA. He married Harriet-⁶ COVERT (# 246) 26 March 1902 at _____ PA. She was the daughter of George L.⁵ COVERT and Mary J. MERRIAM, and was born 1 March 1883; died _____. Cola Walter-⁶ LYON, an attorney, died 1937.

293

Children of Cola Walter[-6] LYON and Harriet COVERT:
Surname **LYON**

552. Margaret	born 9 Jan 1910 PA; died _____
	married Kenneth Eugene BOWLES 11 July 1931 Corning, NY
	(he s/o Miles Leander BOWLES and Mary E. LAMPHIER)
	(he born 4 July 1906; died 12 Dec 1993 Canisteo, NY)

Children: Mary Katherine-[8] born 1 Jan 1933, and Kenneth G-[8] BOWLES born 21 Oct 1934, died 26 Feb 2004

553. Catherine	born 24 Oct 1911; died ___; married Hugh Stanford EDWARDS ca 1927
	(he born 5 July 1906 PA; died 1 May 1991 Coal Grove, OH)
	(he s/o William Hamilton EDWARDS and Mary Moore SMOOT)

Children: Sally Ann-[8] born ca 1928, and Richard Lyon-[8] EDWARDS born 8 June 1935

554. Mary Jane	born 23 July 1924

Reference: Our Harding Family, Pages 101-102

308. WILLARD CLINTON[-6] OWEN, son of Celestia Antoinette [5] CLEVELAND (Mary[-4] LYON; Phebe[-3] KIFF; Andrew[-2]; George[-1]) and William B. OWEN, was born 16 March 1874 IL. He married Alice RAHM ca 1903. She was the daughter of Charles RAHM and Catherine KARCH, and was born 11 Mar 1877 IL; died June 1973 IL. Willard[-6] OWEN, owned a 200 acre farm, called Hillcrest Farm at Frankfort, IL, and died there 31 Jan 1928.

Children of Willard Clinton[-6] OWEN and Alice RAHM:
Surname **OWEN**

555. Margaret	born ca 1906 IL
556. Donald	born 21 April 1907 IL
557. Kingsley Everett	born 12 Dec 1908 IL; died May 1979 Prospect Heights, IL
	married Nellie RIORDAN ca ___
	(she dau/o Patrick Joseph RIORDAN and Elizabeth SHAND)
	(she born 14 July 1910; died July 1992 (buried Joliet, IL)

Children: Nancy-[8] born 3 Jan 1943, married ___ De ROSE, and Maggie-[8] OWEN born 1 Aug 1946, married ___ JOBE

558. Willard Clinton, Jr.	born 9 Aug 1910 IL
559. Marion	born ca 1913 IL
560. Elizabeth Delight	born 6 Mar 1914 IL; died 27 Mar 2003 IL
	married Everett Keith WILSON ca 1938 at Mt. Carroll, IL

Child: Alice-[8] WILSON born ca ___; married David DUGGAN

561. Katherine	born ca 1916-17 IL

310. ARTHUR C[-6] OWEN, brother of above, was born March 1881 IL. He married Evelyn Isabel HAMMOND on 21 June 1905. She was the daughter of _____ HAMMOND and ____, and was born 19 Sept 1881 IL; died 20 Nov 1920. Arthur[-6] OWEN died _____.

Children of Arthur C[-6] OWEN and Evelyn HAMMOND:
Surname **OWEN**

562. William Hammond	born 30 June 1906 IL; died 31 May 1997 Santa Clara, CA
563. Rosamond	born 1908 IL; died 1908
564. John Hammond	born 3 July 1911 IL; died 23 Aug 1943 Muskegon, MI
	married Margaret PRATT 4 April 1936
	(she born 18 June 1910; died 10 Feb 2005 NE)
	(she dau/o Walter Clyde PRATT and Mary M. FINE)
565. Harriet May	born 6 Aug 1914 IL; died 24 Dec 2004 IL

312. AUGUSTUS FRISBEE[-6] CLEVELAND, son of Josiah[-5] CLEVELAND (Mary[-4] LYON; Phebe[-3] KIFF; Andrew[-2]; George[-1]) and Electa PRICE, was born 19 Sept 1874 at Chicago, IL. He married Neira/ Nuice Chandler HATCHER ca 1899. She was the daughter of _____ HATCHER and ____, and was born Jan 1878 OH; died 1930. Augustus[-6] CLEVELAND , a graduate of Yale University Class of 1897, died ___.

Children of Augustus-6 CLEVELAND and Neira C. HATCHER:
Surname **CLEVELAND**

566. Robert Francis	born 29 Jan 1905 OH; died 21 Jan 1985 CA; married Margaret BERGNER (she born 7 Mar 1909 Baltimore, MD; died 4 June 1989 Sonoma, CA)		
567. Augustus F., Jr.	born ca 1908 OH	568. William H.	born ca 1909 OH

314. JOSIAH JUDSON-6 **CLEVELAND**, brother of above, was born 31 July 1882 at Oak Park, IL. He married Grace E. CARR ca ____. She was the daughter of Robert F. CARR and Emily Ann SMICK, and was born October 1880 IL; died 1968. Josiah-6 CLEVELAND died 11 Oct 1948 at Dallas, TX.

Children of Josiah-6 CLEVELAND and Grace CARR:
Surname **CLEVELAND**

569. G. Elizabeth	born ca 1908
570. Judson Carr	born 17 Nov 1909; died 26 March 1964 (3 sons) married Alice Elizabeth MORGAN (she born ca 1908; died 1999)

319. RUTH ANN-6 **GETSINGER,** daughter of Lois Ophelia-5 HAGAR (Sarah-4 LYON; Phebe-3 KIFF; Andrew-2 ; George-1) and Daniel HAGAR, was born 3/9 January 1869 PA. She married first to William Orlando TISDALE ca 1889 OH. He was the son of Martin L. TISDALE and Mary Catherine BROWN, and was born Nov 1866 OH, died 9 March 1933, IL. He worked as a laborer in the oil fields.   Ruth Ann-6 GETSINGER died 25 April 1922.

Children of Ruth-6 GETSINGER and William O. TISDALE:
Surname **TISDALE**

+	**571. BERNICE IRENE**	born 9 Jan 1892 Findlay,OH; died 6 Oct 1959 Findlay married Glenn Robert BOWERS 25 June 1913 (he s/o Emanuel Clement BOWERS and Ellen MC DOUGLE/ MC DOUGAL
	572. Louis Chessrown	born 19 June 1898 OH; died 12 Jan 1965 Parma, OH married Marcella LUZINS 6 June 1927 Ohio (she born ca 1911 OH, died _____) (she dau/o Albert C. LUZINS and Mary WIDOWSKI)

Child: Louis-8 TISDALE, Jr. born 30 Sept 1932 OH, died 9 Dec 2002 Cleveland, OH

	573. Ruth Catherine	born 20 Jan 1904 OH; died 9 Feb 1987 Toledo, OH married Warren William " Doc " DOCHTERMAN ca 1922 (he s/o William Henry DOCHTERMAN and Grace Elizabeth BEACH) (he born 4 Oct 1899; died 24 Oct 1974 Toledo. OH)

Child: Warren Louis-8 DOCHTERMAN born Sept 1929 Findlay, OH; died 2006 Denver CO.)

	574. Virginia L.	born ca 1912 OH

320. LOUIS CHESSROWN-6 **GETSINGER,** brother of above, was born 4 March 1870 at Allegheny, PA. He married to Kathryn A. FABER 30 June 1898 PA. She was the daughter of Louis Charles FABER and Marian G. SCHILLING, and was born 17 Sep 1866 PA; died 3 Sep 1940 PA. Louis-6 died 16 April 1946 at Staunton, VA

Child of Louis C.-6 GETSINGER and Kathryn FABER:
Surname **GETSINGER**

575. Louis Chessrown, Jr.	born 2 Aug 1899 PA; died 24 Sep 1949 1 married Lucille Marie GILLESPIE 10 Nov 1920 PA (she dau/o Philip Collins GILLESPIE and Alice Veronica PITFIELD) (she born 20 May 1899 Pittsburgh, PA; died 20 Sep 1932 Pittsburgh)

Children: (twins) Louis Chessrown III-8 born 14 May 1924 PA; and John Scott-8 GETSINGER born 14 May 1924 PA, died 25 Apr 1970

	2 married Hettie CLERC 20 May 1933 PA (she dau/o Joseph Cornelius CLERC and Pietje VERSCHOOR) (she born 20 Apr 1899 Rotterdam, Holland; died 23 Feb 1989 Pittsburgh)

324. SAMUEL PENN[6] **DAVIDS**, half- brother of above , son of Lois Ophelia-[5] HAGAR (Sarah-[4] LYON; Phebe-[3] KIFF; Andrew-[2]; George-[1]) and William Franklin DAVIDS, was born April 1882 at ____, PA. He married Cora WISE ca 1903. She was the daughter of William WISE and Nancy Miranda CARRIER, and was born November 1881 NY; died ____. They divorced before 1930.

Children of Samuel-[6] DAVIDS and Cora WISE:
Surname **DAVIDS**

576. Dorothy D.	born 6 Sept 1905 PA; died July 1980 Latrobe, PA	
	married _____ JOHNSTONE ca ____; divorced before 1930	
	Child: Cynthia-[8] JOHNSTONE born 1927 PA	
577. C. Miriam.	born ca 1908 PA; died ____;	
	married Ralph E. BIESECKER ca 1926 (divorced before 1930)	
	Child: Hugh-[8] BIESECKER born ca 1927 NY	
578. Daniel Duane	born 18 Apr 1912 PA; died 23 Aug 1989 HI.	

Note: Another grand-daughter of Cora, is listed on the 1930 Census (Yonkers, Westchester, NY) as Constance MC GAYHEY born ca 1925 NY. Unable to determine which daughter was the mother.

326. ROBERT BREWSTER[6] **DAVIDS**, brother of above, was born 6 March 1887 PA. He married Isabell (possibly WHITING) ca 1906. She was born ca 1881 England. She immigrated to America in 1890, and was naturalized in 1897. Robert Brewster-[6] DAVIDS, a clergyman, moved around the country. He died June 1965 MD.

Children of Robert Brewster-[6] DAVIDS and Isabell ____:
Surname **DAVIDS**

579. Lois Eleanor	born 18 Nov 1906 Staten Island, NY; died ____
	married Edward D. PAIGE
580. Clifford Booth	born 10 Aug 1908 PA; died 7 Nov 1995 Riverside, CA
	married Jane ROBERTS
	(she born 9 May 1911 NE; died 28 Aug 1986 Los Angeles, CA)
	(she dau/o Harry ROBERTS and Pearl RITTER) (CA Death Index 1940-77)
581. Robert Maitland	born 17 Aug 1910; died 4 Apr 2002; buried Arlington Cemetery, VA
	1 married ____; 2 married Lily Dorothy LAGUNA 6 June 1987 CA
	Note: Robert M. DAVIDS was a MSG in the US Air Force

327. CHARLES PEARCE[6] **DAVIDS**, brother of above, was born 28 Jan 1889 OH. He married Julia Lucy KLINK on 4 May 1912 OH. She was the daughter of John KLINK and Theresa Flora WHEITOFF, and was born 12 Dec 1890 PA; died ____.. Charles P-[6] DAVIDS died April 1967 Bryan, Ohio

Children of Charles P-[6] DAVIDS and Julia L ____:
Surname **DAVIDS**

582. Thomas C.	born ca 1915 OH
583. Harry R.	born 29 Mar 1917 OH; died ____
	married Florence WALSH 8 Oct 1938 OH (she born 29 Mar 1914 PA)
584. Elaine M.	born 20 Jan 1923 OH; died ____
	married Richard Henry SMITH 3 May 1952 OH
	(he born 14 June 1922; died _____)

336. ANDREW PARKER[6] **" Park " BATEMAN,** son of Evaline Lavencie-[5] HAGAR (Sarah-[4] LYON; Phebe-[3] KIFF; Andrew-[2]; George-[1]) and George P. / Park G. BATEMAN, was born 20 Aug 1876 McIntyre, PA. He married Martha EDDINGS ca ____. She was the daughter of Henry EDDINGS and Martha____, and was born 22 Sept 1881 PA; died Oct 1975 Blossburg, PA. " Park " BATEMAN served in the Spanish American War. He died 4 Dec 1970 Blossburg, PA.

Children of Andrew[-6] BATEMAN and Martha EDDINGS:
Surname **BATEMAN**

585. Evelyn Norton   born ca 1905 Blossburg, PA; died 27 Nov 1998 Blossburg, PA
married Leo Joseph ALLIS ca 1932
(he s/o Adelbert Thomas ALLIS and Anna M. QUINN)
(he born 3 Nov 906 Mansfield, PA; died Apr 1970 Campbell, Steuben, NY
Children: Joe-[8]; Tom-[8]; Park-[8]; and Martha-[8] ALLIS born ca ___, married ___ KIELY

586. Parker Thomas   born 20 Nov 1906 PA; died 25 Feb 2001 NY
587. Howard S.   born 20 Dec 1917; died 24 May 1992; 2nd Lt. U S Army WW 2

340. MARTHA PEARL [-6] **BATEMAN**, sister of above , was born 2 February 1885 at ____, PA. She married Hugh Bruno OELKE 21 Sept 1904 at Weston, WY. He was the son of ____ OELKE and ____, and was born 6 Sept 1876 Germany. He immigrated in 1882, and was naturalized in 1917at Sheridan, WY. He died 12 March 1962 Sheridan, WY. Martha Pearl[-6] BATEMAN died 1 Jan 1977 at Sheridan.

Children of Martha Pearl[-6] BATEMAN and Hugh OELKE:
Surname **OELKE**

588. George W   born 3 Aug1905 NE; died 30 July 1988 Shawnee Mission, Johnson, KS
married Edith Lenore COMPTON
(she born 6 Jan 1913 WA; died 27 Oct 1972 CA)
Children: dau born ____; William Gene-[8] OELKE born 21 Mar 1931 Sheridan, WY; died 2 Mar 2002 MO
589. Julia Evaline   born 3 June 1907 WY
590. James Hugh Berton   born 31 Oct WY; died 1913   EOL
591. Eulalia <u>Marie</u>   born ca 1913 WY; died ____
592. Frank Valoris   born ca 1915 WY; died ____ (served in WW 2)
593. Clayton LaVelle   born ca 1921 WY; presumably died 15 Dec 1945   ++

++ Note: He was a MM Mate 2nd Class in the US Navy , and was killed in action during WW 2. He was awarded the Purple Heart, and there is a monument at Ft. William McKinley in Manila, Phillipines

343. LULA BELLE[-6] **BATEMAN,** sister of above, was born 29 April 1893 _____, NE. She married Wilber Dee Eanos GARRETT ca ____. He was the son of Enos Gilpin GARRETT and Mary Annetta HAMILTON, and was born 31 Aug 1889 Danforth, MO; died 19 Sept 1985 Highland, San Bernardino, CA. Lula Belle[-6] BATEMAN died 23 July 1970 WA.

Children of Lula Belle[-6] BATEMAN and Wilber Dee Enos GARRETT
Surname **GARRETT**

594. Raymond LaVerne   born 27 Apr 1912 WY ; died 18 Aug 1972 FL
1 married Jeanette Wilison LONGWELL ca 1932; divorced 1934 (1 son)
(she born 2 Apr 1912; died ____)
2 married Lillian <u>Josephine</u> RHODES Lamprey
(she dau/o Joseph E. RHODES and Felonise Marie HENRY)
(she born ca 1915; died _____)
Note: she had daughter Dora Marie LAMPREY (born ca 1934) by her 1st husband ____ LAMPREY
595. Edward Elton   born 5 July 1915 WY; died 2 Dec 1949 TX
596. Bernadine Ruth   born 8 Feb 1917 WY; died 28 May 1992 WA.
1 married Erbin Louis GILMORE ca 1932, divorced
(he born 1 Apr 1910; died 3 Apr 1978 WA)
2 married Romey Z. TAYLOR 10 Sept 1948 Spokane, WA; divorced
(he born 1 June 1905; died Oct 1980 Spokane, WA)
597. Wilber Dee   born 12 Jan 1924 WY; died 4 July 1978 BC, Canada
married Clare May NELSON 8 June 1942 Pierce , WA.

346. EDNA IVA [-6] HILL, daughter of Rosa-Belle[-5] HAGAR (Sarah-[4] LYON; Phebe-[3] KIFF; Andrew-[2]; George-[1]) and Wilson C. HILL, was born 8 May 1882 Ward, Tioga, PA. She married Henry Rothland WILCOX (as his 2nd wife) on 10 January 1900 at Ward, Tioga County, PA. He was the son of Hezekiah WILCOX (Isaac) and Mary Elizabeth " Polly " PARKHURST, and was born 19 May 1857 Leroy, Bradford, PA; died 9 Nov 1948. Edna[-6] HILL died 5 Nov 1958 Canton, Bradford, PA.

Note: Henry R. WILCOX was married first to Frances MANDEVILLE on 19 May 1881. She was born ca 1861; died 1897. By that marriage he had 6 children: 1. Ira born July 1884; 2. Edith born Oct 1887; 3. Nettie M. born Nov 1888; 4. Gertrude F. born Nov 1890; 5. Leicester born May 1894; 6. Elam H. born April 1896.

Children of Edna Iva[-6] HILL and Henry WILCOX:
Surname **WILCOX**

598. Laura Naomi	born 31 May 1901 PA; died 20 Apr 1993 Granville Summit, PA	EOL
599. Florence M.	born 5 Feb 1904 Ward, Tioga, PA; died 10 June 1972 Windfall, PA	
600. Edmund <u>Mark</u>	born 24 Feb 1916 Canton, PA; died 27 Nov 1998 Williamsport, PA	
	1 married Terressa Jane SLADE 13 Apr 1941	
	(she born 25 May 1918; died 24 Sept 1985)	
	(she dau/o Philip Franklin SLADE and Mabel Harriett BENEDICT)	

Children: including Kathleen Joyce-[8] WILCOX born 20 Dec 1944 Canton, Bradford, PA
2 married _____ AHLEFELDT 20 June 1948, divorced 1973

349. CLAUDE LYLE[-6] HAGAR, son of John L-[5] HAGAR (Sarah-[4] LYON; Phebe-[3] KIFF; Andrew-[2]; George-[1]) and Sarah SHAW, was born 30 May 1879 Tioga County, PA. He married Jemima/ Jennie Ethel BLY on January 1906. She was the daughter of Edgar Milton BLY and Vina Lucy LUCE, and was born 30 Oct 1881 PA; died 1959 Mansfield, PA. Claude Lyle-[6] LYON died 20 Oct 1952 at Mansfield, PA

Children of Claude Lyle-[6] HAGAR and Jennie BLY:
Surname **HAGAR**

601. Margaret Elizabeth	born 7 Nov 1906 PA; died 23 Sept 1984
	married Lloyd Emerson AUSTIN 24 Dec 1925
	(he born 24 Apr 1901; died 1 Mar 1987)

Children : Richard D-[8] AUSTIN born ca 1927; Lyle-[8] born ca 1928; and Caroline I-[8] AUSTIN born ca 1930

602. Eloise Edith (twin)	born 21 Feb 1908 PA; died 1 Oct 1989 Wellsboro, PA (Ref: Obituary)
	1 married Russell Wheeler WATSON 11 April 1929
	(he born 12 May 1903 Richmond Twsp, Tioga Co., PA; died 26 Oct 1937

Child: Donald R.-[8] WATSON born ca _____ ; resided Syracuse, NY

	2 married Sanford Asahel DYKE 16 Dec 1940
	(he born 15 Aug 1906 Richmond, Tioga, PA; died 6 Feb 1971
	3 married Ross SMITH 1971 (Ref.: Obituary)
603. Elnora Ethel (twin)	born 21 Feb 1908 PA; died 1968
	married Lawrence Aaron COPP 7 Dec 1929 Charleston, Tioga, PA
	(he s/o Sanford George COPP and Martha DOUGLASS)
	(he born 30 March 1906 Asaph, Tioga, PA; died 20 May 971 Mansfield, PA

Children: Norma-[8] who married ___ LING; George-[8]; Eleanor-[8] who married ___ LEE;
and Lawrence Milton-[8] COPP born 19 Feb 1935, died 2000

603. Ina Belle	born 3 Feb 1909 PA; died 20 Dec 2001 Mansfield, PA	EOL
605. Julia Lyle	born 9 April 1910 Richmond Twsp, PA; died 31 Dec 1992	
	1 married Samuel Elias FROST 4 Feb 1928 Tioga, PA	
	(he s/o John S. FROST and _____) ; 2 married Victor JERZAK ca _____	
606. Fordyce John	born 12 April 1912 PA; died 10 March 2000 Tioga, PA	
	1 married Theresa Mary SULLIVAN Hakes 27 Oct 1932	
	(she dau/o Mark Timothy SULLIVAN and Neva Roberts SEYMOUR)	

Children: John M. " Jack "-[8] born ca ___ ; and Joanne-[8] HAGAR born ca ____
2 married Barbara J. BARROWCLIFF Jones

Children of Claude Lyle-⁶ HAGAR and Jennie BLY, continued:
Surname HAGAR

607. Milton Daniel	born 27 April 1917 Richmond, PA; died 24 Mar 1991 Mansfield, PA
	married Marian Arlene BARTLETT 1 Jan 1944 (she born ca 1926; died 2008)
	Child: (male) name unknown born 11 Sept 1954 Mansfield, PA
608. Lois	born 13 Feb 1919 PA; died April 1983 Tioga, PA
	married William HARRIS 13 Feb 1937 Elmira, Chemung, NY
	(he s/o V E HARRIS and _____)
609. Doris Marion	born 12 Dec 1920 PA; died 1 Dec 1979
	married Kenneth Robinson CALVERT 28 Sept 1939
	(he s/o Robert Carl CALVERT and Grace ROBINSON)
	(he born 19 Feb 1917 Wyoming Co., PA; died Jan 1979 Mears, NJ)
610. Lena Adrienne	born 24 June 1922 PA; died 31 Dec 1999 Morris, Tioga, PA
	married William Ramsdell BURROWS 14 April 1951 Mansfield, PA
	(he s/o Franz/ Frank BURROWS and Loula _____)
	(he born 4 May 1919; died 9 March 2007 PA
	Children: David-⁸, Russell-⁸, and Jerald-⁸ BURROWS
611. Claude Willard	born 9 Jan 1924 PA; died ____
	married Carrie Esther EGLI 8 Sept 1957 Montoursville, PA
	(she dau/o Clyde L. EGLI and _____)

359. HAROLD TAYLOR NIVEN-⁶ SMITH, son of Vance Marquis-⁵ SMITH (Harriet-⁴ LYON; Phebe-³ KIFF; Andrew-²; George-¹) and Ida M. _____, was born 5 November 1889 at Brooklyn, NY. He married Ruth E. HARRIS ca 1884 at ____. She was the daughter of Frank Burnside HARRIS and Mary A. ____, and was born June 1890 MA;; died ____. Harold T N-⁶ SMITH died Dec 1975 Brockton, MA.

Children of Harold T N-⁶ SMITH and Ruth E. HARRIS:
Surname SMITH

+ **612. VANCE**	born 8 Aug 1916 MA; died 28 Oct 1988 MA		
MARQUIS II	married Margaret Elizabeth PHINNEY		
613. Susan K.	born ca 1922	614. Sally B.	born ca 1924

361. LOTTA STATIA-⁶ LYON, daughter of Frank Leroy-⁵ LYON (Mason Leroy-⁴; Phebe-³ KIFF; Andrew-²; George-¹) and Mary CAHILL, was born 21 July 1891 at ____, IL. She married George Spencer LYMAN ca 1919. He was the son of William LYMAN and Martha Louise HEAFORD, and was born 29 July 1893, died March 1969, New Liberty, IL. Lotta Statia-⁶ LYON died March 1988.

Children: of Lotta Statia-⁶ LYON and George LYMAN:
Surname LYMAN

615. George Spencer	born 28 Jan 1920 IL; died 9 Feb 1998 Libertyville, IL
	married Florence Hoefer MANSFIELD
	(she born 9 March 1921 IL; died 25 Jan 2001 Libertyville, IL
616. Louise Mary	born ca 1922 IL; died ___ ; married _____ LYONS

362. PAUL LEROY-⁶ LYON, brother of above, was born 29 July 1893. He married Cecile PRANTLE ca ___ . She was the daughter of ____ PRANTLE and ____, and was born 27 Sept 1899, died 15 Jan 1972 Arlington Heights IL. Paul Leroy-⁶ LYON died 6 March 1953 Arlington Hts., IL

Children of Paul-⁶ LYON and Cecile PRANTLE:
Surname LYON

617. Paul Leroy, Jr.	born ca 1933; married Eileen M. ROWADEN 26 Sep 1955 Cook Co., IL
618. Barbara Ann	born ca 1935

363. LE ROY MASON-6 LYON, son of Samuel Mason-5 LYON (Mason LeRoy-4; Phebe-3 KIFF; Andrew-2; George-1) and Wilhelmina Christina SCHROEDER, was born 8 Feb 1891 at Rockford, Winnebago, IL. He married Orelda Grace REEDER on 10 March 1910 at Freeport, Stephenson, IL. She was the daughter of Frank REEDER and Nancy ___, and was born 5 Feb 1894 Freeport, IL; died 18 Dec 1986 Freeport, IL. Presumably they were divorced and he married 2nd to Della GIBBON on 19 Oct 1937. She was born 18 Aug 1894; died 23 Dec 1984 Freeport, IL. Le Roy Mason-6 LYON died 31 August 1986 at Freeport, IL

Children of Le Roy Mason-6 LYON and Orelda REEDER:
Surname **LYON**

619. Orelda Edythe — born 24 January 1914 IL; died ____; married Roland Christian BARES 1941 (he s/o Christian Herman BARES and Antonia K. ARNTZ) (he born 24 Sep 1913 NE; died 5 March 1984 FL)
Child: Stephen-8 BARES born ca ___; and Patricia-8 BARES born 12 June 1943; died 1 July 1943

620. Mason Reeder + — born 17 Nov 1915 Freeport, IL; died 26 Feb 2005 + Note: Conductor on the IL CRR married Katherine BLEHINGER ca 1936
Child: David-8 LYON born ca ___; resided Danville, VA

621. LaVerne Wilbur — born 30 March 1918; died ____; married Anna May MULNIX 14 Feb 1941

622. Patricia Grace — born 10 July 1920 Freeport, IL; died ____ married William Max HOWE 28 Sept 1940 Davenport, Scott, IA. (he born 26 April 1920; died 14 May 1999 Freeport, IL)
Child: Ronald Richard-8 HOWE born 21 Aug 1943; married Patricia Tucker KITCHEN 1971 (2 ch. Myra and Patrick)

364. RUTH VICTORIA-6 LYON, sister of above, as born 8 August 1894 IL. She married Guy Harry MYERS on 22 December 1915 at Freeport, Stephenson, Il. He was the son of Jacob MYERS and Lillian STEVENS, and was born Nov 1893 at Sterling, Whiteside, IL; died ca 1929 Texarkana, TX. Ruth V-6 LYON died 9 March 1974 , IL.

Children of Ruth Victoria-6 LYON and Guy MYERS:
Surname **MYERS**

+   **623. ARTHUR LYON** — born 7 Feb 1917 Freeport, IL; died 20 Nov 2000 Havertown, Delaware, PA married Marion Virginia DIDDENS 6 July 1940 Dubuque, IA. (she born 18 Feb 1919 Freeport, Il; died ____)

365. EDYTHE HENRIETTA-6 LYON, sister of above, was born 10 March 1895 WI. She married Elmer Gotthold. SOMMER on 17 January 1919 at Waukegan, Lake County, IL. He was the son of August F. SOMMER and Lydia Augustine, and was born 9 Oct 1897 Milwaukee, WI; died 11 August 1992 at Venice, Sarasota, FL. Edythe-6 LYON died 7 August 1988 Brookfield, Wisconsin.

Children of Edythe-6 LYON and Elmer SOMMER:
Surname **SOMMER**

624. Jeanne — born 26 Jan 1920; died ____; married Ralph Charles LUCK ca ____ (he born 23 Jan 1918; died Sept 1976 WI)
Children: Ralph Charles-8, Thomas Kent-8, and Susan-8 LUCK

366. CARL DEWEY-6 LYON, brother of above, was born 21 April 1898 at Polo, Ogle, IL. He married first to Hilda Frederica Maria SCHULTZ on 16 October 1920 at La Porte, Indiana. She was the daughter of John William SCHULTZ and Wilhelmina SCHROEDER, and was born 16 April 1898 La Porte, Indiana; died 10 Dec 1954 at Freeport, Stephenson, IL. He married 2nd to Marguerite LANNON ca ___ . She was born 7 July 1907 Arkansas; died ____. Carl D-6 LYON died 6 August 1968 at Jasper, Newton, Arkansas.

Children of Carl Dewey-6 LYON and Hilda SCHULTZ:
Surname **LYON**

+   **625. DORIS ELAINE** — born 2 Oct 1922 Freeport, IL; died 2002 married Ernest Harold STABENOW, Sr. 2 Oct 1945 Red Wing, Minnesota

Children of Carl Dewey-[6] LYON and Hilda SCHULTZ, continued:
Surname **LYON**

625. Cont'd.	(he s/o William Frederick STABENOW and Martha Mary PHILLIPS)	
	(he born 3 May 1920 Winslow, IL; died 8 July 2003 McConnell, IL.	
626. Mary Ellen	born 25 Dec 1924 Freeport, IL; died ____	
	married Donald La Verne KAISER 20 Sept 1946 Morrison, Whiteside, IL	
	(he born 20 Feb 1924 Freeport, IL; died 10 Feb 1957 Freeport)	

Child: Barry Allen -[8] KAISER born 6 July 1947 Freeport, IL

627. Carl Dewey	born 21 Jan 1926 Freeport, IL;	
	married Evelyn Lucille DE NARDO 17 Aug 1946 Chicago, Cook, IL	
	(she born 10 July 1926 Chicago, IL; died ____)	
628. Earl Richard	born 19 July 1927 Freeport, IL; died 10 Feb 1966 Freeport	
	married Darlene Ruth ROEMER Child: Kimberly[8] LYON born ca ___	
629. Beatrice Jane	born ca ____; married Calvin RAHN ca ___	

Children: Dennis Lee-[8] born ca __, and Carl Calvin-[8] RAHN born ca ___

630. Norma Jean	born ca ____; 1 married ____ EELLS ca ___	

Children: Debra-[8] born ca ___ and Cynthia-[8] EELLS born ca ____

2 married Richard R. HAUPT ca ____

Children: Thea-[8] born ca ___ and Brenda-[8] HAUPT born ca ____

370. DONALD EDWARD-[6] **LYON,** brother of above, was born 14 February 1908 Freeport, Stephenson, IL. He married first to Helen Elizabeth VAN DEEST 15 June 1929 at Freeport, IL. She was the daughter of Henry L. VAN DEEST and Florence WINNING, and was born 22 Nov 1910 Freeport, IL; died 21 Apr 1974 West Allis, WI. He married 2nd to Ruth Carolyn ADAMS on 23 Dec 1974 at Vienna, WV. She was born 11 Nov 1918 Pleasants, WV.

Children of Donald Edward-[6] LYON and Helen VAN DEEST:
Surname **LYON**

+	**631. JUNE**	born 15 July 1930 Freeport, IL; died 21 Jan 1996 Rochester, Olmsted, MN
	ELIZABETH	married Elmer Harold PLAETZER 4 June 1955 Milwaukee, WI
		(he born 23 Jan 1931 Milwaukee, WI;
		(he s/o Henry G. PLAETZER and Caroline ____)
+	**632. SONDRA LEE**	born 10 Dec 1936 Freeport, IL; died 18 June 2004 Charleston, WV
		1 married Donald Edward OLM 11 Dec 1954 Milwaukee, WI; divorced
		(he born 9 April 1932 Wauwatosa, WI; died 30 Sept 1971 Milwaukee, WI)
		2 married Carlos Horacio Hipolito BOETSCH, MD 1 Dec 1962 Milwaukee
		(he born 13 August 1934 Bell Ville, Argentina; died _____)
		3 married Cyril Montgomery RADCLIFF 28 Apr 1973 Charleston, WV
		(he born 22 Nov 1928 Miami, FL; died _____)
	633. Donald Edward	born 10 May 1938 Freeport, IL;

373. JEANETTE-[6] **MILLS,** daughter of Harriet-[5] PUTNAM (Harriet-[4] KIFF; Lyman-[3]; Andrew-[2]; George-[1]) and Lewis W. MILLS, was born ca 1853 PA. She married John S. DIETRICH ca 18__. He was the son of ____ DIETRICH and ____, and was born ca 1831 Belgium; died ca 1892. Jeanette-[6] MILLS died ca 1892.

Child of Jeanette-[6] MILLS and John S. DIETRICH:
Surname **DIETRICH**

+	**634. JOHN ALFRED**	born Aug 1872 PA; died 1946
		married Alice SCOHY 22 May 1893 (she born Dec 1874 Germany; died 1955)

391. FRANCES ISABELLE-[6] **PATCHEN,** daughter of Phoebe-[5] KIFF (Samuel-[4]; Lyman-[3]; Andrew-[2]; George-[1]) and Thomas Wilson PATCHEN, was born Dec 1879 PA. She married Charles Henry WERLINE 30 July 1902. He was the son of David R. P. WERLINE and Clara Ellen SHEFFER, and was born 24 May 1877; died 16 Nov 1945, Jersey Shore, Lycoming County, PA. Frances-[6] PATCHEN died 2 May 1963 NC.

Children of Frances-6 Isabelle PATCHEN and Charles Henry WERLINE:
Surname **WERLINE**

	635. Clara Ellen	born 2 Aug 1903 PA; died June 1976; married Arthur William NEFF ca 1928
		(s/o Arthur George NEFF and Martha E. MURRELL)
		(he born 22 Aug 1898; died 7 June 1967 Rochester, Monroe, NY)
		Children: Nancy-8 born, married Warren ALEXANDER; and Arthur Charles-8 NEFF, born13 Aug 1935; died 24 May 2009; married Nancy Lou WYAND 28 May 1957
+	**636. DR. LAURA BELLE**	born 6 Jan 1906 PA; died 12 May 1963 Charlotte, NC
		(he born ca 1900; died 1975)
		married James Almer PALMER; res. Charlotte, NC
	637. Raymond Lamar	born ca 1909; died _____
+	**638. LOUISE MILDRED**	born 1 May 1911 NY; died 6 Jan 1969 NC
		married Dr. Lee John SWEELEY, NC
		(he born ca 1907; died 18 July 1970 NC)
		(he s/o Harry Anthony SWEELEY and Helen Elizabeth LINN)

392. PURLEY IRA-6 PATCHEN, brother of above, was born 15 August 1881. He married Nellie Ada STONE 12 June 1906 Coudersport, PA. She was the daughter of Dellevan R. STONE and Maria Capitolia SLAWSON, and was born 19 Aug 1886, died 21 June 1967 Toledo, Ohio. Purley Ira-6 PATCHEN died 10 Jan 1958 Toledo, Ohio.

Children of Purley Ira-6 PATCHEN and Nellie Ada STONE:
Surname **PATCHEN**

639. Phoebe Ruth	born 20 Jan 1907; died 2 March 1989
	1 married Kenneth YEAGER
	2 married Carl William TSCHAPPAT 23 April 1928
	(he born ca 1901; died 6 May 1942)
640. Purley Kenneth	born 20 Aug 1909 PA; died 17 July 1976 Sylvania, OH
	married Irma Lurlim STEVENS 19 Oct 1929
	(she born 25 Feb 1911; died 31 Dec 1994)
	Child: Robert Kenneth-8 PATCHEN born ca ____
641. Thomas Dellevan	born 22 Feb 1916; died 20 Feb 1995
	married Hazel Pearl DEWITT
	(she dau/o George L. DEWITT and Beulah P. ZERKLE)
	(she born 20 Oct 1919 OH; died 11 Sept 1996 OH)
642. Marie B.	born ca 1922; died _____
	married Spurgeon Roscoe TEDROW 22 Jun 1940
	(he s/o Howard J. Ransom TEDROW and Elsie M. BORN)
	(he born 19 Jan 1914 OH; died 10 Sept 1997 OH)
	Child: Spurgeon Rosco-8 TEDROW, Jr. born 31 Dec 1948 OH
643. Katherine L.	born ca 1924; died _____
644. Vernon Ira	born 30 Sept 1927; died 8 Aug 1998 Owosso, MI.
	Child: Rev. Vernon L-8 PATCHEN born 30 Sept 1968 Owosso, MI

393. MELVINA BLANCHE " Vina"-6 PATCHEN, sister of above, was born 20 Jan 1884. She married Jesse Rumsey FORD ca _____ . He was the son of James C. FORD and Sarah PAUL, and was born 7 Oct 1883 NY ; died 28 Aug 1957. Melvina-6 PATCHEN died 8 April 1927. Jesse R. FORD married second to Louise POTTER.
Children of Melvina-6 PATCHEN and Jesse R. FORD:
Surname **FORD**

645. Harry L.	born 19 Jul 1904; died April 1984
646. Dorothy L.	born 6 June 1906; died May 1977 PA; married Charles BINGMAN
647. Lawrence E.	born 22 Aug 1908; died ____ ; married Elizabeth B. SARVEY
648. Beatrice Eileen.	born 1 Oct 1910; died 27 Oct 2005 NH
	married Harry Robert WHEELER

403. PAULINE EFFIE [-6] BESLEY, daughter of Ruth Evangeline-[5] KIFF (William-[4]; Andrew-[3;2]; George-[1]) and Ernest Monroe BAILEY, was born 26 April 1899/1900 at Austinville, Bradford County, PA. She married James Leon WHEELER 21 August 1920. He was the son of Francis " Frank ' Bradford WHEELER and Elizabeth A. KIFF SMITH, and was born 26 May 1898 Columbia Crossroads, Bradford Co., PA, died. 2 Dec 1978 Elmira, Chemung, NY. Pauline-[6] died 20 February 1960. He married 2nd to _____ HAYES on 2 April 1961.

Children of Pauline Effie-6 BESLEY and James Leon WHEELER:
Surname **WHEELER**   (all children born Elmira, Chemung, NY

649. James Leon	born 19 Oct 1931	651. Carol Ann	born 29 Feb 1936
650. Donald Ernest	born 8 July 1934	652. Virginia Ruth	born 31 Dec 1937

404. KENNETH NELSON-[6] BESLEY, brother of above, was born 25 July 1901/ 02 at Austinville, Bradford Co., PA. He married Irene Mildred MYERS on 27 May 1922 at Elmira, NY. She was the daughter of Charles Henry MYERS and Elizabeth KRISTOF(F), and was born 2 Sept 1903; died 1980. Kenneth-[6] BESLEY died 22 Feb 1988 Elmira Heights, NY

Children of Kenneth Nelson-[6] BESLEY and Mildred MYERS:
Surname **BESLEY**

+	**653. ARLENE ELIZABETH**	born 7 May 1923 Elmira, NY; died 17 Nov 2006 Horseheads, NY married Leon C. BATTERSON 25 Sept 1942 (he s/o Leon E. BATTERSON and Theresa ___) (he born 21 Aug 1921 Elmira, NY; died 6 Jan 2002 Elmira)
+	**654. DELORES HELEN**	born 14 Aug 1926, Elmira, NY; died 12 Oct 2008 married Norton A. BRACE 21 March 1947 (he s/o Adelbert BRACE and Bernice ____) (he born ca 1925 Elmira, NY)
+	**655. RICHARD KENNETH**	born 10 May 1929 Elmira, NY; died 2 March 1994 Elmira, Chemung, NY married Donna Marie TRACY 22 Oct 1956

+   **656. CHARLES HENRY** born 15 July 1936 Elmira, NY; married Carmelita Ann AFFELDT 1 Dec 1956

405. LAWRENCE LA VERNE [-6] BESLEY, brother of above, was born 6 March 1904 at Austinville, Bradford Co., PA. He married Edna May WILSON on 24 Nov 1926 at Elmira, Chemung, NY. She was the daughter of John WILSON and Emma HALL, and was born 28 May 1905 at Gillett, Bradford, PA; died Dec 1977. Lawrence-[6] BESLEY died Sept 1981 Elmira, NY.

Child of LaVerne-[6] BESLEY and Edna WILSON:
Surname **BESLEY**

657. Joan Ruth	bon 12 Sept 1941 Elmira, NY; died ____ married James E. WILSON 19 Jan 1963 Hammondsport, NY (he s/o Charles WILSON and Hazel ____)

407. LILLIAN JUNE-[6] BESLEY, sister of above, was born 25 June 1919 at Austinville, Bradford, PA. She married Arthur J. BOUVIER on 8 March 1941 at Sidney, NY. He was the son of Alfred J. BOUVIER and Eva WOOD, and was born 5 July 1916 at Malone, NY; died 30 Jan 2002 Bainbridge, Chenango Co., NY.

Children of Lillian June-[6] BESLEY and Arthur BOUVIER:
Surname **BOUVIER**   (all children born Sidney, NY)

658. Jeffery	born 5 Aug 1944 ; married Linda _____
659. Michele	born 30 Oct 1946 ; married Kenneth NEWTON; resided Santa Clara, CA
660. Nicole	born 10 Feb 1953; married _____ SHAVER
661. Jacqueline	born 14 Dec 1957; married John PARDEE

412. JOEL METCALF-6 KIFF, son of Arthur David-5 KIFF (Hiram-4; Peter-3; Andrew-2; George-1) and Jennie A. RYER, was born 17 Oct 1892 at Hobart, NY. He married Ester M. RODMAN ca 1917. She was the daughter of Frank RODMAN and Mary WALLACE, and was born ca 1896; died before 1946. Joel M-6 KIFF died March 1972 Kingston, Ulster, NY.

Child of Joel M-6 KIFF and Ester RODMAN:
Surname **KIFF**

> 662. Joel Metcalf, Jr.   born 11 July 1923 NY;   married Dorothy Mae SCHEFFEL 23 June 1946
> (she dau/o Henry L. SCHEFFEL and _____))
> Children: Karen-8 born May 1947, and Pastricia Ann-8 KIFF born 5 Jan 1949 Ashokan NY

416. MILES PERCIVAL -6 FRISBEE, son of Emory P-5 FRISBEE (Frances Estella-4 KIFF; Peter-3; Andrew-2; George-1) and Lena Belle FORSYTH, was born 23 May 1897 Sidney, NY. He married 1st to Juanita BALZA. They divorced 1937. He married 2nd to Ruth Anita HALLOCK on 26 Dec 1937. She was the daughter of Herman Frederick HALLOCK and Gertrude Cecilia ROTHCHILD, and was born 26 Sept 1908 MD, died 11 May 1979 Tampa, FL. He married 3rd to Mary Athelia WELCH on 12 June 1986. Miles-6 FRISBEE died 15 Aug 1994 FL.

Children of Miles-6 FRISBEE and his 2nd wife Ruth HALLOCK:
Surname **FRISBEE**
+   **663. DON ROY**   born 10 Dec 1939; married Lucille YATES 7 Jan 1962

419. ERNEST FORSYTH-6 FRISBEE, brother of above, was born 5 September 1902 at Kortright, Delaware County, NY. He married Doris E. WHITNEY 9 November 1940. She was the daughter of _____ WHITNEY and Vesta J. MILLER, and was born ca 1922 NY; died ____. Ernest-6 FRISBEE died 1 August 1965 Oneonta, NY

Children of Ernest-6 FRISBEE and Doris WHITNEY:
Surname **FRISBEE**
+   **664. LILA MAE**   born 17 May 1944 Oneonta, NY; married Floyd A. SHAW 9 Nov 1962
    665. Sheila Marie   born 1 August 1951 Oneonta, Otsego, NY

420. RUTH LOUISE-6 FRISBEE, sister of above, was born 3 June 1905 Kortright, Delaware County, NY. She married 1st to Rolfe A. MILLER on 1 January 1925. He was the son of George Washington MILLER and Liza THAYER, and was born 2 July 1900, died July 1974 Delhi, NY. They divorced.

She married her 2nd husband , Harold C. CAMPBELL, on 21 August 1937. He was the son of John M. CAMP-BELL and Nancy M. SMITH, and was born Feb 1894, died 1947. She married her 3rd husband, Burr C. HARDEN-BURGH, on 7 Sept 1957. He as the son of Milton HARDENBURGH and Frances E.____, and was born 26 Oct 1887, died ___ NY. Ruth Louise-6 FRISBEE died ___, NY

Child of Ruth Louise-6 FRISBEE and Rolfe MILLER:
Surname **MILLER**

> 666. .Leora Ruth   born 24 September 1924 West Kortright, Delaware, NY
> 663. Lena Elizabeth   born 16 Nov 1925 W. Kortright, NY; died ____

Child of Ruth Louise-6 FRISBEE and Harold CAMPBELL:
Surname **CAMPBELL**

> 668. Emory John   born 23 January 1940 Hobart, Delaware, NY

422. HUGH MIDDLETON-6 FRISBEE, brother of above, was born 7 October 1908 at Kortright, Delaware County, NY. He married Jean Adelia SHELLEY on 6 January 1950. She was the daughter of _____ SHELLEY, and___, and was born ____, died ___. Hugh Middleton-6 FRISBEE died ____.

Children of Hugh[-6] FRISBEE and Jean SHELLEY:
Surname **FRISBEE**

+	**669. WALTER DUANE**	born 16 Oct 1950 Oneonta, NY
		1 married Adele BAUTISTA 1 March 1972 in the Phillipines; annulled
		2 married Joan WILCOX 21 Aug 1972
	670. Ionetta Jane	born 19 March 1953 Oneonta, NY

426. MILDRED AMARILLUS[-6] **KIFF,** daughter of Franklin " Frank " Clayton-[5] KIFF (John Mabie-[4]; Erastus-[3]; Andrew-[2]; George-[1]) and Jennie S. WORDEN, was born 31 December 1899 at Alba Mtn., Alba, Bradford County, PA. She married George Leslie ACOR ca ____ . He was the son of Harry Boyd ACOR and Catherine Elizabeth " Libbie" LAHR, and was born 28 January 1902 Muncy, Lycoming, PA; died by drowning in Seneca Lake (one of the Finger Lakes of NY State) on 18 August 1966. The story of his death was chronicled in the local newspaper as having occurred because, while he was standing in a boat, fishing with a friend, a motor boat passed too close by, causing a wake. It overturned the small fishing boat., thus throwing George ACOR into the water. His body never surfaced according to witnesses, but was later recovered. His friend managed to cling to the overturned boat and was rescued. Unfortunately, the friend suffered a heart attack and died before the rescuers reached shore.

Children of Mildred-[6] KIFF and George ACOR:
Surname **ACOR**

+	**671. BETTY JENNIE**	born 31 Dec 1923 Waterloo, NY; died 30 Sept 1999
		married Charles H. KUMKEY June 1947; divorced
		(he born 28 June 1922; died 12 Jan 2001 Clifton Springs, NY)
	672. Myrtle Marie	born 5 June 1925 Waterloo, NY; died ____
		married James LIEBOLD ca ____ (Child: David-[8] LIEBOLD born ca ___)

428. GERTRUDE LAURA -[6] **KIFF,** sister of above, was born 23 April 1905 Troy, Bradford, PA. She married John Leonard VAN HOESEN 24 July 1926. He was the son of Frank D. VAN HOESEN and Jennie Catherine DECKER, and was born 28 July 1902 East Taghkanic, New York; died 3 Feb 1978 Waterloo, New York. Gertrude-[6] KIFF died 19 December 1994 Penn Yan, Yates County, New York.

Child of Gertrude-[6] KIFF and John Leonard VAN HOESEN:
Surname **VAN HOESEN**

+	**673. BERNICE MAE**	born 30 April 1927 Waterloo, NY; died ___
		1 married Bernard Jesse WARD 11 Oct 1947
		(he s/o Jesse Newell WARD and Ethel Margaret CADE)
		2 married Joseph Gavin DONAHUE 8 Oct 1971 Waterloo, NY
		(he born 10 March 1928 Clyde, Wayne, NY; died ____)

430. HELEN L -[6] **KIFF** , daughter of Delos-[5] KIFF (John-[4]; Erastus-[3]; Andrew-[2]; George-[1]) and Lucy-[5] CEASE, was born ca 1909 at ____ PA. She married James STRAUSS ca ____ .

Children of Helen L-[6] KIFF and James STRAUSS
Surname **STRAUSS**

674. Richard	born ca 1933	676. Linda	born ca 1937
675. John M.	born ca 1935	677. Donna Lou	born ca 1939; died 18 Nov 1940

437. HORACE[-6] **MURRAY,** son of Edson-[5] MURRAY (Ann Eliza-[4] KIFF; Erastus-[3]; Andrew-[2]; George-[1]) and Polly Rowena BOYCE, was born ca 1867 PA.. He married Alice PACKARD 19 Sept 1889 at Canton,

Bradford, PA. She was the daughter of Joel PACKARD and Abigail REYNOLDS, and was born ca 1875; died 3 Jan 1929 Alba, PA. Horace-[6] MURRAY died 20 July 1936 at Alba, PA.; and is buried at the cemetery there.

Child of Horace-[6] MURRAY and Alice PACKARD:
Surname **MURRAY**

+   **678. RAY E.**   born 22 Jan 1900 Alba, PA; died 19 Nov 951 Ward Twsp., Tioga, PA
married Mary JOHNSON ca ___
(she dau/o John JOHNSON and Martha CAMPBELL)
(she born 8 May 1900 Austinville,, PA; died 10 Sept 1956 Troy, Bradford, PA)

439. FRANK MURRAY-[6] JENNER, son of Helen-[5] MURRAY (Ann Eliza-[4] KIFF; Erastus-[3]; Andrew-[2]; George-[1]) and Fred H. JENNER, was born 18 Aug 1887 at Rochester, NY. He married Elizabeth ___ ca ___. She was born ___; died Oct 1974 at Geneva, New York. Frank-[6] JENNER was a Public School Principal, and died Dec 1977 at Canandaigua, Ontario Co., NY.

Children of Frank M-[6] JENNER and Elizabeth ___:
Surname **JENNER**

    679. Frank M., Jr.   born 6 April 1914 NY; died 15 Mar 2002 Longboat Key, Manatee, FL
married Irene R. ____ ca ____;   (he a research physicist)
(she born 10 Aug 1913; died Dec 1978 Pittsford, Monroe, NY)
    680. Helen Elizabeth   born ca 1916 NY; died ____
    681. Frederick E.   born 5 Nov 1917 FL; died 22 June 2008 Webster, Monroe, NY
    682. Pauline   born ca 1925   683. Edward L.   born 4 Oct 1928

440. CHARLES L-[6] CEASE   (see Mc INTOSH section Page 46; # 348 for descendants

445. OWEN-[6] MOORE, George Dudley-[5] MOORE (Harriet-[4] KIFF; Erastus-[3]; Andrew-[2;] George-[1]) and Frances SMITH, was born 25 August 1877 PA. He married Nina May INGERICK ca 1898-99. She was the daughter of George Elmer INGERICK and Minnie Lonella IVES, and was born 20 Dec 1880; died 2 Oct 1950. Owen L-[6] MOORE died 29 July 1948 Canton, Bradford, PA. They are buried at The Turner Cemetery, Grover, PA.

Children of Owen L-[6] MOORE and Nina May INGERICK:
Surname **MOORE**

+   **684. LLOYD W.**   born 10 Aug 1902 Tioga Co., PA; died 1 Sept 1965 Canton, Bradford, PA
married Alta L. BAUMBARGER ca 1923
(she born 27 Jan 1901; died March 1976 Canton)
+   **685. ELOISE A..**   born 17 Aug 1908 PA; died 15 Dec 2000 Canton, PA
married Larue M. LUNDY (he born 16 Apr 1908; died 13 Sept 1966 Canton)
(he s/o Joseph W. LUNDY and Emma REESER)
+   **686. CARLYLE EDWARD**   born 29 Mar 1912 E. Charleston Tioga, PA; died 30 Jan 1995 Canton, PA
1 married Canarisa Rebecca PORTER 24 Nov 1929 Canton, PA
(she dau/o Orwell PORTER and his 2nd wife Lydia NORTON)
(she born 3 Apr 1911 Shunk, Sullivan, PA; died 1975)
2 married Leotta Ruth FOSTER
    687. Marion D.   born ca 1918 PA; died ____

446. EDITH-[6] MOORE, sister of above, was born 22 May 1882 at Armenia Twsp, Bradford, PA. She married Willard-[5] CEASE ca ___. He was the son of Nelson-[4] CEASE and Margaret " Mag" EATON, and was born ca 1874 PA; died 1936. Edith-[6] MOORE died 2 July 1948 at Canton, Bradford, PA (See **page 87** MC INTOSH for children)

448. HARRY LEE -[6] FREEMAN, son of Adell Emma-[5] COSPER (Lucy-[4] KIFF; Erastus-[3]; Andrew-[2]; George-[1]) and Charles Lewis. FREEMAN, was born 9 Aug 1881 Canton, Bradford, PA. He married Pearl H. AUCHENBAUGH ca 1902.She was the daughter of ___ AUCHENBAUGH and ____, and was born ca 1887; died 1959. Harry L-[6] FREEMAN died 27 March 1929, PA.

Children of Harry Lee[-6] FREEMAN and Pearl H. AUCHENBAUGH:
Surname **FREEMAN**

688. Willard L.	born ca 1905 PA	
689. Charles L.	born ca 1907 PA; died ____	
690. Russell R.	born 19 Mar 1912 PA; died 15 July 2001 Glenside, Montgomery, PA	
	married Geraldine R. ENGLISH ca ____	
	(she dau/o Paul ENGLISH and Helen SELLECK)	
	(she born 19 Feb 1913; died 27 Oct 2010)	
691. H. Dwight	born 14 July 1914 Canton, Bradford, PA; died5 June 2003 Williamsport, PA	
	married Geraldine " Deannie" BELLOWS 8 Oct 1940 Canton, PA	
	(she dau/o Luther John BELLOWS and Jennie HOAGLAND)	
	(she born 6 Feb 1917 Leroy Twsp, PA; died 18 June 1992	

Child: Beverly-[8] FREEMAN born ca ___; married Gene SEGUR

692. Merrell Lloyd	born 9 Nov 1921 PA; died ____; served in the USAAC during WW 2

470. MYRTLE FRANCES [-6] **FREEMAN,** daughter of Clara-[5] KIFF (Charles-[4]; Erastus-[3]; Andrew-[2]; George-[1]) and George Phelps FREEMAN, Jr. and was born 31 July 1887 at Alba, Bradford, PA. She married Frank Hamilton-[7] THOMAS ca ____ . He was the son of Alvin [-6] THOMAS (Elizabeth-[5] BECKER; Hannah-[4] KIFF; James-[3]; Andrew-[2]; George-[1]) and his 1st wife Ella F. DEWEY, and was born 17 July 1884; died 10 Jan 1957 Troy, and is buried at Alba, PA .

Children of Myrtle Frances[-6] FREEMAN and Frank-7 THOMAS:
Surname **THOMAS**

+	**693. GEORGE ALVIN**	born 12 Aug 1910 PA; died 19 Sept 1945	
		married Empsie D. WALKER 23 Jan 1933	
		(she born 23 Jan 1914; died 28 April 1992 Indiana, PA)	
		(she dau/o Harry Toland WALKER and Maud Mary ____)	
	694. Wayne Freeman	born 4 Sept 1913; married Helen MILLER no issue	EOL
	695. Francis Paul	born 29 March 1917 PA; died ____; married Ruth JAMES ca ____	
		(she born 24 Nov 1920; died ____) resided New York City	

Children: James H-[8] born ca ___, married Jane MEBUS, and Jane Ann-[8] THOMAS born ca ____

471. IVA ADELL[-6] **FREEMAN ,** sister of above, was born 22 December 1889 at ___, PA. She married Ray W. MC NEAL / MC NEILL on 29 Jan 1912 at ____. He was the son of Edward MC NEAL and Lovina ___, and was born 2 Sept 1889; died February 1921. Iva Adell[-6] FREEMAN died ____. They resided at Elmira, NY.

Children of Iva Adell[-6] FREEMAN and Ray MC NEAL:
Surname **MC NEAL**

696. Jacqueline Clara	born 13 Aug 1914; died Nov 1995 Horseheads, Chemung Co., NY
	married Charles J. ZAWKO, Jr, no issue EOL
	(he born 23 Nov 1916; died 25 Dec 2010 Horseheads, Chemung, NY
697. Gerald Edward	born 16 Jan 1916; died 12 Oct 1949 **** (2 dau)
	married Grace MC ILWAIN ca ____
	(she dau/o Ralph R. MC ILWAIN and Bertha STONE)
	(she born 7 Mar 1916 PA; died 16 June 1988 Canton, PA)
	(she married 2nd Clarence Elwin WOOSTER 19 Sept 1942)
698. Florence Emma	born 22 July 1917; died 1 Aug 2007 Corning, Steuben, NY
	married Eugene H. KRISE 6 April 1934 Alba, Bradford, PA
	(he s/o Charles Edward KRISE and Frances MESSNER)
	(he born 6 May 1915 Pa; died 15 May 1996 Woodhull, Steuben, NY)

**** Note: Newspaper article (PA) 19 Oct 1949
" Gerald MC NEAL, 33, of 366 Walton Place , Elmira (NY) died en route to Soldiers and Sailors Memorial Hospital, Wellsboro, early Wednesday after an automobile accident near Middlebury (PA). Coroner Harry WILLIAMS said Mr. MC NEAL'S death was caused primarily by brain injuries. He also received a fractured left forearm. PA. State Police stated that Mr. MC NEAL was driving North on Route 84, near the home of Mr. and Mrs. Oliver METCALF, when the car failed to make a curve and struck a bridge. The Elmiran was reportedly driving an automobile owned by Mrs. Florence KRISE of 374 Main Street, Elmira. Mrs. KRISE said Mr. MC NEAL had borrowed the car. "

472. FANNIE PEARL-⁶ FREEMAN , sister of above, was born 7 December 1895 at Troy Twsp, Bradford, PA. She married George Albert GARD 13 Jan 1917 at Williamsport, PA. He was the son of George Burgess GARD and Joanna POST, and was born 3 March 1892 PA, died Aug 1978 Towanda, Bradford. PA. Fannie Pearl-⁶ FREEMAN died 8 May 1971 at Towanda, PA.

Child of Fannie-⁶ FREEMAN and George Albert GARD:
Surname **GARD**

699. George E.	born 7 Nov 1918 Wysox Twsp., Bradford, AP; died 6 Feb 2003 Columbia, PA
	married Dorothy JOHNS ca ____
	(she born 8 Dec 1918 PA; died _____)
	(resided Columbia, PA) (2 daus., 1 son)
700. Walter Freeman	born 26 Nov 1922 Bradford, PA; died 8 Feb 1977 Middleton, NY
	married _____ THOMSON (1 son)

473. LEON SHELDON[-7] **THOMAS,** son of Adolphus E-[6] THOMAS (Elizabeth-[5] BECKER ; Hannah-[4] KIFF; James-[3]; Andrew-[2]; George-[1]) and Mary BLAKEMAN, was born 24 December 1881 at Canton, Bradford, PA. He married Maud PACKARD ca 19__. She was the daughter of Winfield PACKARD and Alma FAULKNER, and was born 24 October 1880 PA; died ___. Leon-[7] THOMAS died 23 Oct 1947 at Alba, Bradford, PA., and is buried there.

Children of Leon S-[7] THOMAS and Maud PACKARD:
Surname **THOMAS**

701.	Gerald W.	born 5 Sept 1903 Alba, PA; died 3 Oct 1986 Sayre, Bradford, PA
		married Ella Catherine Cleora "Tot" HERMAN 22 Nov 1930
		(she dau/o Harry HERMAN and Bessie PAGE)
		(she born 27 Nov 1912; died ____; buried Ogdensburg Cemetery

Child: Jack-[8] THOMAS born 1 July 1931; married Ruth Ann ___; resided Binghamton, NY

702.	Alma / Elma	born 17 Nov 1912 PA; died _____
		married Henry Thomas LEHR 1 Nov 1930
		(he born 25 April 1905; died ____) resided Venice, FL

Child: Gerald B-[8] LEHR born 20 Jan 1932

479. ORA LOUISE-[7] **THOMAS,** daughter of Alvin-[6] THOMAS (Elizabeth-[5] BECKER; Hannah-[4] KIFF; James-[3]; Andrew-[2]; George-[1]) and his 1st wife Ella F. DEWEY, and was born 29 November 1881 at Bradford County, PA. She married Matthew Knickerbocker HOLCOMB on 23 Oct 1900 at Leroy, PA. He was the son of Pierson Alonzo HOLCOMB and Sophia Elizabeth MOTT, and was born 15 July 1880 Shunk, Sullivan County, PA; died 4 Jan 1976 Gillett, Bradford Co., PA. Ora Louise-[7] THOMAS died 19 Nov 1953 Sayre, PA

Children of Ora Louise-[7] THOMAS and Matthew HOLCOMB:
Surname **HOLCOMB**

+	**703. ELIZABETH**	born 13 June 1901; died 4 March 1989 Williamsport, Lycoming, PA
		married Mark Leigh AYRES 19 Aug 1918
+	**704. JOSEPHINE E.**	born 13 Aug 1902; died 12 Nov 1994 Gillett, PA
		married Albert " Bert " D. BLODGETT
		(he born 9 May 1899 PA; died 1 May 1957 Troy, PA)
		(he s/o James BLODGETT and Mae S. BARTLETT)
	705. Helen Irene	born 22 July 1903 Alba, PA; died 5 Aug 1993 Elmira, NY
		1 married Horton Erastus BERRY 16 Feb 1922 Canton, PA
		(he s/o Edgar BERRY and Alice M. DOTY)
		(he born 6 Mar 1898; died 6 May 1942 Gillett, PA

Child: Richard Matthew-[9] BERRY born 12 Nov 1928; married Joyce ____

		2 married Francis John WANDELL 3 June 1949
		(he s/o Curtis WANDELL and Clare May ALLEN)
		3 married Clemens ANDRUS ca 1985
		(he born 19 Apr 1904; died 21 Jan 1997)
+	**706. DONALD T.**	born 31 July 1904 PA; died 4 April 1994 Gillett, Bradford, PA
		married Ethel PATTERSON 27 June 1925
	707. Alvin J..	born 4 Oct 1908 PA; died 14 Oct 1933; married Edith Bell CONGDON
		(she dau/o Lynn CONGDON and Delle Voorhees OLDROYD)

480. FRANKLIN HAMILTON-[7] **THOMAS** , brother of above, (see # 470) Myrtle Fances-[6] FREEMAN

483. HARRY ALVIN -[7] **THOMAS** brother of above, was born 28 January 1897 at Bradford County, PA. He married Bernice BERRY ca 1924. She as the daughter of Edgar BERRY and Alice DOTY,and sister of Horton BERRY who married Helen Irene HOLCOMB (# 619) above. She was born 25 April 1901 PA; died May 1980 at Troy, PA. Harry-[7] THOMAS died ca 1979 Alba, Bradford, PA.

Children of Harry Alvin[-7] THOMAS and Bernice BERRY:
Surname **THOMAS**

708. Max   born 13 Oct 1925 ; died _____ (both living 2009; residing Livonia, NY)
married Marjorie Lucille CRANDLE ca _____
(she dau/o James E. CRANDLE and his 2nd wife Hazel Irene MC KEE)
     Child: Bonnie-[8] THOMAS born ca _____

709. Alvin B.   born 30 June 1929 Troy, Bradford, PA; died _____
married Mary Lou GRACE 3 Sept 950 Alba, PA
(she dau/o Arthur Howard GRACE and Florence May AYRES)
(she born ca 1932 Canton, PA; _____)

484. RAYMOND CARLOS[-7] **THOMAS,** half brother of above, son of Alvin[-6] THOMAS and his 2nd wife Mary NEWELL, was born 24 October 1907 At Troy Twsp. Bradford Co., PA. He married Mildred NENNINGER on 4 April 1931. She was the daughter of Charles A. NENNINGER and Virginia _____, and was born 25 April 1911; died ca 1939. Raymond[-7] THOMAS died 23 January 1988 at Burlington, Bradford, PA.

Children of Raymond[-7] THOMAS and Mildred NENNINGER:
Surname **THOMAS**

+   **710. CHARLES RAYMOND**   born 3 July 1932; died 29 June 1992; buried Alba Cemetery PA
married Audrey J. TURNER
(she dau/o Chester TURNER and Bessie SNYDER)

+   **711. RICHARD**   born 8 Jan 1935; died _____
married Virginia BROWN Turner (as her 2nd husband)
(she dau/o John BROWN and Vivian DUART)

485. WILLIAM ALONZO-7 THOMAS, brother of above, was born 12 September 1910 at Bradford County, PA. He married Vadys REESER on 1 June 1935 at Alba, Bradford, PA. She was the daughter of Archie REESER and Ada J. _____, and was born 21 October 1915 PA; died 6 Aug 2008 Hamburg, Berks. PA.

Child of William Alonzo-7 THOMAS and Vadys REESER:
Surname **THOMAS**

712. Lowell Archie   born 20 Aug 1936

487. ALBERT HENRY[-7] **THOMAS,** son of Meade-[6] THOMAS (Elizabeth-[5] BECKER; Hannah-[4] KIFF; James-[3]; Andrew-[2]; George-[1]) and Elizabeth B. NEWELL, was born 16 March 1894 at ___, PA. He married Ruth A. WARREN on 12 Feb 1913 at _____ PA. She was the daughter of Lamarr WARREN and Nellie P. BUNYAN, and was born 16 May 1894; died 27 Feb 1987. Albert H-[7] THOMAS died 7 May 1981. They are both buried at Crown Hill Memorial Park, New Hartford, NY.

Children of Albert-[7] THOMAS and Ruth A. WARREN:
Surname **THOMAS**

713. James Albert   born 13 Nov 1913 PA; died 22 Oct 1923; buried Alba Cemetery, Alba, PA

+   **714. ROBERT SHERMAN**   born 11 March 1925 PA; died _____
married _____

715. Margery Jean   born 15 Oct 1927 PA; died 27 Feb 1990, buried Alba Cemetery
married _____
     Children: (Surname unknown: James Michael-[9] born 26 Feb 1949; Kevin Albert-[9] born 13 Jan 1952;
and Elizabeth Anne-[9] _____ born 24 Nov 1958

716. Anne Elizabeth   born 10 Oct 1929 NY; died 7 May 1962; buried Crown Hill, New Hartford, NY
married _____
     Child: (Surname unknown) Allison Jane-[9] _____ born 10 Feb 1961

491. CHARLES H.-⁷ BECKER, son of Roland-⁶ BECKER (William Henry-⁵; Hannah-⁴ KIFF; James-³; Andrew-²; George-¹) and Julia Etta SMITH, was born 5 Nov 1905 at Blossburg, PA. He married Benita MERRITT ca ___. She was the daughter of Mark M. MERRITT and Bessie G. KITTLE, and was born 7 Dec 1907 Granville, PA, died April 1984 Millerton, Tioga, PA. Charles-⁷ BECKER died 6 February 1974 at Buffalo, New York.

Children of Charles-⁷ BECKER and Benita MERRITT:
Surname **BECKER**
> 717. Merritt Roland   born ca ____; died ____; married Dolores Jean JORALEMON ca ___
>> (she dau/o Paul K. JORALEMON and Irene WARNER)
>>> Children: 1. dau born ca ____; married ____KIPFERL (1 son, 1 dau); 2. dau born ca ____; married KONSOWITZ (2 sons)
>>> 3. son born ca ____; married ____ HUGHES; 4. Gregory David born and died 25 Feb 1957 Troy, PA

500. EUGENE HENRY-⁷ DUMOND, son of Perry Eugene-⁶ DUMOND (William Eugene-⁵; Harriet-⁴ KIFF; James-³; Andrew-²; George-¹) and Edith MASON, as born 24 April 1908 at ___. He married Margaret DUNWORTH on 8 July 1929. She was The daughter of Harry DUNWORTH and _____, and was born 29 April 1911 PA; died May 1974 Richmond, IN. Eugene Henry-⁷ DUMOND died 2 Oct 1988 Billings, Montana.

Children of Eugene H-⁷ DUMOND and Margaret DUNWORTH:
Surname **DUMOND**
> 718. Doris Jean   born 8 June 1932   719. James Wilson   born 1 Sept 1935

509. HELEN HANNAH-⁷ CONGDON, daughter of Clarence Herbert-⁶ CONGDON (Schuyler-⁵; Diantha-⁴ COVERT; Jemima-³ KIFF; Andrew-²; George-¹) and Arian MAPLES, was born 21 March/April 1899 at Oneonta, Otsego, New York. She married George Bernard BENEDICT 21 March 1922. He was the son of ____ BENEDICT and ____, and was born 27 April 1898 at Concepcion, Chile, SA; died 6 Nov 1991 Syracuse, Onondaga, NY. Helen H-⁷ CONGDON died 21 December 1987 Hartwick, NY.

Children of Helen H-⁷ CONGDON and George BENEDICT:
Surname **BENEDICT**
> 720. Patricia Ann   born 9 Jan 1926 Nyack, NY; died ____
>> married Charles Haddon BUCKLAND 23 April 1949 Skaneateles, Onon., NY

> 721. George   born 13 July 1927; died 4 Aug 2010 Onondaga Co., NY
>> 1 married Maria Consuelo BARNOYA 10 Aug 1957
>>> Children Carlos-⁹ born ca ___; nad Michael-⁹ BENEDICT born ca ___
>> 2 married Ruth Ann HANSEN Sitko
>>> Note: He was a well-known Central NY artist and teacher

544. EMMA AGNES-⁷ LYON, daughter of Layton Romain-⁶ LYON (John H-⁵; James-⁴; Jemima-³ KIFF; Andrew-²; George-¹) and Lillie May SHERMAN, was born 3 August 1895 Ward, Tioga, PA. She married Walter Byron EVERTS on 12 April 915. He was the son of Rev. Lawson Ferris EVERTS (Wesleyan minister) and Amy May ___, and was born 13 March 1897 Springfield, Bradford, PA; died 10 Nov 1947 Sayre, Bradford, PA. Emma Agnes died 12 May 1992.

Children of Emma Agnes-⁷ LYON and Walter Byron EVERTS:
Surname **EVERTS**
> 722. Bernard   born 29 May 1916 PA; died Jan 1971
> 723. Hartley L.   born 18 June 1918 PA; died 28 Oct 2008 Troy, PA
> 724. Edna Agnes   born 16 Aug 1920 PA ; died 7 May 1990 NY
>> married Adrian Norman VAN ALSTINE 21 June 1941
>> (he s/o Harold G. VAN ALSTINE and Verdie Otelle THOMPSON
>> (he born ca ____, died 22 May 2001 Corning, NY
> 725. Genevieve   born ca 1923 PA

571. BERNICE IRENE-[7] TISDALE, daughter of Ruth Ann-[6] GETSINGER (Lois Ophelia-[5] HAGAR; Sarah [4] LYON; Phebe-[3] KIFF; Andrew-[2]; George-[1]) and William Orlando TISDALE, was born 9 Jan 1892 Findlay, Hancock, Ohio. She married Glenn Robert BOWERS 25 June 1913 OH. He was the son of Emanuel Clement BOWERS and Elizabeth Ellen MC DOUGLE / MC DOUGAL, and was born 26 Nov 1891 OH; died 21 Sept 1970 Chicago, IL. Bernice-[7] TISDALE died 6 Oct 1959 .

Children of Bernice-[7] TISDALE and Glenn BOWERS:
Surname **BOWERS**

726. William Clement	born 8 May 1914 OH; died 12 Jan 1928 IL	
727. Glenn Robert, Jr.	born 21 Jan 1917 OH; died 19 June 1995 SC	
	married Helen Juanita VAN AUKEN ca _____	
	(she born 4 Sept 1918; died 1987 TX)	
	Child: Glenn Robert -[9] Jr. born 21 Jan 1917; died 19 June 1995 SC	
728. Ruth Ellen	born 22 Feb 1918 OH; died 10 Mar 1997 FL	
729. Elizabeth Louise	born 5 May 1923 IL; died 26 June 1980 FL	
	married Anthony Markas LEAL ca _____	
	(he born 7 Dec 1924 MA; died 2 Sept 1993 MA	
730. Milton Wesley	born ca 1929 Elmhurst, IL; died 1 May 1932 Elmhurst, IL	

612. VANCE MARQUIS-[7] SMITH –II, son of Harold Taylor Niven-[6] SMITH (Vance-[5] SMITH; Harriet-[4] LYON; Phebe-[3] KIFF; Andrew-[2]; George-[1]) and Ruth E. HARRIS, was born 8 Aug 1916 Brooklyn, NY. He married Margaret Elizabeth PHINNEY ca _____ . She was the daughter of Reagh Wilberforce PHINNEY and Gertrude Elizabeth REDDY, and was born 5 Sep 1918 Canada, died 28 Sep 1980 Salem, MA. Vance Marquis-II SMITH died 28 Oct 1988 at Brockton, MA. (Note: They reportedly had 8 children, but I do not have any info on the other 7)

Child of Vance Marquis-7 SMITH and Margaret Elizabeth PHINNEY:
Surname **SMITH**

731. Vance Marquis III	born 18 June 1943 Boston, Suffolk, MA; died 25 Nov 2001 VT	
	married Jane LANGMAID	Child: Vance Marquis-[9] SMITH born 21 Nov 1970

623. ARTHUR LYON -[7] MYERS, son of Ruth Victoria-[6] LYON (Samuel Mason-[5]: Mason LeRoy-[4]; Phebe-[3] KIFF; Andrew-[2;] George-[1]) and Guy Harry MYERS, was born 7 Feb 1917 at Freeport, Stephenson, IL. He married Marion Virginia DIDDENS 6 July 1940 at Dubuque, IA. She was the daughter of _____ DIDDENS and ___ , and was born 18 Feb 1919 Freeport, IL; died___ . Arthur Lyon -[7] MYERS died 20 Nov 2000 Havertown, Delaware, PA

Children of Arthur Lyon-[7] MYERS and Marion DIDDENS:
Surname **MYERS**

732. Arthur Gerald	born 6 Aug 1941 Freeport, IL; died 19 Nov 1943 Freeport, IL	
+ **733. GARY GEORGE**	17 Feb 1945 Freeport, IL	
	1 married Dianne Rae KEHLER 20 January 1968 Lena, Stephenson, IL	
	(she born 10 Oct 1947 Freeport, IL;	
	2 married Gerey May SMITH 12 June 1976 Freeport, IL	
734. Roger Lee	born 25 October 1947 Freeport, IL	
	married Patricia Ann HALBIN 28 March 1969 Freeport	
	(she born 9 July 194 Freeport, IL)	
	Child: Natalie Jean-[9] MYERS born 29 Sept 1969 Freeport, IL	
735. Terry Duane	born 14 June 1953 Freeport, IL	
	married Rose Jeanette WEST 22 Jan 1982 Freeport, IL	
	(she born 23 Sept 1954 Freeport, Il)	
736. Lori Ann	born 15 Aug 1961 Freeport, IL	
	married Steven Clifford TUCKER 10 May 1980 Freeport, IL	
	(he born 16 Nov 1959 Freeport, IL)	
	Child: Brianne Virginia-[9] TUCKER born 16 Aug 1983 at Hill Air Force Base, UT.	

625. DORIS ELAINE[7] **LYON**, daughter of Carl Dewey [6] LYON (Samuel Mason[5]; Mason Leroy[4]; Phebe[3] KIFF; Andrew[2]; George[1]) and Hilda Frederica Maria SCHULTZ, was born 2 October 1922 at Freeport, Stephenson, IL. She married Ernest Harold STABENOW, Sr. on 2 October 1945 at Red Wing, Goodhue, MN. He was the son of William Frederick STABENOW and Martha Mary PHILLIPS, and was born 3 May 1920 in Winslow, Stephenson, IL; died 8 July 2003 McConnell, Stephenson, IL. Doris Elaine[7] LYON died 2 Dec 2002 WI.

Children of Doris Elaine[7] LYON and Ernest STABENOW;
Surname **STABENOW**

+	**737. JEANNE LUCILLE**	born 25 May 1947 Freeport, IL married Billy Joe WIBERG 27 Sept 1969 Lena, Stephenson, IL (he born 14 April 1945 Princeton, Bureau, IL)
+	**738. WILLIAM FREDERICK**	born 30 Nov 1948 Freeport, IL married Marsha Joy RACKOW 4 March 1972 at Freeport, IL (she born 7 Sept 1952 Freeport, IL)
+	**739. ERNEST HAROLD, JR**	born 8 May 1950 Freeport, IL married Cathy Jo RILLIE ca ____ Freeport, IL (she born 2 Sept 1950)
	740. Mary Anne	born 21 Nov 1964 Freeport, IL

631. JUNE ELIZABETH[7] **LYON**, daughter of Donald Edward[6] LYON (Samuel Mason[5]; Mason Leroy[4]; Phebe[3] KIFF; Andrew[2]; George[1]) and Helen Elizabeth VAN DEEST was born 15 July 1930 at Freeport, Stephenson, IL. She married Elmer Harold PLAETZER 4 June 1955 at Milwaukee, WI. He was born 23 January 1931 Milwaukee; died ____ . June Elizabeth[7] LYON died 21 Jan 1996 at Rochester, Olmsted, MN.

Child of June E[7] LYON and Elmer PLAETZER:
Surname **PLAETZER**

741. Scott Alan	born 7 April 1956 Milwaukee, WI married Beth Joanne HAMMER 10 July 1982 Redding, CA (she born 24 Sept 1956 Redding, CA) Child: Alexander William [9] PLAETZER born 27 Feb 1990 Rochester, MN

632. SONDRA LEE[7] **LYON**, sister of above, was born 10 December 1936 at Freeport, Stephenson, IL. She married 1st to Donald Edward OLM on 11 Dec 1954 at Milwaukee, WI. He was the son of ____ OLM and ____, and was born 9 April 1932 at Wauwatosa, Milwaukee, WI; died 30 Sept 1971 at Milwaukee, WI. They were divorced.

Her 2nd husband was Carlos Horacio Hipolito BOETSCH, MD. They married 1 Dec 1962 at West Allis, Milwaukee, WI. He was born 13 August 1934 at Bell Ville, Cordoba, Argentina; died 23 Oct 1969 at Kanawha, WV.

She married 3rd to Cyril Montgomery CRAIG on 28 April 1973 at Charleston, Kanawha, WV. He was born 22 Nov 1928 at Miami, Dade, CA. Sondra[7] LYON died 18 June 2004 at Charleston, WV.

Children of Sondra[7] LYON and her 1st husband Donald OLM:
Surname **OLM** (both children born at Milwaukee, WI)

742. David William	born 10 Nov 1955 (name changed to Boetsch)
743. Debra Lee	born 19 June 1957; died the same day

Children of Sondra[7] LYON and her 2nd husband Carlos BOETSCH:
Surname **BOETSCH**

744. Charles Edward	born 16 Aug 1963 Charleston, WV
745. John Roland	born 8 Sept 1969 Charleston, WV married Elizabeth Ann FETROW 21 Jan 1995 Bedmidji, Beltrami, MN (she born 20 Jan 1970 Omaha, NE)

Child of Sondra-[7] LYON and her 3rd husband Cyril CRAIG:
Surname **CRAIG**

> 746. Chris Montgomery   born 9 Dec 1973 Parkersburg, Wood, WV
> married Karen Suzanne RADCLIFF 1 October 1998 San Diego, CA

634. JOHN ALFRED-[7] DIETRICH, son of Jeanette-[6] MILLS (Harriet-[5] PUTNAM; Harriet-[4] KIFF; Lyman-[3]; Andrew-[2]; George-[1]) and John S. DIETRICH, was born August 1872 at ____, NY. He married Alice SCOHY on 22 May 1893 at Blackford, Indiana. She was the daughter of John Remy SCOHY and Lescadi PANIER, and was born Dec 1874 Germany, immigrated to the US in 1880; died ca 1955. John A-[7] DIETRICH died ca 1946.

Children of John-[7] DIETRICH and Alice SCOHY:
Surname **DIETRICH**

+   **747. DAISY MAY**   born 10 June 1896/7 Elmira, NY; died 8 March 1943 Ft. Smith, Arkansas
    married Vincent Arthur WILSON ca 1913
    (he s/o Lewis WILSON and Sarah M. SMILEY)
    (he born 30 May 1897 Oaks Indian Territory OK; died _____)

748. Vina   born ca Dec 1899 NY; died _____

749. Gladys Adelia   born 25 Apr 1902 PA; died 18 Jan 1997 OK
    married Louis Allen HILL ca _____ (Occupation : Embalmer)
    (he born 20 Oct 1898 OK; died 9 March 1978 El Paso, TX)
    (he s/o Cornelius Dixon HILL and Izora JAMES)
        Children: Louis Allen-[9] Jr. born ca 1927 OK; Doris Carolyn-[9] born ca 1932 OK; and John Dixon-[9] HULL born ca 1939 OK

750. Arlene   born ca 1906; married _____ ABERNATHY ca; divorced before 1940
        Child: Howard D-[9] ABERNATHY born ca 1934 OK

Note: According to the 1940 Census there was another grandchild living with John and Alice DIETRICH His name was John E. DARE and was born ca 1920 Mississippi. Unknown as to which daughter was his mother.

636. LAURA BELLE-[7] WERLINE, daughter of Frances Isabelle-[6] PATCHEN (Phoebe-[5] KIFF; Samuel-[4]; Lyman-[3]; Andrew-[2]; George-[1]) and Charles Henry WERLINE, was born 6 Jan 1906 PA. She was married ca _____ to James Almer PALMER. He was the son of William Samuel PALMER and Rhoda RILEY, and was born 15 Feb 1900 Alabama; died 10 Sept 1975 NC. Both Laura Belle and James were Doctors of Optometry in Charlotte, NC. Laura Belle-7 WERLINE dies 12 May 1963 , NC.

Children of Laura Belle-[7] WERLINE and James PALMER:
Surname **PALMER**

751. JoAnn C.	born ca 1927 NC	753. Mitzi Lee born 27 May 1931 NC.
752. Frances Rhoda	born 26 Feb 1930 NC.; married _____ TODD	

638. LOUISE MILDRED-[7] WERLINE, sister of above, was born 1 May 1911, NY. She married Dr. Lee J. SWEELEY ca ____. He was the son of Harry Anthony SWEELEY and ____, and was born ca 1907; died ____. Louise-[7] WERLINE died 6 Jan 1969 NC.

Children of Louise-[7] WERLINE and Dr. Lee J. SWEELEY:
Surname **SWEELEY**

753. Robert Lee   born ca 1929-30; died ____
755. Thomas David   born ca 1935; died 2005
756. Margaret Elizabeth   born 6 May 1950 Laurinburg, Scotland, NC (NC Birth Records)
757. Sarah Jean   born Dec 1951 Laurinburg, Scotland, NC

653. ARLENE ELIZABETH-[7] BESLEY, daughter of Kenneth-[6] BESLEY (Ruth-[5] KIFF; William-[4]; Andrew-[3;2] George-[1]) and Irene MYERS, was born 7 May 1923 at Elmira, Chemung County, NY. She married Leon C. BATTERSON on 25 Sept 1942. He was the son of Leon E. BATTERSON and Theresa ____, and was born 21 Aug 1921 NY; died 6 Jan 2002. Arlene-[7] BESLEY died 17 Nov 2006 Elmira, NY.

Children of Arlene-[7] BESLEY and Leon BATTERSON:
Surname **BATTERSON**

758. Gary Lee	born 11 Feb 1944 NY; resided Tacoma, WA	
759. Gregory Lynn	born 26 Nov 1946; resided FL	

654. DELORES HELEN-[7] BESLEY, sister of above, was born 14 August 1926 at Elmira, Chemung, NY. She married Norton Augustus BRACE on 21 March 1947. He was the son of Adelbert BRACE and Bernice Dickens TICHENOR, and was born 11 Oct 1924 Elmira Heights, NY; died ____. Delores-[7] BESLEY died 12 Oct 2008 Elmira. NY.

Children of Delores-[7] BESLEY and Norton BRACE:
Surname **BRACE**

760. David John	born 13 Oct 1947	762. Robert Dean	born 18 Jan 1951
761. Susan Irene	born 1 May 1949	763. Thomas Norton	born 5 Sept 1952

655. RICHARD KENNETH-[7] BESLEY, brother of above, was born 10 May 1929 at Elmira, Chemung, NY. He married Donna Marie TRACY on 22 October 1956. She was the daughter of ____ TRACY and ____, and was born ____; died ____. Richard-[7] BESLEY died ____.

Child of Richard K-[7] BESLEY and Donna TRACY:
Surname **BESLEY**

764. Elaine Irene	born 15 Jan 1957 NY

656. CHARLES HENRY-[7] BESLEY, brother of above, was born 15 July 1936 at Elmira, Chemung, NY. He married Carmelita Ann AFFELDT on 1 December 1956. She was the daughter of ____ AFFELDT and ____, and was born ____, died ____. Charles Henry[7] died ____.

Children of Charles Henry-[7] BESLEY and Carmelita AFFELDT:
Surname **BESLEY**

765. Michael Kenneth	born 28 April 1957	767. Sheryl Marie	born 12 Sept 1962
766. Connie Ann	born 22 Sept 1958		

653. DON ROY-[7] FRISBEE, son of Miles Percival-[6] FRISBEE (Emory-[5]; Frances -[4] KIFF; Peter-[3]; Andrew-[2]; George-[1]) and Ruth Anita HALLOCK, was born 10 December 1939 at Lutz, Hillsborough, Florida. He married Lucille Yates 7 January 1962. She was the daughter of ____ YATES and ____, And was born ____.

Children of Don Roy-[7] FRISBEE and Lucille YATES:
Surname **FRISBEE**

768 David Roy	born 29 Dec 1962 Pinellas Park, FL
769. James Robert	born 6 Jan 1964 Pinellas Park, FL
770. Laura Marie	born 20 April 1967 Houston, Harris, TX

664. LILA MAY-[7] FRISBEE, daughter of Ernest Forsyth-[6] FRISBEE (Emory-[5]; Frances Estella-[4] KIFF; Peter-[3]; Andrew-[2], George-[1]) and Doris F. WHITNEY, was born 17 May 1944 at Oneonta, Otsego, NY. She married Floyd A. SHAW 9 Nov 1962.

Children of Lila May-[7] FRISBEE and Floyd A. SHAW:
Surname **SHAW**

771 Raymond Michael	born 10 Nov 1963 Oneonta, NY
772. Darrin Matthew	born 24 March 1965 Oneonta
773 Rebecca Lorraine	born 21 Oct 1970 Delhi, Delaware, NY

669. WALTER DUANE-[7] FRISBEE, son of Hugh Middleton-[6] FRISBEE (Emory-[5]; Frances Estella-[4] KIFF; Peter-[3]; Andrew-[2]; George-[1]) and Jean Adele SHELLEY, was born 16 Oct 1950 at Oneonta, NY. He married 1st to Adele BAUTISTA Mar 1972 in the Philippines. They divorced. He married 2nd to Joan WILCOX on 21 Aug 1972.

Children of Walter Duane-[7] FRISBEE and Joan WILCOX:
Surname **FRISBEE**

774. Walter Duane, Jr.	born 24 May 1973 Tarawa Terrace, NC	
775. Jennifer Lee	born 25 April 1974 Norwich, Chenango, NY	
776. Michael Hugh	born 5 Jan 1976 Jacksonville, SC	
777. Jeffery Gene	born 8 Dec 1976 Jacksonville, SC	
778. Stephanie Ann	born 16 Nov 1977 Jacksonville, SC	
779. Beverly Claudine	born 27 Feb 1979 Hamilton, Madison, NY	
780. Kimberly Lynne	born 12 June 1980 Albany, Albany, NY	

671. BETTY JENNIE-[7] ACOR. daughter of Mildred Amarillus-[6] KIFF (Frank Clayton-[5]; John Mabie-[4]; Erastus-[3]; Andrew-[2;] George-[1]) and George Leslie ACOR, was born 31 December 1923 at Waterloo, NY. She married Charles H. KUMKEY June 1947. They divorced. He was the son of Julius KUMKEY(born Germany) and Bertha H. ____, and was born 28 June 1922 NY; died 12 Jan 2001 Clifton Springs, Ontario, NY. Betty-[7] ACOR died 30 Sept 1999.

Children of Betty Jennie-[7] ACOR and Charles H. KUMKEY:
Surname **KUMKEY**

781. Son (un-named)	born 1947; died 1947	
+ **782. JOYCE ANN**	born 20 June 1948 Waterloo, NY	
	1 married Edward BALDASARI ca 1967/68 Seneca Falls, NY	
	2 married Edward MC CARTY ca ____ (reside Tennessee)	
783. Shirley Mae	born 20 Nov 1950 Waterloo, NY; single	

673. BERNICE MAY-[7] VAN HOESEN, daughter of Gertrude Laura-[6] KIFF (Franklin " Frank"-[5]; John Mabie-[4]; Erastus-[3]; Andrew-[2]; George-[1]) and John Leonard VAN HOESEN, was born 30 April 1927 at Waterloo, NY. She married 1st to Bernard Jesse WARD on 11 Oct 1947. He was the son of Jesse Newell WARD and Ethel Margaret CADE, and was born ____; died ____. Her 2nd marriage was to Joseph Gavin DONAHUE, as his 2nd wife, on 8 Oct 1971 at Waterloo, NY. He was born 10 March 1928 at Clyde, Wayne County, NY.

Children of Bernice-[7] VAN HOESEN and Bernard WARD:
Surname **WARD**

784. Susan Elaine	born 20 July 1948 Waterloo, NY (Child: David James-9 WARD born 23 Nov 1970)	
785. Stephen Brian	born 10 Feb 1952 ; married Susan Jane DONAHUE 5 Nov 1977	
	(she born 30 Sept 1955)	
	Children: Justin John-9 born 2 Jan 979 Geneva, NY, and McKenzie Donahue-9 WARD born 30 May 1981 Geneva	

678. RAY EDD-[7] MURRAY, son of Horace-[6] MURRAY (Edson Allen-[5;] Ann Eliza-[4] KIFF; Erastus-[3]; Andrew-[2]; George-[1]) and Alice PACKARD, was born 23 January 1900 at Alba, Bradford, PA. He married Mary JOHNSON ca 1924. She was the daughter of John JOHNSON and Martha CAMPBELL, and was born 18 May 1900 Austinville, PA; died 10 Sept 1956 at Troy, Bradford, PA. Ray E-[7] MURRAY died 19 Nov 1951 at Ward Twsp., Tioga County, PA. They are buried at the Alba Cemetery.

Child of Ray-[7] MURRAY and Mary JOHNSON:
Surname **MURRAY**

786. William	born ca 1925	
+ **787. CHARLOTTE**	born ____; died ____; married James Murray TILLOTSON ____	
	(he s/o Murray S. TILLOTSON and Edna WILLIAMS)	
	(he born 28 June 1925 Canton, PA; died 24 Aug 1993 Canton, PA)	

684. LLOYD W-[7] MOORE, son of Owen I.-[6] MOORE (George Dudley-[5]; Harriet-[4] KIFF; Erastus-[3]; Andrew-[2]; George-[1]) and Nina May INGERICK, was born 10 Aug. 1902 Tioga County, PA. He married Alta BAUM-BARGER 1923. She was born 27 Jan 1901 PA; died March 1976 Canton, PA. Lloyd-[7] died 1 Sept 1965 Troy, PA.

Children of Lloyd-[7] MOORE and Alta BAUMBARGER:
Surname **MOORE**

788. Ruth V.	born ca 1924	791. Betty M.	born ca 1929
789. Elna L.	born ca 1926	792. Arthur	born 9 Sept 1932; died 1942
790. Lois	born ca 1927	;	

685. ELOISE A-[7] MOORE, sister of above, was born 17 August 1908 PA. She married Larue M. LUNDY ca ___. He was the son of Joseph W. LUNDY and Emma REESER, and was born 16 April 1908; died 13 Sept 1966 Canton, Bradford. PA. Eloise-[7] MOORE died 15 Dec 2000 Canton, PA.

Children of Eloise-[7] MOORE and Larue LUNDY:
Surname **LUNDY**

793. Edward Larue	born 18 Mar 1930 Canton, PA; died 28 Jan 2004 Colton, CA
	married Arlene HANSON
	Children: Hollis Larue-[9] born ca ___, and Cheryl-[9] LUNDY born ca ___, married ___ WYATT
794. Carol	born ca ____, marred Harry JONES; resided Roaring Branch, PA
795. Marilyn	born ca ____, married Frank HUFF; resided Montoursville, PA

686. CARLYLE EDWARD-[7] MOORE, brother of above, was born 29 Mar 1912 at Charleston, Tioga County, PA. He married first to Canarissa Rebecca PORTER on 29 Nov 1929 Canton, PA. She was the daughter of Orwell PORTER and his 2nd wife Lydia NORTON, and was born 3 April 1911 Shunk, Sullivan, PA; died 2 June 1975. He married 2nd to Leotta Ruth FOSTER ca ___. Carlyle-[7] MOORE died 30 Jan 1995 at Canton, Bradford, PA.

Children of Carlyle-[7] MOORE and Canarissa PORTER:
Surname **MOORE**

796. son	born _____
797.	born _____
798. Janet	born _____
799. Canarissa Marie	born 1931; died 1931
800. Duane J.	born 1 Sept 1933
80 . Edward	born ca 1936
801. Joyce Ann	born ca 1939

693. GEORGE ALVIN-[7] THOMAS,, son of Myrtle Frances-[6] FREEMAN (Clara-[5] KIFF; Charles-[4]; Erastus-[3]; Andrew-[2]; George-[1]) and Frank Hamilton THOMAS, was born 12 August 1910 PA. He married Empsie D. WALKER ca ____. She was the daughter of Harry Toland WALKER and Mary Maud ___, and was born 23 Jan 1914 at Danville, Montour, PA; died 28 April 1992 at Indiana, PA. George Alvin-[6] THOMAS died 9 Sept 1945.

Children of George Alvin-[7] THOMAS and Empsie WALKER:
Surname **THOMAS**

802. Ronald Walker	born 18 / 25 April 1937
	married Geri _____
	Children: Greg-[9]; Jeff-[9]; Pam-[9] and Mike-[9] THOMAS

KIFF

703. ELIZABETH-⁸ A. HOLCOMB, daughter of Ora-⁷ THOMAS (Alvin-⁶; Elizabeth-⁵ BECKER; Hannah⁻⁴ KIFF; James-³; Andrew-²; George-¹) and MATTHEW Knickerbocker HOLCOMB, was born 13 June 1901. She married Mark Leigh AYRES on 18 Aug 1918. He was the son of _____ AYRES and ____, and was born 20 Sept 1893 Mainesburg, Tioga, PA; died 11 Nov 1973 Troy, Bradford, PA. Elizabeth-⁸ HOLCOMB died 4 Mar 1989.

Children of Elizabeth⁻⁸ HOLCOMB and Mark AYRES:
Surname **AYRES**

803. Donald Leigh	born 13 April 1920; died 16 May 2005	
804. Oscar Alvin Lanier	born 24 May 1922; died 21 May 2005 Troy, PA; married Helen CRANDLE	

704. JOSEPHINE-⁸ HOLCOMB, sister of above, was born 13 August 1902. She married Albert " Bert " D. BLODGETT on 23 July 1919 at Elmira, NY. He was the son of James BLODGETT and Mae S. BARTLETT, and was born 9 May 1899; died 1 May 1957 Troy, Bradford, PA. Josephine⁻⁸ HOLCOMB died 12 Nov 1991 Gillett, Bradford, PA.

Children of Josephine⁻⁸ HOLCOMB and Bert BLODGETT:
Surname **BLODGETT**

805. Marie	born 9 June 1920	807. Jo Ann	born 3 June 1928; died 1983
806. Phyllis	born 4 Dec 1922		

706. DONALD T⁻⁸ HOLCOMB, brother of above, was born 31 July 1904. He married Ethel PATTERSON on 27 June 1925. She was the daughter of _____ PATTERSON and ____, and was born 1904, died 1991. Donald-⁸ HOLCOMB died 4 April 1994 Gillett, Bradford, PA..

Children of Donald-⁸ HOLCCOMB and Ethel PATTERSON:
Surname **HOLCOMB**

808. Shirley Louise	born 16 March 1928; died ____; married _____ HARKNESS
809. Joyce Mae	born 15 April 1930; 23 Sept 1989 Sayre, PA; married _____ HALL ca 1948

710. CHARLES RAYMOND-⁸ THOMAS, son of Raymond Carlos-⁷ THOMAS (Alvin-⁶; Elizabeth-⁵ BECKER; Hannah-⁴ KIFF; James-³; Andrew-²; George-¹) and Mildred NENNINGER, was born 3 July 1932 at ____. He married Audrey J. TURNER ca ____. She was the daughter of Chester TURNER and Bessie SNYDER, and was born 8 Dec 1933 Canton, died ____. Charles-⁸ THOMAS died 29 June 1992, and is buried at Alba, Bradford, PA.

Children of Charles Raymond-8 THOMAS and Audrey TURNER:
Surname **THOMAS**

810. David R.	born ca ____
811. Daryl	born 22 April 1959; died young Troy, PA
812. Denise	born ca ____; married Paul TOTH
813. De Anna	born ca ____; married Randy E. MAY
814. Dessa	born ca ____; married Brian EARLE
815. Don	born ca ___; married Monika ___

711. RICHARD-⁸ THOMAS, brother of above, was born 18 January 1935 at ____. He married Virginia BROWN Turner ca ____. She was the daughter of John BROWN and Vivian DUART, and was born ____. She was married 1st to Philip TURNER. They divorced.

Children of Richard-[8] THOMAS and Virginia BROWN (Turner):
Surname **THOMAS**

816. Roy	born ca _____	
817. Robin	born ___; married John BRACKMAN ca 1993	
	(he s/o Paul BRACKMAN and _____)	

714. ROBERT SHERMAN-[8] THOMAS, son of Albert-[7] THOMAS (Meade-[6]; Elizabeth-[5] BECKER; Hannah-[4] KIFF; James-[3]; Andrew-[2]; George-[1]) and Ruth WARREN, was born 11 March 1925 at ____. He married _____

Children of Robert S-[8] THOMAS and _____:
Surname **THOMAS**

818. Diane Ruth	born 3 March 1955; died 28 December ___
	buried Crown Hill Memorial Park, New Hartford, NY
819. Donna Anne	born 7 September 1958

733. GARY GEORGE-[8] MYERS, son of Arthur LYON-[7] MYERS (Leroy Mason-[6]; Samuel Mason-[5]; Mason Leroy-[4]; Phebe-[3] KIFF; Andrew-[2]; George-[1]) and Marion Virginia DIDDENS, was born 17 February 1945 at Freeport, Stephenson, Illinois. He married 1st to Dianne Rae KEHLER on 20 January 1968 at Lena, Stephenson, IL. She was the daughter of _____ KEHLER and ____, and was born 10 October 1947 Freeport, IL. He married his 2nd wife Gerey May SMITH on 12 June 1976 at Freeport, IL. She was the daughter of _____ SMITH and ___, and was born 14 May 1953 at Peoria, IL.

Children of Gary George-[8] MYERS and his 1st wife Dianne KEHLER:
Surname **MYERS**

820. Bret Allen	born 24 Feb 1969 Freeport, IL
821. Staci Lyn	born 3 June 1971 Freeport, IL

Children of Gary George-[8] MYERS and his 2nd wife Gerey SMITH:
Surname **MYERS**

822. Erin Marie	born 15 Sept 1978 Freeport, IL
823. Dane Arthur	born 10 Jan 1982 Freeport, IL

737. JEANNE LUCILLE-[8] STABENOW, daughter of Doris Elaine-[7] LYON (Carl Dewey-[6]; Samuel Mason-[5]; Mason Leroy-[4]; Phebe-[3] KIFF; Andrew-[2]; George-[1]) and Ernest Harold STABENOW, was born 25 May 1947 at Freep-ort, Stephenson, Illinois. She married Billy Joe WIBERG on 27 September 1969 at Lena, Stephenson, IL. He was the son of ____ WIBERG and ____, and was born 14 April 1945 at Princeton, Bureau, IL.

Children of Jeanne-[8] STABENOW and Billy Joe WIBERG:
Surname **WIBERG**

824. Andrew Joseph	born 4 Oct 1972 Monroe, Green, Wisconsin
825. Michael James	born 1 June 1976 Monroe, WI
826. Nicholaus Jeffery	born 9 May 1981 Monroe, WI

738. WILLIAM FREDERICK-[8] STABENOW, brother of above, was born 30 November 1948 at Freeport, Stephenson, IL. He married Marsha Joy RACKOW on 4 March 1972 at Freeport, IL. She was the daughter of ____ RACKOW and _____, and was born 7 September 1952 at Freeport, IL.

Children of William F-[8] STABENOW and Marsha RACKOW:
Surname **STABENOW**

827. Blake Le Owen	born 16 June 1973 Freeport, IL
828. Brittany Joy	born 23 March 1975 Monroe, Green, WI

739. ERNEST HAROLD ⁻⁸ STABENOW, JR., brother of above, was born 8 May 1950 at Freeport, Stephenson, IL. He married Cathy Jo RILLIE ca _____ Lena, Stephenson, IL. She was the daughter of _____ RILLIE and _____, and was born 2 September 1950.

Children of Ernest-^{8} STABENOW, Jr. and Cathy RILLIE:
Surname **STABENOW**

      829. Kelly James   born 22 Nov 1970 Freeport, IL
      830. Ernest Harold (III)   born 27 March 1972 Freeport, IL

747. DAISY MAY-^{8} DIETRICH, daughter of John A-^{7} DIETRICH (Jeanette-^{6} MILLS; Harriet-^{5} PUTNAM: Harriet-^{4} KIFF; Lyman-^{3}; Andrew-^{2}; George-^{1}) and Alice SCOHY, was born ca June 1896 Elmira, Chemung County, NY. She married Vincent Arthur WILSON 5 July 1913 at Holdenville, OK. He was the son of Lewis WILSON and Sarah M. SMILEY, and was born 13 May 1888/ 89 Indian Territory, Cherokee, Oklahoma; died _____. Daisy May-^{8} DIETRICH died 8 March 1943 Fort Smith, Arkansas. (reference: Descendants of Wm. ROUNSEVELL)

Children of Daisy May-^{8} DIETRICH and Vincent A. WILSON:
Surname **WILSON**

      831. Lahoma   born 19 May 1914 Okmulgee, OK ; died 27 Aug 2000, CA
                       married Charley HOWARD ca _____
                       (he born 2 / 9 Feb 1909; died 15 Nov 1990 Yuba, CA)
                       (he s/o _____ HOWARD and _____ BARNES)
           Child: Charles Harmon-^{10} HOWARD born 24 Apr 1932 OK; died 1 Aug 1999 Paradise, CA;
           married _____ Apr 1958 OK
      832. Vincent A. Jr.   born ca 1917 OK; died _____
      833. Olive Juanita   born 2 June 1919 OK; died 15 April 1984 CA
                       married Benjamin Franklin JONES (he born 1915; died 2004)
   Children: Benjamin F-^{10}, Jr. born ca 1936, died 1938; John L-^{10} born 1948, died 1948; and John David-^{10} JONES born 1953, died 1974

782. JOYCE ANN-^{8} KUMKEY, daughter of Betty Jennie-^{7} ACOR (Mildred Amarillus-^{6} KIFF; Franklin Clayton-^{5}; John Mabie-^{4}; Erastus-^{3}; Andrew-^{2}; George-^{1}) and Charles H. KUMKEY, was born 20 June 1948 Waterloo, NY. She married 1st to Edward BALDASARI / BALDISARI ca 1966/68 at Seneca Falls, NY. She married 2nd to Edward Mc CARTY, and resides in Tennessee.

Children of Joyce Ann KUMKEY and Edward BALDASARI / BALDISARI:
Surname **BALDASARI/ BALDISARI**

      834. Rhonda Marie   born 1 October 1970
                       1 married _____ ALLEN ca _____
          Children : Rachael-^{10} born ca ___, and Michael-^{10} ALLEN
                       2 married Michael ROBENAULT ca _____
      835. Kimberly Ann   born _____
          Reference: Shirley Mae KUMKEY, personal knowledge

787. CHARLOTTE-^{8} MURRAY, daughter of Ray Edd-^{7} MURRAY (Horace-^{6}; Edson Allen-^{5}; Ann Eliza-^{4} KIFF, Erastus-^{3}; Andrew-^{2}; George-^{1}) and Mary JOHNSON, was born 28 Feb 1932 at _____, PA. She married James Murray TILLOTSON ca _____. He was the son of Murray S. TILLOTSON and Edna I. WILLIAMS, and was born 28 June 1925 PA; died 24 Aug 1993 Canton, PA. He was a veteran of the US Navy in World War 2 They resided Canton, Bradford, PA.

Children of Charlotte-^{8} MURRAY and James TILLOTSON:
Surname **TILLOTSON**

      836. Fay La Rae   born 8 Nov 1948
                       married Bradley Roy PEPPER 18 June 1965
                       (he s/o Lynn A. PEPPER and Martha G. MORSE)   (he born 20 April 1948)

Children of Charlotte-[8] MURRAY and James TILLOTSON, continued:
Surname **TILLOTSON**

837. Patricia Ann	born 21 Dec 1950
	married William Arthur PEPPER 21 Nov 1969
	(he brother of above ; born 23 July 1949)
838. James, Jr.	born ____; married Donna PEPPER ca ____
	(she dau/o Lyle PEPPER and Ella Mae KELLEY)
839. Kay	born ca ____

323

326

328

331

332

333

www.ingramcontent.com/pod-product-compliance
Lightning Source LLC
Chambersburg PA
CBHW080412270326
41929CB00018B/2989